P9-BXW-736

The Singing Church

ISBN: 0-916642-25-9
Printed in the U.S.A.

Hope Publishing Company
CAROL STREAM IL 60188

FOREWORD

People sing about those truths and experiences which are most meaningful to them. Christians sing of their understanding of God, their remembrance of the life, death and resurrection of Christ, and their experiences through the indwelling Holy Spirit. To be sure, ours is a singing faith!

It has been true since the dawn of history. Scripture records that when the worlds were created "the morning stars sang together and all the angels shouted for joy" (Job 38:7). Genesis chapter four suggests that music appeared very early in the cultural development of the human race, and we believe that all of the worship and proclamation texts in the Old Testament were normally sung. In the New Testament we read that Jesus sang with his disciples after the supper in the Upper Room. The epistles speak frequently about music in worship and contain many hymns that were probably used in the early church. In fact, the history of Western music for fifteen hundred years after the birth of Christ is largely a record of music created for Christian worship.

The study of historic hymnology suggests that we should cherish the words spoken and sung by our spiritual forebears, because in doing so we demonstrate the perpetuity of God's covenants with us and the continuity of human response to God's revelation. Like most complete hymnals, THE SINGING CHURCH contains both old and new paraphrases of scripture as well as significant hymns from every period of the church's history. Certain editorial changes have helped to make this possible. In some instances, older texts have been modernized; in others, they have been set to more contemporary tunes.

At the same time, it is important to acknowledge the revolution in hymn singing which has taken place during the past twenty-five years. Beginning in the 1960's new examples of popular hymnody began to appear in fresh literary and musical styles, written by such individuals as Ralph Carmichael, William and Gloria Gaither, Andraé Crouch, Kurt Kaiser, Don Wyrtzen, Ken Medema and Mark Blankenship. Even more recently, we witnessed an "explosion" of new hymns in more traditional forms by authors in both America and Great Britain—Margaret Clarkson, Bryan Jeffery Leech, Timothy Dudley-Smith, Fred Pratt Green, Brian Wren, Erik Routley and Fred Kaan—and a number of them are contained in this book. In addition, a large quantity of spirituals and folk hymns of the American heritage, some contemporary "scripture songs" and a few choral classics, all contribute to the comprehensive and eclectic character of this unique hymnal.

The new hymns presented here support the theological concerns of our day. There are more selections for use in the Advent, Christmas, Easter and Pentecost seasons, and new texts about the second coming of Christ and the call to Christian service in evangelism, missions and social ministry. Tunes have been carefully chosen for their appeal to congregations; in several instances, the same hymn appears with two musical settings.

THE SINGING CHURCH reflects Hope Publishing Company's continuing emphasis on the biblical basis of our worship. Each hymn bears a scripture quotation which focuses on the central meaning of its words. Further, the scripture quotations and allusions found in the hymns are listed on pages 580-585. Finally, eighty scripture readings from eight popular versions and paraphrases are included to meet the many and diverse needs of congregational participation in worship.

In this volume we are also happy to present a more beautiful and more readable hymnbook than ever before. Attractive "divider pages" mark the beginning of each section of hymns, as listed in the Table of Contents. At the top of each hymn page will be found the subject classification, an extra large number and title, and the scripture reference. Below the hymn, at the left, the information about the author/adapter and the composer/arranger is clearly set forth, together with the dates when the words and music first appeared. On the lower right will be found the tune name and the text's meter, the latter for use by those who wish to find an alternate tune.

Many worship leaders have expressed appreciation for the comprehensive hymnic information and references included in our hymnals. In THE SINGING CHURCH we have given fifty pages for a full complement of indexes, using new design and a larger, more readable type face.

We are indebted to many individuals and publishers for use of their copyrighted hymns. Credit is given on the hymnal page, and addresses of copyright owners are listed on pages 586-587. If any acknowledgment has been inadvertently omitted, correction will be made in a subsequent edition.

The Hope Publishing Company will soon celebrate one hundred years of preparing hymnals for America's evangelical churches. With the release of this new book, as with all those that have gone before, we dedicate it to the service of God in public and private worship. May it be used to offer Him a worthy sacrifice of praise.

The Publishers

CONTENTS

THE HYMNS

THE SCRIPTURE READINGS

THE INDEXES

PAGES

Hymns of God The Father

How Great Thou Art 1

Great is the Lord, and greatly to be praised. Psa. 48:1

1. O Lord my God, when I in awe-some won-der Con-sid-er all the worlds* Thy hands have made, I see the stars, I hear the roll-ing* thun-der, Thy pow'r thro'-out the u-ni-verse dis-played.
2. When thro' the woods and for-est glades I wan-der And hear the birds sing sweet-ly in the trees, When I look down from loft-y moun-tain gran-deur, And hear the brook and feel the gen-tle breeze.
3. And when I think that God, His Son not spar-ing, Sent Him to die, I scarce can take it in, That on the cross, my bur-den glad-ly bear-ing, He bled and died to take a-way my sin.
4. When Christ shall come with shout of ac-cla-ma-tion And take me home, what joy shall fill my heart! Then I shall bow in hum-ble ad-o-ra-tion, And there pro-claim, my God, how great Thou art.
Refrain
Then sings my soul, my Sav-ior God, to Thee; How great Thou art, how great Thou art! Then sings my soul, my Sav-ior God, to Thee: How great Thou art, how great Thou art!

WORDS: Stuart K. Hine, 1949
MUSIC: Swedish folk melody; arr. Stuart K. Hine, 1949

HOW GREAT THOU ART
11.10.11.10 Ref.

* *Composer's original words are "works" and "mighty."*

2 Come, Thou Fount of Every Blessing

Blessed be the Lord, who daily loadeth us with benefits. Psa. 68:19

1. Come, Thou Fount of ev - ery bless - ing, Tune my heart to sing Thy grace;
2. Hith - er - to Thy love has blest me; Thou hast bro't me to this place;
3. O to grace how great a debt - or Dai - ly I'm con-strained to be!

Streams of mer - cy, nev - er ceas - ing, Call for songs of loud - est praise.
And I know Thy hand will bring me Safe - ly home by Thy good grace.
Let Thy good - ness, like a fet - ter, Bind my wan-dering heart to Thee:

Teach me some me - lo - dious son - net, Sung by flam - ing tongues a - bove;
Je - sus sought me when a stran - ger, Wan-dering from the fold of God;
Prone to wan - der, Lord, I feel it, Prone to leave the God I love;

Praise His name—I'm fixed up - on it—Name of God's re - deem-ing love.
He, to res - cue me from dan - ger, Bought me with His pre-cious blood.
Here's my heart, O take and seal it; Seal it for Thy courts a - bove. A-men.

WORDS: Robert Robinson, 1758
MUSIC: John Wyeth's *Repository of Sacred Music,* 1813; Traditional American melody

NETTLETON
8.7.8.7 D.

A Mighty Fortress Is Our God 3

God is our refuge and strength. Psa. 46:1

1. A might - y for - tress is our God, A bul - wark nev - er fail - ing;
2. Did we in our own strength con - fide, Our striv - ing would be los - ing,
3. And though this world, with dev - ils filled, Should threat - en to un - do us,
4. That word a - bove all earth - ly powers, No thanks to them, a - bid - eth;
Our help - er He, a - mid the flood Of mor - tal ills pre - vail - ing:
Were not the right Man on our side, The man of God's own choos - ing:
We will not fear, for God hath willed His truth to tri - umph through us:
The Spir - it and the gifts are ours Through him who with us sid - eth:
For still our an - cient foe Doth seek to work us woe; His craft and power are
Dost ask who that may be? Christ Je - sus, it is He; Lord Sab - a - oth His
The Prince of Dark - ness grim, We trem - ble not for him; His rage we can en -
Let goods and kin - dred go, This mor - tal life al - so; The bod - y they may
great, And, armed with cru - el hate, On earth is not his e - qual.
name, From age to age the same, And He must win the bat - tle.
dure, For lo, his doom is sure; One lit - tle word shall fell him.
kill: God's truth a - bid - eth still; His king - dom is for - ev - er. A - men.

WORDS: Martin Luther, 1529; tr. Frederick H. Hedge, 1852; based on Psalm 46
MUSIC: Martin Luther, 1529

EIN' FESTE BURG
8.7.8.7.6.6.6.6.7

4 Praise the Lord! Ye Heavens, Adore Him

Praise ye the Lord from the heavens: praise Him in the heights. Psa. 148:1

1. Praise the Lord! ye heav'ns, a - dore him; Praise him, an - gels in the height;
2. Praise the Lord! for He is glo - rious; Nev - er shall His prom - ise fail;
3. Wor - ship, hon - or, glo - ry, bless - ing, Lord, we of - fer un - to Thee;

Sun and moon, re - joice be - fore Him; Praise Him, all ye stars of light.
God hath made His saints vic - to - rious; Sin and death shall not pre - vail.
Young and old, Thy praise ex - press - ing, In glad hom - age bend the knee.

Praise the Lord! for He hath spo - ken; Worlds His might - y voice o - beyed;
Praise the God of our sal - va - tion! Hosts on high, His pow'r pro - claim;
All the saints in heav'n a - dore Thee; We would bow be - fore Thy throne:

Laws which nev - er shall be bro - ken For their guid - ance He hath made.
Heav'n and earth and all cre - a - tion, Laud and mag - ni - fy His name.
As Thine an - gels serve be - fore Thee, So on earth Thy will be done. A - men.

WORDS: *Foundling Hospital Collection*, 1796; St. 3, Edward Osler, 1836; based on Psalm 148
MUSIC: Franz Joseph Haydn, 1797

AUSTRIAN HYMN
8.7.8.7 D.

Sing Praise to God Who Reigns Above 5

The Lord reigneth; let the earth rejoice . . . Psa. 97:1

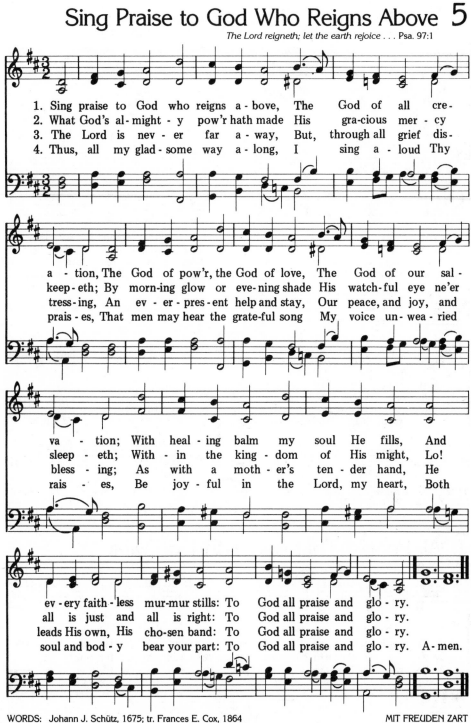

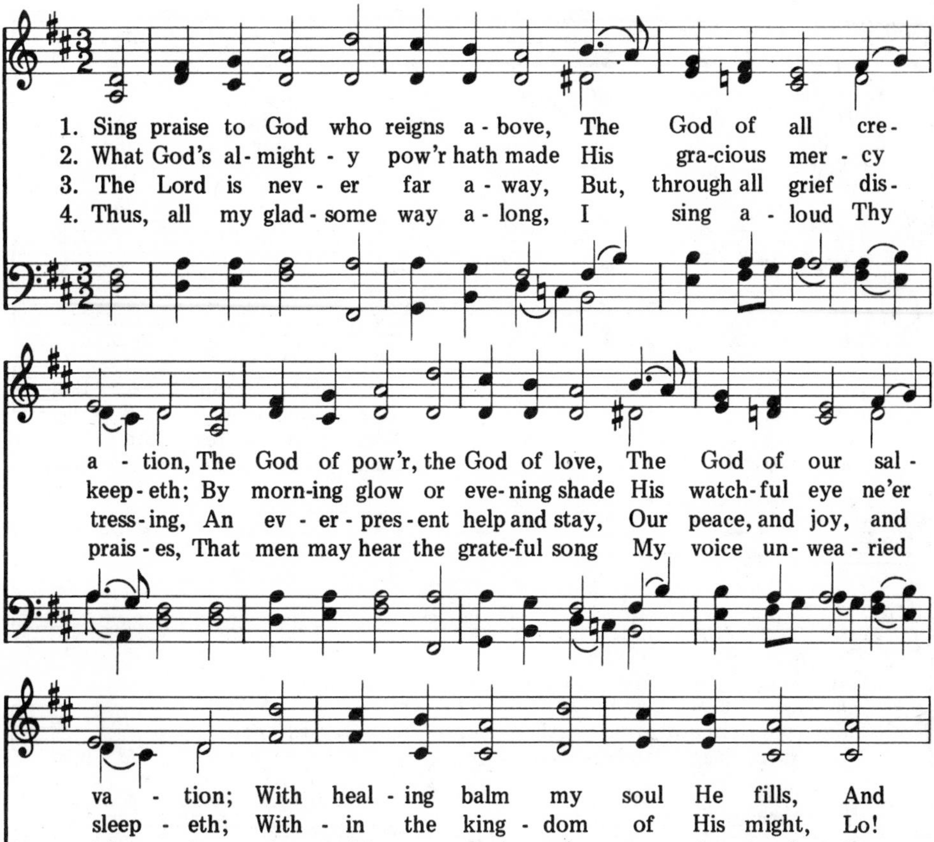

1. Sing praise to God who reigns above,
The God of all creation,
The God of pow'r, the God of love,
The God of our salvation;
With healing balm my soul He fills,
And every faithless murmur stills:
To God all praise and glory.

2. What God's almighty pow'r hath made
His gracious mercy keepeth;
By morning glow or evening shade
His watchful eye ne'er sleepeth;
Within the kingdom of His might,
Lo! all is just and all is right:
To God all praise and glory.

3. The Lord is never far away,
But, through all grief distressing,
An ever-present help and stay,
Our peace, and joy, and blessing;
As with a mother's tender hand,
He leads His own, His chosen band:
To God all praise and glory.

4. Thus, all my gladsome way along,
I sing aloud Thy praises,
That men may hear the grateful song
My voice unwearied raises,
Be joyful in the Lord, my heart,
Both soul and body bear your part:
To God all praise and glory. Amen.

WORDS: Johann J. Schütz, 1675; tr. Frances E. Cox, 1864
MUSIC: Bohemian Brethren's *Kirchengesänge*, Berlin, 1566

MIT FREUDEN ZART
8.7.8.7.8.8.7

6 Stand Up and Bless the Lord

Stand up and bless the Lord your God, for ever and ever. Neh. 9:5

1. Stand up and bless the Lord, Ye people of His choice; Stand up and bless the Lord your God With heart and soul and voice.
2. Though high above all praise, Above all blessing high, Who would not fear His holy name, And laud and magnify?
3. God is our strength and song, And His salvation ours; Then be His love in Christ proclaimed With all our ransomed pow'rs.
4. Stand up and bless the Lord, The Lord your God adore; Stand up and bless His glorious name, Henceforth for evermore. Amen.

WORDS: James Montgomery, 1824
MUSIC: Aaron Williams, 1763

ST. THOMAS
S.M.

7 All People That on Earth Do Dwell

Make a joyful noise unto the Lord, all ye lands. Psa. 100:1

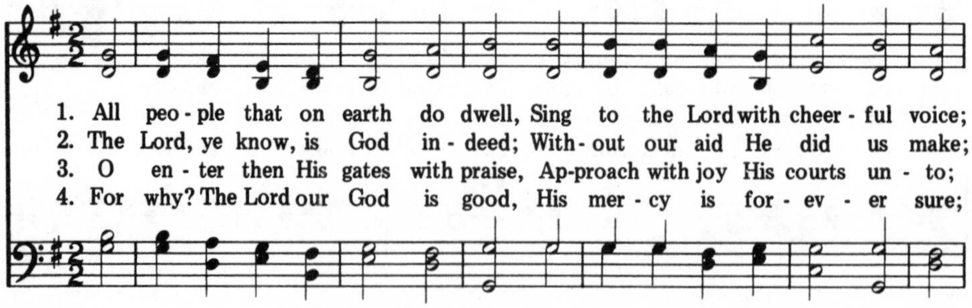

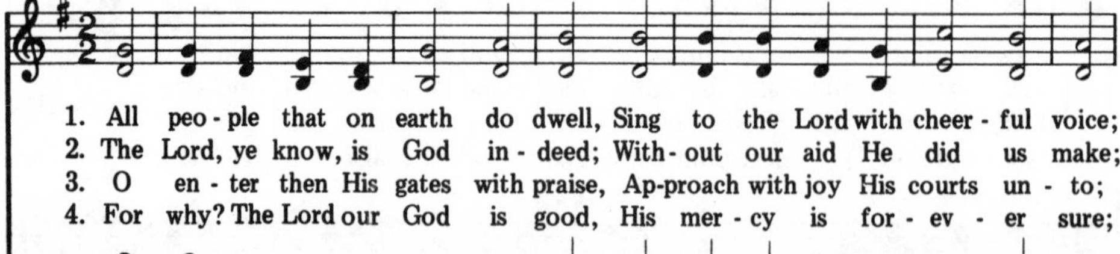
1. All peo - ple that on earth do dwell, Sing to the Lord with cheer - ful voice;
2. The Lord, ye know, is God in - deed; With - out our aid He did us make;
3. O en - ter then His gates with praise, Ap-proach with joy His courts un - to;
4. For why? The Lord our God is good, His mer - cy is for - ev - er sure;

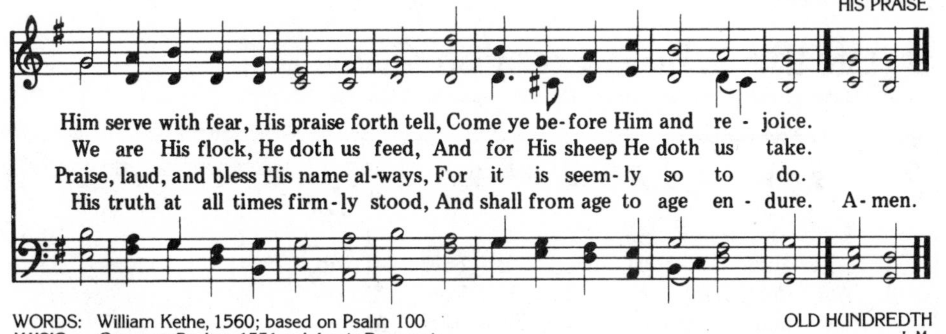
HIS PRAISE
Him serve with fear, His praise forth tell, Come ye be-fore Him and re - joice.
We are His flock, He doth us feed, And for His sheep He doth us take.
Praise, laud, and bless His name al-ways, For it is seem-ly so to do.
His truth at all times firm-ly stood, And shall from age to age en - dure. A-men.

WORDS: William Kethe, 1560; based on Psalm 100
MUSIC: *Genevan Psalter*, 1551, ed. Louis Bourgeois

OLD HUNDREDTH
L.M.

Ye Servants of God, Your Master Proclaim 8

Salvation and glory, and honor, and power, unto the Lord our God. Rev. 19:1

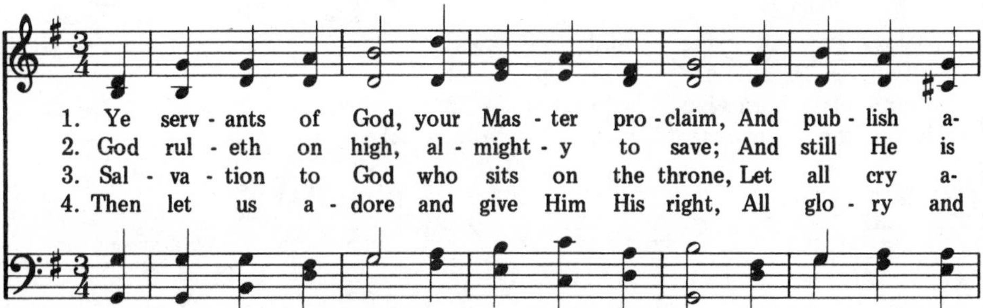

1. Ye serv - ants of God, your Mas - ter pro - claim, And pub - lish a-
2. God rul - eth on high, al - might - y to save; And still He is
3. Sal - va - tion to God who sits on the throne, Let all cry a-
4. Then let us a - dore and give Him His right, All glo - ry and

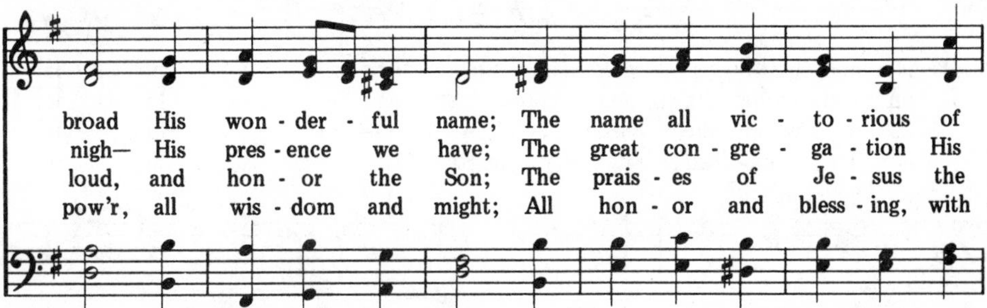

broad His won - der - ful name; The name all vic - to - rious of
nigh— His pres - ence we have; The great con - gre - ga - tion His
loud, and hon - or the Son; The prais - es of Je - sus the
pow'r, all wis - dom and might; All hon - or and bless - ing, with

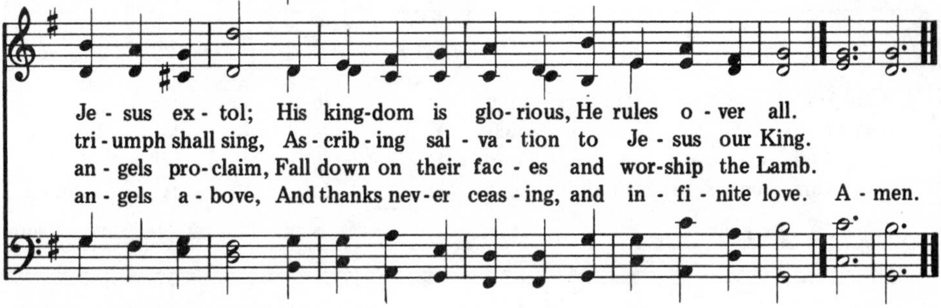

Je - sus ex - tol; His king-dom is glo - rious, He rules o - ver all.
tri - umph shall sing, As - crib - ing sal - va - tion to Je - sus our King.
an - gels pro - claim, Fall down on their fac - es and wor-ship the Lamb.
an - gels a - bove, And thanks nev - er ceas - ing, and in - fi - nite love. A - men.

WORDS: Charles Wesley, 1744
MUSIC: William Croft, 1708

HANOVER
10.10.11.11

9 Let the Whole Creation Cry

Let them praise . . . for He commanded, and they were created. Psa. 148:5

1. Let the whole cre - a - tion cry Al - le - lu - ia!
2. Praise Him, all ye hosts a - bove, Al - le - lu - ia!
3. War - riors fight - ing for the Lord, Al - le - lu - ia!
4. Men and wom - en, young and old, Al - le - lu - ia!
Glo - ry to the Lord on high! Al - le - lu - ia!
Ev - er bright and fair in love! Al - le - lu - ia!
Proph - ets burn - ing with His Word, Al - le - lu - ia!
Raise the an - them man - i - fold; Al - le - lu - ia!
Heav'n and earth, a - wake and sing, Al - le - lu - ia!
Sun and moon, lift up your voice, Al - le - lu - ia!
Those to whom the arts be - long, Al - le - lu - ia!
And let chil - dren's hap - py hearts, Al - le - lu - ia!
God is God and there-fore King, Al - le - lu - ia!
Night and stars in God re - joice, Al - le - lu - ia!
Add their voic - es to the song, Al - le - lu - ia!
In this wor - ship bear their parts: Al - le - lu - ia! A - men.

WORDS: Stopford A. Brooke, 1881; based on Psalm 148
MUSIC: Robert Williams, 1817

LLANFAIR
7.7.7.7 Alleluias

When in Our Music God Is Glorified 10

Let everything that hath breath praise the Lord. Psa. 150:6

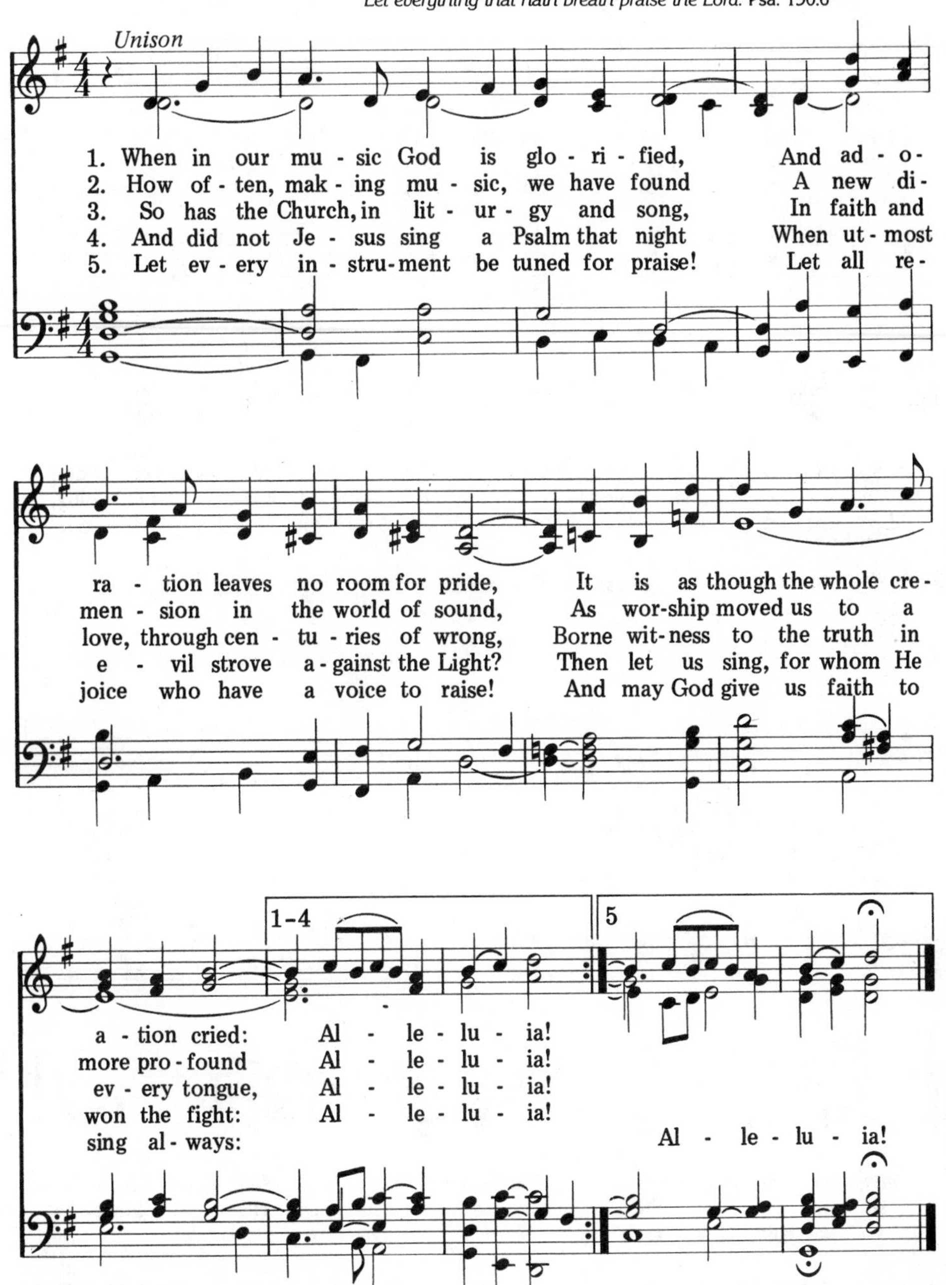
Unison
1. When in our mu - sic God is glo - ri - fied, And ad - o-
2. How of - ten, mak - ing mu - sic, we have found A new di-
3. So has the Church, in lit - ur - gy and song, In faith and
4. And did not Je - sus sing a Psalm that night When ut - most
5. Let ev - ery in - stru - ment be tuned for praise! Let all re-
ra - tion leaves no room for pride, It is as though the whole cre-
men - sion in the world of sound, As wor-ship moved us to a
love, through cen - tu - ries of wrong, Borne wit-ness to the truth in
e - vil strove a - gainst the Light? Then let us sing, for whom He
joice who have a voice to raise! And may God give us faith to
1-4
5
a - tion cried: Al - le - lu - ia!
more pro - found Al - le - lu - ia!
ev - ery tongue, Al - le - lu - ia!
won the fight: Al - le - lu - ia!
sing al - ways: Al - le - lu - ia!

WORDS: Fred Pratt Green, 1972
MUSIC: Charles V. Stanford, 1904

ENGELBERG
10.10.10 Alleluias

11 New Songs of Celebration Render

Sing unto the Lord a new song; for He hath done marvelous things. Psa. 98:1

Unison
1. New songs of cel - e - bra - tion ren - der To Him who has great won - ders done; Awed by His love His foes sur - ren - der And fall be - fore the Might - y One. He has made known His great sal - va - tion Which all His friends with joy con - fess; He has re -
2. Joy - ful - ly, heart - i - ly re - sound - ing, Let ev - ery in - stru - ment and voice Peal out the praise of grace a - bound - ing, Call - ing the whole world to re - joice. Trum - pets and or - gans set in mo - tion Such sounds as make the heav - ens ring: All things that
3. Riv - ers and seas and tor - rents roar - ing, Hon - or the Lord with wild ac - claim; Moun - tains and stones, look up a - dor - ing And find a voice to praise His Name. Righ - teous, com - mand - ing, ev - er glo - rious, Prais - es be His that nev - er cease: Just is our

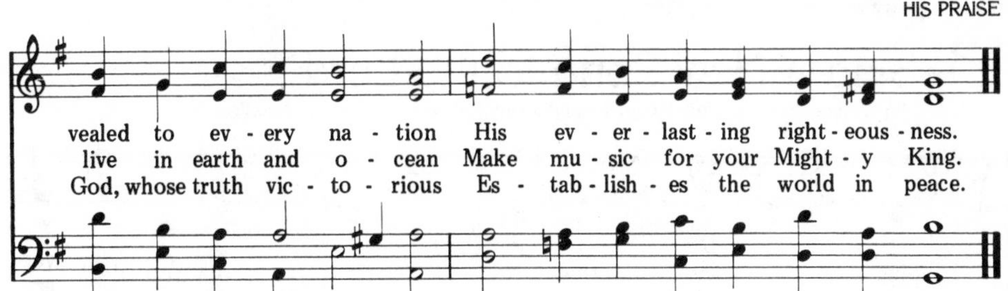
vealed to every nation His everlasting righteousness.
live in earth and ocean Make music for your Mighty King.
God, whose truth victorious Establishes the world in peace.

WORDS: Erik Routley, 1974; based on Psalm 98
MUSIC: Louis Bourgeois, 1543

RENDEZ À DIEU
9.8.9.8 D.

Bless the Lord, O My Soul 12

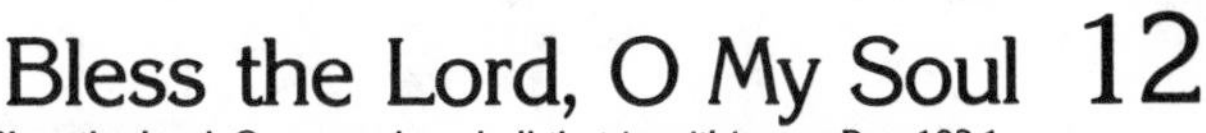

Bless the Lord, O my soul, and all that is within me. Psa. 103:1

Bless the Lord, O my soul, and all that is within me, Bless His

Fine
holy Name. He has done great things, He has done great

D.C. al Fine
things, He has done great things, Bless His holy Name.

WORDS and MUSIC: Andraé Crouch, 1973; based on Psalm 103

BLESS HIS HOLY NAME
Irregular meter

13 Sing a New Song to the Lord

With trumpets and sound of cornet make a joyful noise before the Lord . . . Psa. 98:6

Unison
1. Sing a new song to the Lord, He to whom won-ders be-long! Re-joice in His tri-umph and tell of His pow'r— O sing to the Lord a new song!
2. Now to the ends of the earth See His sal-va-tion is shown; And still He re-mem-bers His mer-cy and truth, Un-chang-ing in love to His own.
3. Sing a new song and re-joice, Pub-lish His prais-es a-broad! Let voic-es in cho-rus, with trum-pet and horn, Re-sound for the joy of the Lord!
4. Join with the hills and the sea Thun-ders of praise to pro-long! In judg-ment and jus-tice He comes to the earth— O sing to the Lord a new song!
1,2,3
D. C.
4

WORDS: Timothy Dudley-Smith, 1971; based on Psalm 98
MUSIC: David G. Wilson, 1973

CANTATE DOMINO
7.7.11.8

Joyful, Joyful, We Adore Thee 14

All Thy works shall praise Thee, O Lord . . . Psa. 145:10

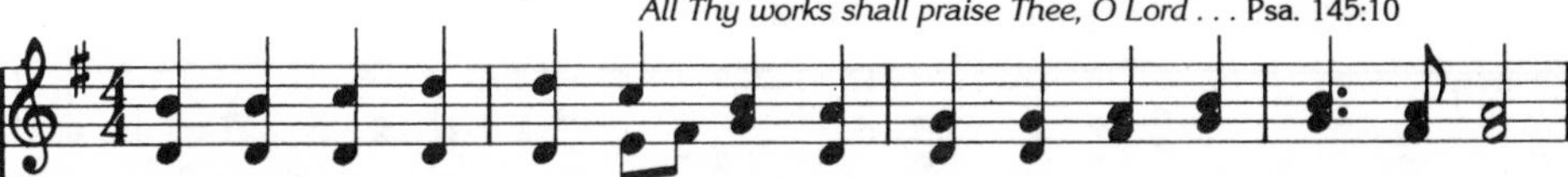

1. Joy - ful, joy - ful, we a - dore Thee, God of glo - ry, Lord of love;
2. All Thy works with joy sur - round Thee, Earth and heav'n re - flect Thy rays,
3. Thou art giv - ing and for - giv - ing, Ev - er bless-ing, ev - er blest,
4. Mor-tals join the might - y cho - rus Which the morn-ing stars be - gan;

Hearts un - fold like flow'rs be - fore Thee, Open-ing to the sun a - bove.
Stars and an - gels sing a - round Thee, Cen - ter of un - bro - ken praise.
Well-spring of the joy of liv - ing, O - cean-depth of hap - py rest!
Fa - ther love is reign - ing o'er us, Broth - er love binds man to man.

Melt the clouds of sin and sad - ness; Drive the dark of doubt a - way;
Field and for - est, vale and moun-tain, Flow - ery mead-ow, flash - ing sea,
Thou our Fa - ther, Christ our Broth - er— All who live in love are Thine;
Ev - er sing - ing, march we on - ward, Vic - tors in the midst of strife;

Giv - er of im - mor-tal glad-ness, Fill us with the light of day!
Chant-ing bird and flow-ing foun-tain Call us to re - joice in Thee.
Teach us how to love each oth - er, Lift us to the joy di - vine.
Joy-ful mu - sic leads us sun-ward In the tri-umph song of life. A - men.

WORDS: Henry van Dyke, 1907
MUSIC: Ludwig van Beethoven, 1824

HYMN TO JOY
8.7.8.7 D.

15 Rejoice, Ye Pure in Heart

Rejoice in the Lord, O ye righteous . . . Psa. 33:1

1. Re - joice, ye pure in heart, Re - joice, give thanks, and sing;
2. Bright youth and snow-crowned age, Strong men and maid - ens fair,
3. With all the an - gel choirs, With all the saints on earth,
4. Yes, on through life's long path, Still chant - ing as ye go;
5. Still lift your stand - ard high, Still march in firm ar - ray;

Your fes - tal ban - ner wave on high, The cross of Christ your King.
Raise high your free, ex - ult - ing song, God's won-drous praise de - clare.
Pour out the strains of joy and bliss, True rap - ture, no - blest mirth!
From youth to age, by night and day, In glad - ness and in woe.
As war - riors through the dark - ness toil Till dawns the gold - en day.

Refrain

Re - joice, re - joice, Re - joice, give thanks, and sing! A-men.
Re - joice, re - joice,

WORDS: Edward H. Plumptre, 1865
MUSIC: Arthur H. Messiter, 1883

MARION
S.M. Ref.

16 Come, We That Love the Lord

Praise the Lord! Sing to the Lord a new song . . . Psa. 149:1

1. Come, we that love the Lord, And let our joys be known; Join
2. Let those re - fuse to sing Who nev - er knew our God; But
3. The men of grace have found Glo - ry be - gun be - low; Ce -
4. The hill of Zi - on yields A thou - sand sa - cred sweets Be -
5. Then let our songs a - bound, And ev - ery tear be dry; We're

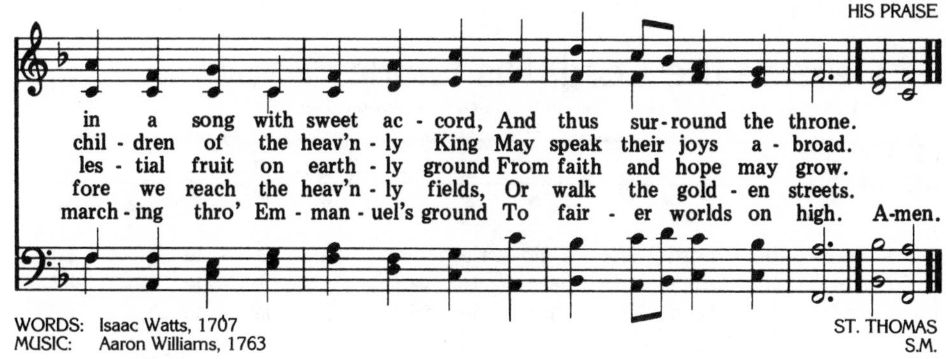
in a song with sweet ac - cord, And thus sur - round the throne.
chil - dren of the heav'n - ly King May speak their joys a - broad.
les - tial fruit on earth - ly ground From faith and hope may grow.
fore we reach the heav'n - ly fields, Or walk the gold - en streets.
march - ing thro' Em - man - uel's ground To fair - er worlds on high. A-men.

WORDS: Isaac Watts, 1707
MUSIC: Aaron Williams, 1763

ST. THOMAS
S.M.

O Worship the King, All Glorious Above 17

O Lord my God . . . Thou art clothed with honor and majesty. Psa. 104:1

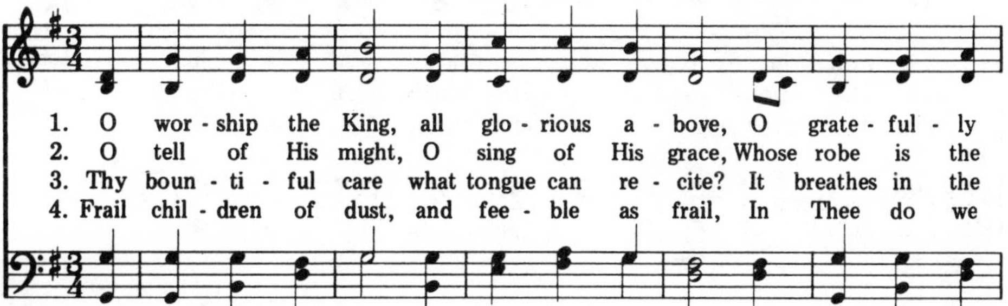

1. O wor - ship the King, all glo - rious a - bove, O grate - ful - ly
2. O tell of His might, O sing of His grace, Whose robe is the
3. Thy boun - ti - ful care what tongue can re - cite? It breathes in the
4. Frail chil - dren of dust, and fee - ble as frail, In Thee do we

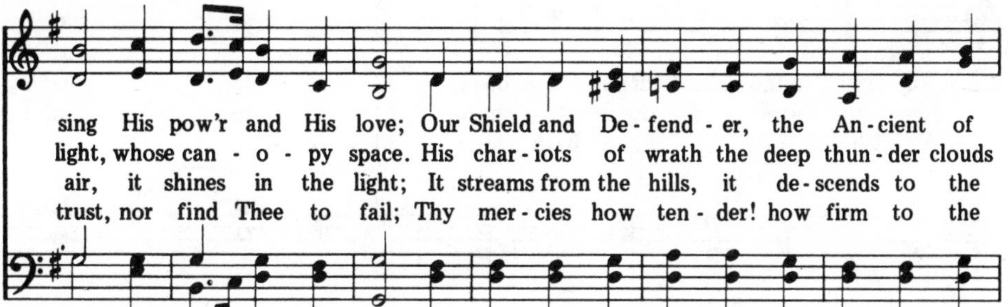

sing His pow'r and His love; Our Shield and De - fend - er, the An - cient of
light, whose can - o - py space. His char - iots of wrath the deep thun - der clouds
air, it shines in the light; It streams from the hills, it de - scends to the
trust, nor find Thee to fail; Thy mer - cies how ten - der! how firm to the

Days, Pa - vil - ioned in splen - dor and gird - ed with praise.
form, And dark is His path on the wings of the storm.
plain, And sweet - ly dis - tills in the dew and the rain.
end! Our Mak - er, De - fend - er, Re - deem - er and Friend. A - men.

WORDS: Robert Grant, 1833; based on Psalm 104
MUSIC: William Gardiner's *Sacred Melodies*, 1815; arr. from Johann M. Haydn, 1737-1806

LYONS
10.10.11.11

18 Praise the Lord, His Glories Show

Bless ye the Lord . . . ye ministers of His, that do His pleasure. Psa. 103:21

1. Praise the Lord, His glo - ries show, Al - le - lu - ia!
Saints with - in His courts be - low, Al - le - lu - ia!
An - gels round His throne a - bove, Al - le - lu - ia!
All that see and share His love, Al - le - lu - ia!

2. Earth to heav'n and heav'n to earth, Al - le - lu - ia!
Tell His won - ders, sing His worth, Al - le - lu - ia!
Age to age and shore to shore, Al - le - lu - ia!
Praise Him, praise Him ev - er - more! Al - le - lu - ia!

3. Praise the Lord, His mer - cies trace, Al - le - lu - ia!
Praise His prov - i - dence and grace, Al - le - lu - ia!
All that He for man hath done, Al - le - lu - ia!
All He sends us through His Son. Al - le - lu - ia! A-men.

WORDS: Henry F. Lyte, 1834; based on Psalm 148
MUSIC: Joseph D. Jones, 1868

GWALCHMAI
7.7.7.7 Alleluias

Praise the Lord Who Reigns Above 19

Praise God in His sanctuary; praise Him in the firmament of His power. Psa. 150:1

1. Praise the Lord who reigns a - bove And keeps His court be - low;
2. Cel - e - brate th'e - ter - nal God With harp and psal - ter - y,
3. Him, in whom they move and live, Let ev - ery crea - ture sing,

Praise the ho - ly God of love, And all His great - ness show;
Tim - brels soft and cym - bals loud In His high praise a - gree;
Glo - ry to their Mak - er give, And hom - age to their King.

Praise Him for His no - ble deeds, Praise Him for His match - less pow'r;
Praise Him ev - ery tune - ful string; All the reach of heav'n - ly art,
Hallow-ed be His name be - neath, As in heav'n on earth a - dored;

Him from whom all good pro - ceeds Let earth and heav'n a - dore.
All the pow'rs of mu - sic bring, The mu - sic of the heart.
Praise the Lord in ev - ery breath, Let all things praise the Lord. A - men.

WORDS: Charles Wesley, 1743; based on Psalm 150
MUSIC: *Foundery Collection*, 1742

AMSTERDAM
7.6.7.6.7.7.7.6

20 O Splendor of God's Glory Bright

That was the true Light, which lighteth every man . . . John 1:9

1. O Splen - dor of God's glo - ry bright, From light e-
2. Come, ver - y Sun of heav - en's love, In last - ing
3. Con - firm our will to do the right, And keep our
4. All praise to God the Fa - ther be, All praise, e-

ter - nal bring - ing light, Thou Light of light, light's
ra - diance from a - bove, And pour the Ho - ly
hearts from en - vy's blight; Let faith her ea - ger
ter - nal Son, to Thee, Whom with the Spir - it

liv - ing Spring, True Day, all days il - lu - min - ing:
Spir - it's ray On all we think or do to - day.
fires re - new, And hate the false, and love the true.
we a - dore For - ev - er and for - ev - er - more. A - men.

WORDS: St. Ambrose of Milan, c. 340-397; tr. composite
MUSIC: Georg Rebenlein's *Musicalisch Handbuch,* Hamburg, 1690; arr. William Havergal, 1847

WINCHESTER NEW
L.M.

21 Lord, We Praise You

Sing unto Him, sing unto Him; talk ye of all His wondrous works . . . Psa. 105:2

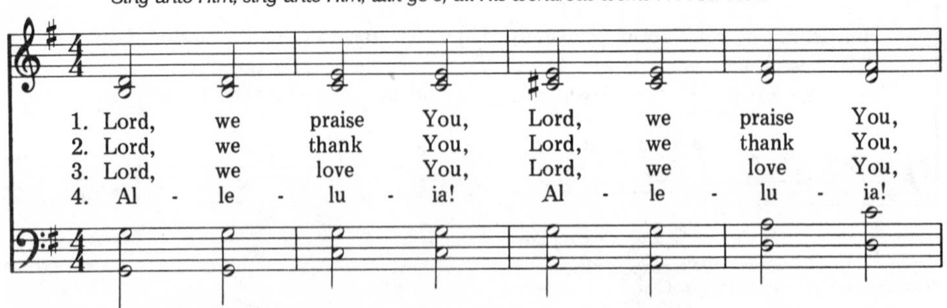
1. Lord, we praise You, Lord, we praise You,
2. Lord, we thank You, Lord, we thank You,
3. Lord, we love You, Lord, we love You,
4. Al - le - lu - ia! Al - le - lu - ia!

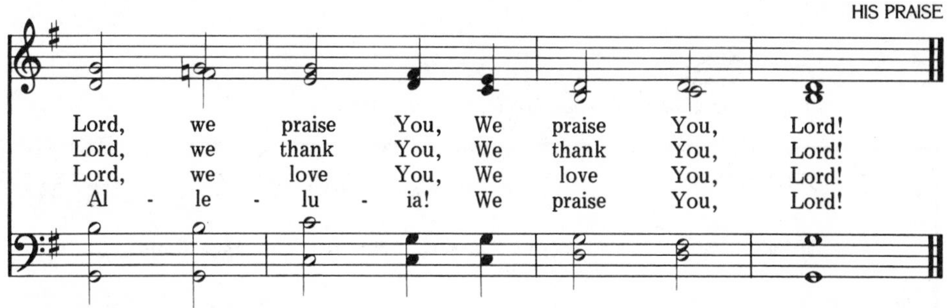
Lord, we praise You, We praise You, Lord!
Lord, we thank You, We thank You, Lord!
Lord, we love You, We love You, Lord!
Al - le - lu - ia! We praise You, Lord!

WORDS and MUSIC: Otis Skillings, 1972

LORD, WE PRAISE YOU
Irregular meter

Let All the World in Every Corner Sing 22

Sing unto the Lord, all the earth. Psa. 96:1

Unison

1. Let all the world in ev - ery cor - ner sing: My God and King! The heav'ns are not too high, His praise may thith - er fly; The earth is not too low, His prais - es there may grow. Let all the world in ev - ery cor - ner sing: My God and King!

2. Let all the world in ev - ery cor - ner sing: My God and King! The church with psalms must shout, No door can keep them out; But, more than all, the heart Must bear the long - est part. Let all the world in ev - ery cor - ner sing: My God and King! A - men.

WORDS: George Herbert, 1633
MUSIC: Robert G. McCutchan, 1934

ALL THE WORLD
14.12.12.14

23 How Can I Say Thanks

To God only wise, be glory through Jesus Christ. Rom. 16:27

How can I say thanks for the things You have done for me?

Things so un-de-served, Yet You gave to prove Your love for me; The

voic-es of a mil-lion an-gels could not ex-press my gra-ti-tude.

All that I am, and ev-er hope to be; I owe it all to Thee.

Refrain

To God be the glo-ry, To God be the glo-ry,

To God be the glo - ry For the things He has done.
With His blood He has saved me; With His power He has raised me;
Fine
To God be the glo - ry For the things He has done.
Just let me live my life; Let it be pleas-ing, Lord, to Thee.
D.S. al Fine
And if I gain an - y praise, Let it go to Cal - va - ry. With His

WORDS and MUSIC: Andraé Crouch, 1971

MY TRIBUTE
Irregular meter

24 Tell Out, My Soul

And Mary said, My soul doth magnify the Lord. Luke 1:46

Unison

1. Tell out, my soul, the great-ness of the Lord! Un - num-bered
2. Tell out, my soul, the great-ness of His Name! Make known His
3. Tell out, my soul, the great-ness of His might! Pow'rs and do -
4. Tell out, my soul, the glo - ries of His word! Firm is His

bless-ings give my spir - it voice; Ten - der to me the
might, the deeds His arm has done; His mer - cy sure, from
min - ions lay their glo - ry by. Proud hearts and stub - born
prom - ise, and His mer - cy sure. Tell out, my soul, the

prom - ise of His word; In God my Sav - ior shall my heart re - joice.
age to age the same; His ho - ly Name, the Lord, the might - y one.
wills are put to flight, The hun - gry fed, the hum - ble lift - ed high.
great - ness of the Lord To chil - dren's chil - dren and for - ev - er - more!

WORDS: Timothy Dudley-Smith, 1961; based on Luke 1:46-55
MUSIC: Walter Greatorex, 1916

WOODLANDS
10.10.10.10

Praise, My Soul, the King of Heaven 25

Bless the Lord, O my soul, and forget not all His benefits. Psa. 103:2

Unison
1. Praise, my soul, the King of heav - en, To His feet thy trib-ute bring; Ran - somed, healed, re - stored, for - giv - en, Ev - er - more His prais - es sing; Al - le - lu - ia! Al - le - lu - ia! Praise the ev - er - last - ing King.
2. Praise Him for his grace and fa - vor To our fa - thers in dis - tress; Praise Him, still the same as ev - er, Slow to chide, and swift to bless; Al - le - lu - ia! Al - le - lu - ia! Glo - rious in His faith - ful - ness.
3. Frail as sum - mer's flow'r we flour - ish; Blows the wind and it is gone; But, while mor - tals rise and per - ish, God en - dures un - chang - ing on: Al - le - lu - ia! Al - le - lu - ia! Praise the high e - ter - nal one.
4. An - gels in the height, a - dore Him; Ye be - hold Him face to face; Saints tri - um - phant, bow be - fore Him; Gath - ered in from ev - ery race; Al - le - lu - ia! Al - le - lu - ia! Praise with us the God of grace.

WORDS: Henry F. Lyte, 1834; based on Psalm 103
MUSIC: Mark Andrews, 1930

ANDREWS
8.7.8.7.8.7

26 My God, How Wonderful Thou Art

I dwell in the high and holy place, with him also that is of a . . . humble spirit. Isa. 57:15

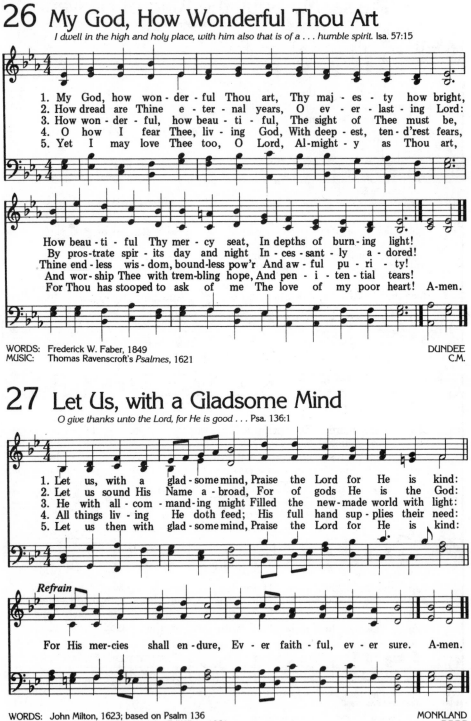

1. My God, how won - der - ful Thou art, Thy maj - es - ty how bright,
2. How dread are Thine e - ter - nal years, O ev - er - last - ing Lord:
3. How won - der - ful, how beau - ti - ful, The sight of Thee must be,
4. O how I fear Thee, liv - ing God, With deep - est, ten - d'rest fears,
5. Yet I may love Thee too, O Lord, Al-might - y as Thou art,

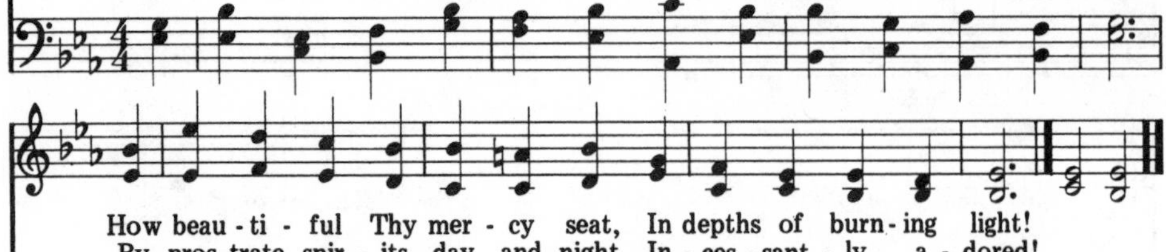

How beau - ti - ful Thy mer - cy seat, In depths of burn - ing light!
By pros-trate spir - its day and night In - ces - sant - ly a - dored!
Thine end - less wis - dom, bound-less pow'r And aw - ful pu - ri - ty!
And wor - ship Thee with trem-bling hope, And pen - i - ten - tial tears!
For Thou has stooped to ask of me The love of my poor heart! A-men.

WORDS: Frederick W. Faber, 1849
MUSIC: Thomas Ravenscroft's *Psalmes*, 1621

DUNDEE
C.M.

27 Let Us, with a Gladsome Mind

O give thanks unto the Lord, for He is good . . . Psa. 136:1

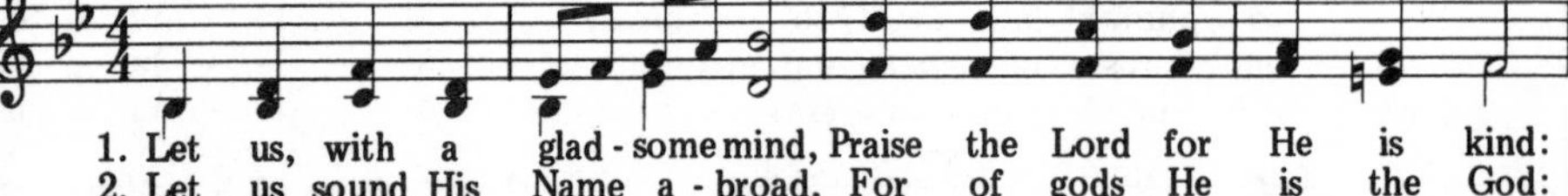

1. Let us, with a glad - some mind, Praise the Lord for He is kind:
2. Let us sound His Name a - broad, For of gods He is the God:
3. He with all - com - mand - ing might Filled the new - made world with light:
4. All things liv - ing He doth feed; His full hand sup - plies their need:
5. Let us then with glad - some mind, Praise the Lord for He is kind:

Refrain

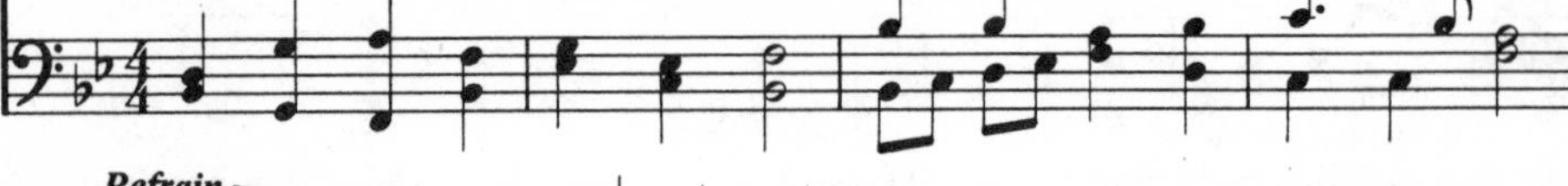

For His mer-cies shall en - dure, Ev - er faith - ful, ev - er sure. A-men.

WORDS: John Milton, 1623; based on Psalm 136
MUSIC: John Antes, c.1790; arr. John B. Wilkes, 1861

MONKLAND
7.7.7.7

Great Is Thy Faithfulness 28

His compassions fail not. They are new every morning. Lam. 3:22, 23

1. Great is Thy faith-ful-ness, O God my Fa-ther, There is no shad-ow of turn-ing with Thee; Thou chang-est not, Thy com-pas-sions they fail not; As Thou hast been Thou for-ev-er wilt be.
2. Sum-mer and win-ter, and springtime and har-vest, Sun, moon and stars in their cours-es a-bove Join with all na-ture in man-i-fold wit-ness To Thy great faith-ful-ness, mer-cy and love.
3. Par-don for sin and a peace that en-dur-eth, Thy own dear pres-ence to cheer and to guide; Strength for to-day and bright hope for to-mor-row, Bless-ings all mine, with ten thou-sand be-side!

Refrain

Great is Thy faith-ful-ness! Great is Thy faith-ful-ness! Morn-ing by morn-ing new mer-cies I see; All I have need-ed Thy hand hath pro-vid-ed—Great is Thy faith-ful-ness, Lord, un-to me!

WORDS: Thomas O. Chisholm, 1923
MUSIC: William M. Runyan, 1923

FAITHFULNESS
11.10.11.10 Ref.

29 The God of Abraham Praise

And God said unto Moses, I AM THAT I AM. Exo. 3:14

1. The God of A - braham praise, Who reigns en - throned a - bove;
2. He by Him - self hath sworn, I on His oath de - pend;
3. The God who reigns on high The great arch - an - gels sing,
4. The whole tri - um - phant host Give thanks to God on high;
An - cient of ev - er - last - ing days, And God of love.
I shall, on ea - gles' wings up - borne, To heav'n as - cend;
And "Ho - ly, ho - ly, ho - ly" cry, "Al - might - y King!"
"Hail, Fa - ther, Son and Ho - ly Ghost!" They ev - er cry.
Je - ho - vah, great I AM, By earth and heav'n con - fessed:
I shall be - hold His face, I shall His pow'r a - dore,
Who was and is the same, And ev - er - more shall be:
Hail, A-braham's God and mine! I join the heav'n - ly lays;
I bow and bless the sa - cred name For - ev - er blest.
And sing the won - ders of His grace For - ev - er - more.
Je - ho - vah, Fa - ther, great I AM, We wor - ship Thee.
All might and maj - es - ty are Thine, And end - less praise. A-men.

WORDS: Thomas Olivers, 1770; based on Jewish *Doxology*
MUSIC: Synagogue melody; arr. Meyer Lyon, 1770

LEONI
6.6.8.4 D.

Immortal, Invisible, God Only Wise 30

Unto the King eternal, immortal, invisible, the only wise God, be honor and glory . . . I Tim. 1:17

1. Im - mor - tal, in - vis - i - ble, God on - ly wise,
2. Un - rest - ing, un - hast - ing, and si - lent as light,
3. To all, life Thou giv - est, to both great and small,
4. Great Fa - ther of glo - ry, pure Fa - ther of light,

In light in - ac - ces - si - ble hid from our eyes,
Nor want - ing, nor wast - ing, Thou rul - est in might;
In all life Thou liv - est, the true life of all.
Thine an - gels a - dore Thee, all veil - ing their sight;

Most bless - ed, most glo - rious, the An - cient of Days,
Thy jus - tice like moun - tains high soar - ing a - bove
We blos - som and flour - ish as leaves on the tree,
All praise we would ren - der; O help us to see

Al - might - y, vic - to - rious, Thy great name we praise.
Thy clouds, which are foun - tains of good - ness and love.
And with - er and per - ish— but naught chang-eth Thee.
'Tis on - ly the splen - dor of light hid - eth Thee! A - men.

WORDS: Walter Chalmers Smith, 1867
MUSIC: Traditional Welsh hymn melody

ST. DENIO
11.11.11.11

31 A Pilgrim Was I and A-wandering

Surely goodness and mercy shall follow me all the days of my life. Psa. 23:6

1. A pilgrim was I and a-wand'ring, In the cold night of sin I did roam, When Jesus the kind Shepherd found me, And now I am on my way home.

2. He restoreth my soul when I'm weary, He giveth me strength day by day; He leads me beside the still waters, He guards me each step of the way.

3. When I walk thro' the dark lonesome valley, My Savior will walk with me there; And safely His great hand will lead me To the mansions He's gone to prepare.

Refrain

Surely goodness and mercy shall follow me All the days, all the days of my life; Surely goodness and mercy shall follow me All the days, all the days of my life.

Coda

And I shall dwell in the house of the Lord for - ev - er, And I shall feast at the ta - ble spread for me; Sure - ly good-ness and mer-cy shall fol - low me All the days, all the days of my life, All the days, all the days of my life.

WORDS and MUSIC: John W. Peterson and Alfred B. Smith, 1958; based on Psalm 23

SURELY GOODNESS AND MERCY
Irregular meter

The King of Love My Shepherd Is 32

I am the good shepherd . . . I lay down My life for the sheep. John 10:14, 15

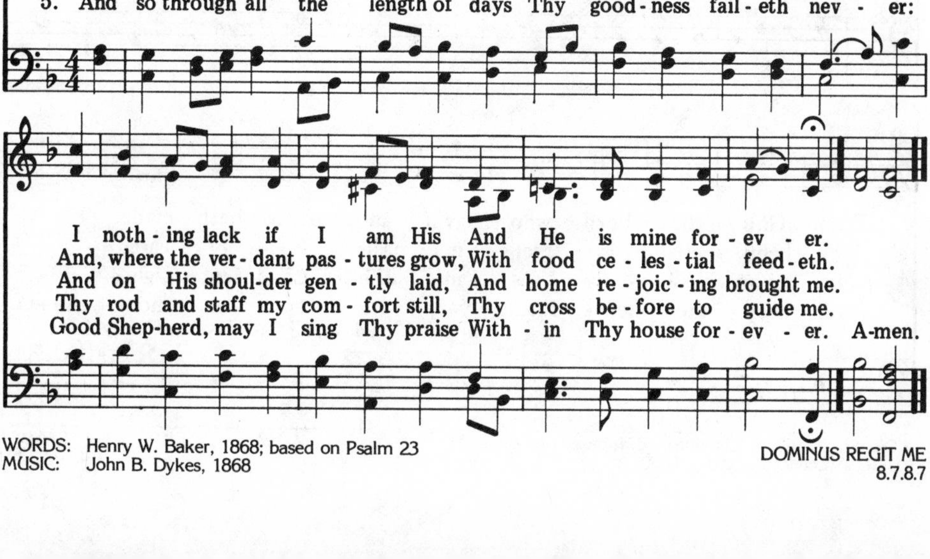

1. The King of love my Shep-herd is, Whose good-ness fail-eth nev - er; I noth-ing lack if I am His And He is mine for - ev - er.
2. Where streams of liv - ing wa - ter flow My ran-somed soul He lead - eth, And, where the ver-dant pas - tures grow, With food ce - les - tial feed-eth.
3. Per-verse and fool - ish oft I strayed But yet in love He sought me. And on His shoul-der gen - tly laid, And home re - joic - ing brought me.
4. In death's dark vale I fear no ill With Thee, dear Lord, be - side me; Thy rod and staff my com - fort still, Thy cross be - fore to guide me.
5. And so through all the length of days Thy good-ness fail-eth nev - er: Good Shep-herd, may I sing Thy praise With - in Thy house for - ev - er. A-men.

WORDS: Henry W. Baker, 1868; based on Psalm 23
MUSIC: John B. Dykes, 1868

DOMINUS REGIT ME
8.7.8.7

33 Unto the Hills Around

I will lift up mine eyes unto the hills. Psa. 121:1

1. Un - to the hills a - round do I lift up My long - ing eyes;
2. He will not suf - fer that thy foot be moved: Safe shalt thou be.
3. Je - ho - vah is Him - self thy keep - er true, Thy change-less shade;
4. From ev - ery e - vil shall He keep thy soul, From ev - ery sin;
O whence for me shall my sal - va - tion come, From whence a - rise?
No care - less slum - ber shall His eye - lids close, Who keep - eth thee.
Je - ho - vah thy de - fense on thy right hand Him - self hath made.
Je - ho - vah shall pre - serve thy go - ing out, Thy com - ing in.
From God the Lord doth come my cer - tain aid,
Be - hold our God the Lord, He slum - bereth ne'er,
And thee no sun by day shall ev - er smite;
A - bove thee watch - ing, He whom we a - dore
From God the Lord who heav'n and earth hath made.
Who keep - eth Is - rael in His ho - ly care.
No moon shall harm thee in the si - lent night.
Shall keep thee hence - forth, yea, for - ev - er - more. A-men.

WORDS: John D. S. Campbell, 1877; based on Psalm 121
MUSIC: Charles H. Purday, 1860

SANDON
10.4.10.4.10.10

Praise to the Lord, the Almighty 34

For then shalt thou have thy delight in the Almighty. Job 22:26

1. Praise to the Lord, the Al - might - y, the King of cre - a - tion! O my soul, praise Him, for He is thy health and sal - va - tion! All ye who hear, Now to His tem - ple draw near; Join me in glad ad - o - ra - tion!
2. Praise to the Lord, who o'er all things so won-drous - ly reign - eth, Shel - ters thee un - der His wings, yea, so gen - tly sus - tain - eth! Hast thou not seen How thy de - sires e'er have been Grant - ed in what He or - dain - eth?
3. Praise to the Lord, who doth pros - per thy work and de - fend thee; Sure - ly His good - ness and mer - cy here dai - ly at - tend thee. Pon - der a - new What the Al - might - y can do, If with His love He be - friend thee.
4. Praise to the Lord! O let all that is in me a - dore Him! All that hath life and breath, come now with prais - es be - fore Him! Let the A - men Sound from His peo - ple a - gain: Glad - ly for aye we a - dore Him. A - men.

WORDS: Joachim Neander, 1680; tr. Catherine Winkworth, 1863
MUSIC: *Stralsund Gesangbuch*, 1665

LOBE DEN HERREN
14.14.4.7.8

35 To God Be the Glory

Give unto the Lord the glory due unto His name. Psa. 29:2

1. To God be the glo - ry, great things He hath done, So loved He the world that He gave us His Son, Who yield-ed His life an a - tone-ment for sin, And o-pened the Life-gate that all may go in.
2. O per-fect re - demp-tion, the pur-chase of blood, To ev - ery be - liev - er the prom-ise of God; The vil - est of - fend - er who tru - ly be-lieves, That mo-ment from Je - sus a par-don re-ceives.
3. Great things He hath taught us, great things He hath done, And great our re-joic - ing thro' Je - sus the Son; But pur - er, and high - er, and great - er will be Our won-der, our trans-port, when Je - sus we see.
Refrain
Praise the Lord, praise the Lord, Let the earth hear His voice! Praise the Lord, praise the Lord, Let the peo - ple re - joice! O come to the Fa - ther thro' Je - sus the Son, And give Him the glo - ry, great things He hath done.

WORDS: Fanny J. Crosby, 1875
MUSIC: William H. Doane, 1875

TO GOD BE THE GLORY
11.11.11.11 Ref.

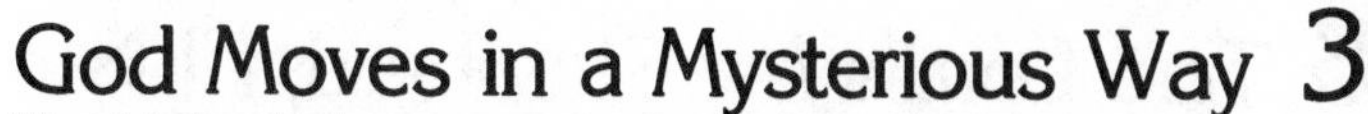

God Moves in a Mysterious Way 36

What I do thou knowest not now; but thou shalt know hereafter. John 13:7

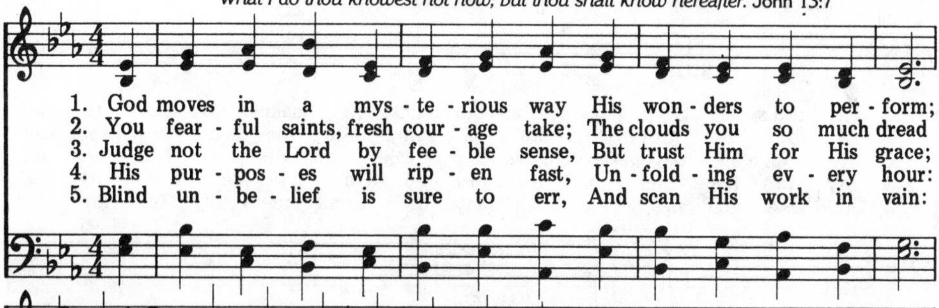

1. God moves in a mys - te - rious way His won - ders to per - form;
2. You fear - ful saints, fresh cour - age take; The clouds you so much dread
3. Judge not the Lord by fee - ble sense, But trust Him for His grace;
4. His pur - pos - es will rip - en fast, Un - fold - ing ev - ery hour:
5. Blind un - be - lief is sure to err, And scan His work in vain:

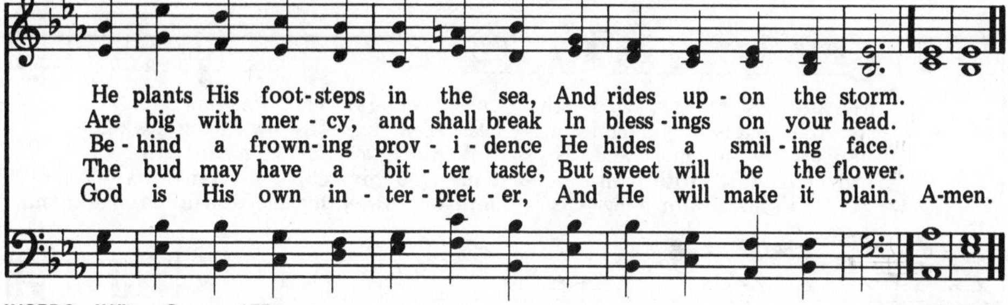

He plants His foot - steps in the sea, And rides up - on the storm.
Are big with mer - cy, and shall break In bless - ings on your head.
Be - hind a frown - ing prov - i - dence He hides a smil - ing face.
The bud may have a bit - ter taste, But sweet will be the flower.
God is His own in - ter - pret - er, And He will make it plain. A-men.

WORDS: William Cowper, 1774
MUSIC: Thomas Ravenscroft's *Psalmes*, 1621

DUNDEE
C.M.

Children of the Heavenly Father 37

As a father pitieth his children, so the Lord pitieth . . . Psa. 103:13

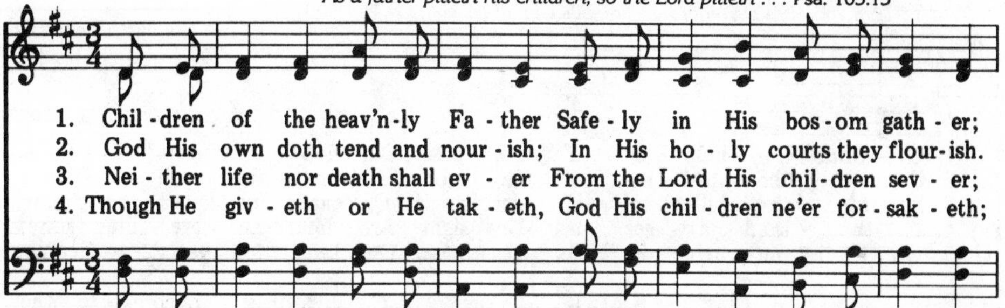

1. Chil - dren of the heav'n - ly Fa - ther Safe - ly in His bos - om gath - er;
2. God His own doth tend and nour - ish; In His ho - ly courts they flour - ish.
3. Nei - ther life nor death shall ev - er From the Lord His chil - dren sev - er;
4. Though He giv - eth or He tak - eth, God His chil - dren ne'er for - sak - eth;

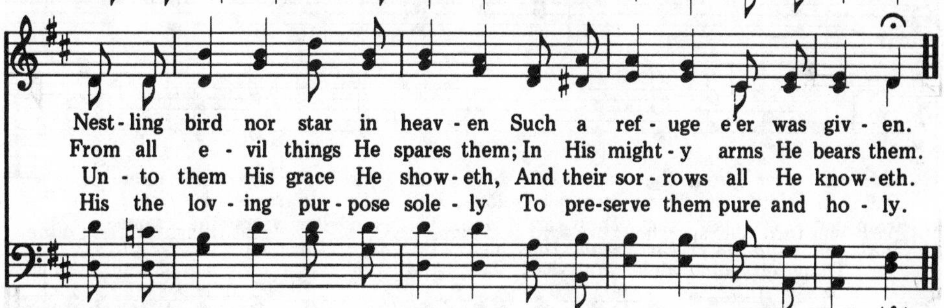

Nest - ling bird nor star in heav - en Such a ref - uge e'er was giv - en.
From all e - vil things He spares them; In His might - y arms He bears them.
Un - to them His grace He show - eth, And their sor - rows all He know - eth.
His the lov - ing pur - pose sole - ly To pre - serve them pure and ho - ly.

WORDS: Carolina Sandell Berg, 1858; tr. Ernst W. Olson, 1925
MUSIC: Traditional Swedish melody

TRYGGARE KAN INGEN VARA
L.M.

38 The Lord's My Shepherd, I'll Not Want

The Lord is my shepherd, I shall not want. Psa. 23:1

1. The Lord's my Shep - herd, I'll not want; He makes me down to lie
2. My soul He doth re - store a - gain; And me to walk doth make
3. Yea, though I walk through death's dark vale, Yet will I fear no ill;
4. My ta - ble Thou hast fur - nish - ed In pres - ence of my foes;
5. Good-ness and mer - cy all my life Shall sure - ly fol - low me;
In pas-tures green; He lead - eth me The qui - et wa - ters by.
With - in the paths of right-eous - ness, E'en for His own name's sake.
For Thou art with me, and Thy rod And staff me com - fort still.
My head Thou dost with oil a - noint, And my cup o - ver-flows.
And in God's house for - ev - er - more My dwell - ing place shall be. A-men.
WORDS: Scottish Psalter, 1650; William Whittingham and others; based on Psalm 23
MUSIC: Jessie S. Irvine, 1871; arr. David Grant, 1872
CRIMOND
C.M.
39 O God, Our Help in Ages Past
Lord, thou has been our dwelling place in all generations. Psa. 90:1
1. O God, our help in a - ges past, Our hope for years to come,
2. Un - der the shad - ow of Thy throne Still may we dwell se - cure;
3. Be - fore the hills in or - der stood, Or earth re - ceived her frame,
4. A thou - sand a - ges in Thy sight Are like an eve - ning gone;
5. O God, our help in a - ges past, Our hope for years to come,
Our shel - ter from the storm - y blast, And our e - ter - nal home!
Suf - fi - cient is Thine arm a - lone, And our de - fense is sure.
From ev - er - last - ing Thou art God, To end - less years the same.
Short as the watch that ends the night, Be - fore the ris - ing sun.
Be Thou our guide while life shall last, And our e - ter - nal home! A-men.

WORDS: Isaac Watts, 1719; based on Psalm 90
MUSIC: William Croft, 1708

ST. ANNE
C.M.

God Be with You till We Meet Again 40

And now, brethren, I commend you to God . . . Acts 20:32
1. God be with you till we meet a - gain; By His coun-sels guide, up-hold you, With His sheep se - cure - ly fold you; God be with you till we meet a - gain.
2. God be with you till we meet a - gain; 'Neath His wings pro-tect-ing hide you, Dai - ly man - na still pro-vide you; God be with you till we meet a - gain.
3. God be with you till we meet a - gain; When life's per-ils thick con-found you, Put His arms un - fail - ing round you; God be with you till we meet a - gain.
4. God be with you till we meet a - gain; Keep love's ban-ner float-ing o'er you, Smite death's threat'ning wave before you; God be with you till we meet a - gain.
WORDS: Jeremiah E. Rankin, 1880
MUSIC: William G. Tomer, 1880
GOD BE WITH YOU
Irregular meter
God Be with You till We Meet Again 41
And now, brethren, I commend you to God . . . Acts 20:32
Unison
(Parts)
(Unison)
1. God be with you till we meet a - gain; By His coun - sels guide, up - hold you, With His sheep se - cure - ly fold you; God be with you till we meet a - gain.
2. God be with you till we meet a - gain; 'Neath His wings pro - tect - ing hide you, Dai - ly man - na still pro - vide you; God be with you till we meet a - gain.
3. God be with you till we meet a - gain; When life's per - ils thick con - found you, Put His lov - ing arms a - round you; God be with you till we meet a - gain.
4. God be with you till we meet a - gain; Keep love's ban - ner float - ing o'er you, Smite death's threat - 'ning wave be - fore you; God be with you till we meet a - gain.

WORDS: Jeremiah E. Rankin, 1880
MUSIC: Ralph Vaughan Williams, 1906

RANDOLPH
Irregular meter

42 All Things Bright and Beautiful

All things were made by Him . . . John 1:3

Unison

(Ref.) All things bright and beau - ti - ful, All crea - tures great and small,
All things wise and won - der - ful; The Lord God made them all.

Fine

1. Each lit - tle flow'r that o - pens, Each lit - tle bird that sings,
He made their glow-ing col - ors, He made their ti - ny wings.

2. The pur - ple - head - ed moun - tain, The riv - er run - ning by,
The sun - set, and the morn - ing That bright - ens up the sky.

3. The cold wind in the win - ter, The pleas - ant sum - mer sun,
The ripe fruits in the gar - den: He made them, ev - ery one.

4. He gave us eyes to see them, And lips that we might tell
How great is God Al - might - y, Who has made all things well.

D.C. Refrain

WORDS: Cecil F. Alexander, 1848
MUSIC: Traditional English melody

ROYAL OAK
7.6.7.6 D.

All Creatures of Our God and King 43

All Thy works shall praise Thee, O Lord. Psa. 145:10

1. All crea-tures of our God and King, Lift up your voice and with us sing
2. Thou rush-ing wind that art so strong, Ye clouds that sail in heav'n a - long,
3. Thou flow-ing wa-ter, pure and clear, Make mu-sic for thy Lord to hear,
4. And all ye men of ten-der heart, For-giv - ing oth - ers, take your part,
5. Let all things their Cre-a - tor bless, And wor-ship Him in hum-ble - ness,
Al-le - lu - ia, Al-le - lu - ia! Thou burn-ing sun with gold - en beam,
O praise Him, Al-le - lu - ia! Thou ris - ing morn in praise re - joice,
Al-le - lu - ia, Al-le - lu - ia! Thou fire so mas - ter - ful and bright,
O sing ye, Al-le - lu - ia! Ye who long pain and sor - row bear,
O praise Him, Al-le - lu - ia! Praise, praise the Fa - ther, praise the Son,
Thou sil - ver moon with soft - er gleam, O praise Him, O praise Him,
Ye lights of eve - ning, find a voice, O praise Him, O praise Him,
That giv - est man both warmth and light, O praise Him, O praise Him,
Praise God and on Him cast your care, O praise Him, O praise Him,
And praise the Spir - it, three in one, O praise Him, O praise Him,
Al-le - lu - ia, al - le - lu - ia, al - le - lu - ia!
Al-le - lu - ia, al - le - lu - ia, al - le - lu - ia!
Al-le - lu - ia, al - le - lu - ia, al - le - lu - ia!
Al-le - lu - ia, al - le - lu - ia, al - le - lu - ia!
Al-le - lu - ia, al - le - lu - ia, al - le - lu - ia! A - men.

WORDS: St. Francis of Assisi, 1225; tr. William H. Draper, 1926
MUSIC: *Geistliche Kirchengesäng,* Cologne, 1623

LASST UNS ERFREUEN
L.M. Alleluias

44 God, Who Stretched the Spangled Heavens

. . . Who stretchest out the heavens like a curtain. Psa. 104:2

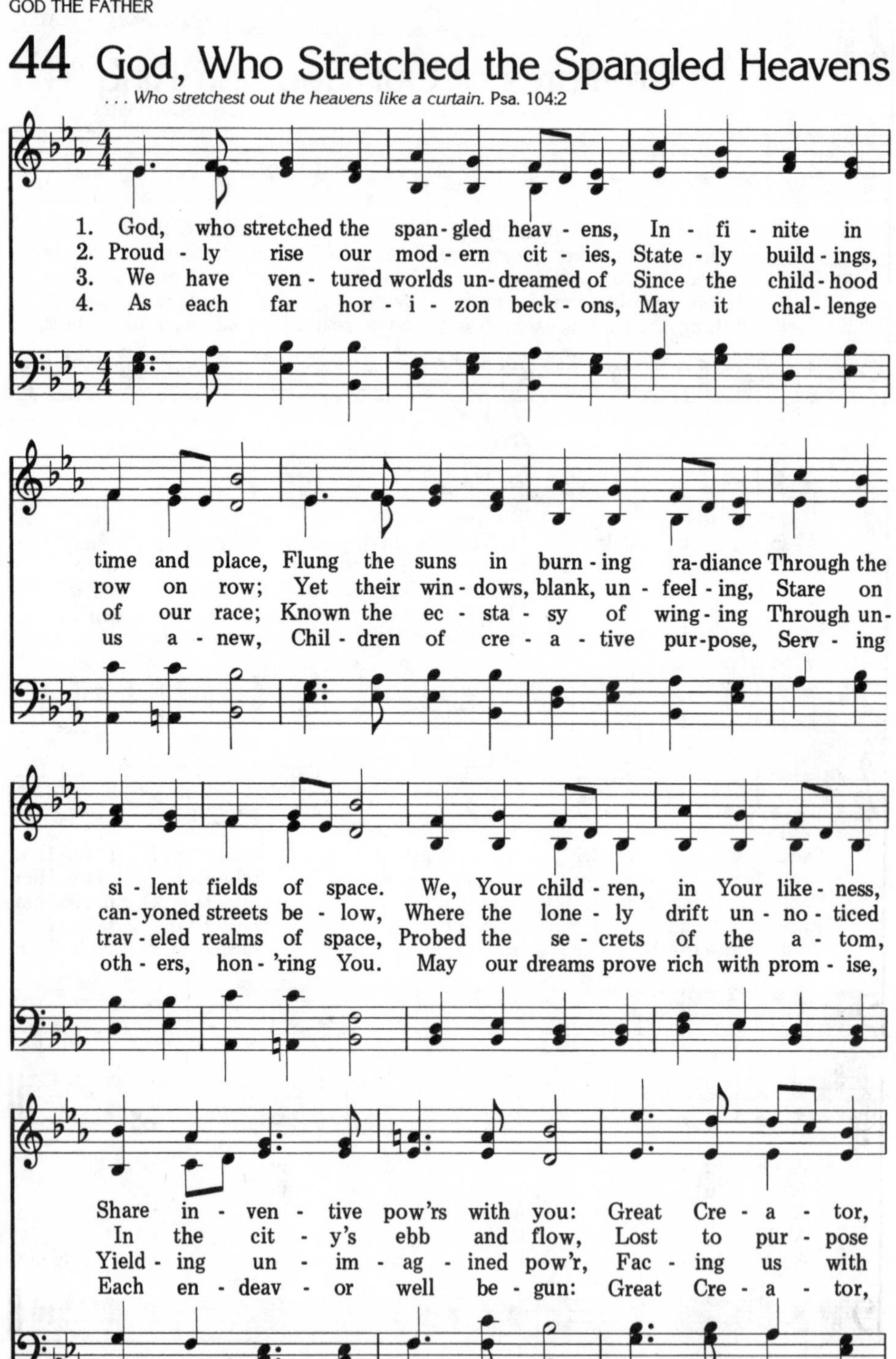
1. God, who stretched the span-gled heav-ens, In-fi-nite in
2. Proud-ly rise our mod-ern cit-ies, State-ly build-ings,
3. We have ven-tured worlds un-dreamed of Since the child-hood
4. As each far hor-i-zon beck-ons, May it chal-lenge
time and place, Flung the suns in burn-ing ra-diance Through the
row on row; Yet their win-dows, blank, un-feel-ing, Stare on
of our race; Known the ec-sta-sy of wing-ing Through un-
us a-new, Chil-dren of cre-a-tive pur-pose, Serv-ing
si-lent fields of space. We, Your child-ren, in Your like-ness,
can-yoned streets be-low, Where the lone-ly drift un-no-ticed
trav-eled realms of space, Probed the se-crets of the a-tom,
oth-ers, hon-'ring You. May our dreams prove rich with prom-ise,
Share in-ven-tive pow'rs with you: Great Cre-a-tor,
In the cit-y's ebb and flow, Lost to pur-pose
Yield-ing un-im-ag-ined pow'r, Fac-ing us with
Each en-deav-or well be-gun: Great Cre-a-tor,

still cre - a - ting, Show us what we yet may do.
and to mean - ing, Scarce - ly car - ing where they go.
life's de - struc - tion Or our most tri - umph - ant hour.
give us guid - ance Till our goals and Yours are one.

AUSTRIAN HYMN
8.7.8.7 D.

WORDS: Catherine Cameron, 1965
MUSIC: Franz Joseph Haydn, 1797

We Search the Starlit Milky Way 45

The fool hath said in his heart, there is no God. Psa. 14:1

1. We search the star - lit Milk - y Way, A mil - lion worlds in rhyth - mic sway, Yet in our blind - ness some will say, "There is no God con - trol - ling!"
2. But as I grope from sphere to sphere, New won - ders crowd the eye, the ear, And faith grows firm - er ev - ery year: "My God is there con - trol - ling!"
3. We probe the a - toms for their cause, Ex - plore the earth for na - ture's laws, Yet sel - dom in our search - ing pause To think of God con - trol - ling!
4. Each flash of fact from out the night, Each burst of truth up - on my sight That quick - ens awe or adds de - light, Re - veals my God con - trol - ling!

GERMANY
L.M.

WORDS: William W. Reid, Jr., 1963
MUSIC: William Gardiner's *Sacred Melodies*, 1815

46 The Spacious Firmament on High

The heavens declare the glory of God, and the firmament showeth His handiwork. Psa.19:1

1. The spa-cious fir - ma - ment on high, With all the blue e - the-real
2. Soon as the eve - ning shades pre - vail, The moon takes up the won-drous
3. What though in sol - emn si - lence all Move round the dark ter - res - trial

sky, And span-gled heav'ns, a shin - ing frame, Their great O - rig - i - nal pro-
tale; And night - ly to the lis-tening earth Re - peats the sto - ry of her
ball? What though no re - al voice nor sound A - mid their ra - diant orbs be

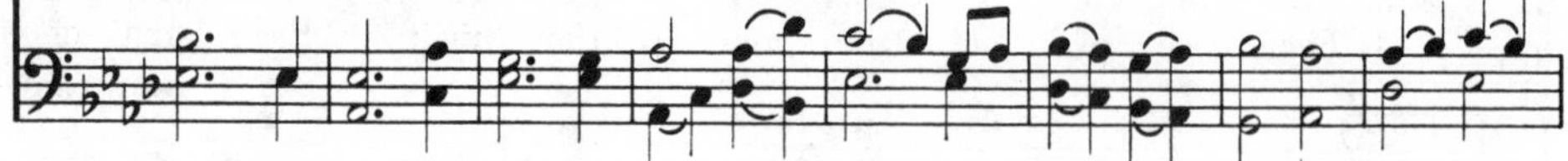

claim. Th'unwearied sun, from day to day, Does his Cre - a - tor's pow'r dis-play; And
birth; While all the stars that round her burn, And all the plan - ets in their turn, Con-
found? In rea-son's ear they all re-joice, And ut - ter forth a glo-rious voice, For-

pub - lish - es to ev - ery land The work of an al-might-y hand.
firm the ti - dings as they roll, And spread the truth from pole to pole.
ev - er sing - ing as they shine, "The hand that made us is di-vine." A-men.

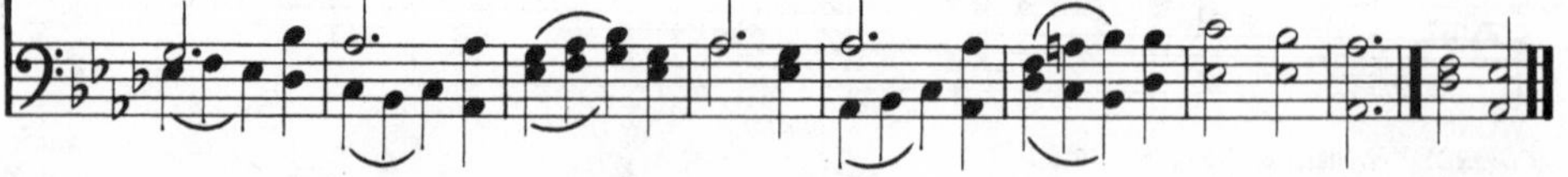

WORDS: Joseph Addison, 1712; based on Psalm 19
MUSIC: Franz Joseph Haydn, 1798

CREATION
L.M.D.

There's the Wonder of Sunset 47

What is man that Thou art mindful of him? Psa. 8:4

1. There's the won - der of sun - set at eve - ning, The won - der as
2. There's the won - der of spring - time and har - vest, The sky, the
sun - rise I see; But the won - der of won - ders that thrills my soul
stars, the sun; But the won - der of won - ders that thrills my soul
Is the won - der that God loves me.
Is a won - der that's on - ly be - gun.
Refrain
O, the won - der of it all! The
won - der of it all! Just to think that God loves me.
O, the won - der of it
all! The won - der of it all! Just to think that God loves me.

WORDS and MUSIC: George Beverly Shea, 1956

WONDER OF IT ALL
Irregular meter

48 I Sing the Almighty Power of God

O come, let us worship . . . let us kneel before the Lord our maker. Psa. 95:6

1. I sing th'al-might - y pow'r of God That made the moun - tains rise,
2. I sing the good - ness of the Lord That filled the earth with food;
3. There's not a plant or flow'r be - low But makes Thy glo - ries known;
That spread the flow - ing seas a - broad And built the loft - y skies.
He formed the crea - tures with His word And then pro-nounced them good.
And clouds a - rise and tem-pests blow By or - der from Thy throne;
I sing the wis - dom that or-dained The sun to rule the day;
Lord, how Thy won - ders are dis-played Where - e'er I turn my eye,
While all that bor - rows life from Thee Is ev - er in Thy care,
The moon shines full at His com-mand And all the stars o - bey.
If I sur - vey the ground I tread Or gaze up - on the sky!
And ev - ery-where that man can be, Thou, God, art pres - ent there.

WORDS: Isaac Watts, 1715
MUSIC: Traditional English melody; arr. Ralph Vaughan Williams, 1906

FOREST GREEN
C.M.D.

For the Beauty of the Earth 49

Every good gift and every perfect gift is from above. James 1:17

1. For the beau - ty of the earth, For the glo - ry of the skies, For the love which from our birth O - ver and a - round us lies, Lord of all, to Thee we raise This our hymn of grate - ful praise.
2. For the beau - ty of each hour Of the day and of the night, Hill and vale, and tree, and flow'r, Sun and moon and stars of light, Lord of all, to Thee we raise This our hymn of grate - ful praise.
3. For the joy of ear and eye, For the heart and mind's de - light, For the mys - tic har - mo - ny Link - ing sense to sound and sight, Lord of all, to Thee we raise This our hymn of grate - ful praise.
4. For the joy of hu - man love, Broth - er, sis - ter, par - ent, child, Friends on earth and friends a - bove, For all gen - tle thoughts and mild, Lord of all, to Thee we raise This our hymn of grate - ful praise.
5. For each per - fect gift of Thine To our race so free - ly giv'n, Grac - es hu - man and di - vine, Flow'rs of earth and buds of heav'n, Lord of all, to Thee we raise This our hymn of grate - ful praise. A - men.

WORDS: Folliott S. Pierpoint, 1864
MUSIC: Conrad Kocher, 1838; arr. William H. Monk, 1861

DIX
7.7.7.7.7.7

50 This Is My Father's World

The morning stars sang together, and all the sons of God shouted for joy. Job 38:7

1. This is my Fa-ther's world, And to my lis-tening ears All
2. This is my Fa-ther's world, The birds their car-ols raise, The
3. This is my Fa-ther's world, O let me ne'er for-get That
na-ture sings, and round me rings The mu-sic of the spheres.
morn-ing light, the lil-y white, De-clare their Mak-er's praise.
though the wrong seems oft so strong, God is the Rul-er yet.
This is my Fa-ther's world: I rest me in the thought Of
This is my Fa-ther's world: He shines in all that's fair; In the
This is my Fa-ther's world: Why should my heart be sad? The
rocks and trees, of skies and seas—His hand the won-ders wrought.
rus-tling grass I hear Him pass, He speaks to me ev-ery-where.
Lord is King: let the heav-ens ring! God reigns: let earth be glad! A-men.

WORDS: Maltbie D. Babcock, 1901
MUSIC: Franklin L. Sheppard, 1915

TERRA BEATA
S.M.D.

Hymns of Jesus Christ

51 At the Name of Jesus

That at the name of Jesus every knee should bow . . . Phil. 2:10

1. At the name of Je - sus Ev - ery knee shall bow,
2. At His voice cre - a - tion Sprang at once to sight,
3. Hum - bled for a sea - son, To re - ceive a name
4. In your hearts en - throne Him; There let Him sub - due
5. Broth - ers, this Lord Je - sus Shall re - turn a - gain,
Ev - ery tongue con - fess Him King of Glo - ry now;
All the an - gel fac - es, All the hosts of light,
From the lips of sin - ners, Un - to whom He came,
All that is not ho - ly, All that is not true:
With His Fa - ther's glo - ry O'er the earth to reign;
'Tis the Fa - ther's pleas - ure We should call Him Lord,
Thrones and dom - i - na - tions, Stars up - on their way,
Faith - ful - ly He bore it Spot - less to the last,
Crown Him as your Cap - tain In temp - ta - tion's hour;
For all wreaths of em - pire Meet up - on His brow,
Who from the be - gin - ning Was the might - y Word.
All the heav'n - ly or - ders In their great ar - ray.
Brought it back vic - to - rious, When from death He passed.
Let His will en - fold you In its light and power.
And our hearts con - fess Him King of Glo - ry now. A - men.

WORDS: Caroline M. Noel, 1870; based on Phillippians 2:5-11
MUSIC: Ralph Vaughan Williams, 1925

KING'S WESTON
6.5.6.5 D.

All Hail the Power of Jesus' Name 52

He hath . . . a name written, King of Kings, and Lord of Lords. Rev. 19:16

1. All hail the pow'r of Je - sus' name! Let an - gels pros-trate
2. Ye cho - sen seed of Is - rael's race, Ye ran-somed of the
3. Let ev - ery kin - dred, ev - ery tribe, On this ter - res - trial
4. O that with yon - der sa - cred throng We at His feet may
fall, Let an - gels pros-trate fall; Bring forth the roy - al di - a-
fall, Ye ran - somed of the fall; Hail Him who saves you by His
ball, On this ter - res - trial ball; To Him all maj - es - ty as-
fall, We at His feet may fall! We'll join the ev - er - last - ing
dem,
grace, And crown Him, crown Him,
cribe,
song,
And crown Him, crown Him, crown Him, crown Him, crown Him,
crown
crown Him, crown Him, And crown Him Lord of all. A-men.
Him, And crown Him

WORDS: Edward Perronet, 1779; adapt. John Rippon, 1787
MUSIC: James Ellor, 1838

DIADEM
C.M. Ref.

53 All Hail the Power of Jesus' Name

He hath . . . a name written, King of Kings, and Lord of Lords. Rev. 19:16

1. All hail the power of Je - sus' name! Let an - gels pros - trate fall;
2. Ye cho - sen seed of Is - rael's race, Ye ran - somed from the fall,
3. Let ev - ery kin - dred, ev - ery tribe, On this ter - res - trial ball,
4. O that with yon - der sa - cred throng We at His feet may fall!
Bring forth the roy - al di - a - dem, And crown Him Lord of all;
Hail Him who saves you by His grace, And crown Him Lord of all;
To Him all maj - es - ty as - cribe, And crown Him Lord of all;
We'll join the ev - er - last - ing song, And crown Him Lord of all;
Bring forth the roy - al di - a - dem, And crown Him Lord of all!
Hail Him who saves you by His grace, And crown Him Lord of all!
To Him all maj - es - ty as - cribe, And crown Him Lord of all!
We'll join the ev - er - last - ing song, And crown Him Lord of all!

WORDS: Edward Perronet, 1779; adapt. John Rippon, 1787
MUSIC: Oliver Holden, 1792

CORONATION
C.M. Repeats

(Second Tune)
1. All hail the power of Je - sus' name! Let angels pros-trate fall; Bring forth the roy - al
di - a - dem, And crown Him, crown Him, crown Him, Crown Him Lord of all!

WORDS: Edward Perronet, 1779; adapt. John Rippon, 1787
MUSIC: William Shrubsole, 1779

MILES LANE
C.M. Repeats

He Is Lord, He Is Lord 54

And that every tongue should confess that Jesus Christ is Lord. Phil. 2:11

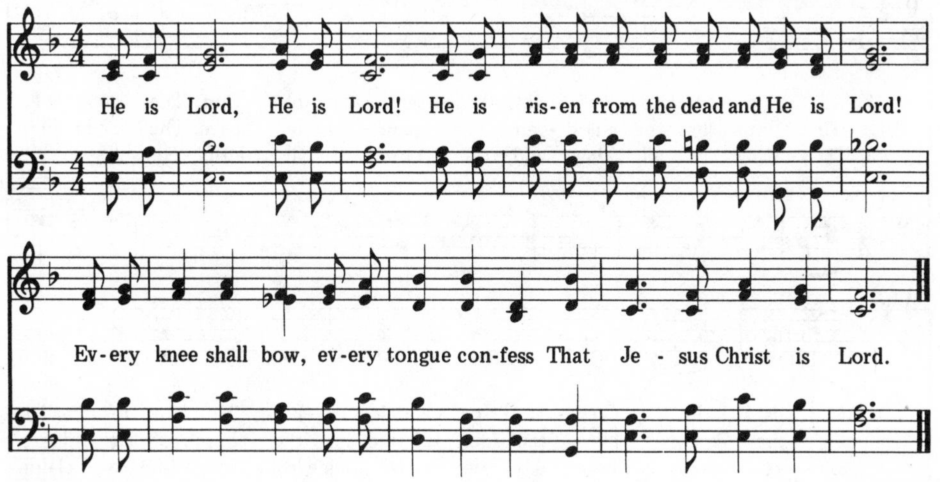
He is Lord, He is Lord! He is ris-en from the dead and He is Lord!
Ev-ery knee shall bow, ev-ery tongue con-fess That Je - sus Christ is Lord.

WORDS: Based on Philippians 2:11
MUSIC: Composer unknown

HE IS LORD
Irregular meter

Jesus, the Very Thought of Thee 55

In whom, though now ye see Him not . . . ye rejoice. I Pet. 1:8

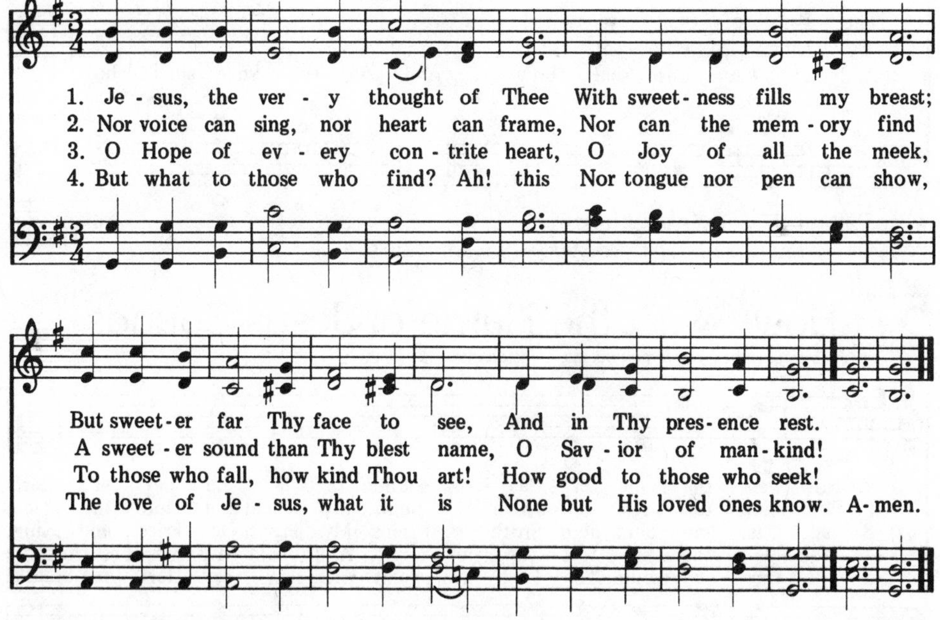
1. Je - sus, the ver - y thought of Thee With sweet-ness fills my breast;
2. Nor voice can sing, nor heart can frame, Nor can the mem - ory find
3. O Hope of ev - ery con - trite heart, O Joy of all the meek,
4. But what to those who find? Ah! this Nor tongue nor pen can show,
But sweet-er far Thy face to see, And in Thy pres-ence rest.
A sweet - er sound than Thy blest name, O Sav - ior of man-kind!
To those who fall, how kind Thou art! How good to those who seek!
The love of Je - sus, what it is None but His loved ones know. A-men.

WORDS: Attr. Bernard of Clairvaux, c.1150; tr. Edward Caswall, 1849
MUSIC: John B. Dykes, 1866

ST. AGNES
C.M.

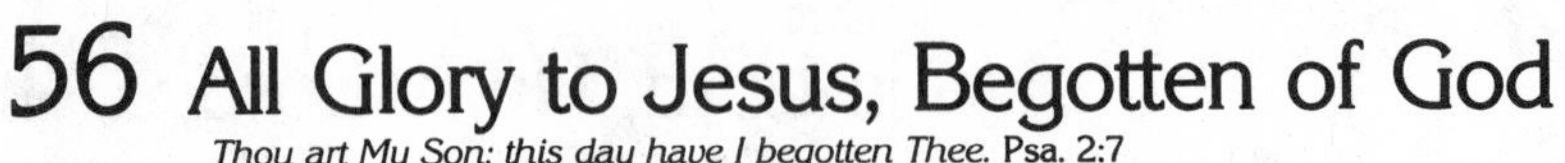

56 All Glory to Jesus, Begotten of God

Thou art My Son; this day have I begotten Thee. Psa. 2:7

1. All glo - ry to Je - sus, be - got - ten of God, The great I
2. To think that the guard - ian of plan - ets in space, The Shep - herd
3. The King of all kings and the Lord of all lords, He reigns in

AM is He; Cre - a - tor, sus - tain - er—but won - der of all,
of the stars, Is ten - der - ly lead - ing the church of His love,
glo - ry now; Some day He is com - ing earth's king - dom to claim,

CODA after last verse

The Lamb of Cal - va - ry!
By hands with crim - son scars!
And ev - ery knee shall bow! And ev - ery knee shall bow!

WORDS and MUSIC: John W. Peterson, 1957

RIDGEMOOR
11.6.11.6

57 How Sweet the Name of Jesus Sounds

Unto you therefore which believe He is precious . . . I Pet. 2:7

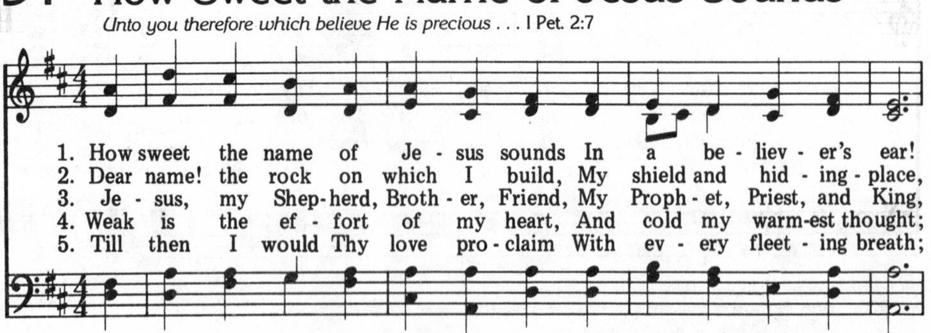
1. How sweet the name of Je - sus sounds In a be - liev - er's ear!
2. Dear name! the rock on which I build, My shield and hid - ing - place,
3. Je - sus, my Shep - herd, Broth - er, Friend, My Proph - et, Priest, and King,
4. Weak is the ef - fort of my heart, And cold my warm - est thought;
5. Till then I would Thy love pro - claim With ev - ery fleet - ing breath;

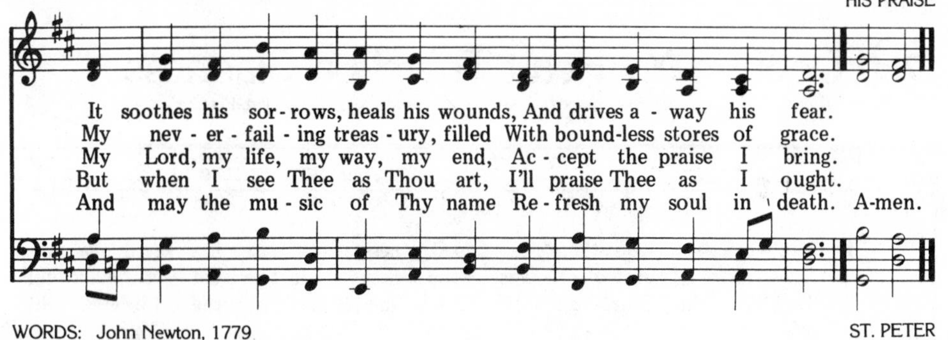
It soothes his sor-rows, heals his wounds, And drives a-way his fear.
My nev-er-fail-ing treas-ury, filled With bound-less stores of grace.
My Lord, my life, my way, my end, Ac-cept the praise I bring.
But when I see Thee as Thou art, I'll praise Thee as I ought.
And may the mu-sic of Thy name Re-fresh my soul in death. A-men.

WORDS: John Newton, 1779
MUSIC: Alexander R. Reinagle, c.1836

ST. PETER
C.M.

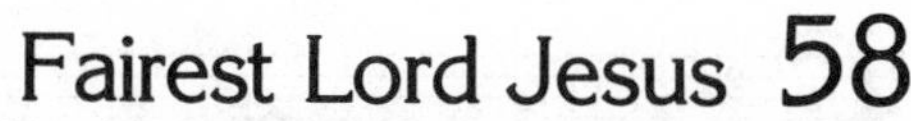

Fairest Lord Jesus 58

Thou art fairer than the children of men . . . Psa. 45:2

1. Fair-est Lord Je-sus! Ru-ler of all na-ture,
2. Fair are the mead-ows, Fair-er still the wood-lands,
3. Fair is the sun-shine, Fair-er still the moon-light,
4. Beau-ti-ful Sav-ior! Lord of the na-tions!

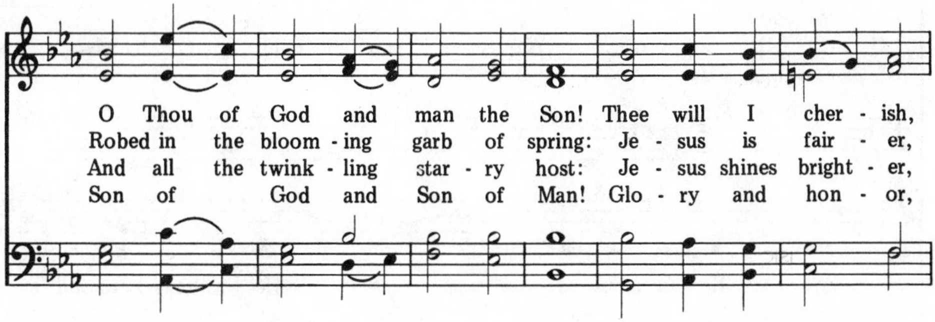

O Thou of God and man the Son! Thee will I cher-ish,
Robed in the bloom-ing garb of spring: Je-sus is fair-er,
And all the twink-ling star-ry host: Je-sus shines bright-er,
Son of God and Son of Man! Glo-ry and hon-or,

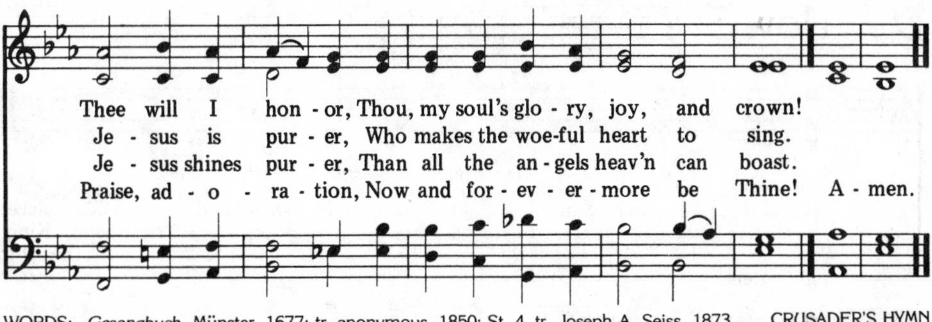

Thee will I hon-or, Thou, my soul's glo-ry, joy, and crown!
Je-sus is pur-er, Who makes the woe-ful heart to sing.
Je-sus shines pur-er, Than all the an-gels heav'n can boast.
Praise, ad-o-ra-tion, Now and for-ev-er-more be Thine! A-men.

WORDS: *Gesangbuch,* Münster, 1677; tr. anonymous, 1850; St. 4, tr. Joseph A. Seiss, 1873
MUSIC: H. A. Hoffman von Fallersleben's *Schlesische Volkslieder,* 1842; arr. Richard S. Willis, 1850

CRUSADER'S HYMN
5.6.8.5.5.8

59 Deep in My Heart There's a Gladness

Therefore my heart greatly rejoiceth; and with my song will I praise Him. Psa. 28:7

1. Deep in my heart there's a glad - ness, Je - sus has saved me from
2. On - ly a glimpse of His good - ness, That was suf - fi - cient for
3. He is the fair - est of fair ones, He is the Lil - y, the

sin! Praise to His name—what a Sav - ior! Cleans - ing with-
me; On - ly one look at the Sav - ior, Then was my
Rose; Riv - ers of mer - cy sur - round Him, Grace, love and

out and with - in.
spir - it set free.
pit - y He shows.

Refrain – Unison or Two Parts

Why do I sing a - bout Je - sus?

Why is He pre-cious to me? He is my Lord and my

Sav - ior, Dy - ing! He set me free!
(set me free!)

WORDS and MUSIC: Albert A. Ketchum, 1923

KETCHUM
8.7.8.7 Ref.

Take the Name of Jesus with You 60

. . . Do all in the name of the Lord Jesus. Col. 3:17

1. Take the name of Je - sus with you, Child of sor - row and of
2. Take the name of Je - sus ev - er, As a shield from ev - ery
3. O the pre - cious name of Je - sus! How it thrills our souls with
4. At the name of Je - sus bow - ing, Fall - ing pros - trate at His

woe; It will joy and com - fort give you, Take it,
snare; If temp - ta - tions 'round you gath - er, Breathe that
joy, When His lov - ing arms re - ceive us, And His
feet, King of kings in heav'n we'll crown Him, When our

Refrain

then, wher - e'er you go.
ho - ly name in prayer. Pre - cious name, O how
songs our tongues em - ploy. Pre - cious name,
jour - ney is com - plete.

sweet! Hope of earth and joy of heav'n; Pre - cious
O how sweet!

name, O how sweet! Hope of earth and joy of heav'n.
Pre-cious name, O how sweet, how sweet!

WORDS: Lydia Baxter, 1870
MUSIC: William H. Doane, 1871

PRECIOUS NAME
8.7.8.7 Ref.

61 I Love Thee, I Love Thee

O love the Lord, all ye His saints. Psa. 31:23

1. I love Thee, I love Thee, I love Thee, my Lord;
I love Thee, my Savior, I love Thee, my God;
I love Thee, I love Thee, and that Thou dost know;
But how much I love Thee my actions will show.
2. I'm happy, I'm happy, O wondrous account!
My joys are immortal, I stand on the mount;
I gaze on my treasure and long to be there,
With Jesus and angels and kindred so dear.
3. O Jesus, my Savior, with Thee I am blest,
My life and salvation, my joy and my rest;
Thy name be my theme, and Thy love be my song;
Thy grace shall inspire both my heart and my tongue.
4. O, who's like my Savior? He's Salem's bright King;
He smiles and He loves me and helps me to sing;
I'll praise Him, I'll praise Him with notes loud and clear,
While rivers of pleasure my spirit shall cheer.
A-men.

WORDS: Source unknown
MUSIC: Ingalls' *Christian Harmony*, 1805

I LOVE THEE
11.11.11.11

Christ Has for Sin Atonement Made 62

. . . And know that this is indeed the Christ, the Savior of the world. John 4:42

1. Christ has for sin a - tone-ment made, What a won-der-ful Sav - ior!
2. I praise Him for the cleans-ing blood, What a won-der-ful Sav - ior!
3. He cleansed my heart from all its sin, What a won-der-ful Sav - ior!
4. He walks be - side me in the way, What a won-der-ful Sav - ior!
We are re-deemed! the price is paid! What a won - der - ful Sav - ior!
That rec - on-ciled my soul to God; What a won - der - ful Sav - ior!
And now He reigns and rules there-in; What a won - der - ful Sav - ior!
And keeps me faith - ful day by day, What a won - der - ful Sav - ior!
Refrain
What a won - der - ful Sav - ior is Je - sus, my Je - sus!
What a won - der - ful Sav - ior is Je - sus, my Lord!

WORDS and MUSIC: Elisha A. Hoffman, 1891

BENTON HARBOR
8.7.8.7 Ref.

63 Praise Him! Praise Him!

Praise Him according to His excellent greatness. Psa. 150:2

1. Praise Him! praise Him! Je - sus, our bless - ed Re - deem - er! Sing, O Earth, His
2. Praise Him! praise Him! Je - sus, our bless - ed Re - deem - er! For our sins He
3. Praise Him! praise Him! Je - sus, our bless - ed Re - deem - er! Heav'n - ly por - tals
won - der - ful love pro - claim! Hail Him! hail Him! high-est arch - an - gels in glo - ry;
suf - fered, and bled and died; He our Rock, our hope of e - ter - nal sal - va - tion,
loud with ho - san - nas ring! Je - sus, Sav - ior, reign-eth for - ev - er and ev - er;
Strength and hon - or give to His ho - ly name! Like a shep - herd Je - sus will
Hail Him! hail Him! Je - sus the Cru - ci - fied. Sound His prais - es! Je - sus who
Crown Him! crown Him! Proph - et and Priest and King! Christ is com - ing! o - ver the
guard His chil - dren, In His arms He car - ries them all day long:
bore our sor - rows; Love un - bound - ed, won - der - ful, deep and strong:
world vic - to - rious, Pow'r and glo - ry un - to the Lord be - long:
Refrain
Praise Him! praise Him!

HIS PRAISE
tell of His ex - cel - lent great - ness; Praise Him! praise Him! ev - er in joy - ful song!

WORDS: Fanny J. Crosby, 1869
MUSIC: Chester G. Allen, 1869

JOYFUL SONG
Irregular meter

Jesus, Thou Joy of Loving Hearts 64

He . . . filleth the hungry soul with goodness. Psa. 107:9

1. Je - sus, Thou Joy of lov - ing hearts, Thou Fount of
2. Thy truth un - changed hath ev - er stood; Thou sav - est
3. We taste Thee, O Thou liv - ing Bread, And long to
4. Our rest - less spir - its yearn for Thee, Where - e'er our
5. O Je - sus, ev - er with us stay, Make all our

life, Thou Light of men, From the best bliss that earth im -
those that on Thee call; To them that seek Thee, Thou art
feast up - on Thee still; We drink of Thee, the Foun - tain -
change - ful lot is cast; Glad, when Thy gra - cious smile we
mo - ments calm and bright; Chase the dark night of sin a -

parts, We turn un - filled to Thee a - gain.
good, To them that find Thee, all in all.
head, And thirst our souls from Thee to fill.
see, Blest, when our faith can hold Thee fast.
way, Shed o'er the world Thy ho - ly light. A - men.

WORDS: Attr. Bernard of Clairvaux, c.1150; tr. Ray Palmer, 1858
MUSIC: Henry Baker, 1854

QUEBEC
L.M.

65 Majestic Sweetness Sits Enthroned

But we see Jesus . . . crowned with glory and honor. Heb. 2:9

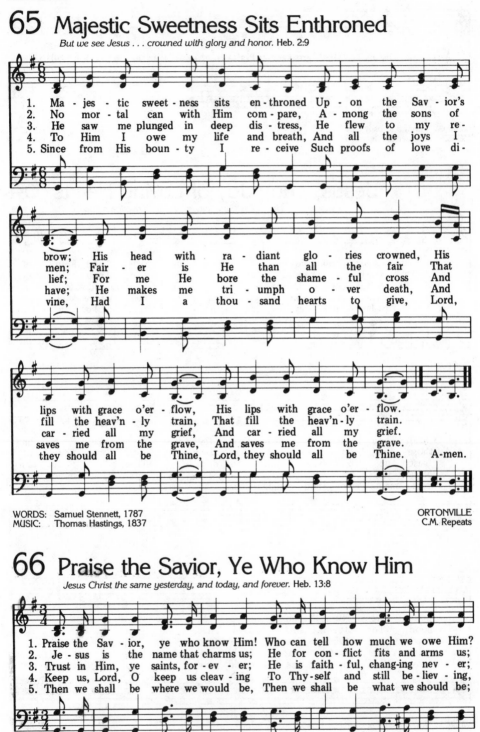

1. Ma - jes - tic sweet - ness sits en - throned Up - on the Sav - ior's
2. No mor - tal can with Him com - pare, A - mong the sons of
3. He saw me plunged in deep dis - tress, He flew to my re -
4. To Him I owe my life and breath, And all the joys I
5. Since from His boun - ty I re - ceive Such proofs of love di -
brow; His head with ra - diant glo - ries crowned, His
men; Fair - er is He than all the fair That
lief; For me He bore the shame - ful cross And
have; He makes me tri - umph o - ver death, And
vine, Had I a thou - sand hearts to give, Lord,
lips with grace o'er - flow, His lips with grace o'er - flow.
fill the heav'n - ly train, That fill the heav'n - ly train.
car - ried all my grief, And car - ried all my grief.
saves me from the grave, And saves me from the grave.
they should all be Thine, Lord, they should all be Thine. A-men.

WORDS: Samuel Stennett, 1787
MUSIC: Thomas Hastings, 1837

ORTONVILLE
C.M. Repeats

66 Praise the Savior, Ye Who Know Him

Jesus Christ the same yesterday, and today, and forever. Heb. 13:8

1. Praise the Sav - ior, ye who know Him! Who can tell how much we owe Him?
2. Je - sus is the name that charms us; He for con - flict fits and arms us;
3. Trust in Him, ye saints, for - ev - er; He is faith - ful, chang-ing nev - er;
4. Keep us, Lord, O keep us cleav - ing To Thy - self and still be - liev - ing,
5. Then we shall be where we would be, Then we shall be what we should be;

Glad - ly let us ren - der to Him All we are and have.
Noth - ing moves and noth - ing harms us While we trust in Him.
Nei - ther force nor guile can sev - er Those He loves from Him.
Till the hour of our re - ceiv - ing Prom - ised joys with Thee.
Things that are not now, nor could be, Soon shall be our own. A - men.

WORDS: Thomas Kelly, 1806
MUSIC: Traditional German melody

ACCLAIM
8.8.8.5

We Come, O Christ, to Thee 67

I am the way, the truth, and the life . . . John 14:6

1. We come, O Christ, to Thee, True Son of God and man, By Whom all things con-
2. Thou art the Way to God, Thy blood our ran - som paid; In Thee we face our
3. Thou art the liv - ing Truth! All wis - dom dwells in Thee, Thou Source of ev - ery
4. Thou on - ly art true Life, To know Thee is to live The more a - bund - ant
5. We wor - ship Thee, Lord Christ, Our Sav - ior and our King, To Thee our youth and

sist, In Whom all life be - gan: In Thee a - lone we
Judge And Mak - er un - a - fraid. Be - fore the throne ab -
skill, E - ter - nal Ver - i - ty! Thou great I Am! In
life That earth can nev - er give: O ris - en Lord! We
strength A - dor - ing - ly we bring: So fill our hearts, that

live and move, And have our be - ing in Thy love.
solved we stand, Thy love has met Thy law's de - mand.
Thee we rest, True an - swer to our ev - ery quest.
live in Thee, And Thou in us e - ter - nal - ly.
men may see Thy life in us, and turn to Thee. A - men.

WORDS: Margaret Clarkson, 1947
MUSIC: John Darwall, 1770

DARWALL
6.6.6.6.8.8

68 We Sing the Boundless Praise

Worthy is the Lamb that was slain . . . Rev. 5:12

1. We sing the bound-less praise Of Him who reigns on high,
2. Thy pre-cious blood a-lone, O Christ, has brought us near;
3. All hail! Re-deem-er, King, Thou Lamb of Cal-va-ry!
And of His glo-rious Son, the Lamb Who brought sal-va-tion nigh.
No long-er stran-gers, God in love Calls us His chil-dren dear.
Let ran-somed sin-ners sing Thy name Thro' all e-ter-ni-ty.
Thine ev-er-last-ing pow'r And maj-es-ty we sing,
The ti-tle of the Lamb Thou bear-est still in heav'n,
When stand the ran-somed throng Be-fore the great I Am,
But with our songs of sov-'reign grace We'll make heav'n's arch-es ring.
Me-mo-rial of Thy sac-ri-fice, And love to sin-ners giv'n.
This shall their end-less an-them be, "All wor-thy is the Lamb!" A-men.
(♮)

WORDS: Joseph C. Macaulay, 1957
MUSIC: Harry D. Loes, 1957

BOUNDLESS PRAISE
S.M.D.

Crown Him with Many Crowns 69

. . . And on His head were many crowns . . . Rev. 19:12

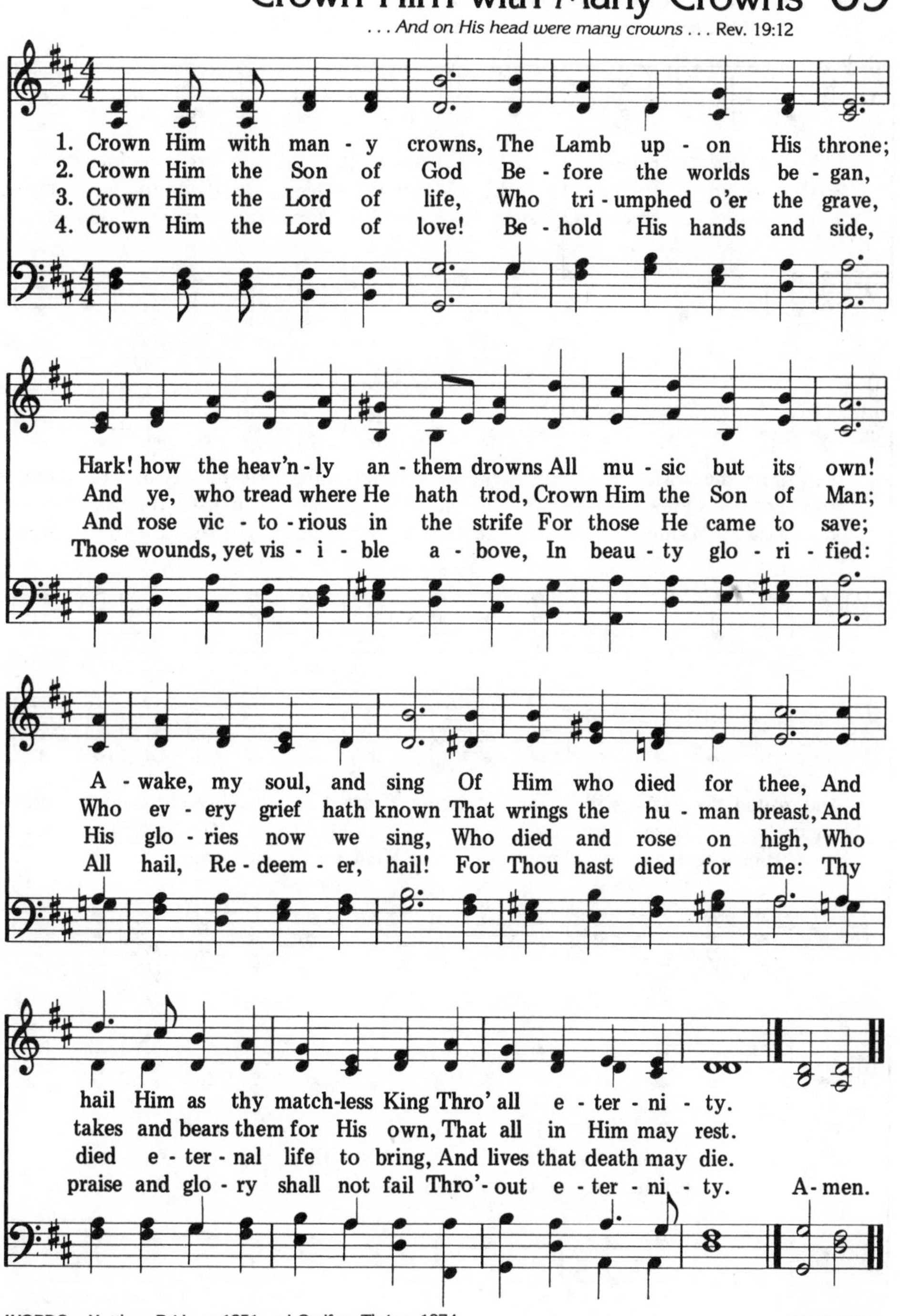
1. Crown Him with man - y crowns, The Lamb up - on His throne;
2. Crown Him the Son of God Be - fore the worlds be - gan,
3. Crown Him the Lord of life, Who tri - umphed o'er the grave,
4. Crown Him the Lord of love! Be - hold His hands and side,
Hark! how the heav'n - ly an - them drowns All mu - sic but its own!
And ye, who tread where He hath trod, Crown Him the Son of Man;
And rose vic - to - rious in the strife For those He came to save;
Those wounds, yet vis - i - ble a - bove, In beau - ty glo - ri - fied:
A - wake, my soul, and sing Of Him who died for thee, And
Who ev - ery grief hath known That wrings the hu - man breast, And
His glo - ries now we sing, Who died and rose on high, Who
All hail, Re - deem - er, hail! For Thou hast died for me: Thy
hail Him as thy match-less King Thro' all e - ter - ni - ty.
takes and bears them for His own, That all in Him may rest.
died e - ter - nal life to bring, And lives that death may die.
praise and glo - ry shall not fail Thro'- out e - ter - ni - ty. A- men.

WORDS: Matthew Bridges, 1851 and Godfrey Thring, 1874
MUSIC: George J. Elvey, 1868

DIADEMATA
S.M.D.

70 I've Found a Friend

Greater love hath no man than this, that a man lay down his life for his friends. John 15:13

1. I've found a Friend, O such a Friend! He loved me ere I knew Him;
2. I've found a Friend, O such a Friend! He bled, He died to save me;
3. I've found a Friend, O such a Friend! So kind and true and ten - der,

He drew me with the cords of love, And thus He bound me to Him.
And not a - lone the gift of life, But His own self He gave me.
So wise a Coun - sel - or and Guide, So might - y a De - fend - er!

And round my heart still close - ly twine Those ties which naught can sev - er,
Naught that I have my own I call, I hold it for the Giv - er;
From Him who loves me now so well, What pow'r my soul can sev - er?

For I am His and He is mine, For - ev - er and for - ev - er.
My heart, my strength, my life, my all Are His, and His for - ev - er.
Shall life or death, or earth or hell? No! I am His for - ev - er.

WORDS: James G. Small, 1863
MUSIC: George C. Stebbins, 1878

FRIEND
8.7.8.7 D.

Come, Christians, Join to Sing 71

O come, let us sing unto the Lord. Psa.95:1

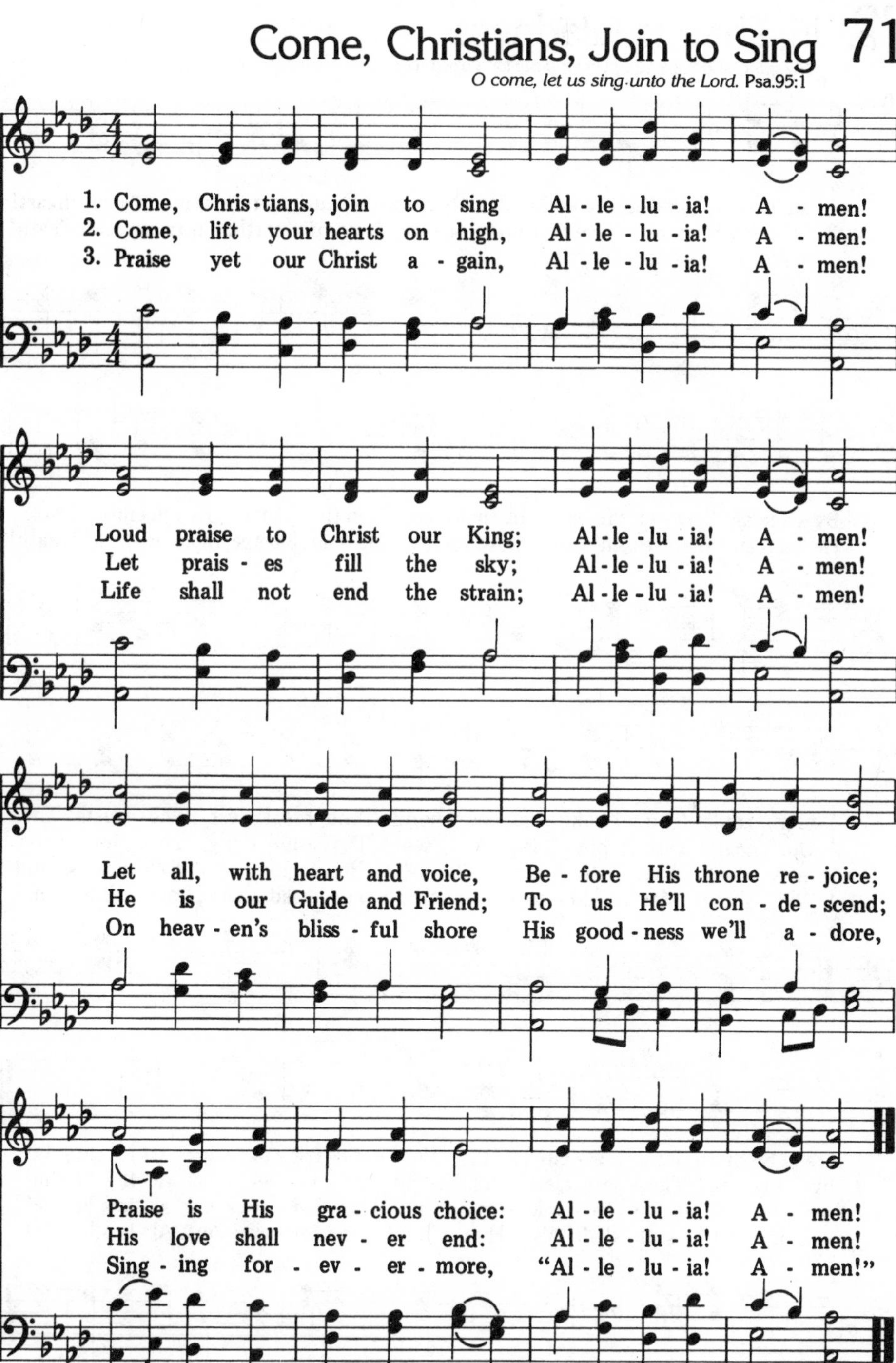
1. Come, Chris-tians, join to sing Al - le - lu - ia! A - men!
2. Come, lift your hearts on high, Al - le - lu - ia! A - men!
3. Praise yet our Christ a - gain, Al - le - lu - ia! A - men!
Loud praise to Christ our King; Al - le - lu - ia! A - men!
Let prais - es fill the sky; Al - le - lu - ia! A - men!
Life shall not end the strain; Al - le - lu - ia! A - men!
Let all, with heart and voice, Be - fore His throne re - joice;
He is our Guide and Friend; To us He'll con - de - scend;
On heav - en's bliss - ful shore His good - ness we'll a - dore,
Praise is His gra - cious choice: Al - le - lu - ia! A - men!
His love shall nev - er end: Al - le - lu - ia! A - men!
Sing - ing for - ev - er - more, "Al - le - lu - ia! A - men!"

WORDS: Christian H. Bateman, 1843
MUSIC: Traditional Spanish melody; arr. David Evans, 1927

MADRID
6.6.6.6 D.

72 In Thee Is Gladness

My spirit hath rejoiced in God my Savior. Luke 1:47

1. In Thee is gladness amid all sadness, Jesus, sunshine of my heart! By Thee are given the gifts of heaven, Thou the true Redeemer art! Our souls Thou wakest, our bonds Thou breakest, Who trusts Thee surely hath built securely, He stands forever: Alleluia! Our hearts are pining to see Thy shining, Dying or living, to Thee are cleaving, Naught can us sever: Alleluia!

2. If He is ours we fear no powers, Not of earth, nor sin, nor death! He sees and blesses in worst distresses, He can change them with a breath! Wherefore the story tell of His glory With hearts and voices; all heav'n rejoices In Him forever: Alleluia! We shout for gladness, triumph o'er sadness, Love Him and praise Him and still shall raise Him Glad hymns forever: Alleluia!

WORDS: Johann Lindemann, 1598; tr. Catherine Winkworth, 1858 and 1863
MUSIC: Giovanni Gastoldi, 1591

IN DIR IST FREUDE
Irregular meter

Jesus, Jesus, Jesus 73

. . . Thou shalt call His name Jesus . . . Matt. 1:23

Je - sus, Je - sus, Je - sus; There's just some - thing a - bout that
name! Mas - ter, Sav - ior, Je - sus, Like the fra - grance
af - ter the rain; Je - sus, Je - sus, Je - sus, Let all
Heav - en and earth pro - claim: Kings and king - doms will
all pass a - way, But there's some - thing a - bout that name!

WORDS: Gloria Gaither and William J. Gaither, 1970
MUSIC: William J. Gaither, 1970

THAT NAME
Irregular meter

74 Love Divine, All Loves Excelling

Above all these things put on charity, which is the bond of perfectness. Col. 3:14

1. Love di - vine, all loves ex - cel - ling, Joy of heav'n, to earth come down;
2. Breathe, O breathe Thy lov - ing Spir - it In - to ev - ery trou-bled breast!
3. Come, Al - might - y to de - liv - er, Let us all Thy life re - ceive;
4. Fin - ish then Thy new cre - a - tion, Pure and spot-less let us be;

Fix in us Thy hum-ble dwell-ing, All Thy faith - ful mer-cies crown.
Let us all in Thee in - her - it, Let us find the prom-ised rest.
Sud-den - ly re - turn, and nev - er, Nev - er - more Thy tem-ples leave:
Let us see Thy great sal - va - tion Per-fect - ly re-stored in Thee:

Je - sus, Thou art all com - pas - sion, Pure, un-bound-ed love Thou art;
Take a - way the love of sin-ning, Al - pha and O - me - ga be;
Thee we would be al - ways bless-ing, Serve Thee as Thy hosts a - bove,
Changed from glo - ry in - to glo - ry, Till in heav'n we take our place,

Vis - it us with Thy sal - va - tion; En - ter ev - ery trem-bling heart.
End of faith, as its be - gin-ning, Set our hearts at lib - er - ty.
Pray, and praise Thee with-out ceas-ing, Glo - ry in Thy per-fect love.
Till we cast our crowns be-fore Thee, Lost in won-der, love, and praise. A-men.

WORDS: Charles Wesley, 1747
MUSIC: John Zundel, 1870

BEECHER
8.7.8.7 D.

Jesus! What a Friend for Sinners 75

Behold . . . a friend of publicans and sinners! Luke 7:34

1. Je - sus! what a Friend for sin - ners! Je - sus! Lov - er of my soul;
2. Je - sus! what a Strength in weak - ness! Let me hide my - self in Him;
3. Je - sus! what a Help in sor - row! While the bil - lows o'er me roll,
4. Je - sus! what a Guide and Keep - er! While the tem - pest still is high,
5. Je - sus! I do now re - ceive Him, More than all in Him I find,
Friends may fail me, foes as - sail me, He, my Sav - ior, makes me whole.
Tempt-ed, tried, and some-times fail - ing, He, my Strength, my vic-t'ry wins.
E - ven when my heart is break-ing, He, my Com - fort, helps my soul.
Storms a - bout me, night o'er - takes me, He, my Pi - lot, hears my cry.
He hath grant - ed me for - give - ness, I am His, and He is mine.
Refrain
Hal - le - lu - jah! what a Sav - ior! Hal - le - lu - jah! what a Friend!
Sav - ing, help - ing, keep - ing, lov - ing, He is with me to the end.

WORDS: J. Wilbur Chapman, 1910
MUSIC: Rowland H. Prichard, c.1830; arr. Robert Harkness, 1910

HYFRYDOL
8.7.8.7 D.

76 Shepherd of Eager Youth

. . . Our Lord Jesus, that great shepherd of the sheep . . . Heb. 13:20

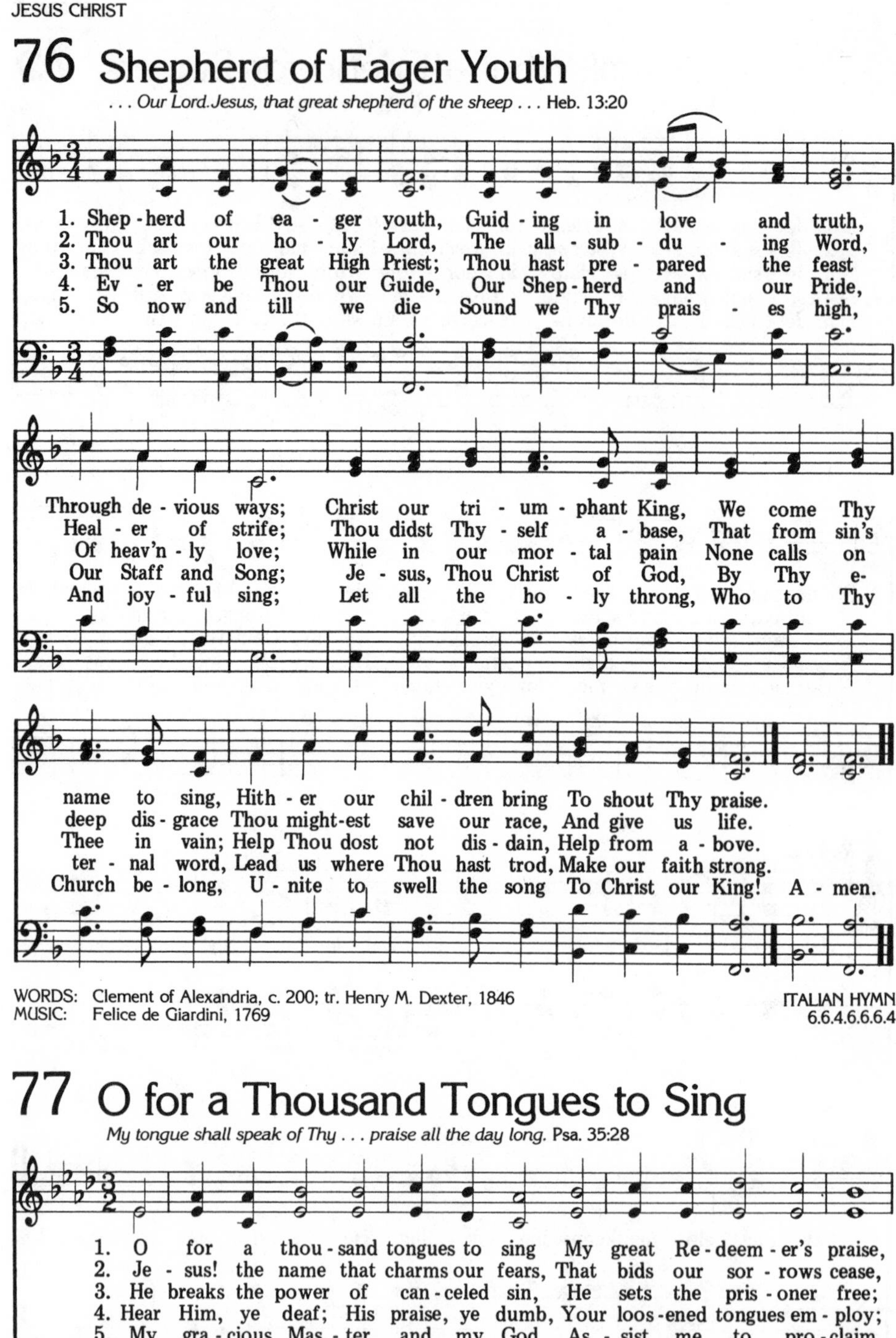
1. Shep - herd of ea - ger youth, Guid - ing in love and truth, Through de - vious ways; Christ our tri - um - phant King, We come Thy name to sing, Hith - er our chil - dren bring To shout Thy praise.
2. Thou art our ho - ly Lord, The all - sub - du - ing Word, Heal - er of strife; Thou didst Thy - self a - base, That from sin's deep dis - grace Thou might-est save our race, And give us life.
3. Thou art the great High Priest; Thou hast pre - pared the feast Of heav'n - ly love; While in our mor - tal pain None calls on Thee in vain; Help Thou dost not dis - dain, Help from a - bove.
4. Ev - er be Thou our Guide, Our Shep - herd and our Pride, Our Staff and Song; Je - sus, Thou Christ of God, By Thy e - ter - nal word, Lead us where Thou hast trod, Make our faith strong.
5. So now and till we die Sound we Thy prais - es high, And joy - ful sing; Let all the ho - ly throng, Who to Thy Church be - long, U - nite to swell the song To Christ our King! A - men.

WORDS: Clement of Alexandria, c. 200; tr. Henry M. Dexter, 1846
MUSIC: Felice de Giardini, 1769

ITALIAN HYMN
6.6.4.6.6.6.4

77 O for a Thousand Tongues to Sing

My tongue shall speak of Thy . . . praise all the day long. Psa. 35:28

1. O for a thou - sand tongues to sing My great Re - deem - er's praise,
2. Je - sus! the name that charms our fears, That bids our sor - rows cease,
3. He breaks the power of can - celed sin, He sets the pris - oner free;
4. Hear Him, ye deaf; His praise, ye dumb, Your loos - ened tongues em - ploy;
5. My gra - cious Mas - ter and my God, As - sist me to pro - claim,

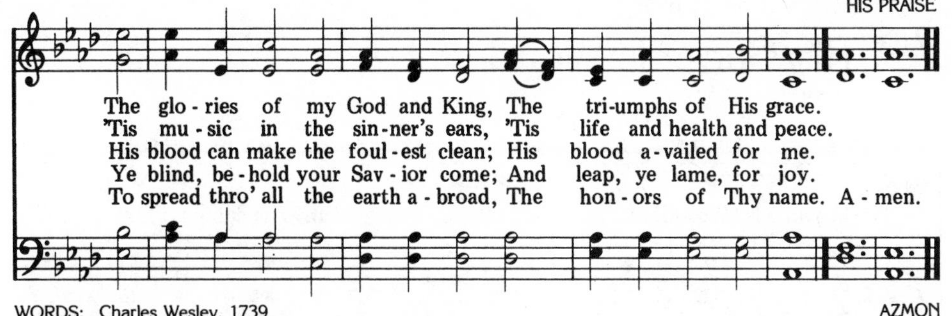
The glo - ries of my God and King, The tri-umphs of His grace.
'Tis mu - sic in the sin-ner's ears, 'Tis life and health and peace.
His blood can make the foul - est clean; His blood a-vailed for me.
Ye blind, be - hold your Sav - ior come; And leap, ye lame, for joy.
To spread thro' all the earth a - broad, The hon - ors of Thy name. A - men.

WORDS: Charles Wesley, 1739
MUSIC: Carl G. Gläser, 1784-1829; arr. Lowell Mason, 1839

AZMON
C.M.

My Jesus, I Love Thee 78

We love Him because He first loved us. I John 4:19

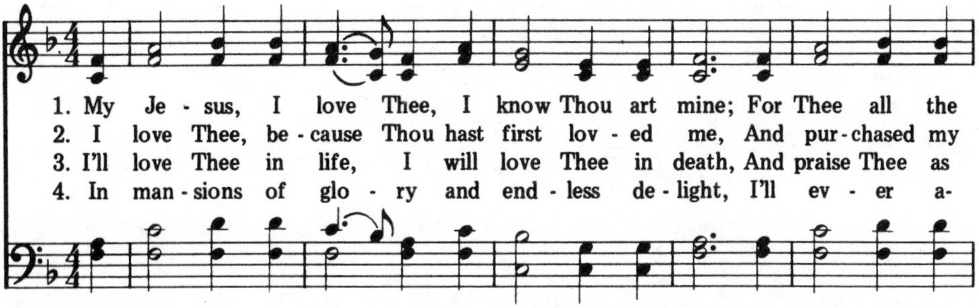

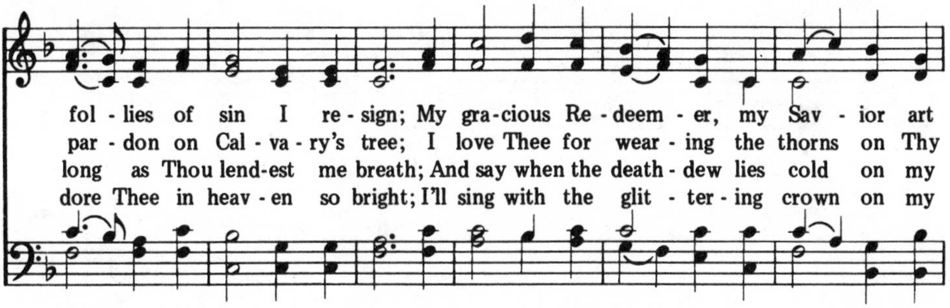

1. My Je - sus, I love Thee, I know Thou art mine; For Thee all the fol - lies of sin I re - sign; My gra-cious Re - deem - er, my Sav - ior art Thou; If ev - er I loved Thee, my Je - sus, 'tis now.

2. I love Thee, be - cause Thou hast first lov - ed me, And pur-chased my par - don on Cal - va - ry's tree; I love Thee for wear - ing the thorns on Thy brow; If ev - er I loved Thee, my Je - sus, 'tis now.

3. I'll love Thee in life, I will love Thee in death, And praise Thee as long as Thou lend-est me breath; And say when the death - dew lies cold on my brow; If ev - er I loved Thee, my Je - sus, 'tis now.

4. In man - sions of glo - ry and end - less de - light, I'll ev - er a - dore Thee in heav - en so bright; I'll sing with the glit - ter - ing crown on my brow; If ev - er I loved Thee, my Je - sus, 'tis now. A - men.

WORDS: William R. Featherstone, c.1862
MUSIC: Adoniram J. Gordon, 1876

GORDON
11.11.11.11

79 His Name Is Wonderful

His name shall be called Wonderful . . . Isa. 9:6

His name is Won-der-ful, His name is Won-der-ful, His name is Won-der-ful,
Je-sus, my Lord; He is the might-y King, Mas-ter of ev-ery-thing,
His name is Won-der-ful, Je-sus, my Lord. He's the great Shep-herd, the
Rock of all a-ges, Al-might-y God is He; Bow down be-
fore Him, Love and a-dore Him, His name is Won-der-ful, Je-sus my Lord.

WORDS and MUSIC: Audrey Meir, 1959

MIEIR
Irregular meter

There's a Spirit in the Air 80

Where the Spirit of the Lord is, there is liberty. II Cor. 3:17

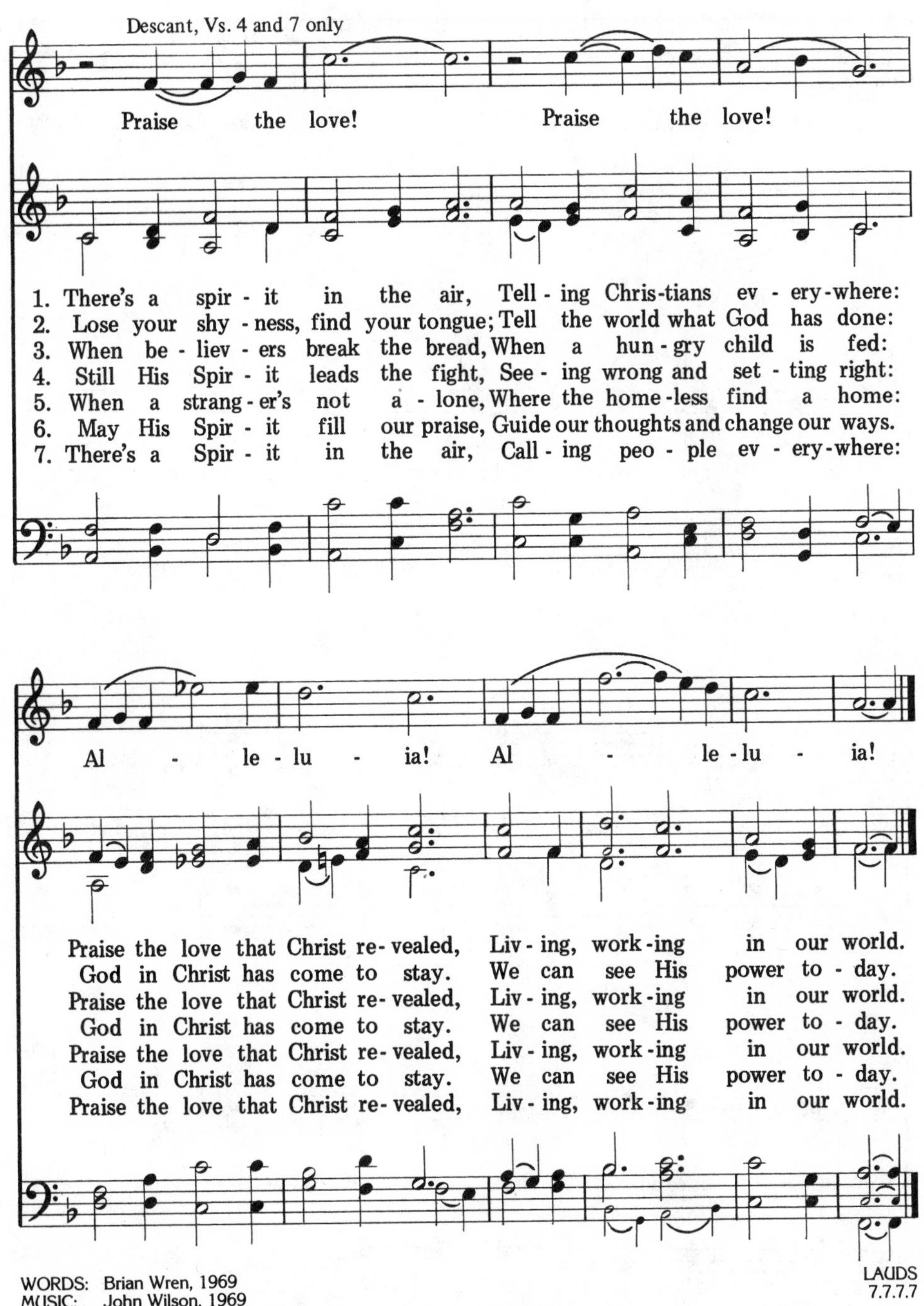
Descant, Vs. 4 and 7 only
Praise the love! Praise the love!
1. There's a spir - it in the air, Tell - ing Chris-tians ev - ery-where:
2. Lose your shy - ness, find your tongue; Tell the world what God has done:
3. When be - liev - ers break the bread, When a hun - gry child is fed:
4. Still His Spir - it leads the fight, See - ing wrong and set - ting right:
5. When a strang - er's not a - lone, Where the home - less find a home:
6. May His Spir - it fill our praise, Guide our thoughts and change our ways.
7. There's a Spir - it in the air, Call - ing peo - ple ev - ery-where:
Al - le - lu - ia! Al - le - lu - ia!
Praise the love that Christ re- vealed, Liv - ing, work - ing in our world.
God in Christ has come to stay. We can see His power to - day.
Praise the love that Christ re- vealed, Liv - ing, work - ing in our world.
God in Christ has come to stay. We can see His power to - day.
Praise the love that Christ re- vealed, Liv - ing, work - ing in our world.
God in Christ has come to stay. We can see His power to - day.
Praise the love that Christ re- vealed, Liv - ing, work - ing in our world.

WORDS: Brian Wren, 1969
MUSIC: John Wilson, 1969

LAUDS
7.7.7.7

81 Let's Just Praise the Lord

The Lord Jehovah is my strength and my song . . . Isa. 12:2

Let's just praise the Lord! Praise the Lord! Let's just

lift our hearts* to heav - en and praise the

Lord; Let's just praise the Lord, Praise the Lord, Let's just

lift our hearts* to heav - en and praise the Lord!

Fine

*Alternate words: "voice," "hands."

HIS PRAISE
1. O, we thank You for Your kind - ness, We thank You for Your love, We have been in heaven-ly plac - es, felt bless-ings from a - bove; We've been shar - ing all the good things, the fam - ily can af - ford. Let's just turn our praise toward heav - en and praise the Lord.
2. Just the pre - cious name of Je - sus is worth - y of our praise. Let us bow our knees be - fore Him, our hands to heav - en raise: When He comes in clouds of glo - ry, with Him to ev - er reign, Let's just lift our hap - py voic - es, and praise His name.
D.C.

WORDS: Gloria Gaither and William J. Gaither, 1972
MUSIC: William J. Gaither, 1972

LET'S JUST PRAISE THE LORD
Irregular meter

82 Worthy Is the Lamb

Worthy is the Lamb that was slain . . . Rev. 5:12

Unison

1. Wor - thy is the Lamb who died in awe - some grief;
2. Wor - thy is the Lamb who paid the price of death;
3. Wor - thy is the Lamb, though dead all else should be;
4. Wor - thy is the Lamb to live my life a - lone;

Wor - thy is the Lamb who saved a dy - ing thief.
Wor - thy is the Lamb who gave my soul its breath;
Wor - thy is the Lamb to live in you and me;
Wor - thy is the Lamb to make my soul His own,

Wor - thy is the Lamb to make up for my fall; Yes,
Wor - thy is the Lamb to grant my life the call; Yes,
Wor - thy is the Lamb to take our bit - ter gall; Yes,
Wor - thy is the Lamb to change our lives, like Paul; Yes,

wor - thy is the Lamb, praise God, He is all!
wor - thy is the Lamb, praise God, He is all!
wor - thy is the Lamb, praise God, He is all!
wor - thy is the Lamb, praise God, He is all!

WORDS and MUSIC: Stephen Leddy, 1967

WORTHY LAMB
Irregular meter

Join All the Glorious Names 83

Far above . . . every name that is named. Eph. 1:21

1. Join all the glo - rious names. Of wis - dom, love, and pow'r,
2. Great Proph - et of my God, My tongue would bless Thy name:
3. Je - sus, my great High Priest, Of - fered His blood, and died;
4. Thou art my Coun - sel - lor, My Pat - tern, and my Guide,
5. My Sav - ior and my Lord, My Con-qu'ror and my King,
That ev - er mor - tals knew, That an - gels
By Thee the joy - ful news Of our sal -
My guilt - y con - science seeks No sac - ri -
And Thou my Shep - herd art; O, keep me
Thy scep - tre and Thy sword, Thy reign - ing
ev - er bore: All are too poor to speak His worth,
va - tion came, The joy - ful news of sins for - giv'n,
fice be - side: His pow'r - ful blood did once a - tone
near Thy side; Nor let my feet e'er turn a - stray
grace, I sing: Thine is the pow'r; be - hold I sit
Too poor to set my Sav - ior forth.
Of hell sub - dued and peace with heav'n.
And now it pleads be - fore the throne.
To wan - der in the crook - ed way.
In will - ing bonds be - neath Thy feet. A - men.

WORDS: Isaac Watts, 1707
MUSIC: John Darwall, 1770

DARWALL
6.6.6.6.8.8

84 Christ Is the World's Light

In Him was life . . . the light of men. John 1:4

Unison

1. Christ is the world's light; Christ and none oth - er;
2. Christ is the world's peace: Christ and none oth - er;
3. Christ is the world's life, Christ and none oth - er;
4. Give God the glo - ry, God and none oth - er;
Born in our dark - ness, He be - came our broth - er.
No one can serve Him and de - spise an - oth - er.
Sold once for sil - ver, mur - dered here, our broth - er—
Give God the glo - ry, Spir - it, Son and Fa - ther;
If we have seen Him, we have seen the Fa - ther:
Who else u - nites us, one in God the Fa - ther?
He, who re - deems us, reigns with God the Fa - ther:
Give God the glo - ry, God in Man my broth - er:
Glo - ry to God on high!
Glo - ry to God on high!
Glo - ry to God on high!
Glo - ry to God on high! A - men.

WORDS: Fred Pratt Green, 1968
MUSIC: Melody from *Paris Antiphoner,* 1681; harm. *Cantate Domino,* 1980

CHRISTE SANCTORUM
10.11.11.6

All Praise to Him Who Reigns Above 85

Blessed be the name of the Lord. Job 1:21

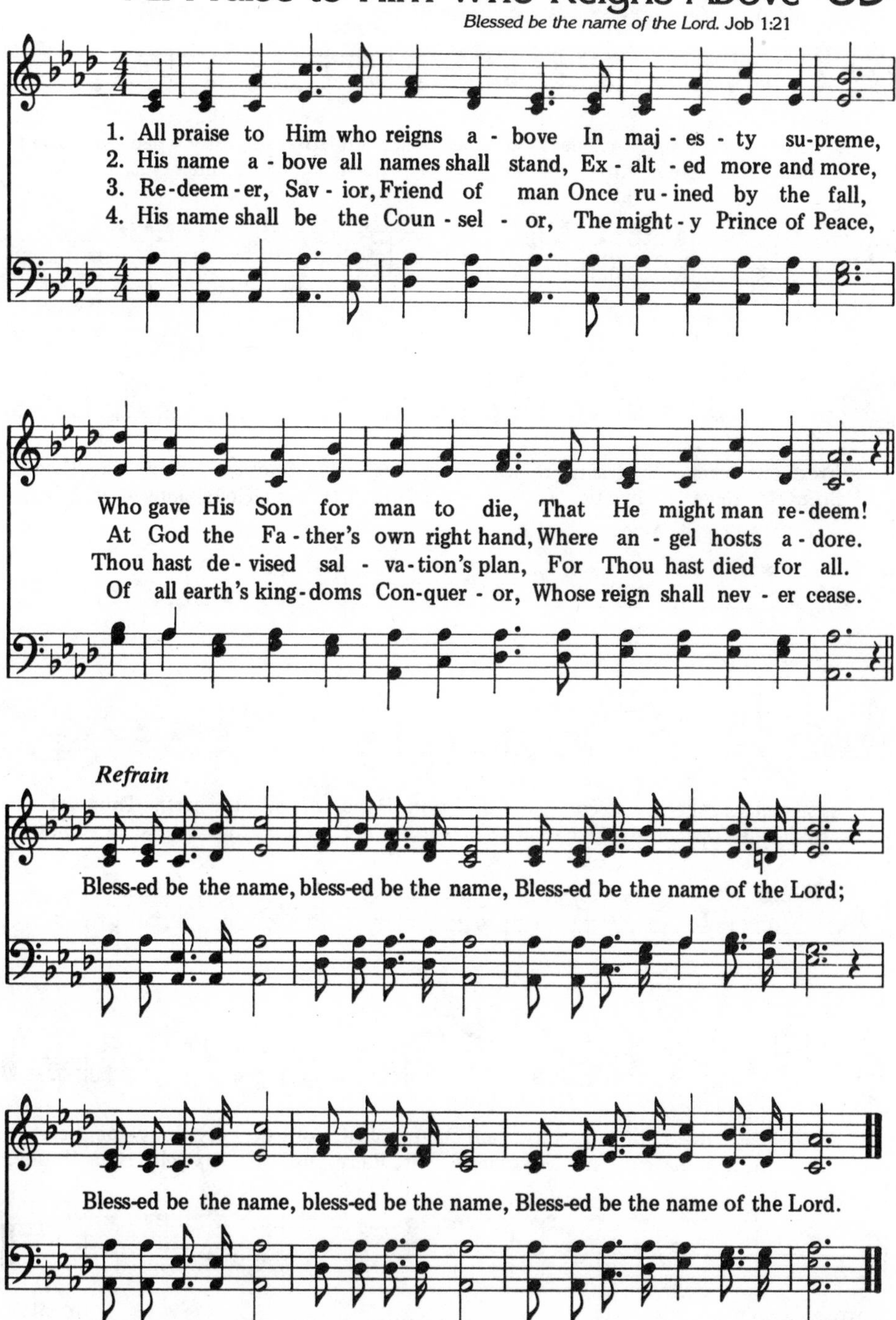
1. All praise to Him who reigns a - bove In maj - es - ty su-preme,
2. His name a - bove all names shall stand, Ex - alt - ed more and more,
3. Re-deem - er, Sav - ior, Friend of man Once ru - ined by the fall,
4. His name shall be the Coun - sel - or, The might - y Prince of Peace,
Who gave His Son for man to die, That He might man re-deem!
At God the Fa - ther's own right hand, Where an - gel hosts a - dore.
Thou hast de - vised sal - va-tion's plan, For Thou hast died for all.
Of all earth's king-doms Con-quer - or, Whose reign shall nev - er cease.
Refrain
Bless-ed be the name, bless-ed be the name, Bless-ed be the name of the Lord;
Bless-ed be the name, bless-ed be the name, Bless-ed be the name of the Lord.

WORDS: William H. Clark, 19th century; refrain, Ralph E. Hudson, 1887
MUSIC: Source unknown; arr. Ralph E. Hudson, 1887, and William J. Kirkpatrick, 1888

BLESSED NAME
L.M. Ref.

86 Come, Thou Long Expected Jesus

The desire of all nations shall come . . . Haggai 2:7

1. Come, Thou long ex-pect - ed Je - sus, Born to set Thy peo - ple free;
2. Born Thy peo - ple to de - liv - er, Born a child and yet a king.
From our fears and sins re - lease us; Let us find our rest in Thee.
Born to reign in us for - ev - er, Now Thy gra-cious king-dom bring.
Is - rael's strength and con - so - la - tion, Hope of all the earth Thou art;
By Thine own e - ter - nal Spir - it Rule in all our hearts a - lone;
Dear De - sire of ev - ery na - tion, Joy of ev - ery long - ing heart.
By Thine all suf - fi - cient mer - it, Raise us to Thy glo - rious throne.

WORDS: Charles Wesley, 1744
MUSIC: Rowland H. Prichard, c.1830; harm. by Ralph Vaughan Williams, 1906

HYFRYDOL
8.7.8.7 D.

O Come, O Come, Emmanuel 87

Behold a virgin shall . . . bear a son, and shall call His name Immanuel. Isa. 7:14

Unison
1. O come, O come, Em - man - u - el, And ran - som cap - tive Is - ra - el, That mourns in lone - ly ex - ile here Un - til the Son of God ap - pear.
2. O come, Thou Rod of Jes - se, free Thine own from Sa - tan's tyr - an - ny; From depths of hell Thy peo - ple save And give them vic - t'ry o'er the grave.
3. O come, Thou Day-spring, come and cheer Our spir - its by Thine ad - vent here; And drive a - way the shades of night, And pierce the clouds and bring us light!
4. O come, Thou Key of Da - vid, come, And o - pen wide our heav'n - ly home; Make safe the way that leads on high, And close the path to mis - er - y.
5. O come, De - sire of na - tions, bind All peo - ples in one heart and mind; Bid en - vy, strife and quar - rels cease; Fill all the world with heav - en's peace.
Re - joice! re - joice! Em - man - u - el Shall come to thee, O Is - ra - el!
A - men.

WORDS: Latin hymn; tr. John M. Neale, 1851; St. 5, Henry Sloane Coffin, 1916
MUSIC: Thomas Helmore, 1854; based on plainsong phrases

VENI EMMANUEL
8.8.8.8.8.8

88 Rejoice, Rejoice, Believers

Behold the bridegroom cometh, go ye out to meet him. Matt. 25:6

1. Re - joice, re - joice, be - liev - ers, And let your light ap - pear;
The eve - ning is ad - van - cing, And dark - er night is near:
The Bride-groom is a - ris - ing, And soon He draw - eth nigh;
Up, pray and watch and wres - tle: At mid-night comes the cry.

2. See that your lamps are burn - ing; Re - plen - ish them with oil,
And wait for your sal - va - tion— The end of earth - ly toil.
The watch - ers on the moun - tain Pro - claim the Bride-groom near,
Go meet Him as He com - eth, With al - le - lu - ias clear.

3. Our hope and ex - pec - ta - tion, O Je - sus, now ap - pear!
A - rise, thou Sun so longed for, O'er this be - night - ed sphere!
With hearts and hands up - lift - ed, We plead, O Lord, to see
The day of earth's re - demp - tion That brings us un - to Thee.

WORDS: Laurentius Laurenti, 1700; tr. Sarah B. Findlater, 1854; based on Matt. 25:1-13
MUSIC: Henry Smart, 1836

LANCASHIRE
7.6.7.6 D.

Jesus Came, the Heavens Adoring 89

And being found in fashion as a man, He humbled himself . . . Phil. 2:8

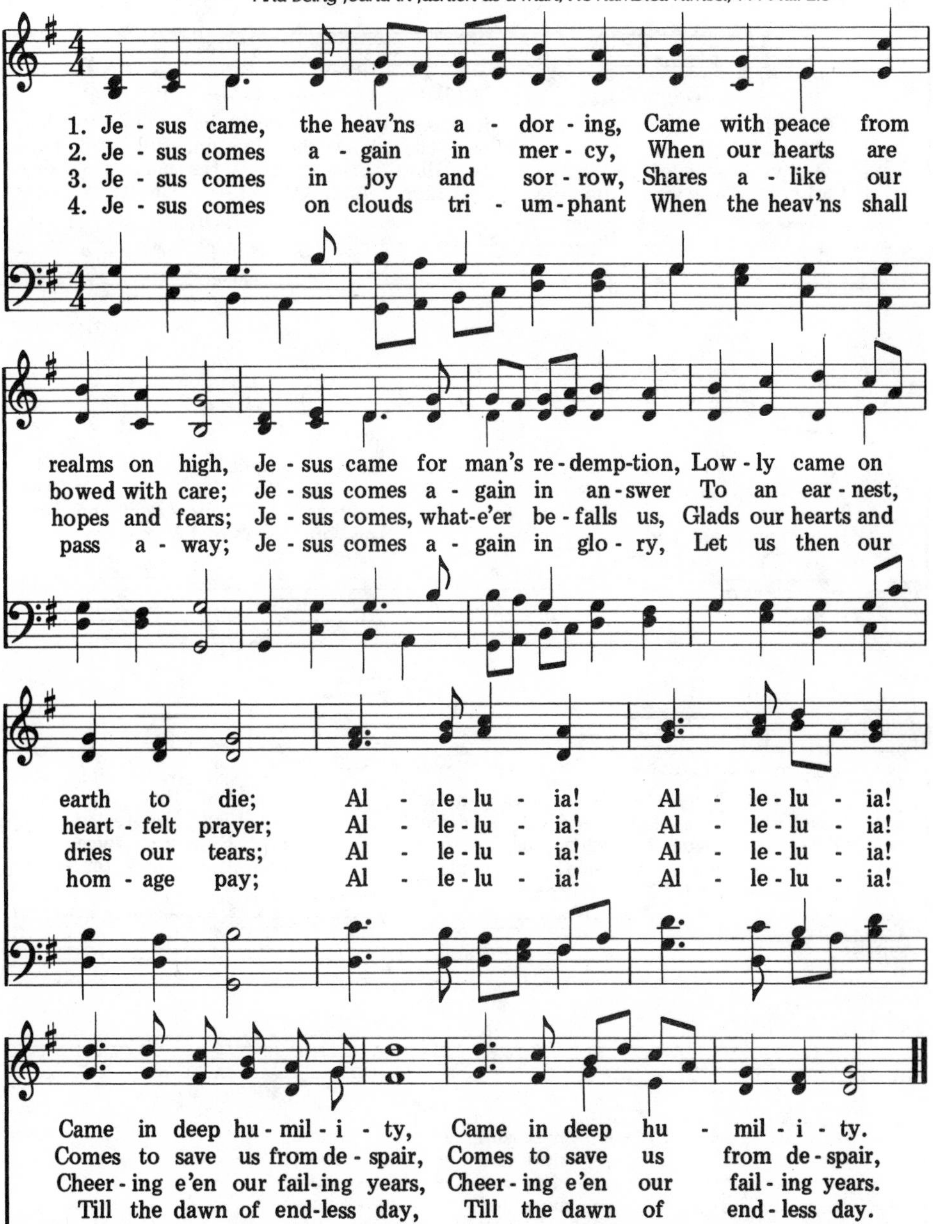

1. Je - sus came, the heav'ns a - dor - ing, Came with peace from
2. Je - sus comes a - gain in mer - cy, When our hearts are
3. Je - sus comes in joy and sor - row, Shares a - like our
4. Je - sus comes on clouds tri - um - phant When the heav'ns shall

realms on high, Je - sus came for man's re - demp - tion, Low - ly came on
bowed with care; Je - sus comes a - gain in an - swer To an ear - nest,
hopes and fears; Je - sus comes, what - e'er be - falls us, Glads our hearts and
pass a - way; Je - sus comes a - gain in glo - ry, Let us then our

earth to die; Al - le - lu - ia! Al - le - lu - ia!
heart - felt prayer; Al - le - lu - ia! Al - le - lu - ia!
dries our tears; Al - le - lu - ia! Al - le - lu - ia!
hom - age pay; Al - le - lu - ia! Al - le - lu - ia!

Came in deep hu - mil - i - ty, Came in deep hu - mil - i - ty.
Comes to save us from de - spair, Comes to save us from de - spair,
Cheer - ing e'en our fail - ing years, Cheer - ing e'en our fail - ing years.
Till the dawn of end - less day, Till the dawn of end - less day.

WORDS: Godfrey Thring, 1864
MUSIC: John Hughes, 1905

CWM RHONDDA
8.7.8.7.8.7.7

90 Of the Father's Love Begotten

In the beginning was the Word . . . and the Word was God. John 1:1

Unison
1. Of the Fa - ther's love be - got - ten, Ere the worlds be - gan to be,
2. O that birth for - ev - er bless - ed, When the Vir - gin, full of grace,
3. O ye heights of heav'n, a - dore Him; An - gel hosts, His prais - es sing,
4. Christ, to Thee with God the Fa - ther, And, O Ho - ly Ghost, to Thee,
He is Al - pha and O - me - ga, He the Source, the End - ing He,
By the Ho - ly Ghost con - ceiv - ing, Bare the Sav - ior of our race;
Pow'rs, do - min - ions, bow be - fore Him, And ex - tol our God and King;
Hymn and chant and high thanks-giv - ing And un - wea - ried prais - es be:
Of the things that are, that have been, And that fu - ture
And the Babe, the world's Re - deem - er, First re - vealed His
Let no tongue on earth be si - lent, Ev - ery voice in
Hon - or, glo - ry, and do - min - ion, And e - ter - nal
years shall see, Ev - er - more and ev - er - more!
sa - cred face, Ev - er - more and ev - er - more!
con - cert ring, Ev - er - more and ev - er - more!
vic - to - ry, Ev - er - more and ev - er - more! A - men.

WORDS: Aurelius C. Prudentius, 4th century; tr. John M. Neale, 1854, and Henry W. Baker, 1859
MUSIC: Plainsong, 13th century; arr. C. Winfred Douglas, 1916

DIVINUM MYSTERIUM
8.7.8.7.8.7.7

O Come, All Ye Faithful 91

Let us now go even unto Bethlehem . . . Luke 2:15

1. O come, all ye faith - ful, joy - ful and tri - um - phant,
2. God of God, and Light of Light be - got - ten,
3. Sing, choirs of an - gels, sing in ex - ul - ta - tion!
4. Yea, Lord, we greet Thee, born this hap - py morn - ing,
O come ye, O come ye to Beth - le - hem!
Lo, He ab - hors not the Vir - gin's womb;
O sing, all ye cit - i - zens of heav'n a - bove;
Je - sus, to Thee be all glo - ry giv'n;
Come and be - hold Him, born the King of an - gels;
Ver - y God, be - got - ten, not cre - a - ted;
Glo - ry to God, all glo - ry in the high - est;
Word of the Fa - ther, now in flesh ap - pear - ing;
Refrain
O come, let us a - dore Him, O come, let us a - dore Him,
O come, let us a - dore Him, Christ the Lord. A-men.

WORDS: Latin hymn; attr. John F. Wade, 1751; tr. Frederick Oakeley, 1841, and others
MUSIC: John F. Wade's *Cantus Diversi,* 1751

ADESTE FIDELES
Irregular meter

92 Joy to the World! The Lord Is Come

Make a joyful noise unto the Lord, all the earth . . . Psa. 98:4

1. Joy to the world! the Lord is come; Let earth receive her King; Let every heart prepare Him room, And heav'n and nature sing, And heav'n and nature sing, And heav'n, and heav'n and nature sing.
2. Joy to the earth! the Savior reigns; Let men their songs employ; While fields and floods, rocks, hills, and plains Repeat the sounding joy, Repeat the sounding joy, Repeat, repeat the sounding joy.
3. No more let sins and sorrows grow, Nor thorns infest the ground; He comes to make His blessings flow Far as the curse is found, Far as the curse is found, Far as, far as the curse is found.
4. He rules the world with truth and grace, And makes the nations prove The glories of His righteousness, And wonders of His love, And wonders of His love, And wonders, wonders of His love.
1. And heav'n and nature sing,
heav'n and nature sing,
1. And

WORDS: Isaac Watts, 1719; based on Psalm 98
MUSIC: George Frederick Handel, 1742; arr. Lowell Mason, 1839

ANTIOCH
C.M.

Angels We Have Heard on High 93

Glory to God in the highest and on earth peace . . . Luke 2:14

1. An-gels we have heard on high, Sweet-ly sing-ing o'er the plains,
2. Shepherds, why this ju-bi-lee? Why your joy-ous strains pro-long?
3. Come to Beth-le-hem, and see Him whose birth the an-gels sing;
4. See with-in a man-ger laid Je-sus, Lord of heav'n and earth!
And the moun-tains in re-ply Ech-o back their joy-ous strains.
Say what may the ti-dings be, Which in-spire your heav'n-ly song?
Come, a-dore on bend-ed knee Christ the Lord, the new-born King.
Ma-ry, Jo-seph, lend your aid, With us sing our Sav-ior's birth.
Refrain
Glo - - - ri-a in ex-cel-sis De-o,
Glo - - - ri-a in ex-cel-sis De - o.

WORDS: Traditional French carol
MUSIC: Traditional French melody

GLORIA
7.7.7.7 Ref.

94 The First Noel, the Angel Did Say

And there were in the same country shepherds abiding in the field . . . Luke 2:8

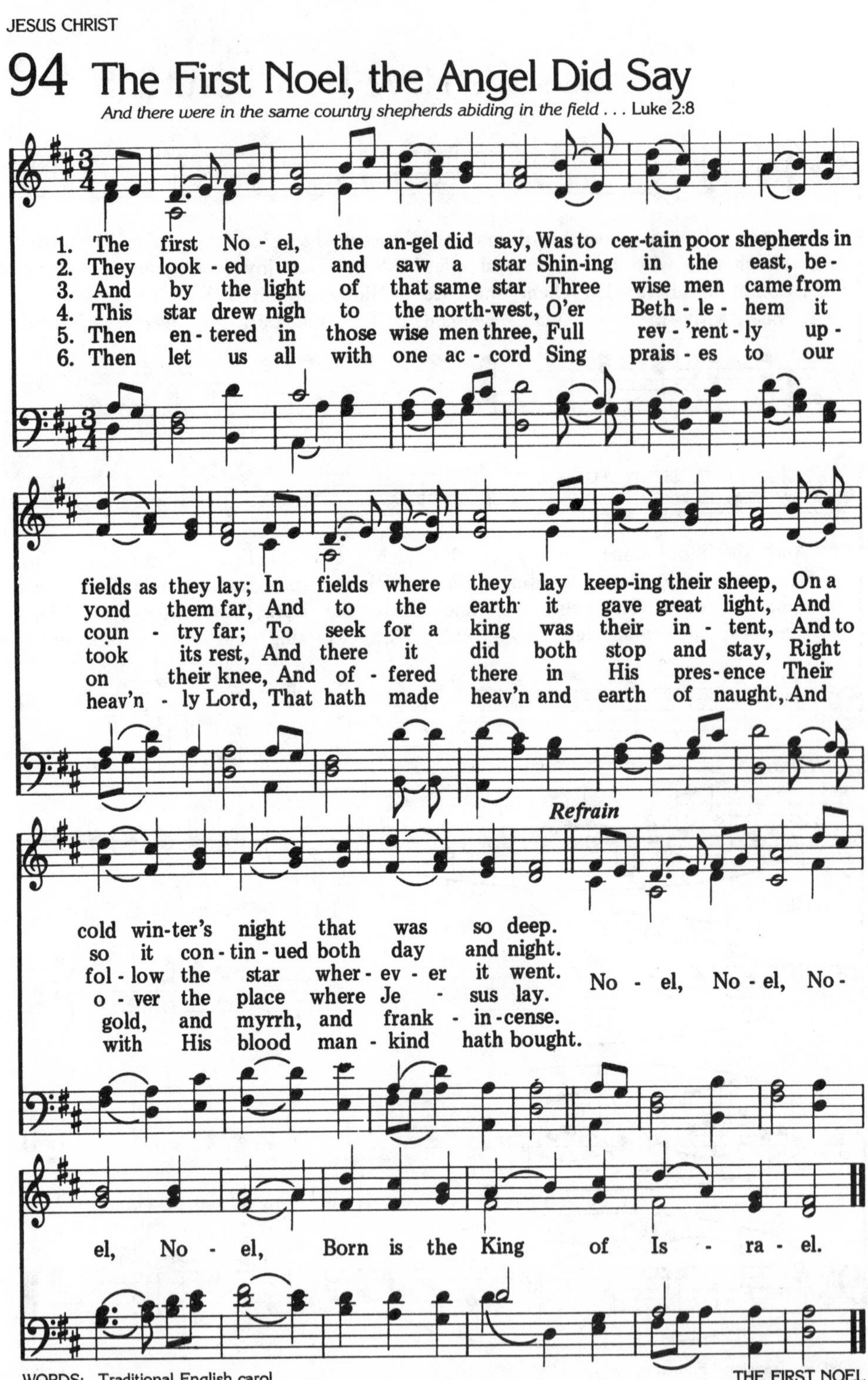
1. The first No - el, the an-gel did say, Was to cer-tain poor shepherds in
2. They look - ed up and saw a star Shin-ing in the east, be -
3. And by the light of that same star Three wise men came from
4. This star drew nigh to the north-west, O'er Beth - le - hem it
5. Then en - tered in those wise men three, Full rev - 'rent - ly up -
6. Then let us all with one ac - cord Sing prais - es to our
fields as they lay; In fields where they lay keep-ing their sheep, On a
yond them far, And to the earth it gave great light, And
coun - try far; To seek for a king was their in - tent, And to
took its rest, And there it did both stop and stay, Right
on their knee, And of - fered there in His pres-ence Their
heav'n - ly Lord, That hath made heav'n and earth of naught, And
Refrain
cold win-ter's night that was so deep.
so it con - tin - ued both day and night.
fol - low the star wher - ev - er it went.
o - ver the place where Je - sus lay.
gold, and myrrh, and frank - in-cense.
with His blood man - kind hath bought.
No - el, No - el, No -
el, No - el, Born is the King of Is - ra - el.

WORDS: Traditional English carol
MUSIC: W. Sandys' *Christmas Carols*, 1833; arr. John Stainer, 1871

THE FIRST NOEL
Irregular meter

It Came upon the Midnight Clear 95

Glory to God in the highest, and on earth peace . . . Luke 2:14

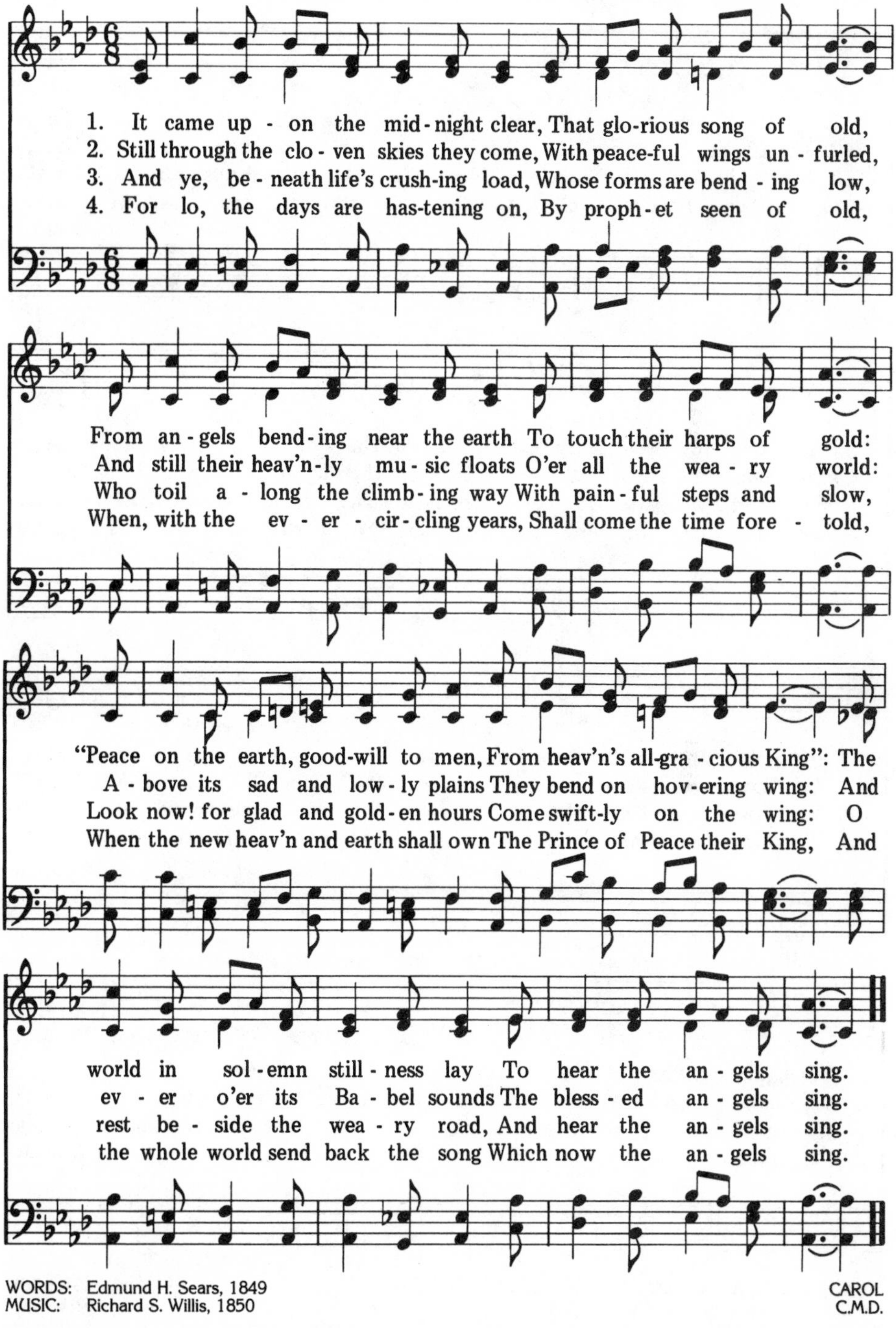

1. It came up - on the mid - night clear, That glo-rious song of old,
2. Still through the clo - ven skies they come, With peace-ful wings un - furled,
3. And ye, be - neath life's crush-ing load, Whose forms are bend - ing low,
4. For lo, the days are has-tening on, By proph - et seen of old,

From an - gels bend - ing near the earth To touch their harps of gold:
And still their heav'n - ly mu - sic floats O'er all the wea - ry world:
Who toil a - long the climb - ing way With pain - ful steps and slow,
When, with the ev - er - cir - cling years, Shall come the time fore - told,

"Peace on the earth, good-will to men, From heav'n's all-gra - cious King": The
A - bove its sad and low - ly plains They bend on hov-ering wing: And
Look now! for glad and gold - en hours Come swift-ly on the wing: O
When the new heav'n and earth shall own The Prince of Peace their King, And

world in sol - emn still - ness lay To hear the an - gels sing.
ev - er o'er its Ba - bel sounds The bless - ed an - gels sing.
rest be - side the wea - ry road, And hear the an - gels sing.
the whole world send back the song Which now the an - gels sing.

WORDS: Edmund H. Sears, 1849
MUSIC: Richard S. Willis, 1850

CAROL
C.M.D.

96 O Little Town of Bethlehem

Thou, Bethlehem . . . though thou be little . . . out of thee shall He come. Micah 5:2

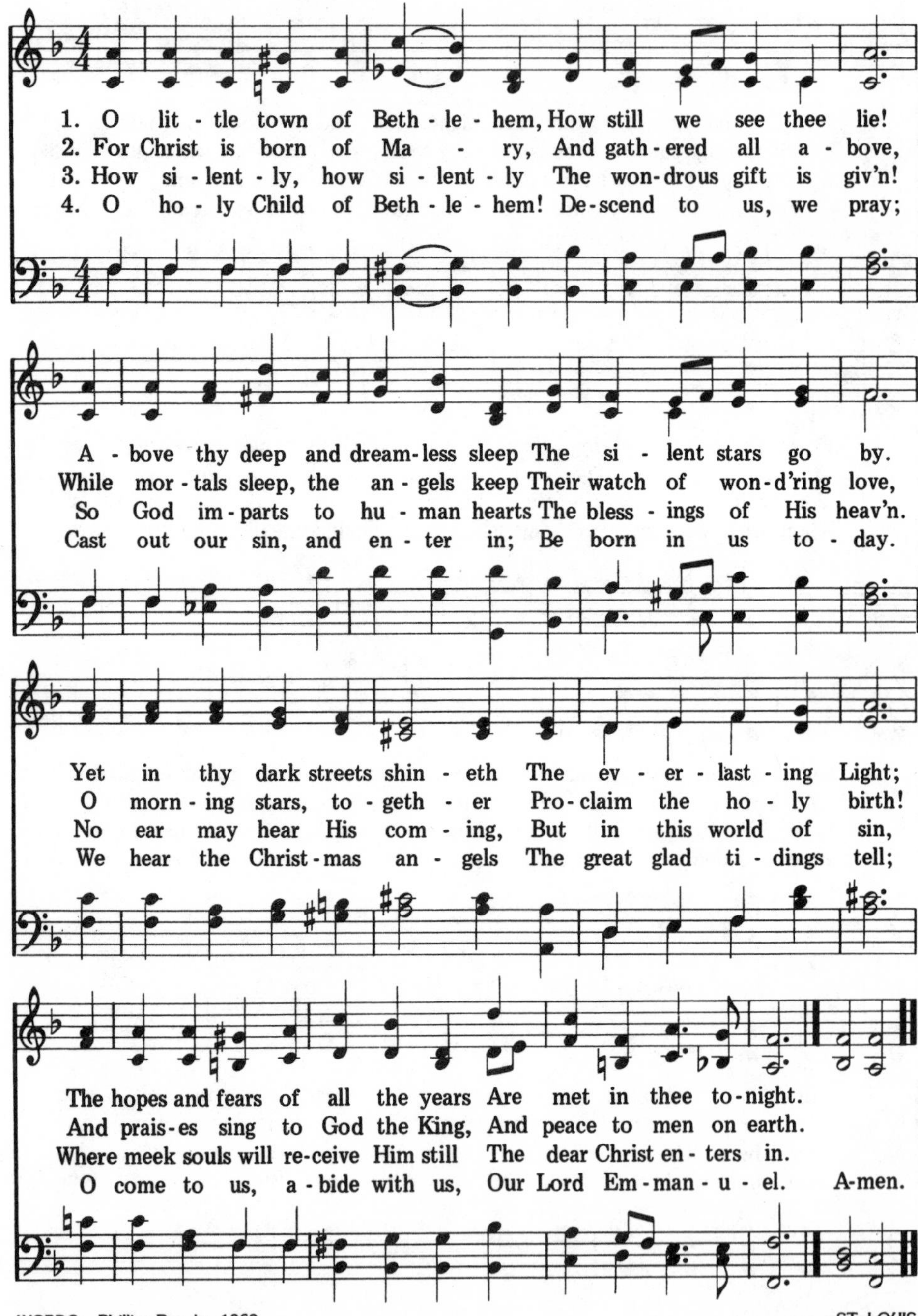
1. O lit - tle town of Beth - le - hem, How still we see thee lie!
2. For Christ is born of Ma - ry, And gath - ered all a - bove,
3. How si - lent - ly, how si - lent - ly The won - drous gift is giv'n!
4. O ho - ly Child of Beth - le - hem! De - scend to us, we pray;
A - bove thy deep and dream - less sleep The si - lent stars go by.
While mor - tals sleep, the an - gels keep Their watch of won - d'ring love,
So God im - parts to hu - man hearts The bless - ings of His heav'n.
Cast out our sin, and en - ter in; Be born in us to - day.
Yet in thy dark streets shin - eth The ev - er - last - ing Light;
O morn - ing stars, to - geth - er Pro - claim the ho - ly birth!
No ear may hear His com - ing, But in this world of sin,
We hear the Christ - mas an - gels The great glad ti - dings tell;
The hopes and fears of all the years Are met in thee to - night.
And prais - es sing to God the King, And peace to men on earth.
Where meek souls will re - ceive Him still The dear Christ en - ters in.
O come to us, a - bide with us, Our Lord Em - man - u - el. A - men.

WORDS: Phillips Brooks, 1868
MUSIC: Lewis H. Redner, 1868

ST. LOUIS
8.6.8.6.7.6.8.6

Hark! the Herald Angels Sing 97

And suddenly there was . . . a multitude of the heavenly host praising God . . . Luke 2:13

1. Hark! the her - ald an - gels sing, "Glo - ry to the new - born King:
2. Christ, by high - est heav'n a - dored; Christ, the ev - er - last - ing Lord!
3. Hail the heav'n - born Prince of Peace! Hail the Sun of Right - eous - ness!
Peace on earth, and mer - cy mild, God and sin - ners rec - on - ciled!"
Late in time be - hold Him come, Off - spring of the Vir - gin's womb:
Light and life to all He brings, Ris'n with heal - ing in His wings.
Joy - ful, all ye na - tions, rise, Join the tri - umph of the skies;
Veiled in flesh the God - head see; Hail th'in - car - nate De - i - ty,
Mild He lays His glo - ry by, Born that man no more may die,
With th'an - gel - ic host pro - claim, "Christ is born in Beth - le - hem!"
Pleased as man with men to dwell, Je - sus, our Em - man - u - el.
Born to raise the sons of earth, Born to give them sec - ond birth.
Hark! the her - ald an - gels sing, "Glo - ry to the new - born King." A - men.

WORDS: Charles Wesley, 1739
MUSIC: Felix Mendelssohn, 1840; arr. William H. Cummings, 1856

MENDELSSOHN
7.7.7.7 D. Ref.

98 Good Christian Men, Rejoice

Unto you is born this day . . . a Savior, which is Christ the Lord. Luke 2:11

1. Good Chris - tian men, re - joice With heart and soul and voice!
2. Good Chris - tian men, re - joice With heart and soul and voice!
3. Good Chris - tian men, re - joice With heart and soul and voice!
Give ye heed to what we say: Je - sus Christ is born to - day;
Now ye hear of end - less bliss; Je - sus Christ was born for this!
Now ye need not fear the grave; Je - sus Christ was born to save!
Ox and ass be - fore Him bow, And He is in the man - ger now.
He hath oped the heav'n - ly door, And man is blest for - ev - er - more.
Calls you one and calls you all To gain His ev - er - last - ing hall.
Christ is born to - day! Christ is born to - day!
Christ was born for this! Christ was born for this!
Christ was born to save! Christ was born to save!

WORDS: Latin carol, 14th century; tr. John M. Neale, 1853
MUSIC: Traditional German melody

IN DULCI JUBILO
Irregular meter

While by the Sheep We Watched 99

Therefore with joy shall they draw water out of the wells of salvation . . . Isa. 12:3

1. While by the sheep we watched at night,
Glad tidings brought an angel bright.
How great our joy! Great our joy!
Joy, joy, joy! Joy, joy, joy!
Praise we the Lord in heav'n on high!
Praise we the Lord in heav'n on high!

2. There shall be born, so he did say,
In Bethlehem a Child today.
How great our joy! Great our joy!
Joy, joy, joy! Joy, joy, joy!
Praise we the Lord in heav'n on high!
Praise we the Lord in heav'n on high!

3. There shall the Child lie in a stall,
This Child who shall redeem us all.
How great our joy! Great our joy!
Joy, joy, joy! Joy, joy, joy!
Praise we the Lord in heav'n on high!
Praise we the Lord in heav'n on high!

4. This gift of God we'll cherish well,
That ever joy our hearts shall fill.
How great our joy! Great our joy!
Joy, joy, joy! Joy, joy, joy!
Praise we the Lord in heav'n on high!
Praise we the Lord in heav'n on high!

WORDS: Traditional German carol
MUSIC: Traditional German melody; arr. Hugo Jungst, c.1890

JUNGST
Irregular meter

100 Gentle Mary Laid Her Child

And she brought forth her firstborn son . . . and laid Him in a manger. Luke 2:7

1. Gen - tle Ma - ry laid her Child Low - ly in a man - ger;
There He lay, the un - de - filed, To the world a stran - ger:
Such a Babe in such a place, Can He be the Sav - ior?
Ask the saved of all the race Who have found His fa - vor.

2. An - gels sang a - bout His birth; Wise Men sought and found Him;
Heav - en's star shone bright - ly forth, Glo - ry all a - round Him:
Shep - herds saw the won - drous sight, Heard the an - gels sing - ing;
All the plains were lit that night, All the hills were ring - ing.

3. Gen - tle Ma - ry laid her Child Low - ly in a man - ger;
He is still the un - de - filed, But no more a stran - ger:
Son of God, of hum - ble birth, Beau - ti - ful the sto - ry;
Praise His name in all the earth, Hail the King of glo - ry!

WORDS: Joseph S. Cook, 1919
MUSIC: *Piae Cantiones*, 1582; arr. Ernest Macmillan, 1930

TEMPUS ADEST FLORIDUM
7.6.7.6 D.

Infant Holy, Infant Lowly 101

For He is Lord of lords, and King of kings . . . and they that are with Him are called, and chosen, and faithful. Rev. 17:14

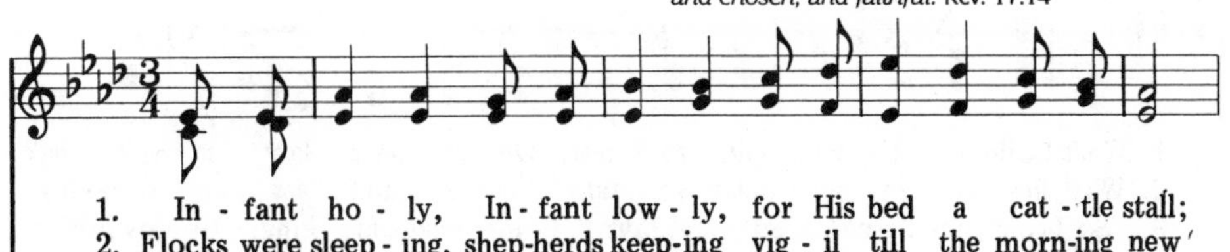
1. In - fant ho - ly, In - fant low - ly, for His bed a cat - tle stall;
2. Flocks were sleep - ing, shep-herds keep-ing vig - il till the morn-ing new

Ox - en low - ing, lit - tle know-ing Christ the babe is Lord of all.
Saw the glo - ry, heard the sto - ry, tid - ings of a gos - pel true.

Swift are wing - ing an - gels sing - ing, no - els ring - ing,
Thus re - joic - ing, free from sor - row, prais - es voic - ing,

tid - ings bring - ing: Christ the babe is Lord of all.
greet the mor - row: Christ the babe was born for you.

WORDS: Polish carol; paraphrase by Edith E. M. Reed, c.1925
MUSIC: Traditional Polish carol

W ZLOBIE LEZY
8.7.8.7.8.8.7

102 What Child Is This, Who, Laid to Rest

Where is He that is born King of the Jews? Matt. 2:2

1. What Child is this, who, laid to rest, On Ma - ry's lap is sleep-ing?
2. Why lies He in such mean es - tate Where ox and ass are feed - ing?
3. So bring Him in - cense, gold and myrrh, Come, peas-ant, king, to own Him;
Whom an - gels greet with an - thems sweet, While shep-herds watch are keep-ing?
Good Chris - tian, fear; for sin - ners here The si - lent Word is plead - ing.
The King of kings sal - va - tion brings, Let lov - ing hearts en-throne Him.
Refrain
This, this is Christ the King, Whom shep-herds guard and an - gels sing:
This, this is Christ the King, The babe, the Son of Ma - ry.

WORDS: William C. Dix, c.1865
MUSIC: Traditional English melody, 16th century

GREENSLEEVES
8.7.8.7 Ref.

Long Years Ago on a Deep Winter Night 103

When they saw the star, they rejoiced . . . Matt. 2:10

1. Long years a - go on a deep win - ter night,
2. Je - sus, the Lord, was that Ba - by so small,
3. Dear Ba - by Je - sus, how ti - ny Thou art,
High in the heav'ns a star shone bright,
Laid down to sleep in a hum - ble stall;
I'll make a place for Thee in my heart,
While in a man - ger a wee Ba - by lay,
Then came the star and it stood o - ver - head,
And when the stars in the heav - ens I see,
Sweet - ly a - sleep on a bed of hay.
Shed - ding its light 'round His lit - tle bed.
Ev - er and al - ways I think of Thee.

WORDS: Wihla Hutson, 1954
MUSIC: Alfred S. Burt, 1954

STAR CAROL
10.8.10.8

104 I Wonder as I Wander

And all they that heard it wondered at those things which were told them . . . Luke 2:18

Unison
1. I won - der as I wan - der, out un - der the sky, How Je - sus the Sav - ior did come for to die For poor ord' - nary peo - ple like you and like I; I won-der as I wan-der, out un - der the sky.
2. When Ma - ry birthed Je - sus, 'twas in a cow's stall, With wise men and farm - ers and shep-herds and all. But high from God's heav - en a star's light did fall, The prom-ise of a - ges it then did re - call.
3. If Je - sus had want - ed for an - y wee thing, A star in the sky or a bird on the wing, Or all of God's an - gels in heav'n for to sing, He sure - ly could have it, 'cause He was the King.
4. I won - der as I wan - der, out un - der the sky, How Je - sus the Sav - ior did come for to die For poor ord' - nary peo - ple like you and like I; I won-der as I wan-der, out un - der the sky. Out un-der the sky.
(Optional Coda)

WORDS: Appalachian carol; John Jacob Niles, 1934
MUSIC: John Jacob Niles, 1934; arr. Donald P. Hustad, 1984

I WONDER AS I WANDER
Irregular meter

That Boy-Child of Mary 105

A virgin shall . . . bear a son . . . and shall call His name Immanuel. Isa. 7:14

Refrain
Unison
That boy-child of Ma - ry was born in a sta - ble, A
man-ger His cra - dle in Beth - le-hem.
Fine
1. What shall we call Him, child of the man - ger?
2. His name is Je - su, God ev - er with us,
3. How can He save us, how can He help us,
4. Gift of the Fa - ther, to hu-man moth - er,
5. One with the Fa - ther, He is our Sav - ior,
6. Glad-ly we praise Him, love and a-dore Him,
What name is giv - en in Beth - le - hem?
God giv - en for us, in Beth - le - hem.
Born here a - mong us, in Beth - le - hem?
Makes Him our broth - er of Beth - le - hem.
Heav - en - sent Help - er of Beth - le - hem.
Give our-selves to Him, of Beth - le - hem.
D. C. al Fine

WORDS: Tom Colvin, 1969
MUSIC: Traditional Malawi melody; adapt. Tom Colvin, 1969

BLANTYRE
Irregular meter

106 Mary, Mary

Behold, thou shalt . . . bring forth a son, and shalt call His name Jesus. Luke 1:31

Unison
Ma - ry, Ma - ry, what you gon - na name that ba - by?
What you gon - na call that ho - ly ba - by?
Fine
1. Slaves are we and look - ing for a mas - ter: Why don't you
2. We, like our sheep, need some - one to guide us, Why don't you
3. Hun - gry and poor, we need some - one to save us, Why don't you
4. Kings of the world, we seek some - one to rule us, Why don't you
1,2,3
4
D.C. al Fine
call Him Lord? Sh! Let's all call Him Lord!
call Him Shep - herd? Sh! Let's all call Him Shep - herd!
call Him Sav - ior? Sh! Let's all call Him Sav - ior!
call Him King? Sh! Let's all call Him King!

WORDS and MUSIC: Richard Avery and Donald Marsh, 1967

ROSECHESTER
Irregular meter

Go, Tell It on the Mountain 107

. . . They made known abroad the saying . . . concerning this child. Luke 2:17

Unison
(Ref.) Go, tell it on the moun-tain, O-ver the hills and ev-ery-where;
Go, tell it on the moun-tain That Je-sus Christ is born.
Fine
1. While shep-herds kept their watch-ing O'er si-lent flocks by night, Be-hold, through-out the heav-ens There shone a ho-ly light.
2. The shep-herds feared and trem-bled When, lo! a-bove the earth Rang out the an-gel cho-rus That hailed our Sav-ior's birth.
3. Down in a low-ly man-ger Our hum-ble Christ was born, And God sent us sal-va-tion That bless-ed Christ-mas morn.
D.C.

WORDS: John W. Work, 1907
MUSIC: Traditional Spiritual

GO TELL IT
Irregular meter

108 Angels from the Realms of Glory

We . . . are come to worship Him. Matt. 2:2

1. An - gels from the realms of glo - ry, Wing your flight o'er all the earth;
2. Shep-herds in the fields a - bid - ing, Watch-ing o'er your flocks by night,
3. Sag - es, leave your con - tem - pla - tions, Bright-er vi - sions beam a - far;
4. Saints be - fore the al - tar bend - ing, Watch-ing long in hope and fear,

Ye who sang cre - a - tion's sto - ry, Now pro-claim Mes - si - ah's birth:
God with man is now re - sid - ing, Yon - der shines the in - fant Light:
Seek the great De - sire of na - tions, Ye have seen His na - tal star:
Sud - den - ly the Lord, de - scend - ing, In His tem - ple shall ap - pear:

Refrain

Come and wor-ship, come and wor-ship, Wor-ship Christ, the new-born King. A-men.

WORDS: James Montgomery, 1816
MUSIC: Henry T. Smart, 1867

REGENT SQUARE
8.7.8.7.8.7

109 From Heaven Above to Earth I Come

I bring you good tidings of great joy . . . Luke 2:10

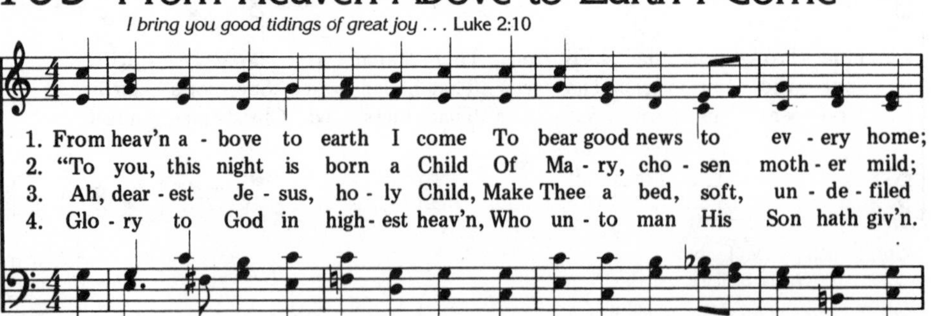
1. From heav'n a - bove to earth I come To bear good news to ev - ery home;
2. "To you, this night is born a Child Of Ma - ry, cho - sen moth - er mild;
3. Ah, dear - est Je - sus, ho - ly Child, Make Thee a bed, soft, un - de - filed
4. Glo - ry to God in high - est heav'n, Who un - to man His Son hath giv'n.

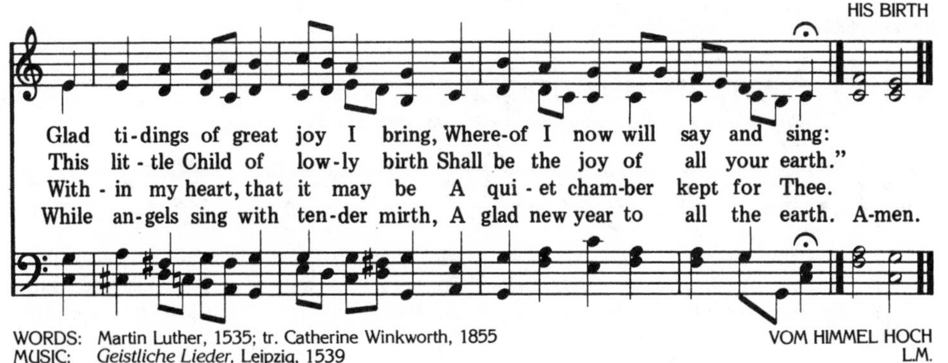
Glad ti-dings of great joy I bring, Where-of I now will say and sing:
This lit - tle Child of low-ly birth Shall be the joy of all your earth."
With - in my heart, that it may be A qui - et cham-ber kept for Thee.
While an-gels sing with ten-der mirth, A glad new year to all the earth. A-men.

WORDS: Martin Luther, 1535; tr. Catherine Winkworth, 1855
MUSIC: *Geistliche Lieder*, Leipzig, 1539

VOM HIMMEL HOCH
L.M.

While Shepherds Watched Their Flocks 110

There were shepherds abiding in the field, keeping watch over their flocks . . . Luke 2:8

1. While shep-herds watched their flocks by night, All seat - ed on the
2. "Fear not!" said he; for might - y dread Had seized their troub - led
3. "To you, in Da - vid's town this day, Is born of Da - vid's
4. "The heav'n-ly Babe you there shall find To hu - man view dis -
5. "All glo - ry be to God on high, And to the earth be

ground, The an - gel of the Lord came down, And
mind, "Glad ti - dings of great joy I bring To
line, The Sav - ior who is Christ the Lord, And
played, All mean - ly wrapped in swath - ing bands, And
peace: Good will hence - forth from heav'n to men, Be -

glo - ry shone a - round, And glo - ry shone a - round.
you and all man - kind, To you and all man - kind.
this shall be the sign: And this shall be the sign:
in a man - ger laid; And in a man - ger laid.
gin and nev - er cease, Be - gin and nev - er cease." A-men.

WORDS: Nahum Tate, 1700; based on Luke 2:8-14
MUSIC: George Frederick Handel, 1728; arr. in Weyman's *Melodia Sacra*, 1815

CHRISTMAS
C.M. Repeats

111 Away in a Manger

She brought forth her firstborn son . . . and laid Him in a manger. Luke 2:7

Unison

1. A - way in a man - ger, no crib for a bed, The lit - tle Lord Je - sus laid down His sweet head; The stars in the bright sky looked down where He lay, The lit - tle Lord Je - sus a - sleep on the hay.
2. The cat - tle are low - ing, the Ba - by a - wakes, But lit - tle Lord Je - sus, no cry - ing He makes. I love Thee, Lord Je - sus, look down from the sky, And stay by my cra - dle till morn - ing is nigh.
3. Be near me, Lord Je - sus; I ask Thee to stay Close by me for - ev - er, and love me, I pray. Bless all the dear chil - dren in Thy ten - der care, And fit us for heav - en, to live with Thee there.

WORDS: Source unknown, 1885, 1892
MUSIC: William J. Kirkpatrick, 1895

CRADLE SONG
11.11.11.11

112 Away in a Manger

She brought forth her firstborn son . . . and laid Him in a manger. Luke 2:7

1. A - way in a man - ger, no crib for a bed, The lit - tle Lord
2. The cat - tle are low - ing, the Ba - by a - wakes, But lit - tle Lord
3. Be near me, Lord Je - sus; I ask Thee to stay Close by me for -

Je - sus laid down His sweet head; The stars in the sky looked
Je - sus, no cry - ing He makes; I love Thee, Lord Je - sus, look
ev - er, and love me, I pray. Bless all the dear chil - dren in
down where He lay, The lit - tle Lord Je - sus a - sleep on the hay.
down from the sky, And stay by my cra - dle till morn - ing is nigh.
Thy ten - der care, And fit us for heav - en, to live with Thee there.
WORDS: Source unknown, 1885, 1892
MUSIC: James R. Murray, 1887
MUELLER
11.11.11.11
Silent Night! Holy Night! 113
And they . . . found Mary, and Joseph, and the babe lying in a manger. Luke 2:16
1. Si - lent night! ho - ly night! All is calm, all is bright
2. Si - lent night! ho - ly night! Shep - herds quake at the sight,
3. Si - lent night! ho - ly night! Son of God, love's pure light,
'Round yon vir - gin moth - er and Child, Ho - ly In - fant so ten - der and mild,
Glo - ries stream from heav - en a - far, Heav'n-ly hosts sing Al - le - lu - ia;
Ra - diant beams from Thy ho - ly face, With the dawn of re - deem - ing grace,
Sleep in heav - en - ly peace, Sleep in heav - en - ly peace.
Christ the Sav - ior is born, Christ the Sav - ior is born.
Je - sus, Lord, at Thy birth, Je - sus, Lord, at Thy birth. A-men.

WORDS: Joseph Mohr, 1818; tr. John F. Young, 1863
MUSIC: Franz Grüber, 1818

STILLE NACHT
Irregular meter

114 Let All Mortal Flesh Keep Silence

Let all the earth keep silence . . . Heb. 2:20

Unison
1. Let all mor - tal flesh keep si - lence, And with fear and
2. King of kings, yet born of Ma - ry, As of old on
3. Rank on rank the host of heav - en Spreads its van - guard
4. At his feet the six - winged Ser - aph, Cher - u - bim, with
trem - bling stand; Pon - der noth-ing earth - ly mind - ed,
earth He stood, Lord of lords, in hu - man ves - ture,
on the way, As the Light of light de - scend - eth
sleep - less eye, Veil their fac - es to the pres - ence,
For with bless - ing in His hand, Christ our God to
In the bod - y and the blood, He will give to
From the realms of end - less day, That the pow'rs of
As with cease - less voice they cry, Al - le - lu - ia,
earth de - scend - eth, Our full hom-age to de - mand.
all the faith - ful His own self for heav'n - ly food.
hell may van - ish As the dark-ness clears a - way.
Al - le - lu - ia, Al - le - lu - ia, Lord most high! A - men.

WORDS: *Liturgy of St. James*, 5th century; adapt. Gerard Moultrie, 1864
MUSIC: Traditional French melody, 17th century; Hymn version, 1906

PICARDY
8.7.8.7.8.7

As with Gladness Men of Old 115

When they saw the star, they rejoiced . . . Matt. 2:10

1. As with glad - ness men of old Did the guid - ing star be - hold; As with joy they hailed its light, Lead - ing on - ward, beam - ing bright, So, most gra - cious Lord, may we Ev - er - more be led to Thee.
2. As with joy - ful steps they sped To that low - ly man - ger bed, There to bend the knee be - fore Him Whom heav'n and earth a - dore, So, may we with will - ing feet Ev - er seek the mer - cy seat.
3. As they of - fered gifts most rare At that man - ger rude and bare, So may we with ho - ly joy, Pure and free from sin's al - loy, All our cost - liest treas - ures bring, Christ, to Thee our heav'n - ly King.
4. Ho - ly Je - sus, ev - ery day Keep us in the nar - row way; And when earth - ly things are past, Bring our ran - somed souls at last Where they need no star to guide, Where no clouds Thy glo - ry hide. A - men.

WORDS: William C. Dix, 1858
MUSIC: Conrad Kocher, 1838

DIX
7.7.7.7.7.7

116 We Three Kings of Orient Are

Behold, there came wise men from the east . . . Matt. 2:1

1. We three kings of O - ri - ent are, Bear - ing gifts we trav - erse a - far Field and foun - tain, moor and moun - tain, Fol - low - ing yon - der star.
2. Born a King on Beth - le - hem's plain, Gold I bring to crown Him a - gain, King for - ev - er, ceas - ing nev - er O - ver us all to reign.
3. Frank - in - cense to of - fer have I, In - cense owns a De - i - ty nigh; Prayer and prais - ing, all men rais - ing, Wor - ship Him, God on high.
4. Myrrh is mine; its bit - ter per - fume Breathes a life of gath - er - ing gloom; Sor - rowing, sigh - ing, bleed - ing, dy - ing, Sealed in the stone - cold tomb.
5. Glo - rious now be - hold Him a - rise, King and God and Sac - ri - fice; Al - le - lu - ia, Al - le - lu - ia! Peals through the earth and skies.
Refrain
O star of won - der, star of night, Star with roy - al beau - ty bright, West - ward lead - ing, still pro - ceed - ing, Guide us to thy per - fect light.

WORDS and MUSIC: John H. Hopkins, 1857

THREE KINGS OF ORIENT
8.8.4.4.6 Ref.

Lo! How a Rose E'er Blooming 117

I am the rose of Sharon, the lily of the valley. S. of Sol. 2:1

1. Lo! how a rose e'er bloom - ing From ten - der stem hath
2. I - sa - iah 'twas fore - told it, The rose I have in
3. This flower, whose fra - grance ten - der With sweet - ness fills the
sprung! Of Jes - se's lin - eage com - ing As men of old have
mind; With Mar - y we be - hold it, The vir - gin moth - er
air, Dis - pels with glo - rious splen - dor The dark - ness ev - ery -
sung. It came, a flow - eret bright, A - mid the
kind. To show God's love a - right She bore to
where. True man, yet ver - y God, From sin and
cold of win - ter, When half - spent was the night.
men a Sav - ior, When half - spent was the night.
death He saves us And light - ens ev - ery load.

WORDS: German carol, 16th century; Sts. 1, 2, tr. Theodore Baker, 1894; St. 3, tr. Harriet Krauth Spaeth, 1875
MUSIC: *Geistliche Kirchengesäng*, 1599; harm. Michael Praetorius, 1609

ES IST EIN' ROS' ENTSPRUNGEN
Irregular meter

118 Thou Didst Leave Thy Throne

He came unto His own and His own received Him not. John 1:11

1. Thou didst leave Thy throne and Thy king - ly crown When Thou
2. Heav - en's arch - es rang when the an - gels sang, Pro -
3. The fox - es found rest and the birds their nest In the
4. Thou cam - est, O Lord, with the liv - ing Word That should
5. When the heav - ens shall ring, and the an - gels sing, At Thy
cam - est to earth for me; But in Beth - le - hem's home
claim - ing Thy roy - al de - gree; But in low - ly birth
shade of the for - est tree; But thy couch was the sod,
set Thy peo - ple free; But with mock - ing scorn,
com - ing to vic - to - ry, Let Thy voice call me home,
there was found no room For Thy ho - ly na - tiv - i - ty:
Thou didst come to earth, And in great hu - mil - i - ty:
O Thou Son of God, In the des - ert of Gal - i - lee:
and with crown of thorn, They bore Thee to Cal - va - ry:
say - ing, "Yet there is room, There is room at My side for thee:"
Refrain
1-4. O come to my heart, Lord Je - sus! There is room in my heart for Thee.
5. My heart shall re-joice, Lord Je - sus! When Thou com-est and call-est for me. A-men.

WORDS: Emily E. S. Elliott, 1864
MUSIC: Timothy R. Matthews, 1876

MARGARET
Irregular meter

Tell Me the Story of Jesus 119

He expounded unto them . . . the things concerning Himself. Luke 24:27

1. Tell me the sto-ry of Je-sus, Write on my heart ev-ery word;
2. Fast-ing a-lone in the des-ert, Tell of the days that are past,
3. Tell of the cross where they nailed Him, Writhing in an-guish and pain;
Ref. Tell me the sto-ry of Je-sus, Write on my heart ev-ery word;
Fine
Tell me the sto-ry most pre-cious, Sweet-est that ev-er was heard.
How for our sins He was tempt-ed, Yet was tri-um-phant at last.
Tell of the grave where they laid Him, Tell how He liv-eth a-gain.
Tell me the sto-ry most pre-cious, Sweet-est that ev-er was heard.
Tell how the an-gels in cho-rus Sang as they wel-comed His birth,
Tell of the years of His la-bor, Tell of the sor-row He bore,
Love in that sto-ry so ten-der Clear-er than ev-er I see:
D.C. for Refrain
"Glo-ry to God in the high-est! Peace and good ti-dings to earth."
He was de-spised and af-flict-ed, Home-less, re-ject-ed and poor.
Stay, let me weep while you whis-per, Love paid the ran-som for me.

WORDS: Fanny J. Crosby, 1880
MUSIC: John R. Sweney, 1880

STORY OF JESUS
8.7.8.7 D. Ref.

120 Amen, Amen!

And the Word was made flesh and dwelt among us. John 1:14

A - men, A - men, A -
Solo
1. See the lit - tle ba - by
2. See Him in the tem - ple
3. See Him at the sea - shore
4. See Him in the gar - den
5. See Him on the cross
6. Yes, He died to save us
7. Al - le - lu - ia!
men, A - men, A - men!
A -
ly - ing in a man - ger
talk - ing to the el - ders;
preach-ing to the peo - ple,
pray - ing to the Fa - ther
bear - ing all my sins
and He rose on Eas - ter,
Je - sus is my Sav - ior
on Christ - mas morn - ing,
how they all mar - velled!
heal-ing all the sick ones!
in deep - est sor - row!
in bit - ter ag - o - ny,
now He lives for-ev - er!
for He lives for-ev - er!
men,
A - men,
last time
A - men, A - men, A - men!

WORDS and MUSIC: Traditional Spiritual; adapt. John F. Wilson, 1970

AMEN
Irregular meter

O Sing a Song of Bethlehem 121

To this end was I born, and for this cause came I into the world. John 18:37

1. O sing a song of Beth-le-hem, Of shep-herds watch-ing there,
2. O sing a song of Naz-a-reth, Of sun-ny days of joy,
3. O sing a song of Gal-i-lee, Of lake and woods and hill,
4. O sing a song of Cal-va-ry, Its glo-ry and dis-may;
And of the news that came to them From an-gels in the air:
O sing of fra-grant flow-ers' breath, And of the sin-less Boy:
Of Him who walked up-on the sea And bade the waves be still:
Of Him who hung up-on the tree, And took our sins a-way:
The light that shone on Beth-le-hem Fills all the world to-day;
For now the flowers of Naz-a-reth In ev-ery heart may grow;
For though like waves on Gal-i-lee, Dark seas of trou-ble roll,
For He who died on Cal-va-ry Is ris-en from the grave,
Of Je-sus' birth and peace on earth The an-gels sing al-way.
Now spreads the fame of His dear name On all the winds that blow.
When faith has heard the Mas-ter's word, Falls peace up-on the soul.
And Christ, our Lord, by heav'n a-dored, Is might-y now to save.

WORDS: Louis F. Benson, 1899
MUSIC: Traditional English melody; arr. Ralph Vaughan Williams, 1906

KINGSFOLD
C.M.D.

122 One Day When Heaven Was Filled

When the fulness of the time was come, God sent forth His Son . . . Gal. 4:4

1. One day when heav - en was filled with His prais - es, One day when
2. One day they led Him up Cal - va - ry's moun - tain, One day they
3. One day they left Him a - lone in the gar - den, One day He
4. One day the grave could con - ceal Him no long - er, One day the
5. One day the trum - pet will sound for His com - ing, One day the

sin was as black as could be, Je - sus came forth to be
nailed Him to die on the tree; Suf - fer - ing an - guish, de-
rest - ed, from suf - fer - ing free; An - gels came down o'er His
stone rolled a - way from the door; Then He a - rose, o - ver
skies with His glo - ry will shine; Won - der - ful day, my be-

born of a vir - gin, Dwelt a - mong men, my ex - am - ple is He!
spised and re - ject - ed, Bear - ing our sins, my Re - deem - er is He!
tomb to keep vig - il; Hope of the hope - less, my Sav - ior is He!
death He has con-quered; Now is as - cend - ed, my Lord ev - er - more!
lov - ed ones bring - ing; Glo - ri - ous Sav - ior, this Je - sus is mine!

Refrain

Liv - ing, He loved me; dy - ing, He saved me; Bur - ied, He

car - ried my sins far a - way; Ris - ing, He jus - ti - fied

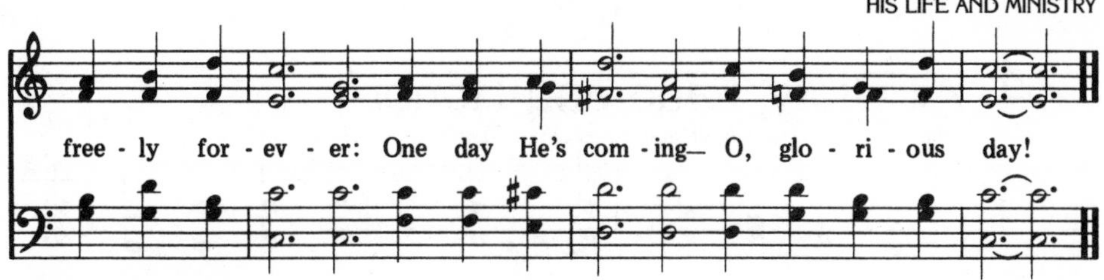
free - ly for - ev - er: One day He's com - ing— O, glo - ri - ous day!

WORDS: J. Wilbur Chapman, 1910
MUSIC: Charles H. Marsh, 1910

CHAPMAN
11.10.11.10 Ref.

Who Is He in Yonder Stall? 123

He is Lord of lords and King of kings. Rev. 17:14

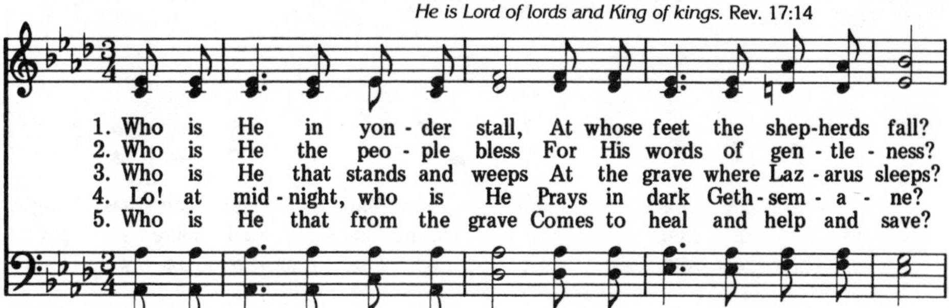

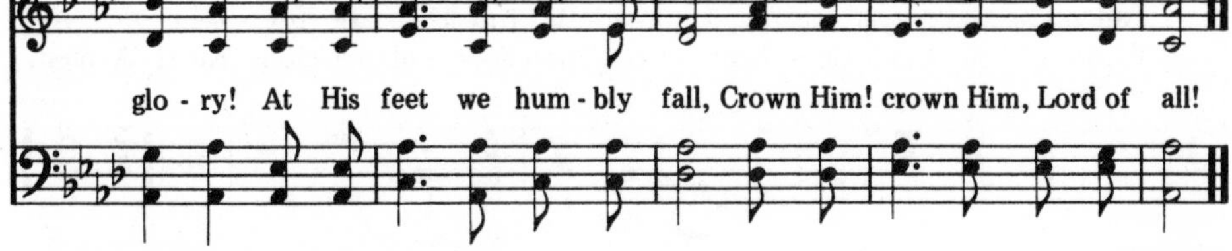

1. Who is He in yon - der stall, At whose feet the shep-herds fall?
2. Who is He the peo - ple bless For His words of gen - tle - ness?
3. Who is He that stands and weeps At the grave where Laz - arus sleeps?
4. Lo! at mid - night, who is He Prays in dark Geth - sem - a - ne?
5. Who is He that from the grave Comes to heal and help and save?

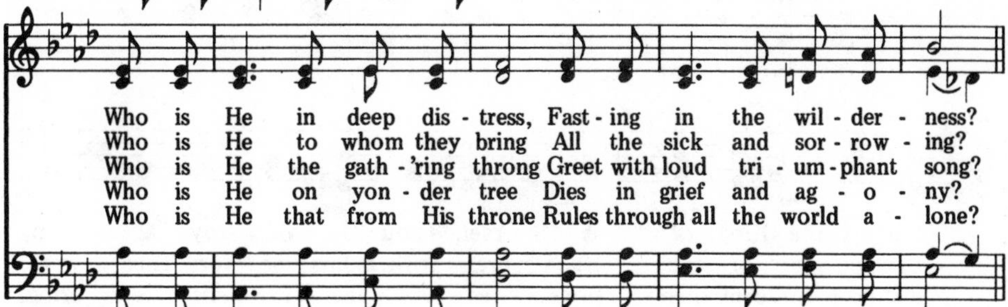

Who is He in deep dis - tress, Fast - ing in the wil - der - ness?
Who is He to whom they bring All the sick and sor - row - ing?
Who is He the gath - 'ring throng Greet with loud tri - um - phant song?
Who is He on yon - der tree Dies in grief and ag - o - ny?
Who is He that from His throne Rules through all the world a - lone?

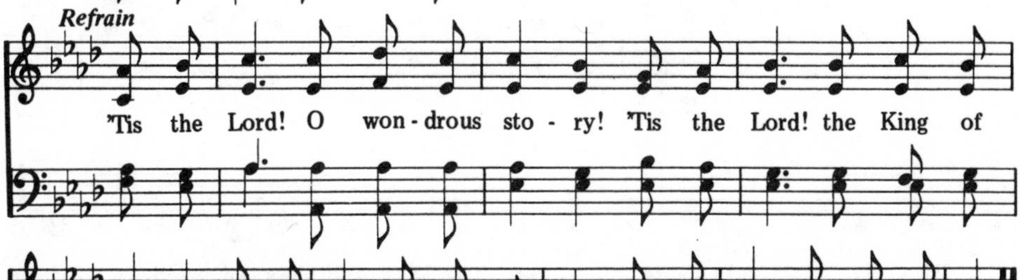

Refrain

'Tis the Lord! O won - drous sto - ry! 'Tis the Lord! the King of glo - ry! At His feet we hum - bly fall, Crown Him! crown Him, Lord of all!

WORDS and MUSIC: Benjamin R. Hanby, 1866

LOWLINESS
7.7.7.7 Ref.

124 All Glory, Laud and Honor

Blessed is the King of Israel that cometh in the name of the Lord. John 12:13

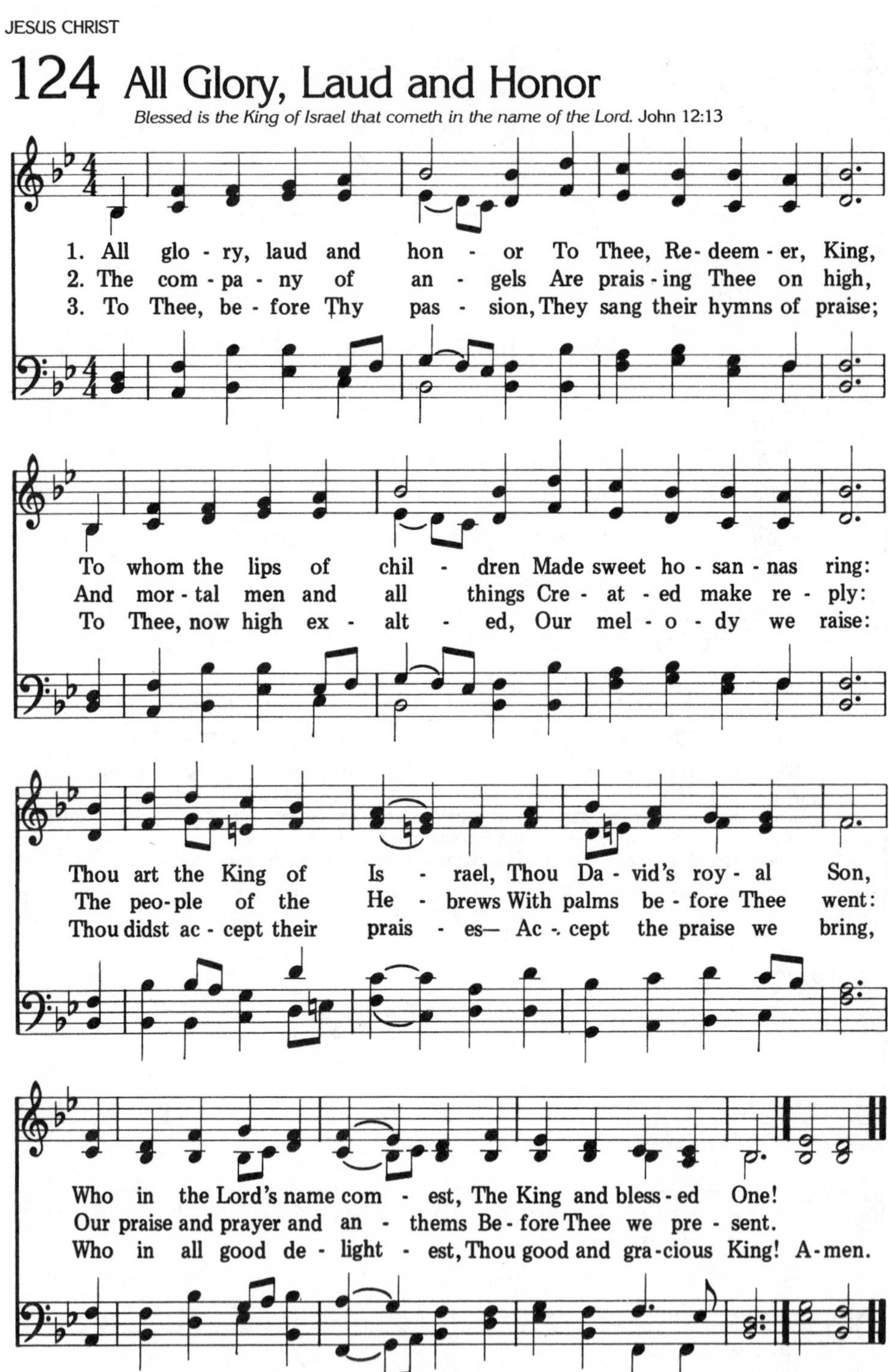
1. All glo - ry, laud and hon - or To Thee, Re- deem - er, King,
2. The com - pa - ny of an - gels Are prais - ing Thee on high,
3. To Thee, be - fore Thy pas - sion, They sang their hymns of praise;
To whom the lips of chil - dren Made sweet ho - san - nas ring:
And mor - tal men and all things Cre - at - ed make re - ply:
To Thee, now high ex - alt - ed, Our mel - o - dy we raise:
Thou art the King of Is - rael, Thou Da - vid's roy - al Son,
The peo- ple of the He - brews With palms be - fore Thee went:
Thou didst ac - cept their prais - es— Ac - cept the praise we bring,
Who in the Lord's name com - est, The King and bless - ed One!
Our praise and prayer and an - thems Be - fore Thee we pre - sent.
Who in all good de - light - est, Thou good and gra - cious King! A - men.

WORDS: Theodulph of Orleans, c. 800; tr. John M. Neale, 1854
MUSIC: Melchior Teschner, c.1613

ST. THEODULPH
7.6.7.6 D.

Ride On, Ride On, O Savior King 125

. . . Behold, thy King cometh unto thee, meek, and sitting upon an ass . . . Matt. 21:5

1. Ride on, ride on, O Sav - ior King, To set the sin - ner free!
2. Ride on, ride on, O Sav - ior King, To claim the hearts of men!
3. Ride on, ride on, O Sav - ior King! Ride on o'er land and sea,
To sin-cursed souls sal - va - tion bring And peace e - ter - nal - ly!
Now death has lost its dread - ful sting And hope is born a - gain.
For You a - lone to man can bring E - ter - nal lib - er - ty.
Ride on to dark Geth - sem - a - ne, To un - told ag - o - ny,
O come, in hu - man hearts to reign; Sup - press the pow'r of sin!
Ride on to sin - bound na - tions, Lord, Un - til each heart shall own
And on the cross of Cal - va - ry Pro - cure our vic - to - ry!
Our own en - deav - or is in vain; Lord, You must help us win!
Your sav - ing, sanc - ti - fy - ing word, And bow be - fore Your throne!

WORDS: Carl K. Solberg, c.1930
MUSIC: Henry S. Cutler, 1872

ALL SAINTS, NEW
C.M.D.

126 Hosanna, Loud Hosanna

Hosanna; Blessed is He that cometh in the name of the Lord. Mark 11:9

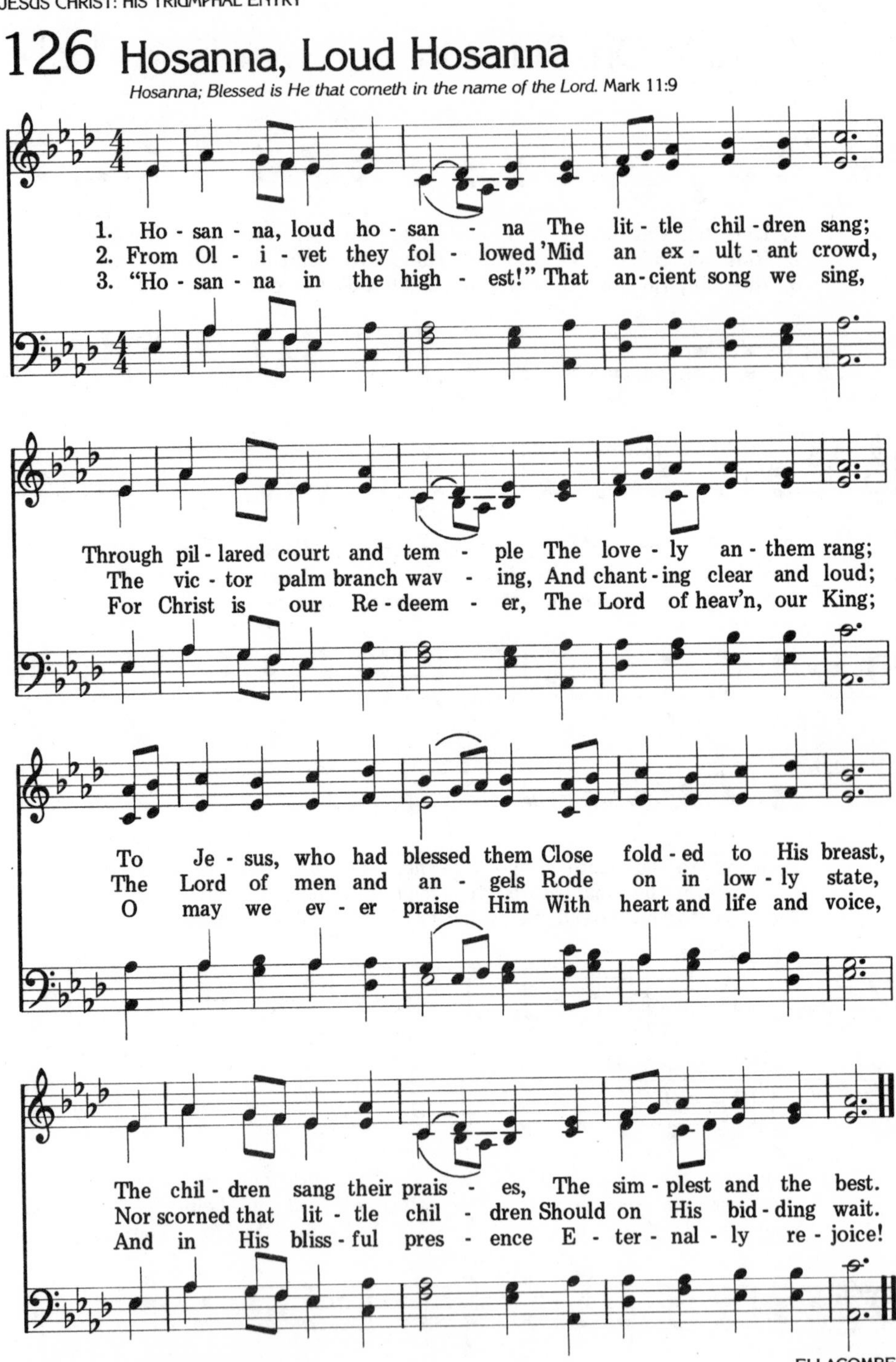
1. Ho - san - na, loud ho - san - na The lit - tle chil - dren sang;
2. From Ol - i - vet they fol - lowed 'Mid an ex - ult - ant crowd,
3. "Ho - san - na in the high - est!" That an - cient song we sing,
Through pil - lared court and tem - ple The love - ly an - them rang;
The vic - tor palm branch wav - ing, And chant - ing clear and loud;
For Christ is our Re - deem - er, The Lord of heav'n, our King;
To Je - sus, who had blessed them Close fold - ed to His breast,
The Lord of men and an - gels Rode on in low - ly state,
O may we ev - er praise Him With heart and life and voice,
The chil - dren sang their prais - es, The sim - plest and the best.
Nor scorned that lit - tle chil - dren Should on His bid - ding wait.
And in His bliss - ful pres - ence E - ter - nal - ly re - joice!

WORDS: Jennette Threlfall, 1873
MUSIC: *Gesangbuch*, Wirtemberg, 1784

ELLACOMBE
7.6.7.6 D.

Beneath the Cross of Jesus 127

Now there stood by the cross of Jesus . . . John 19:25

1. Be - neath the cross of Je - sus I fain would take my stand—
2. Up - on that cross of Je - sus Mine eye at times can see
3. I take, O cross, thy shad - ow For my a - bid - ing place;

The shad - ow of a might - y Rock With - in a wea - ry land;
The ver - y dy - ing form of One Who suf - fered there for me;
I ask no oth - er sun - shine than The sun - shine of His face;

A home with - in the wil - der - ness, A rest up - on the way,
And from my smit - ten heart with tears Two won - ders I con - fess—
Con - tent to let the world go by, To know no gain nor loss,

From the burn - ing of the noon - tide heat, And the bur - den of the day.
The won - ders of re - deem - ing love And my un - wor - thi - ness.
My sin - ful self my on - ly shame, My glo - ry all the cross. A - men.

WORDS: Elizabeth C. Clephane, 1872
MUSIC: Frederick C. Maker, 1881

ST. CHRISTOPHER
7.6.8.6.8.6.8.6

128 I Saw One Hanging on a Tree

Who . . . bare our sins in His own body on the tree. I Pet. 2:24

1. I saw One hang - ing on a tree, In ag - o - ny and blood;
2. Sure, nev - er till my lat - est breath, Can I for - get that look;
3. My con-science felt and owned the guilt, And plunged me in de - spair;
4. A sec - ond look He gave, which said, "I free - ly all for - give:
He fixed His lov - ing eyes on me, As near His cross I stood.
It seemed to charge me with His death, Though not a word He spoke.
I saw my sins His blood had spilt And helped to nail Him there.
This blood is for your ran - som paid, I die that you may live."
Refrain
O, can it be, up - on a tree The Sav - ior died for me?
My soul is thrilled, my heart is filled, To think He died for me!

WORDS: John Newton, 1779
MUSIC: Edwin O. Excell, 1917

EXCELL
C.M. Ref.

Were You There? 129

It was the third hour, and they crucified Him. Mark 15:25

1. Were you there when they cru - ci - fied my Lord? (Were you there?)
2. Were you there when they nailed Him to the tree? (Were you there?)
3. Were you there when they pierced Him in the side? (Were you there?)
4. Were you there when they laid Him in the tomb? (Were you there?)
5. Were you there when He rose up from the dead? (Were you there?)
Were you there when they cru - ci - fied my Lord? (Were you there?)
Were you there when they nailed Him to the tree? (Were you there?)
Were you there when they pierced Him in the side? (Were you there?)
Were you there when they laid Him in the tomb? (Were you there?)
Were you there when He rose up from the dead? (Were you there?)
Oh! Some-times it caus - es me to trem-ble, trem-ble,
(5. Some-times I feel like shout-ing glo - ry, glo - ry,)
trem-ble, Were you there when they cru - ci - fied my Lord? (Were you there?)
trem-ble, Were you there when they nailed Him to the tree? (Were you there?)
trem-ble, Were you there when they pierced Him in the side? (Were you there?)
trem-ble, Were you there when they laid Him in the tomb? (Were you there?)
glo - ry! Were you there when He rose up from the dead? (Were you there?)

WORDS and MUSIC: Traditional Spiritual

WERE YOU THERE?
Irregular meter

130 Deep Were His Wounds, and Red

. . . And with His stripes we are healed. Isa. 53:5

Unison
1. Deep were His wounds, and red, On cru - el Cal - va - ry,
2. He suf - fered shame and scorn, And wretch-ed, dire dis - grace;
3. His life, His all He gave When He was cru - ci - fied;
As on the cross He bled In bit - ter ag - o - ny;
For - sak - en and for - lorn, He hung there in our place.
Our bur-dened souls to save, What fear - ful death He died!
But they, whom sin has wound-ed sore, Find heal - ing in the wounds He bore.
But such as would from sin be free, Look to His Cross for vic - to - ry.
But each of us, though dead in sin, Through Him e - ter - nal life may win. A-men.
1. Cross of Je - sus, cross of sor - row, Where the blood of Christ was shed,
2. Here the King of all the a - ges, Throned in light ere worlds could be,
3. O mys - te - rious con - de - scend-ing! O a - ban - don - ment sub - lime!
4. Ev - er - more for hu - man fail - ure By His pas - sion we can plead;

WORDS: William Johnson, 1958
MUSIC: Leland B. Sateren, 1958

MARLEE
6.6.6.6.8.8

131 Cross of Jesus, Cross of Sorrow

Christ also . . . suffered for sins, the just for the unjust. I Pet. 3:18

Per-fect man on thee did suf - fer, Per - fect God on thee has bled!
Robed in mor - tal flesh is dy - ing, Cru - ci - fied by sin for me.
Ver - y God Him - self is bear - ing All the suf - fer - ings of time!
God has borne all mor - tal an - guish, Sure - ly He will know our need. A-men.

WORDS: William J. Sparrow-Simpson, 1887
MUSIC: John Stainer, 1887

CROSS OF JESUS
8.7.8.7

Ask Ye What Great Thing I Know 132

I determined not to know anything . . . save Jesus Christ, and Him crucified. I Cor. 2:2

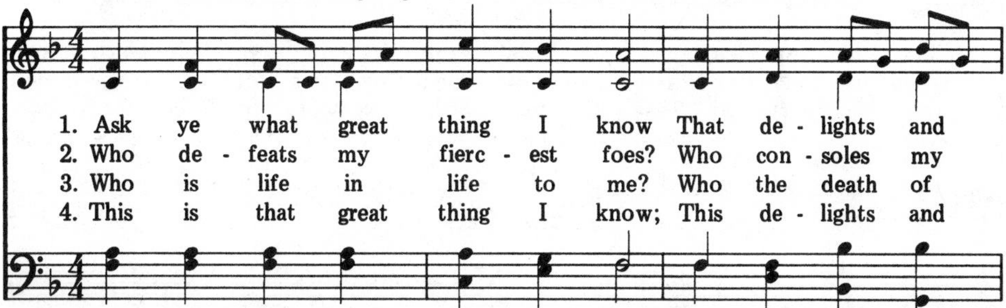

1. Ask ye what great thing I know That de - lights and
2. Who de - feats my fierc - est foes? Who con - soles my
3. Who is life in life to me? Who the death of
4. This is that great thing I know; This de - lights and

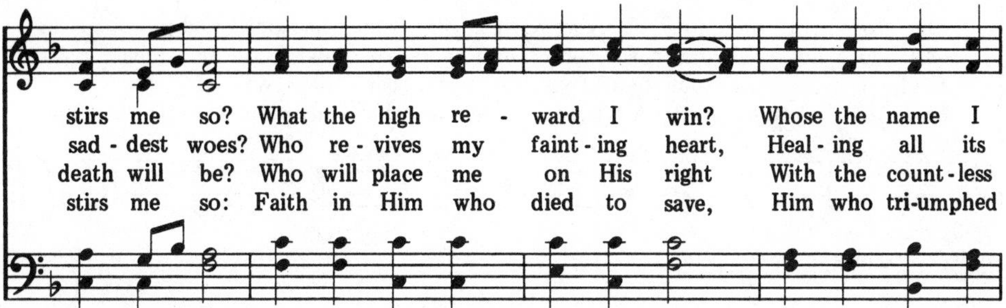

stirs me so? What the high re - ward I win? Whose the name I
sad - dest woes? Who re - vives my faint - ing heart, Heal - ing all its
death will be? Who will place me on His right With the count - less
stirs me so: Faith in Him who died to save, Him who tri-umphed

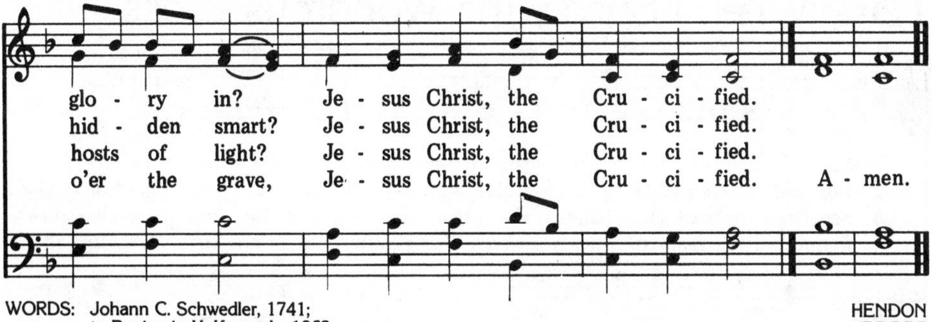

glo - ry in? Je - sus Christ, the Cru - ci - fied.
hid - den smart? Je - sus Christ, the Cru - ci - fied.
hosts of light? Je - sus Christ, the Cru - ci - fied.
o'er the grave, Je - sus Christ, the Cru - ci - fied. A - men.

WORDS: Johann C. Schwedler, 1741;
tr. Benjamin H. Kennedy, 1863
MUSIC: Henri A. César Malan, 1827

HENDON
7.7.7.7.7

133 Rock of Ages, Cleft for Me

I will put thee in a cleft of the rock, and will cover thee . . . Exo. 33:22

1. Rock of A - ges, cleft for me, Let me hide my - self in Thee;
2. Not the la - bors of my hands Can ful - fill Thy law's de - mands;
3. Noth - ing in my hand I bring, Sim - ply to Thy cross I cling;
4. While I draw this fleet - ing breath, When my eyes shall close in death,

Let the wa - ter and the blood, From Thy riv - en side which flowed,
Could my zeal no res - pite know, Could my tears for - ev - er flow,
Na - ked, come to Thee for dress, Help - less, look to Thee for grace;
When I soar to worlds un - known, See Thee on Thy judg - ment throne,

Be of sin the dou - ble cure, Cleanse me from its guilt and pow'r.
All for sin could not a - tone; Thou must save and Thou a - lone.
Foul, I to the foun - tain fly, Wash me, Sav - ior, or I die!
Rock of A - ges, cleft for me, Let me hide my - self in Thee. A-men.

WORDS: Augustus M. Toplady, 1776
MUSIC: Thomas Hastings, 1830

TOPLADY
7.7.7.7.7.7

134 When I Survey the Wondrous Cross

What things were gain to me, those I counted loss for Christ. Phil. 3:7

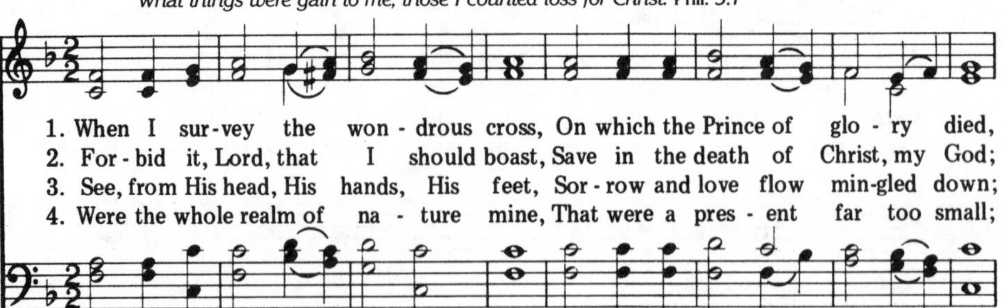
1. When I sur - vey the won - drous cross, On which the Prince of glo - ry died,
2. For - bid it, Lord, that I should boast, Save in the death of Christ, my God;
3. See, from His head, His hands, His feet, Sor - row and love flow min - gled down;
4. Were the whole realm of na - ture mine, That were a pres - ent far too small;

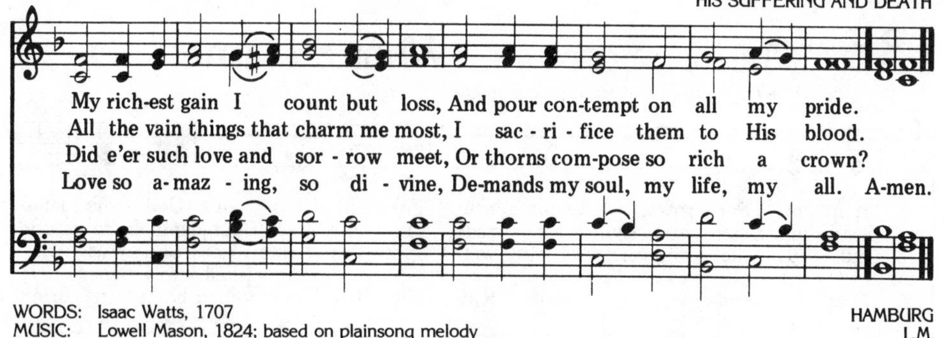
My rich-est gain I count but loss, And pour con-tempt on all my pride.
All the vain things that charm me most, I sac-ri-fice them to His blood.
Did e'er such love and sor-row meet, Or thorns com-pose so rich a crown?
Love so a-maz-ing, so di-vine, De-mands my soul, my life, my all. A-men.

WORDS: Isaac Watts, 1707
MUSIC: Lowell Mason, 1824; based on plainsong melody

HAMBURG
L.M.

Go To Dark Gethsemane 135

Then cometh Jesus with them unto a place called Gethsemane . . . Matt. 26:36

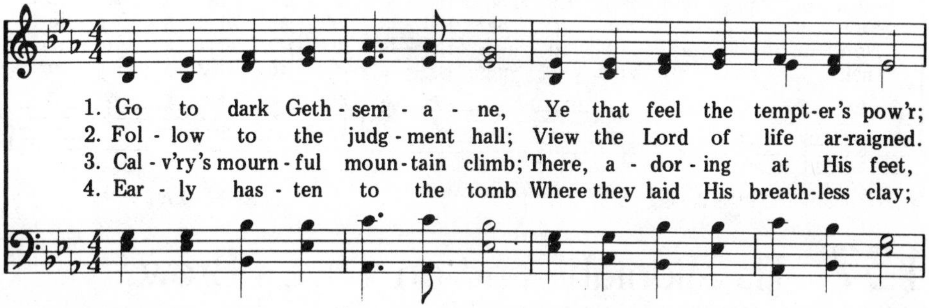

1. Go to dark Geth-sem-a-ne, Ye that feel the tempt-er's pow'r;
2. Fol-low to the judg-ment hall; View the Lord of life ar-raigned.
3. Cal-v'ry's mourn-ful moun-tain climb; There, a-dor-ing at His feet,
4. Ear-ly has-ten to the tomb Where they laid His breath-less clay;

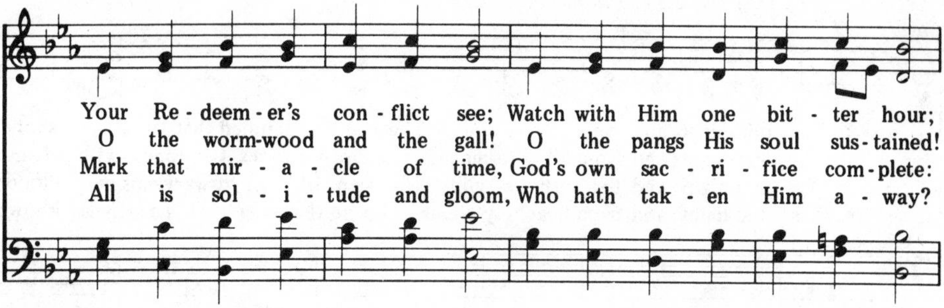

Your Re-deem-er's con-flict see; Watch with Him one bit-ter hour;
O the worm-wood and the gall! O the pangs His soul sus-tained!
Mark that mir-a-cle of time, God's own sac-ri-fice com-plete:
All is sol-i-tude and gloom, Who hath tak-en Him a-way?

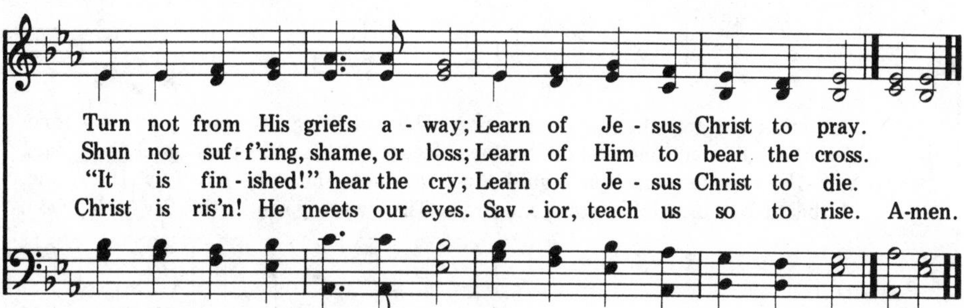

Turn not from His griefs a-way; Learn of Je-sus Christ to pray.
Shun not suf-f'ring, shame, or loss; Learn of Him to bear the cross.
"It is fin-ished!" hear the cry; Learn of Je-sus Christ to die.
Christ is ris'n! He meets our eyes. Sav-ior, teach us so to rise. A-men.

WORDS: James Montgomery, 1825
MUSIC: Richard Redhead, 1853

REDHEAD
7.7.7.7.7.7

136 "Man of Sorrows," What a Name

A man of sorrows and acquainted with grief . . . Isa. 53:3

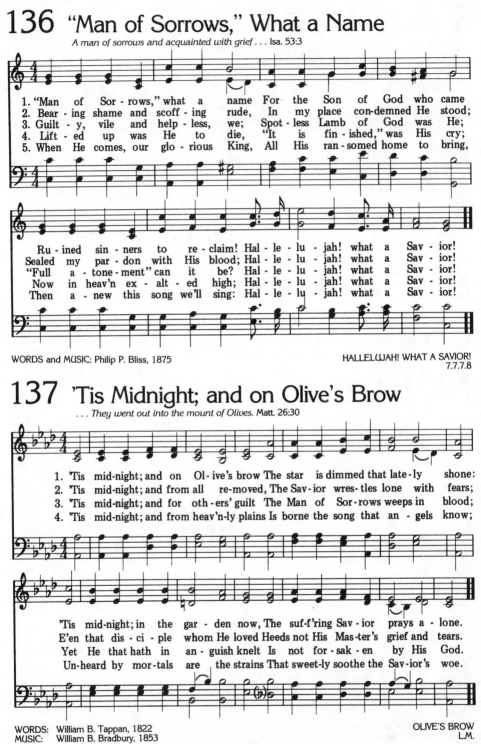

1. "Man of Sor - rows," what a name For the Son of God who came
2. Bear - ing shame and scoff - ing rude, In my place con-demned He stood;
3. Guilt - y, vile and help - less, we; Spot - less Lamb of God was He;
4. Lift - ed up was He to die, "It is fin - ished," was His cry;
5. When He comes, our glo - rious King, All His ran - somed home to bring,

Ru - ined sin - ners to re - claim! Hal - le - lu - jah! what a Sav - ior!
Sealed my par - don with His blood; Hal - le - lu - jah! what a Sav - ior!
"Full a - tone - ment" can it be? Hal - le - lu - jah! what a Sav - ior!
Now in heav'n ex - alt - ed high; Hal - le - lu - jah! what a Sav - ior!
Then a - new this song we'll sing: Hal - le - lu - jah! what a Sav - ior!

WORDS and MUSIC: Philip P. Bliss, 1875

HALLELUJAH! WHAT A SAVIOR!
7.7.7.8

137 'Tis Midnight; and on Olive's Brow

. . . They went out into the mount of Olives. Matt. 26:30

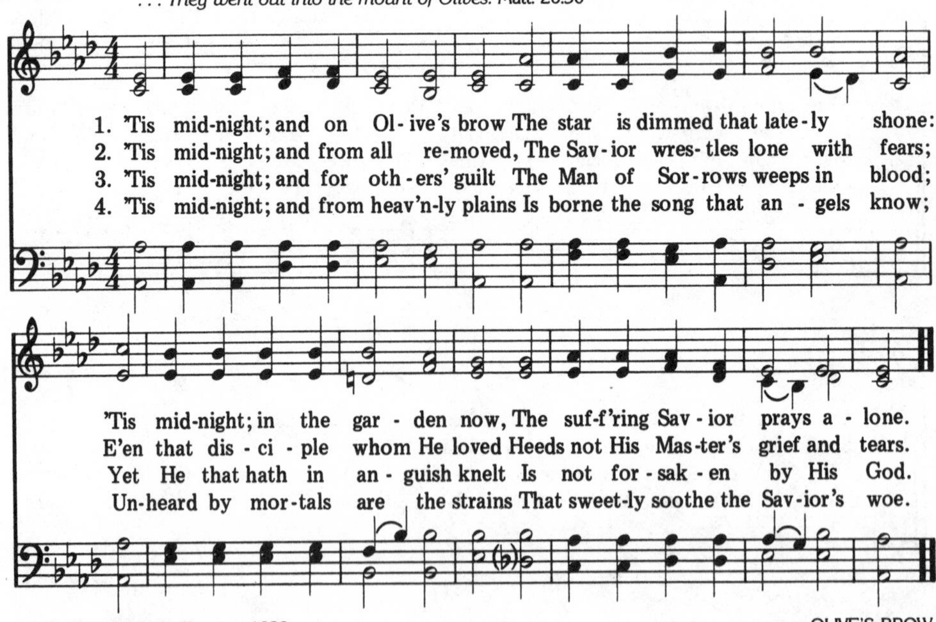

1. 'Tis mid-night; and on Ol - ive's brow The star is dimmed that late - ly shone:
2. 'Tis mid-night; and from all re-moved, The Sav - ior wres - tles lone with fears;
3. 'Tis mid-night; and for oth - ers' guilt The Man of Sor - rows weeps in blood;
4. 'Tis mid-night; and from heav'n-ly plains Is borne the song that an - gels know;
'Tis mid-night; in the gar - den now, The suf-f'ring Sav - ior prays a - lone.
E'en that dis - ci - ple whom He loved Heeds not His Mas-ter's grief and tears.
Yet He that hath in an - guish knelt Is not for - sak - en by His God.
Un-heard by mor-tals are the strains That sweet-ly soothe the Sav-ior's woe.

WORDS: William B. Tappan, 1822
MUSIC: William B. Bradbury, 1853

OLIVE'S BROW
L.M.

Up Calvary's Mountain One Dreadful Morn 138

They were come to the place called Calvary . . . Luke 23:33

1. Up Cal-vary's moun-tain one dread-ful morn, Walked Christ my Sav - ior, wea - ry and worn; Fac - ing for sin - ners death on the cross, That He might save them from end - less loss.
2. "Fa - ther, for - give them!" thus did He pray, E'en while His life-blood flowed fast a - way; Pray - ing for sin - ners while such woe— No one but Je - sus ev - er loved so.
3. O how I love Him, Sav - ior and Friend, How can my prais - es ev - er find end! Thro' years un - num - bered on heav - en's shore, My tongue shall praise Him for - ev - er - more.
Refrain
Bless - ed Re - deem - er! pre-cious Re-deem - er! Seems now I see Him on Cal - va - ry's tree;
Wound-ed and bleed-ing, for sin-ners plead-ing, Blind and un-heed-ing— dy-ing for me!

WORDS: Avis B. Christiansen, 1920
MUSIC: Harry D. Loes, 1920

REDEEMER
Irregular meter

139 What Wondrous Love Is This

What manner of love the Father hath bestowed upon us . . . I John 3:1

1. What won-drous love is this, O my soul, O my soul, What
2. To God and to the Lamb I will sing, I will sing, To
3. And when from death I'm free, I'll sing on, I'll sing on, And
won-drous love is this, O my soul! What won-drous love is
God and to the Lamb I will sing; To God and to the
when from death I'm free, I'll sing on; And when from death I'm
this that caused the Lord of bliss To bear the dread-ful curse for my
Lamb, who is the great "I Am," While mil-lions join the theme, I will
free, I'll sing and joy-ful be, And through e-ter-ni-ty I'll sing
soul, for my soul, To bear the dread-ful curse for my soul!
sing, I will sing, While mil-lions join the theme, I will sing!
on, I'll sing on, And through e-ter-ni-ty I'll sing on!

WORDS: American folk hymn
MUSIC: *Southern Harmony*, 1835

WONDROUS LOVE
12.9.12.12.9

He Was Wounded for Our Transgressions 140

He was wounded for our transgressions . . . Isa. 53:5

1. He was wound - ed for our trans - gress - ions, He bore our sins in His bod - y on the tree; For our guilt He gave us peace, From our bond - age gave re - lease, And with His stripes, and with His stripes, And with His stripes our souls are healed.
2. He was num - bered a - mong trans - gress - ors, We did es - teem Him for - sak - en by His God; As our sac - ri - fice He died, That the law be sat - is - fied, And all our sin, and all our sin, And all our sin was laid on Him.
3. We had wan - dered, we all had wan - dered Far from the fold of "the Shep - herd of the sheep;" But He sought us where we were, On the moun - tains bleak and bare, And brought us home, and brought us home, And brought us safe - ly home to God.
4. Who can num - ber His gen - er - a - tion? Who shall de - clare all the tri - umphs of His cross? Mil - lions dead now live a - gain, Myr - iads fol - low in His train! Vic - to - rious Lord, vic - to - rious Lord, Vic - to - rious Lord and com - ing King!

WORDS: Thomas O. Chisholm, 1941
MUSIC: Merrill Dunlop, 1941

OAK PARK
Irregular meter

141 My Lord Has Garments So Wondrous Fine

. . . Out of the ivory palaces, whereby they have made thee glad. Psa. 45:8

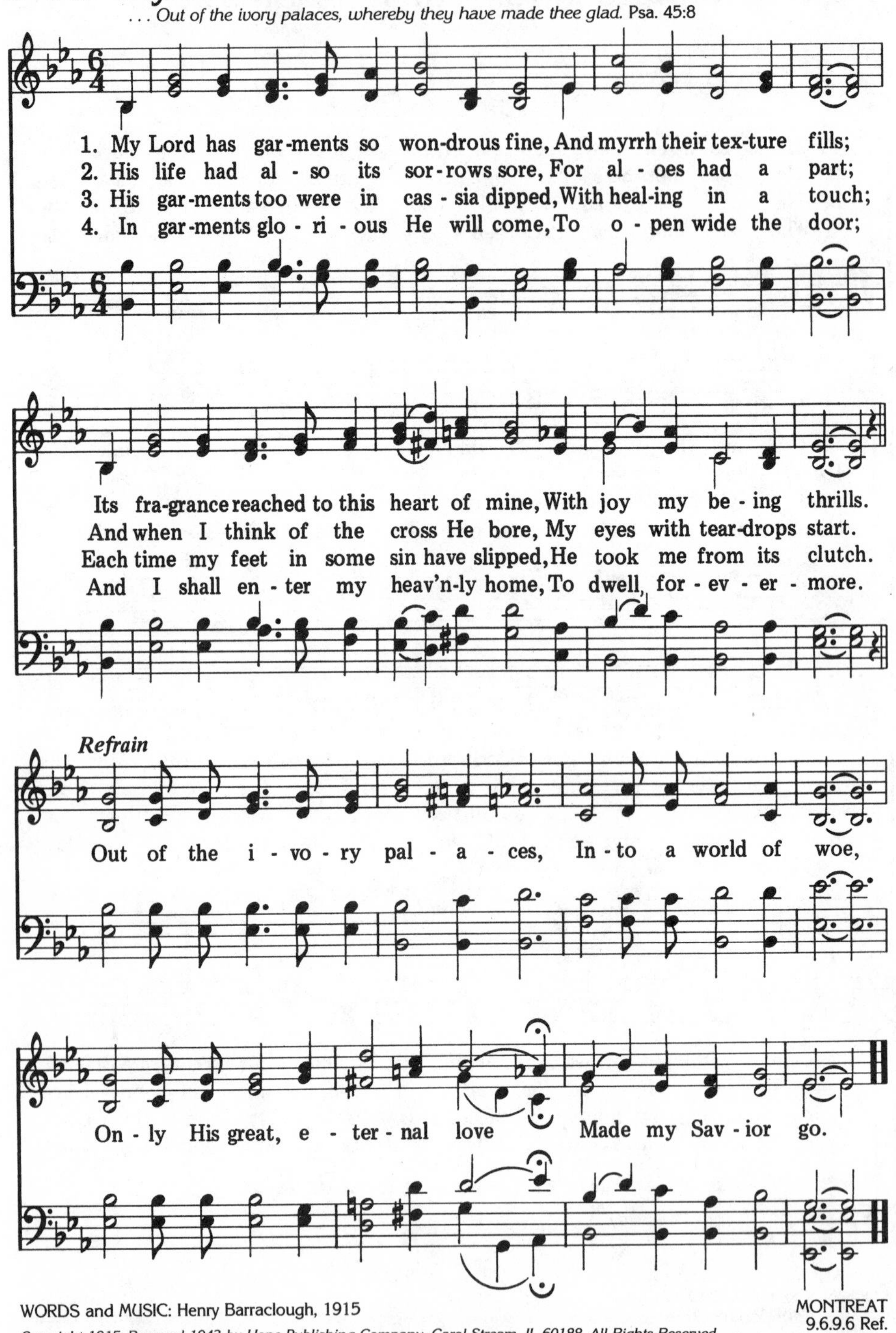
1. My Lord has gar-ments so won-drous fine, And myrrh their tex-ture fills;
2. His life had al - so its sor-rows sore, For al - oes had a part;
3. His gar-ments too were in cas - sia dipped, With heal-ing in a touch;
4. In gar-ments glo - ri - ous He will come, To o - pen wide the door;
Its fra-grance reached to this heart of mine, With joy my be - ing thrills.
And when I think of the cross He bore, My eyes with tear-drops start.
Each time my feet in some sin have slipped, He took me from its clutch.
And I shall en - ter my heav'n-ly home, To dwell for - ev - er - more.
Refrain
Out of the i - vo - ry pal - a - ces, In - to a world of woe,
On - ly His great, e - ter - nal love Made my Sav - ior go.

WORDS and MUSIC: Henry Barraclough, 1915

MONTREAT
9.6.9.6 Ref.

O Sacred Head, Now Wounded 142

When they had platted a crown of thorns, they put it upon His head . . . Matt. 27:29

1. O sa - cred Head, now wound - ed, With grief and shame weighed down,
2. What Thou, my Lord, hast suf - fered Was all for sin - ners' gain;
3. What lan - guage shall I bor - row To thank Thee, dear - est friend,
Now scorn - ful - ly sur - round - ed With thorns, Thine on - ly crown:
Mine, mine was the trans - gres - sion, But Thine the dead - ly pain.
For this Thy dy - ing sor - row, Thy pit - y with - out end?
O sa - cred Head, what glo - ry, What bliss till now was Thine!
Lo, here I fall, my Sav - ior! 'Tis I de - serve Thy place;
O make me Thine for - ev - er; And should I faint - ing be,
Yet, though de - spised and go - ry, I joy to call Thee mine.
Look on me with Thy fa - vor, Vouch - safe to me Thy grace.
Lord, let me nev - er, nev - er Out - live my love to Thee. A - men.

WORDS: Attr. Bernard of Clairvaux, 12th century; tr. (German) Paul Gerhardt, 1656; tr. (English) James W. Alexander, 1830
MUSIC: Hans Leo Hassler, 1601; arr. J. S. Bach, 1729

PASSION CHORALE
7.6.7.6 D.

143 Lift High the Cross

I, if I be lifted up from the earth, will draw all men unto Me. John 12:32

Unison
Fine
D.C.
(Ref.) Lift high the Cross, the love of Christ pro-claim, Till all the world a - dore His sa - cred name.
1. Come, breth - ren, fol - low where our Sav - ior trod, Our King vic - to - rious, Christ, the Son of God.
2. Led on their way by this tri - um - phant sign, The hosts of God in con-qu'ring ranks com-bine.
3. O Lord, once lift - ed on the glo - rious Tree, As Thou hast prom - ised, draw men un - to Thee.
4. Set up Thy throne, that earth's de - spair may cease Be - neath the shad - ow of its heal - ing peace.
5. For Thy blest Cross which doth for all a - tone, Cre - a - tion's prais - es rise be - fore Thy throne.

WORDS: George W. Kitchin and Michael R. Newbolt, 1916
MUSIC: Sydney H. Nicholson, 1916

CRUCIFER
Irregular meter

In the Cross of Christ I Glory 144

God forbid that I should glory, save in the cross . . . Gal. 6:14

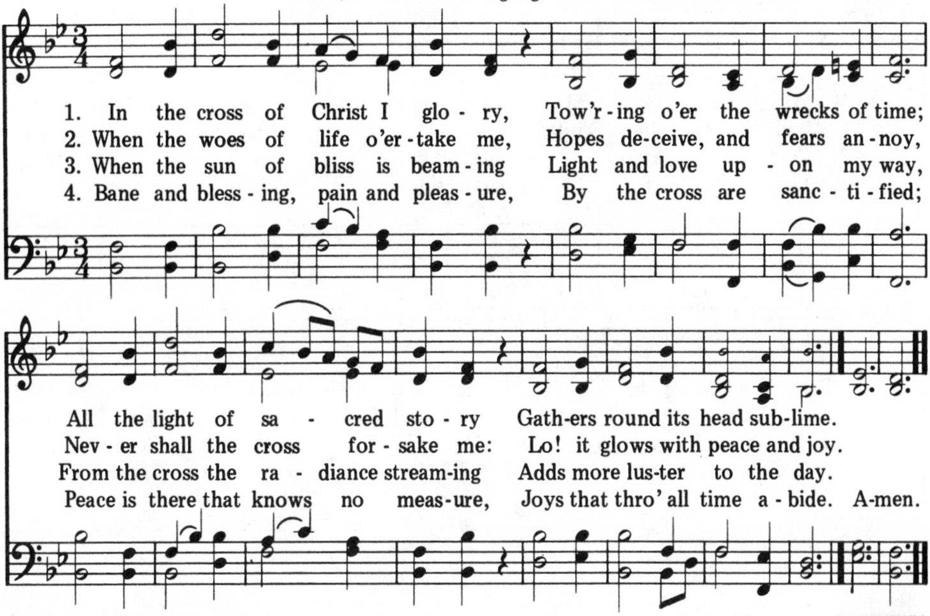

1. In the cross of Christ I glory, Tow'r-ing o'er the wrecks of time;
2. When the woes of life o'er-take me, Hopes de-ceive, and fears an-noy,
3. When the sun of bliss is beam-ing Light and love up-on my way,
4. Bane and bless-ing, pain and pleas-ure, By the cross are sanc-ti-fied;

All the light of sa-cred sto-ry Gath-ers round its head sub-lime.
Nev-er shall the cross for-sake me: Lo! it glows with peace and joy.
From the cross the ra-diance stream-ing Adds more lus-ter to the day.
Peace is there that knows no meas-ure, Joys that thro' all time a-bide. A-men.

WORDS: John Bowring, 1825
MUSIC: Ithamar Conkey, 1849

RATHBUN
8.7.8.7

Alas! and Did My Savior Bleed? 145

. . . He was bruised for our iniquities . . . Isa. 53:5

1. A-las! and did my Sav-ior bleed, And did my Sov'reign die? Would He de-vote that sa-cred head For sin-ners such as I?
2. Was it for crimes that I have done, He groaned up-on the tree? A-maz-ing pit-y! grace un-known! And love be-yond de-gree!
3. Well might the sun in dark-ness hide And shut his glo-ries in, When God, the might-y Mak-er, died For man the crea-ture's sin.
4. But drops of grief can ne'er re-pay The debt of love I owe; Here, Lord, I give my-self a-way; 'Tis all that I can do. A-men.

WORDS: Isaac Watts, 1707
MUSIC: Hugh Wilson, c.1800

MARTYRDOM
C.M.

146 Ah, Holy Jesus, How Hast Thou Offended?

He is despised and rejected of men . . . Isa. 53:3

1. Ah, ho - ly Je - sus, how hast Thou of - fend - ed,
2. Who was the guilt - y? Who brought this up - on Thee?
3. For me, kind Je - sus, was Thy in - car - na - tion,
4. There - fore, kind Je - sus, since I can - not pay Thee,

That man to judge Thee hath in hate pre - tend - ed? By foes de -
A - las, my trea - son, Je - sus, hath un - done Thee! 'Twas I, Lord
Thy mor - tal sor - row, and Thy life's ob - la - tion; Thy death of
I do a - dore Thee, and will ev - er pray Thee, Think on Thy

rid - ed, by Thine own re - ject - ed, O most af - flict - ed!
Je - sus, I it was de - nied Thee; I cru - ci - fied Thee.
an - guish and Thy bit - ter pas - sion, For my sal - va - tion.
pit - y and Thy love un - swerv - ing, Not my de - serv - ing. A - men.

WORDS: Johann Heermann, c. 1630; tr. Robert S. Bridges, 1899; based on Jean de Fecamp. d.1078
MUSIC: Johann Crüger, 1640

HERZLIEBSTER JESU
11.11.11.5

147 A Purple Robe, a Crown of Thorn

. . . And they put on Him a purple robe . . . John 19:2

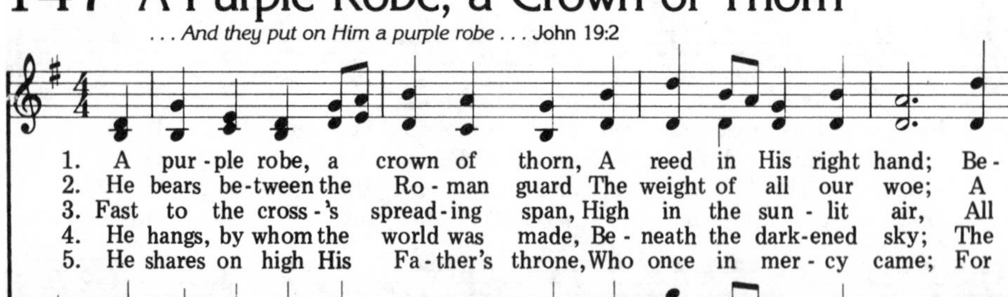
1. A pur - ple robe, a crown of thorn, A reed in His right hand; Be -
2. He bears be - tween the Ro - man guard The weight of all our woe; A
3. Fast to the cross - 's spread - ing span, High in the sun - lit air, All
4. He hangs, by whom the world was made, Be - neath the dark - ened sky; The
5. He shares on high His Fa - ther's throne, Who once in mer - cy came; For

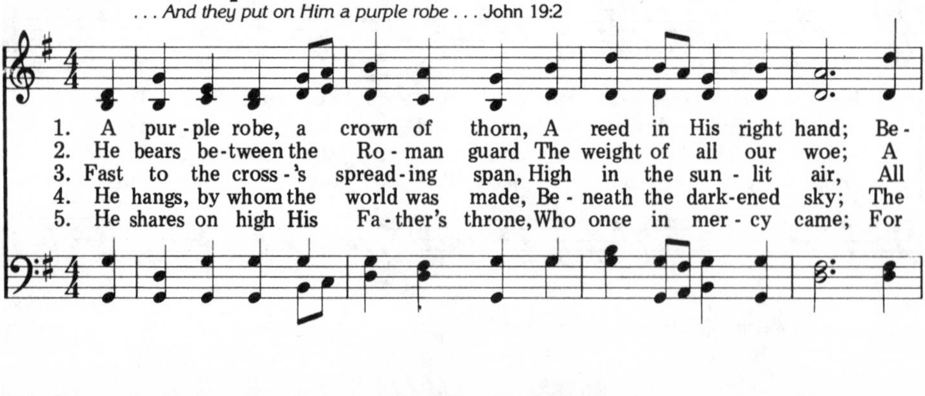

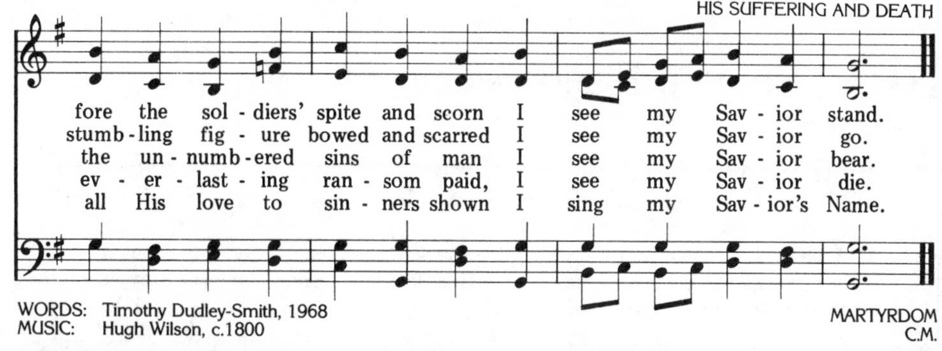
fore the sol - diers' spite and scorn I see my Sav - ior stand.
stumb - ling fig - ure bowed and scarred I see my Sav - ior go.
the un - numb - ered sins of man I see my Sav - ior bear.
ev - er - last - ing ran - som paid, I see my Sav - ior die.
all His love to sin - ners shown I sing my Sav - ior's Name.

WORDS: Timothy Dudley-Smith, 1968
MUSIC: Hugh Wilson, c.1800

MARTYRDOM
C.M.

King of My Life, I Crown Thee Now 148

Consider Him that endured such contradiction of sinners against Himself. Heb. 12:3

1. King of my life, I crown Thee now, Thine shall the glo - ry be;
2. Show me the tomb where Thou wast laid, Ten - der - ly mourned and wept;
3. Let me, like Ma - ry thro' the gloom, Come with a gift to Thee;
4. May I be will - ing, Lord, to bear Dai - ly my cross for Thee;

Lest I for - get Thy thorn-crowned brow, Lead me to Cal - va - ry.
An - gels in robes of light ar - rayed Guard - ed Thee whilst Thou slept.
Show to me now the emp - ty tomb, Lead me to Cal - va - ry.
E - ven Thy cup of grief to share, Thou hast borne all for me.

Refrain

Lest I for - get Geth - sem - a - ne; Lest I for - get Thine ag - o - ny;
Lest I for - get Thy love for me, Lead me to Cal - va - ry.

WORDS: Jennie E. Hussey, 1921
MUSIC: William J. Kirkpatrick, 1921

DUNCANNON
C.M. Ref.

149 I Serve a Risen Savior

. . . That I may know Him, and the power of His resurrection. Phil. 3:10

1. I serve a ris - en Sav - ior, He's in the world to - day; I know that He is liv - ing, what - ev - er men may say; I see His hand of mer - cy, I hear His voice of cheer, And just the time I need Him He's al - ways near.
2. In all the world a-round me I see His lov-ing care, And tho' my heart grows wea - ry, I nev - er will de - spair; I know that He is lead - ing thro' all the storm - y blast, The day of His ap - pear - ing will come at last.
3. Re-joice, re-joice, O Christ-ian, lift up your voice and sing E - ter - nal hal - le- lu - jahs to Je - sus Christ the King! The Hope of all who seek Him, the Help of all who find, None oth - er is so lov - ing, so good and kind.
Refrain
He lives, He lives, Christ Je - sus lives to - day! He walks with me and talks with me a - long life's nar-row way. He lives, He lives, sal-
He lives, He lives,
He lives, He lives,

va - tion to im - part! You ask me how I know He lives? He lives within my heart.

WORDS and MUSIC: Alfred H. Ackley, 1933

ACKLEY
Irregular meter

Good Christian Men, Rejoice and Sing 150

With great power gave the apostles witness of the resurrection . . . Acts 4:33

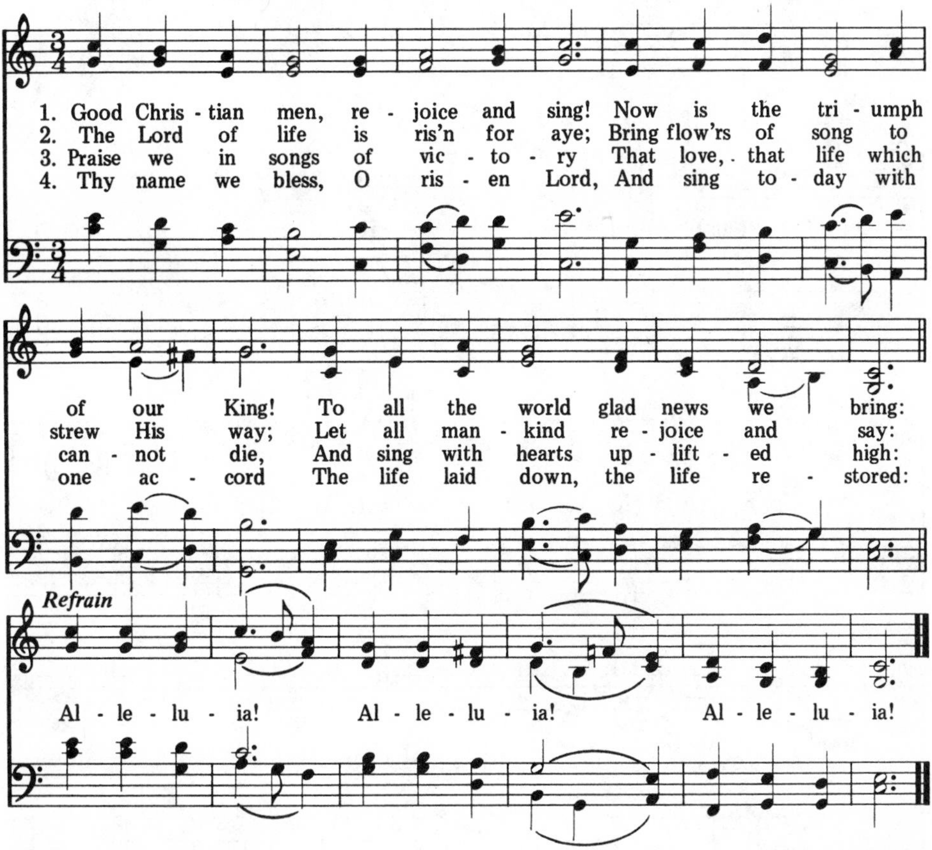

1. Good Chris - tian men, re - joice and sing! Now is the tri - umph of our King! To all the world glad news we bring:
2. The Lord of life is ris'n for aye; Bring flow'rs of song to strew His way; Let all man - kind re - joice and say:
3. Praise we in songs of vic - to - ry That love, that life which can - not die, And sing with hearts up - lift - ed high:
4. Thy name we bless, O ris - en Lord, And sing to - day with one ac - cord The life laid down, the life re - stored:

Refrain

Al - le - lu - ia! Al - le - lu - ia! Al - le - lu - ia!

WORDS: Cyril A. Alington, 1931
MUSIC: Melchior Vulpius, 1609

GELOBT SEI GOTT
8.8.8 Alleluias

151 Low in the Grave He Lay

The angel of the Lord . . . rolled back the stone from the door. Matt. 28:2

1. Low in the grave He lay—Je - sus my Sav - ior! Wait-ing the com-ing day—Je - sus my Lord!
2. Vain - ly they watch His bed—Je - sus my Sav - ior! Vain - ly they seal the dead—Je - sus my Lord!
3. Death can-not keep his prey—Je - sus my Sav - ior! He tore the bars a - way—Je - sus my Lord!
Refrain
Up from the grave He a - rose, He a - rose, With a might - y tri-umph o'er His foes; He a-rose! He a - rose a vic - tor from the dark do - main, And He lives for - ev - er with His saints to reign. He a - rose! He a - rose! He a - rose! He a - rose! Hal - le - lu - jah! Christ a - rose!

WORDS and MUSIC: Robert Lowry, 1874

CHRIST AROSE
6.5.6.5 Ref.

Christ the Lord Is Risen Today 152

Now is Christ risen . . . and become the first fruits of them that slept. I Cor. 15:20

1. Christ the Lord is risen to - day, Al - le - lu - ia!
2. Lives a - gain our glo - rious King; Al - le - lu - ia!
3. Love's re - deem - ing work is done, Al - le - lu - ia!
4. Soar we now where Christ has led, Al - le - lu - ia!
Sons of men and an - gels say: Al - le - lu - ia!
Where, O death, is now thy sting? Al - le - lu - ia!
Fought the fight, the bat - tle won; Al - le - lu - ia!
Fol-lowing our ex - alt - ed Head; Al - le - lu - ia!
Raise your joys and tri - umphs high, Al - le - lu - ia!
Dy - ing once, He all doth save: Al - le - lu - ia!
Death in vain for - bids Him rise; Al - le - lu - ia!
Made like Him, like Him we rise; Al - le - lu - ia!
Sing, ye heav'ns, and earth re - ply, Al - le - lu - ia!
Where thy vic - to - ry, O grave? Al - le - lu - ia!
Christ has o - pened Par - a - dise. Al - le - lu - ia!
Ours the cross, the grave, the skies. Al - le - lu - ia! A-men.

WORDS: Charles Wesley, 1739
MUSIC: Arr. from *Lyra Davidica*, London, 1708

EASTER HYMN
7.7.7.7 Alleluias

153 Hear the Bells Ringing

He is not here: for He is risen, as He said. Matt. 28:6

Hear the bells ring - ing, they're sing - ing that we can be
born a - gain.
Hear the bells ring - ing, they're sing - ing "Christ is ris - en from the
dead."
The an - gel
up on the tomb-stone said "He is ris - en just as He said.

Quick - ly now, go tell His dis - ci - ples that Je - sus Christ is
no long - er dead!" Joy to the world, He is
ris - en, al - le - lu - ia, He's ris - en, al -
le - lu - ia; He's ris - en, al - le - lu -
ia! Al - le - lu - ia!

WORDS and MUSIC: Anne Herring, 1974

EASTER SONG
Irregular meter

154 O Sons and Daughters, Let Us Sing

He is not here, but is risen . . . Luke 24:6

1. O sons and daugh - ters, let us sing! The King of heav'n, the glo - rious King, O'er death to - day rose tri - umph - ing, Al - le - lu - ia! Al - le - lu - ia!
2. That Eas - ter morn at break of day, The faith - ful wom - en went their way To seek the tomb where Je - sus lay,
3. An an - gel clad in white they see, Who sat and spake un - to the three, "Your Lord doth go to Gal - i - lee,"
4. How blest are they who have not seen, And yet whose faith hath con - stant been; For they e - ter - nal life shall win,
5. On this most ho - ly day of days, Our hearts and voic - es, Lord, we raise To Thee, in ju - bi - lee and praise,

Al - le - lu - ia! Al - le - lu - ia! A - men.

WORDS: Jean Tisserand, c.1490; tr. John M. Neale, 1851
MUSIC: Traditional French melody, 17th century

O FILII ET FILIAE
8.8.8 Alleluias

155 The Strife Is O'er, the Battle Done

Death is swallowed up in victory. I Cor. 15:54

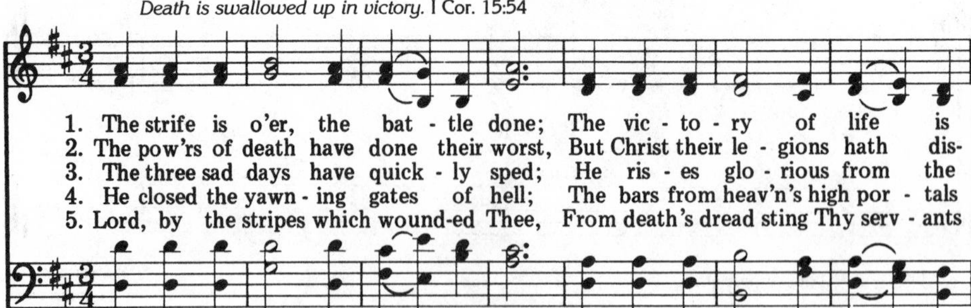
1. The strife is o'er, the bat - tle done; The vic - to - ry of life is
2. The pow'rs of death have done their worst, But Christ their le - gions hath dis-
3. The three sad days have quick - ly sped; He ris - es glo - rious from the
4. He closed the yawn - ing gates of hell; The bars from heav'n's high por - tals
5. Lord, by the stripes which wound-ed Thee, From death's dread sting Thy serv - ants

won; The song of tri - umph has be - gun. Al - le - lu - ia!
persed: Let shouts of ho - ly joy out - burst. Al - le - lu - ia!
dead: All glo - ry to our ris - en Head! Al - le - lu - ia!
fell: Let hymns of praise His tri - umphs tell. Al - le - lu - ia!
free, That we may live and sing to Thee. Al - le - lu - ia!

WORDS: Latin hymn, c.1695; tr. Francis Pott, 1859
MUSIC: Giovanni P. da Palestrina, 1591; arr. William H. Monk, 1861

VICTORY
8.8.8.4 Alleluias

Jesus Lives and So Shall I 156

O Death, where is thy sting? I Cor. 15:55

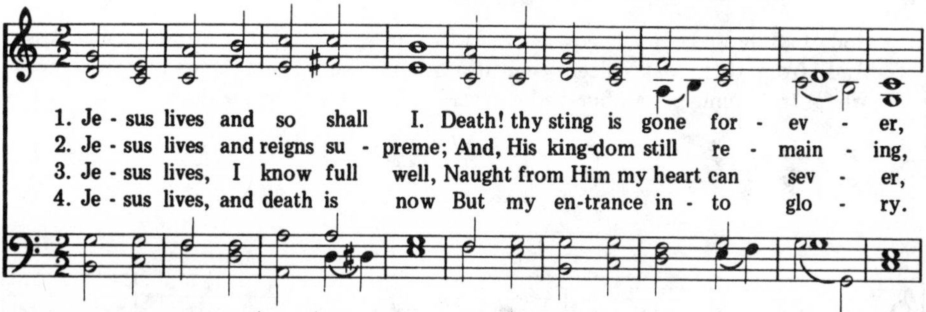

1. Je - sus lives and so shall I. Death! thy sting is gone for - ev - er,
2. Je - sus lives and reigns su - preme; And, His king-dom still re - main - ing,
3. Je - sus lives, I know full well, Naught from Him my heart can sev - er,
4. Je - sus lives, and death is now But my en-trance in - to glo - ry.

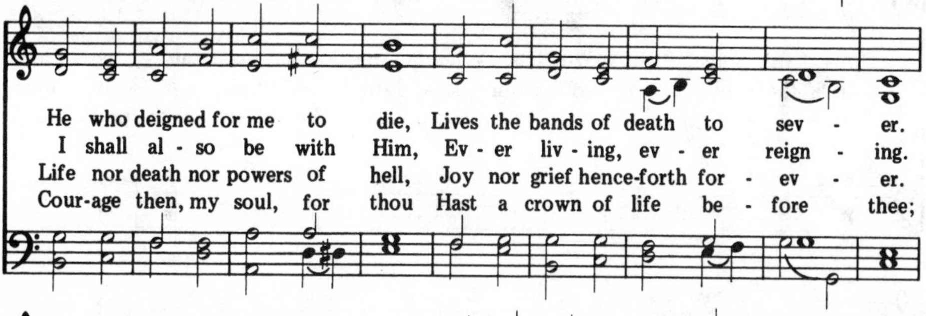

He who deigned for me to die, Lives the bands of death to sev - er.
I shall al - so be with Him, Ev - er liv - ing, ev - er reign - ing.
Life nor death nor powers of hell, Joy nor grief hence-forth for - ev - er.
Cour-age then, my soul, for thou Hast a crown of life be - fore thee;

He shall raise me with the just; Je - sus is my Hope and Trust.
God has prom-ised: be it must; Je - sus is my Hope and Trust.
None of all His saints is lost; Je - sus is my Hope and Trust.
Thou shalt find thy hopes were just; Je - sus is the Chris-tian's Trust. A - men.

WORDS: Christian F. Gellert, 1757; tr. Philip Schaff, c. 1870
MUSIC: Johann Crüger, 1653

ZUVERSICHT
7.8.7.8.7.7

157 Come, Ye Faithful, Raise the Strain

Thou hast ascended on high, Thou hast led captivity captive. Psa. 68:18

1. Come, ye faith - ful, raise the strain Of tri - um - phant glad - ness;
2. 'Tis the spring of souls to - day, Christ hath burst His pris - on,
3. "Al - le - lu - ia!" now we cry To our King Im - mor - tal,
God hath brought His peo - ple forth In - to joy from sad - ness.
And from three day's sleep in death As a sun hath ris - en.
Who, tri - um - phant, burst the bars Of the tomb's dark por - tal;
Now re - joice, Je - ru - sa - lem, And with true af - fec - tion
All the win - ter of our sins, Long and dark, is fly - ing
"Al - le - lu - ia!" with the Son, God the Fa - ther prais - ing;
Wel - come in un - wea - ried strains Je - sus' res - ur - rec - tion.
From His light, to whom we give Laud and praise un - dy - ing.
"Al - le - lu - ia!" yet a - gain To the Spir - it rais - ing. A-men.

WORDS: John of Damascus, 8th century; tr. John M. Neale, 1859
MUSIC: Arthur S. Sullivan, 1872

ST. KEVIN
7.6.7.6 D.

I Know that My Redeemer Lives 158

I know that my Redeemer liveth . . . Job 19:25

Unison
1. I know that my Re - deem - er lives; Glo - ry, hal - le - lu - jah!
2. He lives, He lives, who once was dead, Glo - ry, hal - le - lu - jah!
3. He lives to bless me with His love, Glo - ry, hal - le - lu - jah!
4. He lives, all glo - ry to His name! Glo - ry, hal - le - lu - jah!
What com - fort this sweet sen - tence gives, Glo - ry, hal - le - lu - jah!
He lives, my ev - er - last - ing head, Glo - ry, hal - le - lu - jah!
He lives to plead for me a - bove, Glo - ry, hal - le - lu - jah!
He lives, my Je - sus, still the same, Glo - ry, hal - le - lu - jah!
Refrain
Shout on, pray on, we're gain - ing ground, Glo - ry, hal - le - lu - jah! The
dead's a - live and the lost is found, Glo - ry, hal - le - lu - jah!

WORDS: Samuel Medley, 1775; Refrain anonymous
MUSIC: American folk hymn, 19th century

SHOUT ON
8.6.8.6 Ref.

159 God Sent His Son, They Called Him Jesus

Because I live, ye shall live also. John 14:19

1. God sent His Son, they called Him Je - sus; He came to love,
2. How sweet to hold a new-born ba - by, And feel the pride
3. And then one day I'll cross the riv - er; I'll fight life's fi -
heal, and for - give; He lived and died to buy my
and joy He gives; But great - er still the calm as -
nal war with pain; And then as death gives way to
par - don, An emp - ty grave is there to prove my Sav - ior lives.
sur - ance, This child can face un - cer - tain days be - cause He lives.
vic - tory, I'll see the lights of glo - ry and I'll know He lives.
Refrain
Be - cause He lives I can face to - mor - row; Be - cause He lives
all fear is gone; Be - cause I know He holds the fu - ture,

HIS RESURRECTION
And life is worth the liv - ing just be-cause He lives.

WORDS: Gloria Gaither and William J. Gaither, 1971
MUSIC: William J. Gaither, 1971

RESURRECTION
Irregular meter

160 The Day of Resurrection

Jesus met them, saying, All hail. Matt. 28:9

1. The day of res - ur - rec - tion! Earth, tell it out a - broad;
2. Our hearts be pure from e - vil, That we may see a - right
3. Now let the heav'ns be joy - ful! Let earth her song be - gin!

The Pass - o - ver of glad - ness, The Pass - o - ver of God.
The Lord in rays e - ter - nal Of res - ur - rec - tion light;
The world re-sound in tri - umph, And all that is there - in;

From death to life e - ter - nal, From earth un - to the sky,
And, lis-t'ning to His ac - cents, May hear, so calm and plain,
Let all things seen and un - seen Their notes of glad-ness blend;

Our Christ hath brought us o - ver With hymns of vic - to - ry.
His own "All hail!" and, hear - ing, May raise the vic - tor strain.
For Christ the Lord hath ris - en, Our Joy that hath no end.

WORDS: John of Damascus, 8th Century; tr. John M. Neale, 1862
MUSIC: Henry T. Smart, 1835

LANCASHIRE
7.6.7.6 D.

161 Thine Is the Glory, Risen Conquering Son

O grave, where is thy victory? I Cor. 15:55

1. Thine is the glo - ry, Ris - en, con-qu'ring Son; End - less is the vic - t'ry Thou o'er death hast won. An - gels in bright rai - ment Rolled the stone a - way, Kept the fold - ed grave-clothes Where Thy bod - y lay.
2. Lo! Je - sus meets us, Ris - en, from the tomb; Lov - ing - ly He greets us, Scat - ters fear and gloom; Let His church with glad - ness Hymns of tri - umph sing, For her Lord now liv - eth; Death hath lost its sting.
3. No more we doubt Thee, Glo-rious Prince of Life! Life is naught with- out Thee; Aid us in our strife; Make us more than con-qu'rors, Through Thy death - less love; Bring us safe through Jor - dan To Thy home a - bove.
Refrain
Thine is the glo - ry, Ris - en, con-qu'ring Son; End - less is the vic - t'ry Thou o'er death hast won. A - men.

WORDS: Edmond L. Budry, 1884; tr. Richard B. Hoyle, 1923
MUSIC: George Frederick Handel, 1746

MACCABEUS
10.11.11.11 Ref.

Jesus Christ Is Risen Today 162

He is not here; for He is risen . . . Matt. 28:6

1. Je - sus Christ is ris'n to - day, Al - le - lu - ia!
2. Hymns of praise then let us sing, Al - le - lu - ia!
3. But the pains which He en - dured, Al - le - lu - ia!
4. Sing we to our God a - bove, Al - le - lu - ia!
Our tri - um - phant ho - ly day, Al - le - lu - ia!
Un - to Christ, our heav'n - ly King, Al - le - lu - ia!
Our sal - va - tion have pro - cured; Al - le - lu - ia!
Praise e - ter - nal as His love; Al - le - lu - ia!
Who did once, up - on the cross, Al - le - lu - ia!
Who en - dured the cross and grave, Al - le - lu - ia!
Now a - bove the sky He's King, Al - le - lu - ia!
Praise Him, all ye heav'n - ly host, Al - le - lu - ia!
Suf - fer to re - deem our loss, Al - le - lu - ia!
Sin - ners to re - deem and save, Al - le - lu - ia!
Where the an - gels ev - er sing: Al - le - lu - ia!
Fa - ther, Son, and Ho - ly Ghost, Al - le - lu - ia!

WORDS: St. 1, 14th century Latin hymn; tr. *Lyra Davidica,* 1708;
St. 2, 3, Arnold's *Compleat Psalmodist,* 1749; St. 4, Charles Wesley, 1740
MUSIC: Robert Williams, 1817

LLANFAIR
7.7.7.7 Alleluias

163 Hail the Day That Sees Him Rise

Lift up your heads, O ye gates . . . and the King of glory shall come in. Psa. 24:7

1. Hail the day that sees Him rise, Al - le - lu - ia!
2. There for Him high tri - umph waits; Al - le - lu - ia!
3. See, He lifts His hands a - bove! Al - le - lu - ia!
4. Lord, be - yond our mor - tal sight, Al - le - lu - ia!
To His throne a - bove the skies; Al - le - lu - ia!
Lift your heads, e - ter - nal gates, Al - le - lu - ia!
See, He shows the prints of love! Al - le - lu - ia!
Raise our hearts to reach Thy height, Al - le - lu - ia!
Christ, the Lamb for sin - ners giv'n, Al - le - lu - ia!
He hath con-quered death and sin, Al - le - lu - ia!
Hark! His gra - cious lips be - stow, Al - le - lu - ia!
There Thy face un - cloud - ed see, Al - le - lu - ia!
En - ters now the high - est heav'n. Al - le - lu - ia!
Take the King of glo - ry in! Al - le - lu - ia!
Bless-ings on His church be - low. Al - le - lu - ia!
Find our heav'n of heav'ns in Thee! Al - le - lu - ia! A - men.

WORDS: Charles Wesley, 1739
MUSIC: Welsh hymn melody; arr. John Roberts, 1837

LLANFAIR
7.7.7.7 Alleluias

A Hymn of Glory Let Us Sing! 164

Who . . . sat down on the right hand of the majesty on high. Heb. 1:3

Unison
1. A hymn of glo - ry let us sing! New hymns through-out the world shall ring: Al-le - lu - ia! Al-le-lu - ia! Christ, by a road be-fore un-trod, As-cends un-to the throne of God. Al-le-lu - ia!
2. The ho - ly ap - os - tol - ic band Up - on the Mount of Ol - ives stand. Al-le - lu - ia! Al-le-lu - ia! And with his faith-ful fol-l'wers see Their Lord as-cend in maj-es - ty. Al-le-lu - ia!
3. O Lord our home-ward path-way bend, That our un - wear - ied hearts as-cend. Al-le - lu - ia! Al-le-lu - ia! Where, seat - ed on Your Fa-ther's throne, You reign as King of kings a - lone. Al-le-lu - ia!
4. O ris - en Christ, as - cend - ed Lord, All praise to You let earth ac-cord: Al-le - lu - ia! Al-le-lu - ia! You are, while end-less ag - es run, With Fa-ther and with Spir - it one. Al-le-lu - ia!
Al-le - lu - ia! Al-le - lu - ia, al-le - lu - ia, al-le - lu - ia!

WORDS: The Venerable Bede, 673-735; tr. *Lutheran Book of Worship,* 1978
MUSIC: *Geistliche Kirchengesäng;* Cologne, 1623; harm. Ralph Vaughan Williams, 1906

LASST UNS ERFREUEN
8.8.4.4.8.8 Alleluias

165 Rejoice, the Lord is King

But we see Jesus . . . crowned with glory and honor. Heb. 2:9

1. Re - joice, the Lord is King: Your Lord and King a - dore! Re-
2. Je - sus the Sav - ior reigns, The God of truth and love; When
3. His king - dom can - not fail, He rules o'er earth and heav'n; The
4. Re - joice in glo - rious hope! Our Lord the Judge shall come, And

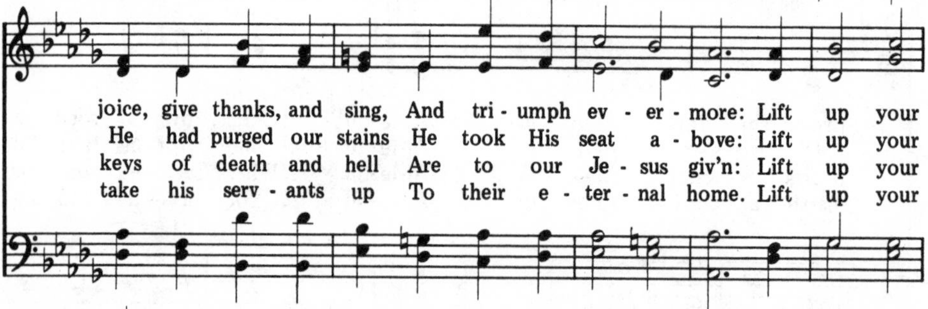

joice, give thanks, and sing, And tri - umph ev - er - more: Lift up your
He had purged our stains He took His seat a - bove: Lift up your
keys of death and hell Are to our Je - sus giv'n: Lift up your
take his serv - ants up To their e - ter - nal home. Lift up your

heart, lift up your voice! Re - joice, a - gain I say, re - joice!
heart, lift up your voice! Re - joice, a - gain I say, re - joice!
heart, lift up your voice! Re - joice, a - gain I say, re - joice!
heart, lift up your voice! Re - joice, a - gain I say, re - joice! A - men.

WORDS: Charles Wesley, 1746
MUSIC: John Darwall, 1770

DARWALL
6.6.6.6.8.8

166 The Head That Once Was Crowned

Wherefore God also hath highly exalted Him . . . Phil. 2:9

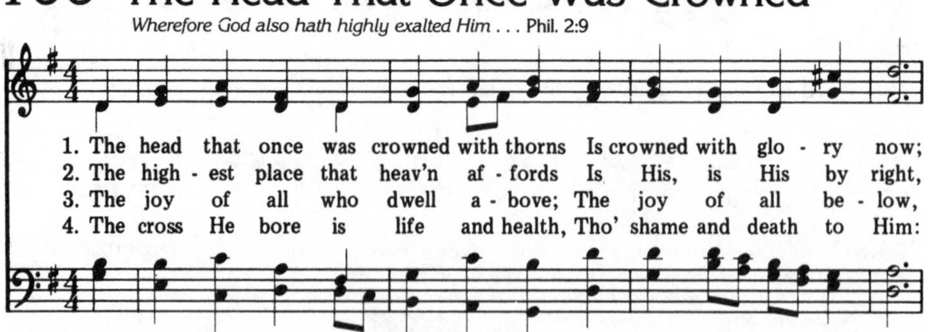
1. The head that once was crowned with thorns Is crowned with glo - ry now;
2. The high - est place that heav'n af - fords Is His, is His by right,
3. The joy of all who dwell a - bove; The joy of all be - low,
4. The cross He bore is life and health, Tho' shame and death to Him:

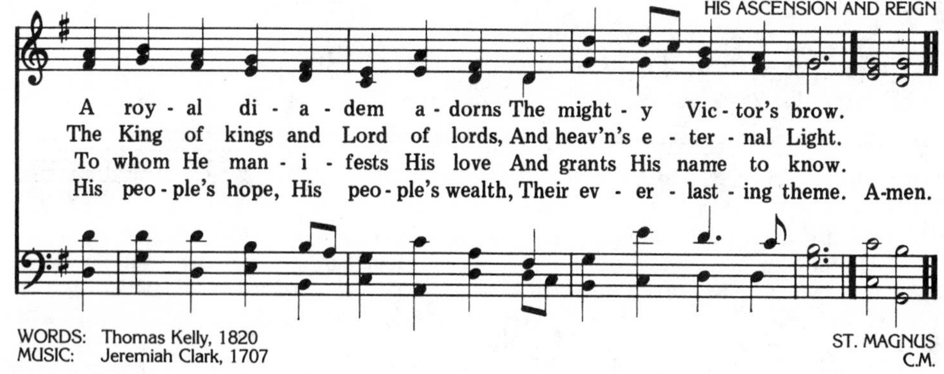
A roy - al di - a - dem a - dorns The might - y Vic - tor's brow.
The King of kings and Lord of lords, And heav'n's e - ter - nal Light.
To whom He man - i - fests His love And grants His name to know.
His peo - ple's hope, His peo - ple's wealth, Their ev - er - last - ing theme. A-men.

WORDS: Thomas Kelly, 1820
MUSIC: Jeremiah Clark, 1707

ST. MAGNUS
C.M.

Look, Ye Saints! the Sight Is Glorious 167

God hath made that same Jesus . . . both Lord and Christ. Acts 2:36

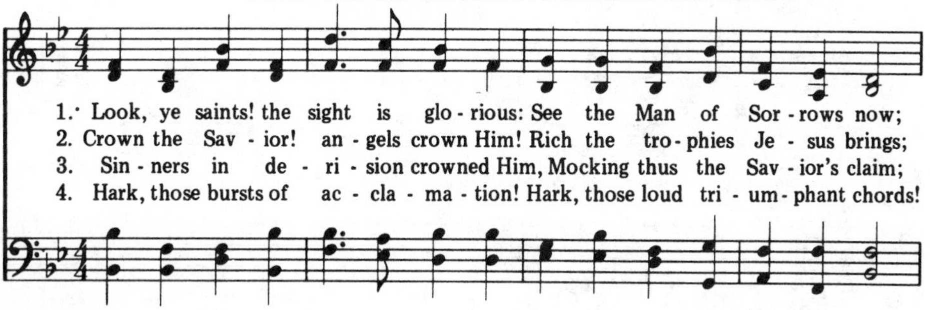

1.· Look, ye saints! the sight is glo - rious: See the Man of Sor - rows now;
2. Crown the Sav - ior! an - gels crown Him! Rich the tro - phies Je - sus brings;
3. Sin - ners in de - ri - sion crowned Him, Mocking thus the Sav - ior's claim;
4. Hark, those bursts of ac - cla - ma - tion! Hark, those loud tri - um - phant chords!

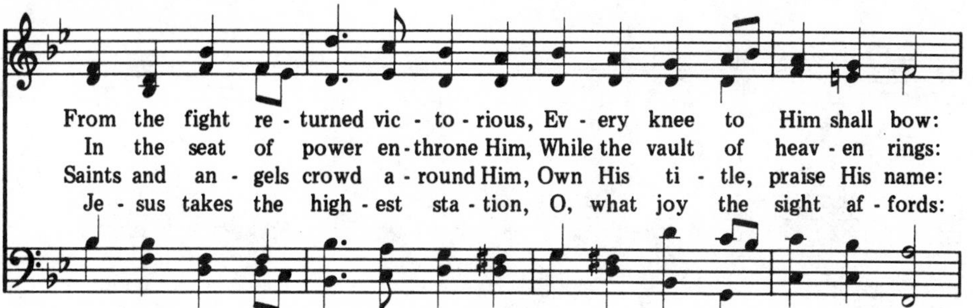

From the fight re - turned vic - to - rious, Ev - ery knee to Him shall bow:
In the seat of power en - throne Him, While the vault of heav - en rings:
Saints and an - gels crowd a - round Him, Own His ti - tle, praise His name:
Je - sus takes the high - est sta - tion, O, what joy the sight af - fords:

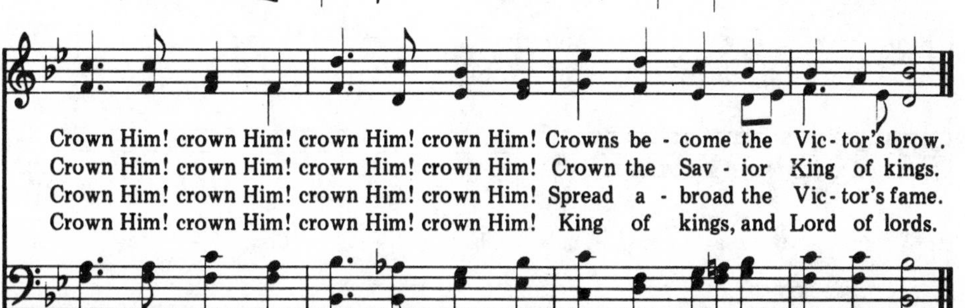

Crown Him! crown Him! crown Him! crown Him! Crowns be - come the Vic - tor's brow.
Crown Him! crown Him! crown Him! crown Him! Crown the Sav - ior King of kings.
Crown Him! crown Him! crown Him! crown Him! Spread a - broad the Vic - tor's fame.
Crown Him! crown Him! crown Him! crown Him! King of kings, and Lord of lords.

WORDS: Thomas Kelly, 1809
MUSIC: Henry T. Smart, 1867

REGENT SQUARE
8.7.8.7.8.7

168 Marvelous Message We Bring

Watch therefore, for ye know neither the day nor the hour . . . Matt. 25:13

1. Mar - vel - ous mes - sage we bring, Glo - ri - ous car - ol we sing,
2. For - est and flow - er ex - claim, Moun-tain and mead - ow the same,
3. Stand - ing be - fore Him at last, Tri - al and trou - ble all past,
Won - der - ful word of the King— Je - sus is com - ing a - gain! (a-gain!)
All earth and heav - en pro - claim— Je - sus is com - ing a - gain! (a-gain!)
Crowns at His feet we will cast— Je - sus is com - ing a - gain! (a-gain!)
Refrain – Unison
Com - ing a - gain, Com - ing a-
gain; May - be morn - ing, may - be noon,
May - be eve - ning and may - be soon! Com - ing a -

gain, Com - ing a - gain;
Parts
O what a won - der - ful day it will be— Je - sus is com - ing a - gain!
1. Christ is com - ing! let cre - a - tion From her groans and tra - vail cease;
2. Earth can now but tell the sto - ry Of Thy bit - ter cross and pain;
3. Long Thine ex - iles have been pin - ing, Far from rest, and home, and Thee:
4. With that bless - ed hope be - fore us, Let no harp re - main un - strung;
Let the glo - rious proc - la - ma - tion Hope re - store and faith in - crease:
She shall yet be - hold Thy glo - ry, When Thou com - est back to reign:
But in heav'n - ly ves - tures shin - ing, They their lov - ing Lord shall see:
Let the might - y ad - vent cho - rus On - ward roll from tongue to tongue:
Christ is com - ing! Christ is com - ing! Come, Thou bless - ed Prince of Peace.
Christ is com - ing! Christ is com - ing! Let each heart re - peat the strain.
Christ is com - ing! Christ is com - ing! Haste the joy - ous ju - bi - lee.
Christ is com - ing! Christ is com - ing! Come, Lord Je - sus, quick - ly come! A - men.

WORDS and MUSIC: John W. Peterson, 1957

COMING AGAIN
7.7.7.7 Ref.

Christ Is Coming! Let Creation 169

Looking for that blessed hope, and the glorious appearing of . . . Jesus Christ. Titus 2:13

WORDS: John R. Macduff, 1853
MUSIC: Joachim Neander, 1680

UNSER HERRSCHER
8.7.8.7.8.7

170 Jesus Is Coming to Earth Again

The Lord Himself shall descend from heaven with a shout . . . I Thess. 4:16

1. Je - sus is com - ing to earth a - gain, What if it were to - day?
2. Sa - tan's do - min - ion will soon be o'er, O, that it were to - day!
3. Faith - ful and true would He find us here, If He should come to - day?

Com - ing in pow - er and love to reign, What if it were to - day?
Sor - row and sigh - ing shall be no more, O, that it were to - day!
Watch - ing in glad - ness and not in fear, If He should come to - day?

Com - ing to claim His cho - sen Bride, All the re - deemed and pu - ri - fied,
Then shall the dead in Christ a - rise, Caught up to meet Him in the skies,
Signs of His com - ing mul - ti - ply, Morn - ing light breaks in east - ern sky,

O - ver this whole earth scat - tered wide, What if it were to - day?
When shall these glo - ries meet our eyes? What if it were to - day?
Watch, for that time is draw - ing nigh, What if it were to - day?

Refrain

Glo - ry, glo - ry! Joy to my heart 'twill bring; Glo - ry,
Joy to my heart 'twill bring;

glo - ry! When we shall crown Him King; Glo - ry, glo - ry!
When we shall crown Him King;
Haste to pre-pare the way; Glo - ry, glo - ry! Je-sus will come some day.
Haste to pre-pare the way;

WORDS and MUSIC: Lelia N. Morris, 1912

SECOND COMING
Irregular meter

He Is Coming Again 171

. . . The Son of man coming in a cloud with power and great glory. Luke 21:27

He is com - ing a - gain, He is com - ing a - gain, The ver - y same
Je - sus re - ject - ed of men; He is com - ing a - gain, He is
com - ing a - gain, With pow'r and great glo - ry He is com-ing a - gain!

WORDS and MUSIC: Mabel Johnston Camp, 1913; based on Luke 21:27

CAMP
Irregular meter

172 When He Comes

For the Lord Himself shall descend from heaven with a shout. I Thess. 4:16

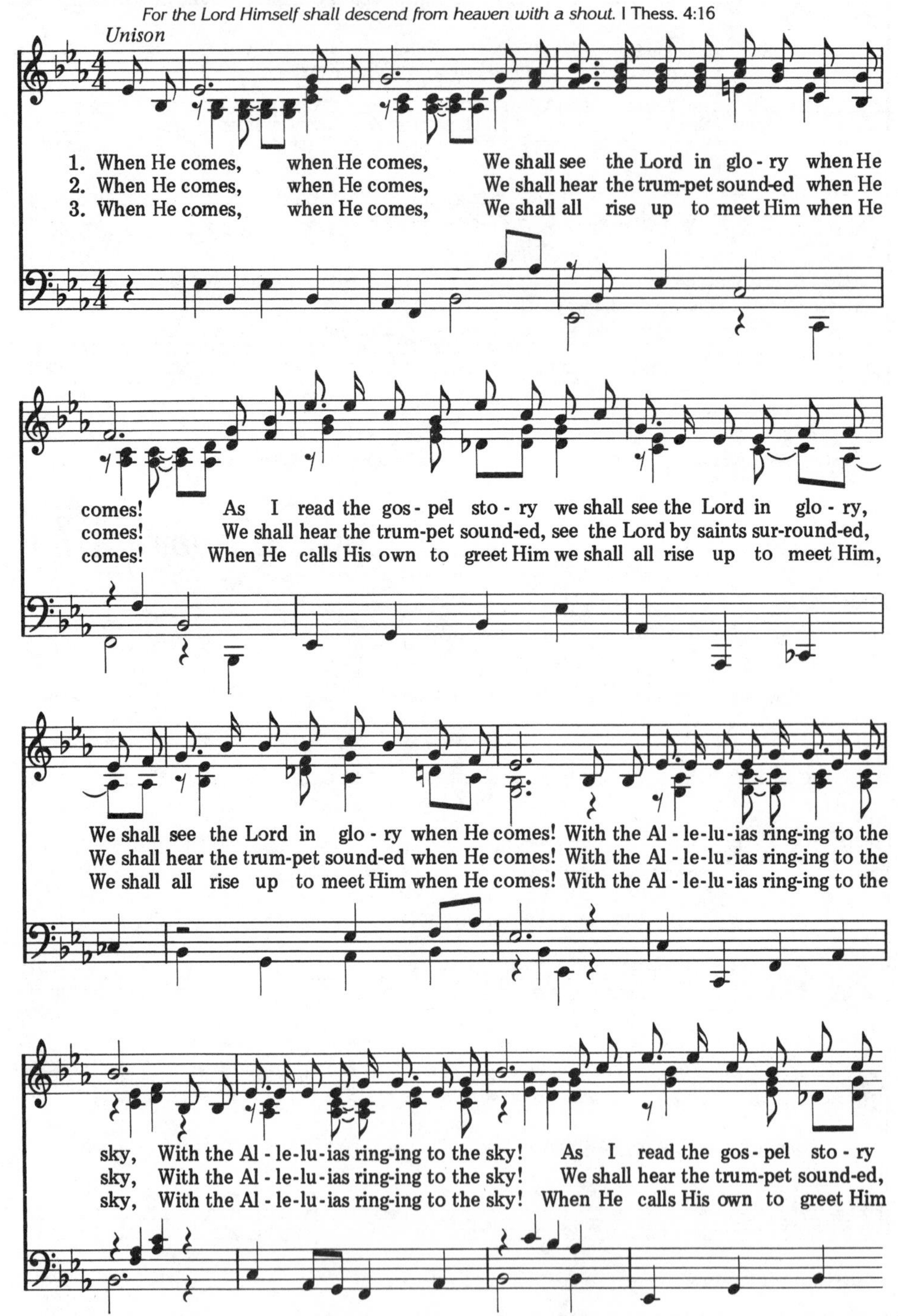
Unison
1. When He comes, when He comes, We shall see the Lord in glo - ry when He
2. When He comes, when He comes, We shall hear the trum-pet sound-ed when He
3. When He comes, when He comes, We shall all rise up to meet Him when He
comes! As I read the gos - pel sto - ry we shall see the Lord in glo - ry,
comes! We shall hear the trum-pet sound-ed, see the Lord by saints sur-round-ed,
comes! When He calls His own to greet Him we shall all rise up to meet Him,
We shall see the Lord in glo - ry when He comes! With the Al - le-lu-ias ring-ing to the
We shall hear the trum-pet sound-ed when He comes! With the Al - le-lu-ias ring-ing to the
We shall all rise up to meet Him when He comes! With the Al - le-lu-ias ring-ing to the
sky, With the Al - le-lu-ias ring-ing to the sky! As I read the gos - pel sto - ry
sky, With the Al - le-lu-ias ring-ing to the sky! We shall hear the trum-pet sound-ed,
sky, With the Al - le-lu-ias ring-ing to the sky! When He calls His own to greet Him

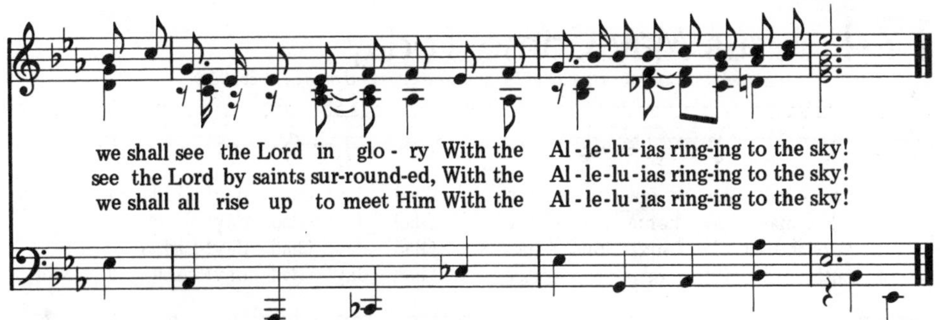
we shall see the Lord in glo - ry With the Al - le - lu - ias ring-ing to the sky!
see the Lord by saints sur-round-ed, With the Al - le - lu - ias ring-ing to the sky!
we shall all rise up to meet Him With the Al - le - lu - ias ring-ing to the sky!

WORDS: Timothy Dudley-Smith, 1967; based on 1 Thess. 4:14-17
MUSIC: James D. Thornton, 1969

THORNTON
Irregular meter

Lift Up the Trumpet 173

He which testifieth . . . saith, Surely I come quickly. Rev. 22:20

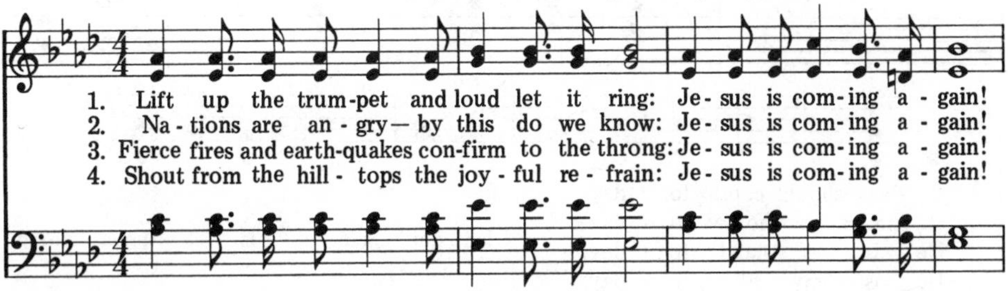

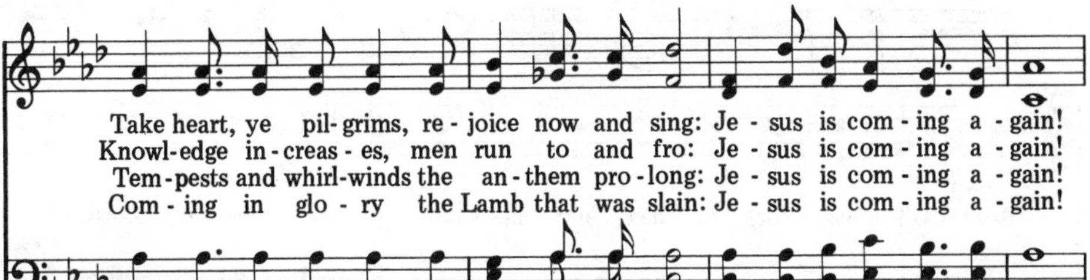

1. Lift up the trum-pet and loud let it ring: Je - sus is com - ing a - gain!
2. Na - tions are an - gry— by this do we know: Je - sus is com - ing a - gain!
3. Fierce fires and earth-quakes con-firm to the throng: Je - sus is com - ing a - gain!
4. Shout from the hill - tops the joy - ful re - frain: Je - sus is com - ing a - gain!

Take heart, ye pil - grims, re - joice now and sing: Je - sus is com - ing a - gain!
Knowl-edge in - creas - es, men run to and fro: Je - sus is com - ing a - gain!
Tem-pests and whirl-winds the an - them pro - long: Je - sus is com - ing a - gain!
Com - ing in glo - ry the Lamb that was slain: Je - sus is com - ing a - gain!

Com - ing a-gain, com - ing a-gain, Je - sus is com - ing a - gain!

WORDS: Jessie E. Strout, 19th century; alt. Eldon Burkwall, 1979
MUSIC: George E. Lee, 19th century; arr. Eldon Burkwall, 1979

TRUMPET
10.7.10.7 Ref.

174 Jesus May Come Today

Unto them that look for Him shall He appear the second time . . . Heb. 9:28

1. Je - sus may come to - day, Glad day! Glad day! And I would see my Friend; Dan - gers and trou - bles would end If Je - sus should come to - day.
2. I may go home to - day, Glad day! Glad day! Seem - eth I hear their song; Hail to the ra - di - ant throng! If I should go home to - day.
3. Why should I anx - ious be? Glad day! Glad day! Lights ap - pear on the shore, Storms will af - fright nev - er - more, For He is "at hand" to - day.
4. Faith - ful I'll be to - day, Glad day! Glad day! And I will free - ly tell Why I should love Him so well, For He is my all to - day.
Refrain
Glad day! Glad day! Is it the crown-ing day? I'll live for to - day, nor anx - ious be, Je - sus my Lord I soon shall see; Glad day! Glad day! Is it the crown - ing day?

WORDS: Henry Ostrom, 1910
MUSIC: Charles H. Marsh, 1910

CROWNING DAY
Irregular meter

It May Be at Morn 175

Ye shall see the Son of man . . . coming in the clouds of heaven. Mark 14:62

1. It may be at morn, when the day is a - wak - ing, When sun - light through dark - ness and shad - ow is break - ing, That Je - sus will come in the full - ness of glo - ry, To re - ceive from the world His own.
2. It may be at mid - day, it may be at twi - light, It may be, per - chance, that the black - ness of mid - night Will burst in - to light in the blaze of His glo - ry, When Je - sus re - ceives His own.
3. While hosts cry Ho - san - na, from heav - en de - scend - ing, With glo - ri - fied saints and the an - gels at - tend - ing, With grace on His brow, like a ha - lo of glo - ry, Will Je - sus re - ceive His own.
4. O joy! O de - light! should we go with - out dy - ing, No sick - ness, no sad - ness, no dread and no cry - ing, Caught up through the clouds with our Lord in - to glo - ry, When Je - sus re - ceives His own.
Refrain
O Lord Je - sus, how long, how long Ere we shout the glad song, Christ re - turn - eth! Hal - le - lu - jah! hal - le - lu - jah! A - men, Hal - le - lu - jah! A - men.

WORDS: H. L. Turner, 1878
MUSIC: James McGranahan, 1878

CHRIST RETURNETH
Irregular meter

176 Lo, He Comes with Clouds Descending

Behold, He cometh with clouds; and every eye shall see Him. Rev. 1:7

1. Lo, He comes with clouds de - scend - ing, Once for fa - vored sin - ners slain;
2. Ev - ery eye shall now be - hold Him, Robed in dread - ful maj - es - ty;
3. Now re - demp-tion, long ex - pect - ed, See in sol - emn pomp ap - pear:
4. Yea, A - men! let all a - dore Thee, High on Thine e - ter - nal throne;
Thou-sand thou-sand saints at - tend - ing Swell the tri - umph of His train:
Those who set at naught and sold Him, Pierced and nailed Him to the tree,
All His saints, by men re - ject - ed, Now shall meet Him in the air:
Sav - ior, take the pow'r and glo - ry, Claim the king - dom for Thine own:
Al - le - lu - ia! al - le - lu - ia! God ap - pears on earth to reign.
Deep - ly wail - ing, deep - ly wail - ing, Shall the true Mes - si - ah see.
Al - le - lu - ia! al - le - lu - ia! See the day of God ap - pear.
O, come quick-ly, O, come quick-ly! Ev - er - last - ing God, come down. A-men.

WORDS: Charles Wesley, 1758, and Martin Madan, 1760; based on John Cennick, 1752
MUSIC: Henry T. Smart, 1867

REGENT SQUARE
8.7.8.7.8.7

177 The King Shall Come

Surely, I come quickly . . . Even so, come, Lord Jesus. Rev. 22:20

Unison

1. The King shall come when morn - ing dawns And light tri - um-phant breaks, When
2. Not as of old a lit - tle child To bear and fight and die, But
3. O bright - er than the ris - ing morn When He, vic - to - rious, rose And
4. O bright - er than that glo - rious morn Shall this fair morn - ing be, When
5. The King shall come when morn - ing dawns And light and beau - ty brings. Hail,

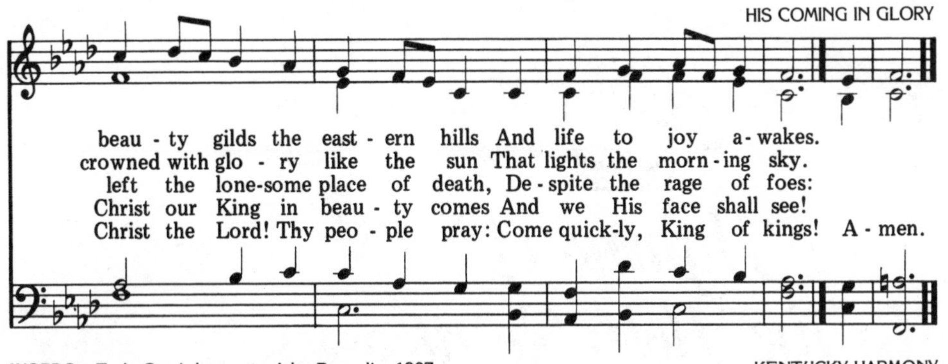
beau - ty gilds the east - ern hills And life to joy a-wakes.
crowned with glo - ry like the sun That lights the morn-ing sky.
left the lone-some place of death, De-spite the rage of foes:
Christ our King in beau - ty comes And we His face shall see!
Christ the Lord! Thy peo - ple pray: Come quick-ly, King of kings! A - men.

WORDS: Early Greek hymn; tr. John Brownlie, 1907
MUSIC: Traditional American melody; *Kentucky Harmony*, 1816

KENTUCKY HARMONY
C.M.

When He Shall Come 178

And they shall walk with me in white. Rev. 3:4

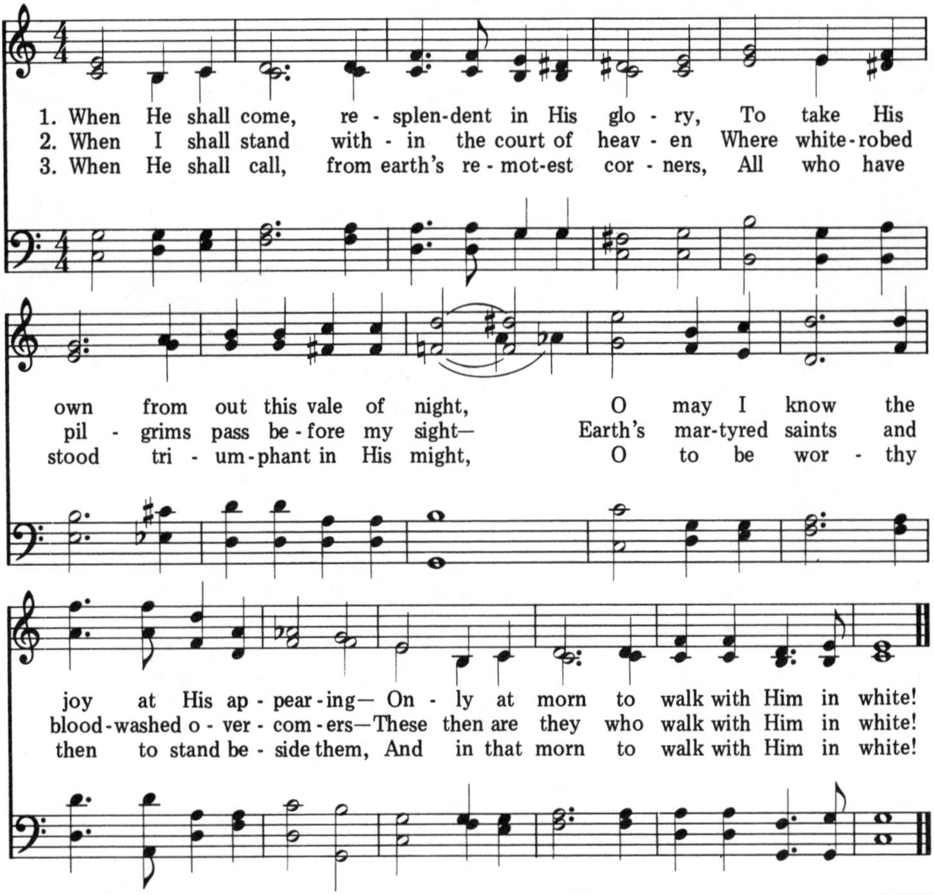

1. When He shall come, re - splen-dent in His glo - ry, To take His own from out this vale of night, O may I know the joy at His ap - pear-ing— On - ly at morn to walk with Him in white!

2. When I shall stand with - in the court of heav - en Where white-robed pil - grims pass be - fore my sight— Earth's mar-tyred saints and blood-washed o - ver - com - ers—These then are they who walk with Him in white!

3. When He shall call, from earth's re - mot-est cor - ners, All who have stood tri - um-phant in His might, O to be wor - thy then to stand be - side them, And in that morn to walk with Him in white!

WORDS and MUSIC: Almeda J. Pearce, 1934; based on Rev. 3:4 and 7:9

PEARCE
11.10.11.10

Hymns of The Holy Spirit

Breathe on Me, Breath of God 179

He breathed on them, and saith, Receive ye the Holy Ghost. John 20:22

1. Breathe on me, Breath of God, Fill me with life anew, That I may love what Thou dost love, And do what Thou wouldst do.
2. Breathe on me, Breath of God, Until my heart is pure, Until my will is one with Thine, To do and to endure.
3. Breathe on me, Breath of God, Till I am wholly Thine, Until this earthly part of me Glows with Thy fire divine.
4. Breathe on me, Breath of God, So shall I never die, But live with Thee the perfect life Of Thine eternity. Amen.

WORDS: Edwin Hatch, 1878
MUSIC: Robert Jackson, 1888

TRENTHAM
S.M.

Come, Holy Ghost, Our Souls Inspire 180

. . . The love of God is shed abroad in our hearts by the Holy Ghost . . . Rom. 5:5

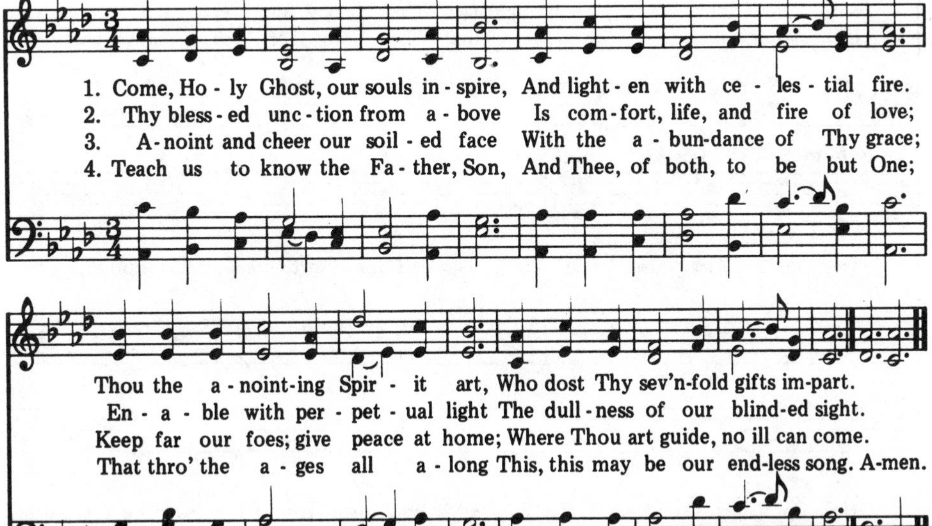
1. Come, Ho - ly Ghost, our souls in - spire, And light - en with ce - les - tial fire.
2. Thy bless - ed unc - tion from a - bove Is com - fort, life, and fire of love;
3. A - noint and cheer our soil - ed face With the a - bun - dance of Thy grace;
4. Teach us to know the Fa - ther, Son, And Thee, of both, to be but One;
Thou the a - noint - ing Spir - it art, Who dost Thy sev'n - fold gifts im - part.
En - a - ble with per - pet - ual light The dull - ness of our blind - ed sight.
Keep far our foes; give peace at home; Where Thou art guide, no ill can come.
That thro' the a - ges all a - long This, this may be our end - less song. A - men.

WORDS: Attr. Rabanus Maurus, c.776-856; tr. John Cosin, 1627
MUSIC: Traditional German melody; arr. Samuel Dyer, 1824

MENDON
L.M.

181 O Spread the Tidings 'Round

I will pray the Father, and He will give you another Comforter. John 14:16

1. O spread the ti - dings 'round wher - ev - er man is found, Wher - ev - er hu - man hearts and hu - man woes a - bound; Let ev - ery Chris - tian tongue pro - claim the joy - ful sound: The Com - fort - er has come!
2. The long, long night is past, the morn - ing breaks at last, And hushed the dread - ful wail and fu - ry of the blast, As o'er the gold - en hills the day ad - vanc - es fast! The Com - fort - er has come!
3. Lo, the great King of kings with heal - ing in His wings, To ev - ery cap - tive soul a full de - liv-'rance brings; And through the va - cant cells the song of tri - umph rings; The Com - fort - er has come!
4. O bound - less love di - vine! how shall this tongue of mine To wond-'ring mor - tals tell the match - less grace di - vine—That I, a child of hell, should in His im - age shine! The Com - fort - er has come!
Refrain
The Com - fort - er has come, the Com - fort - er has come! The Ho - ly Ghost from Heav'n, the Fa - ther's pro - mise giv'n; O spread the ti - dings

'round wher - ev - er man is found—The Com - fort - er has come!

WORDS: Frank Bottome, 1890
MUSIC: William J. Kirkpatrick, 1890

COMFORTER
12.12.12.6 Ref.

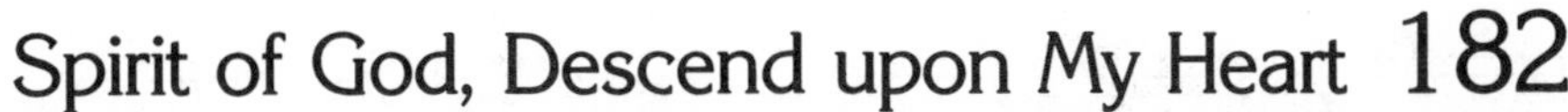

Spirit of God, Descend upon My Heart 182

If we live in the Spirit, let us also walk in the Spirit. Gal. 5:25

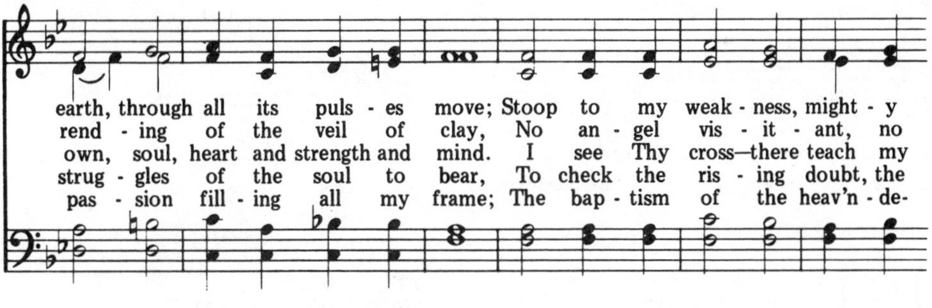

1. Spirit of God, descend upon my heart; Wean it from earth, through all its pulses move; Stoop to my weakness, mighty as Thou art, And make me love Thee as I ought to love.

2. I ask no dream, no prophet ecstasies, No sudden rending of the veil of clay, No angel visitant, no o-p'ning skies; But take the dimness of my soul away.

3. Hast Thou not bid us love Thee, God and King? All, all Thine own, soul, heart and strength and mind. I see Thy cross—there teach my heart to cling: O let me seek Thee, and O let me find.

4. Teach me to feel that Thou art always nigh; Teach me the struggles of the soul to bear, To check the rising doubt, the rebel sigh; Teach me the patience of unanswered prayer.

5. Teach me to love Thee as Thine angels love, One holy passion filling all my frame; The baptism of the heav'n-descended Dove, My heart an altar, and Thy love the flame. A-men.

WORDS: George Croly, 1867
MUSIC: Frederick C. Atkinson, 1870

MORECAMBE
10.10.10.10

183 Spirit of the Living God

I will pour out in those days of my Spirit . . . Acts 2:18

Spir - it of the liv - ing God, Fall fresh on me. Spir - it of the

liv - ing God, Fall fresh on me. Melt me, mold me, fill me,

use me. Spir - it of the liv - ing God, Fall fresh on me.

WORDS and MUSIC: Daniel Iverson, 1926

IVERSON
Irregular meter

184 Come, Holy Spirit, Heavenly Dove

The love of God is shed abroad in our hearts by the Holy Ghost . . . Romans 5:5

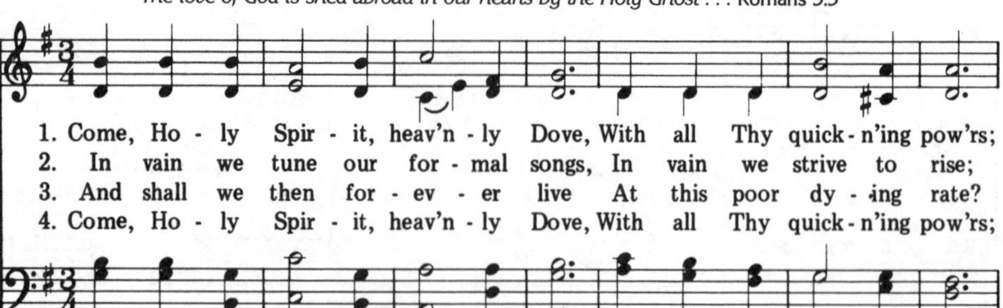
1. Come, Ho - ly Spir - it, heav'n - ly Dove, With all Thy quick - n'ing pow'rs;
2. In vain we tune our for - mal songs, In vain we strive to rise;
3. And shall we then for - ev - er live At this poor dy - ing rate?
4. Come, Ho - ly Spir - it, heav'n - ly Dove, With all Thy quick - n'ing pow'rs;

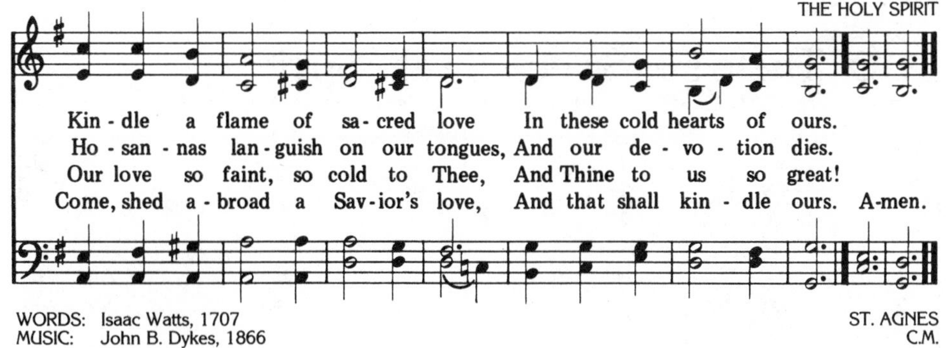
Kin - dle a flame of sa - cred love In these cold hearts of ours.
Ho - san - nas lan - guish on our tongues, And our de - vo - tion dies.
Our love so faint, so cold to Thee, And Thine to us so great!
Come, shed a - broad a Sav - ior's love, And that shall kin - dle ours. A-men.

WORDS: Isaac Watts, 1707
MUSIC: John B. Dykes, 1866

ST. AGNES
C.M.

Gracious Spirit, Dwell with Me 185

A new spirit will I put within you. Ezek. 36:26

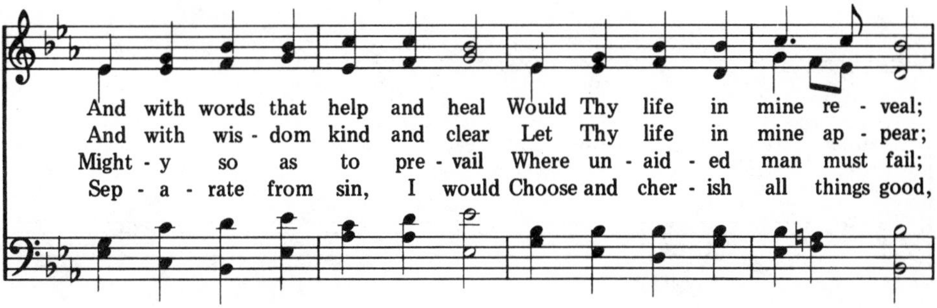

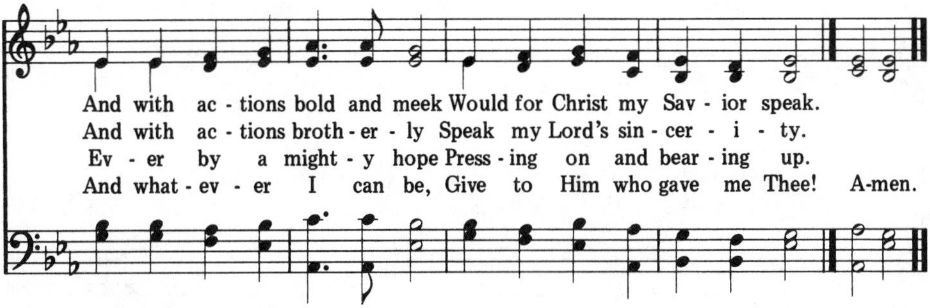

1. Gra - cious Spir - it, dwell with me: I my - self would gra - cious be;
And with words that help and heal Would Thy life in mine re - veal;
And with ac - tions bold and meek Would for Christ my Sav - ior speak.

2. Truth - ful Spir - it, dwell with me: I my - self would truth - ful be;
And with wis - dom kind and clear Let Thy life in mine ap - pear;
And with ac - tions broth - er - ly Speak my Lord's sin - cer - i - ty.

3. Might - y Spir - it, dwell with me: I my - self would might - y be;
Might - y so as to pre - vail Where un - aid - ed man must fail;
Ev - er by a might - y hope Press - ing on and bear - ing up.

4. Ho - ly Spir - it, dwell with me: I my - self would ho - ly be;
Sep - a - rate from sin, I would Choose and cher - ish all things good,
And what - ev - er I can be, Give to Him who gave me Thee! A-men.

WORDS: Thomas T. Lynch, 1855
MUSIC: Richard Redhead, 1853

REDHEAD
7.7.7.7.7.7

186 There's a Sweet, Sweet Spirit

Behold, how good and how pleasant it is for brethren to dwell together in unity! Psa. 133:1

Unison
1. There's a sweet, sweet Spir - it in this place, And I
2. There are bless - ings you can - not re - ceive Till you
know that it's the Spir - it of the Lord; There are
know Him in His full - ness, and be - lieve. You're the
sweet ex - pres - sions on each face, And I
one to pro - fit when you say, "I am
know they feel the pres - ence of the Lord.
going to walk with Je - sus all the way."

Refrain
Sweet Ho - ly Spir - it, Sweet heav-en-ly Dove, Stay right here
with us, Fill - ing us with your love, And for these
bless - ings we lift our hearts in praise; With-out a
doubt we'll know that we have been re - vived When we shall leave this place.

WORDS and MUSIC: Doris Akers, 1962

SWEET, SWEET SPIRIT
Irregular meter

187 Where the Spirit of the Lord Is

Where the Spirit of the Lord is . . . II Cor. 3:17

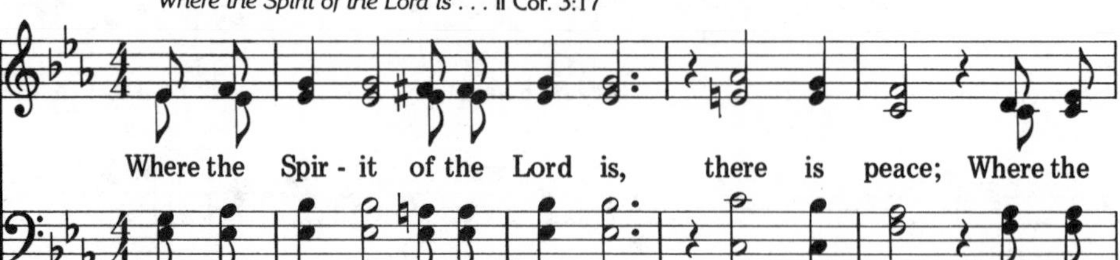
Where the Spir - it of the Lord is, there is peace; Where the

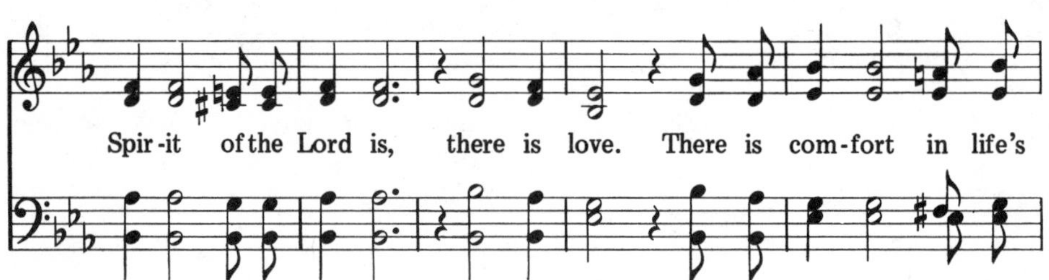
Spir-it of the Lord is, there is love. There is com-fort in life's

dark - est hour, there is light and life; There is help and

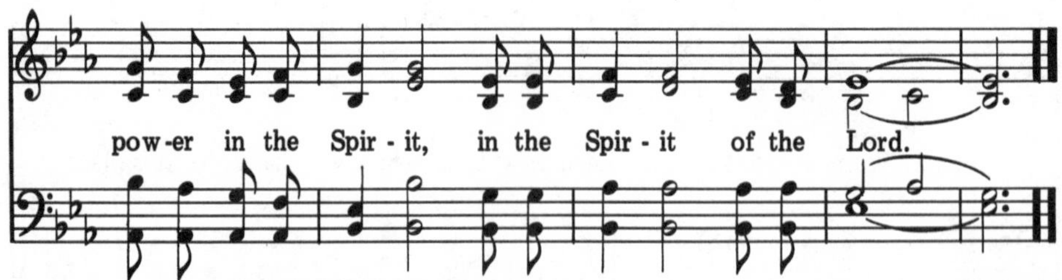
pow-er in the Spir - it, in the Spir - it of the Lord.

WORDS and MUSIC: Stephen R. Adams, 1973

ADAMS
Irregular meter

Joys Are Flowing Like a River 188

He shall give you another Comforter, that He may abide with you forever. John 14:16

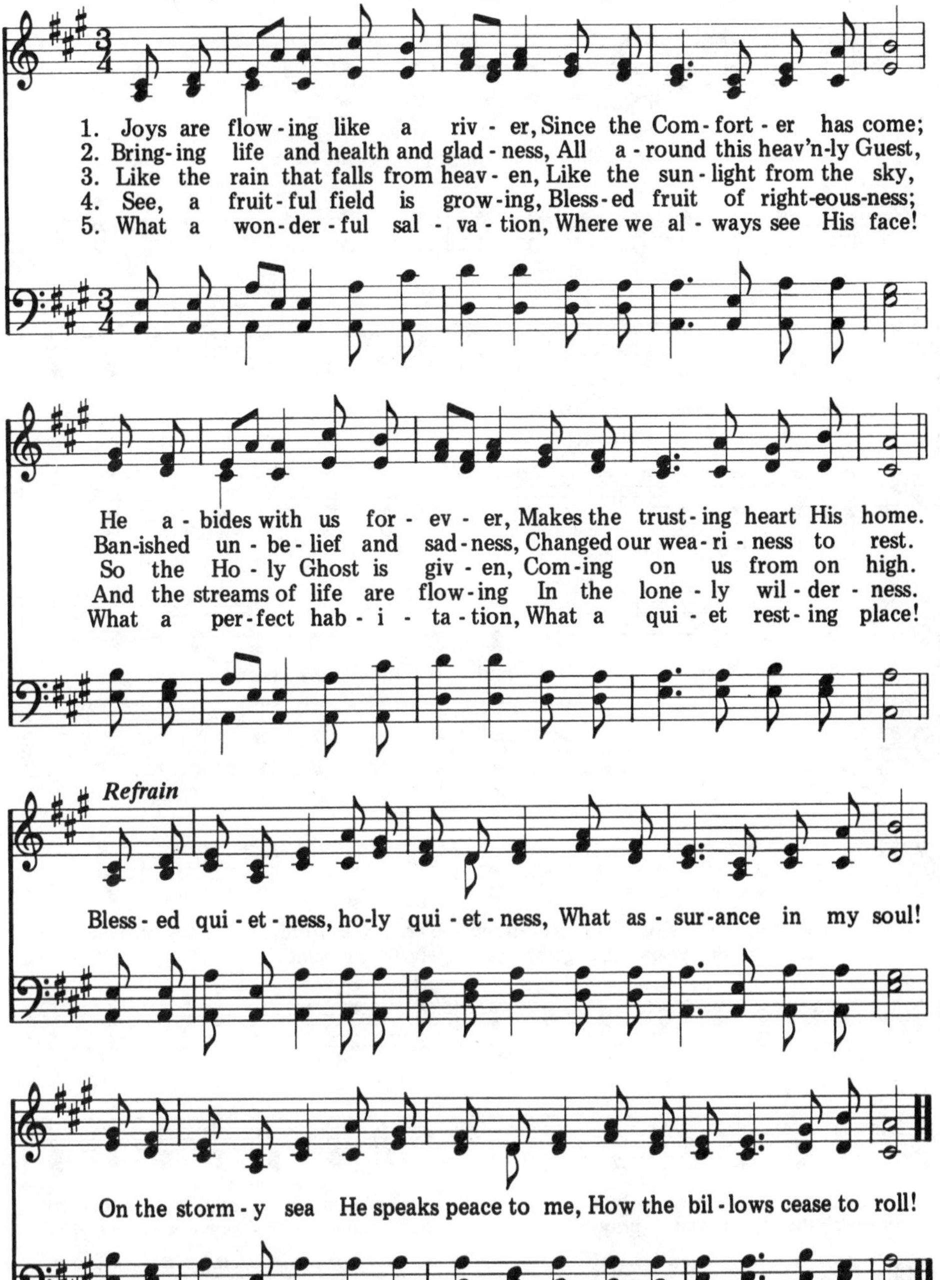

1. Joys are flow-ing like a riv-er, Since the Com-fort-er has come;
He a-bides with us for-ev-er, Makes the trust-ing heart His home.

2. Bring-ing life and health and glad-ness, All a-round this heav'n-ly Guest,
Ban-ished un-be-lief and sad-ness, Changed our wea-ri-ness to rest.

3. Like the rain that falls from heav-en, Like the sun-light from the sky,
So the Ho-ly Ghost is giv-en, Com-ing on us from on high.

4. See, a fruit-ful field is grow-ing, Bless-ed fruit of right-eous-ness;
And the streams of life are flow-ing In the lone-ly wil-der-ness.

5. What a won-der-ful sal-va-tion, Where we al-ways see His face!
What a per-fect hab-i-ta-tion, What a qui-et rest-ing place!

Refrain

Bless-ed qui-et-ness, ho-ly qui-et-ness, What as-sur-ance in my soul!
On the storm-y sea He speaks peace to me, How the bil-lows cease to roll!

WORDS: Manie P. Ferguson, 1900
MUSIC: W. S. Marshall, 19th century; arr. James M. Kirk, 1900

BLESSED QUIETNESS
8.7.8.7 Ref.

189 The Holy Spirit Came at Pentecost

In the last days . . . I will pour out of my Spirit upon all flesh. Acts 2:17

1. The Ho-ly Spir-it came at Pen-te-cost, He came in might-y full-ness then; His wit-ness thro' be-liev-ers won the lost, And mul-ti-tudes were born a-gain.
2. Then in an age when dark-ness gripped the earth, "The just shall live by faith" was learned; The Ho-ly Spir-it gave the Church new birth As ref-or-ma-tion fires burned.
The ear-ly Chris-tians scat-tered o'er the world, They preached the Gos-pel fear-less-ly; Tho' some were mar-tyred and to
In lat-er years the great re-viv-als came, When saints would seek the Lord and pray; O, once a-gain we need that

li - ons hurled, They marched a - long in vic - to - ry!
ho - ly flame To meet the chal - lenge of to - day!
Refrain
Come, Ho - ly Spir - it, Dark is the hour, We need Your fill - ing, Your
love and Your might - y pow'r; Move now a - mong us, Stir us, we
D. C.
pray, Come, Ho - ly Spir - it, Re - vive the church to - day!
Coda
Re - vive the church to - day! Re - vive the church to - day!

WORDS and MUSIC: John W. Peterson, 1971

COME, HOLY SPIRIT
Irregular meter

190 O Breath of Life

Wilt Thou not revive us again . . . ? Psa. 85:6

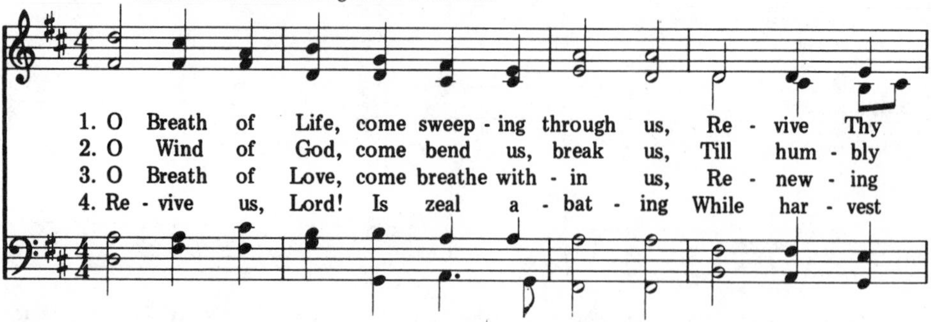

1. O Breath of Life, come sweep - ing through us, Re - vive Thy
2. O Wind of God, come bend us, break us, Till hum - bly
3. O Breath of Love, come breathe with - in us, Re - new - ing
4. Re - vive us, Lord! Is zeal a - bat - ing While har - vest

church with life and pow'r; O Breath of Life, come, cleanse, re -
we con - fess our need; Then in Thy ten - der - ness re -
thought and will and heart; Come, Love of Christ, a - fresh to
fields are vast and white? Re - vive us, Lord, the world is

new us, And fit Thy church to meet this hour.
make us, Re - vive, re - store, for this we plead.
win us, Re - vive Thy church in ev - ery part.
wait - ing, E - quip Thy church to spread the light. A-men.

WORDS: Bessie P. Head, c.1914
MUSIC: Mary J. Hammond, c.1920

SPIRITUS VITAE
9.8.9.8

191 Holy Spirit, Light Divine

He . . . shall also quicken your mortal bodies by His Spirit. Rom. 8:11

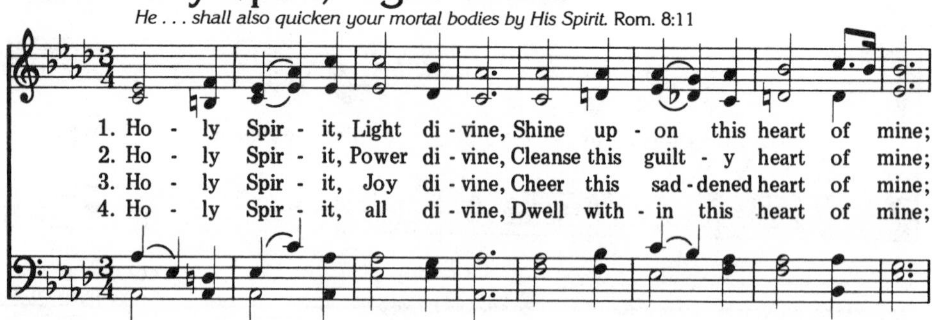
1. Ho - ly Spir - it, Light di - vine, Shine up - on this heart of mine;
2. Ho - ly Spir - it, Power di - vine, Cleanse this guilt - y heart of mine;
3. Ho - ly Spir - it, Joy di - vine, Cheer this sad - dened heart of mine;
4. Ho - ly Spir - it, all di - vine, Dwell with - in this heart of mine;

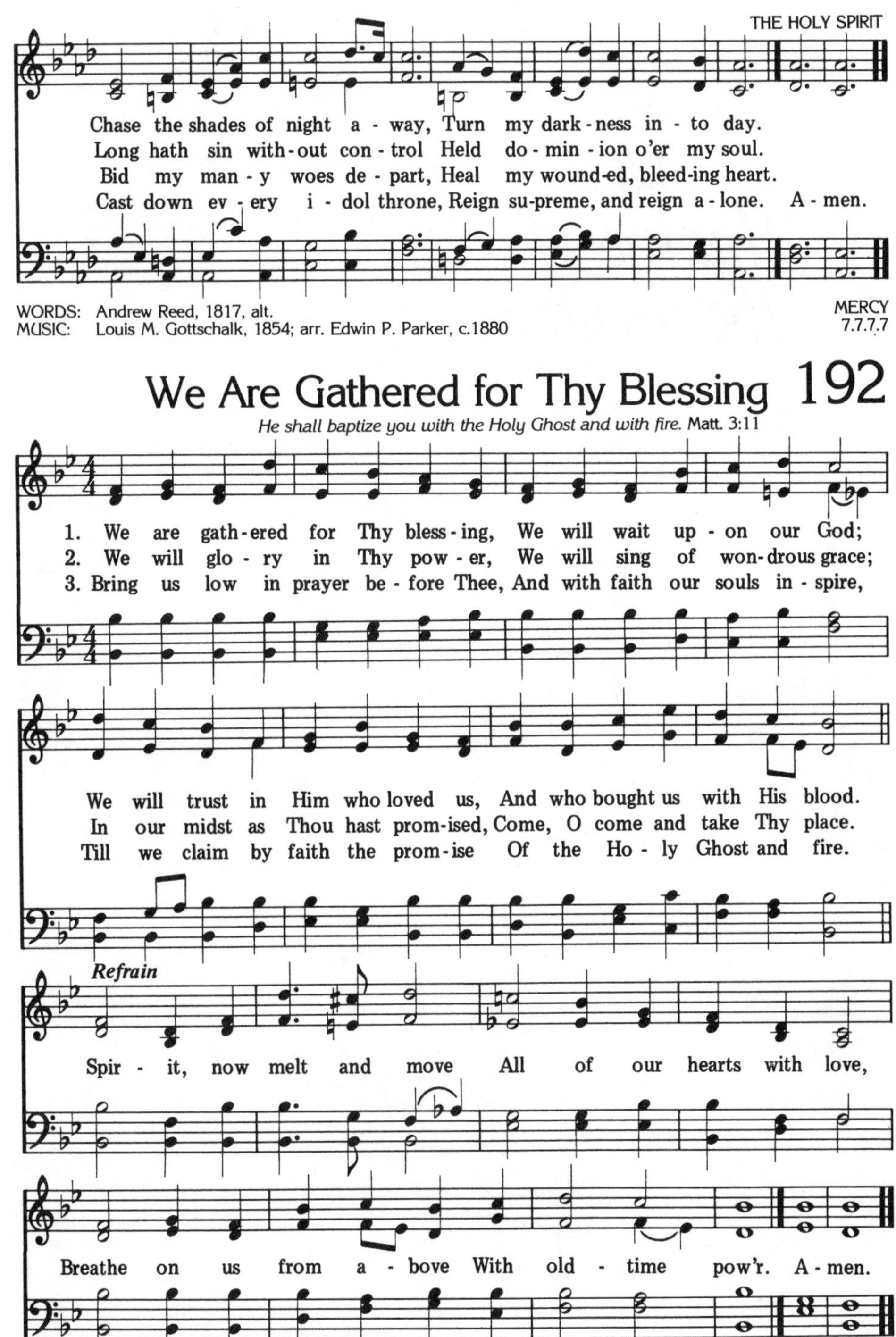
THE HOLY SPIRIT
Chase the shades of night a - way, Turn my dark - ness in - to day.
Long hath sin with - out con - trol Held do - min - ion o'er my soul.
Bid my man - y woes de - part, Heal my wound-ed, bleed-ing heart.
Cast down ev - ery i - dol throne, Reign su-preme, and reign a - lone. A - men.
WORDS: Andrew Reed, 1817, alt.
MUSIC: Louis M. Gottschalk, 1854; arr. Edwin P. Parker, c.1880
MERCY
7.7.7.7
We Are Gathered for Thy Blessing 192
He shall baptize you with the Holy Ghost and with fire. Matt. 3:11
1. We are gath - ered for Thy bless - ing, We will wait up - on our God;
2. We will glo - ry in Thy pow - er, We will sing of won - drous grace;
3. Bring us low in prayer be - fore Thee, And with faith our souls in - spire,
We will trust in Him who loved us, And who bought us with His blood.
In our midst as Thou hast prom - ised, Come, O come and take Thy place.
Till we claim by faith the prom - ise Of the Ho - ly Ghost and fire.
Refrain
Spir - it, now melt and move All of our hearts with love,
Breathe on us from a - bove With old - time pow'r. A - men.
WORDS and MUSIC: Paul Rader, 1920
TABERNACLE
8.7.8.7 Ref.

Hymns of The Trinity

Holy, Holy, Holy! Lord God Almighty 193

They rest not day and night, saying, Holy, holy, holy, Lord God almighty. Rev. 4:8

1. Ho - ly, ho - ly, ho - ly! Lord God Al - might - y!
2. Ho - ly, ho - ly, ho - ly! all the saints a - dore Thee,
3. Ho - ly, ho - ly, ho - ly! though the dark - ness hide Thee,
4. Ho - ly, ho - ly, ho - ly! Lord God Al - might - y!

Ear - ly in the morn - ing our song shall rise to Thee;
Cast - ing down their gold - en crowns a - round the glass - y sea;
Though the eye of sin - ful man Thy glo - ry may not see,
All Thy works shall praise Thy name, in earth, and sky, and sea;

Ho - ly, ho - ly, ho - ly! mer - ci - ful and might - y!
Cher - u - bim and ser - a - phim fall - ing down be - fore Thee,
On - ly Thou art ho - ly; there is none be - side Thee,
Ho - ly, ho - ly, ho - ly! mer - ci - ful and might - y!

God in three per - sons, bless - ed Trin - i - ty!
Which wert and art, and ev - er - more shalt be.
Per - fect in pow'r, in love, and pu - ri - ty.
God in three per - sons, bless - ed Trin - i - ty! A-men.

WORDS: Reginald Heber, 1826
MUSIC: John B. Dykes, 1861

NICAEA
11.12.12.10

194 I Bind Unto Myself Today

. . . The Father, the Word, and the Holy Ghost: and these three are one. I John 5:7

Unison
1. I bind un - to my - self to - day The strong name of the Trin - i - ty, By in - vo - ca - tion of the same, The Three in One and One in Three, Of whom all na - ture hath cre - a - tion, E - ter - nal Fa - ther, Spir - it,
2. I bind this day to me for - ev - er, By pow'r of faith Christ's in - car - na-tion; His bap - tism in the Jor - dan riv-er; His death on cross for my sal - va - tion. His burst - ing from the spic - ed tomb; His rid - ing up the heav'n - ly
3. I bind un - to my - self to - day The pow'r of God to hold and lead, His eye to watch, His might to stay, His ear to heark - en to my need; The wis - dom of my God to teach, His hand to guide, His shield to

Word, Praise to the Lord of my sal - va - tion: Sal - va - tion is of Christ the Lord.
way; His com - ing at the day of doom: I bind un - to my - self to - day.
ward, The word of God to give me speech, His heav'n - ly host to be my guard.

Fine

Coda

Christ be with me, Christ with - in me, Christ be - hind me, Christ be - fore me,
Christ be - side me, Christ to win me, Christ to com - fort and re - store me,

Christ be - neath me, Christ a - bove me, Christ in qui - et, Christ in dan - ger,
Christ in hearts of all that love me, Christ in mouth of friend and strang - er.

Repeat stanza 1.

WORDS: St. Patrick, 5th c.; tr. Cecil F. Alexander, 1889
MUSIC: Traditional Irish melody; arr. Donald Hustad, 1984

ST. PATRICK'S BREASTPLATE
Irregular meter

195 Come, Thou Almighty King

Give unto the Lord the glory due unto His name . . . Psa. 29:2

1. Come, Thou Al - might - y King, Help us Thy name to sing, Help us to praise: Fa - ther, all glo - ri - ous, O'er all vic - to - ri - ous, Come, and reign o - ver us, An - cient of Days.
2. Come, Thou In - car - nate Word, Gird on Thy might - y sword, Our prayer at - tend: Come, and Thy peo - ple bless, And give Thy word suc - cess: Spir - it of ho - li - ness, On us de - scend.
3. Come, Ho - ly Com - fort - er, Thy sa - cred wit - ness bear In this glad hour: Thou who al - might - y art, Now rule in ev - ery heart, And ne'er from us de - part, Spir - it of pow'r.
4. To Thee, great One in Three, E - ter - nal prais - es be Hence, ev - er - more! Thy sov - ereign maj - es - ty May we in glo - ry see, And to e - ter - ni - ty Love and a - dore! A - men.

WORDS: Source unknown, c.1757
MUSIC: Felice de Giardini, 1769

ITALIAN HYMN
6.6.4.6.6.6.4

196 Glory Be to God on High

Unto God and our Father be glory for ever and ever. Phil. 4:20

1. Glo - ry be to God on high, Al - le - lu - ia!
2. Praise the Fa - ther, Spir - it, Son, Al - le - lu - ia!
3. Glo - ry be to God on high, Al - le - lu - ia!
4. Sing we prais - es un - to Thee, Al - le - lu - ia!
5. Glo - ry be to God on high, Al - le - lu - ia!

Glo - ry be to God on high, Al - le - lu - ia!
Praise the God - head, Three - in - One, Al - le - lu - ia!
Glo - ry be to God on high, Al - le - lu - ia!
For the truth that sets us free, Al - le - lu - ia!
Glo - ry be to God on high, Al - le - lu - ia!

WORDS: Author unknown
MUSIC: Traditional melody

MICHAEL'S BOAT
7.4.7.4

Glory Be to God the Father 197

To Him be glory and dominion for ever and ever. Rev. 1:6

1. Glo - ry be to God the Fa - ther, Glo - ry be to God the Son,
2. Glo - ry be to Him who loved us, Washed us from each spot and stain:
3. Glo - ry to the King of an - gels, Glo - ry to the Church - 's King,
4. Glo - ry, bless - ing, praise e - ter - nal! Thus the choir of an - gels sings;

Glo - ry be to God the Spir - it: Great Je - ho - vah, Three in One!
Glo - ry be to Him who bought us, Made us kings with Him to reign!
Glo - ry to the King of na - tions; Heav'n and earth, your prais - es bring!
Hon - or, rich - es, pow'r, do - min - ion! Thus its praise cre - a - tion brings.

Glo - ry, glo - ry, glo - ry, glo - ry, While e - ter - nal a - ges run!
Glo - ry, glo - ry, glo - ry, glo - ry, To the Lamb that once was slain!
Glo - ry, glo - ry, glo - ry, glo - ry, To the King of glo - ry sing!
Glo - ry, glo - ry, glo - ry, glo - ry, Glo - ry to the King of kings!

WORDS: Horatius Bonar, 1866
MUSIC: Henry T. Smart, 1867

REGENT SQUARE
8.7.8.7.8.7

198 Holy, Holy

. . . Holy, holy, holy, Lord God Almighty, which was, and is, and is to come. Rev. 4:8

1. Ho - ly, ho - ly, ho - ly, ho - ly, Ho - ly, ho - ly,
2. Gra-cious Fa - ther, gra-cious Fa - ther, We're so blest to be your
3. Pre-cious Je - sus, pre-cious Je - sus, We're so glad that you've re-
4. Ho - ly Spir - it, Ho - ly Spir - it, Come and fill our hearts a-
5. Ho - ly, ho - ly, ho - ly, ho - ly, Ho - ly, ho - ly,
Lord God al - might - y; And we lift our hearts be - fore You as a
chil-dren, gra-cious Fa - ther; And we lift our heads be - fore You as a
deemed us, pre-cious Je - sus; And we lift our hands be - fore You as a
new, Ho - ly Spir - it; And we lift our voice be - fore You as a
Lord God al - might - y; And we lift our hearts be - fore You as a
to - ken of our love, Ho - ly, ho - ly, ho - ly, ho - ly.
to - ken of our love, Gra-cious Fa - ther, gra-cious Fa - ther.
to - ken of our love, Pre-cious Je - sus, pre-cious Je - sus.
to - ken of our love, Ho - ly Spir - it, Ho - ly Spir - it.
to - ken of our love, Ho - ly, ho - ly, ho - ly, ho - ly.

WORDS and MUSIC: Jimmy Owens, 1972

HOLY, HOLY
Irregular meter

God, Our Father, We Adore Thee 199

Ye have received the Spirit of adoption, whereby we cry, Abba, Father. Rom. 8:15

1. God, our Fa - ther, we a - dore Thee! We, Thy chil - dren, bless Thy name!
2. Son E - ter - nal, we a - dore Thee! Lamb up - on the throne on high!
3. Ho - ly Spir - it, we a - dore Thee! Par - a - clete and heav'n - ly guest!
4. Fa - ther, Son, and Ho - ly Spir - it— Three in One! we give Thee praise!
Cho - sen in the Christ be - fore Thee, We are "ho - ly with - out blame."
Lamb of God, we bow be - fore Thee, Thou hast brought Thy peo - ple nigh!
Sent from God and from the Sav - ior, Thou hast led us in - to rest.
For the rich - es we in - her - it, Heart and voice to Thee we raise!
We a - dore Thee! we a - dore Thee! Ab - ba's prais - es we pro - claim!
We a - dore Thee! we a - dore Thee! Son of God, who came to die!
We a - dore Thee! we a - dore Thee! By Thy grace for - ev - er blest:
We a - dore Thee! we a - dore Thee! Thee we bless, thro' end - less days!
We a - dore Thee! we a - dore Thee! Ab-ba's prais-es we pro-claim!
We a - dore Thee! we a - dore Thee! Son of God, who came to die!
We a - dore Thee! we a - dore Thee! By Thy grace for-ev - er blest!
We a - dore Thee! we a - dore Thee! Thee we bless, thro' end-less days! A - men.

WORDS: George W. Frazer, 1904; St. 3, Alfred S. Loizeaux, 1952
MUSIC: John Zundel, 1870

BEECHER
8.7.8.7 D.

200 Holy God, We Praise Thy Name

. . . Holy, Holy, Holy is the Lord of hosts . . . Isa. 6:3

1. Ho - ly God, we praise Thy name; Lord of all, we bow be - fore Thee; All on earth Thy scep - ter claim; All in heav'n a - bove a - dore Thee. In - fi - nite Thy vast do - main, Ev - er - last - ing is Thy reign.
2. Hark! the loud ce - les - tial hymn An - gel choirs a - bove are rais - ing; Cher - u - bim and ser - a - phim In un - ceas - ing cho - rus prais - ing, Fill the heav'ns with sweet ac - cord: Ho - ly, ho - ly, ho - ly Lord.
3. Lo! the ap - os - tol - ic train Join Thy sa - cred name to hal - low; Proph - ets swell the glad re - frain, And the white - robed mar - tyrs fol - low; And from morn to set of sun, Through the Church the song goes on.
4. Ho - ly Fa - ther, Ho - ly Son, Ho - ly Spir - it, Three we name Thee; While in es - sence on - ly One, Un - di - vid - ed God we claim Thee, And a - dor - ing bend the knee, While we sing our praise to Thee.

WORDS: Attr. Ignace Franz, c. 1774; tr. Clarence A. Walworth, 1853; based on *Te Deum,* c.4th century
MUSIC: *Katholisches Gesangbuch,* Vienna, c.1774

GROSSER GOTT, WIR LOBEN DICH
7.8.7.8.7.7

Praise Ye the Father 201

I will . . . praise Thy name for Thy lovingkindness. Psa. 138:2

1. Praise ye the Fa - ther! for His lov - ing kind - ness, Ten - der - ly
2. Praise ye the Sav - ior! great is His com - pas - sion, Gra - cious - ly
3. Praise ye the Spir - it! Com-fort - er of Is - rael, Sent of the

cares He for His err - ing chil - dren; Praise Him, ye an - gels,
cares He for His cho - sen peo - ple; Young men and maid - ens,
Fa - ther and the Son to bless us; Praise ye the Fa - ther,

praise Him in the heav - ens, Praise ye Je - ho - vah!
ye old men and chil - dren, Praise ye the Sav - ior!
Son and Ho - ly Spir - it, Praise ye the tri - une God!

WORDS: Elizabeth R. Charles, c.1859
MUSIC: Friedrich F. Flemming, 1811

FLEMMING
11.11.11.6

Father, I Adore You 202

We love Him because He first loved us. I John 4:19

Three-part round (in unison)
1
2
3
1. Fa - ther, I a - dore You, Lay my life be - fore You, How I love You.
2. Je - sus, I a - dore You, Lay my life be - fore You, How I love You.
3. Spir - it, I a - dore You, Lay my life be - fore You, How I love You.

WORDS and MUSIC: Terrye Coelho, 1973

MARANATHA
Irregular meter

203 All Glory Be to God on High

Glory to God in the highest, and on earth peace, good will toward men. Luke 2:14

1. All glo - ry be to God on high And thanks to Him for - ev - er! What - ev - er Sa - tan's host may try, God foils their dark en - deav - or. He bends his ear to ev - ery call And of - fers peace, good - will to all, And calms the trou - bled spir - it.
2. O Fa - ther, for Your lord - ship true We give You praise and hon - or; We wor - ship You, we trust in You, We give You thanks for - ev - er. Your will is per - fect, and Your might Re - lent - less - ly con - firms the right; Your lord - ship is our bless - ing.
3. Lord Je - sus Christ, the on - ly Son Of God, cre - a - tion's au - thor, Re - deem - er of Your wan - d'ring ones, And source of all true plea - sure: O Lamb of God, O Lord di - vine, Con - form our lives to Your de - sign, And on us all have mer - cy.
4. O Ho - ly Spir - it, per - fect gift, Who brings us con - so - la - tion: To men and wo - men saved by Christ As - sure Your in - spi - ra - tion. Through sick - ness, need, and bit - ter death, Grant us Your warm, life - giv - ing breath; Our lives are in Your keep - ing.

WORDS: Nicolaus Decius, 1522; tr. Gilbert E. Doan, 1978; based on *Gloria in Excelsis*
MUSIC: Bohemian Brethren's *Kirchengesänge*, Berlin, 1566

MIT FREUDEN ZART
8.7.8.7.8.8.7

Hymns of The Church

204 Renew Thy Church, Her Ministries

O Lord, revive Thy work in the midst of the years. Heb. 3:2

1. Re - new Thy church, her min - is - tries re - store: Both to serve and a - dore.
2. Teach us Thy Word, re - veal its truth di - vine, On our path let it shine;
3. Teach us to pray, for Thou art ev - er near, Thy still voice let us hear.
4. Teach us to love, with strength of heart and mind, Ev - ery - one, all man-kind,
Make her a - gain as salt through-out the land, And as light from a stand.
Tell of Thy works, Thy might - y acts of grace, From each page show Thy face.
Our souls are rest - less till they rest in Thee, This our glad des - ti - ny.
Break down old walls of prej - u - dice and hate, Leave us not to our fate.
'Mid som-ber shad - ows of the night, Where greed and ha - treds spread their blight,
As Thou hast loved us, sent Thy Son, And our sal - va - tion now is won,
Be - fore Thy pres - ence keep us still That we may find for us Thy will,
As Thou hast loved and giv'n Thy life To end hos - til - i - ty and strife,
O send us forth with pow'r en - dued, Help us, Lord, be re - newed.
O let our hearts with love be stirred, Help us, Lord, know thy Word.
And seek Thy guid - ance ev - ery day, Teach us, Lord, how to pray.
O share Thy grace from heav'n a - bove, Teach us, Lord, how to love. A - men.

WORDS: Kenneth L. Cober, 1960
MUSIC: Traditional English melody; *The Sacred Harp*, 1844

ALL IS WELL
10.6.10.6.8.8.8.6

There's a Quiet Understanding 205

Where two or three are gathered in My name, there am I . . . Matt. 18:20

1. There's a quiet understanding when we're gathered in the Spirit, It's a promise that He gives us, when we gather in His name. There's a love we feel in Jesus, there's a manna that He feeds us, It's a promise that He gives us
2. And we know when we're together, sharing love and understanding, That our brothers and our sisters feel the oneness that He brings. Thank You, thank You, thank You, Jesus, for the way You love and feed us, For the many ways You lead us,
1
When we gather in His name.
2 (Repeat, ad lib.)
Thank You, thank You, Lord.

WORDS and MUSIC: Tedd Smith, 1973

QUIET UNDERSTANDING
Irregular meter

206 The Church's One Foundation

Other foundation can no man lay than that is laid . . . Jesus Christ. I Cor. 3:11

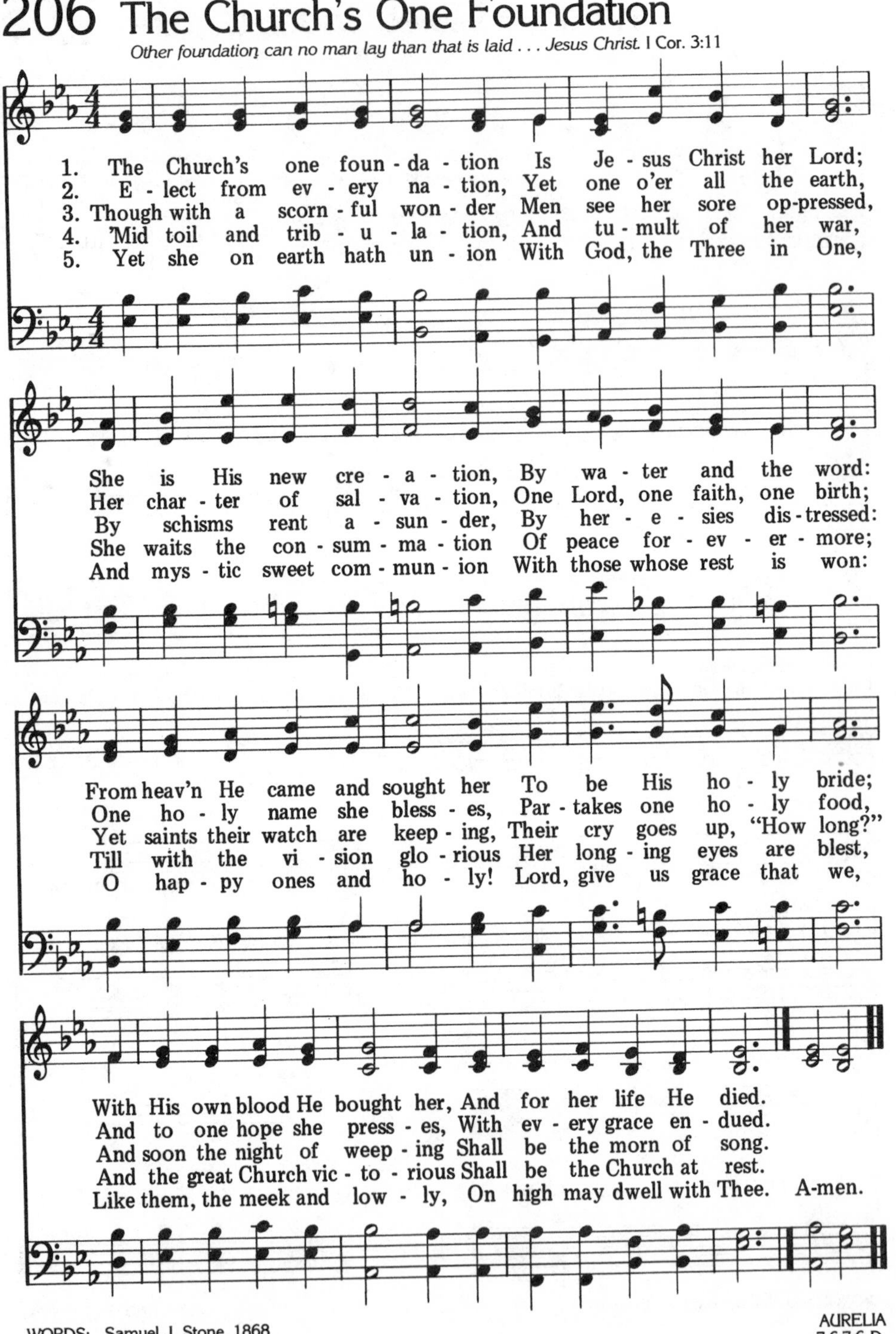
1. The Church's one foun - da - tion Is Je - sus Christ her Lord;
2. E - lect from ev - ery na - tion, Yet one o'er all the earth,
3. Though with a scorn - ful won - der Men see her sore op-pressed,
4. 'Mid toil and trib - u - la - tion, And tu - mult of her war,
5. Yet she on earth hath un - ion With God, the Three in One,
She is His new cre - a - tion, By wa - ter and the word:
Her char - ter of sal - va - tion, One Lord, one faith, one birth;
By schisms rent a - sun - der, By her - e - sies dis - tressed:
She waits the con - sum - ma - tion Of peace for - ev - er - more;
And mys - tic sweet com - mun - ion With those whose rest is won:
From heav'n He came and sought her To be His ho - ly bride;
One ho - ly name she bless - es, Par - takes one ho - ly food,
Yet saints their watch are keep - ing, Their cry goes up, "How long?"
Till with the vi - sion glo - rious Her long - ing eyes are blest,
O hap - py ones and ho - ly! Lord, give us grace that we,
With His own blood He bought her, And for her life He died.
And to one hope she press - es, With ev - ery grace en - dued.
And soon the night of weep - ing Shall be the morn of song.
And the great Church vic - to - rious Shall be the Church at rest.
Like them, the meek and low - ly, On high may dwell with Thee. A-men.

WORDS: Samuel J. Stone, 1868
MUSIC: Samuel S. Wesley, 1864

AURELIA
7.6.7.6 D.

Christ Is Made the Sure Foundation 207

Are built upon the foundation . . . Jesus Christ Himself being the chief cornerstone. Eph 2:20

1. Christ is made the sure foun - da - tion, Christ the head and cor - ner - stone, Chos - en of the Lord and pre - cious, Bind - ing all the Church in one, Ho - ly Zi - on's help for - ev - er, And her con - fi - dence a - lone.
2. To this tem - ple, where we call Thee, Come, O Lord of hosts, to - day; With ac - cus - tomed lov - ing - kind - ness Hear Thy peo - ple as they pray, And Thy full - est ben - e - dic - tion Shed with - in its walls al - way.
3. Here vouch - safe to all Thy serv - ants What they ask of Thee to gain, What they gain from Thee for - ev - er With the bless - ed to re - tain, And here - aft - er in Thy glo - ry Ev - er - more with Thee to reign.
4. Laud and hon - or to the Fa - ther, Laud and hon - or to the Son, Laud and hon - or to the Spir - it, Ev - er three and ev - er one, One in might and one in glo - ry While un - end - ing a - ges run. A - men.

WORDS: Latin hymn, 7th century; tr. John M. Neale, 1851
MUSIC: Henry T. Smart, 1867

REGENT SQUARE
8.7.8.7.8.7

208 We Are One in the Bond of Love

By this shall all men know . . . if ye have love one to another. John 13:35

1. We are one in the bond of love; We are one in the bond of love. We have joined our spir - it with the Spir - it of God; We are one in the bond of love.
2. Let us sing now, ev - ery - one; Let us feel His love be - gun. Let us join our hands that the world will know We are one in the bond of love.

WORDS and MUSIC: Otis Skillings, 1971

SKILLINGS
Irregular meter

209 Blest Be the Tie That Binds

For ye are all one in Christ Jesus. Gal. 3:28

1. Blest be the tie that binds Our hearts in Chris - tian love;
2. Be - fore our Fa - ther's throne We pour our ar - dent prayers;
3. We share our mu - tual woes, Our mu - tual bur - dens bear;
4. When we a - sun - der part, It gives us in - ward pain;

The fel - low - ship of kin - dred minds Is like to that a - bove.
Our fears, our hopes, our aims are one, Our com - forts and our cares.
And oft - en for each oth - er flows The sym - pa - thiz - ing tear.
But we shall still be joined in heart, And hope to meet a - gain. A - men.

WORDS: John Fawcett, 1782
MUSIC: Johann G. Nägeli, 1773-1836; arr. Lowell Mason, 1845

DENNIS
S.M.

There's a Church within Us, O Lord 210

For, behold, the kingdom of God is within you. Luke 17:21

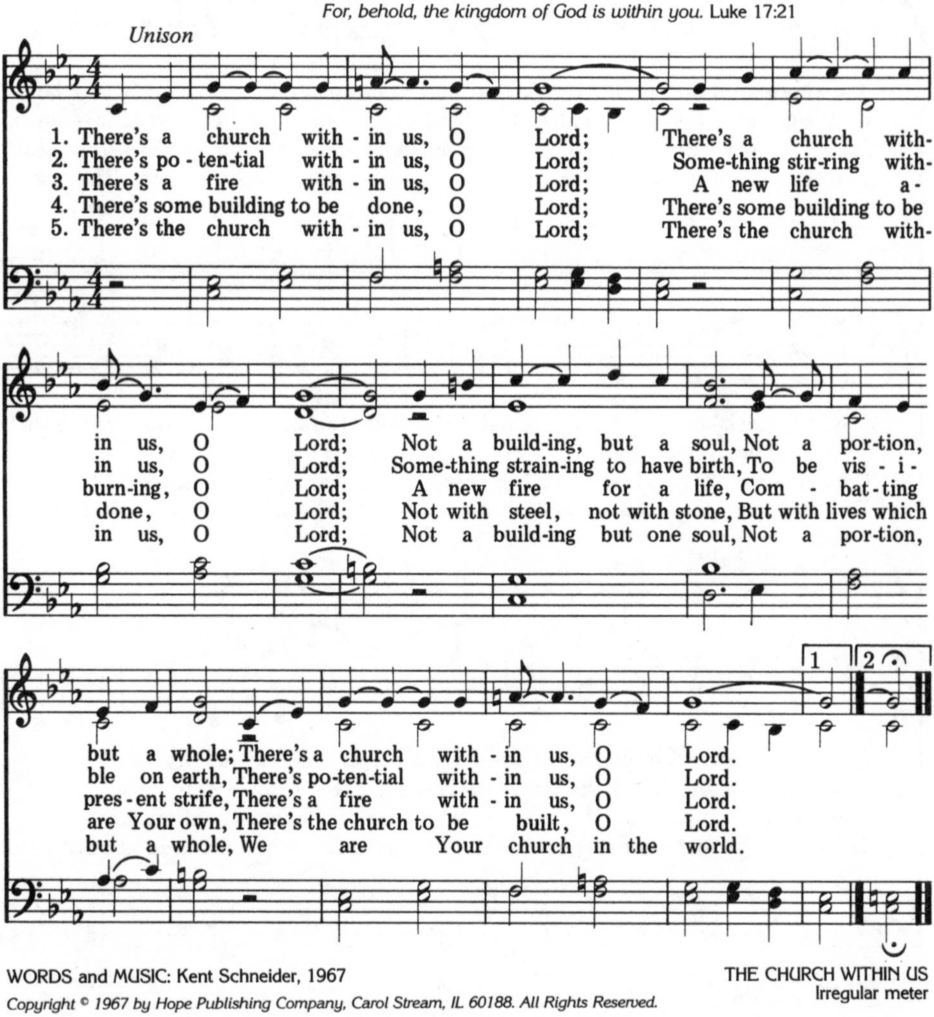

Unison

1. There's a church with - in us, O Lord; There's a church with - in us, O Lord; Not a build - ing, but a soul, Not a por - tion, but a whole; There's a church with - in us, O Lord.
2. There's po - ten - tial with - in us, O Lord; Some - thing stir - ring with - in us, O Lord; Some - thing strain - ing to have birth, To be vis - i - ble on earth, There's po - ten - tial with - in us, O Lord.
3. There's a fire with - in us, O Lord; A new life a - burn - ing, O Lord; A new fire for a life, Com - bat - ing pres - ent strife, There's a fire with - in us, O Lord.
4. There's some building to be done, O Lord; There's some building to be done, O Lord; Not with steel, not with stone, But with lives which are Your own, There's the church to be built, O Lord.
5. There's the church with - in us, O Lord; There's the church with - in us, O Lord; Not a build - ing but one soul, Not a por - tion, but a whole, We are Your church in the world.

WORDS and MUSIC: Kent Schneider, 1967

THE CHURCH WITHIN US
Irregular meter

211 Glorious Things of Thee Are Spoken

Glorious things are spoken of thee, O city of God. Psa. 87:3

1. Glo - rious things of thee are spo - ken, Zi - on, cit - y of our God;
2. See the streams of liv - ing wa - ters, Spring-ing from e - ter - nal love,
3. Round each hab - i - ta - tion hov - ering, See the cloud and fire ap - pear
4. Sav - ior, if of Zi - on's cit - y, I through grace a mem-ber am,
He whose word can - not be bro - ken Formed thee for His own a - bode;
Well sup - ply thy sons and daugh - ters, And all fear of want re - move:
For a glo - ry and a cov - ering, Show - ing that the Lord is near!
Let the world de - ride or pit - y, I will glo - ry in Thy name;
On the Rock of A - ges found - ed, What can shake thy sure re - pose?
Who can faint, while such a riv - er Ev - er will their thirst as - suage?
Thus de - riv - ing from their ban - ner Light by night and shade by day;
Fad - ing is the world's best pleas-ure, All its boast - ed pomp and show;
With sal - va - tion's walls sur-round-ed, Thou mayst smile at all thy foes.
Grace which, like the Lord, the Giv - er, Nev - er fails from age to age.
Safe they feed up - on the man - na Which He gives them when they pray.
Sol - id joys and last - ing treas - ure None but Zi - on's chil-dren know. A-men.

WORDS: John Newton, 1779
MUSIC: Franz Joseph Haydn, 1797

AUSTRIAN HYMN
8.7.8.7 D.

We Are One in the Spirit 212

By this shall all men know . . . if ye have love one to another. John 13:35

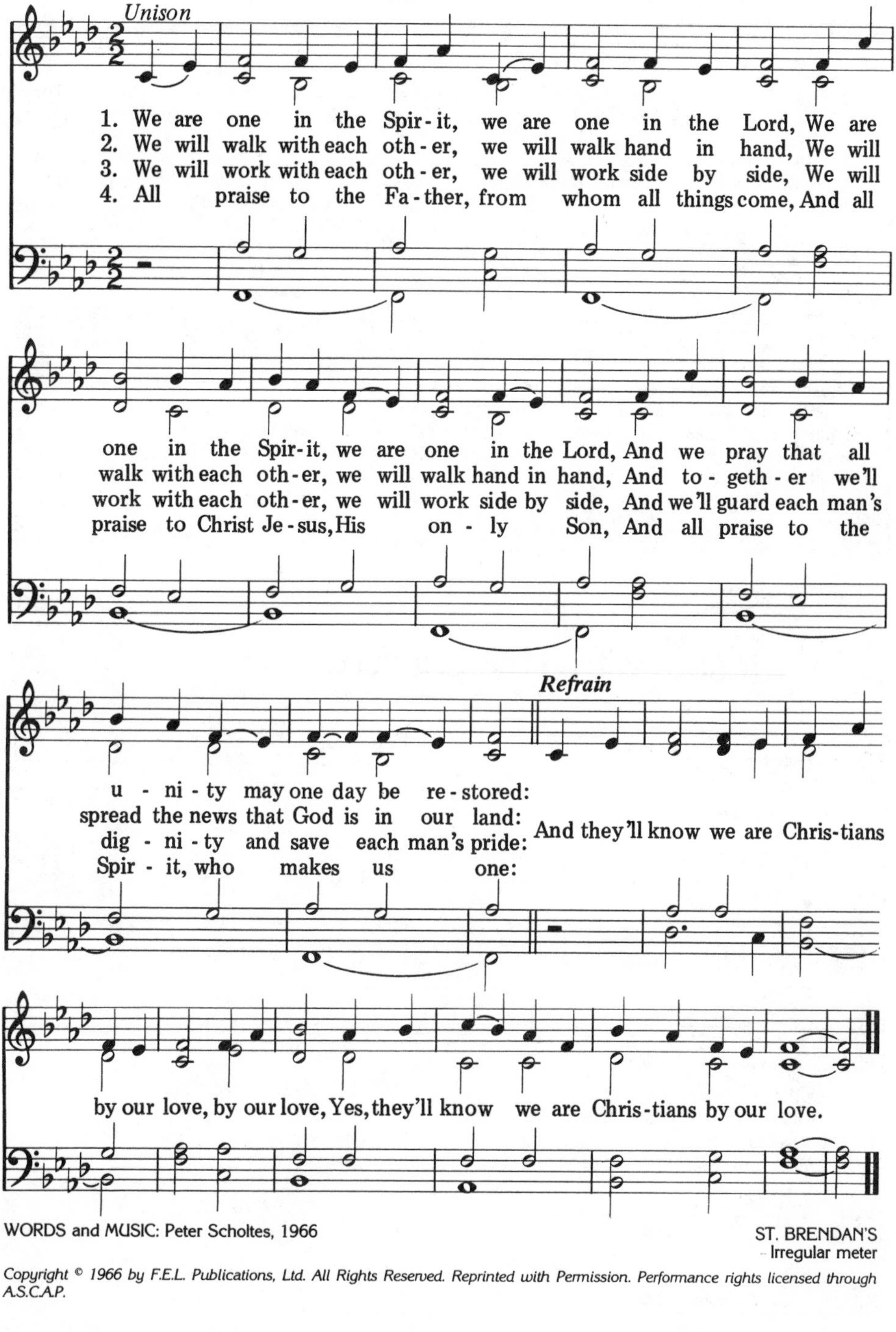

Unison

1. We are one in the Spir-it, we are one in the Lord, We are one in the Spir-it, we are one in the Lord, And we pray that all u-ni-ty may one day be re-stored:
2. We will walk with each oth-er, we will walk hand in hand, We will walk with each oth-er, we will walk hand in hand, And to-geth-er we'll spread the news that God is in our land:
3. We will work with each oth-er, we will work side by side, We will work with each oth-er, we will work side by side, And we'll guard each man's dig-ni-ty and save each man's pride:
4. All praise to the Fa-ther, from whom all things come, And all praise to Christ Je-sus, His on-ly Son, And all praise to the Spir-it, who makes us one:
Refrain
And they'll know we are Chris-tians by our love, by our love, Yes, they'll know we are Chris-tians by our love.

WORDS and MUSIC: Peter Scholtes, 1966

ST. BRENDAN'S
Irregular meter

213 I Love Thy Kingdom, Lord

Lord, I have loved the habitation of Thy house. Psa. 26:8

1. I love Thy king - dom, Lord, The house of Thine a - bode, The
2. I love Thy Church, O God! Her walls be - fore Thee stand, Dear
3. For her my tears shall fall; For her my prayers as - cend; To
4. Be - yond my high - est joy I prize her heav'n - ly ways, Her
5. Sure as Thy truth shall last, To Zi - on shall be giv'n The
Church our blest Re - deem - er saved With His own pre - cious blood.
as the ap - ple of Thine eye, And grav - en on Thy hand.
her my cares and toils be giv'n, Till toils and cares shall end.
sweet com - mun - ion, sol - emn vows, Her hymns of love and praise.
bright - est glo - ries earth can yield, And bright - er bliss of heav'n. A-men.

WORDS: Timothy Dwight, 1800
MUSIC: Aaron Williams, 1763

ST. THOMAS
S.M.

214 Jesus, with Thy Church Abide

The church of the living God, the pillar and ground of the truth. I Tim.3:15

1. Je - sus, with Thy church a - bide, Be her Sav - ior, Lord, and Guide,
2. May she guide the poor and blind, Seek the lost un - til she find,
3. Keep her life and doc - trine pure, Help her, pa - tient to en - dure,
4. May the grace of Him who died, And the Fa - ther's love a - bide,
While on earth her faith is tried: We be - seech Thee, hear us.
And the bro - ken - heart - ed bind: We be - seech Thee, hear us.
Trust - ing in Thy prom - ise sure: We be - seech Thee, hear us.
And the Spir - it ev - er guide: We be - seech Thee, hear us.

WORDS: Thomas B. Pollock, 1871
MUSIC: Orlando Gibbons, 1623

SONG 13
7.7.7.6

Built on the Rock the Church Doth Stand 215

And upon this rock I will build My church. Matt. 16:18

1. Built on the Rock the church doth stand, E - ven when stee - ples are fall - ing; Crum-bled have spires in ev - ery land, Bells still are chim - ing and call - ing, Call - ing the young and old to rest, But a - bove all the soul dis-tressed, Long-ing for life ev - er - last - ing.
2. Sure - ly in tem - ples made with hands, God the most high is not dwell - ing; High a - bove earth His tem - ple stands, All earth - ly tem - ples ex - cel - ling. Yet He whom heav'ns can - not con - tain Chose to a - bide on earth with men, Built in our bod - ies His tem - ple.
3. We are God's house of liv - ing stones, Built for His own hab - i - ta - tion; He fills our hearts, his hum - ble thrones, Grant-ing us life and sal - va - tion; Were two or three to seek His face, He in their midst would show His grace, Bless-ings up - on them be - stow - ing.
4. Now we may gath - er with our King E'en in the low - li - est dwell - ing; Prais - es to Him we there may bring, His won-drous mer - cy forth - tell - ing. Je - sus His grace to us ac - cords; Spir - it and life are all His words; His truth doth hal - low the tem - ple. A - men.

WORDS: Nicolai F. S. Grundtvig, 1837; tr. Carl Doving, 1909; adapt. Fred C. M. Hansen, c.1927
MUSIC: Ludvig M. Lindeman, 1840

KIRKEN DEN ER ET
8.8.8.8.8.8.8

216 Faith of Our Fathers

Earnestly contend for the faith which was once delivered unto the saints. Jude 3

1. Faith of our fa - thers! liv - ing still In spite of dun - geon,
2. Our fa - thers, chained in pris - ons dark, Were still in heart and
3. Faith of our fa - thers! we will strive To win all na - tions
4. Faith of our fa - thers! we will love Both friend and foe in
fire and sword: O how our hearts beat high with joy
con - science free: How sweet would be their chil - dren's fate,
un - to thee, And thro' the truth that comes from God,
all our strife: And preach thee too as love knows how,
When-e'er we hear that glo - rious word! Faith of our fa - thers,
If they like them could die for thee! Faith of our fa - thers,
Man-kind shall then be tru - ly free. Faith of our fa - thers,
By kind - ly words and vir - tuous life: Faith of our fa - thers,
ho - ly faith! We will be true to thee till death!
ho - ly faith! We will be true to thee till death!
ho - ly faith! We will be true to thee till death!
ho - ly faith! We will be true to thee till death!

WORDS: Frederick W. Faber, 1849
MUSIC: Henri F. Hemy, 1864; arr. James G. Walton, 1874

ST. CATHERINE
8.8.8.8.8.8

I Am the Church 217

Ye also, as lively stones, are built up a spiritual house. I Pet. 2:5

Unison
I am the church! You are the church! We are the church to - geth - er!
Fine
All who fol-low Je-sus All a-round the world! Yes, we're the church to - geth-er!
1. The church is not a build-ing, The church is not a stee - ple, The church is not a rest - ing place, The church is a peo - ple!
2. We're man - y kinds of peo - ple, With man - y kinds of fac - es, All col - ors and all a - ges, too, From all times and plac - es.
3. Some-times the church is march-ing, Some-times it's brave - ly burn-ing, Some-times it's rid - ing, some-times hid - ing, Al - ways it's learn - ing:
4. And when the peo - ple gath - er There's sing - ing and there's pray-ing, There's laugh - ing and there's cry - ing some - times, All of it say - ing:
5. At Pen - te - cost some peo - ple Re - ceived the Ho - ly Spir - it And told the Good News thro' the world To all who would hear it.
6. I count if I am nine - ty, Or nine or just a ba - by; There's one thing I am sure a - bout And I don't mean may - be:
D.C.

WORDS and MUSIC: Richard Avery and Donald Marsh, 1972

WE ARE THE CHURCH
Irregular meter

218 We Come As Guests Invited

And the Spirit and the Bride say, Come. Rev. 22:17

1. We come as guests in - vit - ed When Je - sus bids us dine,
2. We eat and drink, re - ceiv - ing From Christ the grace we need,
3. One bread is ours for shar - ing, One sin - gle, fruit - ful vine,
His friends on earth u - nit - ed To share the bread and wine;
And in our hearts be - liev - ing On Him by faith we feed;
Our fel - low - ship de - clar - ing Re - newed in bread and wine—
The bread of life is bro - ken, The wine is free - ly poured
With won - der and thanks - giv - ing For love that knows no end,
Re - newed, sus - tained and giv - en By to - ken, sign and word,
For us, in sol - emn to - ken Of Christ our dy - ing Lord.
We find in Je - sus liv - ing Our ev - er - pres - ent friend.
The pledge and seal of heav - en, The love of Christ our Lord.

WORDS: Timothy Dudley-Smith, 1975
MUSIC: Hans Leo Hassler, 1601; arr. J. S. Bach, 1729

PASSION CHORALE
7.6.7.6 D.

Here, O My Lord, I See Thee 219

The things which are not seen are eternal. II Cor. 4:18

1. Here, O my Lord, I see Thee face to face;
2. Here would I feed up - on the bread of God;
3. I have no help but Thine; nor do I need
4. Mine is the sin, but Thine the right-eous - ness;

Here would I touch and han - dle things un - seen,
Here drink with Thee the roy - al wine of heav'n;
An - oth - er arm save Thine to lean up - on;
Mine is the guilt, but Thine the cleans - ing blood.

Here grasp with firm - er hand th'e - ter - nal grace,
Here would I lay a - side each earth - ly load,
It is e - nough, my Lord, e - nough in - deed;
Here is my robe, my ref - uge, and my peace;

And all my wea - ri - ness up - on Thee lean.
Here taste a - fresh the calm of sin for - giv'n.
My strength is in Thy might, Thy might a - lone.
Thy blood, Thy right - eous - ness, O Lord, my God.

WORDS: Horatius Bonar, 1855
MUSIC: Frederick C. Atkinson, 1870

MORECAMBE
10.10.10.10

220 Bread of the World in Mercy Broken

Take, eat: this is My body which is broken for you. I Cor. 11:24

1. Bread of the world in mer - cy bro - ken, Wine of the soul in mer - cy shed, By whom the words of life were spo - ken, And in whose death our sins are dead:

2. Look on the heart by sor - row bro - ken, Look on the tears by sin - ners shed; And be Thy feast to us the to - ken That by Thy grace our souls are fed!

WORDS: Reginald Heber, 1827
MUSIC: John S. B. Hodges, 1868

EUCHARISTIC HYMN
9.8.9.8

221 According to Thy Gracious Word

This do in remembrance of Me. Luke 22:19

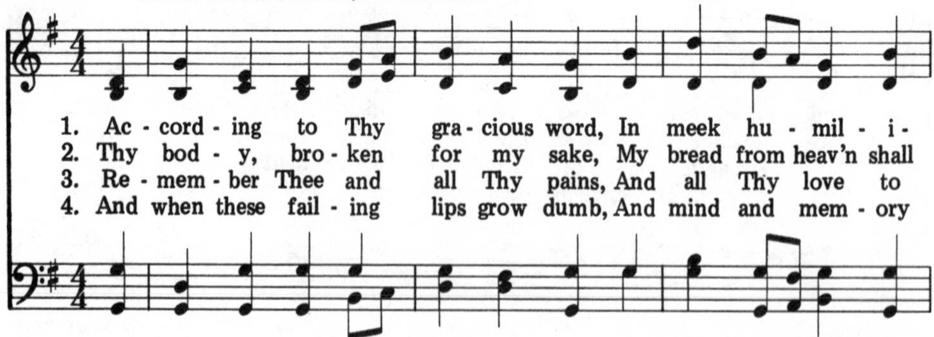
1. Ac - cord - ing to Thy gra - cious word, In meek hu - mil - i -
2. Thy bod - y, bro - ken for my sake, My bread from heav'n shall
3. Re - mem - ber Thee and all Thy pains, And all Thy love to
4. And when these fail - ing lips grow dumb, And mind and mem - ory

ty, This will I do, my dy-ing Lord, I will re-mem-ber Thee.
be; Thy cup of bless-ing I will take, And thus re-mem-ber Thee.
me: Yea, while a breath, a pulse re-mains, Will I re-mem-ber Thee.
flee, When Thou shalt in Thy king-dom come, Je-sus, re-mem-ber me.

WORDS: James Montgomery, 1825
MUSIC: Hugh Wilson, c.1800

MARTYRDOM
C.M.

Let Us Break Bread Together 222

He took bread, and blessed it, and brake, and gave to them. Luke 24:30

Unison

1. Let us break bread to-geth-er on our knees; Let us break bread to-geth-er on our knees.
2. Let us drink the cup to-geth-er on our knees; Let us drink the cup to-geth-er on our knees.
3. Let us praise God to-geth-er on our knees; Let us praise God to-geth-er on our knees.

Refrain

When I fall on my knees, With my face to the ris-ing sun, O Lord, have mer-cy on me.

WORDS: Traditional Spiritual
MUSIC: Traditional Spiritual; arr. Carlton R. Young

LET US BREAK BREAD
Irregular meter

223 As We Gather Around the Table

This do in remembrance of Me. I Cor. 11:24

Unison

1. As we gath - er a - round the ta - ble of our Lord,
2. As we gath - er a - round the ta - ble of our Lord,
3. As we gath - er a - round the ta - ble of our Lord,

We re - call His hum - ble birth in Beth - le - hem,
We re - call His ag - o - ny up - on the cross.
We re - call the emp - ty tomb where He was laid.

As the an - gels sang, As the shep - herds came, Let us a -
There our Sav - ior died; A - lone was cru - ci - fied; Let us a -
He is liv - ing still; Our long - ing hearts to fill; Let us a -

dore and wor - ship the Lord, Let us re - mem - ber Him.
dore and wor - ship the Lord, Let us re - mem - ber Him.
dore and wor - ship the Lord, Let us re - mem - ber Him.

WORDS and MUSIC: Mark Blankenship, 1974

NORTH PHOENIX
Irregular meter

I Come with Joy 224

My soul shall be joyful in the Lord. Psa. 35:9

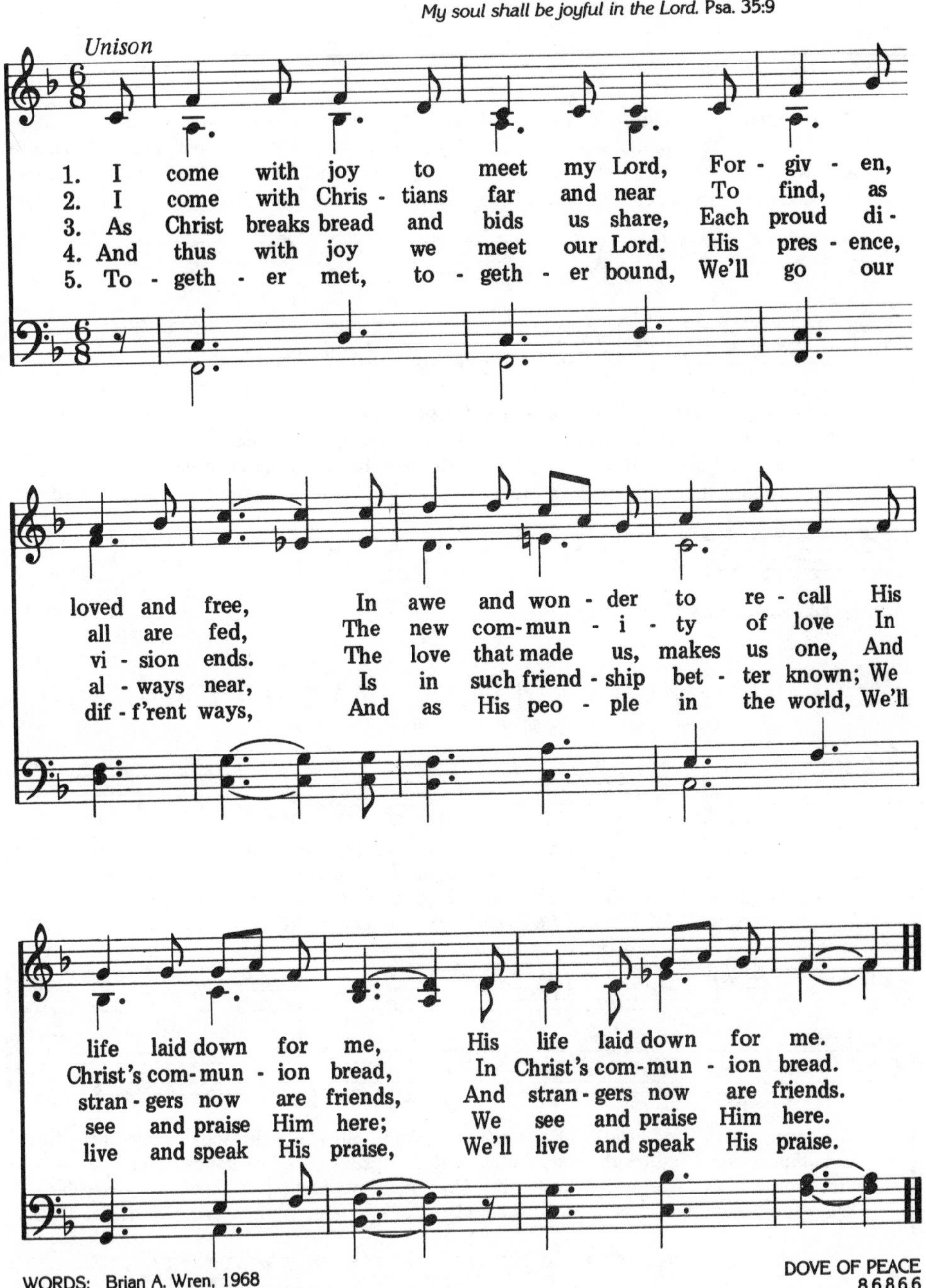
Unison
1. I come with joy to meet my Lord, Forgiven, loved and free, In awe and wonder to recall His life laid down for me, His life laid down for me.
2. I come with Christians far and near To find, as all are fed, The new community of love In Christ's communion bread, In Christ's communion bread.
3. As Christ breaks bread and bids us share, Each proud division ends. The love that made us, makes us one, And strangers now are friends, And strangers now are friends.
4. And thus with joy we meet our Lord. His presence, always near, Is in such friendship better known; We see and praise Him here; We see and praise Him here.
5. Together met, together bound, We'll go our diff'rent ways, And as His people in the world, We'll live and speak His praise, We'll live and speak His praise.

WORDS: Brian A. Wren, 1968
MUSIC: American melody;
arr. Austin C. Lovelace, 1977

DOVE OF PEACE
8.6.8.6.6

225 Come, Holy Spirit, Dove Divine

We are buried with Him by baptism . . . Rom. 6:4

1. Come, Ho - ly Spir - it, Dove di - vine, On these bap - tis - mal wa - ters shine,
2. We love Thy name, we love Thy laws, And joy - ful - ly em - brace Thy cause;
3. We sink be-neath the wa - ter's face; And thank Thee for Thy sav - ing grace;
4. And as we rise with Thee to live, O let the Ho - ly Spir - it give

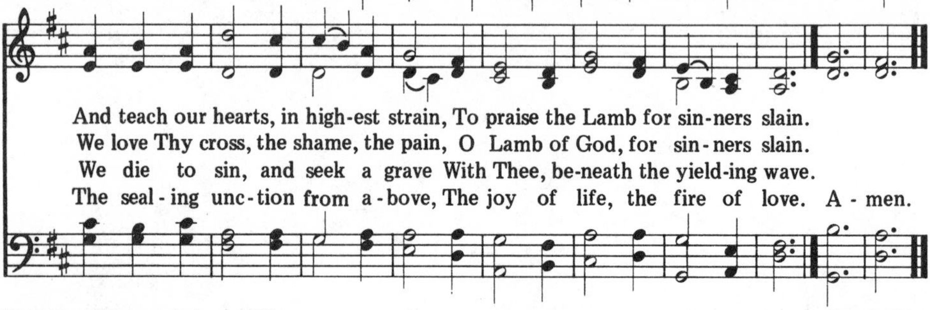

And teach our hearts, in high-est strain, To praise the Lamb for sin-ners slain.
We love Thy cross, the shame, the pain, O Lamb of God, for sin-ners slain.
We die to sin, and seek a grave With Thee, be-neath the yield-ing wave.
The seal - ing unc-tion from a-bove, The joy of life, the fire of love. A - men.

WORDS: Adoniram Judson, 1832
MUSIC: H. Percy Smith, 1876

MARYTON
L.M.

226 We Bless the Name of Christ the Lord

For thus it becometh us to fulfill all righteousness. Matt. 3:15

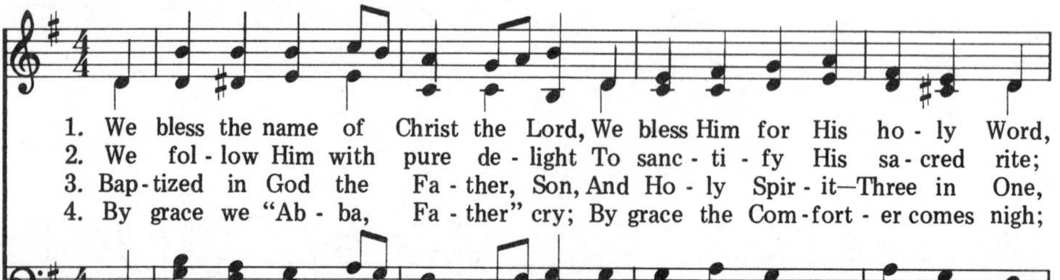

1. We bless the name of Christ the Lord, We bless Him for His ho - ly Word,
2. We fol - low Him with pure de - light To sanc - ti - fy His sa - cred rite;
3. Bap - tized in God the Fa - ther, Son, And Ho - ly Spir - it—Three in One,
4. By grace we "Ab - ba, Fa - ther" cry; By grace the Com - fort - er comes nigh;
Who loved to do His Fa - ther's will, And all His right-eous - ness ful - fill.
And thus our faith with wa - ter seal, To prove o - be - dience that we feel.
With con-science free, we rest in God, In love and peace thro' Je - sus' blood.
And for Thy grace our love shall be For - ev - er, on - ly, Lord, for Thee.

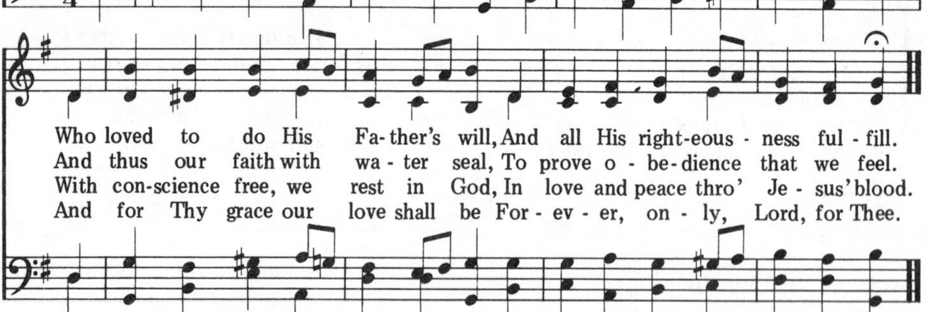

WORDS: Samuel F. Coffman, 1926
MUSIC: Robert A. Schumann, 1839

CANONBURY
L.M.

This Child We Dedicate to Thee 227

And the child . . . was in favor both with the Lord, and also with men. I Sam. 2:26

1. This child we ded - i - cate to Thee, O God of grace and pu - ri - ty!
2. O may Thy Spir - it gen - tly draw Its will-ing soul to keep Thy law;
In Thy great love its life pro - long, Shield it, we pray, from sin and wrong.
May vir - tue, pi - e - ty, and truth Dawn e-ven with its dawn-ing youth.

WORDS: From the German; tr. Samuel Gilman, c.1820
MUSIC: Henry K. Oliver, 1832

FEDERAL STREET
L.M.

See Israel's Gentle Shepherd Stand 228

And He took them up in His arms . . . and blessed them. Mark 10:16

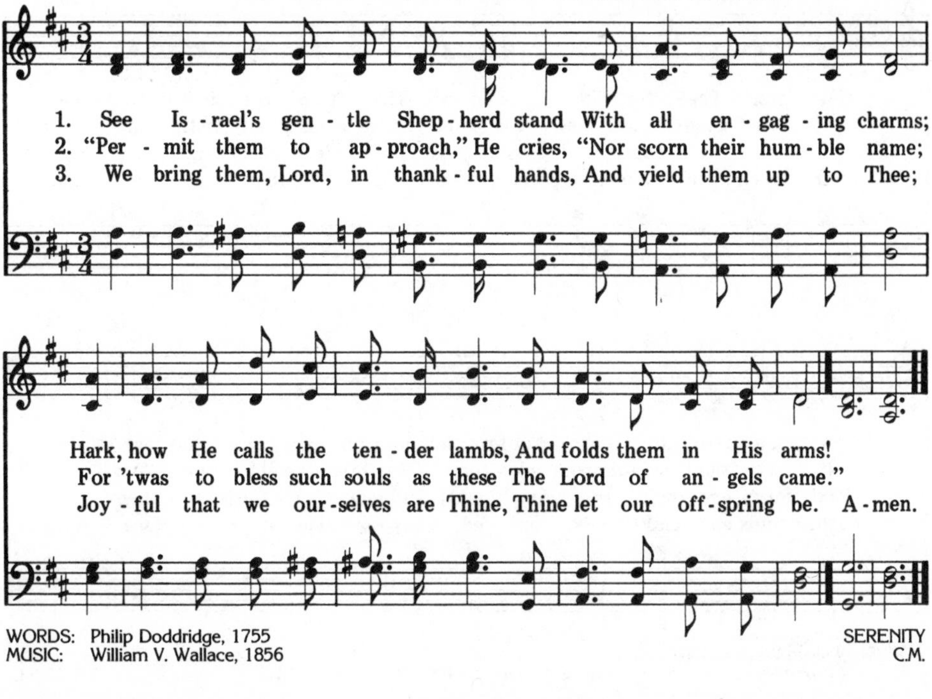

1. See Is - rael's gen - tle Shep - herd stand With all en - gag - ing charms;
Hark, how He calls the ten - der lambs, And folds them in His arms!

2. "Per - mit them to ap - proach," He cries, "Nor scorn their hum - ble name;
For 'twas to bless such souls as these The Lord of an - gels came."

3. We bring them, Lord, in thank - ful hands, And yield them up to Thee;
Joy - ful that we our-selves are Thine, Thine let our off-spring be. A - men.

WORDS: Philip Doddridge, 1755
MUSIC: William V. Wallace, 1856

SERENITY
C.M.

229 O Word of God Incarnate

The entrance of Thy words giveth light . . . Psa. 119:130

1. O Word of God in - car - nate, O Wis - dom from on high,
2. The Church from her dear Mas - ter Re - ceived the gift di - vine,
3. It float - eth like a ban - ner Be - fore God's host un - furled;
4. O make Thy Church, dear Sav - ior, A lamp of pur - est gold,
O Truth un - changed, un - chang - ing, O Light of our dark sky;
And still that light she lift - eth O'er all the earth to shine.
It shin - eth like a bea - con A - bove the dark - ling world.
To bear be - fore the na - tions Thy true light as of old.
We praise Thee for the ra - diance That from the hal - lowed page,
It is the gold - en cas - ket Where gems of truth are stored;
It is the chart and com - pass That o'er life's surg - ing sea,
O teach Thy wan - d'ring pil - grims By this their path to trace,
A lan - tern to our foot-steps, Shines on from age to age.
It is the heav'n-drawn pic - ture Of Christ, the liv - ing Word.
'Mid mists and rocks and quick-sands, Still guides, O Christ, to Thee.
Till, clouds and dark - ness end - ed, They see Thee face to face. A-men.

WORDS: William W. How, 1867
MUSIC: *Neuvermehrtes Gesangbuch,* Meiningen, 1693; arr. Felix Mendelssohn, 1847

MUNICH
7.6.7.6 D.

Holy Bible, Book Divine 230

O how I love Thy law! It is my meditation all the day! Psa. 119:97

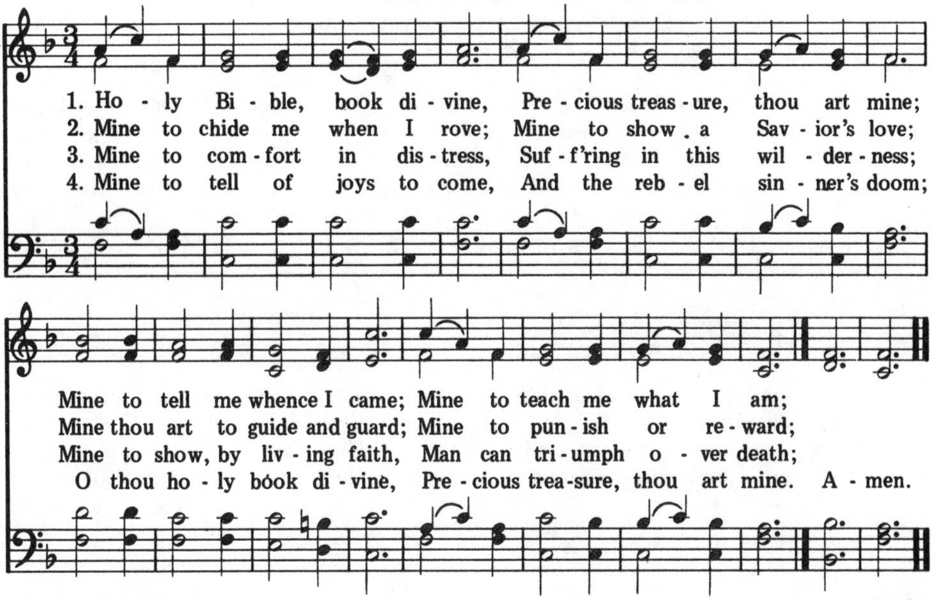

1. Ho - ly Bi - ble, book di - vine, Pre - cious treas - ure, thou art mine;
Mine to tell me whence I came; Mine to teach me what I am;

2. Mine to chide me when I rove; Mine to show a Sav - ior's love;
Mine thou art to guide and guard; Mine to pun - ish or re - ward;

3. Mine to com - fort in dis - tress, Suf - f'ring in this wil - der - ness;
Mine to show, by liv - ing faith, Man can tri - umph o - ver death;

4. Mine to tell of joys to come, And the reb - el sin - ner's doom;
O thou ho - ly book di - vine, Pre - cious trea - sure, thou art mine. A - men.

WORDS John Burton, 1803
MUSIC: William B. Bradbury, 1858

ALETTA
7.7.7.7

How Precious Is the Book Divine 231

All scripture is given by inspiration of God . . . II Tim. 3:16

1. How pre - cious is the book di - vine, By in - spi - ra - tion giv'n!
2. Its light, de - scend - ing from a - bove, Our gloom - y world to cheer,
3. It shows to us our wan - d'ring ways And where our feet have trod,
Bright as a lamp its teach - ings shine To guide our souls to heav'n.
Dis - plays our Sav - ior's bound - less love And brings His glo - ries near.
And brings to view the match - less grace Of our for - giv - ing God.

WORDS: John Fawcett, 1782
MUSIC: Early American melody

CAMPMEETING
C.M.

232 Break Thou the Bread of Life

He looked up to heaven, and blessed, and brake the loaves . . . Mark 6:41

1. Break Thou the bread of life, Dear Lord, to me, As Thou didst
2. Bless Thou the truth, dear Lord, To me, to me, As Thou didst
3. Thou art the bread of life, O Lord, to me, Thy ho - ly
4. O send Thy Spir - it, Lord, Now un - to me, That He may

break the loaves Be - side the sea; Be - yond the sa - cred page
bless the bread By Gal - i - lee; Then shall all bond - age cease,
Word the truth That sav - eth me; Give me to eat and live
touch my eyes And make me see: Show me the truth con - cealed

I seek Thee, Lord, My spir - it pants for Thee, O liv - ing Word.
All fet - ters fall; And I shall find my peace, My All in all.
With Thee a - bove; Teach me to love Thy truth, For Thou art love.
With - in Thy Word, And in Thy Book re - vealed I see the Lord. A-men.

WORDS: Mary A. Lathbury, 1877
MUSIC: William F. Sherwin, 1877

BREAD OF LIFE
6.4.6.4 D.

233 The Heavens Declare Thy Glory, Lord

The law of the Lord is perfect, converting the soul. Psa. 19:7

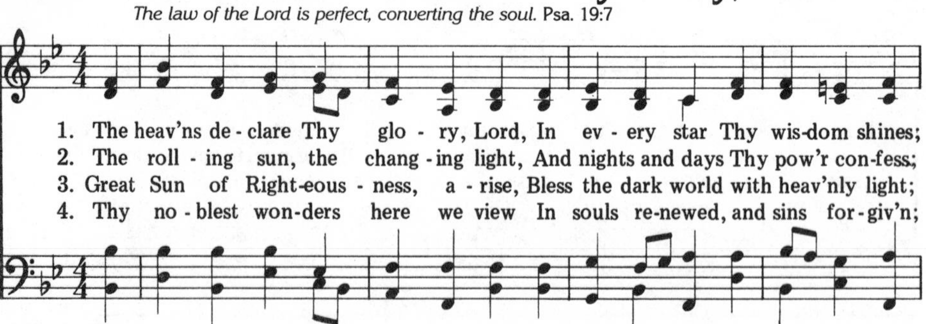
1. The heav'ns de - clare Thy glo - ry, Lord, In ev - ery star Thy wis-dom shines;
2. The roll - ing sun, the chang - ing light, And nights and days Thy pow'r con-fess;
3. Great Sun of Right-eous - ness, a - rise, Bless the dark world with heav'nly light;
4. Thy no - blest won-ders here we view In souls re-newed, and sins for - giv'n;

But when our eyes be - hold Thy Word, We read Thy name in fair - er lines.
But the blest vol - ume Thou hast writ, Re - veals Thy jus - tice and Thy grace.
Thy gos - pel makes the sim - ple wise, Thy laws are pure, Thy judg - ments right.
Lord, cleanse my sins, my soul re - new, And make Thy Word my guide to heav'n. A - men.
WORDS: Isaac Watts, 1719; based on Psalm 19
MUSIC: Georg Rebenlein's Musicalisch Handbuch, Hamburg, 1690; arr. William H. Havergal, 1847
WINCHESTER NEW
L.M.
Sing Them Over Again to Me
234
Lord, to whom shall we go? Thou hast the words of eternal life. John 6:68
1. Sing them o - ver a - gain to me, Won - der - ful words of Life;
2. Christ, the bless - ed One, gives to all Won - der - ful words of Life;
3. Sweet - ly ech - o the gos - pel call, Won - der - ful words of Life;
Let me more of their beau - ty see, Won - der - ful words of Life.
Sin - ner, list to the lov - ing call, Won - der - ful words of Life.
Of - fer par - don and peace to all, Won - der - ful words of Life.
Words of life and beau - ty, Teach me faith and du - ty:
All so free - ly giv - en, Woo - ing us to Heav - en:
Je - sus, on - ly Sav - ior, Sanc - ti - fy for - ev - er:
Refrain
Beau - ti - ful words, won - der - ful words, Won - der - ful words of Life. Life.
WORDS and MUSIC: Philip P. Bliss, 1874
WORDS OF LIFE
8.6.8.6.6.6 Ref.

235 The Bible Stands Like a Rock Undaunted

Unison . . . *The word of God, which liveth and abideth forever.* I Pet. 1:23

1. The Bi - ble stands like a rock un-daunt - ed 'Mid the rag - ing storms of time; Its pag - es burn with the truth e - ter - nal, And they glow with a light sub-lime.
2. The Bi - ble stands like a moun - tain tow - 'ring Far a - bove the works of man; Its truth by none ev - er was re - fut - ed, And de - stroy it they nev - er can.
3. The Bi - ble stands and it will for - ev - er, When the world has passed a - way; By in - spi - ra - tion it has been giv - en, All its pre-cepts I will o - bey.
4. The Bi - ble stands ev - ery test we give it, For its Au - thor is di - vine; By grace a - lone I ex - pect to live it, And to prove it and make it mine.
Refrain
The Bi - ble stands tho' the hills may tum - ble, It will firm - ly stand when the earth shall crum - ble; I will plant my feet on its firm foun - da - tion, For the Bi - ble stands, The Bi - ble stands.

WORDS: Haldor Lillenas, 1917
MUSIC: Donald P. Hustad, 1973

RIDGE LINE
Irregular meter

Standing on the Promises 236

Whereby are given unto us exceeding great and precious promises . . . II Pet. 1:4

1. Stand-ing on the prom-is-es of Christ my King, Thro' e-ter-nal a-ges let His prais-es ring; Glo-ry in the high-est, I will shout and sing,
2. Stand-ing on the prom-is-es that can-not fail, When the howl-ing storms of doubt and fear as-sail, By the liv-ing Word of God I shall pre-vail,
3. Stand-ing on the prom-is-es of Christ the Lord, Bound to Him e-ter-nal-ly by love's strong cord, O-ver-com-ing dai-ly with the Spir-it's sword,
4. Stand-ing on the prom-is-es I can-not fall, Lis-t'ning ev-ery moment to the Spir-it's call, Rest-ing in my Sav-ior as my all in all,
Stand-ing on the prom-is-es of God.
Refrain
Stand-ing, stand-ing,
stand-ing on the prom-is-es,
Stand-ing on the prom-is-es of God my Sav-ior; Stand-ing,
stand-ing,
stand-ing on the prom-is-es,
I'm stand-ing on the prom-is-es of God.

WORDS and MUSIC: R. Kelso Carter, 1886

PROMISES
11.11.11.9 Ref.

237 How Firm a Foundation

Heaven and earth shall pass away: but My words shall not . . . Luke 21:33

1. How firm a foun - da - tion, ye saints of the Lord,
2. "Fear not, I am with thee; O be not dis - mayed,
3. "When through the deep wa - ters I call thee to go,
4. "When through fier - y tri - als thy path - way shall lie,
5. "The soul that on Je - sus hath leaned for re - pose,
Is laid for your faith in His ex - cel - lent Word!
For I am thy God, and will still give thee aid;
The riv - ers of sor - row shall not o - ver - flow;
My grace, all suf - fi - cient, shall be thy sup - ply:
I will not, I will not de - sert to his foes;
What more can He say than to you He hath said,
I'll strength - en thee, help thee, and cause thee to stand,
For I will be with thee, thy trou - bles to bless,
The flame shall not hurt thee; I on - ly de - sign
That soul, though all hell should en - deav - or to shake,
To you who for ref - uge to Je - sus have fled?
Up - held by my right - eous, om - nip - o - tent hand.
And sanc - ti - fy to thee thy deep - est dis - tress.
Thy dross to con - sume, and thy gold to re - fine.
I'll nev - er, no, nev - er, no, nev - er for - sake!" A - men.

WORDS: Rippon's *Selection of Hymns,* 1787
MUSIC: Traditional American melody; Caldwell's *Union Harmony,* 1837

FOUNDATION
11.11.11.11

Thanks to God 238

For He spake and it was done; He commanded and it stood fast. Psa. 33:9

Unison

1. Thanks to God whose Word was spo - ken
In the deed that made the earth.
His the voice that called a na - tion;
His the fires that tried her worth.
God has spo - ken:
Praise Him for His o - pen Word.

2. Thanks to God whose Word in - car - nate
Glo - ri - fied the flesh of man.
Deeds and words and death and ris - ing
Tell the grace in heav - en's plan.
God has spo - ken:
Praise Him for His o - pen Word.

3. Thanks to God whose Word was writ - ten
In the Bi - ble's sa - cred page,
Rec - ord of the rev - e - la - tion
Show - ing God to ev - ery age.
God has spo - ken:
Praise Him for His o - pen Word.

4. Thanks to God whose Word is pub - lished
In the tongues of ev - ery race.
See its glo - ry un - dim - in - ished
By the change of time or place.
God has spo - ken:
Praise Him for His o - pen Word.

5. Thanks to God whose Word is an - swered
By the Spir - it's voice with - in.
Here we drink of joy un - mea - sured,
Life re - deemed from death and sin.
God is speak - ing;
Praise Him for His o - pen Word.

WORDS: R. T. Brooks, 1954
MUSIC: Peter Cutts, 1966

WYLDE GREEN
8.7.8.7.4.7

239 God Hath Spoken by His Prophets

God . . . spake in time past unto the fathers by the prophets . . . Heb. 1:1

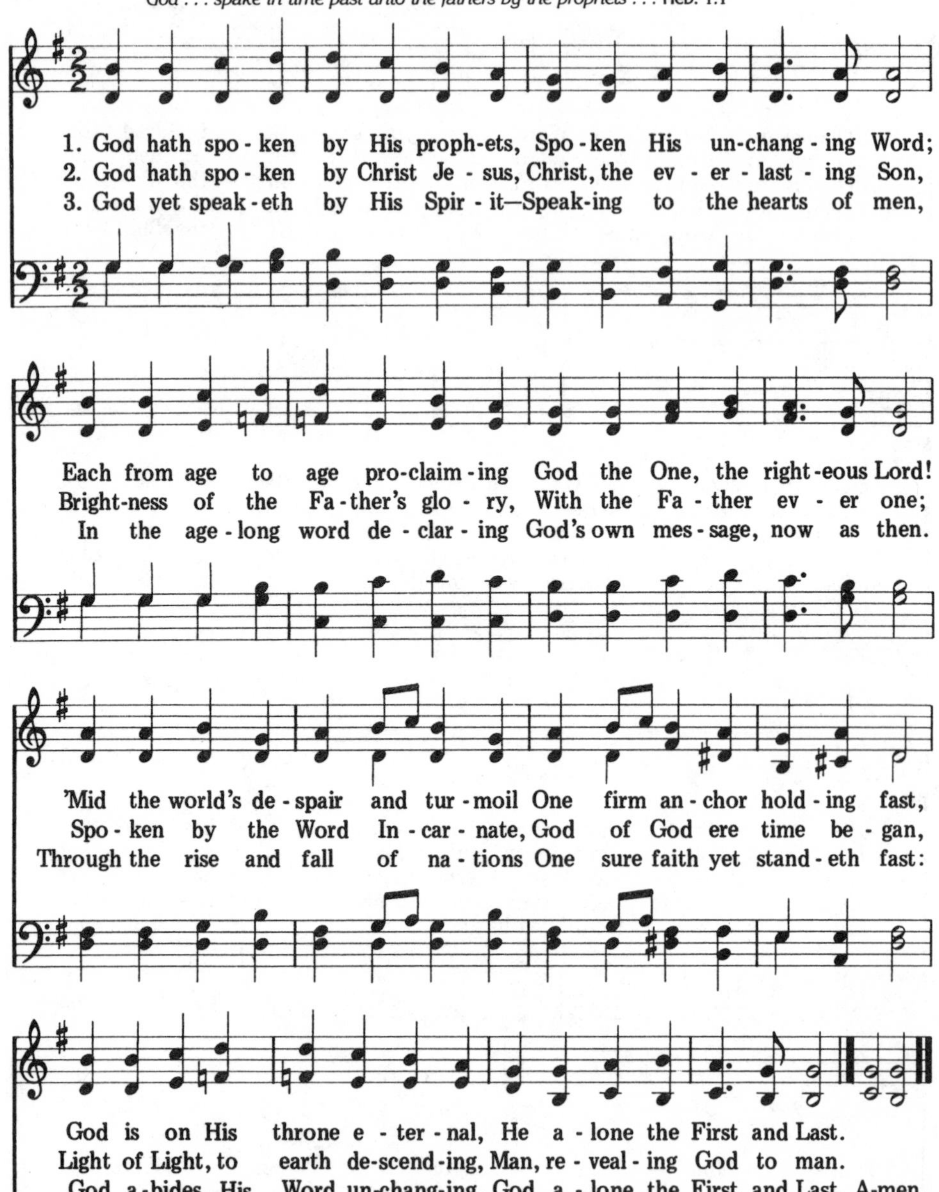
1. God hath spo - ken by His proph-ets, Spo - ken His un-chang - ing Word;
2. God hath spo - ken by Christ Je - sus, Christ, the ev - er - last - ing Son,
3. God yet speak - eth by His Spir - it—Speak-ing to the hearts of men,
Each from age to age pro-claim - ing God the One, the right-eous Lord!
Bright-ness of the Fa - ther's glo - ry, With the Fa - ther ev - er one;
In the age - long word de - clar - ing God's own mes - sage, now as then.
'Mid the world's de - spair and tur - moil One firm an - chor hold - ing fast,
Spo - ken by the Word In - car - nate, God of God ere time be - gan,
Through the rise and fall of na - tions One sure faith yet stand - eth fast:
God is on His throne e - ter - nal, He a - lone the First and Last.
Light of Light, to earth de-scend-ing, Man, re - veal - ing God to man.
God a - bides, His Word un-chang-ing, God a - lone the First and Last. A-men.

WORDS: George W. Briggs, 1952
MUSIC: Ludwig van Beethoven, 1824

HYMN TO JOY
8.7.8.7 D.

Hymns of The Gospel

240 You Said You'd Come

And God shall wipe away all tears from their eyes. Rev. 7:17

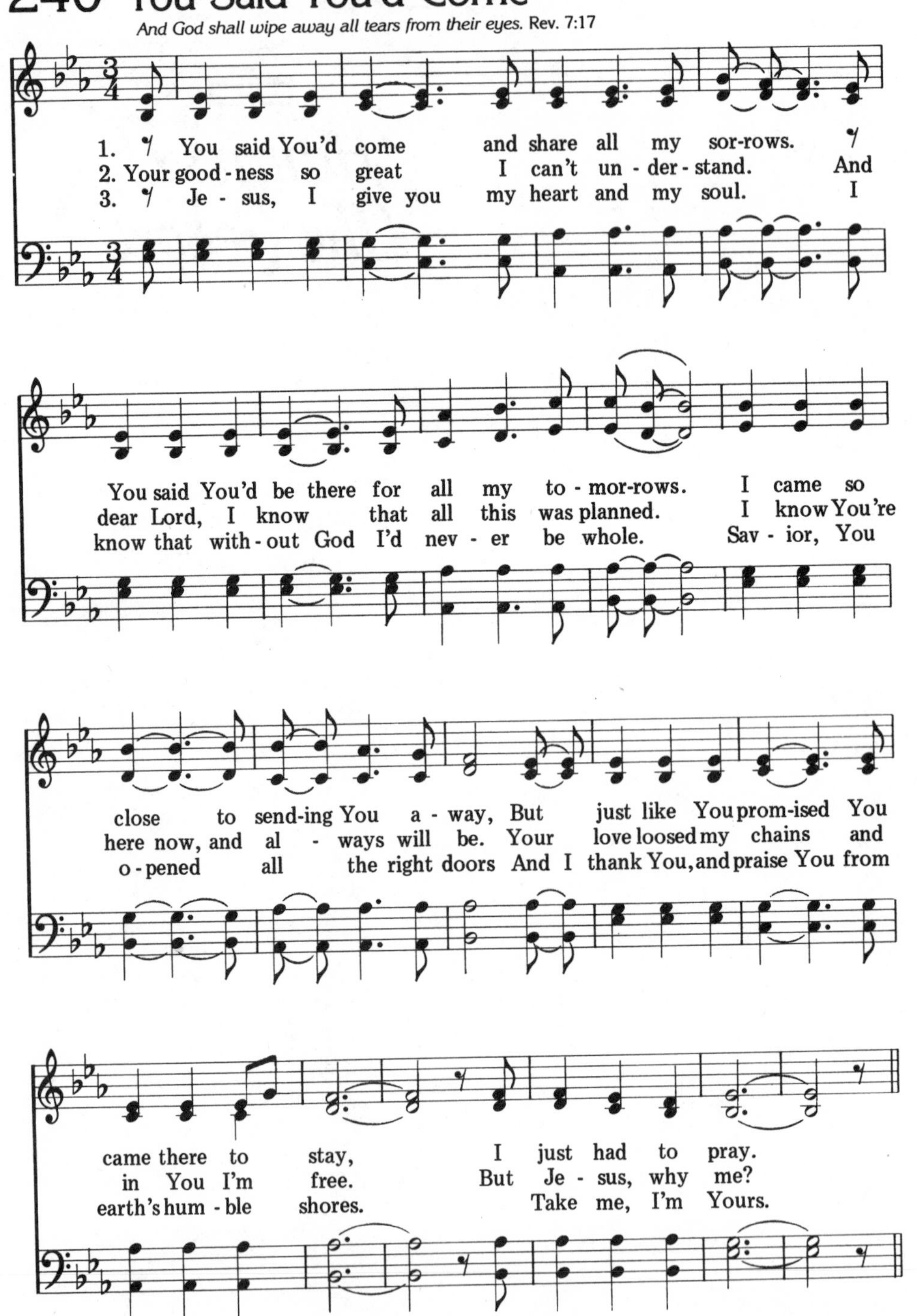
1. You said You'd come and share all my sor-rows.
2. Your good-ness so great I can't un-der-stand. And
3. Je-sus, I give you my heart and my soul. I
You said You'd be there for all my to-mor-rows. I came so
dear Lord, I know that all this was planned. I know You're
know that with-out God I'd nev-er be whole. Sav-ior, You
close to send-ing You a-way, But just like You prom-ised You
here now, and al-ways will be. Your love loosed my chains and
o-pened all the right doors And I thank You, and praise You from
came there to stay, I just had to pray.
in You I'm free. But Je-sus, why me?
earth's hum-ble shores. Take me, I'm Yours.

Refrain
And Je - sus said, "Come to the wa - ter, stand by my
side. I know you are thirst - y, you won't be de -
nied. I felt ev - ery tear - drop when in
dark - ness you cried, And I strove to re -
mind you that for those tears I died."

WORDS and MUSIC: Marsha J. Stevens, 1969

FOR THOSE TEARS
Irregular meter

241 I Lay My Sins on Jesus

Who . . . bare our sins in His own body on the tree . . . I Pet. 2:24

1. I lay my sins on Jesus, The spotless Lamb of God;
He bears them all, and frees us From the accursed load:
I bring my guilt to Jesus, To wash my crimson stains
White in His blood most precious, Till not a stain remains.

2. I lay my wants on Jesus; All fulness dwells in Him;
He heals all my diseases, He doth my soul redeem:
I lay my griefs on Jesus, My burdens and my cares;
He from them all releases, He all my sorrows shares.

3. I rest my soul on Jesus, This weary soul of mine;
His right hand me embraces, I on His breast recline:
I love the name of Jesus, Immanuel, Christ the Lord;
Like fragrance on the breezes, His name abroad is poured.

4. I long to be like Jesus, Meek, loving, lowly, mild;
I long to be like Jesus, The Father's holy Child:
I long to be with Jesus, Amid the heav'nly throng,
To sing with saints His praises, To learn the angels' song. Amen.

WORDS: Horatius Bonar, 1843
MUSIC: Samuel S. Wesley, 1864

AURELIA
7.6.7.6 D.

O the Deep, Deep Love of Jesus 242

Having loved His own . . . He loved them unto the end. John 13:1

1. O the deep, deep love of Je - sus, Vast, un - meas-ured, bound-less, free!
2. O the deep, deep love of Je - sus, Spread His praise from shore to shore!
3. O the deep, deep love of Je - sus, Love of ev - ery love the best;
Roll - ing as a might - y o - cean In its full - ness o - ver me,
How He lov - eth, ev - er lov - eth, Chang-eth nev - er, nev - er - more;
'Tis an o - cean vast of bless-ing, 'Tis a ha - ven sweet of rest,
Un - der - neath me, all a - round me, Is the cur - rent of Thy love;
How He watch - es o'er His loved ones, Died to call them all His own;
O the deep, deep love of Je - sus, 'Tis a Heav'n of Heav'ns to me;
Lead - ing on-ward, lead-ing home-ward To my glo-rious rest a-bove.
How for them He in - ter - ced-eth, Watch-eth o'er them from the throne.
And it lifts me up to glo - ry, For it lifts me up to Thee. A-men.

WORDS: S. Trevor Francis, c.1890
MUSIC: Thomas J. Williams, 1890

TON-Y-BOTEL
8.7.8.7 D.

243 The Blood That Jesus Shed for Me

Thou . . . has redeemed us to God by Thy blood . . . Rev. 5:9

1. The blood that Je - sus shed for me, 'Way back on Cal - va - ry; The blood that gives me strength from day to day, It will nev - er lose its power.
2. It soothes my doubts and calms my fears, And it dries all my tears; The blood that gives me strength from day to day, It will nev - er lose its power.
Refrain
It reach - es to the high - est moun - tain. It flows to the

low - est val - ley. The blood that gives me strength from
day to day, It will nev - er lose its power.

WORDS and MUSIC: Andraé Crouch, 1966

THE BLOOD
Irregular meter

Jesus, Thy Blood and Righteousness 244

He hath clothed me with the garments of salvation . . . Isa. 61:10

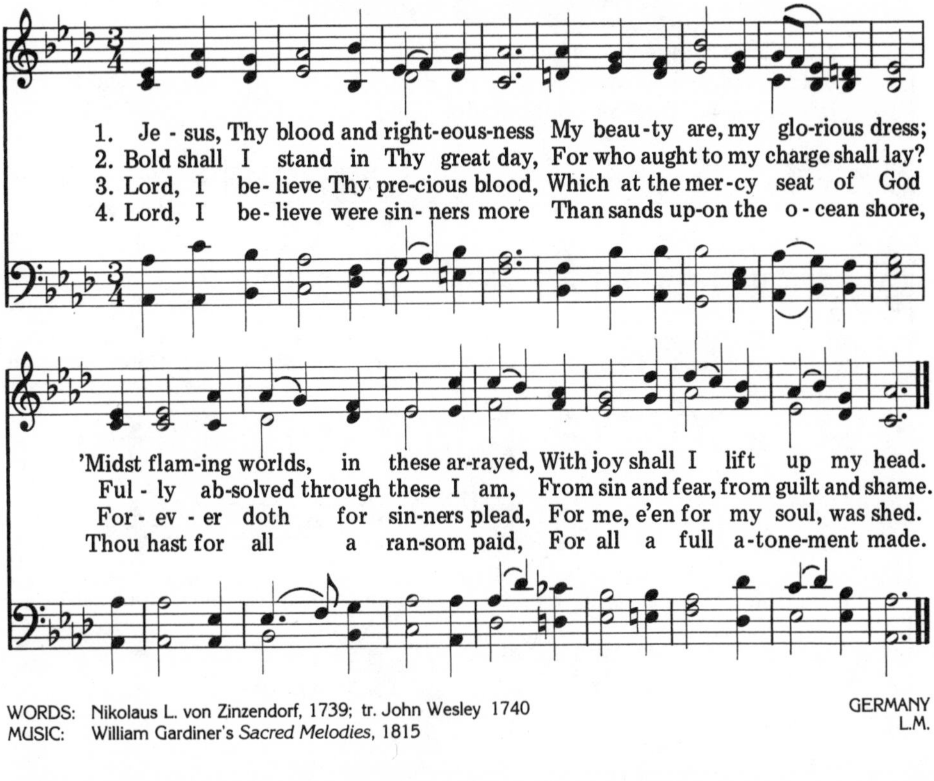

1. Je - sus, Thy blood and right-eous-ness My beau-ty are, my glo-rious dress;
'Midst flam-ing worlds, in these ar-rayed, With joy shall I lift up my head.

2. Bold shall I stand in Thy great day, For who aught to my charge shall lay?
Ful - ly ab-solved through these I am, From sin and fear, from guilt and shame.

3. Lord, I be- lieve Thy pre-cious blood, Which at the mer-cy seat of God
For - ev - er doth for sin-ners plead, For me, e'en for my soul, was shed.

4. Lord, I be- lieve were sin- ners more Than sands up-on the o - cean shore,
Thou hast for all a ran-som paid, For all a full a-tone-ment made.

WORDS: Nikolaus L. von Zinzendorf, 1739; tr. John Wesley 1740
MUSIC: William Gardiner's *Sacred Melodies*, 1815

GERMANY
L.M.

245 Free from the Law, O Happy Condition

Christ hath redeemed us from the curse of the law. Gal. 3:13

1. Free from the law, O hap - py con - di - tion, Je - sus hath
2. Now are we free—there's no con - dem - na - tion, Je - sus pro-
3. Chil - dren of God, O glo - ri - ous call - ing, Sure - ly His
bled, and there is re - mis - sion; Cursed by the law and bruised by the
vides a per - fect sal - va - tion; "Come un - to Me," O hear His sweet
grace will keep us from fall - ing; Pass - ing from death to life at His
Refrain
fall, Grace hath re-deemed us once for all.
call, Come, and He saves us once for all. Once for all— O sin - ner, recall, Bless-ed sal - va - tion once for all.
ceive it; Once for all— O broth - er, be - lieve it; Cling to the
cross, the bur - den will fall, Christ hath re-deemed us once for all.

WORDS and MUSIC: Philip P. Bliss, 1873

ONCE FOR ALL
10.10.9.8 Ref.

There Is a Fountain Filled with Blood 246

In that day there shall be a fountain opened . . . for sin and for uncleanness. Zech. 13:1

1. There is a foun-tain filled with blood Drawn from Im - man-uel's veins;
2. The dy - ing thief re-joiced to see That foun-tain in his day;
3. Dear dy - ing Lamb, Thy pre-cious blood Shall nev - er lose its pow'r,
4. E'er since by faith I saw the stream Thy flow - ing wounds sup - ply,
5. When this poor lisp - ing, stamm'ring tongue Lies si - lent in the grave,

And sin - ners, plunged be-neath that flood, Lose all their guilt - y stains:
And there may I, though vile as he, Wash all my sins a - way:
Till all the ran-somed Church of God Be saved, to sin no more:
Re - deem - ing love has been my theme, And shall be till I die:
Then in a no - bler, sweet - er song, I'll sing Thy pow'r to save:

Lose all their guilt - y stains, Lose all their guilt - y stains; And
Wash all my sins a - way, Wash all my sins a - way; And
Be saved, to sin no more, Be saved, to sin no more; Till
And shall be till I die, And shall be till I die; Re -
I'll sing Thy pow'r to save, I'll sing Thy pow'r to save; Then

sin - ners, plunged be-neath that flood, Lose all their guilt - y stains.
there may I, though vile as he, Wash all my sins a - way.
all the ran-somed Church of God Be saved, to sin no more.
deem - ing love has been my theme, And shall be till I die.
in a no - bler, sweet-er song I'll sing Thy pow'r to save. A-men.

WORDS: William Cowper, 1771
MUSIC: Traditional American melody; arr. Lowell Mason, 1830

CLEANSING FOUNTAIN
C.M.D.

247 And Can It Be That I Should Gain

While we were yet sinners, Christ died for us. Rom. 5:8

1. And can it be that I should gain An in - t'rest in the
2. 'Tis mys - tery all! Th'Im - mor - tal dies! Who can ex - plore His
3. He left His Fa - ther's throne a - bove, So free, so in - fi-
4. Long my im - pris - oned spir - it lay Fast bound in sin and
5. No con - dem - na - tion now I dread; Je - sus, and all in

Sav - ior's blood? Died He for me, who caused His pain? For me, who
strange de - sign? In vain the first - born ser - aph tries To sound the
nite His grace; Emp - tied Him - self of all but love, And bled for
na - ture's night; Thine eye dif - fused a quick-'ning ray, I woke, the
Him, is mine! A - live in Him, my liv - ing Head, And clothed in

Him to death pur - sued? A - maz - ing love! how can it be That
depths of love di - vine! 'Tis mer - cy all! let earth a - dore, Let
Ad - am's help - less race; 'Tis mer - cy all, im - mense and free; For,
dun-geon flamed with light; My chains fell off, my heart was free; I
right-eous - ness di - vine, Bold I ap - proach th'e - ter - nal throne, And

Thou, my God, shouldst die for me?
an - gel minds in - quire no more.
O my God, it found out me.
rose, went forth and fol - lowed Thee.
claim the crown, through Christ my own.

Refrain

A - maz - ing love! how
A - maz-ing love!

can it be That Thou, my God, shouldst die for me. A - men.
How can it be That Thou, my God,
WORDS: Charles Wesley, 1738
MUSIC: Thomas Campbell, 1825
SAGINA
L.M.D.
There Shall Be Showers of Blessing
248
There shall be showers of blessing . . . Ezek. 34:26
1. There shall be show-ers of bless - ing: This is the prom-ise of love;
2. There shall be show-ers of bless - ing — Pre-cious re - viv - ing a - gain;
3. There shall be show-ers of bless - ing: Send them up - on us, O Lord;
4. There shall be show-ers of bless - ing: O, that to - day they might fall,
There shall be sea - sons re - fresh - ing, Sent from the Sav - ior a - bove.
O - ver the hills and the val - leys, Sound of a - bun-dance of rain.
Grant to us now a re - fresh - ing, Come, and now hon - or Thy Word.
Now as to God we're con - fess - ing, Now, as on Je - sus we call!
Refrain
Show - ers of bless - ing, Show - ers of bless - ing we need:
Show - ers, show - ers of bless - ing,
Mer - cy - drops 'round us are fall - ing, But for the show - ers we plead.

WORDS: Daniel W. Whittle, 1883
MUSIC: James McGranahan, 1883

SHOWERS OF BLESSING
8.7.8.7 Ref.

249 Wonderful Grace of Jesus

For ye know the grace of our Lord Jesus Christ . . . II Cor. 8:9

1. Won - der - ful grace of Je - sus, Great - er than all my sin;
2. Won - der - ful grace of Je - sus, Reach - ing to all the lost,
3. Won - der - ful grace of Je - sus, Reach - ing the most de - filed,
How shall my tongue de - scribe it, Where shall its praise be - gin?
By it I have been par - doned, Saved to the ut - ter - most;
By its trans - form - ing pow - er Mak - ing him God's dear child,
Tak - ing a - way my bur - den, Set - ting my spir - it free,
Chains have been torn a - sun - der, Giv - ing me lib - er - ty,
Pur - chas - ing peace and heav - en For all e - ter - ni - ty—
For the won - der - ful grace of Je - sus reach - es me.
For the won - der - ful grace of Je - sus reach - es me.
And the won - der - ful grace of Je - sus reach - es me.
Refrain
the match-less grace of Je - sus,
Won - der - ful the match-less grace of Je - sus, Deep - er than the

might - y roll - ing sea; the roll - ing sea;
Won - der - ful
High - er than the moun - tain,
grace, all suf - fi - cient for
spark - ling like a foun - tain, All suf - fi - cient grace for e - ven
me, for e - ven me;
me;
Broad - er than the scope of my trans-
trans-
gres - sions, Great - er far than all my sin and shame;
gres - sions, sing it!
my sin and shame;
O mag - ni - fy the pre - cious name of Je - sus, Praise His name!

WORDS and MUSIC: Haldor Lillenas, 1918

WONDERFUL GRACE
Irregular meter

250 Marvelous Grace of Our Loving Lord

Where sin abounded, grace did much more abound. Rom. 5:20

1. Mar - vel - ous grace of our lov - ing Lord, Grace that ex - ceeds our sin and our guilt, Yon - der on Cal - va - ry's mount out - poured, There where the blood of the Lamb was spilt.
2. Sin and de - spair like the sea waves cold, Threat - en the soul with in - fi - nite loss; Grace that is great - er, yes, grace un - told, Points to the ref - uge, the might - y cross.
3. Dark is the stain that we can - not hide, What can a - vail to wash it a - way? Look! there is flow - ing a crim - son tide; Whit - er than snow you may be to - day.
4. Mar - vel - ous, in - fi - nite, match - less grace, Free - ly be - stowed on all who be - lieve; All who are long - ing to see His face, Will you this mo - ment His grace re - ceive?
Refrain
Grace, grace, God's grace, Grace that will par - don and cleanse with - in; Grace, grace, God's grace, Grace that is great - er than all our sin.
Mar - vel - ous grace, in - fi - nite grace, Mar - vel - ous grace, in - fi - nite grace,

WORDS: Julia H. Johnston, 1910
MUSIC: Daniel B. Towner, 1910

MOODY
9.9.9.9 Ref.

On a Hill Far Away 251

Who for the joy that was set before Him endured the cross, despising the shame . . . Heb. 12:2

1. On a hill far a - way stood an old rug - ged cross, The em - blem of suf - fering and shame; And I love that old cross where the dear - est and best For a world of lost sin - ners was slain.
2. O that old rug - ged cross, so de - spised by the world, Has a won - drous at - trac - tion for me; For the dear Lamb of God left His glo - ry a - bove To bear it to dark Cal - va - ry.
3. In the old rug - ged cross, stained with blood so di - vine, A won - drous beau - ty I see; For 'twas on that old cross Je - sus suf - fered and died To par - don and sanc - ti - fy me.
4. To the old rug - ged cross I will ev - er be true, Its shame and re - proach glad - ly bear; Then He'll call me some day to my home far a - way, Where His glo - ry for - ev - er I'll share.
Refrain
So I'll cher - ish the old rug - ged cross, the old rug - ged cross, Till my tro - phies at last I lay down; I will cling to the old rug - ged cross, the old rug - ged cross, And ex - change it some day for a crown.

WORDS and MUSIC: George Bennard, 1913

OLD RUGGED CROSS
Irregular meter

252 I Hear the Savior Say

Though your sins be as scarlet, they shall be as white as snow. Isa. 1:18

1. I hear the Sav - ior say, "Thy strength in - deed is small, Child of
2. Lord, now in - deed I find Thy pow'r and Thine a - lone Can
3. For noth - ing good have I Where - by Thy grace to claim— I'll
4. And when be - fore the throne I stand in Him com - plete, "Je - sus

weak-ness, watch and pray, Find in Me thine all in all."
change the lep - er's spots And melt the heart of stone.
wash my gar-ments white In the blood of Cal-v'ry's Lamb.
died my soul to save," My lips shall still re - peat.

Refrain

Je - sus paid it all,
All to Him I owe; Sin had left a crim - son stain, He washed it white as snow.

WORDS: Elvina M. Hall, 1865
MUSIC: John T. Grape, 1868

ALL TO CHRIST
6.6.7.7 Ref.

253 Depth of Mercy! Can There Be

Thy mercy is great above the heavens . . . Psa. 108:4

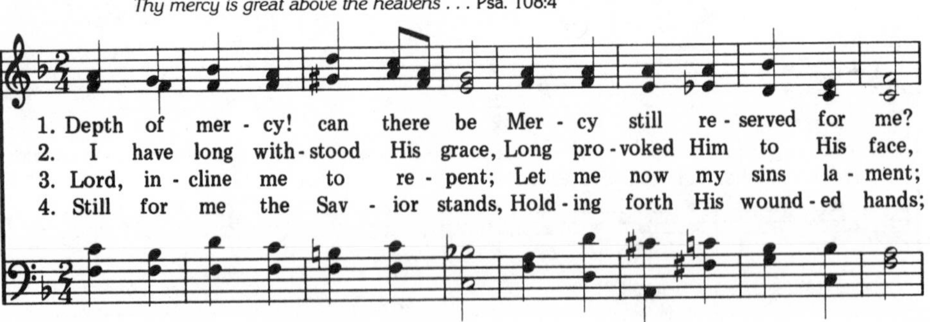
1. Depth of mer - cy! can there be Mer - cy still re - served for me?
2. I have long with - stood His grace, Long pro - voked Him to His face,
3. Lord, in - cline me to re - pent; Let me now my sins la - ment;
4. Still for me the Sav - ior stands, Hold - ing forth His wound - ed hands;

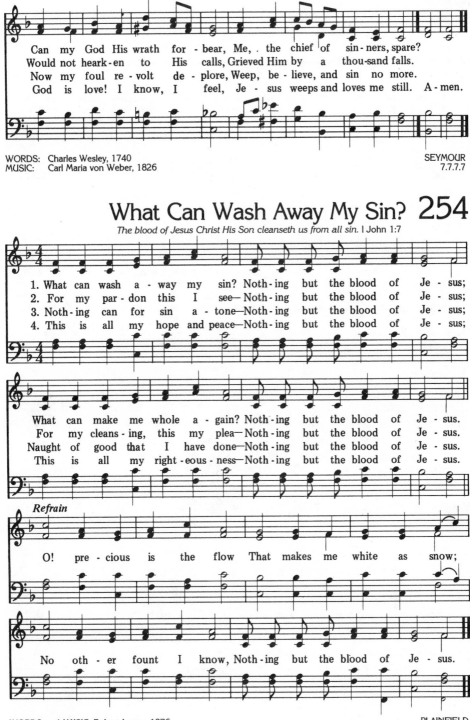

Can my God His wrath for - bear, Me, the chief of sin - ners, spare?
Would not heark - en to His calls, Grieved Him by a thou - sand falls.
Now my foul re - volt de - plore, Weep, be - lieve, and sin no more.
God is love! I know, I feel, Je - sus weeps and loves me still. A - men.

WORDS: Charles Wesley, 1740
MUSIC: Carl Maria von Weber, 1826

SEYMOUR
7.7.7.7

What Can Wash Away My Sin? 254

The blood of Jesus Christ His Son cleanseth us from all sin. I John 1:7

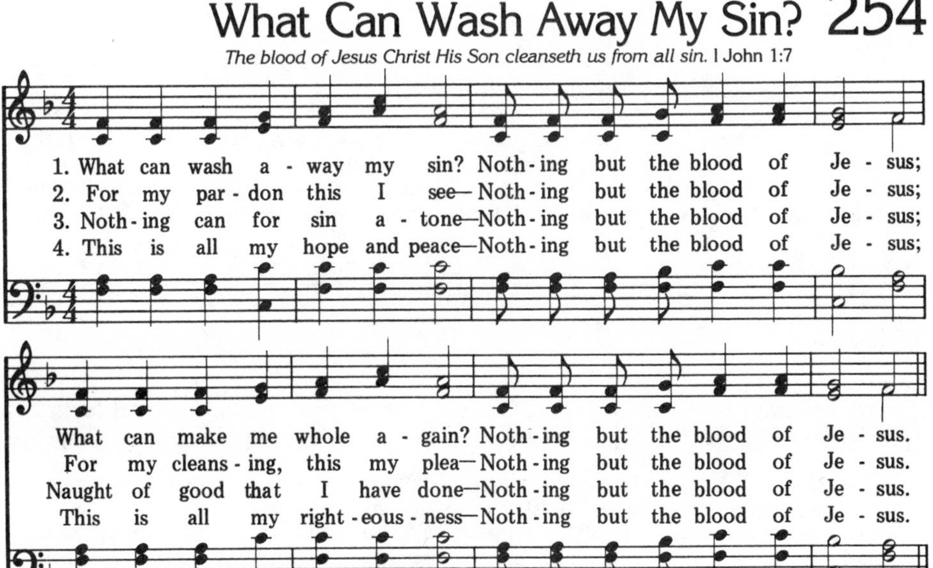

1. What can wash a - way my sin? Noth - ing but the blood of Je - sus;
What can make me whole a - gain? Noth - ing but the blood of Je - sus.

2. For my par - don this I see—Noth - ing but the blood of Je - sus;
For my cleans - ing, this my plea—Noth - ing but the blood of Je - sus.

3. Noth - ing can for sin a - tone—Noth - ing but the blood of Je - sus;
Naught of good that I have done—Noth - ing but the blood of Je - sus.

4. This is all my hope and peace—Noth - ing but the blood of Je - sus;
This is all my right - eous - ness—Noth - ing but the blood of Je - sus.

Refrain

O! pre - cious is the flow That makes me white as snow;
No oth - er fount I know, Noth - ing but the blood of Je - sus.

WORDS and MUSIC: Robert Lowry, 1876

PLAINFIELD
7.8.7.8 Ref.

255 Jesus, Lover of My Soul

Thou hast been . . . a refuge from the storm . . . Isa. 25:4

1. Je - sus, Lov - er of my soul, Let me to Thy bos - om fly,
2. Oth - er ref - uge have I none; Hangs my help - less soul on Thee;
3. Thou, O Christ, art all I want; More than all in Thee I find;
4. Plen - teous grace with Thee is found, Grace to cov - er all my sin;
While the near - er wa - ters roll, While the tem - pest still is high;
Leave, ah! leave me not a - lone, Still sup - port and com - fort me.
Raise the fall - en, cheer the faint, Heal the sick, and lead the blind.
Let the heal - ing streams a - bound; Make and keep me pure with - in.
Hide me, O my Sav - ior, hide, Till the storm of life is past;
All my trust on Thee is stayed, All my help from Thee I bring;
Just and ho - ly is Thy name, I am all un - right - eous - ness;
Thou of life the foun - tain art, Free - ly let me take of Thee;
Safe in - to the ha - ven guide; O re - ceive my soul at last!
Cov - er my de - fense - less head With the shad - ow of Thy wing.
False and full of sin I am, Thou art full of truth and grace.
Spring Thou up with - in my heart, Rise to all e - ter - ni - ty.

WORDS: Charles Wesley, 1740
MUSIC: Joseph Parry, 1879

ABERYSTWYTH
7.7.7.7 D.

Love Was When God Became a Man 256

. . . And was made in the likeness of men . . . Phil. 2:7

1. Love was when God be-came a man Locked in time and space with-out rank or place;
Love was God born of Jew-ish kin, Just a car-pen-ter with some fish-er-men.
2. Love was when God be-came a man Down where I could see love that reached to me;
Love was God dy-ing for my sin— And so trapped was I, my whole world caved in.
Love was when Je-sus walked in his-to-ry— Lov-ing-ly He brought a new life that's free;
Love was when Je-sus rose to walk with me— Lov-ing-ly He brought a new life that's free;
Love was God nailed to bleed and die To reach and love one such as I.
Love was God— on-ly He would try To reach and love one such as I.

WORDS: John E. Walvoord, 1970
MUSIC: Don Wyrtzen, 1970

LOVE WAS WHEN
Irregular meter

257 O How He Loves You and Me!

Greater love hath no man than this . . . John 15:13

1. O how He loves you and me, O how He loves you and
2. Je - sus to Cal - v'ry did go, His love for man-kind to

me; He gave His life—what more could He give? O how He
show; What He did there bro't hope from de - spair: O how He

loves you, O how He loves me, O how He loves you and me!
loves you, O how He loves me, O how He loves you and me!

WORDS and MUSIC: Kurt Kaiser, 1975

HE LOVES YOU AND ME
Irregular meter

258 There's a Wideness in God's Mercy

Thou, O Lord, art a God . . . plenteous in mercy and truth. Psa. 86:15

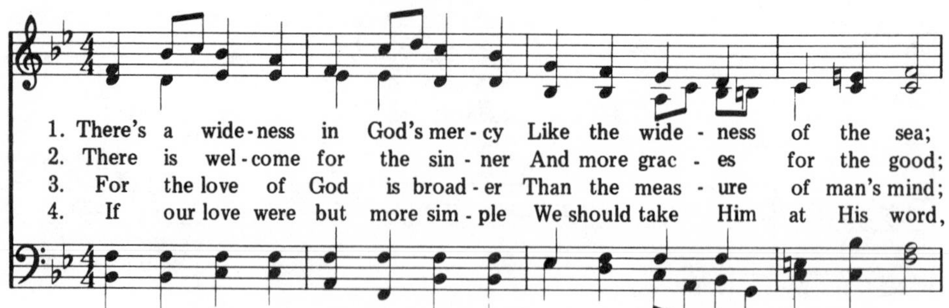
1. There's a wide-ness in God's mer-cy Like the wide - ness of the sea;
2. There is wel-come for the sin - ner And more grac - es for the good;
3. For the love of God is broad - er Than the meas - ure of man's mind;
4. If our love were but more sim - ple We should take Him at His word,

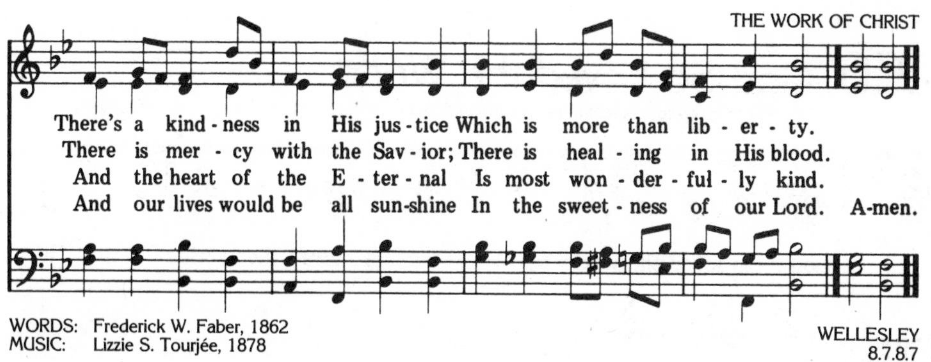
There's a kind-ness in His jus-tice Which is more than lib-er-ty.
There is mer-cy with the Sav-ior; There is heal-ing in His blood.
And the heart of the E-ter-nal Is most won-der-ful-ly kind.
And our lives would be all sun-shine In the sweet-ness of our Lord. A-men.

WORDS: Frederick W. Faber, 1862
MUSIC: Lizzie S. Tourjée, 1878

WELLESLEY
8.7.8.7

O Happy Day That Fixed My Choice 259

This day is salvation come to this house . . . Luke 19:9

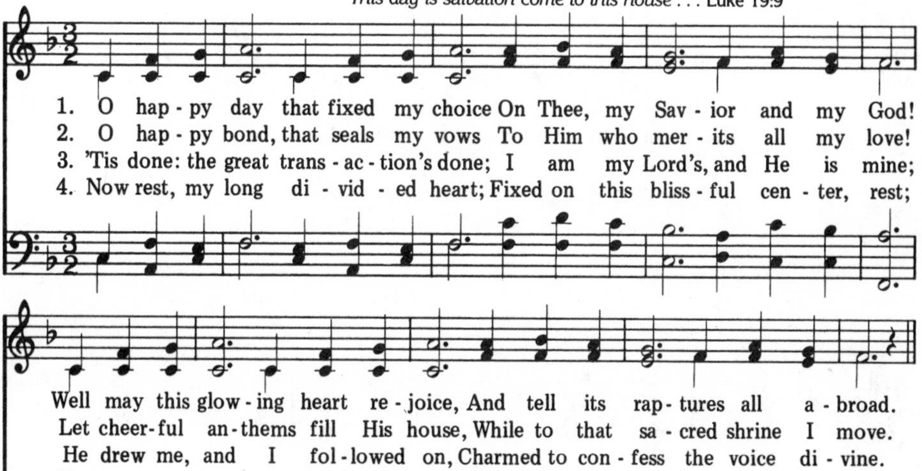

1. O hap-py day that fixed my choice On Thee, my Sav-ior and my God!
Well may this glow-ing heart re-joice, And tell its rap-tures all a-broad.

2. O hap-py bond, that seals my vows To Him who mer-its all my love!
Let cheer-ful an-thems fill His house, While to that sa-cred shrine I move.

3. 'Tis done: the great trans-ac-tion's done; I am my Lord's, and He is mine;
He drew me, and I fol-lowed on, Charmed to con-fess the voice di-vine.

4. Now rest, my long di-vid-ed heart; Fixed on this bliss-ful cen-ter, rest;
Nor ev-er from my Lord de-part, With Him of ev-ery good pos-sessed.

Refrain
Hap-py day, hap-py day, When Je-sus washed my sins a-way! *Fine*
He taught me how to watch and pray, And live re-joic-ing ev-ery day; *D.S.*

WORDS: Philip Doddridge, 1755
MUSIC: Edward F. Rimbault, 1854

HAPPY DAY
L.M. Ref.

260 God So Loved the World

God hath given to us eternal life, and this life is in His Son. I John 5:11

God so loved the world, God so loved the world, that He
gave His on - ly be - got - ten Son, that who - so be -
liev - eth, be - liev - eth in Him should not per - ish, should not
per - ish but have ev - er - last - ing life. For God sent not His
1

Son in - to the world to con - demn the world, God sent not His
Son in - to the world to con - demn the world; But that the
D. C.
2
world through Him might be sav - ed. life, ev - er - last - ing
life, ev - er - last - ing, ev - er - last - ing life. God so loved the
world, God so loved the world, God so loved the world.

WORDS: John 3:16, 17
MUSIC: John Stainer, 1887

STAINER
Irregular meter

261 The Whole World Was Lost

I am the light of the world . . . John 8:12

1. The whole world was lost in the dark-ness of sin; The Light of the world is Je - sus; Like sun-shine at noon-day His glo - ry shone in,
2. No dark - ness have we who in Je - sus a - bide, The Light of the world is Je - sus; We walk in the Light when we fol - low our Guide,
3. Ye dwell - ers in dark-ness with sin-blind - ed eyes, The Light of the world is Je - sus; Go wash at His bid - ding and light will a - rise,
4. No need of the sun-light in heav - en, we're told, The Light of the world is Je - sus; The Lamb is the Light in the Cit - y of Gold,
The Light of the world is Je - sus.
Refrain
Come to the Light, 'tis shin - ing for thee; Sweet - ly the Light has dawned up - on me;
Once I was blind, but now I can see; The Light of the world is Je - sus.

WORDS and MUSIC: Philip P. Bliss, 1875

LIGHT OF THE WORLD
11.8.11.8 Ref.

O Jesus, Thou Art Standing 262

If any man . . . open the door, I will come in to him. Rev. 3:20

1. O Je - sus, Thou art stand - ing Out - side the fast - closed door,
2. O Je - sus, Thou art knock - ing; And lo! that hand is scarred,
3. O Je - sus, Thou art plead - ing In ac - cents meek and low,
In low - ly pa - tience wait - ing To pass the thresh - old o'er:
And thorns Thy brow en - cir - cle, And tears Thy face have marred:
"I died for you, My chil - dren, And will ye treat Me so?"
Shame on us, Chris - tian bro - thers, His Name and sign who bear,
O love that pass - eth knowl-edge, So pa - tient - ly to wait!
O Lord, with shame and sor - row We o - pen now the door;
O shame, thrice shame up - on us, To keep Him stand-ing there!
O sin that hath no e - qual, So fast to bar the gate!
Dear Sav - ior, en - ter, en - ter, And leave us nev - er - more! A-men.

WORDS: William W. How, 1867
MUSIC: Justin H. Knecht, 1799, and Edward Husband, 1871

ST. HILDA
7.6.7.6 D.

263 Softly and Tenderly Jesus Is Calling

Come unto Me, all ye that labor and are heavy laden . . . Matt. 11:28

Refrain
1. Soft - ly and ten - der - ly Je - sus is call - ing, Call - ing for you and for me; See, on the por - tals He's wait - ing and watch - ing, Watch - ing for you and for me.
2. Why should we tar - ry when Je - sus is plead - ing, Plead - ing for you and for me? Why should we lin - ger and heed not His mer - cies, Mer - cies for you and for me?
3. Time is now fleet - ing, the mo - ments are pass - ing, Pass - ing from you and from me; Shad - ows are gath - er - ing, death's night is com - ing, Com - ing for you and for me.
4. O for the won - der - ful love He has prom - ised, Prom - ised for you and for me! Though we have sinned, He has mer - cy and par - don, Par - don for you and for me.
Come home, come home,
Come home, come home,
Ye who are wea - ry, come home; Ear - nest - ly, ten - der - ly, Je - sus is call - ing, Call - ing, O sin - ner, come home!

WORDS and MUSIC: Will L. Thompson, 1880

THOMPSON
11.7.11.7 Ref.

Have You Any Room for Jesus? 264

Today if ye will hear His voice, harden not your hearts . . . Heb. 3:15

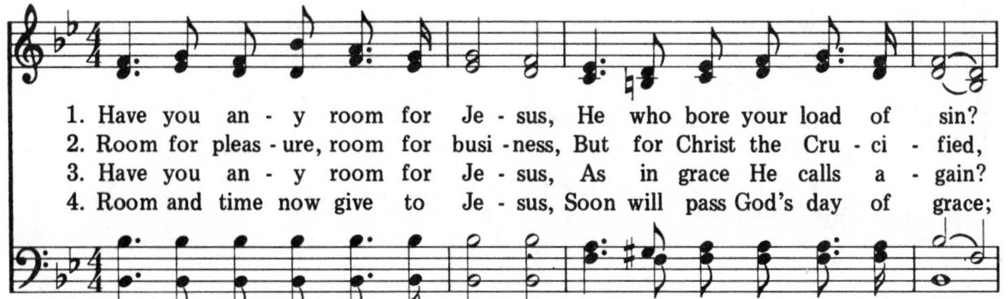
1. Have you an - y room for Je - sus, He who bore your load of sin?
2. Room for pleas - ure, room for busi - ness, But for Christ the Cru - ci - fied,
3. Have you an - y room for Je - sus, As in grace He calls a - gain?
4. Room and time now give to Je - sus, Soon will pass God's day of grace;

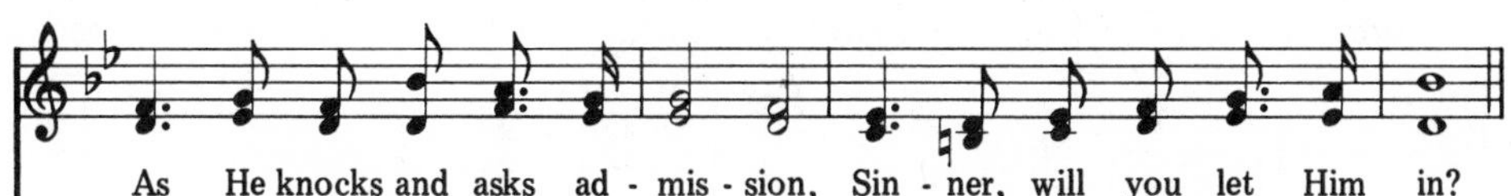

As He knocks and asks ad - mis - sion, Sin - ner, will you let Him in?
Not a place that He can en - ter, In the heart for which He died?
O, to - day is time ac - cept - ed, You will nev - er call in vain.
Soon your heart left cold and si - lent, And the Sav - ior's plead - ing cease.

Refrain

Room for Je - sus, King of glo - ry! Has - ten now, His word o - bey;

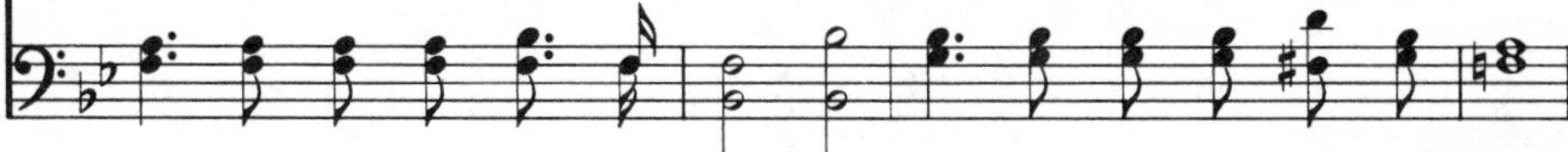

Swing the heart's door wide - ly o - pen, Bid Him en - ter while you may.

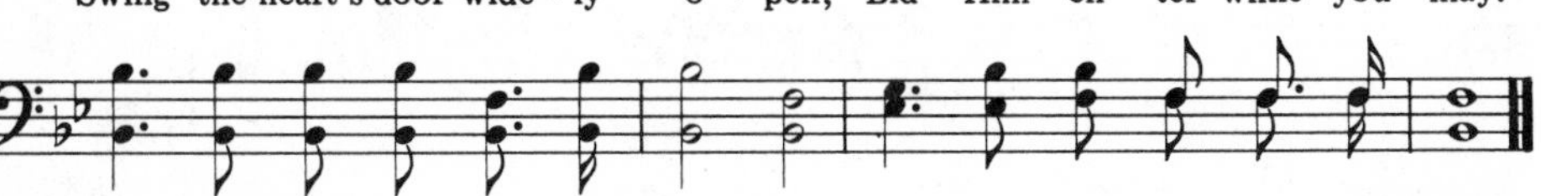

WORDS: Source unknown; adapt. Daniel W. Whittle, 1878
MUSIC: C. C. Williams, 1878

ANY ROOM
8.7.8.7 Ref.

265 The Savior Is Waiting

Behold, I stand at the door, and knock . . . Rev. 3:20

1. The Sav - ior is wait - ing to en - ter your heart, Why don't you let Him come in? There's noth-ing in this world to keep you a - part, What is your an - swer to Him?
2. If you'll take one step t'ward the Sav - ior, my friend, You'll find His arms o - pen wide; Re-ceive Him, and all of your dark-ness will end, With - in your heart He'll a - bide.
Refrain
Time af - ter time He has wait - ed be - fore, And now He is wait - ing a - gain To see if you're will-ing to o - pen the door, O, how He wants to come in.

WORDS and MUSIC: Ralph Carmichael, 1958

CARMICHAEL
11.7.11.7 Ref.

O Soul, Are You Weary and Troubled? 266

Look unto Me, and be ye saved, all the ends of the earth. Isa. 45:22

1. O soul, are you wea - ry and troub - led? No light in the dark-ness you see? There's light for a look at the Sav - ior, And life more a - bun - dant and free!
2. Through death in - to life ev - er - last - ing He passed, and we fol - low Him there; O - ver us sin no more hath do - min - ion— For more than con-qu'rors we are!
3. His word shall not fail you— He prom - ised; Be - lieve Him and all will be well: Then go to a world that is dy - ing, His per - fect sal - va - tion to tell!
Refrain
Turn your eyes up-on Je - sus, Look full in His won - der - ful face; And the things of earth will grow strange-ly dim In the light of His glo - ry and grace.

WORDS and MUSIC: Helen H. Lemmel, 1922

LEMMEL
9.8.9.8 Ref.

267 Come, Every Soul by Sin Oppressed

He is able also to save them to the uttermost . . . Heb. 7:25

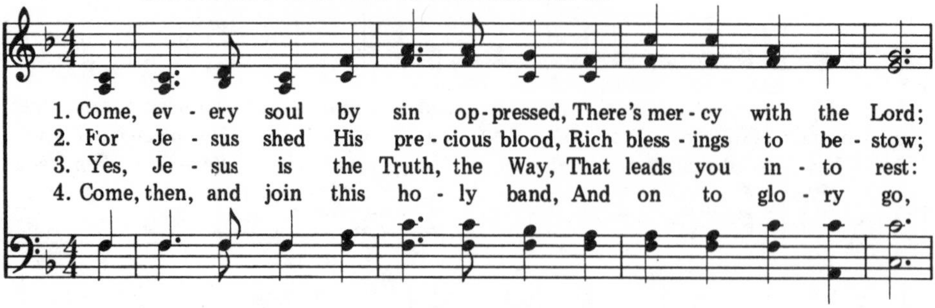

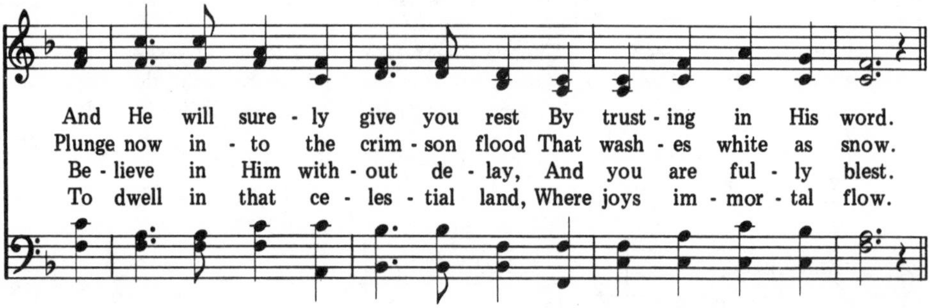

1. Come, ev - ery soul by sin op-pressed, There's mer - cy with the Lord;
And He will sure - ly give you rest By trust - ing in His word.

2. For Je - sus shed His pre - cious blood, Rich bless - ings to be - stow;
Plunge now in - to the crim - son flood That wash - es white as snow.

3. Yes, Je - sus is the Truth, the Way, That leads you in - to rest:
Be - lieve in Him with - out de - lay, And you are ful - ly blest.

4. Come, then, and join this ho - ly band, And on to glo - ry go,
To dwell in that ce - les - tial land, Where joys im - mor - tal flow.

Refrain
On - ly trust Him, on - ly trust Him, On - ly trust Him now.
He will save you, He will save you, He will save you now.

WORDS and MUSIC: John H. Stockton, 1874

MINERVA
C.M. Ref.

268 Come, Ye Sinners, Poor and Needy

Come unto Me, all ye that labor . . . and I will give you rest. Matt. 11:28

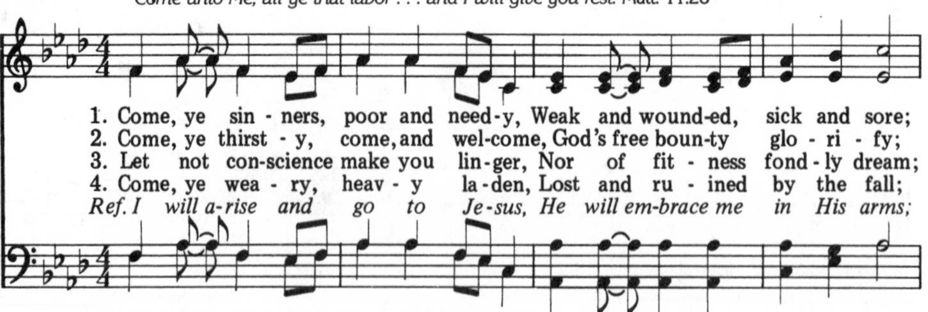
1. Come, ye sin - ners, poor and need-y, Weak and wound-ed, sick and sore;
2. Come, ye thirst - y, come, and wel-come, God's free boun-ty glo - ri - fy;
3. Let not con-science make you lin-ger, Nor of fit - ness fond-ly dream;
4. Come, ye wea - ry, heav - y la-den, Lost and ru - ined by the fall;
Ref. I will a-rise and go to Je-sus, He will em-brace me in His arms;

THE CALL OF CHRIST
D.C. Refrain
Je - sus read - y stands to save you, Full of pit - y, love, and pow'r.
True be - lief and true re - pent-ance, Ev - ery grace that brings you nigh.
All the fit - ness He re - quir - eth Is to feel your need of Him.
If you tar - ry till you're bet - ter, You will nev - er come at all.
In the arms of my dear Sav - ior, O, there are ten thou-sand charms.

WORDS: Joseph Hart, 1759; refrain, source unknown
MUSIC: Traditional American melody

ARISE
8.7.8.7 Ref.

Just As I Am, without One Plea 269

Him that cometh to Me I will in no wise cast out. John 6:37

1. Just as I am, with - out one plea But that Thy blood was shed for me, And that Thou bidd'st me come to Thee, O Lamb of God, I come! I come!
2. Just as I am, and wait - ing not To rid my soul of one dark blot, To Thee whose blood can cleanse each spot, O Lamb of God, I come! I come!
3. Just as I am, though tossed a - bout With man - y a con - flict, man - y a doubt, Fight-ings and fears with - in, with - out, O Lamb of God, I come! I come!
4. Just as I am, poor, wretch - ed, blind; Sight, rich - es, heal - ing of the mind, Yea, all I need, in Thee I find, O Lamb of God, I come! I come!
5. Just as I am, Thou wilt re - ceive, Wilt wel - come, par - don, cleanse, re - lieve; Be - cause Thy prom - ise I be - lieve, O Lamb of God, I come! I come!

Coda (after last stanza)

O Lamb of God, I come. A-men.

WORDS: Charlotte Elliott, 1834
MUSIC: William B. Bradbury, 1849

WOODWORTH
L.M. Coda

270 Seek Ye First the Kingdom of God

Seek ye first the kingdom of God and His righteousness . . . Matt. 6:33

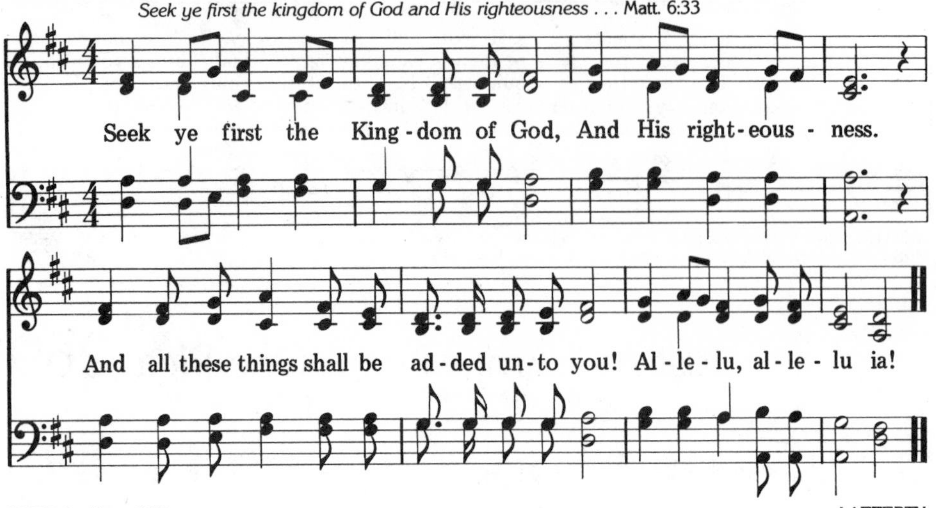
Seek ye first the King-dom of God, And His right-eous - ness.
And all these things shall be ad-ded un-to you! Al-le-lu, al-le-lu ia!

WORDS: Matt. 6:33
MUSIC: Karen Lafferty, 1972

LAFFERTY
Irregular meter

271 Are You Weary, Heavy Laden?

Come unto Me, all ye that labor and are heavy laden . . . Matt. 11:28

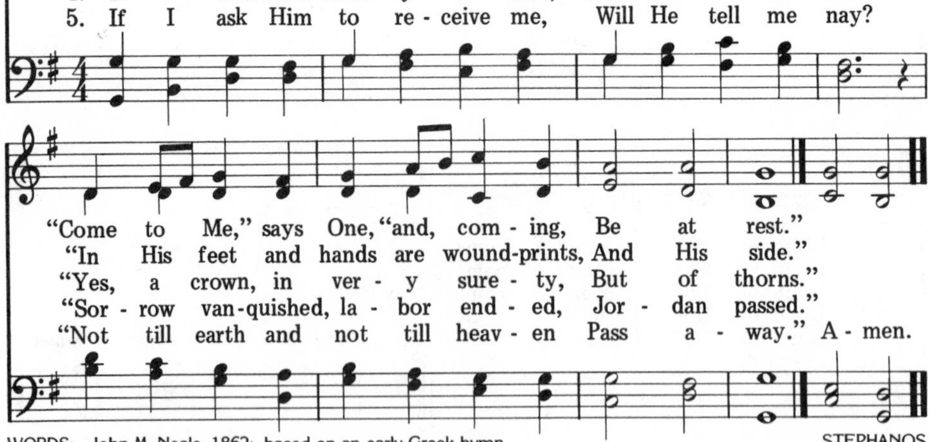

1. Are you wea - ry, heav - y lad - en, Are you sore dis - tressed?
"Come to Me," says One, "and, com - ing, Be at rest."

2. Has He marks to lead me to Him, If He be my Guide?
"In His feet and hands are wound-prints, And His side."

3. Is there di - a - dem, as Mon-arch, That His brow a - dorns?
"Yes, a crown, in ver - y sure - ty, But of thorns."

4. If I still hold close - ly to Him, What has He at last?
"Sor - row van-quished, la - bor end - ed, Jor - dan passed."

5. If I ask Him to re - ceive me, Will He tell me nay?
"Not till earth and not till heav - en Pass a - way." A - men.

WORDS: John M. Neale, 1862; based on an early Greek hymn
MUSIC: Henry W. Baker, 1868

STEPHANOS
8.5.8.3

Out of My Bondage, Sorrow and Night 272

He hath sent Me . . . to proclaim liberty to the captives . . . Isa. 61:1

1. Out of my bond-age, sor-row and night, Je-sus, I come, Je-sus, I come;
2. Out of my shame-ful fail-ure and loss, Je-sus, I come, Je-sus, I come;
3. Out of un-rest and ar-ro-gant pride, Je-sus, I come, Je-sus, I come;
4. Out of the fear and dread of the tomb, Je-sus, I come, Je-sus, I come;
In-to Thy free-dom, glad-ness and light, Je-sus, I come to Thee.
In-to the glo-rious gain of Thy cross, Je-sus, I come to Thee.
In-to Thy bless-ed will to a-bide, Je-sus, I come to Thee.
In-to the joy and light of Thy home, Je-sus, I come to Thee.
Out of my sick-ness in-to Thy health, Out of my want and in-to Thy wealth,
Out of earth's sor-rows in-to Thy balm, Out of life's storms and in-to Thy calm,
Out of my-self to dwell in Thy love, Out of de-spair in-to rap-tures a-bove,
Out of the depths of ru-in un-told, In-to the peace of Thy shel-ter-ing fold,
Out of my sin and in-to Thy-self, Je-sus, I come to Thee.
Out of dis-tress to ju-bi-lant psalm, Je-sus, I come to Thee.
Up-ward for aye on wings like a dove, Je-sus, I come to Thee.
Ev-er Thy glo-rious face to be-hold, Je-sus, I come to Thee.

WORDS: William T. Sleeper, 1887
MUSIC: George C. Stebbins, 1887

JESUS, I COME
Irregular meter

273 I Stand Amazed in the Presence

God, who is rich in mercy, for His great love wherewith He loved us . . . Eph. 2:4

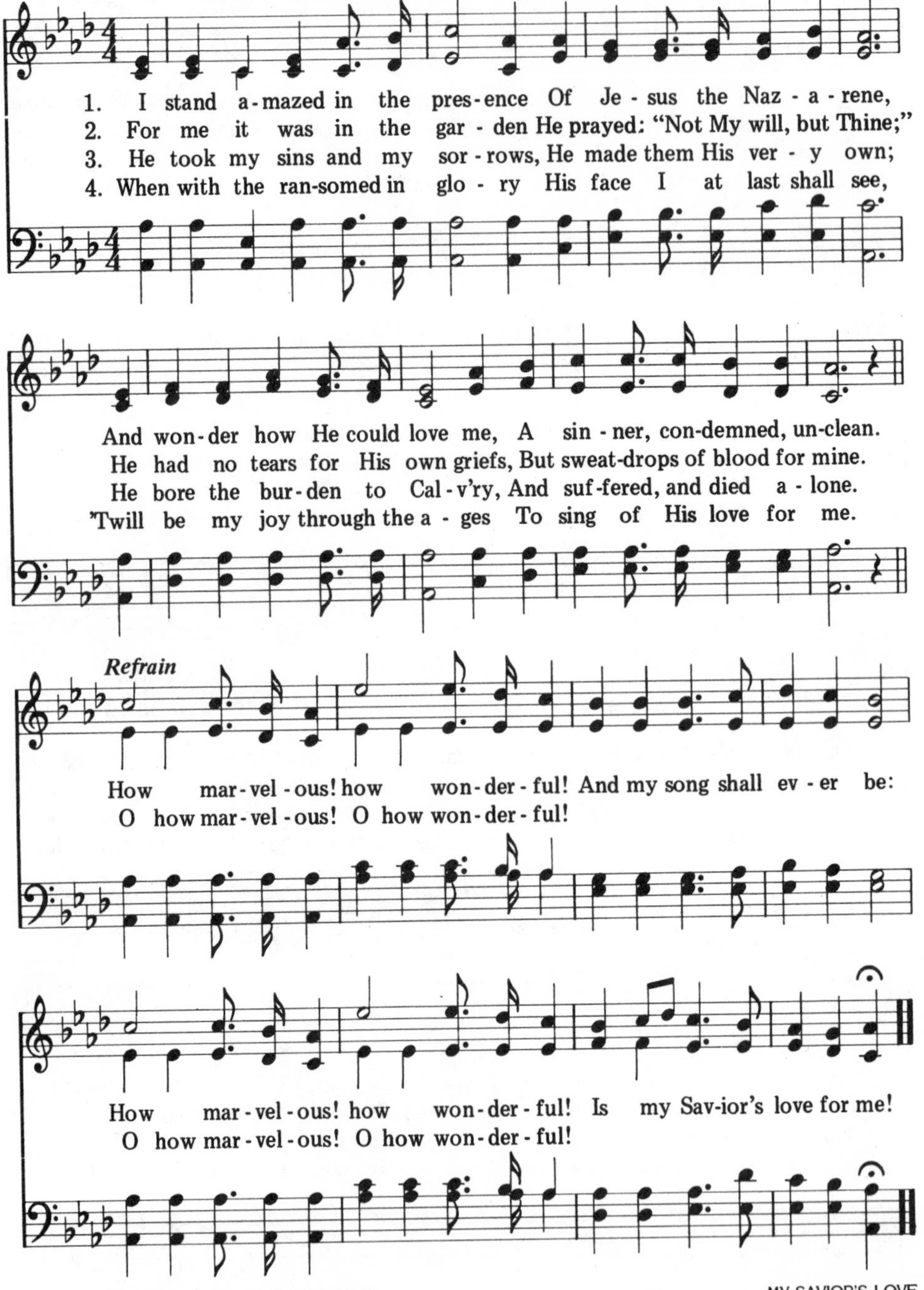
1. I stand a-mazed in the pres-ence Of Je-sus the Naz-a-rene,
2. For me it was in the gar-den He prayed: "Not My will, but Thine;"
3. He took my sins and my sor-rows, He made them His ver-y own;
4. When with the ran-somed in glo-ry His face I at last shall see,
And won-der how He could love me, A sin-ner, con-demned, un-clean.
He had no tears for His own griefs, But sweat-drops of blood for mine.
He bore the bur-den to Cal-v'ry, And suf-fered, and died a-lone.
'Twill be my joy through the a-ges To sing of His love for me.
Refrain
How mar-vel-ous! how won-der-ful! And my song shall ev-er be:
O how mar-vel-ous! O how won-der-ful!
How mar-vel-ous! how won-der-ful! Is my Sav-ior's love for me!
O how mar-vel-ous! O how won-der-ful!

WORDS and MUSIC: Charles H. Gabriel, 1905

MY SAVIOR'S LOVE
8.7.8.7 Ref.

Alas! and Did My Savior Bleed? 274

Surely He hath borne our griefs, and carried our sorrows. Isa. 53:4

1. A - las! and did my Sav - ior bleed? And did my Sov - 'reign die?
Would He de - vote that sa - cred head For sin - ners such as I?

2. Was it for crimes that I have done He groaned up - on the tree?
A - maz - ing pit - y! grace un - known! And love be - yond de - gree!

3. Well might the sun in dark - ness hide, And shut his glo - ries in,
When Christ, the might - y Mak - er, died For man the crea - ture's sin.

4. But drops of grief can ne'er re - pay The debt of love I owe:
Here, Lord, I give my - self a - way, 'Tis all that I can do!

Refrain

At the cross, at the cross where I first saw the light, And the bur - den of my heart rolled a - way, (rolled a - way,) It was there by faith I re - ceived my sight, And now I am hap - py all the day!

WORDS: Isaac Watts, 1707; refrain, Ralph E. Hudson, 1885
MUSIC: Ralph E. Hudson, 1885; refrain melody by John Hill Hewitt, 1864

HUDSON
C.M. Ref.

275 I Heard the Voice of Jesus Say

Come unto Me, all ye that labor . . . and I will give you rest. Matt. 11:28

1. I heard the voice of Je - sus say, "Come un - to Me and rest;
2. I heard the voice of Je - sus say, "Be - hold, I free - ly give
3. I heard the voice of Je - sus say, "I am this dark world's Light;
Lay down, thou wea - ry one, lay down Thy head up - on My breast."
The liv - ing wa - ter; thirst - y one, Stoop down, and drink, and live."
Look un - to Me, thy morn shall rise, And all thy day be bright."
I came to Je - sus as I was, Wea - ry, and worn, and sad;
I came to Je - sus, and I drank Of that life - giv - ing stream;
I looked to Je - sus, and I found In Him my Star, my Sun;
I found in Him a rest - ing place, And He has made me glad.
My thirst was quenched, my soul re - vived, And now I live in Him.
And in that Light of life I'll walk, Till trav-'ling days are done.

WORDS: Horatius Bonar, 1846
MUSIC: John B. Dykes, 1868

VOX DILECTI
C.M.D.

I Know Not Why God's Wondrous Grace 276

For I know whom I have believed . . . II Tim. 1:12

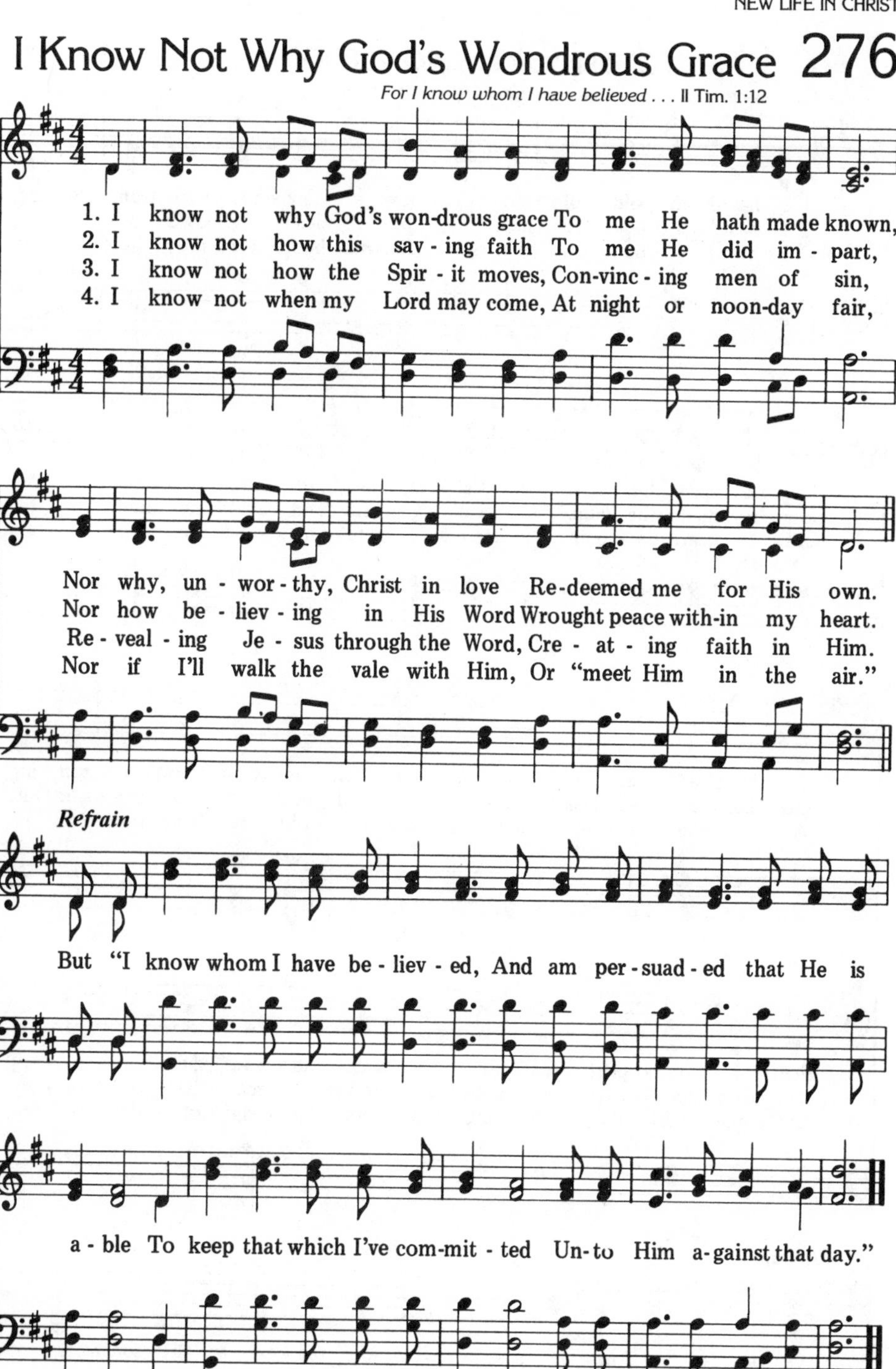
1. I know not why God's won-drous grace To me He hath made known,
2. I know not how this sav - ing faith To me He did im - part,
3. I know not how the Spir - it moves, Con-vinc - ing men of sin,
4. I know not when my Lord may come, At night or noon-day fair,
Nor why, un - wor - thy, Christ in love Re-deemed me for His own.
Nor how be - liev - ing in His Word Wrought peace with-in my heart.
Re - veal - ing Je - sus through the Word, Cre - at - ing faith in Him.
Nor if I'll walk the vale with Him, Or "meet Him in the air."
Refrain
But "I know whom I have be - liev - ed, And am per - suad - ed that He is
a - ble To keep that which I've com-mit - ted Un- to Him a - gainst that day."

WORDS: Daniel W. Whittle, 1883
MUSIC: James McGranahan, 1883

EL NATHAN
C.M. Ref.

277 I Heard an Old, Old Story

Victory . . . through our Lord Jesus Christ. I Cor. 15:57

1. I heard an old, old sto - ry, how a Sav - ior came from glo - ry,
2. I heard a - bout His heal - ing, of His cleans - ing pow'r re - veal - ing,
3. I heard a - bout a man - sion He has built for me in glo - ry,
How He gave his life on Cal - va - ry to save a wretch like me;
How He made the lame to walk a - gain and caused the blind to see;
And I heard a - bout the streets of gold be - yond the crys - tal sea;
I heard a - bout His groan - ing, of His pre - cious blood's a - ton - ing,
And then I cried "Dear Je - sus, come and heal my bro - ken spir - it,"
A - bout the an - gels sing - ing, and the old re - demp - tion sto - ry,
Then I re - pent - ed of my sins and won the vic - to - ry.
And some - how Je - sus came and bro't to me the vic - to - ry.
And some sweet day I'll sing up there the song of vic - to - ry.
Refrain
O vic - to - ry in Je - sus, my Sav - ior, for - ev - er, He sought me and

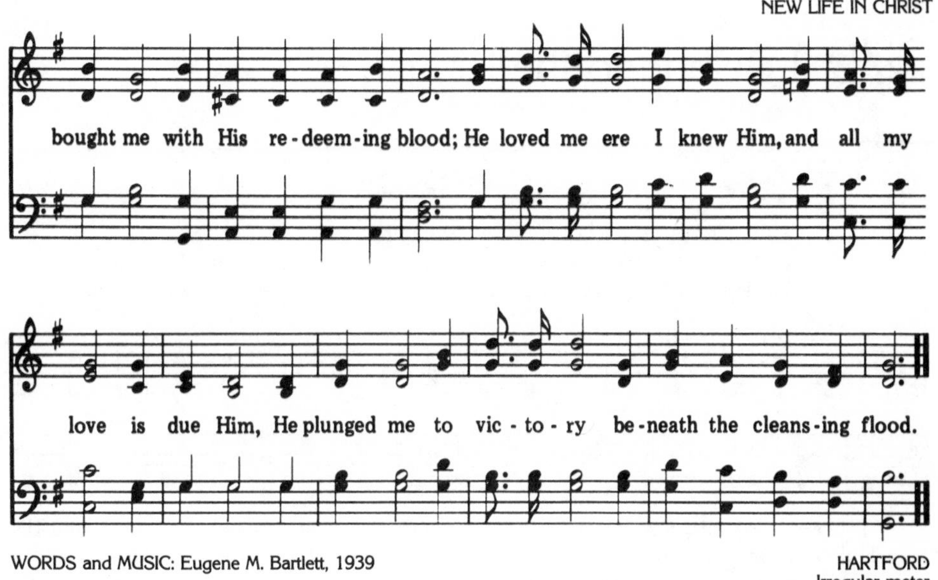
bought me with His re-deem-ing blood; He loved me ere I knew Him, and all my
love is due Him, He plunged me to vic-to-ry be-neath the cleans-ing flood.

WORDS and MUSIC: Eugene M. Bartlett, 1939

HARTFORD
Irregular meter

Amazing Grace! How Sweet the Sound 278

God is able to make all grace abound toward you . . . II Cor. 9:8

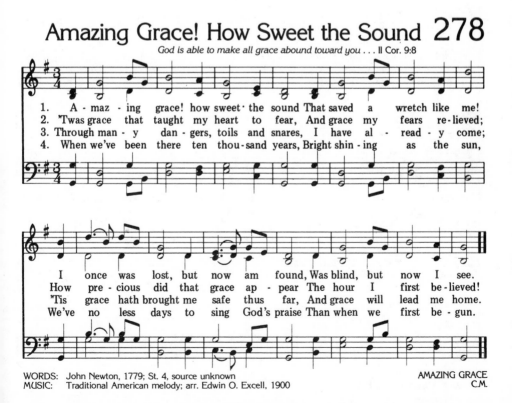

1. A - maz - ing grace! how sweet the sound That saved a wretch like me!
2. 'Twas grace that taught my heart to fear, And grace my fears re - lieved;
3. Through man - y dan - gers, toils and snares, I have al - read - y come;
4. When we've been there ten thou - sand years, Bright shin - ing as the sun,

I once was lost, but now am found, Was blind, but now I see.
How pre - cious did that grace ap - pear The hour I first be - lieved!
'Tis grace hath brought me safe thus far, And grace will lead me home.
We've no less days to sing God's praise Than when we first be - gun.

WORDS: John Newton, 1779; St. 4, source unknown
MUSIC: Traditional American melody; arr. Edwin O. Excell, 1900

AMAZING GRACE
C.M.

279 I Belong to the King

... We are the children of God. Rom. 8:16

1. I be-long to the King, I'm a child of His love, I shall dwell in His
2. I be-long to the King, and He loves me, I know, For His mer-cy and
3. I be-long to the King, and His prom-ise is sure, That we all shall be
pal-ace so fair; For He tells of its bliss in yon heav-en a-bove, And His
kind-ness, so free, Are un-ceas-ing-ly mine where-so-ev-er I go, And my
gath-ered at last In His king-dom a-bove, by life's wa-ters so pure, When this
chil-dren its splen-dors shall share.
ref-uge un-fail-ing is He.
life with its tri-als is past.
Refrain
I be-long to the King, I'm a
child of His love, And He nev-er for-sak-eth His own; He will call me some
day to His pal-ace a-bove, I shall dwell by His glo-ri-fied throne.

WORDS: Ida R. Smith, 1896
MUSIC: J. Lincoln Hall, 1896

CLIFTON
Irregular meter

I'd Rather Have Jesus 280

. . . I count all things but loss for the excellency of the knowledge of Christ Jesus . . . Phil. 3:8

1. I'd rath - er have Je - sus than sil - ver or gold, I'd rath - er be
2. I'd rath - er have Je - sus than men's ap - plause, I'd rath - er be
3. He's fair - er than lil - ies of rar - est bloom, He's sweet - er than
His than have rich - es un - told; I'd rath - er have Je - sus than
faith - ful to His dear cause; I'd rath - er have Je - sus than
hon - ey from out the comb; He's all that my hun - ger - ing
hous - es or lands, I'd rath - er be led by His nail-pierced hand
world - wide fame, I'd rath - er be true to His ho - ly name
spir - it needs, I'd rath - er have Je - sus and let Him lead
Than to be the king of a vast do - main Or be held in sin's dread sway; I'd
rath - er have Je - sus than an - y - thing This world af - fords to - day.

WORDS: Rhea F. Miller, 1922
MUSIC: George Beverly Shea, 1939

I'D RATHER HAVE JESUS
Irregular meter

281 Shackled by a Heavy Burden

Jesus put forth His hand and touched him, saying, I will; be thou clean. Matt. 8:3

1. Shack - led by a heav - y bur - den, 'Neath a load of
2. Since I met this bless - ed Sav - ior, Since He cleansed and
guilt and shame; Then the hand of Je - sus touched me,
made me whole; I will nev - er cease to praise Him,
And now I am no long - er the same.
I'll shout it while e - ter - ni - ty rolls.
Refrain
He touched me, O, He
touched me, And O, the joy that floods my soul; Some-thing
hap - pened, and now I know, He touched me and made me whole.

WORDS and MUSIC: William J. Gaither, 1963

HE TOUCHED ME
Irregular meter

Redeemed, How I Love to Proclaim It 282

In whom we have redemption through His blood ... Eph. 1:7

Unison
1. Re - deemed, how I love to pro - claim it! Re - deemed by the blood of the Lamb; Re-deemed thro' His in - fi - nite mer - cy, His child, and for - ev - er, I am.
2. Re - deemed and so hap - py in Je - sus, No lan - guage my rap - ture can tell; I know that the light of His pres - ence With me doth con - tin - ual - ly dwell.
3. I think of my bless - ed Re - deem - er, I think of Him all the day long; I sing, for I can - not be si - lent; His love is the theme of my song.
Refrain
Re - deemed, re - deemed, Re - deemed by the blood of the Lamb; Re - deemed thro' His in - fi - nite mer - cy, His child, and for - ev - er, I am.

WORDS: Fanny J. Crosby, 1882
MUSIC: A. L. Butler, 1966

ADA
9.8.9.8 Ref.

283 I Have a Song I Love to Sing

Let the redeemed of the Lord say so . . . Psa. 107:2

Refrain
1. I have a song I love to sing, Since I have been re - deemed,
2. I have a Christ who sat - is - fies, Since I have been re - deemed;
3. I have a wit - ness bright and clear, Since I have been re - deemed,
4. I have a home pre - pared for me, Since I have been re - deemed,
Of my Re - deem - er, Sav - ior, King, Since I have been re - deemed.
To do His will my high - est prize, Since I have been re - deemed.
Dis - pel - ling ev - ery doubt and fear, Since I have been re - deemed.
Where I shall dwell e - ter - nal - ly, Since I have been re - deemed.
Since I have been re - deemed, Since I have been re-
Since I have been re-deemed, Since I have been re-deemed,
deemed, I will glo - ry in His name; Since I have been re-
Since I have been re-deemed, Since
deemed, I will glo - ry in my Sav - ior's name.
I have been re - deemed,

WORDS and MUSIC: Edwin O. Excell, 1884

OTHELLO
C.M. Ref.

I Will Sing the Wondrous Story 284

And they sing the song . . . of the Lamb, saying, great and marvelous are Thy works. Rev. 15:3

1. I will sing the won-drous sto - ry Of the Christ who died for me,
2. I was lost but Je - sus found me, Found the sheep that went a - stray,
3. I was bruised but Je - sus healed me; Faint was I from man - y a fall;
4. Days of dark - ness still come o'er me, Sor - row's paths I oft - en tread,
How He left His home in glo - ry For the cross of Cal - va - ry.
Threw His lov - ing arms a - round me, Drew me back in - to His way.
Sight was gone, and fears pos-sessed me, But He freed me from them all.
But the Sav - ior still is with me; By His hand I'm safe - ly led.
Refrain
Yes, I'll sing the won-drous sto - ry Of the
Yes, I'll sing the won-drous sto - ry
Christ who died for me, Sing it with the saints in
Of the Christ who died for me, Sing it with
glo - ry Gath-ered by the crys-tal sea.
the saints in glo - ry, Gath-ered by the crys-tal sea.

WORDS: Francis H. Rowley, 1886
MUSIC: Peter P. Bilhorn, 1886

WONDROUS STORY
8.7.8.7 Ref.

285 My Father Is Omnipotent

Greater love hath no man than this . . . John 15:13

1. My Father is omnipotent, And that you can't deny;
A God of might and miracles—'Tis written in the sky.

2. Tho' here His glory has been shown, We still can't fully see
The wonders of His might, His throne, 'Twill take eternity.

3. The Bible tells us of His pow'r And wisdom all way thro';
And every little bird and flow'r Are testimonies, too.

Refrain

It took a miracle to put the stars in place, It took a miracle to hang the world in space; But when He saved my soul, Cleansed and made me whole, It took a miracle of love and grace!

WORDS and MUSIC: John W. Peterson, 1948

MONTROSE
Irregular meter

Naught Have I Gotten 286

For by grace are ye saved through faith . . . Eph. 2:8

1. Naught have I got - ten but what I re-ceived; Grace hath be-stowed it since I have be - lieved; Boast - ing ex - clud - ed, pride I a - base; I'm on - ly a sin - ner saved by grace!
2. Once I was fool - ish, and sin ruled my heart, Caus - ing my foot-steps from God to de - part; Je - sus hath found me, hap - py my case; I now am a sin - ner saved by grace!
3. Tears un - a - vail - ing, no mer - it had I; Mer - cy had saved me, or else I must die; Sin had a - larmed me, fear - ing God's face; But now I'm a sin - ner saved by grace!
4. Suf - fer a sin - ner whose heart o - ver-flows, Lov - ing his Sav - ior to tell what he knows; Once more to tell it would I em - brace—I'm on - ly a sin - ner saved by grace!
Refrain
On - ly a sin - ner saved by grace! On - ly a sin - ner saved by grace! This is my sto - ry, to God be the glo - ry— I'm on - ly a sin - ner saved by grace!

WORDS: James M. Gray, 1905
MUSIC: Daniel B. Towner, 1905

ONLY A SINNER
10.10.9.9 Ref.

287 What a Wonderful Change in My Life

If any man be in Christ, he is a new creature . . . II Cor. 5:17

1. What a won-der-ful change in my life has been wrought Since Je-sus came in-to my heart! I have light in my soul for which long I have sought, Since Je-sus came in-to my heart!
2. I have ceased from my wand-'ring and go-ing a-stray, Since Je-sus came in-to my heart! And my sins, which were man-y, are all washed a-way,
3. There's a light in the val-ley of death now for me, Since Je-sus came in-to my heart! And the gates of the Cit-y be-yond I can see,
4. I shall go there to dwell in that Cit-y, I know, Since Je-sus came in-to my heart! And I'm hap-py, so hap-py, as on-ward I go,
Refrain
Since Je-sus came in-to my heart, Since Je-sus came in-to my heart,
Since Je-sus came in, came in-to my heart, Since Je-sus came in, came in-to my heart,
Floods of joy o'er my soul like the sea bil-lows roll, Since Je-sus came in-to my heart.

WORDS: Rufus H. McDaniel, 1914
MUSIC: Charles H. Gabriel, 1914

McDANIEL
12.8.12.8 Ref.

Out of the Depths to the Glory Above 288

I will extol Thee, O Lord; for Thou hast lifted me up. Psa. 30:1

1. Out of the depths to the glo - ry a - bove, I have been lift - ed in won - der - ful love; From ev - ery fet - ter my spir - it is free— For Je - sus has lift - ed me!
2. Out of the world in - to heav - en - ly rest, In - to the land of the ran - somed and blest; There in the glo - ry with Him I shall be— For Je - sus has lift - ed me!
3. Out of my - self in - to Him I a - dore, There to a - bide in His love ev - er - more; Thro' end - less a - ges His glo - ry to see— My Je - sus has lift - ed me!
Refrain
Je - sus has lift - ed me! lift - ed me! Je - sus has lift - ed me! lift - ed me!
Out of the night in - to glo - ri - ous light, Yes, Je - sus has lift - ed me! lift - ed me!

WORDS: Avis B. Christiansen, 1918
MUSIC: Haldor Lillenas, 1918

LILLENAS
10.10.10.7 Ref.

289 I've Heard the King

I will come in to him, and will sup with him, and he with Me. Rev. 3:20

Refrain
1. I've heard the King! The King of heav - en! Nor can I e'er for - get the mu - sic of His voice. I've heard the King! His call I've an-swered. I've made the King of heav'n my ev - er - last - ing choice.
2. I've heard the King! The King of glo - ry; For whom my heart's door o - pened wide and He came in. I've heard the King! O, bless-ed hear - ing, His voice spoke peace and par - don for my guilt and sin.
3. I've heard the King! O, had I missed Him, My life for - ev - er - more could not re - gain the loss. From heav'n He came, the world to ran - som, And this He did one day on Cal-v'ry's cru - el cross.
4. I've heard the King! and now I'm tell - ing To all the world the gos - pel of un - dy - ing love, That oth - ers too may catch the mu - sic His voice can bring, and find their way to heav'n a - bove.
He came to me, and with Him came a bless - ing. He spoke to me, and glo - ry filled my soul; His voice I heard, so charm-ing and so won - drous. I've heard the King, and hear - ing am made whole.

WORDS: Grant C. Tullar, 1953
MUSIC: Donald P. Hustad, 1953

HIGHLANDS
9.12.9.12 Ref.

Come, We That Love the Lord 290

Let the children of Zion be joyful in their King. Psa. 149:2

1. Come, we that love the Lord, And let our joys be known,
2. Let those re - fuse to sing Who nev - er knew our God,
3. The hill of Zi - on yields A thou - sand sa - cred sweets
4. Then let our songs a - bound, And ev - ery tear be dry;
Join in a song with sweet ac - cord, Join in a song with sweet ac - cord
But chil - dren of the heav'n - ly King, But chil - dren of the heav'n - ly King
Be - fore we reach the heav'n - ly fields, Be - fore we reach the heav'n - ly fields
We're march-ing thro' Im-manuel's ground, We're march - ing thro' Im-manuel's ground
And thus sur - round the throne, And thus sur - round the throne.
May speak their joys a - broad, May speak their joys a - broad.
Or walk the gold - en streets, Or walk the gold - en streets.
To fair - er worlds on high, To fair - er worlds on high.
Refrain
We're march - ing to Zi - on, Beau - ti - ful, beau - ti - ful Zi - on;
We're march - ing on to Zi - on,
We're march - ing up - ward to Zi - on, The beau - ti - ful cit - y of God.

WORDS: Isaac Watts, 1707; refrain, Robert Lowry, 1867
MUSIC: Robert Lowry, 1867

MARCHING TO ZION
6.6.8.8.6.6 Ref.

291 He Giveth More Grace

God is able to make all grace abound toward you . . . II Cor. 9:8

1. He giv-eth more grace when the bur-dens grow great-er; He send-eth more strength when the la-bors in-crease. To add-ed af-flic-tion He add-eth His mer-cy; To mul-ti-plied tri-als, His mul-ti-plied peace.
2. When we have ex-haust-ed our store of en-dur-ance, When our strength has failed ere the day is half done, When we reach the end of our hoard-ed re-sourc-es, Our Fa-ther's full giv-ing is on-ly be-gun.
Refrain
His love has no lim-it; His grace has no meas-ure; His pow'r has no bound-a-ry known un-to men. For out of His in-fi-nite

rich-es in Je-sus, He giv-eth, and giv-eth, and giv-eth a-gain!

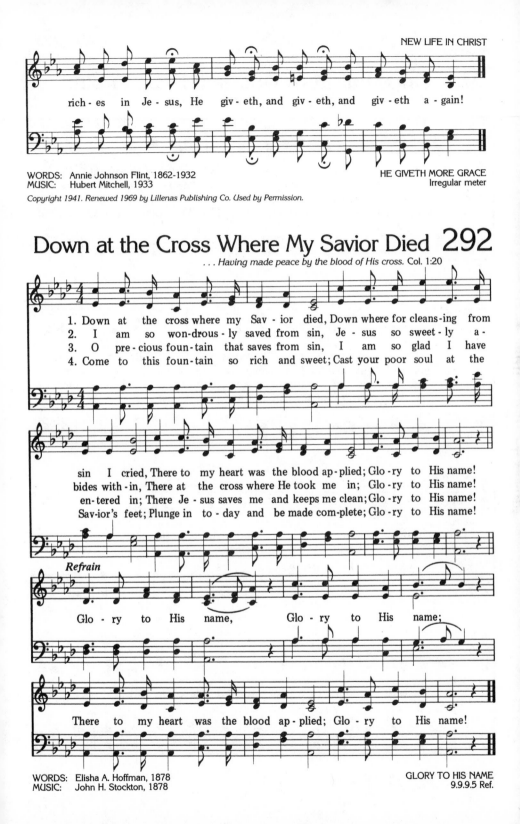

WORDS: Annie Johnson Flint, 1862-1932
MUSIC: Hubert Mitchell, 1933

HE GIVETH MORE GRACE
Irregular meter

Down at the Cross Where My Savior Died 292

. . . Having made peace by the blood of His cross. Col. 1:20

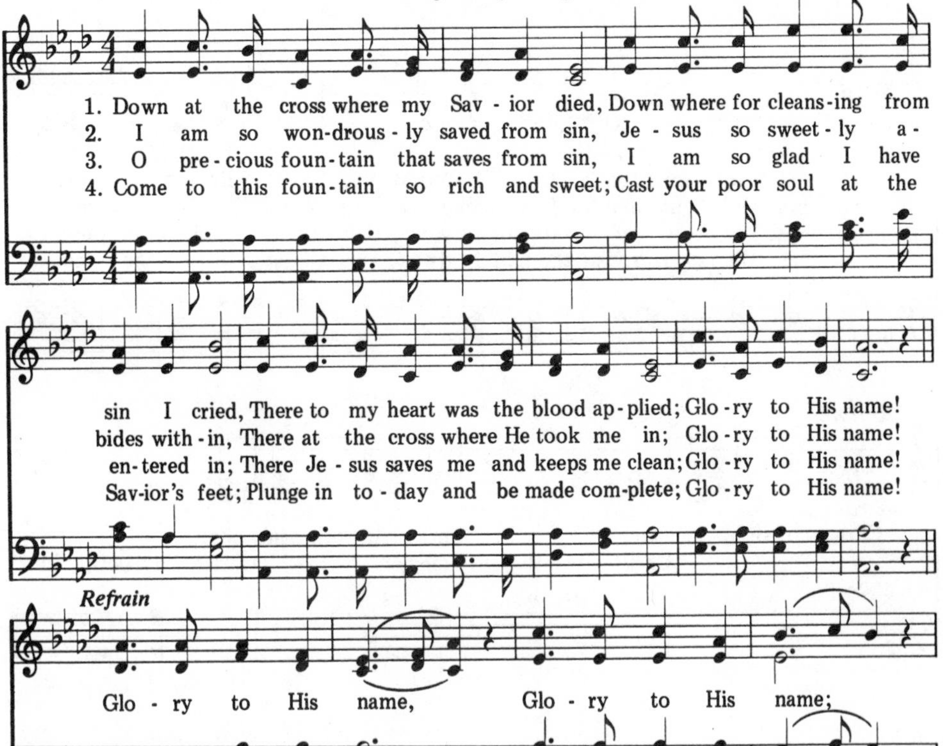

1. Down at the cross where my Sav-ior died, Down where for cleans-ing from sin I cried, There to my heart was the blood ap-plied; Glo-ry to His name!
2. I am so won-drous-ly saved from sin, Je-sus so sweet-ly a-bides with-in, There at the cross where He took me in; Glo-ry to His name!
3. O pre-cious foun-tain that saves from sin, I am so glad I have en-tered in; There Je-sus saves me and keeps me clean; Glo-ry to His name!
4. Come to this foun-tain so rich and sweet; Cast your poor soul at the Sav-ior's feet; Plunge in to-day and be made com-plete; Glo-ry to His name!

Refrain

Glo-ry to His name, Glo-ry to His name; There to my heart was the blood ap-plied; Glo-ry to His name!

WORDS: Elisha A. Hoffman, 1878
MUSIC: John H. Stockton, 1878

GLORY TO HIS NAME
9.9.9.5 Ref.

293 Once Far from God and Dead in Sin

Nevertheless I live; yet not I, but Christ liveth in me . . . Gal. 2:20

1. Once far from God and dead in sin, No light my heart could see,
2. As rays of light from yon - der sun The flow'rs of earth set free,
3. As lives the flow'r with - in the seed, As in the cone the tree,
4. With long - ing all my heart is filled That like Him I may be,
But in God's Word the light I found, Now Christ liv - eth in me.
So life and light and love came forth From Christ liv - ing in me.
So, praise the God of truth and grace, His Spir - it dwell-eth in me.
As on the won-drous thought I dwell, That Christ liv - eth in me.
Refrain
Christ liv - eth in me, Christ liv - eth in me;
Christ liv - eth in me, Christ liv - eth in
O what a sal - va - tion this—That Christ liv - eth in me.
me; O

WORDS: Daniel W. Whittle, 1891
MUSIC: James McGranahan, 1891

CHRIST LIVETH
C.M. Ref.

There's Not a Friend 294

There is a friend that sticketh closer than a brother. Prov. 18:24

1. There's not a friend like the low - ly Je - sus, No, not one! no, not one!
2. No friend like Him is so high and ho - ly, No, not one! no, not one!
3. There's not an hour that He is not near us, No, not one! no, not one!
4. Did ev - er saint find this friend for-sake him? No, not one! no, not one!
5. Was e'er a gift like the Sav - ior giv - en? No, not one! no, not one!
None else could heal all our soul's dis - eas - es, No, not one! no, not one!
And yet no friend is so meek and low - ly, No, not one! no, not one!
No night so dark but His love can cheer us, No, not one! no, not one!
Or sin - ner find that He would not take him? No, not one! no, not one!
Will He re - fuse us a home in heav - en? No, not one! no, not one!
Refrain
Je - sus knows all a - bout our strug-gles, He will guide till the day is done;
There's not a friend like the low - ly Je - sus, No, not one! no, not one!

WORDS: Johnson Oatman, Jr., c.1890
MUSIC: George C. Hugg, c.1890

NO, NOT ONE
10.6.10.6 Ref.

295 In the Stars His Handiwork I See

When I consider Thy heavens . . . what is man, that Thou art mindful of him? Psa. 8:3,4

Unison
1. In the stars His hand-i-work I see, On the wind He speaks in maj-es-ty,
2. I will cel - e- brate na-tiv - i - ty For it has a place in his-to-ry,
Though He ruleth o - ver land and sea, What is that to me?
Sure, He came to set His people free, What is that to
1
2
me? Till by faith I met Him face to face, And I felt the won-der of His grace,
Then I knew that He was more than just a God who did-n't care, who lived a-way out
there, And now He walks be-side me day by day, Ev-er watch-ing o'er me lest I stray,

Help-ing me to find that nar-row way, He's ev-ery-thing to me.

WORDS and MUSIC: Ralph Carmichael, 1964

HE'S EVERYTHING TO ME
Irregular meter

In Loving Kindness Jesus Came 296

He brought me up also out of an horrible pit . . . Psa. 40:2

1. In lov-ing kind-ness Je-sus came My soul in mer-cy to re-claim, And from the depths of sin and shame Thro' grace He lift-ed me.
2. He called me long be-fore I heard, Be-fore my sin-ful heart was stirred, But when I took Him at His word, For-giv'n He lift-ed me.
3. His brow was pierced with man-y a thorn, His hands by cru-el nails were torn, When from my guilt and grief, for-lorn, In love He lift-ed me.
4. Now on a high-er plane I dwell, And with my soul I know 'tis well; Yet how or why, I can-not tell, He should have lift-ed me.

(He lift-ed me.)

Refrain

From sink-ing sand He lift-ed me, With ten-der hand He lift-ed me, From shades of night to plains of light, O praise His name, He lift-ed me!

WORDS and MUSIC: Charles H. Gabriel, 1905

HE LIFTED ME
8.8.8.6 Ref.

297 Years I Spent in Vanity and Pride

And when they were come to . . . Calvary, there they crucified Him. Luke 23:33

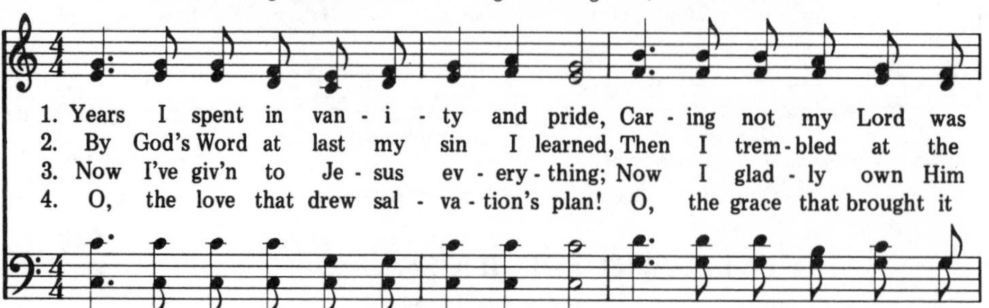
1. Years I spent in van - i - ty and pride, Car - ing not my Lord was
2. By God's Word at last my sin I learned, Then I trem - bled at the
3. Now I've giv'n to Je - sus ev - ery - thing; Now I glad - ly own Him
4. O, the love that drew sal - va - tion's plan! O, the grace that brought it

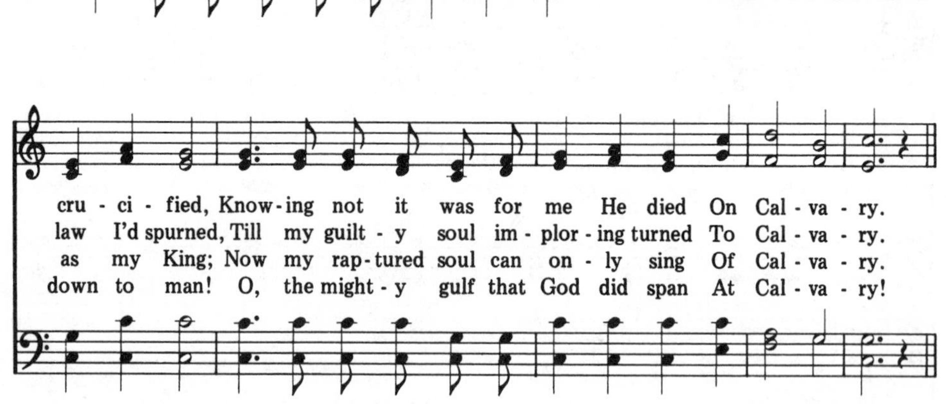
cru - ci - fied, Know - ing not it was for me He died On Cal - va - ry.
law I'd spurned, Till my guilt - y soul im - plor - ing turned To Cal - va - ry.
as my King; Now my rap - tured soul can on - ly sing Of Cal - va - ry.
down to man! O, the might - y gulf that God did span At Cal - va - ry!

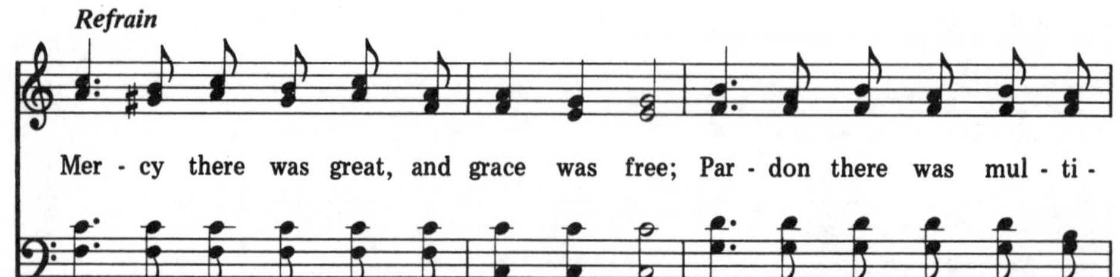
Refrain
Mer - cy there was great, and grace was free; Par - don there was mul - ti -

plied to me; There my bur - dened soul found lib - er - ty, At Cal - va - ry.

WORDS: William R. Newell, 1895
MUSIC: Daniel B. Towner, 1895

CALVARY
9.9.9.4 Ref.

In Tenderness He Sought Me 298

Rejoice with me; for I have found my sheep which was lost. Luke 15:6

1. In ten - der - ness He sought me, Wea - ry and sick with sin,
2. He washed the bleed - ing sin - wounds And poured in oil and wine;
3. He point - ed to the nail - prints, For me His blood was shed,
4. I'm sit - ting in His pres - ence, The sun - shine of His face,
5. So while the hours are pass - ing All now is per - fect rest;

And on His shoul - ders brought me Back to His fold a - gain. While
He whis - pered to as - sure me, "I've found thee, thou art Mine;" I
A mock - ing crown so thorn - y Was placed up - on His head: I
While with a - dor - ing won - der His bless - ings I re - trace: It
I'm wait - ing for the morn - ing, The bright - est and the best, When

an - gels in His pres - ence sang Un - til the courts of heav - en rang.
nev - er heard a sweet - er voice; It made my ach - ing heart re - joice!
won-dered what He saw in me To suf - fer such deep ag - o - ny.
seems as if e - ter - nal days Are far too short to sound His praise.
He will call us to His side, To be with Him, His spot - less bride.

Refrain

O the love that sought me! O the blood that bought me! O the grace that brought me to the fold, Won - drous grace that brought me to the fold!

WORDS: W. Spencer Walton, 1894
MUSIC: Adoniram J. Gordon, 1894

CLARENDON
7.6.7.6.8.8 Ref.

299 My Faith Has Found a Resting Place

While we were yet sinners, Christ died for us. Rom. 5:8

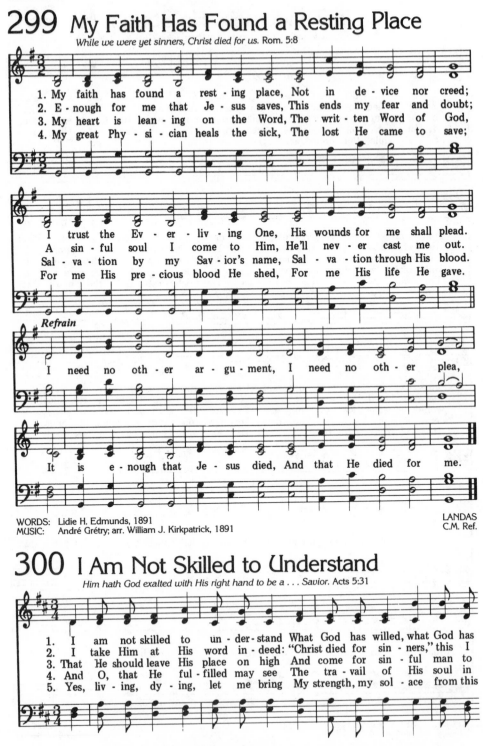

1. My faith has found a rest - ing place, Not in de - vice nor creed;
2. E - nough for me that Je - sus saves, This ends my fear and doubt;
3. My heart is lean - ing on the Word, The writ - ten Word of God,
4. My great Phy - si - cian heals the sick, The lost He came to save;

I trust the Ev - er - liv - ing One, His wounds for me shall plead.
A sin - ful soul I come to Him, He'll nev - er cast me out.
Sal - va - tion by my Sav - ior's name, Sal - va - tion through His blood.
For me His pre - cious blood He shed, For me His life He gave.

Refrain

I need no oth - er ar - gu - ment, I need no oth - er plea,
It is e - nough that Je - sus died, And that He died for me.

WORDS: Lidie H. Edmunds, 1891
MUSIC: André Grétry; arr. William J. Kirkpatrick, 1891

LANDAS
C.M. Ref.

300 I Am Not Skilled to Understand

Him hath God exalted with His right hand to be a . . . Savior. Acts 5:31

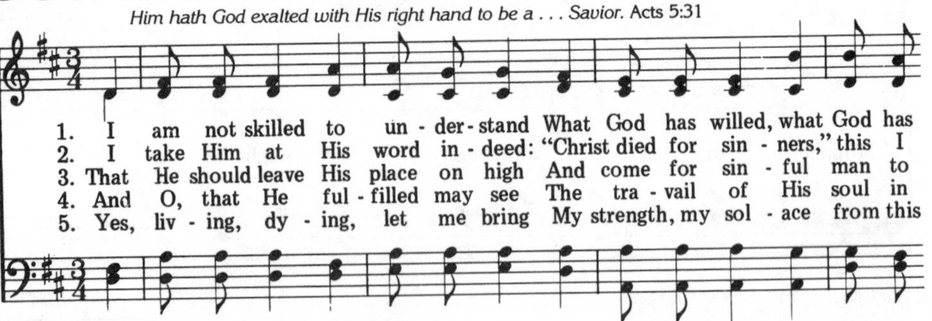

1. I am not skilled to un - der - stand What God has willed, what God has
2. I take Him at His word in - deed: "Christ died for sin - ners," this I
3. That He should leave His place on high And come for sin - ful man to
4. And O, that He ful - filled may see The tra - vail of His soul in
5. Yes, liv - ing, dy - ing, let me bring My strength, my sol - ace from this

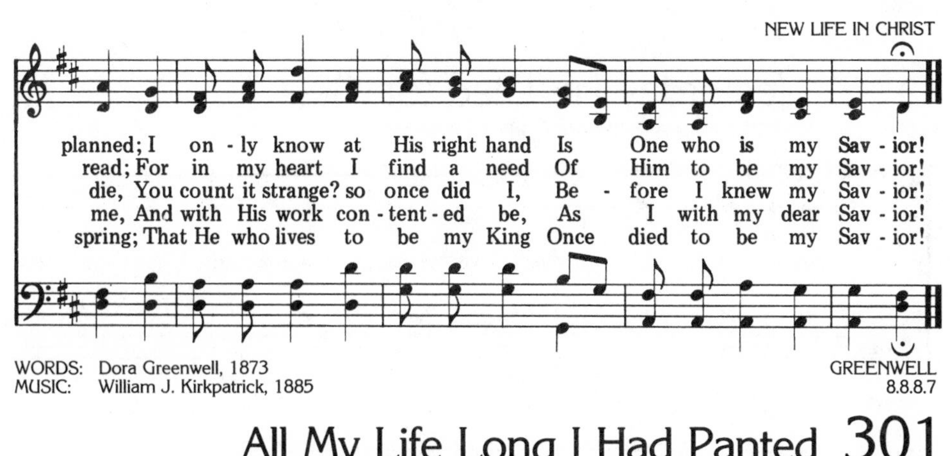
planned; I on - ly know at His right hand Is One who is my Sav - ior!
read; For in my heart I find a need Of Him to be my Sav - ior!
die, You count it strange? so once did I, Be - fore I knew my Sav - ior!
me, And with His work con - tent - ed be, As I with my dear Sav - ior!
spring; That He who lives to be my King Once died to be my Sav - ior!

WORDS: Dora Greenwell, 1873
MUSIC: William J. Kirkpatrick, 1885

GREENWELL
8.8.8.7

All My Life Long I Had Panted 301

He satisfieth the longing soul, and filleth the hungry soul with goodness. Psa. 107:9

1. All my life long I had pant - ed For a drink from some cool spring
2. Feed - ing on the husks a - round me Till my strength was al - most gone,
3. Poor I was, and sought for rich - es, Some-thing that would sat - is - fy;
4. Well of wa - ter, ev - er spring - ing, Bread of life, so rich and free,

That I hoped would quench the burn - ing Of the thirst I felt with - in.
Longed my soul for some-thing bet - ter, On - ly still to hun - ger on.
But the dust I gath-ered round me On - ly mocked my soul's sad cry.
Un - told wealth that nev - er fail - eth, My Re - deem - er is to me.

Refrain

Hal - le - lu - jah! I have found Him—Whom my soul so long has craved!
Je - sus sat - is - fies my long - ings; Thro' His blood I now am saved.

WORDS: Clara T. Williams, 1881
MUSIC: Ralph E. Hudson, 1881

SATISFIED
8.7.8.7 Ref.

302 Yesterday He Died for Me

Christ died for our sins according to the scriptures . . . I Cor. 15:3

Unison

Yes-ter-day He died for me, yes-ter-day, yes-ter-day, Yes-ter-day He died for me, yes-ter-day, Yes-ter-day He died for me, died for me— This is his-to-ry. To-day He lives for me, to-day, to-day, To-day He lives for me, to-day, To-day He lives for me, lives for me— This is vic-to-ry.

To - mor-row He comes for me, He comes, He comes, To-mor-row He
comes for me, He comes, To - mor-row He comes for me, comes for me—
This is mys - ter - y. O friend, do you know Him? know Him?
know Him? O friend, do you know Him? know Him?
O friend, do you know Him, do you know Him? Je - sus Christ the
Lord. Je - sus Christ the Lord. Je - sus Christ the Lord.

WORDS: Jack Wyrtzen, 1966
MUSIC: Don Wyrtzen, 1966

YESTERDAY, TODAY AND TOMORROW
Irregular meter

303 I Love to Tell the Story

And they sang a new song saying, Thou art worthy . . . Rev. 5:9

1. I love to tell the sto - ry Of un - seen things a -
2. I love to tell the sto - ry, More won - der - ful it
3. I love to tell the sto - ry, 'Tis pleas - ant to re -
4. I love to tell the sto - ry, For those who know it
bove, Of Je - sus and His glo - ry, Of Je - sus and His
seems Than all the gold - en fan - cies Of all our gold - en
peat What seems, each time I tell it, More won - der - ful - ly
best Seem hun - ger - ing and thirst - ing To hear it like the
love. I love to tell the sto - ry Be - cause I know 'tis
dreams. I love to tell the sto - ry, It did so much for
sweet. I love to tell the sto - ry, For some have nev - er
rest. And when, in scenes of glo - ry, I sing the new, new
true; It sat - is - fies my long - ings As noth - ing else can do.
me; And that is just the rea - son I tell it now to thee.
heard The mes - sage of sal - va - tion From God's own Ho - ly Word.
song, 'Twill be the old, old sto - ry That I have loved so long.
Refrain
I love to tell the sto - ry, 'Twill be my theme in glo - ry,

To tell the old, old sto - ry Of Je - sus and His love.

WORDS: A. Catherine Hankey, 1866
MUSIC: William G. Fischer, 1869

HANKEY
7.6.7.6 D. Ref.

Jesus My Lord Will Love Me Forever 304

Whether we live, therefore, or die, we are the Lord's. Rom. 14:8

1. Je - sus my Lord will love me for - ev - er, From Him no pow'r of e - vil can sev - er, He gave His life to ran - som my soul, Now I be - long to Him;
2. Once I was lost in sin's deg - ra - da - tion, Je - sus came down to bring me sal - va - tion, Lift - ed me up from sor - row and shame, Now I be - long to Him;
3. Joy floods my soul for Je - sus has saved me, Freed me from sin that long had en - slaved me, His pre - cious blood He gave to re - deem, Now I be - long to Him;

Refrain

Now I be - long to Je - sus, Je - sus be - longs to me, Not for the years of time a - lone, But for e - ter - ni - ty.

WORDS and MUSIC: Norman J. Clayton, 1943

ELLSWORTH
10.10.9.6 Ref.

305 Saved! Saved! Saved!

For there is none other name under heaven . . . whereby we must be saved. Acts 4:12

Unison
1. Saved! saved! saved! my sins are all for - giv'n; Christ is mine! I'm on my way to heav'n; Once a guilt - y sin - ner, lost, un - done, Now a child of God, saved thro' His Son.
2. Saved! saved! saved! by grace and grace a - lone; O, what won - drous love to me was shown, In my stead Christ Je - sus bled and died, Bore my sins, for me was cru - ci - fied.
3. Saved! saved! saved! O, joy be - yond com - pare! Christ my life and I His con - stant care; Yield - ing all and trust - ing Him a - lone, Liv - ing now each mo-ment as His own.
Refrain - parts
Saved! I'm saved thro' Christ, my all in all; Saved! I'm saved, what-
my all in all;
ev - er may be - fall, He died up - on the cross for me, He bore the aw - ful

pen - al - ty; And now I'm saved e - ter - nal - ly—I'm saved! saved! saved!

WORDS: Oswald J. Smith, 1918
MUSIC: Roger M. Hickman, 1918

HICKMAN
9.9.9.9 Ref.

Something Beautiful 306

If any man be in Christ, he is a new creature. II Cor. 5:17

Some-thing beau-ti-ful, some-thing good; All my con - fu - sion

He un - der - stood; All I had to of - fer Him was bro - ken - ness and

strife, But He made some - thing beau - ti - ful of my life.

WORDS: Gloria Gaither, 1971
MUSIC: William J. Gaither, 1971

SOMETHING BEAUTIFUL
Irregular meter

307 There Is a Name I Love to Hear

We love Him, because He first loved us. I John 4:19

1. There is a name I love to hear, I love to sing its worth; It sounds like mu - sic in my ear, The sweet-est name on earth.
2. It tells me of a Sav - ior's love, Who died to set me free; It tells me of His pre - cious blood, The sin - ner's per - fect plea.
3. It tells me what my Fa - ther hath In store for ev - ery day, And though I tread a dark - some path, Yields sun-shine all the way.
4. It tells of One whose lov - ing heart Can feel my deep - est woe, Who in each sor - row bears a part, That none can bear be - low.

Refrain

O how I love Je - sus, O, how I love Je - sus,
O, how I love Je - sus, Be - cause He first loved me!

WORDS: Frederick Whitfield, 1855
MUSIC: Traditional American melody

O, HOW I LOVE JESUS
C.M. Ref.

308 Born by the Holy Spirit's Breath

. . . That which is born of the Spirit is spirit. John 3:6

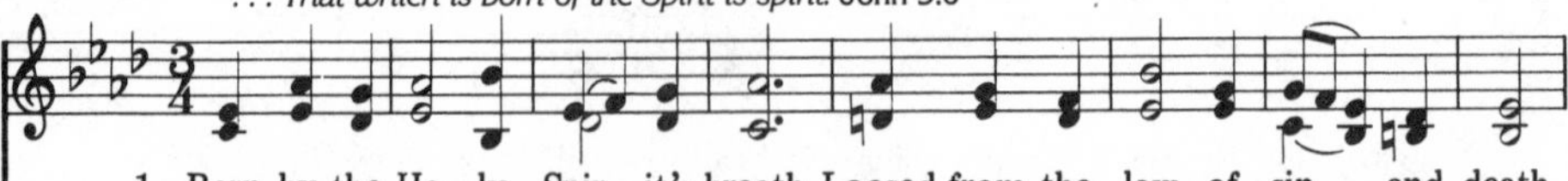

1. Born by the Ho - ly Spir - it's breath, Loosed from the law of sin and death,
2. In us the Spir - it makes His home That we in Him may o - ver - come;
3. Sons, then, and heirs of God most high, We by His Spir - it "Fa - ther" cry;
4. One is His love, His pur - pose one; To form the like-ness of His Son
5. Nor death nor life, nor powers un - seen, Nor height nor depth can come be - tween;

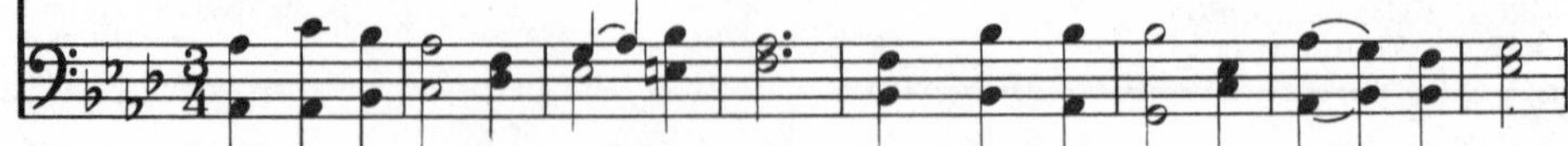

NEW LIFE IN CHRIST
Now cleared in Christ from ev - ery claim, No judg-ment stands a - gainst our name.
Christ's ris - en life, in all its powers, Its all - pre - vail - ing strength, is ours.
That Spir - it with our spir - it shares To frame and breathe our word - less prayers.
In all who, called and just - i - fied, Shall reign in glo - ry at His side.
We know through per - il, pain and sword, The love of God in Christ our Lord.
WORDS: Timothy Dudley-Smith, 1972
MUSIC: William Gardiner's Sacred Melodies, 1815
GERMANY
L.M.
Words Copyright © 1984 by Hope Publishing Company, Carol Stream, IL 60188. All Rights Reserved.
Talk About a Soul 309
I will declare what He hath done for my soul. Psa. 66:16
Unison
1. Talk a - bout a soul that's been con - vert - ed, Here's one, here's one,
2. Talk a - bout a soul that loves his Je - sus, Here's one, here's one,
Talk a - bout a soul that's been con - vert - ed, Here's one, here's one,
Talk a - bout a soul that loves his Je - sus, Here's one, here's one,
Ev - er since I heard the Gos - pel sto - ry, I've been walk-ing up the
In old Sa - tan's snares I once was fall - ing Till I heard the voice of
path to glo - ry, Talk a - bout a soul that's been con-vert-ed, Here's one.
my Lord call - ing, Talk a - bout a soul that's been con-vert-ed, Here's one.
WORDS and MUSIC: Traditional Spiritual; adapt. John F. Wilson, 1966
HERE'S ONE
Irregular meter

310 Jesus Is All the World to Me

I have called you friends. John 15:15

1. Je - sus is all the world to me, My life, my joy, my all;
2. Je - sus is all the world to me, My Friend in tri - als sore;
3. Je - sus is all the world to me, And true to Him I'll be;
4. Je - sus is all the world to me, I want no bet - ter friend;
He is my strength from day to day, With - out Him I would fall.
I go to Him for bless - ings, and He gives them o'er and o'er.
O, how could I this Friend de - ny, When He's so true to me?
I trust Him now, I'll trust Him when Life's fleet - ing days shall end.
When I am sad to Him I go, No oth - er one can cheer me so;
He sends the sun-shine and the rain, He sends the har-vest's gold - en grain;
Fol - low - ing Him I know I'm right, He watch - es o'er me day and night;
Beau - ti - ful life with such a Friend; Beau - ti - ful life that has no end;
When I am sad He makes me glad, He's my Friend.
Sun - shine and rain, har - vest of grain, He's my Friend.
Fol - low - ing Him by day and night, He's my Friend.
E - ter - nal life, e - ter - nal joy, He's my Friend.

WORDS and MUSIC: Will L. Thompson, 1904

ELIZABETH
Irregular meter

My Hope Is in the Lord 311

Christ in you, the hope of glory. Col. 1:27

Refrain
1. My hope is in the Lord Who gave Him - self for me,
And paid the price of all my sin at Cal - va - ry.
2. No mer - it of my own His an - ger to sup - press,
My on - ly hope is found in Je - sus' right - eous - ness.
3. And now for me He stands Be - fore the Fa - ther's throne,
He shows His wound - ed hands, and names me as His own.
4. His grace has planned it all, 'Tis mine but to be - lieve,
And rec - og - nize His work of love and Christ re - ceive.
For me He died, For me He lives,
For me He died, For me He lives,
And ev - er - last - ing life and light He free - ly gives.

WORDS and MUSIC: Norman J. Clayton, 1945

WAKEFIELD
6.6.6.6 Ref.

Hymns of The Christian Life

Simply Trusting Every Day 312

Commit thy way unto the Lord; trust also in Him . . . Psa. 37:5

1. Sim - ply trust - ing ev - ery day, Trust - ing through a storm - y way;
2. Bright - ly doth His Spir - it shine In - to this poor heart of mine;
3. Sing - ing if my way is clear, Pray - ing if the path be drear;
4. Trust - ing Him while life shall last, Trust - ing Him till earth be past;
E - ven when my faith is small, Trust - ing Je - sus—that is all.
While He leads I can - not fall, Trust - ing Je - sus—that is all.
If in dan - ger, for Him call, Trust - ing Je - sus—that is all.
Till with - in the jas - per wall, Trust - ing Je - sus—that is all.
Refrain
Trust - ing as the mo - ments fly, Trust - ing as the days go by;
Trust - ing Him what - e'er be - fall, Trust - ing Je - sus—that is all.

WORDS: Edgar P. Stites, 1876
MUSIC: Ira D. Sankey, 1876

TRUSTING JESUS
7.7.7.7 Ref.

313 Anywhere with Jesus I Can Safely Go

Lo, I am with you always . . . Matt. 28:20

1. An - y - where with Je - sus I can safe - ly go; An - y - where He leads me in this world be - low; An - y - where with - out Him dear - est joys would fade; An - y - where with Je - sus I am not a - fraid.
2. An - y - where with Je - sus I am not a - lone, Oth - er friends may fail me, He is still my own; Though His hand may lead me o - ver drear - y ways, An - y - where with Je - sus is a house of praise.
3. An - y - where with Je - sus o - ver land and sea, Tell - ing souls in dark - ness of sal - va - tion free; Read - y as He sum - mons me to go or stay, An - y - where with Je - sus when He points the way.
Refrain
An - y - where! an - y - where! Fear I can - not know; An - y - where with Je - sus I can safe - ly go.

WORDS: St. 1, 2, Jessie B. Pounds, 1887; St. 3, Helen C. Dixon, c.1915
MUSIC: Daniel B. Towner, 1887

SECURITY
11.11.11.11 Ref.

Blessed Assurance, Jesus Is Mine 314

I will sing praises unto my God while I have my being. Psa. 146:2

1. Bless - ed as - sur - ance, Je - sus is mine! O, what a fore - taste of glo - ry di - vine! Heir of sal - va - tion, pur - chase of God, Born of His Spir - it, washed in His blood.
2. Per - fect sub - mis - sion, per - fect de - light, Vi - sions of rap - ture now burst on my sight; An - gels de - scend - ing, bring from a - bove Ech - oes of mer - cy, whis - pers of love.
3. Per - fect sub - mis - sion, all is at rest, I in my Sav - ior am hap - py and blest; Watch - ing and wait - ing, look - ing a - bove, Filled with His good - ness, lost in His love.
Refrain
This is my sto - ry, this is my song, Prais - ing my Sav - ior all the day long; This is my sto - ry, this is my song, Prais - ing my Sav - ior all the day long.

WORDS: Fanny J. Crosby, 1873
MUSIC: Phoebe P. Knapp, 1873

ASSURANCE
9.10.9.9 Ref.

315 Dying with Jesus, by Death Reckoned

Who are kept by the power of God through faith unto salvation. I Pet. 1:5

1. Dy - ing with Je - sus, by death reck-oned mine; Liv - ing with Je - sus a
2. Nev - er a tri - al that He is not there, Nev - er a bur - den that
3. Nev - er a heart-ache and nev - er a groan, Nev - er a tear-drop and
4. Nev - er a weak-ness that He doth not feel, Nev - er a sick-ness that
new life di - vine; Look-ing to Je - sus till glo - ry doth shine, Mo-ment by
He doth not bear, Nev - er a sor - row that He doth not share, Mo-ment by
nev - er a moan; Nev - er a dan - ger, but there on the throne, Mo-ment by
He can - not heal; Mo-ment by mo-ment, in woe or in weal, Je - sus my
mo-ment, O Lord, I am Thine.
mo-ment, I'm un - der His care.
mo-ment, He thinks of His own.
Sav - ior a - bides with me still.
Refrain
Mo-ment by mo-ment I'm kept in His love;
Mo - ment by mo - ment I've life from a - bove; Look-ing to Je - sus till
glo - ry doth shine; Mo - ment by mo - ment, O Lord, I am Thine.

WORDS: Daniel W. Whittle, 1893
MUSIC: May W. Moody, 1893

WHITTLE
10.10.10.10 Ref.

Trust in the Lord with All Your Heart 316

Trust in the Lord with all thine heart . . . Prov. 3:5

1. Trust in the Lord with all your heart, This is God's gra-cious com-mand;
2. Trust in the Lord who rul-eth all, See-eth all things as they are,
3. Trust in the Lord—His eye will guide All thro' your path-way a-head,
In all your ways ac-knowl-edge Him, So shall you dwell in the land.
Be it a bird-ling in its nest, Or yon-der ut-ter-most star.
He hath re-deemed and He will keep, Trust Him and be not a-fraid.
Refrain
Trust in the Lord, O trou-bled soul, Rest in the arms of His care; What-
care, of His care;
ev-er your lot, it mat-ter-eth not, For noth-ing can trou-ble you there;
Trust in the Lord, O trou-bled soul, Noth-ing can trou-ble you there.

WORDS: Thomas O. Chisholm, 1937
MUSIC: Wendell P. Loveless, 1937

LOVELESS
8.7.8.7 Ref.

317 My Father Is Rich in Houses and Lands

We are the children of God; and if children, then heirs. Rom. 8:16,17

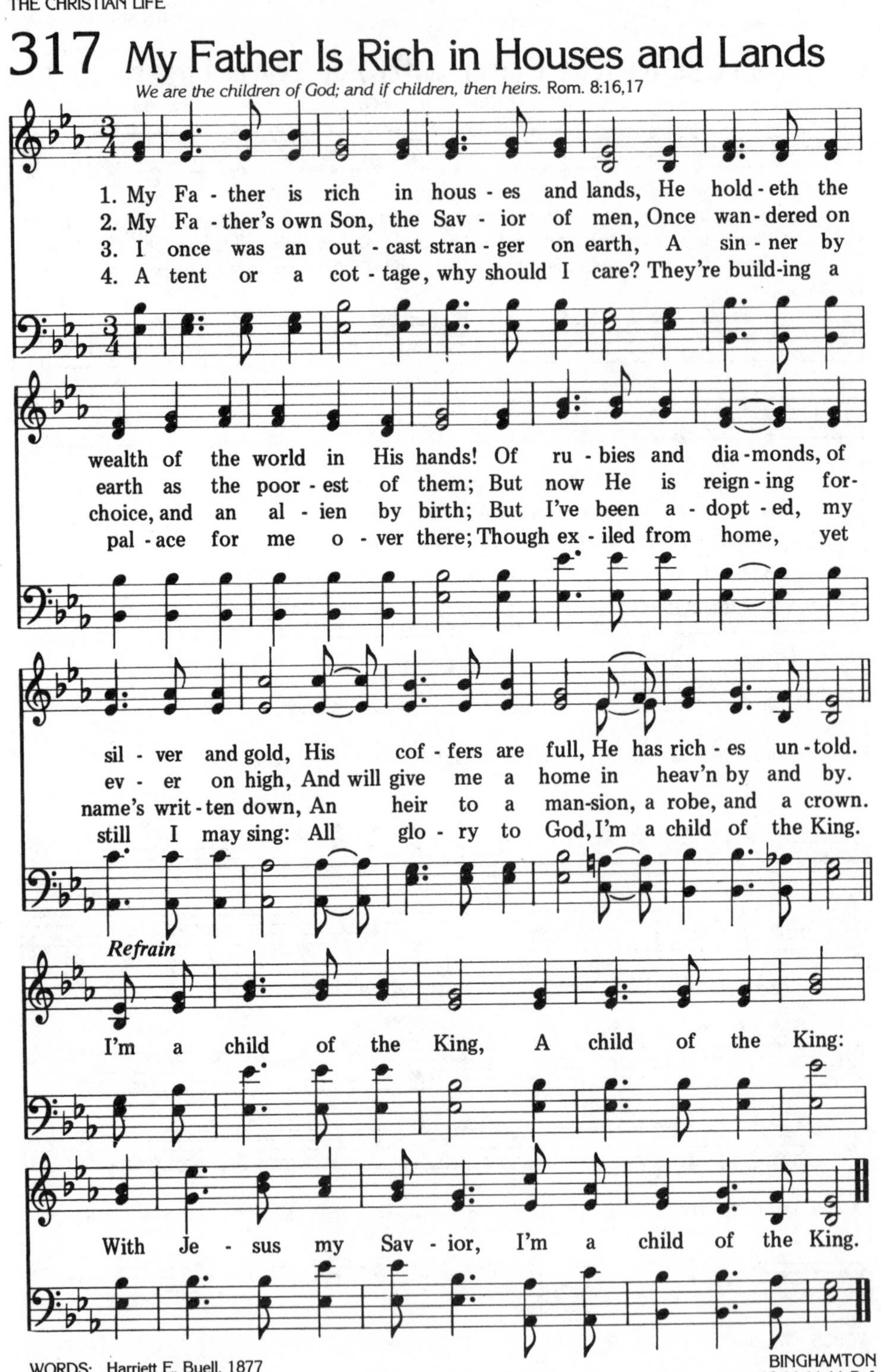
1. My Fa - ther is rich in hous - es and lands, He hold - eth the
2. My Fa - ther's own Son, the Sav - ior of men, Once wan - dered on
3. I once was an out - cast stran - ger on earth, A sin - ner by
4. A tent or a cot - tage, why should I care? They're build - ing a
wealth of the world in His hands! Of ru - bies and dia - monds, of
earth as the poor - est of them; But now He is reign - ing for-
choice, and an al - ien by birth; But I've been a - dopt - ed, my
pal - ace for me o - ver there; Though ex - iled from home, yet
sil - ver and gold, His cof - fers are full, He has rich - es un - told.
ev - er on high, And will give me a home in heav'n by and by.
name's writ - ten down, An heir to a man - sion, a robe, and a crown.
still I may sing: All glo - ry to God, I'm a child of the King.
Refrain
I'm a child of the King, A child of the King:
With Je - sus my Sav - ior, I'm a child of the King.

WORDS: Harriett E. Buell, 1877
MUSIC: John B. Sumner, 1877

BINGHAMTON
10.11.11.11 Ref.

Be Still, My Soul 318

Be still, and know that I am God. Psa. 46:10

1. Be still, my soul! the Lord is on thy side: Bear pa-tient-ly the cross of grief or pain; Leave to thy God to or-der and pro-vide; In ev-ery change He faith-ful will re-main. Be still, my soul! thy best, thy heav'n-ly Friend Thro' thorn-y ways leads to a joy-ful end.
2. Be still, my soul! thy God doth un-der-take To guide the fu-ture as He has the past. Thy hope, thy con-fi-dence let noth-ing shake; All now mys-te-rious shall be bright at last. Be still, my soul! the waves and winds still know His voice who ruled them while He dwelt be-low.
3. Be still, my soul! the hour is has-t'ning on When we shall be for-ev-er with the Lord, When dis-ap-point-ment, grief and fear are gone, Sor-row for-got, love's pur-est joys re-stored. Be still, my soul! when change and tears are past, All safe and bless-ed we shall meet at last.

WORDS: Katharina A. von Schlegel, 1752; tr. Jane L. Borthwick, 1855
MUSIC: Jean Sibelius, 1899

FINLANDIA
10.10.10.10.10.10

319 Savior, Like a Shepherd Lead Us

When He putteth forth His own sheep, He goeth before them. John 10:4

1. Sav - ior, like a shep-herd lead us, Much we need Thy ten- der care;
2. We are Thine, do Thou be-friend us, Be the guard-ian of our way;
3. Thou hast prom-ised to re - ceive us, Poor and sin - ful though we be;
4. Ear - ly let us seek Thy fa - vor, Ear - ly let us do Thy will;
In Thy pleas- ant- pas-tures feed us, For our use Thy folds pre-pare:
Keep Thy flock, from sin de - fend us, Seek us when we go a - stray:
Thou hast mer - cy to re - lieve us, Grace to cleanse, and pow'r to free:
Bless - ed Lord and on - ly Sav - ior, With Thy love our bos - oms fill:
Bless - ed Je - sus, bless - ed Je - sus, Thou hast bought us, Thine we are;
Bless - ed Je - sus, bless - ed Je - sus, Hear, O hear us when we pray;
Bless - ed Je - sus, bless - ed Je - sus, Ear - ly let us turn to Thee;
Bless - ed Je - sus, bless - ed Je - sus, Thou hast loved us, love us still;
Bless - ed Je - sus, bless - ed Je - sus, Thou hast bought us, Thine we are.
Bless - ed Je - sus, bless - ed Je - sus, Hear, O hear us when we pray.
Bless - ed Je - sus, bless - ed Je - sus, Ear - ly let us turn to Thee.
Bless - ed Je - sus, bless - ed Je - sus, Thou hast loved us, love us still.

WORDS: *Hymns for the Young,* 1836; attr. Dorothy A. Thrupp
MUSIC: William B. Bradbury, 1859

BRADBURY
8.7.8.7 D.

Under His Wings I Am Safely Abiding 320

Under His wings shalt thou trust. Psa. 91:4

1. Un - der His wings I am safe - ly a - bid - ing; Though the night deep - ens and tem - pests are wild, Still I can trust Him— I know He will keep me; He has re-deemed me and I am His child.
2. Un - der His wings, what a ref - uge in sor - row! How the heart yearn - ing - ly turns to His rest! Oft - en when earth has no balm for my heal - ing, There I find com-fort and there I am blest.
3. Un - der His wings, O what pre-cious en - joy-ment! There will I hide till life's tri - als are o'er; Shel-tered, pro-tect - ed, no e - vil can harm me; Rest-ing in Je - sus I'm safe ev - er-more.
Refrain
Un-der His wings, un-der His wings, Who from His love can sev - er? Un-der His wings my soul shall a - bide, Safe-ly a - bide for - ev - er.

WORDS: William O. Cushing, c.1896
MUSIC: Ira D. Sankey, 1896

HINGHAM
11.10.11.10 Ref.

321 When We Walk with the Lord

If ye continue in My word, then are ye My disciples indeed. John 8:31

1. When we walk with the Lord in the light of His Word, What a glo - ry He sheds on our way! While we do His good will He a - bides with us still, And with all who will trust and o - bey.
2. Not a shad - ow can rise, not a cloud in the skies, But His smile quick - ly drives it a - way; Not a doubt nor a fear, not a sigh nor a tear, Can a - bide while we trust and o - bey.
3. Not a bur - den we bear, not a sor - row we share, But our toil He doth rich - ly re - pay; Not a grief nor a loss, not a frown nor a cross, But is blest if we trust and o - bey.
4. But we nev - er can prove the de - lights of His love Un - til all on the al - tar we lay; For the fa - vor He shows and the joy He be - stows Are for them who will trust and o - bey.
5. Then in fel - low - ship sweet we will sit at His feet, Or we'll walk by His side in the way; What He says we will do, where He sends we will go— Nev - er fear, on - ly trust and o - bey.
Refrain
Trust and o - bey, for there's no oth - er way To be hap - py in Je - sus, But to trust and o - bey.

WORDS: John H. Sammis, 1887
MUSIC: Daniel B. Towner, 1887

TRUST AND OBEY
6.6.9 D. Ref.

My Hope Is Built on Nothing Less 322

Other foundation can no man lay than that is laid, which is Jesus Christ. I Cor. 3:11

1. My hope is built on noth-ing less Than Je - sus' blood and right-eous-ness;
2. When dark-ness veils His love - ly face, I rest on His un-chang-ing grace;
3. His oath, His cov - e - nant, His blood Sup - port me in the whelm-ing flood;
4. When He shall come with trum - pet sound, O may I then in Him be found;
I dare not trust the sweet-est frame, But whol - ly lean on Je - sus' name.
In ev - ery high and storm - y gale, My an - chor holds with - in the veil.
When all a - round my soul gives way He then is all my hope and stay.
Dressed in His right - eous - ness a - lone, Fault - less to stand be - fore the throne.
Refrain
On Christ the sol - id Rock I stand; All oth - er ground
is sink - ing sand, All oth - er ground is sink - ing sand.

WORDS: Edward Mote, 1834
MUSIC: William B. Bradbury, 1863

SOLID ROCK
L.M. Ref.

323 In Heavenly Love Abiding

If ye keep My commandments, ye shall abide in My love. John 15:10

1. In heav'n - ly love a - bid - ing, No change my heart shall fear;
2. Wher - ev - er He may guide me No want shall turn me back;
3. Green pas - tures are be - fore me Which yet I have not seen;

And safe is such con - fid - ing, For noth - ing chang - es here.
My Shep - herd is be - side me And noth - ing can I lack.
Bright skies will soon be o'er me Where dark - est clouds have been.

The storm may roar with - out me, My heart may low be laid;
His wis - dom ev - er wak - eth, His sight is nev - er dim;
My hope I can - not meas - ure, My path to life is free;

But God is round a - bout me, And can I be dis - mayed?
He knows the way He tak - eth, And I will walk with Him.
My Sav - ior has my treas - ure, And He will walk with me. A-men.

WORDS: Anna L. Waring, 1850
MUSIC: Traditional Finnish melody; arr. David Evans, 1927

NYLAND
7.6.7.6 D.

The Lord's Our Rock, in Him We Hide 324

A man shall be . . . like the shadow of a great rock in a weary land. Isa. 32:2

1. The Lord's our rock, in Him we hide, A shel - ter in the time of storm;
2. A shade by day, de-fense by night, A shel - ter in the time of storm;
3. The rag - ing storms may round us beat, A shel - ter in the time of storm;
4. O Rock di - vine, O Ref - uge dear, A shel - ter in the time of storm;
Se - cure what-ev - er ill be - tide, A shel - ter in the time of storm.
No fears a - larm, no foes af - fright, A shel - ter in the time of storm.
We'll nev - er leave our safe re - treat, A shel - ter in the time of storm.
Be Thou our help - er ev - er near, A shel - ter in the time of storm.
Refrain
O, Je - sus is a rock in a wea-ry land, A wea-ry land, a wea-ry land;
O, Je - sus is a rock in a wea-ry land, A shel-ter in the time of storm.

WORDS: Vernon J. Charlesworth, c.1880; adapt. Ira D. Sankey, 1885
MUSIC: Ira D. Sankey, 1885

SHELTER
L.M. Ref.

325 He's Got the Whole World in His Hands

In whose hand is the soul of every living thing . . . Job 12:10

Unison

1. He's got the whole world in His hands, He's got the whole world in His hands, He's got the whole world in His hands, He's got the whole world in His hands.
2. He's got the wind and the rain in His hands, He's got the wind and the rain in His hands, He's got the wind and the rain in His hands, He's got the whole world in His hands.
3. He's got the ti - ny lit - tle ba - by in His hands, He's got the ti - ny lit - tle ba - by in His hands, He's got the ti - ny lit - tle ba - by in His hands, He's got the whole world in His hands.
4. He's got you and me, broth-er, in His hands, He's got you and me, sis - ter, in His hands, He's got you and me, broth-er, in His hands, He's got the whole world in His hands.

Coda (after last stanza)

He's got the whole world in His hands.

WORDS and MUSIC: Traditional Spiritual

WHOLE WORLD
Irregular meter

326 O for a Faith That Will Not Shrink

Lord, I believe; help Thou my unbelief. Mark 9:24

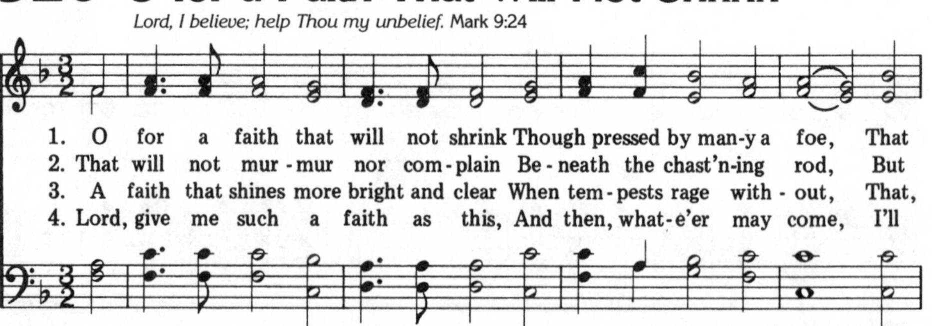
1. O for a faith that will not shrink Though pressed by man-y a foe, That
2. That will not mur - mur nor com - plain Be - neath the chast'n-ing rod, But
3. A faith that shines more bright and clear When tem - pests rage with - out, That,
4. Lord, give me such a faith as this, And then, what - e'er may come, I'll

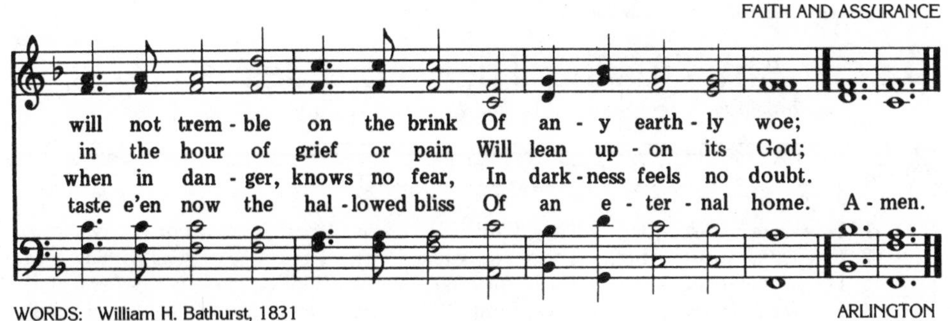
will not trem - ble on the brink Of an - y earth - ly woe;
in the hour of grief or pain Will lean up - on its God;
when in dan - ger, knows no fear, In dark - ness feels no doubt.
taste e'en now the hal - lowed bliss Of an e - ter - nal home. A - men.

WORDS: William H. Bathurst, 1831
MUSIC: Thomas A. Arne, 1762

ARLINGTON
C.M.

'Tis So Sweet to Trust in Jesus 327

That we should be to the praise of His glory, who first trusted in Christ. Eph. 1:12

1. 'Tis so sweet to trust in Je - sus, Just to take Him at His word;
2. O how sweet to trust in Je - sus, Just to trust His cleans - ing blood;
3. Yes, 'tis sweet to trust in Je - sus, Just from sin and self to cease;
4. I'm so glad I learned to trust Thee, Pre - cious Je - sus, Sav - ior, Friend;
Just to rest up - on His prom - ise; Just to know, "Thus saith the Lord."
Just in sim - ple faith to plunge me 'Neath the heal - ing, cleans - ing flood!
Just from Je - sus sim - ply tak - ing Life and rest, and joy and peace.
And I know that Thou art with me, Wilt be with me to the end.

Refrain
Je - sus, Je - sus, how I trust Him! How I've proved Him o'er and o'er!

Je - sus, Je - sus, pre - cious Je - sus! O for grace to trust Him more!

WORDS: Louisa M. R. Stead, 1882
MUSIC: William J. Kirkpatrick, 1882

TRUST IN JESUS
8.7.8.7 Ref.

328 I Am Trusting Thee, Lord Jesus

Trust ye in the Lord for ever . . . Isa. 26:4

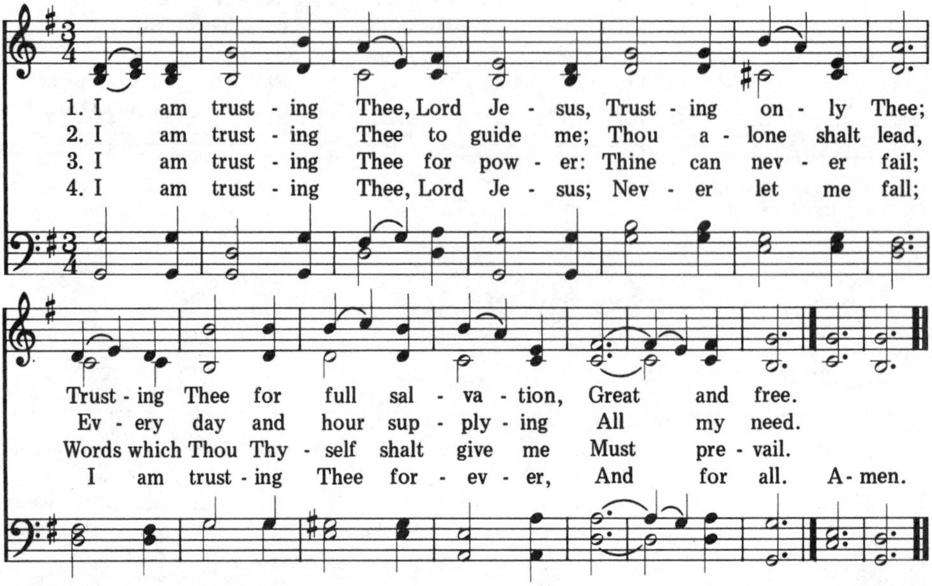

1. I am trust - ing Thee, Lord Je - sus, Trust - ing on - ly Thee;
2. I am trust - ing Thee to guide me; Thou a - lone shalt lead,
3. I am trust - ing Thee for pow - er: Thine can nev - er fail;
4. I am trust - ing Thee, Lord Je - sus; Nev - er let me fall;

Trust - ing Thee for full sal - va - tion, Great and free.
Ev - ery day and hour sup - ply - ing All my need.
Words which Thou Thy - self shalt give me Must pre - vail.
I am trust - ing Thee for - ev - er, And for all. A - men.

WORDS: Frances R. Havergal, 1874
MUSIC: Ethelbert W. Bullinger, 1874

BULLINGER
8.5.8.3

329 O Holy Savior, Friend Unseen

It is better to trust in the Lord than to put confidence in man. Psa. 118:8

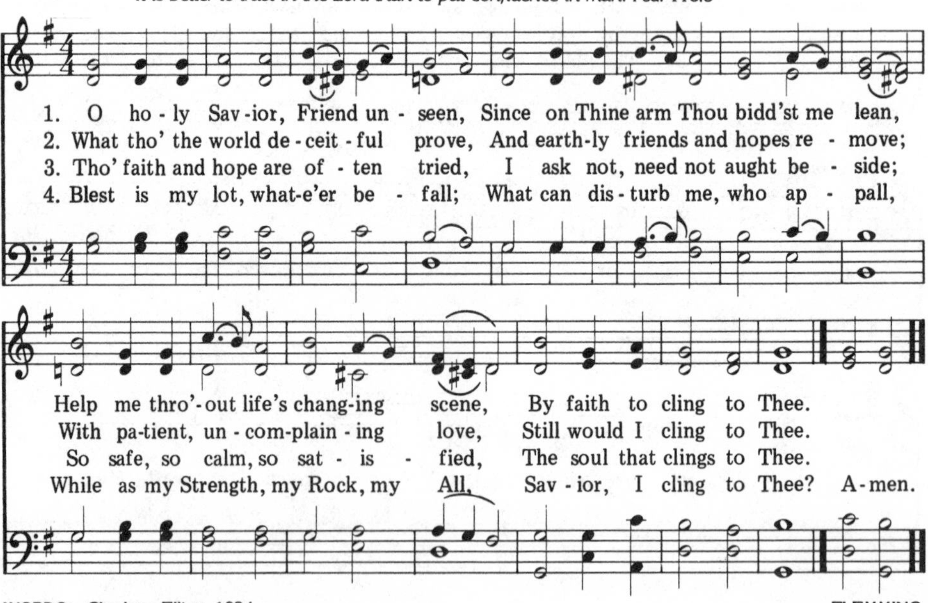
1. O ho - ly Sav - ior, Friend un - seen, Since on Thine arm Thou bidd'st me lean,
2. What tho' the world de - ceit - ful prove, And earth - ly friends and hopes re - move;
3. Tho' faith and hope are of - ten tried, I ask not, need not aught be - side;
4. Blest is my lot, what - e'er be - fall; What can dis - turb me, who ap - pall,
Help me thro' - out life's chang - ing scene, By faith to cling to Thee.
With pa - tient, un - com - plain - ing love, Still would I cling to Thee.
So safe, so calm, so sat - is - fied, The soul that clings to Thee.
While as my Strength, my Rock, my All, Sav - ior, I cling to Thee? A - men.

WORDS: Charlotte Elliott, 1834
MUSIC: Friedrich F. Flemming, 1811

FLEMMING
8.8.8.6

When Peace Like a River Attendeth 330

Bless the Lord, O my soul, and forget not all His benefits . . . Psa. 103:2

1. When peace like a riv - er at - tend - eth my way, When sor - rows like
2. Though Sa - tan should buf - fet, tho' tri - als should come, Let this blest as -
3. My sin— O, the bliss of this glo - ri - ous thought, My sin— not in
4. And, Lord, haste the day when the faith shall be sight, The clouds be rolled
sea - bil - lows roll; What - ev - er my lot, Thou hast taught me to say,
sur - ance con - trol, That Christ has re - gard - ed my help - less es - tate,
part but the whole, Is nailed to the cross and I bear it no more,
back as a scroll, The trump shall re - sound and the Lord shall de - scend,
Refrain
"It is well, it is well with my soul."
And hath shed His own blood for my soul.
Praise the Lord, praise the Lord, O my soul!
"E - ven so"— it is well with my soul.
It is well with my
It is well
soul, It is well, it is well with my soul.
with my soul,

WORDS: Horatio G. Spafford, 1873
MUSIC: Philip P. Bliss, 1876

VILLE DU HAVRE
11.8.11.9 Ref.

331 O What a Wonderful, Wonderful Day

If any man be in Christ, he is a new creature. II Cor. 5:17

1. O what a won - der - ful, won - der - ful day— Day I will
2. Born of the Spir - it with life from a - bove In - to God's
3. Now I've a hope that will sure - ly en - dure Aft - er the
nev - er for - get; Aft - er I'd wan - dered in dark - ness a - way,
fam - ily di - vine, Jus - ti - fied ful - ly thro' Cal - va - ry's love,
pass - ing of time; I have a fu - ture in heav - en for sure,
Je - sus my Sav - ior I met. O what a ten - der, com - pas - sion-ate friend—
O what a stand - ing is mine! And the trans - ac - tion so quick - ly was made
There in those man-sions sub - lime. And it's be - cause of that won - der - ful day
He met the need of my heart; Shad - ows dis - pel - ling, With
When as a sin - ner I came, Took of the of - fer Of
When at the cross I be - lieved; Rich - es e - ter - nal And

joy I am tell - ing, He made all the dark - ness de - part!
grace He did prof - fer— He saved me, O praise His dear name!
bless - ings su - per - nal From His pre - cious hand I re - ceived.
Refrain
Heav - en came down and glo - ry filled my soul, (filled my soul,)
When at the cross the Sav - ior made me whole; (made me whole;) My
sins were washed a - way And my night was turned to day—
Heav - en came down and glo - ry filled my soul! (filled my soul!)

WORDS and MUSIC: John W. Peterson, 1961

HEAVEN CAME DOWN
Irregular meter

332 Jesus, I Am Resting, Resting

Looking unto Jesus the author and finisher of our faith. Heb. 12:2

1. Je - sus, I am rest - ing, rest - ing In the joy of what Thou art;
2. O, how great Thy lov - ing kind - ness, Vast - er, broad - er than the sea!
3. Sim - ply trust - ing Thee, Lord Je - sus, I be - hold Thee as Thou art,
4. Ev - er lift Thy face up - on me As I work and wait for Thee;
(Ref.) Je - sus, I am rest - ing, rest - ing In the joy of what Thou art;
Fine
I am find - ing out the great - ness Of Thy lov - ing heart.
O, how mar - vel - ous Thy good - ness, Lav - ished all on me!
And Thy love, so pure, so change - less, Sat - is - fies my heart;
Rest - ing 'neath Thy smile, Lord Je - sus, Earth's dark shad - ows flee.
I am find - ing out the great - ness Of Thy lov - ing heart.
Thou hast bid me gaze up - on Thee, And Thy beau - ty fills my soul,
Yes, I rest in Thee, Be - lov - ed, Know what wealth of grace is Thine,
Sat - is - fies its deep - est long - ings, Meets, sup - plies its ev - ery need,
Bright - ness of my Fa - ther's glo - ry, Sun - shine of my Fa - ther's face,
D.C. Refrain
For by Thy trans - form - ing pow - er, Thou hast made me whole.
Know Thy cer - tain - ty of prom - ise, And have made it mine.
Com - pass - eth me round with bless - ings: Thine is love in - deed!
Keep me ev - er trust - ing, rest - ing, Fill me with Thy grace.

WORDS: Jean S. Pigott, 1876
MUSIC: James Mountain, 1876

TRANQUILLITY
8.7.8.5 D. Ref.

Loved with Everlasting Love 333

I am persuaded that (nothing) shall be able to separate us from the love of God. Rom. 8:38,39

1. Loved with ev - er - last - ing love, Led by grace that love to know;
2. Heav'n a - bove is soft - er blue, Earth a - round is sweet - er green!
3. Things that once were wild a - larms Can - not now dis - turb my rest;
4. His for - ev - er, on - ly His; Who the Lord and me shall part?

Gra - cious Spir - it from a - bove, Thou hast taught me it is so!
Some-thing lives in ev - ery hue Christ - less eyes have nev - er seen:
Closed in ev - er - last - ing arms, Pil - lowed on the lov - ing breast.
Ah, with what a rest of bliss Christ can fill the lov - ing heart!

O, this full and per - fect peace! O, this trans - port all di - vine!
Birds with glad - der songs o'er - flow, Flow'rs with deep - er beau - ties shine,
O, to lie for - ev - er here, Doubt and care and self re - sign,
Heav'n and earth may fade and flee, First - born light in gloom de - cline;

In a love which can - not cease, I am His, and He is mine. mine.
Since I know, as now I know, I am His, and He is mine. mine.
While He whis - pers in my ear, I am His, and He is mine. mine.
But while God and I shall be, I am His, and He is mine. mine.

WORDS: George W. Robinson, 1890
MUSIC: James Mountain, c.1890

EVERLASTING LOVE
7.7.7.7 D.

334 There's a Peace in My Heart

I will never leave thee, nor forsake thee. Heb. 13:5

1. There's a peace in my heart that the world nev - er gave, A peace it can not take a - way; Tho' the tri - als of life may sur-round like a cloud, I've a peace that has come there to stay!
2. All the world seemed to sing of a Sav - ior and King, When peace sweetly came to my heart; Troub-les all fled a - way and my night turned to day, Bless-ed Je - sus, how glorious Thou art!
3 This treas - ure I have in a tem - ple of clay, While here on His foot-stool I roam: But He's com - ing to take me some glo - ri - ous day, O - ver there to my heav-en - ly home!

Refrain

Con - stant-ly a - bid - ing, Je - sus is mine;
Constant-ly a - bid - ing, constant - ly a - bid - ing, Je - sus is mine, yes, Je - sus is mine;
Con - stant-ly a - bid - ing, rap - ture di -
Con-stant-ly a - bid - ing, con-stant-ly a - bid - ing, rap-ture di-vine, O

vine; He nev - er leaves me lone - ly, whis-pers,
rap-ture di-vine; He nev - er leaves me, nev-er leaves me lone-ly, whis-pers,
O so kind: "I will nev - er leave thee," Je - sus is mine.
whis-pers, O so kind: nev - er leave thee, Je - sus, Je - sus is mine.

WORDS and MUSIC: Anne S. Murphy, 1908

CONSTANTLY ABIDING
12.8.12.9 Ref.

Have No Fear, Little Flock 335

Fear not, little flock, for it is your Father's good pleasure to give you the Kingdom. Luke 12:32

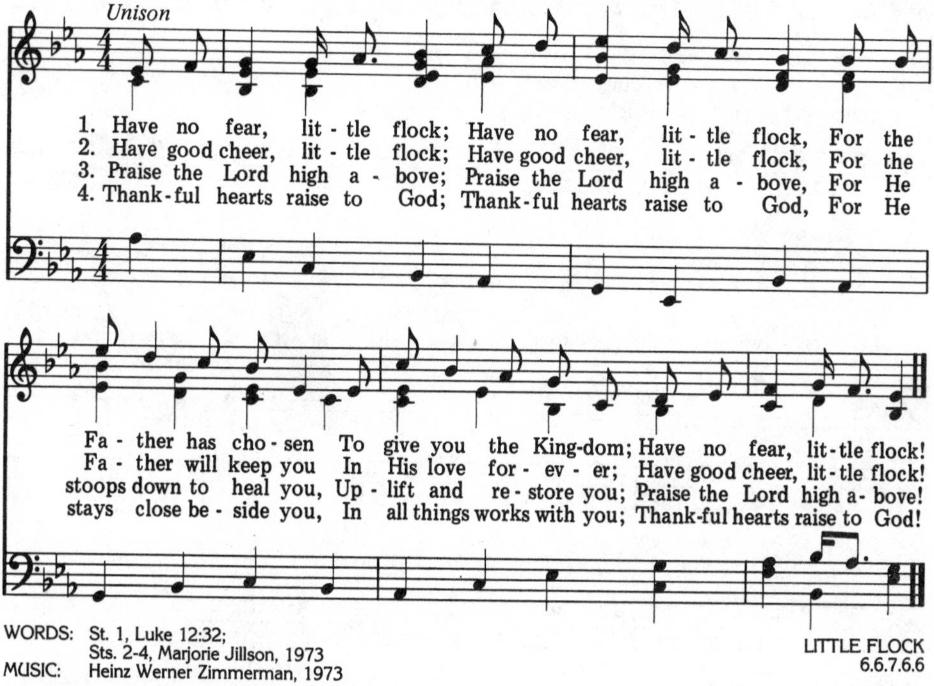

Unison

1. Have no fear, lit - tle flock; Have no fear, lit - tle flock, For the Fa - ther has cho - sen To give you the King-dom; Have no fear, lit-tle flock!
2. Have good cheer, lit - tle flock; Have good cheer, lit - tle flock, For the Fa - ther will keep you In His love for - ev - er; Have good cheer, lit-tle flock!
3. Praise the Lord high a - bove; Praise the Lord high a - bove, For He stoops down to heal you, Up - lift and re - store you; Praise the Lord high a- bove!
4. Thank-ful hearts raise to God; Thank-ful hearts raise to God, For He stays close be - side you, In all things works with you; Thank-ful hearts raise to God!

WORDS: St. 1, Luke 12:32;
Sts. 2-4, Marjorie Jillson, 1973
MUSIC: Heinz Werner Zimmerman, 1973

LITTLE FLOCK
6.6.7.6.6

336 Walking in Sunlight All of My Journey

He that followeth Me shall not walk in darkness . . . John 8:12

1. Walk - ing in sun - light all of my jour - ney, O - ver the moun-tains,
2. Shad - ows a - round me, shad - ows a - bove me Nev - er con - ceal my
3. In the bright sun - light, ev - er re - joic - ing, Press - ing my way to
through the deep vale; Je - sus has said, "I'll nev - er for - sake thee,"
Sav - ior and Guide; He is the Light, in Him is no dark - ness;
man - sions a - bove; Sing - ing His prais - es glad - ly I'm walk - ing,
Refrain
Prom - ise di - vine that nev - er can fail.
Ev - er I'm walk - ing close to His side. Heav - en - ly sun - light,
Walk - ing in sun - light, sun - light of love.
heav - en - ly sun - light, Flood-ing my soul with glo - ry di - vine; Hal - le -
lu - jah! I am re - joic - ing, Sing - ing His prais - es, Je - sus is mine.

WORDS: Henry J. Zelley, 1899
MUSIC: George H. Cook, 1899

HEAVENLY SUNLIGHT
10.9.10.9 Ref.

A Wonderful Savior Is Jesus My Lord 337

I will put thee in a cleft of the rock, and will cover thee with My hand. Exo. 33:22

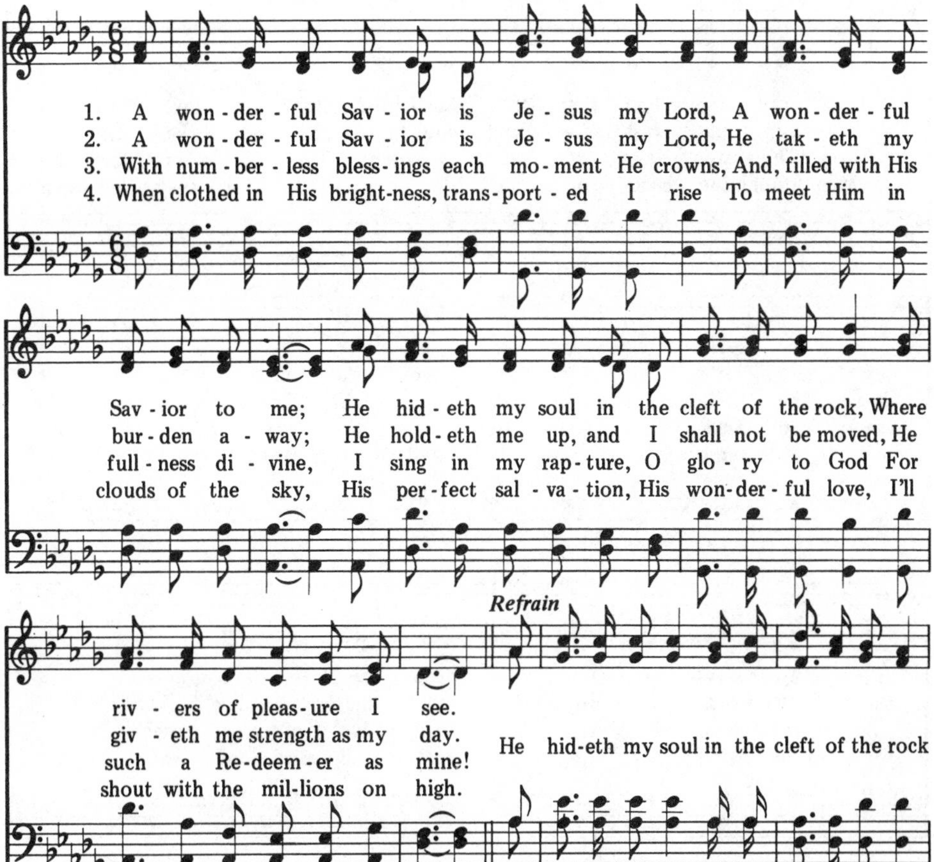

1. A won - der - ful Sav - ior is Je - sus my Lord, A won - der - ful
2. A won - der - ful Sav - ior is Je - sus my Lord, He tak - eth my
3. With num - ber - less bless - ings each mo - ment He crowns, And, filled with His
4. When clothed in His bright-ness, trans - port - ed I rise To meet Him in

Sav - ior to me; He hid - eth my soul in the cleft of the rock, Where
bur - den a - way; He hold - eth me up, and I shall not be moved, He
full - ness di - vine, I sing in my rap - ture, O glo - ry to God For
clouds of the sky, His per - fect sal - va - tion, His won - der - ful love, I'll

riv - ers of pleas - ure I see.
giv - eth me strength as my day.
such a Re - deem - er as mine!
shout with the mil - lions on high.

Refrain

He hid-eth my soul in the cleft of the rock
That shad - ows a dry, thirst - y land; He hid - eth my life in the depths of His love,
And cov - ers me there with His hand, And cov - ers me there with His hand.

WORDS: Fanny J. Crosby, 1890
MUSIC: William J. Kirkpatrick, 1890

KIRKPATRICK
11.8.11.8 Ref.

338 Dear Lord and Father of Mankind

. . . Sitting at the feet of Jesus, clothed, and in his right mind. Luke 8:35

1. Dear Lord and Fa - ther of man - kind, For - give our fool - ish
2. In sim - ple trust like theirs who heard, Be - side the Syr - ian
3. Drop Thy still dews of qui - et - ness, Till all our striv - ings
4. Breathe through the heats of our de - sire Thy cool - ness and Thy
ways! Re - clothe us in our right - ful mind; In pur - er
Sea, The gra - cious call - ing of the Lord, Let us, like
cease; Take from our souls the strain and stress, And let our
balm; Let sense be dumb, let flesh re - tire; Speak through the
lives Thy serv - ice find, In deep - er rev - 'rence, praise.
them, with - out a word, Rise up and fol - low Thee.
or - dered lives con - fess The beau - ty of Thy peace.
earth - quake, wind, and fire, O still small voice of calm! A-men.

WORDS: John G. Whittier, 1872
MUSIC: Frederick C. Maker, 1887

REST
8.6.8.8.6

339 Peace, Perfect Peace

Thou wilt keep him in perfect peace, whose mind is stayed on Thee. Isa. 26:3

1. Peace, per - fect peace, in this dark world of sin?
2. Peace, per - fect peace, by throng - ing du - ties pressed?
3. Peace, per - fect peace, with sor - rows surg - ing round?
4. Peace, per - fect peace, our fu - ture all un - known?
5. Peace, per - fect peace, death shad - owing us and ours?
6. It is e - nough: earth's strug - gles soon shall cease,

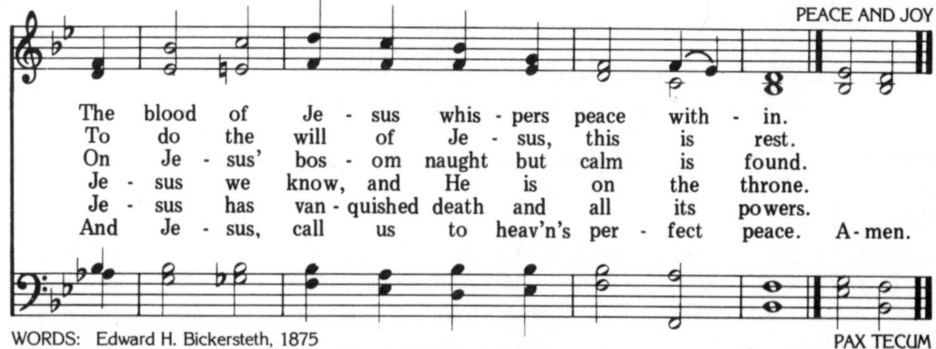

PEACE AND JOY
The blood of Je - sus whis - pers peace with - in.
To do the will of Je - sus, this is rest.
On Je - sus' bos - om naught but calm is found.
Je - sus we know, and He is on the throne.
Je - sus has van - quished death and all its powers.
And Je - sus, call us to heav'n's per - fect peace. A - men.

WORDS: Edward H. Bickersteth, 1875
MUSIC: George T. Caldbeck, 1877; arr. Charles J. Vincent, 1877

Music used by permission of the Trustees of Vincent (Hazeon) Trust, England.

PAX TECUM
Irregular meter

Like a River Glorious 340

Then had Thy peace been as a river . . . Isa. 48:18

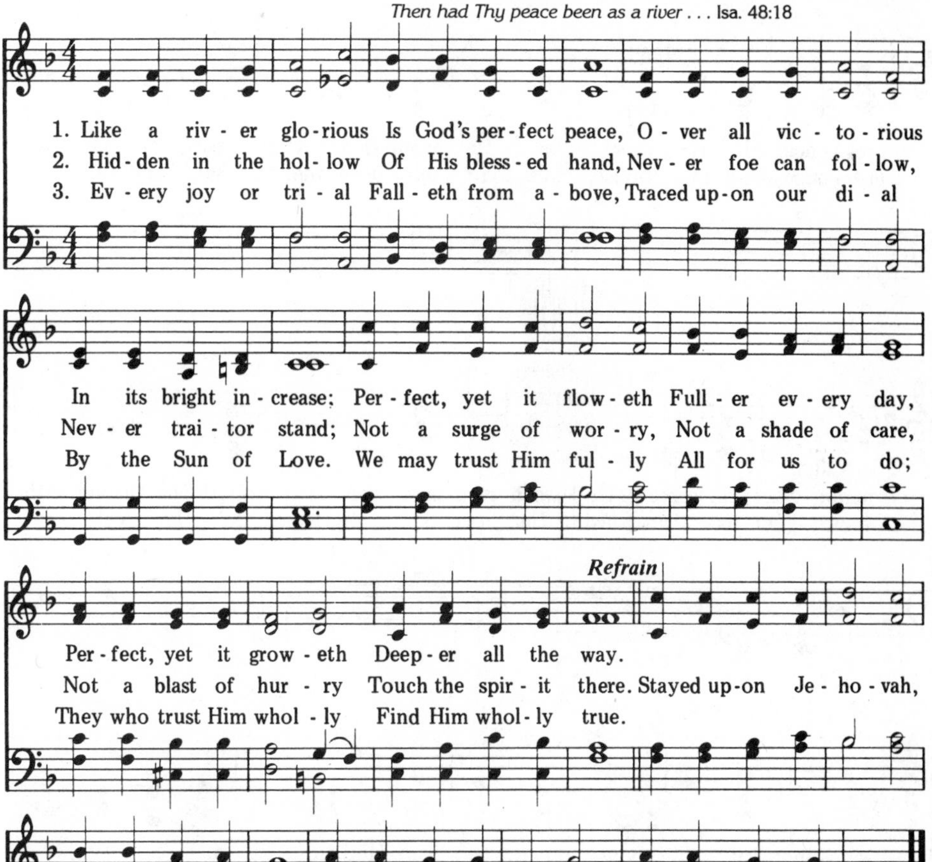

1. Like a riv - er glo - rious Is God's per - fect peace, O - ver all vic - to - rious
2. Hid - den in the hol - low Of His bless - ed hand, Nev - er foe can fol - low,
3. Ev - ery joy or tri - al Fall - eth from a - bove, Traced up - on our di - al

In its bright in - crease; Per - fect, yet it flow - eth Full - er ev - ery day,
Nev - er trai - tor stand; Not a surge of wor - ry, Not a shade of care,
By the Sun of Love. We may trust Him ful - ly All for us to do;

Per - fect, yet it grow - eth Deep - er all the way.
Not a blast of hur - ry Touch the spir - it there.
They who trust Him whol - ly Find Him whol - ly true.

Refrain

Stayed up - on Je - ho - vah, Hearts are ful - ly blest; Find - ing, as He prom - ised, Per - fect peace and rest.

WORDS: Frances R. Havergal, 1874
MUSIC: James Mountain, 1876

WYE VALLEY
6.5.6.5 D. Ref.

341 Let's Enjoy God Together

O magnify the Lord with me and let us exalt His name together! Psa. 34:3

Unison
1. Let's en - joy God to - geth - er as we wor - ship in His
2. Let's en - joy God to - geth - er as we wor - ship in His
pres - ence, He is here as He prom - ised, for we gath - er in His
pres - ence, One in praise, one in pur - pose, one in heart and one in
name; Let us serve God with glad - ness and sur - round His throne with
hand; Let us rise from His ta - ble strong from ho - ly cel - e -
sing - ing; Let us bow down be - fore Him and His maj - es - ty ac -
bra - tion; In the pow'r of His Spir - it to o - bey His last com -

claim!
mand!
Let's en - joy God to - geth - er in the full - ness of His Spir - it;
Let's re - joice in the one - ness He has giv - en through His Son, Let us
break bread as broth - ers at our Fa - ther's ho - ly ta - ble; Let's en -
joy God to - geth - er, for His fam - i - ly is one! Let's en -
1
2
fam - i - ly is one!

WORDS: Margaret Clarkson, 1979
MUSIC: Tedd Smith, 1979

LET'S ENJOY GOD
Irregular meter

342 I Will Sing of My Redeemer

Jesus Christ; who gave Himself for us, that He might redeem us . . . Titus 2:13,14

1. I will sing of my Re - deem-er And His won-drous love to me;
2. I will tell the won-drous sto - ry, How my lost es - tate to save,
3. I will praise my dear Re - deem-er, His tri - umph-ant power I'll tell,
4. I will sing of my Re - deem-er And His heav'n-ly love for me;
On the cru - el cross He suf-fered, From the curse to set me free.
In His bound-less love and mer - cy, He the ran-som free-ly gave.
How the vic - to - ry He giv - eth O - ver sin and death and hell.
He from death to life hath brought me, Son of God, with Him to be.
Refrain
Sing, O sing of my Re - deem-er, With His blood He pur-chased me,
On the cross He sealed my par - don, Paid the debt, and made me free.

WORDS: Philip P. Bliss, 1876
MUSIC: Rowland H. Prichard, c.1830

HYFRYDOL
8.7.8.7 Ref.

Come, Come, Ye Saints 343

All things work together for good to them that love God . . . Rom. 8:28

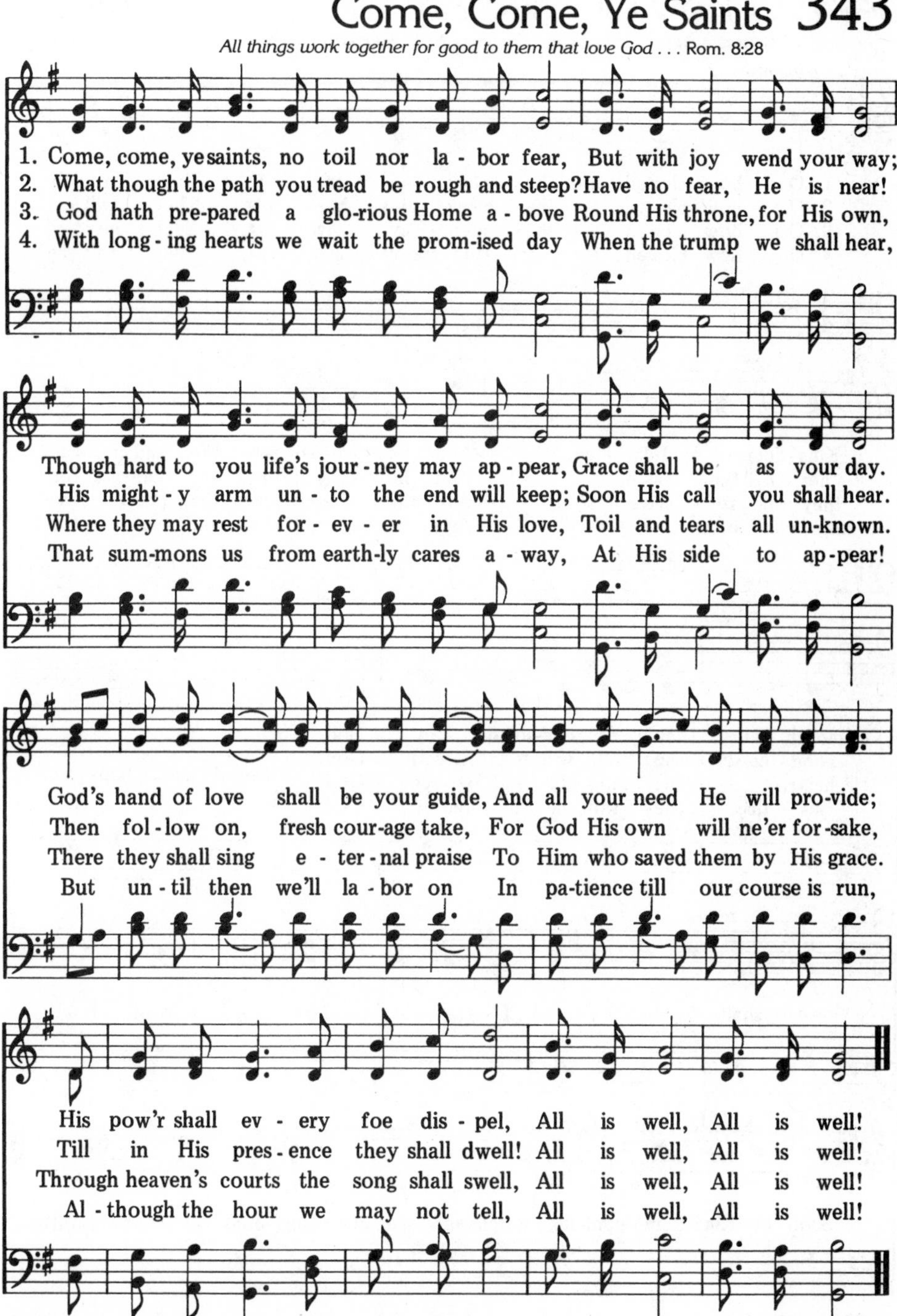
1. Come, come, ye saints, no toil nor la - bor fear, But with joy wend your way;
2. What though the path you tread be rough and steep? Have no fear, He is near!
3. God hath pre-pared a glo-rious Home a - bove Round His throne, for His own,
4. With long - ing hearts we wait the prom-ised day When the trump we shall hear,
Though hard to you life's jour - ney may ap - pear, Grace shall be as your day.
His might - y arm un - to the end will keep; Soon His call you shall hear.
Where they may rest for - ev - er in His love, Toil and tears all un-known.
That sum-mons us from earth-ly cares a - way, At His side to ap-pear!
God's hand of love shall be your guide, And all your need He will pro-vide;
Then fol - low on, fresh cour-age take, For God His own will ne'er for-sake,
There they shall sing e - ter - nal praise To Him who saved them by His grace.
But un - til then we'll la - bor on In pa-tience till our course is run,
His pow'r shall ev - ery foe dis - pel, All is well, All is well!
Till in His pres - ence they shall dwell! All is well, All is well!
Through heaven's courts the song shall swell, All is well, All is well!
Al - though the hour we may not tell, All is well, All is well!

WORDS: Avis B. Christiansen, 1966; based on William Clayton, 1846
MUSIC: Traditional English melody; *The Sacred Harp*, 1844

ALL IS WELL
10.6.10.6.8.8.8.6

344 O How Blessed Are the Poor in Spirit

Blessed are the poor in spirit; for theirs is the kingdom of heaven. Matt. 5:3

Unison
1. O how blessed are the poor in spir - it, Theirs is the King-dom of Heav - en. And how blessed are the sad and mourn - ful; They'll be con-soled by God.
2. O how blessed are the meek and hum - ble, They will in - her - it the earth. And how blessed those who hun-ger for good - ness, They all will feast with God.
3. O how blessed are the mer - cy giv - ers, Such mer - cy they will re - ceive. And how blessed are the pure in heart, They sure - ly will see God.
4. O how blessed are the true peace - mak - ers, They will be known as God's chil - dren. And how blessed those who suf - fer for jus - tice, They will be hon-ored by God.
Refrain
Blessed and hap - py we shall be. Lis - ten to the Mas - ter's word! Soon the King-dom's com-ing—watch and see: the King-dom of the Lord!

WORDS and MUSIC: Richard Avery and Donald Marsh, 1979

BEATITUDES
Irregular meter

There Is Sunshine in My Soul Today 345

For God, who commanded the light to shine out of darkness, hath shined in our hearts . . . II Cor. 4:6

1. There is sun - shine in my soul to - day, More glo - ri - ous and bright
2. There is mu - sic in my soul to - day, A car - ol to my King,
3. There is spring - time in my soul to - day, For when the Lord is near
4. There is glad - ness in my soul to - day, And hope and praise and love,
Than glows in an - y earth - ly sky, For Je - sus is my light.
And Je - sus, lis - ten - ing can hear The songs I can - not sing.
The dove of peace sings in my heart, The flow'rs of grace ap - pear.
For bless - ings which He gives me now, For joys "laid up a - bove."
Refrain
O there's sun - shine, bless - ed sun - shine, When the peace - ful, hap - py mo-ments
roll; When Je - sus shows His smil-ing face, There is sun-shine in my soul.
3

WORDS: Eliza E. Hewitt, 1887
MUSIC: John R. Sweney, 1887

SUNSHINE
9.6.8.6 Ref.

346 There's within My Heart a Melody

We know that we have passed from death to life . . . I John 3:14

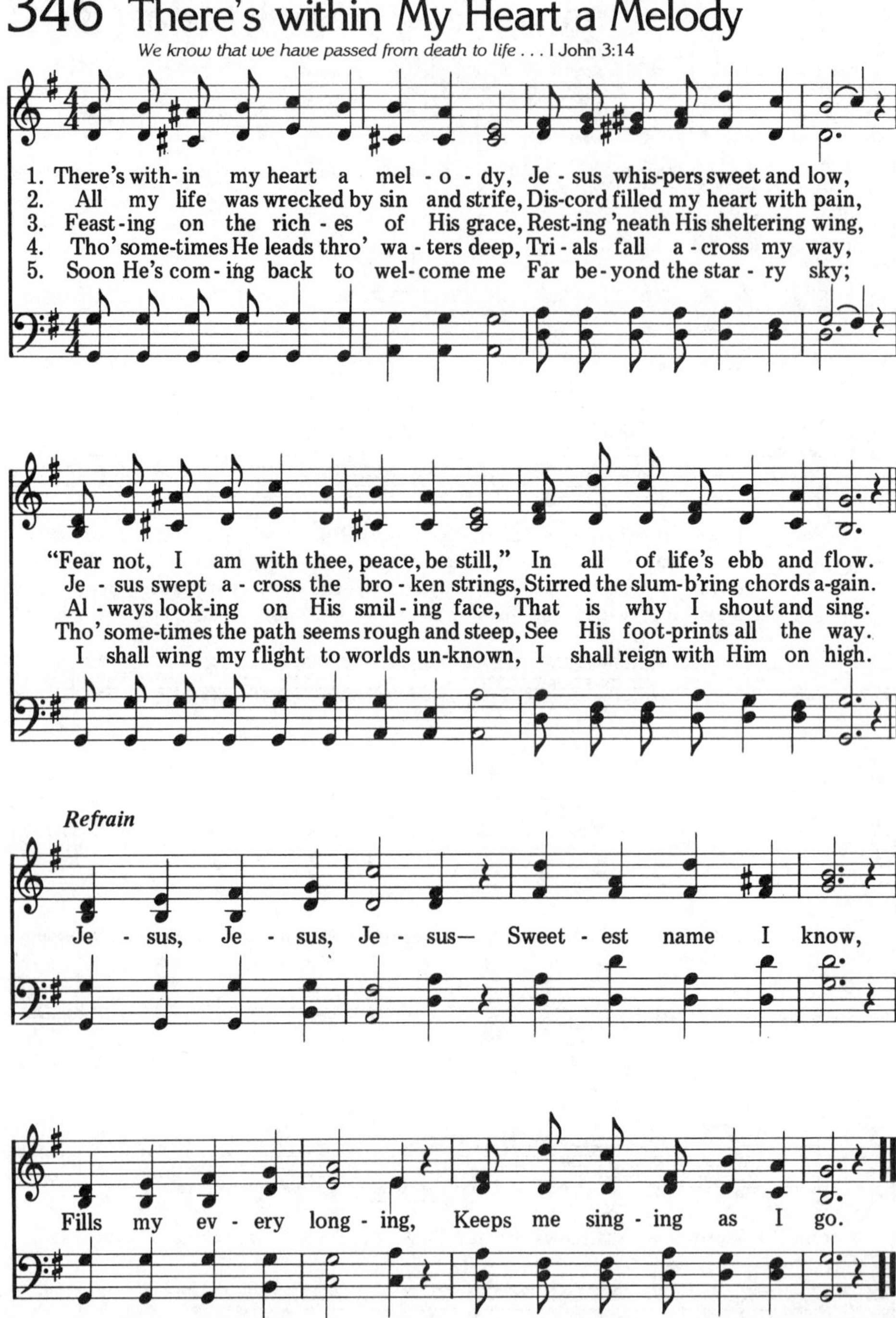
1. There's with-in my heart a mel-o-dy, Je-sus whis-pers sweet and low, "Fear not, I am with thee, peace, be still," In all of life's ebb and flow.
2. All my life was wrecked by sin and strife, Dis-cord filled my heart with pain, Je-sus swept a-cross the bro-ken strings, Stirred the slum-b'ring chords a-gain.
3. Feast-ing on the rich-es of His grace, Rest-ing 'neath His sheltering wing, Al-ways look-ing on His smil-ing face, That is why I shout and sing.
4. Tho' some-times He leads thro' wa-ters deep, Tri-als fall a-cross my way, Tho' some-times the path seems rough and steep, See His foot-prints all the way.
5. Soon He's com-ing back to wel-come me Far be-yond the star-ry sky; I shall wing my flight to worlds un-known, I shall reign with Him on high.
Refrain
Je-sus, Je-sus, Je-sus— Sweet-est name I know, Fills my ev-ery long-ing, Keeps me sing-ing as I go.

WORDS and MUSIC: Luther B. Bridgers, 1909

SWEETEST NAME
9.7.9.7 Ref.

I Have a Song That Jesus Gave Me 347

Singing and making melody in your heart to the Lord. Eph. 5:19

1. I have a song that Je - sus gave me, It was sent from heav'n a - bove; There nev - er was a sweet - er mel - o - dy, 'Tis a mel - o - dy of love.
2. I love the Christ who died on Cal - v'ry, For He washed my sins a - way; He put with - in my heart a mel - o - dy, And I know it's there to stay.
3. 'Twill be my end - less theme in glo - ry, With the an - gels I will sing; 'Twill be a song with glo - rious har - mo - ny, When the courts of heav - en ring.
Refrain
In my heart there rings a mel - o - dy, There rings a mel - o - dy with heav - en's har - mo - ny; In my heart there rings a mel - o - dy; There rings a mel - o - dy of love.

WORDS and MUSIC: Elton M. Roth, 1924

HEART MELODY
Irregular meter

348 O Safe to the Rock That Is Higher than I

Lead me to the rock that is higher than I. Psa. 61:2

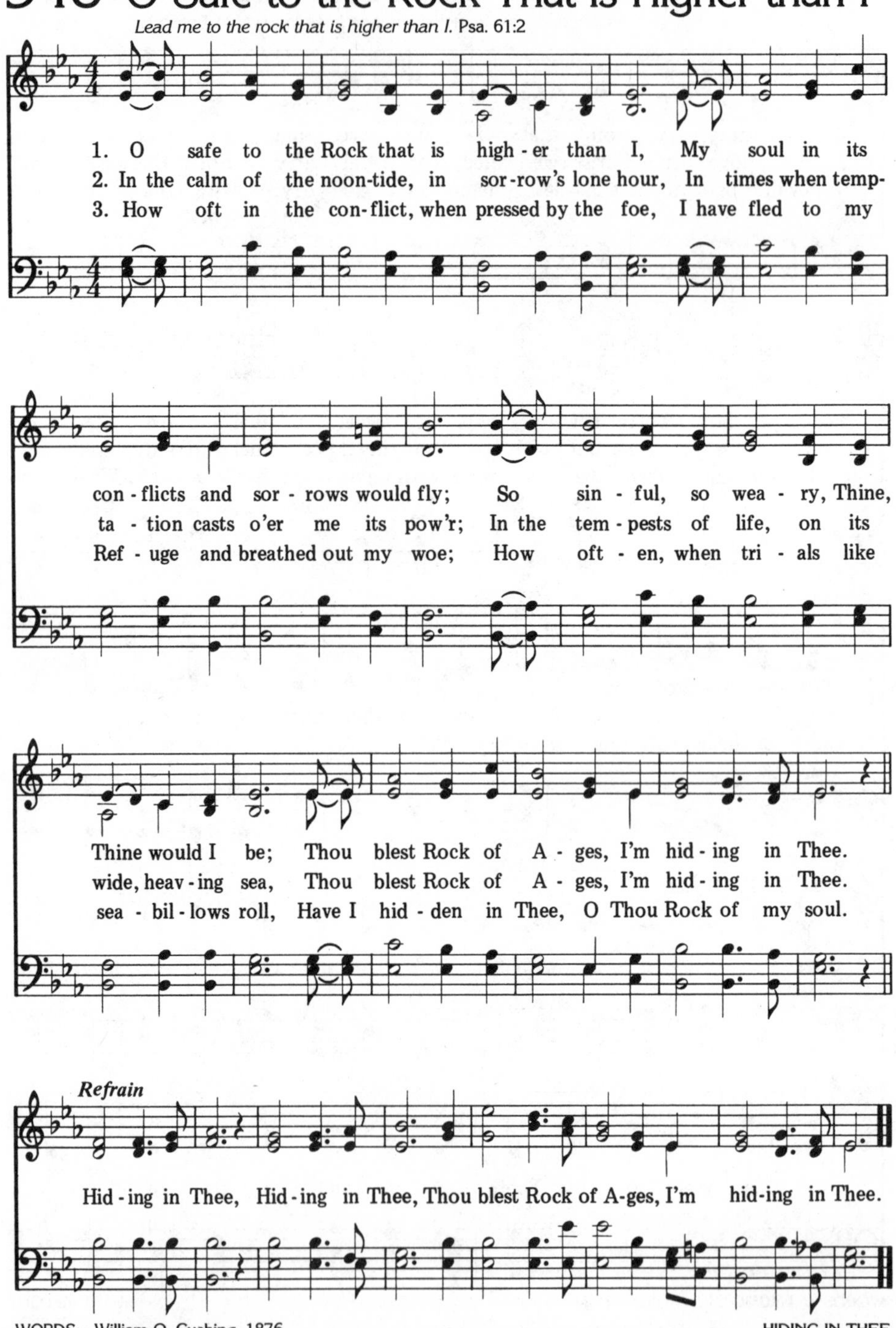
1. O safe to the Rock that is high - er than I, My soul in its con - flicts and sor - rows would fly; So sin - ful, so wea - ry, Thine, Thine would I be; Thou blest Rock of A - ges, I'm hid - ing in Thee.
2. In the calm of the noon-tide, in sor-row's lone hour, In times when temp - ta - tion casts o'er me its pow'r; In the tem - pests of life, on its wide, heav - ing sea, Thou blest Rock of A - ges, I'm hid - ing in Thee.
3. How oft in the con - flict, when pressed by the foe, I have fled to my Ref - uge and breathed out my woe; How oft - en, when tri - als like sea - bil - lows roll, Have I hid - den in Thee, O Thou Rock of my soul.
Refrain
Hid - ing in Thee, Hid - ing in Thee, Thou blest Rock of A-ges, I'm hid-ing in Thee.

WORDS: William O. Cushing, 1876
MUSIC: Ira D. Sankey, 1877

HIDING IN THEE
11.11.11.11 Ref.

I Come to the Garden Alone 349

Mary Magdalene came and told the disciples that she had seen the Lord. John 20:18

1. I come to the gar - den a - lone, While the dew is still on the ros - es; And the voice I hear, fall - ing on my ear, The Son of God dis - clos - es.
2. He speaks, and the sound of His voice Is so sweet the birds hush their sing - ing, And the mel - o - dy that He gave to me With- in my heart is ring - ing.
3. I'd stay in the gar - den with Him Though the night a - round me be fall - ing, But He bids me go; through the voice of woe, His voice to me is call - ing.
Refrain
And He walks with me, and He talks with me, And He tells me I am His own, And the joy we share as we tar - ry there, None oth - er has ev - er known.

WORDS and MUSIC: C. Austin Miles, 1912

GARDEN
Irregular meter

350 We Praise Thee, O God

Wilt Thou not revive us again: that Thy people may rejoice in Thee? Psa. 85:6

1. We praise Thee, O God, for the Son of Thy love, For Je - sus who
2. We praise Thee, O God, for Thy Spir - it of light, Who has shown us our
3. All glo - ry and praise to the Lamb that was slain, Who has borne all our
4. Re - vive us a - gain, fill each heart with Thy love; May each soul be re-

died and is now gone a - bove.
Sav - ior and scat - tered our night.
sins, and has cleansed ev - ery stain.
kin - dled with fire from a - bove.

Refrain

Hal - le - lu - jah! Thine the glo - ry, Hal - le - lu - jah! A - men; Hal - le - lu - jah! Thine the glo - ry; Re - vive us a - gain.

WORDS: William P. Mackay, 1863
MUSIC John J. Husband, c.1880

REVIVE US AGAIN
11.11 Ref.

351 O for a Heart to Praise My God

I will praise Thee, O Lord, with my whole heart. Psa. 9:1

1. O for a heart to praise my God, A heart from sin set free,
2. A hum - ble, low - ly, con - trite heart, Be - liev - ing, true and clean;
3. A heart in ev - ery thought re - newed, And full of love di - vine;
4. Thy na - ture, gra - cious Lord, im - part; Come quick - ly from a - bove,

A heart that al - ways feels Thy blood So free - ly shed for me!
Which neith-er life nor death can part From Him that dwells with - in.
Per - fect and right and pure and good, A cop - y, Lord, of Thine!
Write Thy new name up - on my heart, Thy new best name of Love. A - men.

WORDS: Charles Wesley, 1742
MUSIC: Carl G. Gläser, 1784-1829; arr. Lowell Mason, 1839

AZMON
C.M.

Jesus, Thy Boundless Love to Me 352

. . . And to know the love of Christ, which passeth knowledge. Eph. 3:19

1. Je - sus, Thy bound-less love to me No thought can reach, no tongue de-clare;
2. O Love, how cheer-ing is Thy ray! All fear be - fore Thy pres-ence flies;
3. In suf-fering be Thy love my peace; In weak - ness be Thy love my pow'r;
O knit my thank-ful heart to Thee, And reign with - out a ri - val there!
Care, an-guish, sor - row, melt a - way, Wher-e'er Thy heal - ing beams a - rise:
And when the storms of life shall cease, O Je - sus, in that sol - emn hour,
Thine whol-ly, Thine a - lone, I'd live, My - self to Thee en - tire - ly give.
O Je - sus, noth-ing may I see, Noth-ing de - sire, or seek, but Thee!
In death as life be Thou my guide, And save me, who for me hast died. A-men.

WORDS: Paul Gerhardt, 1653; tr. John Wesley, 1739
MUSIC: Henri F. Hemy, 1864; arr. James G. Walton, 1874

ST. CATHERINE
8.8.8.8.8.8

353 I Am Thine, O Lord

Let us draw near with a true heart . . . Heb. 10:22

1. I am Thine, O Lord, I have heard Thy voice, And it told Thy love to me; But I long to rise in the arms of faith, And be clos - er drawn to Thee.
2. Con - se - crate me now to Thy serv - ice, Lord, By the pow'r of grace di - vine; Let my soul look up with a stead - fast hope, And my will be lost in Thine.
3. O, the pure de - light of a sin - gle hour That be - fore Thy throne I spend, When I kneel in prayer, and with Thee, my God, I com - mune as friend with friend!
4. There are depths of love that I can - not know Till I cross the nar - row sea; There are heights of joy that I may not reach Till I rest in peace with Thee.
Refrain
Draw me near - er, near - er, bless - ed Lord, To the cross where Thou hast died; Draw me near - er, near - er, near - er, bless - ed Lord, To Thy pre - cious, bleed - ing side.

WORDS: Fanny J. Crosby, 1875
MUSIC: William H. Doane, 1875

I AM THINE
10.7.10.7 Ref.

O to Be Like Thee! Blessed Redeemer 354

... *To be conformed to the image of His Son.* Rom. 8:29

1. O to be like Thee! bless-ed Re-deem-er, This is my con-stant long-ing and prayer. Glad-ly I'll for-feit all of earth's treas-ures, Je-sus, Thy per-fect like-ness to wear.
2. O to be like Thee! full of com-pas-sion, Lov-ing, for-giv-ing, ten-der and kind, Help-ing the help-less, cheer-ing the faint-ing, Seek-ing the wan-d'ring sin-ner to find.
3. O to be like Thee! low-ly in spir-it, Ho-ly and harm-less, pa-tient and brave; Meek-ly en-dur-ing cru-el re-proach-es, Will-ing to suf-fer 'oth-ers to save.
4. O to be like Thee! while I am plead-ing, Pour out Thy Spir-it, fill with Thy love; Make me a tem-ple meet for Thy dwell-ing, Fit me for life and heav-en a-bove.
Refrain
O to be like Thee! O to be like Thee, Bless-ed Re-deem-er, pure as Thou art! Come in Thy sweet-ness, come in Thy full-ness; Stamp Thine own im-age deep on my heart.

WORDS: Thomas O. Chisholm, 1897
MUSIC: William J. Kirkpatrick, 1897

RONDINELLA
10.9.10.9 Ref.

355 I Need Thee Every Hour

Bow down Thine ear, O Lord, and hear me: for I am poor and needy. Psa. 86:1

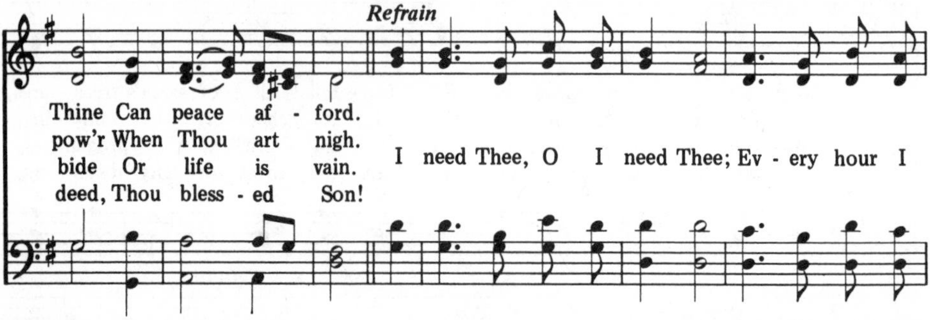

1. I need Thee ev - ery hour, Most gra - cious Lord; No ten - der voice like Thine Can peace af - ford.
2. I need Thee ev - ery hour, Stay Thou near by; Temp - ta - tions lose their pow'r When Thou art nigh.
3. I need Thee ev - ery hour In joy or pain; Come quick - ly and a - bide Or life is vain.
4. I need Thee ev - ery hour, Most Ho - ly One; O make me Thine in - deed, Thou bless - ed Son!

Refrain

I need Thee, O I need Thee; Ev - ery hour I need Thee; O bless me now, my Sav - ior, I come to Thee!

WORDS: Annie S. Hawks, 1872
MUSIC: Robert Lowry, 1872

NEED
6.4.6.4 Ref.

356 I Am Weak, but Thou Art Strong

Let the weak say, I am strong. Joel 3:10

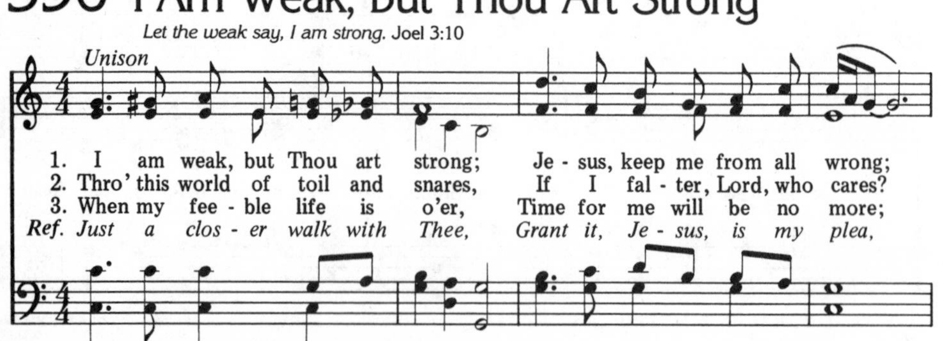
Unison
1. I am weak, but Thou art strong; Je - sus, keep me from all wrong;
2. Thro' this world of toil and snares, If I fal - ter, Lord, who cares?
3. When my fee - ble life is o'er, Time for me will be no more;
Ref. Just a clos - er walk with Thee, Grant it, Je - sus, is my plea,

D.C. Refrain
I'll be sat - is - fied as long As I walk, let me walk close to Thee.
Who with me my bur - den shares? None but Thee, dear Lord, none but Thee.
Guide me gent - ly, safe - ly o'er To Thy king - dom shore, to Thy shore.
Dai - ly walk - ing close to Thee, Let it be, dear Lord, let it be.

WORDS and MUSIC: Source unknown

CLOSER WALK
Irregular meter

There Is a Place of Quiet Rest 357

Draw nigh to God, and He will draw nigh to you. James 4:8

1. There is a place of qui - et rest Near to the heart of God,
   A place where sin can - not mo - lest, Near to the heart of God.

2. There is a place of com - fort sweet Near to the heart of God,
   A place where we our Sav - ior meet, Near to the heart of God.

3. There is a place of full re - lease Near to the heart of God,
   A place where all is joy and peace, Near to the heart of God.

Refrain

O Je - sus, blest Re - deem - er Sent from the heart of God,
Hold us who wait be - fore Thee Near to the heart of God.

WORDS and MUSIC: Cleland B. McAfee, 1901

McAFEE
C.M. Ref.

358 I Would Be True

Be thou an example of the believers . . . I Tim. 4:12

1. I would be true, for there are those who trust me; I would be
2. I would be friend of all— the foe, the friend - less; I would be
3. I would be learn - ing day by day the les - sons My heav'n-ly
4. I would be prayer - ful through each bus - y mo - ment; I would be

pure, for there are those who care: I would be strong, for there is
giv - ing, and for - get the gift; I would be hum - ble, for I
Fa - ther gives me in His Word; I would be quick to hear His
con - stant - ly in touch with God; I would be tuned to hear His

much to suf - fer; I would be brave, for there is much to
know my weak - ness; I would look up, and laugh, and love, and
light - est whis - per, And prompt and glad to do the things I've
slight - est whis - per, I would have faith to keep the path Christ

dare; I would be brave, for there is much to dare.
lift; I would look up, and laugh, and love, and lift.
heard; And prompt and glad to do the things I've heard.
trod; I would have faith to keep the path Christ trod. A-men.

WORDS: Howard A. Walter, 1907
MUSIC: Joseph Y. Peek, 1909

PEEK
11.10.11.10.10

Be Thou My Vision 359

What things were gain to me, those I counted loss for Christ. Phil. 3:7

Unison
1. Be Thou my Vi - sion, O Lord of my heart;
2. Be Thou my Wis - dom, and Thou my true Word;
3. Rich - es I heed not, nor man's emp - ty praise,
4. High King of heav - en, my vic - to - ry won,
Naught be all else to me, save that Thou art—
I ev - er with Thee and Thou with me, Lord;
Thou mine in - her - i - tance, now and al - ways;
May I reach heav - en's joys, O bright heav'n's Sun!
Thou my best thought, by day or by night,
Thou my great Fa - ther, I Thy true son;
Thou and Thou on - ly, first in my heart,
Heart of my own heart, what - ev - er be - fall,
Wak - ing or sleep - ing, Thy pres - ence my light.
Thou in me dwell - ing, and I with Thee one.
High King of heav - en, my Treas - ure Thou art.
Still be my Vi - sion, O Rul - er of all. A - men.

WORDS: Irish hymn, c. 8th century; tr. Mary E. Byrne, 1905; versified Eleanor H. Hull, 1912
MUSIC: Traditional Irish melody; arr. Donald P. Hustad, 1973

SLANE
10.10.10.10

360 More Love to Thee, O Christ

This I pray, that your love may abound yet more and more. Phil. 1:9

1. More love to Thee, O Christ, More love to Thee! Hear Thou the prayer I make On bend - ed knee; This is my ear - nest plea:
2. Once earth - ly joy I craved, Sought peace and rest; Now Thee a - lone I seek, Give what is best; This all my prayer shall be:
3. Let sor - row do its work, Send grief and pain; Sweet are Thy mes - sen - gers, Sweet their re - frain, When they can sing with me:
4. Then shall my lat - est breath Whis - per Thy praise; This be the part - ing cry My heart shall raise; This still its prayer shall be:

More love, O Christ, to Thee, More love to Thee, More love to Thee! A-men.

WORDS: Elizabeth P. Prentiss, 1856
MUSIC: William H. Doane, 1870

MORE LOVE TO THEE
6.4.6.4.6.6.4.4

361 Lord Jesus, Think on Me

According to Thy mercy remember Thou me . . . Psa. 25:7

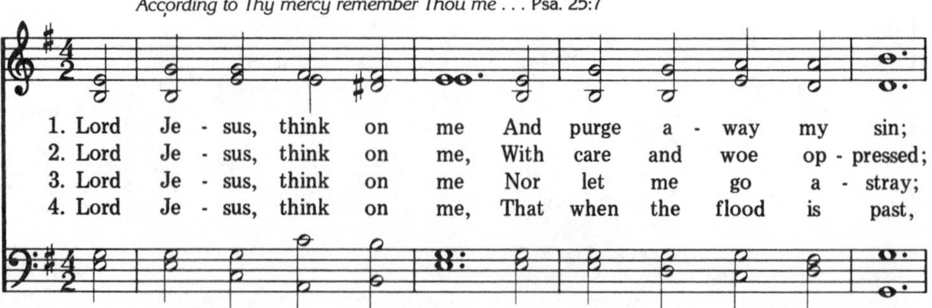
1. Lord Je - sus, think on me And purge a - way my sin;
2. Lord Je - sus, think on me, With care and woe op - pressed;
3. Lord Je - sus, think on me Nor let me go a - stray;
4. Lord Je - sus, think on me, That when the flood is past,

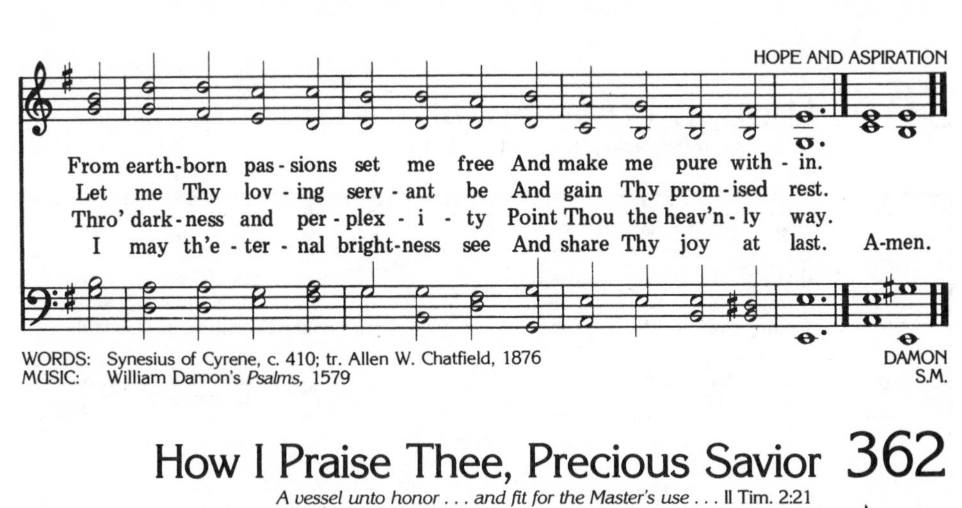
From earth-born pas-sions set me free And make me pure with-in.
Let me Thy lov-ing serv-ant be And gain Thy prom-ised rest.
Thro' dark-ness and per-plex-i-ty Point Thou the heav'n-ly way.
I may th'e-ter-nal bright-ness see And share Thy joy at last. A-men.

WORDS: Synesius of Cyrene, c. 410; tr. Allen W. Chatfield, 1876
MUSIC: William Damon's *Psalms*, 1579

DAMON
S.M.

How I Praise Thee, Precious Savior 362

A vessel unto honor . . . and fit for the Master's use . . . II Tim. 2:21

1. How I praise Thee, pre-cious Sav-ior, That Thy love laid hold of me;
Thou hast saved and cleansed and filled me That I might Thy chan-nel be.

2. Emp-tied that Thou should-est fill me, A clean ves-sel in Thy hand;
With no pow'r but as Thou giv-est Gra-cious-ly with each com-mand.

3. Wit-ness-ing Thy pow'r to save me, Set-ting free from self and sin;
Thou who bought me to pos-sess me, In Thy full-ness, Lord, come in.

4. Je-sus, fill now with Thy Spir-it Hearts that full sur-ren-der know;
That the streams of liv-ing wa-ter From our in-ner man may flow.

Refrain

Chan-nels on-ly, bless-ed Mas-ter, But with all Thy won-drous pow'r
Flow-ing through us, Thou canst use us Ev-ery day and ev-ery hour.

WORDS: Mary E. Maxwell, 1910
MUSIC: Ada R. Gibbs, 1910

CHANNELS
8.7.8.7 Ref.

363 Though I May Speak

... But the greatest of these is love. I Cor. 13:13

Unison
1. Though I may speak with brav - est fire,
2. Though I may give all I pos - sess,
3. Come, Spir - it, come, our hearts con - trol,
And have the gift to all in - spire,
And striv - ing so my love pro - fess,
Our spir - its long to be made whole.
And have not love; my words are vain;
But not be giv'n by love with - in.
Let in - ward love guide ev - ery deed;
As sound - ing brass, and hope - less gain.
The prof - it soon turns strange - ly thin.
By this we wor - ship, and are freed.

WORDS: Hal Hopson, 1972; based on I Corinthians 13
MUSIC: Hal Hopson, 1972; based on an American Folk Tune

GIFT OF LOVE
L.M.

I'm Pressing on the Upward Way 364

I press toward the mark for the prize . . . Phil. 3:14

1. I'm press - ing on the up - ward way, New heights I'm gain - ing ev - ery day; Still pray - ing as I'm on - ward bound, "Lord, plant my feet on high - er ground."
2. My heart has no de - sire to stay Where doubts a - rise and fears dis- may; Though some may dwell where these a - bound, My prayer, my aim is high - er ground.
3. I want to live a - bove the world, Though Sa-tan's darts at me are hurled; For faith has caught the joy - ful sound, The song of saints on high - er ground.
4. I want to scale the ut - most height, And catch a gleam of glo - ry bright; But still I'll pray till heav'n I've found, "Lord, lead me on to high - er ground."
Refrain
Lord, lift me up and let me stand By faith on heav - en's ta - ble - land, A high - er plane than I have found; Lord, plant my feet on high - er ground.

WORDS: Johnson Oatman, Jr., 1898
MUSIC: Charles H. Gabriel, 1898

HIGHER GROUND
L.M. Ref.

365 Nearer, Still Nearer

For to me to live is Christ, and to die is gain. Phil. 1:21

1. Near-er, still near-er, close to Thy heart, Draw me, my Sav-ior, so pre-cious Thou art; Fold me, O fold me close to Thy breast, Shel-ter me safe in that "Ha-ven of Rest," Shel-ter me safe in that "Ha-ven of Rest."
2. Near-er, still near-er, noth-ing I bring, Naught as an of-f'ring to Je-sus my King; On-ly my sin-ful, now con-trite heart, Grant me the cleans-ing Thy blood doth im-part, Grant me the cleans-ing Thy blood doth im-part.
3. Near-er, still near-er, Lord, to be Thine, Sin with its fol-lies I glad-ly re-sign; All of its pleas-ures, pomp and its pride, Give me but Je-sus, my Lord cru-ci-fied, Give me but Je-sus, my Lord cru-ci-fied.
4. Near-er, still near-er, while life shall last, Till safe in glo-ry my an-chor is cast; Thro' end-less a-ges, ev-er to be Near-er, my Sav-ior, still near-er to Thee, Near-er, my Sav-ior, still near-er to Thee. A-men.

WORDS and MUSIC: Lelia N. Morris, 1898

MORRIS
9.10.9.10

366 Speak, Lord, in the Stillness

Speak, Lord; for Thy servant heareth. I Sam. 3:9

1. Speak, Lord, in the still-ness While I wait on Thee;
2. Speak, O bless-ed Mas-ter, In this qui-et hour;
3. For the words Thou speak-est, They are life in-deed;
4. All to Thee is yield-ed, I am not my own;
5. Fill me with the know-ledge Of Thy glo-rious will;

HOPE AND ASPIRATION
Hushed my heart tc lis - ten In ex - pect - an - cy.
Let me see Thy face, Lord, Feel Thy touch of power.
Liv - ing bread from heav - en, Now my spir - it feed!
Bliss - ful, glad sur - ren - der, I am Thine a - lone.
All Thine own good pleas - ure In Thy child ful - fill. A-men.
WORDS: E. May Grimes, 1920
MUSIC: Harold Green, c.1925
QUIETUDE
6.5.6.5
Open My Eyes, That I May See 367
Open Thou mine eyes, that I may behold wondrous things out of Thy law. Psa. 119:18
1. O - pen my eyes, that I may see Glimps-es of truth Thou hast for me;
2. O - pen my ears, that I may hear Voic - es of truth Thou send - est clear;
3. O - pen my mouth, and let me bear Glad - ly the warm truth ev - ery-where;
Place in my hands the won - der - ful key That shall un - clasp and set me free.
And while the wave-notes fall on my ear, Ev - ery-thing false will dis - ap - pear.
O - pen my heart, and let me pre - pare Love with Thy chil - dren thus to share.
Refrain
Si - lent - ly now I wait for Thee, Read - y, my God, Thy will to see;
O - pen my eyes, il - lu - mine me, Spir - it di - vine!
O - pen my ears, il - lu - mine me, Spir - it di - vine!
O - pen my heart, il - lu - mine me, Spir - it di - vine! A-men.
WORDS and MUSIC: Clara H. Scott, 1895
SCOTT
Irregular meter

368 Lord, I Want to Be a Christian

Desire the sincere milk of the Word, that ye may grow thereby. I Pet. 2:2

1. Lord, I want to be a Chris-tian In - a my heart, in - a my heart, Lord, I want to be a Chris-tian In - a my heart.
2. Lord, I want to be more lov - ing In - a my heart, in - a my heart, Lord, I want to be more lov - ing In - a my heart.
3. Lord, I want to be more ho - ly In - a my heart, in - a my heart, Lord, I want to be more ho - ly In - a my heart.
4. Lord, I want to be like Je - sus In - a my heart, in - a my heart, Lord, I want to be like Je - sus In - a my heart.
Refrain
In - a my heart, In - a my heart,
In - a my heart, In - a my heart,
Lord, I want to be a Chris-tian In - a my heart.
Lord, I want to be more lov - ing In - a my heart.
Lord, I want to be more ho - ly In - a my heart.
Lord, I want to be like Je - sus In - a my heart.

WORDS and MUSIC: Traditional Spiritual

I WANT TO BE A CHRISTIAN
Irregular meter

I Want a Principle Within 369

I exercise myself, to have always a conscience void of offense . . . Acts 24:16

1. I want a prin - ci - ple with - in Of watch - ful, god - ly fear,
2. From Thee that I no more may stray, No more Thy good - ness grieve,
3. Al - might - y God of truth and love, To me Thy pow'r im - part;
A sen - si - bil - i - ty of sin, A pain to feel it near.
Grant me the fil - ial awe, I pray, The ten - der con-science give.
The bur - den from my soul re - move, The hard - ness from my heart.
Help me the first ap - proach to feel Of pride or wrong de - sire;
Quick as the ap - ple of an eye, O God, my con-science make!
O may the least o - mis - sion pain My re - a - wak-ened soul,
To catch the wan-dering of my will, And quench the kind-ling fire.
A - wake my soul when sin is nigh, And keep it still a - wake.
And drive me to that grace a - gain, Which makes the wound-ed whole. A-men.

WORDS: Charles Wesley, 1749
MUSIC: Traditional Welsh melody

LLANGLOFFAN
C.M.D.

370 Savior, Thy Dying Love

. . . Faith which worketh by love. Gal. 5:6

1. Sav - ior, Thy dy - ing love Thou gav - est me, Nor should I aught with-hold, Dear Lord, from Thee: In love my soul would bow, My heart ful- fill its vow, Some of - fering bring Thee now, Some-thing for Thee.
2. At the blest mer - cy - seat Plead-ing for me, My fee - ble faith looks up, Je - sus, to Thee: Help me the cross to bear, Thy won-drous love de-clare, Some song to raise, or prayer, Some-thing for Thee.
3. Give me a faith - ful heart, Like-ness to Thee, That each de - part - ing day Henceforth may see Some work of love be - gun, Some deed of kind - ness done, Some wan - d'rer sought and won, Some-thing for Thee.
4. All that I am and have— Thy gifts so free— In joy, in grief, thro' life, Dear Lord, for Thee! And when Thy face I see, My ran-somed soul shall be Through all e - ter - ni - ty, Some-thing for Thee. A - men.

WORDS: Sylvanus D. Phelps, 1862
MUSIC: Robert Lowry, 1871

SOMETHING FOR THEE
6.4.6.4.6.6.6.4

371 "Take Up Your Cross," the Savior Said

If any man will come after Me, let him . . . take up his cross, and follow Me. Matt. 16:24

1. "Take up your cross," the Sav - ior said, "If you would My dis - ci - ple be;
2. Take up your cross; let not its weight Fill your weak soul with vain a - larm;
3. Take up your cross, nor heed the shame, And let your fool - ish pride be still:
4. Take up your cross, then, in His strength, And calm - ly ev - ery dan - ger brave;
5. Take up your cross, and fol - low Christ, Nor think till death to lay it down;

Take up your cross with wil - ling heart, And hum-bly fol - low af - ter Me."
His strength shall bear your spir - it up, And brace your heart and nerve your arm.
Your Lord re-fused not e'en to die Up - on a cross on Cal - v'ry's hill.
'Twill guide you to a bet - ter home, And lead to vic - t'ry o'er the grave.
For on - ly he who bears the cross May hope to wear the glo-rious crown.
WORDS: Charles W. Everest, 1833
MUSIC: Henry Baker, 1854
QUEBEC
L.M.
Jesus, Keep Me Near the Cross
372
God forbid that I should glory, save in the cross . . . Gal. 6:14
1. Je - sus, keep me near the cross, There a pre - cious foun - tain
2. Near the cross, a trem - bling soul, Love and mer - cy found me;
3. Near the cross! O Lamb of God, Bring its scenes be - fore me;
4. Near the cross I'll watch and wait, Hop - ing, trust - ing ev - er,
Free to all, a heal - ing stream, Flows from Cal - v'ry's moun - tain.
There the Bright and Morn - ing Star Sheds its beams a - round me.
Help me walk from day to day With its shad - ows o'er me.
Till I reach the gold - en strand Just be - yond the riv - er.
Refrain
In the cross, in the cross Be my glo - ry ev - er;
Till my rap - tured soul shall find Rest be - yond the riv - er.

WORDS: Fanny J. Crosby, 1869
MUSIC: William H. Doane, 1869

NEAR THE CROSS
7.6.7.6 Ref.

373 More About Jesus Would I Know

But grow in grace, and in the knowledge of our Lord and Savior Jesus Christ. II Pet. 3:18

1. More a - bout Je - sus would I know, More of His grace to oth - ers show;
2. More a - bout Je - sus let me learn, More of His ho - ly will dis - cern;
3. More a - bout Je - sus; in His Word, Hold-ing com-mun-ion with my Lord;
4. More a - bout Je - sus on His throne, Rich-es in glo - ry all His own;
More of His sav - ing ful - ness see, More of His love who died for me.
Spir - it of God, my teach - er be, Show-ing the things of Christ to me.
Hear - ing His voice in ev - ery line, Mak - ing each faith - ful say - ing mine.
More of His king-dom's sure in-crease; More of His com - ing, Prince of Peace.
Refrain
More, more a - bout Je - sus, More, more a - bout Je - sus;
More of His sav - ing ful - ness see, More of His love who died for me.

WORDS: Eliza E. Hewitt, 1887
MUSIC: John R. Sweney, 1887

SWENEY
L.M. Ref.

Earthly Pleasures Vainly Call Me 374

We . . . are changed into the same image from glory to glory. II Cor. 3:18

1. Earth-ly pleas-ures vain - ly call me, I would be like Je - sus;
2. He has bro-ken ev - ery fet - ter, I would be like Je - sus;
3. All the way from earth to glo - ry, I would be like Je - sus;
4. That in heav - en He may meet me, I would be like Je - sus;
would be like Je - sus;
Noth - ing world - ly shall en - thrall me, I would be like Je - sus.
That my soul may serve Him bet - ter, I would be like Je - sus.
Tell - ing o'er and o'er the sto - ry, I would be like Je - sus.
That His words "Well done" may greet me, I would be like Je - sus.
would be like Je - sus.
Refrain
Be like Je - sus, this my song, In the home and in the throng;
Be like Je - sus, all day long! I would be like Je - sus.

WORDS: James Rowe, 1912
MUSIC: Bentley D. Ackley, 1912

SPRING HILL
C.M. Ref.

375 My Faith Looks Up to Thee

Looking unto Jesus the author and finisher of our faith. Heb. 12:2

1. My faith looks up to Thee, Thou Lamb of Cal - va - ry,
2. May Thy rich grace im - part Strength to my faint - ing heart,
3. While life's dark maze I tread, And griefs a - round me spread,
4. When ends life's tran - sient dream, When death's cold, sul - len stream

Sav - ior di - vine! Now hear me while I pray, Take all my
My zeal in - spire; As Thou hast died for me, O may my
Be Thou my guide; Bid dark - ness turn to day, Wipe sor - row's
Shall o'er me roll; Blest Sav - ior, then, in love, Fear and dis -

guilt a - way, O let me from this day Be whol - ly Thine!
love to Thee Pure, warm, and change - less be, A liv - ing fire!
tears a - way, Nor let me ev - er stray From Thee a - side.
trust re - move; O bear me safe a - bove, A ran - somed soul! A-men.

WORDS: Ray Palmer, 1830
MUSIC: Lowell Mason, 1832

OLIVET
6.6.4.6.6.6.4

376 May the Mind of Christ My Savior

Let this mind be in you which was also in Christ Jesus . . . Phil. 2:5

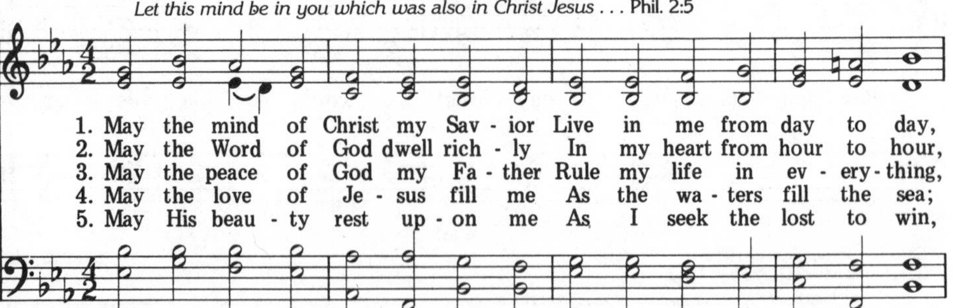
1. May the mind of Christ my Sav - ior Live in me from day to day,
2. May the Word of God dwell rich - ly In my heart from hour to hour,
3. May the peace of God my Fa - ther Rule my life in ev - ery - thing,
4. May the love of Je - sus fill me As the wa - ters fill the sea;
5. May His beau - ty rest up - on me As I seek the lost to win,

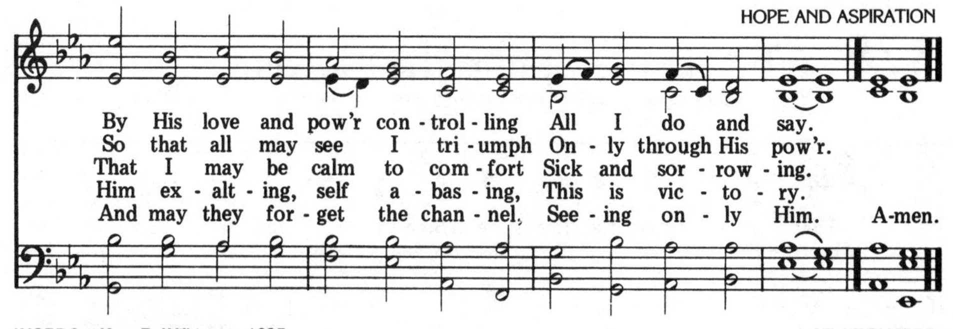
By His love and pow'r con - trol - ling All I do and say.
So that all may see I tri - umph On - ly through His pow'r.
That I may be calm to com - fort Sick and sor - row - ing.
Him ex - alt - ing, self a - bas - ing, This is vic - to - ry.
And may they for - get the chan - nel, See - ing on - ly Him. A-men.

WORDS: Kate B. Wilkinson, 1925
MUSIC: A. Cyril Barham-Gould, 1925

ST. LEONARDS
8.7.8.5

O Love That Will Not Let Me Go 377

The Lord hath appeared . . . saying, Yea, I have loved thee with an everlasting love. Jer. 31:3

1. O Love that will not let me go,
I rest my weary soul in Thee;
I give Thee back the life I owe,
That in Thine ocean depths its flow
May richer, fuller be.

2. O Light that fol - l'west all my way,
I yield my flick - 'ring torch to Thee;
My heart restores its borrowed ray,
That in Thy sunshine's blaze its day
May brighter, fairer be.

3. O Joy that seekest me through pain,
I cannot close my heart to Thee;
I trace the rainbow through the rain,
And feel the promise is not vain
That morn shall tearless be.

4. O Cross that liftest up my head,
I dare not ask to fly from Thee;
I lay in dust life's glory dead,
And from the ground there blossoms red
Life that shall endless be. A-men.

WORDS: George Matheson, 1882
MUSIC: Albert L. Peace, 1884

ST. MARGARET
8.8.8.8.6

378 When in the Spring the Flowers

Lo, the winter is past . . . the time of the singing of birds is come. S. of Sol. 2:11, 12

1. When in the spring the flow'rs are bloom-ing bright and fair Aft - er the gray of win-ter's gone, Once a - gain the lark be - gins its tun - ing Back in the mead - ows of my home.
2. Lord, make me like that stream that flows so cool and clear Down from the moun-tains high a - bove; I will tell the world the won-drous sto - ry Of the pre - cious stream filled with your love.
(♭)
Refrain
Lord, to my heart bring back the spring - time, Take a-way the cold and dark of sin; O re-turn to me, sweet Ho - ly

Spir - it, May I warm and ten- der be a - gain.

WORDS and MUSIC: Kurt Kaiser, 1970

SPRINGTIME
Irregular meter

Nearer, My God, to Thee 379

It is good for me to draw near to God . . . Psa. 73:28

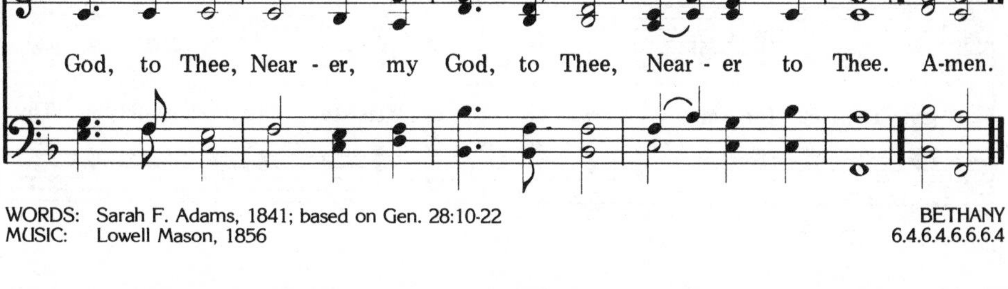

1. Near - er, my God, to Thee, Near - er to Thee! E'en though it
2. Though like the wan - der - er, The sun gone down, Dark - ness be
3. There let the way ap - pear Steps un - to heav'n; All that Thou
4. Then, with my wak - ing thoughts Bright with Thy praise, Out of my
5. Or if on joy - ful wing, Cleav - ing the sky, Sun, moon, and

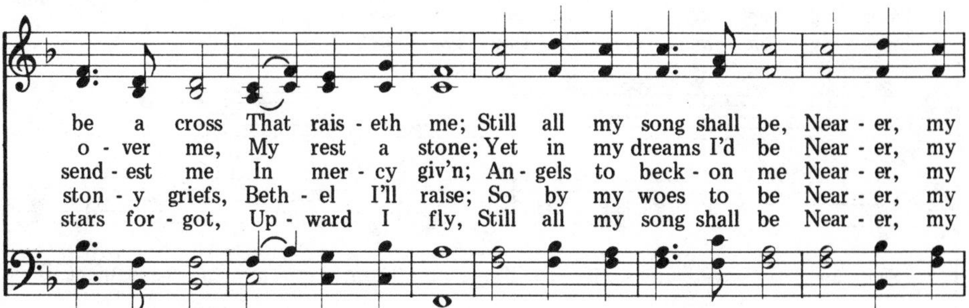

be a cross That rais - eth me; Still all my song shall be, Near - er, my
o - ver me, My rest a stone; Yet in my dreams I'd be Near - er, my
send - est me In mer - cy giv'n; An - gels to beck - on me Near - er, my
ston - y griefs, Beth - el I'll raise; So by my woes to be Near - er, my
stars for - got, Up - ward I fly, Still all my song shall be Near - er, my

God, to Thee, Near - er, my God, to Thee, Near - er to Thee. A-men.

WORDS: Sarah F. Adams, 1841; based on Gen. 28:10-22
MUSIC: Lowell Mason, 1856

BETHANY
6.4.6.4.6.6.6.4

380 Living for Jesus a Life That Is True

That ye might walk worthy of the Lord . . . Col. 1:10

1. Liv - ing for Je - sus a life that is true, Striv - ing to please Him in all that I do; Yield - ing al - le - giance, glad - heart - ed and free, This is the path - way of bless - ing for me.
2. Liv - ing for Je - sus who died in my place, Bear - ing on Cal - v'ry my sin and dis - grace; Such love con - strains me to an - swer His call, Fol - low His lead - ing and give Him my all.
3. Liv - ing for Je - sus wher - ev - er I am, Do - ing each du - ty in His ho - ly name; Will - ing to suf - fer af - flic - tion and loss, Deem - ing each tri - al a part of my cross.
4. Liv - ing for Je - sus through earth's lit - tle while, My dear - est treas - ure, the light of His smile; Seek - ing the lost ones He died to re - deem, Bring - ing the wea - ry to find rest in Him.
Refrain
O Je - sus, Lord and Sav - ior, I give my - self to Thee, For Thou, in Thy a - tone - ment, Didst give Thy - self for me; I own no oth - er Mas - ter, My heart shall be Thy

throne; My life I give, hence-forth to live, O Christ, for Thee a - lone.

WORDS: Thomas O. Chisholm, 1917
MUSIC: C. Harold Lowden, 1915

LIVING
10.10.10.10 Ref.

Teach Me Thy Will, O Lord 381

Teach me to do Thy will; for Thou art my God. Psa. 143:10

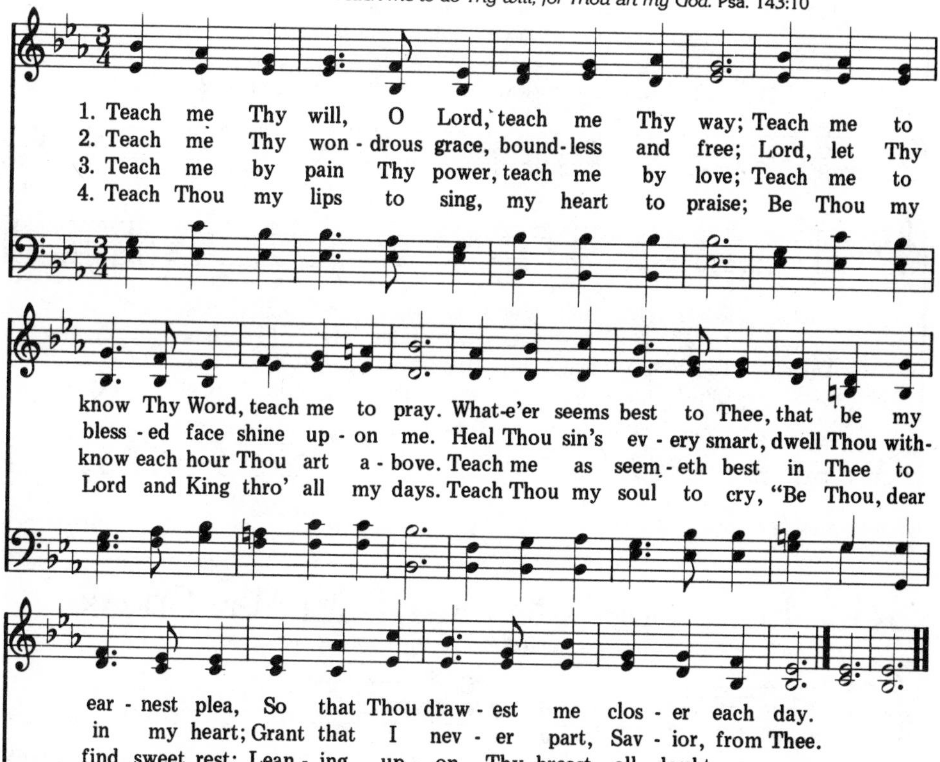

1. Teach me Thy will, O Lord, teach me Thy way; Teach me to
2. Teach me Thy won - drous grace, bound - less and free; Lord, let Thy
3. Teach me by pain Thy power, teach me by love; Teach me to
4. Teach Thou my lips to sing, my heart to praise; Be Thou my

know Thy Word, teach me to pray. What-e'er seems best to Thee, that be my
bless - ed face shine up - on me. Heal Thou sin's ev - ery smart, dwell Thou with-
know each hour Thou art a - bove. Teach me as seem - eth best in Thee to
Lord and King thro' all my days. Teach Thou my soul to cry, "Be Thou, dear

ear - nest plea, So that Thou draw - est me clos - er each day.
in my heart; Grant that I nev - er part, Sav - ior, from Thee.
find sweet rest; Lean - ing up - on Thy breast, all doubt re - move.
Sav - ior, nigh, Teach me to live, to die, saved by Thy grace." A - men.

WORDS: Katherine A. Grimes, 1935
MUSIC: William M. Runyan, 1935

TEACH ME
6.4.6.4.6.6.6.4

382 Have Thine Own Way, Lord

We are the clay, and Thou our potter . . . Isa. 64:8

1. Have Thine own way, Lord! Have Thine own way! Thou art the
2. Have Thine own way, Lord! Have Thine own way! Search me and
3. Have Thine own way, Lord! Have Thine own way! Wound - ed and
4. Have Thine own way, Lord! Have Thine own way! Hold o'er my

Pot - ter, I am the clay. Mold me and make me aft - er Thy
try me, Mas - ter, to - day! Whit - er than snow, Lord, wash me just
wea - ry, help me, I pray! Pow - er— all pow - er— sure - ly is
be - ing ab - so - lute sway! Fill with Thy Spir - it till all shall

will, While I am wait - ing yield - ed and still.
now, As in Thy pres - ence hum - bly I bow.
Thine! Touch me and heal me, Sav - ior di - vine!
see Christ on - ly, al - ways, liv - ing in me! A - men.

WORDS: Adelaide A. Pollard, 1902
MUSIC: George C. Stebbins, 1907

ADELAIDE
5.4.5.4 D.

383 Lord, Speak to Me, That I May Speak

The things that thou hast heard of Me . . . commit thou to faithful men. II Tim. 2:2

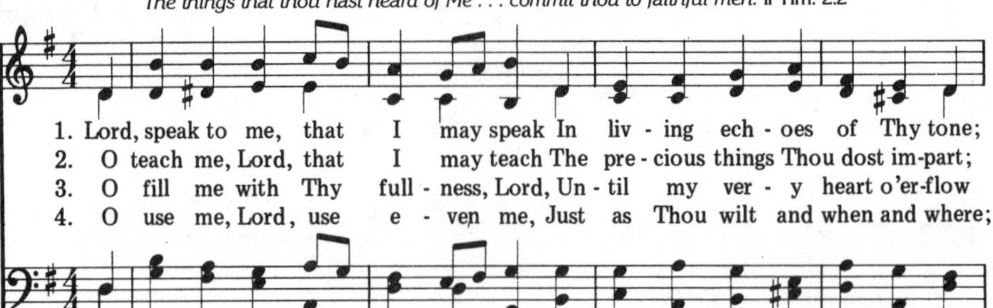
1. Lord, speak to me, that I may speak In liv - ing ech - oes of Thy tone;
2. O teach me, Lord, that I may teach The pre - cious things Thou dost im-part;
3. O fill me with Thy full - ness, Lord, Un - til my ver - y heart o'er-flow
4. O use me, Lord, use e - ven me, Just as Thou wilt and when and where;

As Thou hast sought, so let me seek Thy err-ing chil-dren lost and lone.
And wing my words, that they may reach The hid-den depths of many a heart.
In kind-ling thought and glow-ing word Thy love to tell, Thy praise to show.
Un-til Thy bless-ed face I see, Thy rest, Thy joy, Thy glo-ry share. A-men.

WORDS: Frances R. Havergal, 1872
MUSIC: Robert A. Schumann, 1839

CANONBURY
L.M.

Jesus, Savior, All I Have Is Thine 384

. . . A vessel unto honor . . . meet for the Master's use. II Tim. 2:21

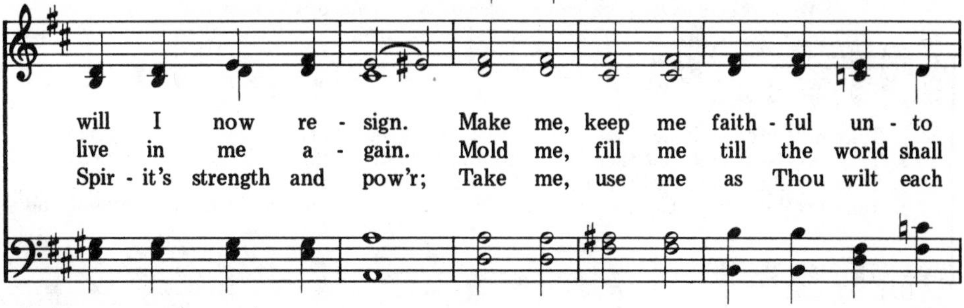

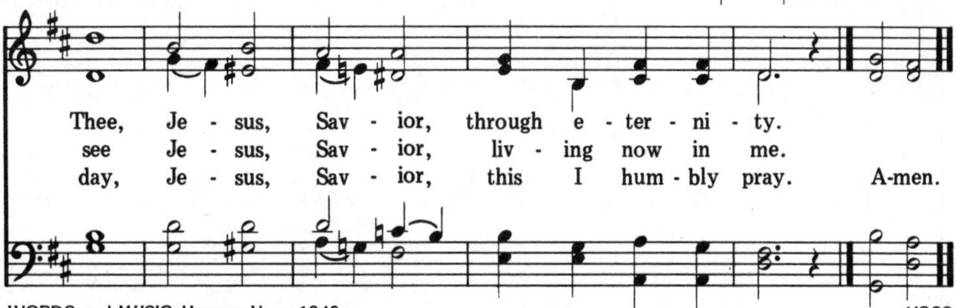

1. Je - sus, Sav - ior, all I have is Thine, Bod - y, soul and will I now re - sign. Make me, keep me faith - ful un - to Thee, Je - sus, Sav - ior, through e - ter - ni - ty.

2. Je - sus, Sav - ior, I would die to sin, Come, O come and live in me a - gain. Mold me, fill me till the world shall see Je - sus, Sav - ior, liv - ing now in me.

3. Je - sus, Sav - ior, in this qui - et hour, May I feel Thy Spir - it's strength and pow'r; Take me, use me as Thou wilt each day, Je - sus, Sav - ior, this I hum - bly pray. A-men.

WORDS and MUSIC: Herman Voss, 1940

VOSS
Irregular meter

385 I Can Hear My Savior Calling

Master, I will follow Thee whithersoever Thou goest. Matt. 8:19

1. I can hear my Sav - ior call - ing, I can hear my Sav - ior call - ing,
2. I'll go with Him thro' the gar - den, I'll go with Him thro' the gar - den,
3. I'll go with Him thro' the judg - ment, I'll go with Him thro' the judg-ment,
4. He will give me grace and glo - ry, He will give me grace and glo - ry,
Ref. – Where He leads me I will fol - low, Where He leads me I will fol - low,
D.C. Refrain
I can hear my Sav - ior call - ing, "Take thy cross and fol - low, fol - low Me."
I'll go with Him thro' the gar - den, I'll go with Him, with Him all the way.
I'll go with Him thro' the judg-ment, I'll go with Him, with Him all the way.
He will give me grace and glo - ry, And go with me, with me all the way.
Where He leads me I will fol - low, I'll go with Him, with Him all the way.
1. Take my life and let it be Con - se - crat - ed, Lord, to Thee; Take my hands and
2. Take my feet and let them be Swift and beau - ti - ful for Thee; Take my voice and
3. Take my lips and let them be Filled with mes - sa - ges for Thee; Take my sil - ver
4. Take my love, my God, I pour At Thy feet its treas-ure store; Take my-self and
let them move At the im-pulse of Thy love, At the im - pulse of Thy love.
let me sing Al - ways, on - ly, for my King, Al - ways, on - ly, for my King.
and my gold, Not a mite would I with-hold, Not a mite would I with-hold.
I will be Ev - er, on - ly, all for Thee, Ev - er, on - ly, all for Thee.

WORDS: E. W. Blandy, 1890
MUSIC: John S. Norris, 1890

NORRIS
8.8.8.9 Ref.

386 Take My Life and Let It Be

Ye are bought with a price; therefore glorify God in your body . . . I Cor. 6:20

WORDS: Frances R. Havergal, 1874
MUSIC: Henri A. César Malan, 1827

HENDON
7.7.7.7.7

My Life, My Love I Give to Thee 387
That they might live . . . unto Him which died for them. II Cor. 5:15
1. My life, my love I give to Thee, Thou Lamb of God who died for me;
2. I now be-lieve Thou dost re-ceive, For Thou hast died that I might live;
3. O Thou who died on Cal-va-ry, To save my soul and make me free,
Ref. – I'll live for Him who died for me, How hap-py then my life shall be!
O may I ev-er faith-ful be, My Sav-ior and my God!
And now hence-forth I'll trust in Thee, My Sav-ior and my God!
I'll con-se-crate my life to Thee, My Sav-ior and my God!
I'll live for Him who died for me, My Sav-ior and my God!
D.C. Refrain
WORDS: Ralph E. Hudson, 1882
MUSIC: C. R. Dunbar, 1882
DUNBAR
8.8.8.6 Ref.
All for Jesus! All for Jesus! 388
Present your bodies a living sacrifice . . . Rom. 12:1
1. All for Je-sus! All for Je-sus! All my be-ing's ran-somed pow'rs;
2. Let my hands per-form His bid-ding, Let my feet run in His ways;
3. Since my eyes were fixed on Je-sus, I've lost sight of all be-side;
4. O, what won-der! how a-maz-ing! Je-sus, glo-rious King of kings,
All my thoughts and words and do-ings, All my days and all my hours.
Let my eyes see Je-sus on-ly, Let my lips speak forth His praise.
So en-chained my spir-it's vi-sion, Look-ing at the Cru-ci-fied.
Deigns to call me His be-lov-ed, Lets me rest be-neath His wings. A-men.
WORDS: Mary D. James, 1889
MUSIC: John Stainer, 1887
WYCLIFF
8.7.8.7

389 "Are Ye Able," Said the Master

Jesus said . . . Can ye drink of the cup that I drink of? Mark 10:38

1. "Are ye a - ble," said the Mas - ter, "To be cru - ci - fied with me?"
"Yea," the stur - dy dream - ers an - swered, "To the death we fol - low Thee."

2. "Are ye a - ble," to re - mem - ber, When a thief lifts up his eyes,
That his par - doned soul is wor - thy Of a place in par - a - dise?

3. "Are ye a - ble," when the shad - ows Close a - round you with the sod,
To be - lieve that spir - it tri - umphs, To com - mend your soul to God?

4. "Are ye a - ble?" still the Mas - ter Whis - pers down e - ter - ni - ty,
And he - ro - ic spir - its an - swer Now, as then in Gal - i - lee.

Refrain

"Lord, we are a - ble," our spir - its are Thine. Re - mold them, make us like Thee, di - vine: Thy guid - ing ra - diance a - bove us shall be A bea - con to God, To love and loy - al - ty. A - men.

WORDS: Earl Marlatt, 1925
MUSIC: Harry S. Mason, 1924

BEACON HILL
8.7.8.7 Ref.

Make Me a Captive, Lord 390

. . . He that loseth his life for My sake shall find it. Matt. 10:39

1. Make me a cap - tive, Lord, And then I shall be free;
2. My heart is weak and poor Un - til it mas - ter find;
3. My pow'r is faint and low Till I have learned to serve;
4. My will is not my own Till Thou hast made it Thine;
Force me to ren - der up my sword, And I shall con-queror be;
It has no spring of ac - tion sure— It var - ies with the wind;
It wants the need - ed fire to glow, It wants the breeze to nerve;
If it would reach the mon-arch's throne It must its crown re - sign:
I sink in life's a - larms When by my - self I stand;
It can - not free - ly move Till Thou hast wrought its chain;
It can - not drive the world Un - til it - self be driv'n;
It on - ly stands un - bent, A - mid the clash - ing strife,
Im - pris - on me with - in Thine arms, And strong shall be my hand.
En - slave it with Thy match- less love, And death - less it shall reign.
Its flag can on - ly be un-furled When Thou shalt breathe from heav'n.
When on Thy bos - om it has leaned, And found in Thee its life.

WORDS: George Matheson, 1890
MUSIC: Donald P. Hustad, 1953

PARADOXY
S.M.D.

391 God Himself Is with Us

The Lord is in His holy temple: let all the earth keep silence before Him. Hab. 2:20

1. God Him-self is with us; Let us all a - dore Him, And with awe ap-
2. Come, a - bide with - in me; Let my soul, like Ma - ry, Be Thine earth-ly
3. Glad - ly we sur - ren - der Earth's de-ceit - ful treas-ures, Pride of life and
pear be - fore Him. God is here with - in us; Soul, in si - lence
sanc - tu - ar - y. Come, in - dwell - ing Spir - it, With trans - fig - ured
sin - ful pleas - ures; Glad - ly, Lord, we of - fer Thine to be for-
fear Him, Hum-bly, fer-vent - ly draw near Him. Now His own who have known
splen-dor; Love and hon-or will I ren - der. Where I go here be - low
ev - er, Soul and life and each en - deav - or. Thou a - lone shalt be known
God, in wor - ship low - ly, Yield their spir - its whol - ly.
Let me bow be - fore Thee, Know Thee and a - dore Thee.
Lord of all our be - ing, Life's true way de - cree - ing. A - men.

WORDS: Gerhard Tersteegen, 1729; tr. *Hymnal*, 1940
MUSIC: Joachim Neander's *Bundes-lieder*, 1680

WUNDERBARER KÖNIG
6.6.8.D.3.3.6.6

Take Thou Our Minds, Dear Lord 392

Thou shalt love the Lord thy God . . . with all thy mind. Matt. 22:37

1. Take Thou our minds, dear Lord, we hum - bly pray;
2. Take Thou our hearts, O Christ, they are Thine own;
3. Take Thou our wills, Most High! hold Thou full sway;
4. Take Thou our - selves, O Lord, heart, mind and will;
Give us the mind of Christ each pass - ing day;
Come Thou with - in our souls and claim Thy throne;
Have in our in - most souls Thy per - fect way;
Through our sur - ren - dered souls Thy plans ful - fill.
Teach us to know the truth that sets us free;
Help us to shed a - broad Thy death - less love;
Guard Thou each sa - cred hour from self - ish ease;
We yield our - selves to Thee— time, tal - ents, all!
Grant us in all our thoughts to hon - or Thee.
Use us to make the earth like heav'n a - bove.
Guide Thou our or - dered lives as Thou dost please.
We hear, and hence - forth heed Thy sov - ereign call. A-men.

WORDS: William H. Foulkes, 1918
MUSIC: Calvin W. Laufer, 1918

HALL
10.10.10.10

393 All to Jesus I Surrender

Lo, we have left all, and have followed Thee. Mark 10:28

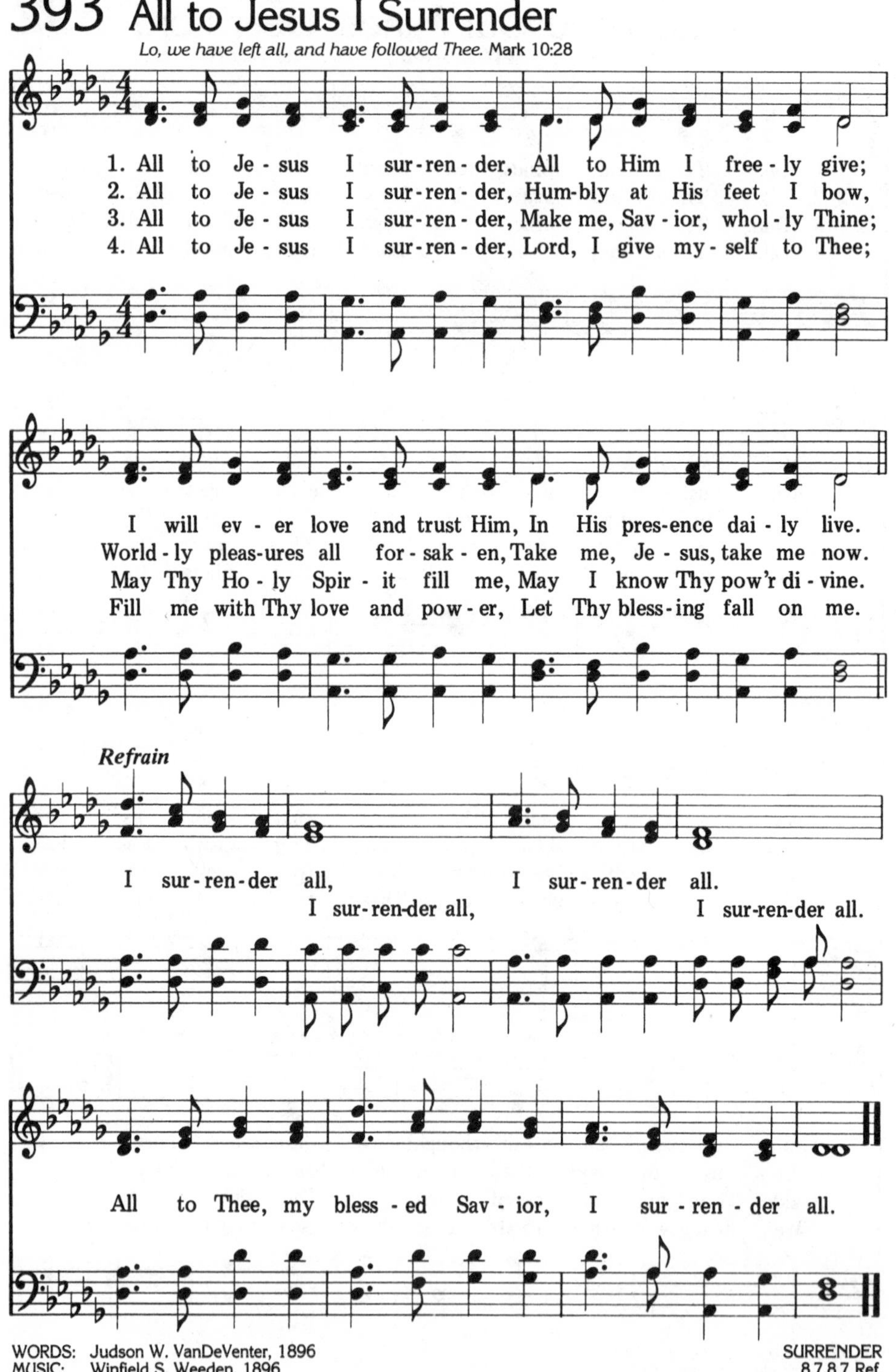
1. All to Je - sus I sur-ren - der, All to Him I free - ly give;
2. All to Je - sus I sur-ren - der, Hum-bly at His feet I bow,
3. All to Je - sus I sur-ren - der, Make me, Sav - ior, whol - ly Thine;
4. All to Je - sus I sur-ren - der, Lord, I give my - self to Thee;
I will ev - er love and trust Him, In His pres-ence dai - ly live.
World - ly pleas-ures all for - sak - en, Take me, Je - sus, take me now.
May Thy Ho - ly Spir - it fill me, May I know Thy pow'r di - vine.
Fill me with Thy love and pow - er, Let Thy bless - ing fall on me.
Refrain
I sur - ren - der all, I sur - ren - der all.
I sur-ren-der all, I sur-ren-der all.
All to Thee, my bless - ed Sav - ior, I sur - ren - der all.

WORDS: Judson W. VanDeVenter, 1896
MUSIC: Winfield S. Weeden, 1896

SURRENDER
8.7.8.7 Ref.

Only One Life to Offer 394

But this I say, brethren, the time is short . . . I Cor. 7:29

1. On - ly one life to of - fer— Je - sus, my Lord and King;
2. On - ly this hour is mine, Lord—May it be used for Thee;
3. On - ly one life to of - fer— Take it, dear Lord, I pray;
On - ly one tongue to praise Thee And of Thy mer - cy sing (for-ev - er);
May ev - ery pass - ing mo-ment Count for e - ter - ni - ty (my Sav-ior);
Noth-ing from Thee with-hold - ing, Thy will I now o - bey (my Je - sus);
On - ly one heart's de - vo - tion—Sav - ior, O may it be Con - se -
Souls all a - bout are dy - ing, Dy - ing in sin and shame; Help me
Thou who hast free - ly giv - en Thine all in all for me, Claim this
crat - ed a - lone to Thy match - less glo - ry, Yield - ed ful - ly to Thee.
bring them the mes - sage of Cal - v'ry's re-demp-tion In Thy glo - ri - ous name.
life for Thine own, to be used, my Sav - ior, Ev - ery mo-ment for Thee.

WORDS: Avis B. Christiansen, 1937
MUSIC: Merrill Dunlop, 1937

ONLY ONE LIFE
Irregular meter

395 We Rest on Thee

For we rest on Thee, and in Thy name we go against this multitude. II Chron. 14:11

1. "We rest on Thee"— our Shield and our De - fen - der! We go not
2. Yea, "in Thy Name," O Cap - tain of sal - va - tion! In Thy dear
3. "We go" in faith, our own great weak-ness feel - ing, And need - ing
4. "We rest on Thee"— our Shield and our De - fen - der! Thine is the
forth a - lone a - gainst the foe; Strong in Thy strength, safe
Name, all oth - er names a - bove; Je - sus our Right - eous-
more each day Thy grace to know: Yet from our hearts a
bat - tle, Thine shall be the praise! When pass - ing through the
in Thy keep - ing ten - der, "We rest on Thee, and
ness, our sure foun - da - tion, Our Prince of glo - ry
song of tri - umph peal - ing; "We rest on Thee, and
gates of pearl - y splen - dor, Vic - tors— we rest with
in Thy Name we go," Strong in Thy strength, safe in Thy keep - ing
and our King of love, Je - sus our Right - eous-ness, our sure foun-
in Thy Name we go," Yet from our hearts a song of tri - umph
Thee, thro' end - less days, When pass - ing through the gates of pearl - y

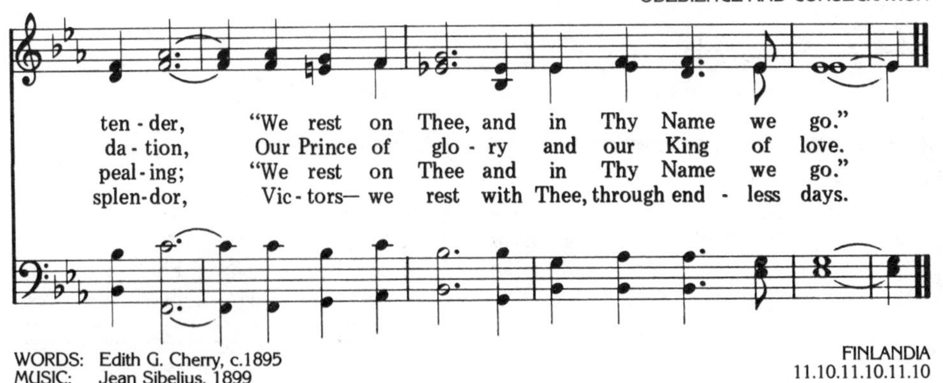
ten - der, "We rest on Thee, and in Thy Name we go."
da - tion, Our Prince of glo - ry and our King of love.
peal - ing; "We rest on Thee and in Thy Name we go."
splen-dor, Vic - tors— we rest with Thee, through end - less days.

WORDS: Edith G. Cherry, c.1895
MUSIC: Jean Sibelius, 1899

FINLANDIA
11.10.11.10.11.10

Teach Me Thy Way, O Lord 396

Teach me Thy way, O Lord, and lead me in a plain path. Psa. 27:11

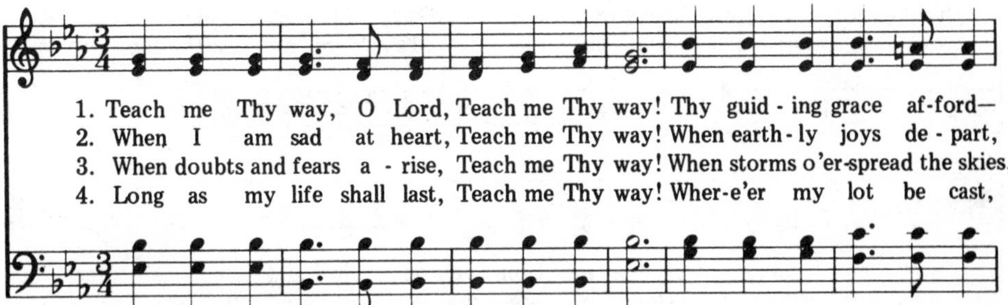

1. Teach me Thy way, O Lord, Teach me Thy way! Thy guid - ing grace af-ford—
2. When I am sad at heart, Teach me Thy way! When earth - ly joys de - part,
3. When doubts and fears a - rise, Teach me Thy way! When storms o'er-spread the skies,
4. Long as my life shall last, Teach me Thy way! Wher-e'er my lot be cast,

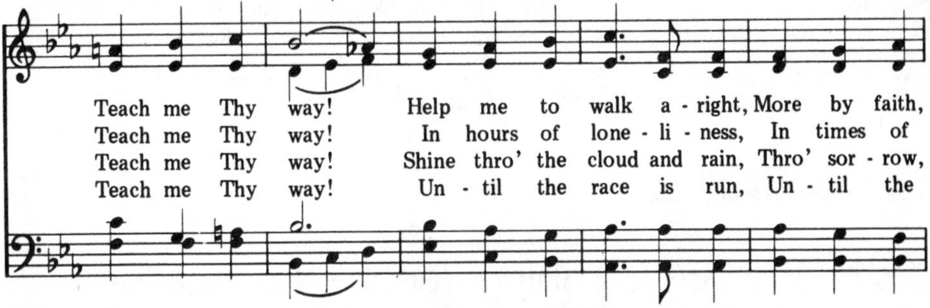

Teach me Thy way! Help me to walk a - right, More by faith,
Teach me Thy way! In hours of lone - li - ness, In times of
Teach me Thy way! Shine thro' the cloud and rain, Thro' sor - row,
Teach me Thy way! Un - til the race is run, Un - til the

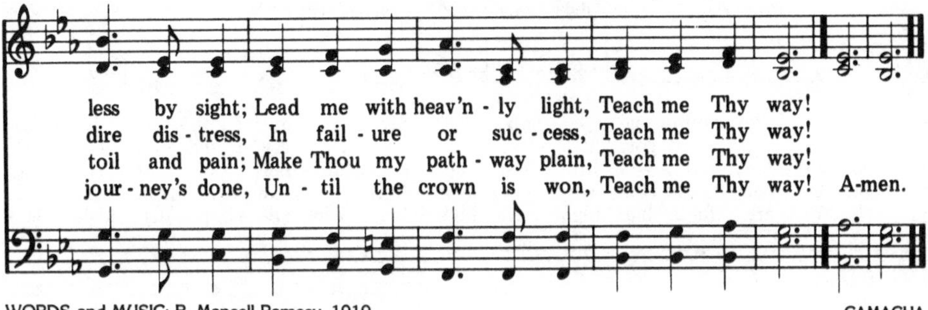

less by sight; Lead me with heav'n - ly light, Teach me Thy way!
dire dis - tress, In fail - ure or suc - cess, Teach me Thy way!
toil and pain; Make Thou my path - way plain, Teach me Thy way!
jour - ney's done, Un - til the crown is won, Teach me Thy way! A-men.

WORDS and MUSIC: B. Mansell Ramsey, 1919

CAMACHA
6.4.6.4.6.6.6.4

397 Search Me, O God

Search me, O God, and know my heart . . . Psa. 139:23

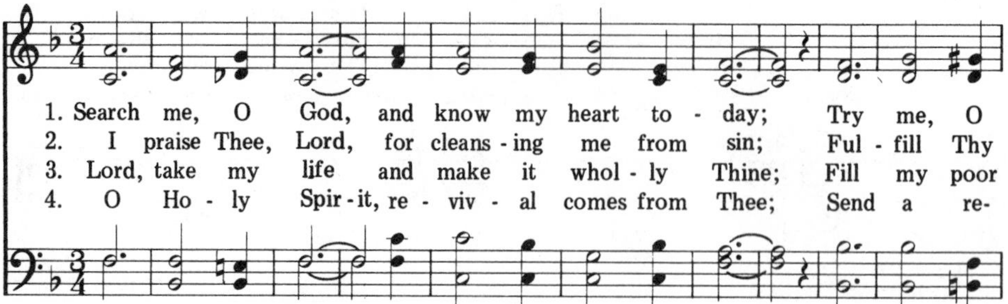

1. Search me, O God, and know my heart to - day; Try me, O
2. I praise Thee, Lord, for cleans - ing me from sin; Ful - fill Thy
3. Lord, take my life and make it whol - ly Thine; Fill my poor
4. O Ho - ly Spir - it, re - viv - al comes from Thee; Send a re-

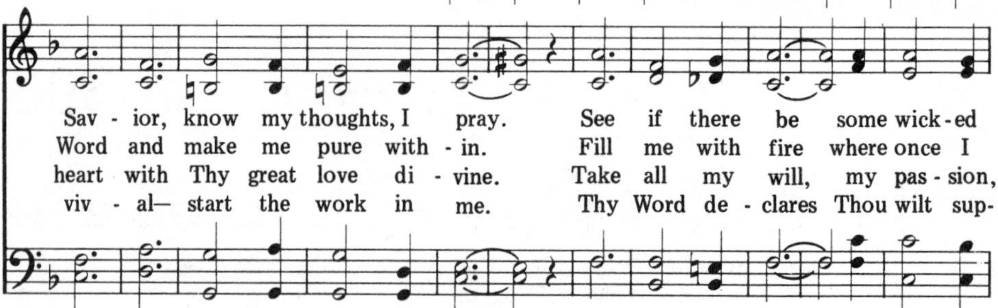

Sav - ior, know my thoughts, I pray. See if there be some wick - ed
Word and make me pure with - in. Fill me with fire where once I
heart with Thy great love di - vine. Take all my will, my pas - sion,
viv - al— start the work in me. Thy Word de - clares Thou wilt sup-

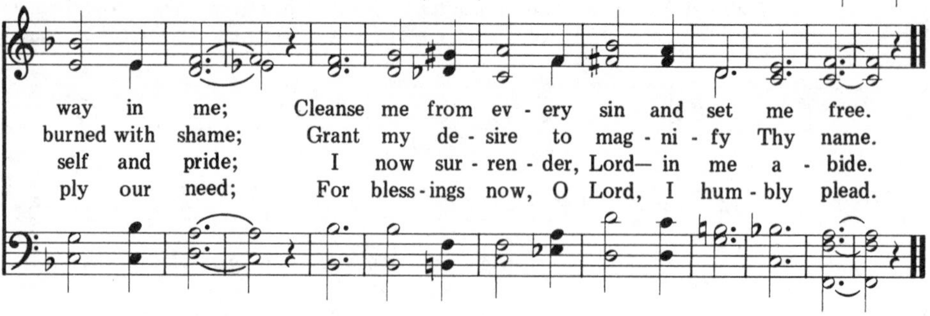

way in me; Cleanse me from ev - ery sin and set me free.
burned with shame; Grant my de - sire to mag - ni - fy Thy name.
self and pride; I now sur - ren - der, Lord— in me a - bide.
ply our need; For bless - ings now, O Lord, I hum - bly plead.

WORDS: J. Edwin Orr, 1936
MUSIC: Traditional Maori melody

MAORI
10.10.10.10

398 We Are Climbing Jacob's Ladder

Behold a ladder . . . and the top of it reached to heaven. Gen. 28:12

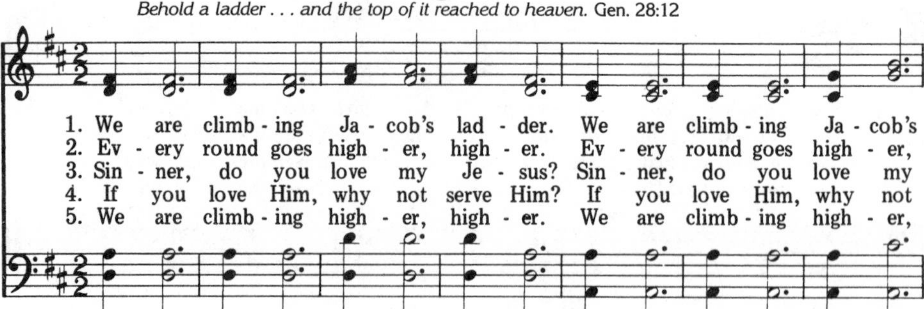
1. We are climb - ing Ja - cob's lad - der. We are climb - ing Ja - cob's
2. Ev - ery round goes high - er, high - er. Ev - ery round goes high - er,
3. Sin - ner, do you love my Je - sus? Sin - ner, do you love my
4. If you love Him, why not serve Him? If you love Him, why not
5. We are climb - ing high - er, high - er. We are climb - ing high - er,

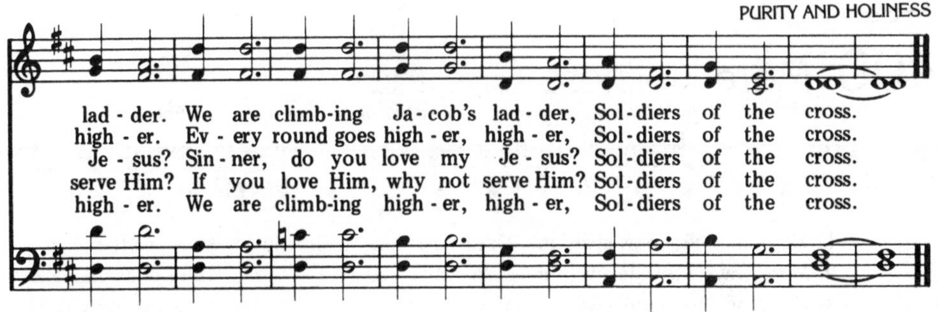

lad - der. We are climb-ing Ja - cob's lad - der, Sol - diers of the cross.
high - er. Ev - ery round goes high - er, high - er, Sol - diers of the cross.
Je - sus? Sin - ner, do you love my Je - sus? Sol - diers of the cross.
serve Him? If you love Him, why not serve Him? Sol - diers of the cross.
high - er. We are climb-ing high - er, high - er, Sol - diers of the cross.

WORDS and MUSIC: Traditional Spiritual

JACOB'S LADDER
8.8.8.5

Purer in Heart, O God 399

Every man that hath this hope in Him purifieth himself . . . I John 3:3

1. Pur - er in heart, O God, Help me to be; May I de - vote my life Whol - ly to Thee: Watch Thou my way - ward feet, Guide me with coun - sel sweet; Pur - er in heart Help me to be.

2. Pur - er in heart, O God, Help me to be; Teach me to do Thy will Most lov - ing - ly: Be Thou my friend and guide, Let me with Thee a - bide; Pur - er in heart Help me to be.

3. Pur - er in heart, O God, Help me to be; Un - til Thy ho - ly face One day I see: Keep me from se - cret sin, Reign Thou my soul with - in; Pur - er in heart Help me to be.

WORDS: Fannie E. Davison, 1877
MUSIC: James H. Fillmore, 1877

PURER IN HEART
6.4.6.4.6.6.4.4

400 More Holiness Give Me

Till we all come . . . unto the measure of the stature of the fulness of Christ. Eph. 4:13

1. More ho - li - ness give me, More striv - ing with - in; More patience in
2. More grat - i - tude give me, More trust in the Lord; More pride in His
3. More pu - ri - ty give me, More strength to o'er - come; More free-dom from

suf - f'ring, More sor - row for sin; More faith in my Sav - ior,
glo - ry, More hope in His word; More tears for His sor - rows,
earth - stains, More long - ings for home; More fit for the king - dom,

More sense of His care; More joy in His ser - vice, More pur - pose in prayer.
More pain at His grief; More meek-ness in tri - al, More praise for re - lief.
More used would I be; More bless-ed and ho - ly, More, Sav - ior, like Thee.

WORDS and MUSIC: Philip P. Bliss, 1873

MY PRAYER
6.5.6.5 D.

401 God Who Touches Earth with Beauty

He hath made every thing beautiful in His time. Eccl. 3:11

1. God who touch - es earth with beau - ty, Make my heart a - new;
2. Like Your springs and run - ning wa - ters Make me crys - tal pure,
3. Like Your danc - ing waves in sun - light Make me glad and free,
4. Like the arch - ing of the heav - ens Lift my thoughts a - bove,
5. God who touch - es earth with beau - ty, Make my heart a - new;

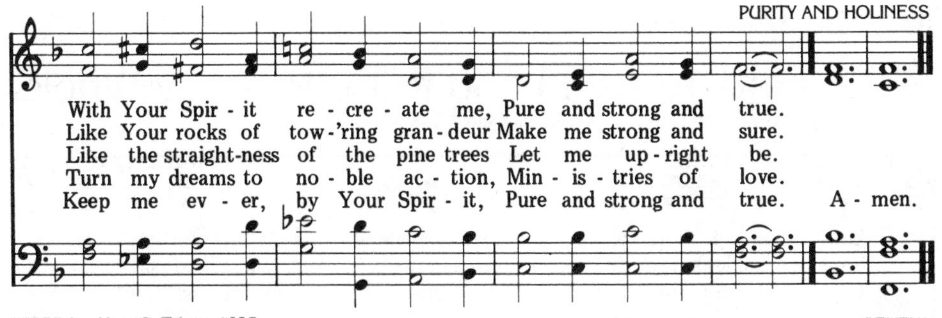
With Your Spir - it re - cre - ate me, Pure and strong and true.
Like Your rocks of tow-'ring gran - deur Make me strong and sure.
Like the straight-ness of the pine trees Let me up - right be.
Turn my dreams to no - ble ac - tion, Min - is - tries of love.
Keep me ev - er, by Your Spir - it, Pure and strong and true. A - men.

WORDS: Mary S. Edgar, 1925
MUSIC: C. Harold Lowden, 1925

GENEVA
8.5.8.5

Take Time to Be Holy 402

Follow peace with all men, and holiness . . . Heb. 12:14

1. Take time to be ho - ly, Speak oft with thy Lord; A - bide in Him
2. Take time to be ho - ly, The world rush - es on; Spend much time in
3. Take time to be ho - ly, Let Him be thy guide, And run not be-
4. Take time to be ho - ly, Be calm in thy soul; Each thought and each

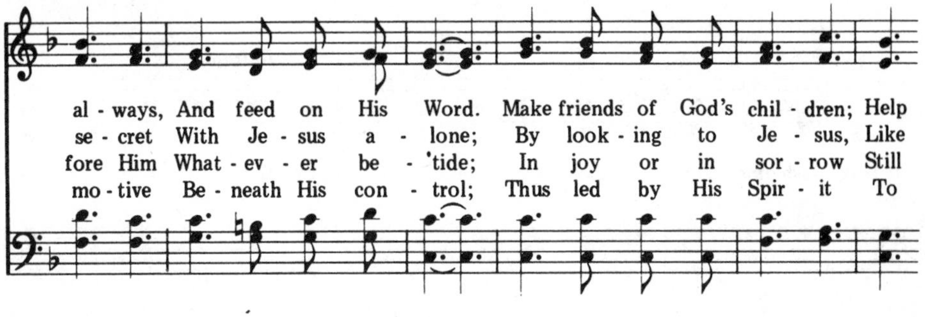

al - ways, And feed on His Word. Make friends of God's chil - dren; Help
se - cret With Je - sus a - lone; By look - ing to Je - sus, Like
fore Him What - ev - er be - 'tide; In joy or in sor - row Still
mo - tive Be - neath His con - trol; Thus led by His Spir - it To

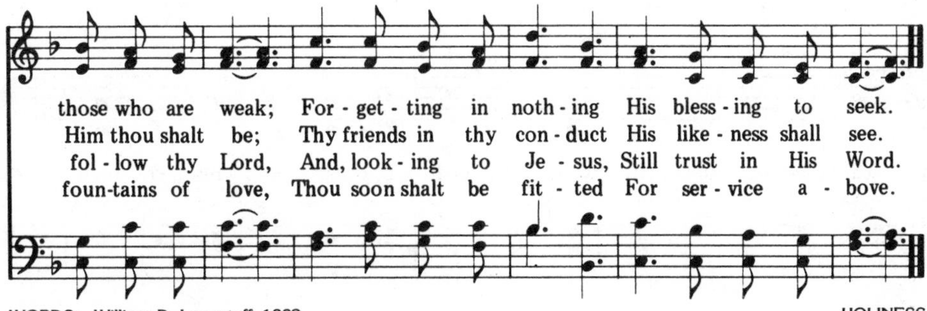

those who are weak; For - get - ting in noth - ing His bless - ing to seek.
Him thou shalt be; Thy friends in thy con - duct His like - ness shall see.
fol - low thy Lord, And, look - ing to Je - sus, Still trust in His Word.
foun-tains of love, Thou soon shalt be fit - ted For ser - vice a - bove.

WORDS: William D. Longstaff, 1882
MUSIC: George C. Stebbins, 1890

HOLINESS
6.5.6.5 D.

403 Lord Jesus, I Long to Be Perfectly Whole

Wash me, and I shall be whiter than snow. Psa. 51:7

1. Lord Je-sus, I long to be per-fect-ly whole; I want You for-ev-er to live in my soul, Break down ev-ery i-dol, cast out ev-ery foe; Now wash me and I shall be whit-er than snow.
2. Lord Je-sus, look down from Your throne in the skies, And help me to make a com-plete sac-ri-fice; I give up my-self, and what-ev-er I know, Now wash me and I shall be whit-er than snow.
3. Lord Je-sus, for this I most hum-bly en-treat, I wait, bless-ed Lord, at Your cru-ci-fied feet; By faith, for my cleans-ing I see Your blood flow, Now wash me and I shall be whit-er than snow.
4. Lord Je-sus, You see that I pa-tient-ly wait, Come now, and with-in me a new heart cre-ate; To those who have sought You, You nev-er said "No," Now wash me and I shall be whit-er than snow.

Refrain

Whit-er than snow, yes, whit-er than snow; Now wash me, and I shall be whit-er than snow.

WORDS: James L. Nicholson, 1872
MUSIC: William G. Fischer, 1872

FISCHER
11.11.11.11 Ref.

Be Not Dismayed Whate'er Betide 404

Casting all your care on Him; for He careth for you. I Pet. 5:7

1. Be not dis-mayed what-e'er be-tide, God will take care of you;
2. Thro' days of toil when heart doth fail, God will take care of you;
3. All you may need He will pro-vide, God will take care of you;
4. No mat-ter what may be the test, God will take care of you;
Be-neath His wings of love a-bide, God will take care of you.
When dan-gers fierce your path as-sail, God will take care of you.
Noth-ing you ask will be de-nied, God will take care of you.
Lean, wea-ry one, up-on His breast, God will take care of you.
Refrain
God will take care of you, Thro' ev-ery day, o'er all the way;
He will take care of you, God will take care of you.

WORDS: Civilla D. Martin, 1904
MUSIC: W. Stillman Martin, 1904

GOD CARES
C.M. Ref.

405 Give to the Winds Your Fears

Commit thy way unto the Lord . . . and He shall bring it to pass. Psa. 37:5

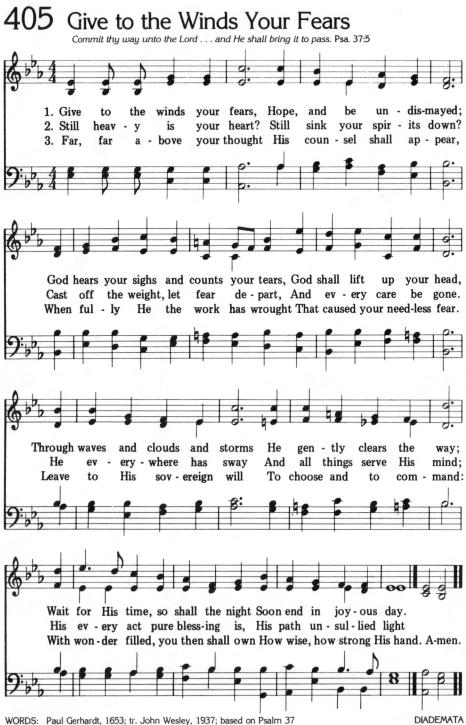

1. Give to the winds your fears, Hope, and be un - dis-mayed;
2. Still heav - y is your heart? Still sink your spir - its down?
3. Far, far a - bove your thought His coun - sel shall ap - pear,

God hears your sighs and counts your tears, God shall lift up your head,
Cast off the weight, let fear de - part, And ev - ery care be gone.
When ful - ly He the work has wrought That caused your need-less fear.

Through waves and clouds and storms He gen - tly clears the way;
He ev - ery - where has sway And all things serve His mind;
Leave to His sov - ereign will To choose and to com - mand:

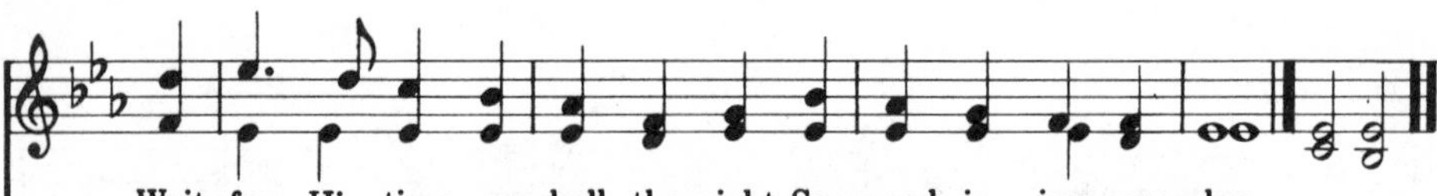

Wait for His time, so shall the night Soon end in joy - ous day.
His ev - ery act pure bless-ing is, His path un - sul - lied light
With won - der filled, you then shall own How wise, how strong His hand. A-men.

WORDS: Paul Gerhardt, 1653; tr. John Wesley, 1937; based on Psalm 37
MUSIC: George J. Elvey, 1868

DIADEMATA
S.M.D.

Days Are Filled with Sorrow and Care 406

Cast thy burden upon the Lord, and He shall sustain thee. Psa. 55:22

1. Days are filled with sor-row and care, Hearts are lone-ly and drear;
2. Cast your care on Je-sus to-day, Leave your wor-ry and fear;
3. Trou-bled soul, the Sav-ior can see Ev-ery heart-ache and tear;
Bur-dens are lift-ed at Cal-va-ry, Je-sus is ver-y near.
Bur-dens are lift-ed at Cal-va-ry, Je-sus is ver-y near.
Bur-dens are lift-ed at Cal-va-ry, Je-sus is ver-y near.
Refrain
Bur-dens are lift-ed at Cal-va-ry, Cal-va-ry, Cal-va-ry;
Bur-dens are lift-ed at Cal-va-ry, Je-sus is ver-y near.

WORDS and MUSIC: John M. Moore, 1952

BURDENS LIFTED
Irregular meter

407 Is Your Burden Heavy?

Surely He hath borne our griefs and carried our sorrows . . . Isa. 53:4

Unison
1. Is your bur-den heav-y as you bear it all a-lone? Does the road you trav-el har-bor dan-ger yet un-known? Are you grow-ing wea-ry in the strug-gle of it all? Je-sus will help you when on His name you call.
2. Is the life you're liv-ing filled with sor-row and de-spair? Does the fu-ture press you with its wor-ry and its care? Are you tired and friend-less, have you al-most lost your way? Je-sus will help you—just come to Him to-day.
He is al-ways there hear-ing ev-ery prayer, Faith-ful and true, Walk-ing by our side, in His love we hide all the day
3

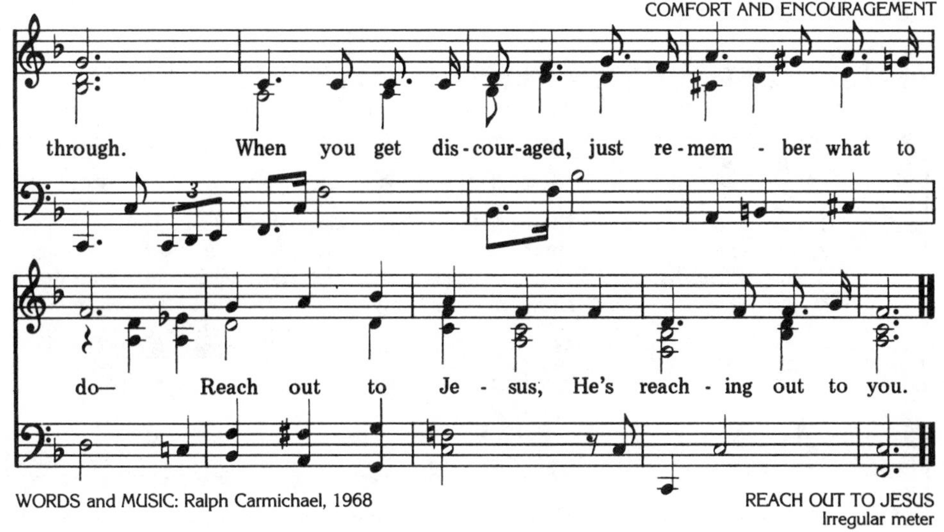
through. When you get dis-cour-aged, just re-mem - ber what to
do— Reach out to Je - sus, He's reach - ing out to you.

WORDS and MUSIC: Ralph Carmichael, 1968

REACH OUT TO JESUS
Irregular meter

God Is My Strong Salvation 408

The Lord is my light and my salvation; whom shall I fear? Psa. 27:1

Unison

1. God is my strong sal - va - tion: What foe have I to fear? In darkness and temp - ta - tion, My light, my help is near. Tho' hosts en-camp a - round me, Firm in the fight I stand; What ter - ror can con-found me, With God at my right hand?

2. Place on the Lord re - li - ance; My soul, with cour-age wait; His truth be thine af - fi - ance, When faint and des - o - late. His might thy heart shall strengthen, His love thy joy in-crease; Mer - cy thy days shall length-en; The Lord will give thee peace. A-men.

WORDS: James Montgomery, 1822
MUSIC: Traditional American melody; *The Sacred Harp,* 1844; arr. Donald P. Hustad, 1973

WEDLOCK
7.6.7.6

409 Just When I Need Him Jesus Is Near

God is our refuge and strength, a very present help in trouble. Psa. 46:1

1. Just when I need Him Je - sus is near, Just when I fal - ter,
2. Just when I need Him Je - sus is true, Nev - er for - sak - ing
3. Just when I need Him Je - sus is strong, Bear - ing my bur - dens
4. Just when I need Him He is my all, An - swer - ing when up -
just when I fear; Read - y to help me, read - y to cheer,
all the way through; Giv - ing for bur - dens pleas - ures a - new,
all the day long; For all my sor - row giv - ing a song,
on Him I call; Ten - der - ly watch - ing lest I should fall,
Just when I need Him most.
Refrain
Just when I need Him most,
Just when I need Him most;
Je - sus is near to
com - fort and cheer, Just when I need Him most.

WORDS: William C. Poole, 1907
MUSIC: Charles H. Gabriel, 1907

GABRIEL
9.9.9.6 Ref.

What a Fellowship, What a Joy Divine 410

The eternal God is thy refuge, and underneath are the everlasting arms. Deut. 33:27

1. What a fel-low-ship, what a joy di-vine, Lean-ing on the ev-er-last-ing arms; What a bless-ed-ness, what a peace is mine, Lean-ing on the ev-er-last-ing arms.
2. O how sweet to walk in this pil-grim way, Lean-ing on the ev-er-last-ing arms; O, how bright the path grows from day to day, Lean-ing on the ev-er-last-ing arms.
3. What have I to dread, what have I to fear, Lean-ing on the ev-er-last-ing arms? I have bless-ed peace with my Lord so near, Lean-ing on the ev-er-last-ing arms.
Refrain
Lean-ing, lean-ing, Safe and se-cure from all a-larms; Lean-ing, lean-ing, Lean-ing on the ev-er-last-ing arms.
Lean-ing on Je-sus, lean-ing on Je-sus, Lean-ing on Je-sus, lean-ing on Je-sus,

WORDS: Elisha A. Hoffman, 1887
MUSIC: Anthony J. Showalter, 1887

SHOWALTER
10.9.10.9 Ref.

411 In the Hour of Trial

God is faithful, who will not suffer you to be tempted above that ye are able . . . I Cor. 10:13

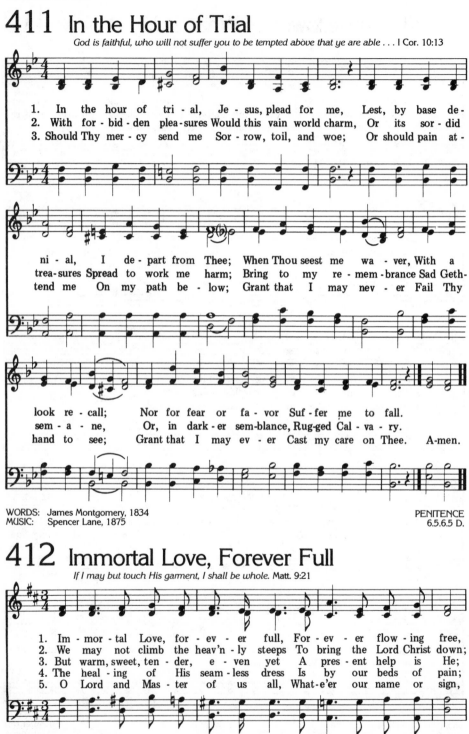

1. In the hour of tri - al, Je - sus, plead for me, Lest, by base de -
2. With for - bid - den plea - sures Would this vain world charm, Or its sor - did
3. Should Thy mer - cy send me Sor - row, toil, and woe; Or should pain at -

ni - al, I de - part from Thee; When Thou seest me wa - ver, With a
trea - sures Spread to work me harm; Bring to my re - mem - brance Sad Geth-
tend me On my path be - low; Grant that I may nev - er Fail Thy

look re - call; Nor for fear or fa - vor Suf - fer me to fall.
sem - a - ne, Or, in dark - er sem - blance, Rug - ged Cal - va - ry.
hand to see; Grant that I may ev - er Cast my care on Thee. A - men.

WORDS: James Montgomery, 1834
MUSIC: Spencer Lane, 1875

PENITENCE
6.5.6.5 D.

412 Immortal Love, Forever Full

If I may but touch His garment, I shall be whole. Matt. 9:21

1. Im - mor - tal Love, for - ev - er full, For - ev - er flow - ing free,
2. We may not climb the heav'n - ly steeps To bring the Lord Christ down;
3. But warm, sweet, ten - der, e - ven yet A pres - ent help is He;
4. The heal - ing of His seam - less dress Is by our beds of pain;
5. O Lord and Mas - ter of us all, What - e'er our name or sign,

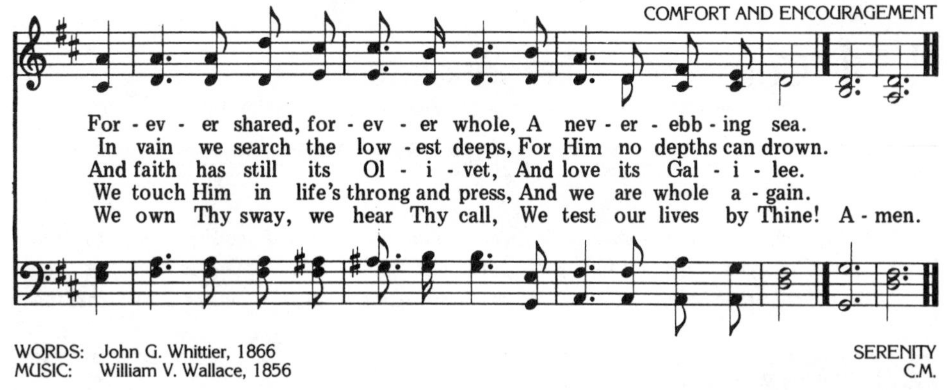
For - ev - er shared, for - ev - er whole, A nev - er - ebb - ing sea.
In vain we search the low - est deeps, For Him no depths can drown.
And faith has still its Ol - i - vet, And love its Gal - i - lee.
We touch Him in life's throng and press, And we are whole a - gain.
We own Thy sway, we hear Thy call, We test our lives by Thine! A - men.

WORDS: John G. Whittier, 1866
MUSIC: William V. Wallace, 1856

SERENITY
C.M.

There Is a Balm in Gilead 413

Is there no balm in Gilead; is there no physician there? Jer. 8:22

(Ref.) There is a balm in Gil - e - ad To make the wound - ed whole,
There is a balm in Gil - e - ad To heal the sin - sick soul. *Fine*

1. Some - times I feel dis - cour - aged, And think my work's in vain,
2. If you can - not preach like Pe - ter, If you can - not pray like Paul,

But then the Ho - ly Spir - it Re - vives my soul a - gain.
You can tell the love of Je - sus, And say, "He died for all."
D.C. Refrain

WORDS and MUSIC: Traditional Spiritual

BALM IN GILEAD
Irregular meter

414 Come, Ye Disconsolate

Let us then with confidence draw near to the throne of grace . . . Heb. 4:16

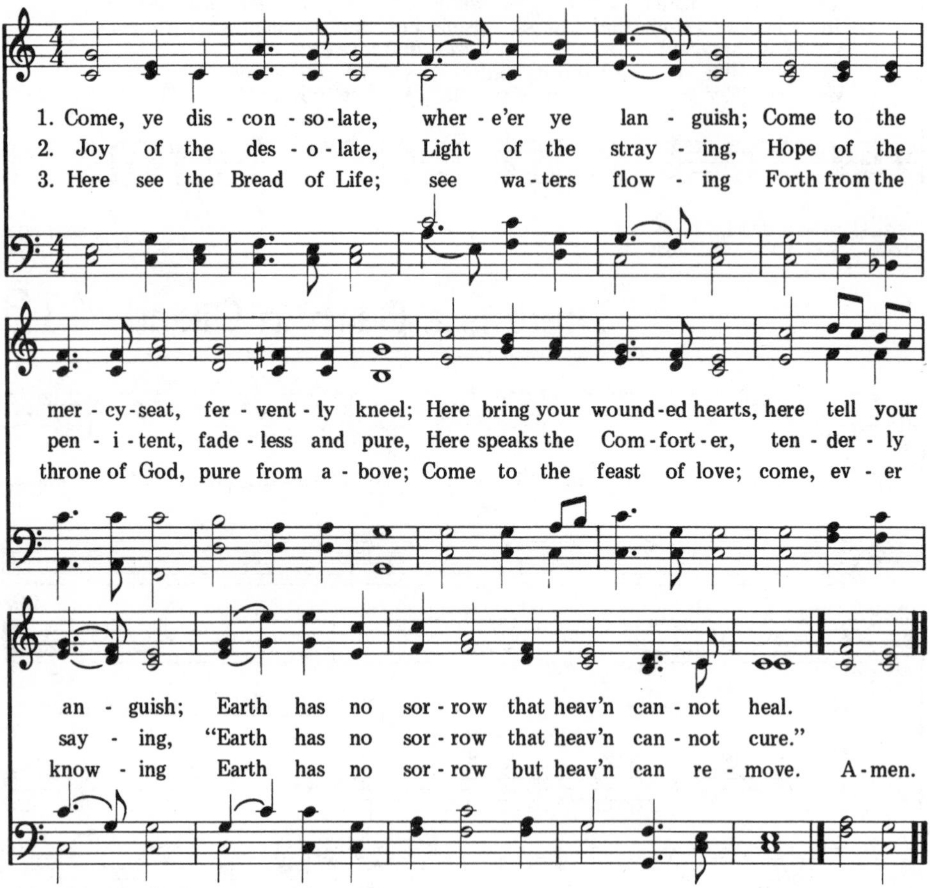

1. Come, ye dis - con - so - late, wher - e'er ye lan - guish; Come to the
2. Joy of the des - o - late, Light of the stray - ing, Hope of the
3. Here see the Bread of Life; see wa - ters flow - ing Forth from the

mer - cy - seat, fer - vent - ly kneel; Here bring your wound - ed hearts, here tell your
pen - i - tent, fade - less and pure, Here speaks the Com - fort - er, ten - der - ly
throne of God, pure from a - bove; Come to the feast of love; come, ev - er

an - guish; Earth has no sor - row that heav'n can - not heal.
say - ing, "Earth has no sor - row that heav'n can - not cure."
know - ing Earth has no sor - row but heav'n can re - move. A - men.

WORDS: St. 1, 2, Thomas Moore, 1824;
St. 3, Thomas Hastings, 1831
MUSIC: Samuel Webbe, 1792

CONSOLATOR
11.10.11.10

415 I Know Not What the Future Has

My times are in Thy hand. Psa. 31:15

1. I know not what the fu - ture has Of mar - vel or sur - prise,
2. And if my heart and flesh are weak To bear an un - tried pain,
3. And so be - side the si - lent sea I wait the muf - fled oar:
4. I know not where His is - lands lift Their frond - ed palms in air;

COMFORT AND ENCOURAGEMENT

As - sured a - lone that life and death God's mer - cy un - der - lies.
The bruis - ed reed He will not break, But strength - en and sus - tain.
No harm from Him can come to me On o - cean or on shore.
I on - ly know I can - not drift Be - yond His love and care.

WORDS: John G. Whittier, 1867
MUSIC: William V. Wallace, 1856

SERENITY
C.M.

If You Will Only Let God Guide You 416

Cast thy burden upon the Lord, and He shall sustain thee. Psa. 55:22

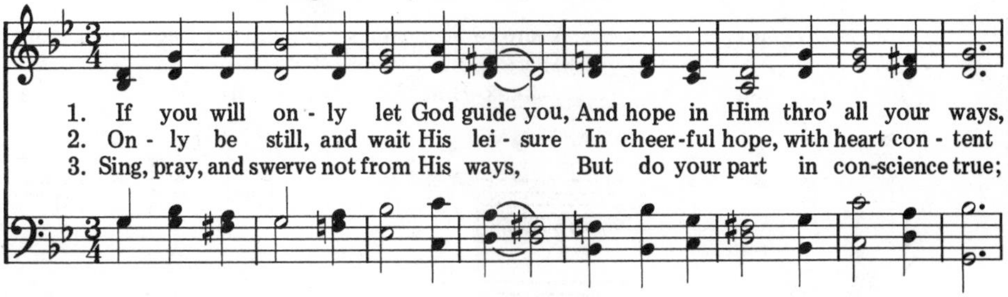

1. If you will on - ly let God guide you, And hope in Him thro' all your ways,
2. On - ly be still, and wait His lei - sure In cheer-ful hope, with heart con - tent
3. Sing, pray, and swerve not from His ways, But do your part in con-science true;

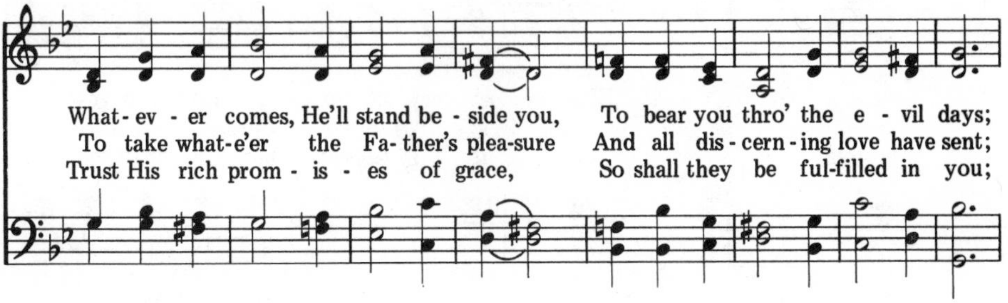

What - ev - er comes, He'll stand be - side you, To bear you thro' the e - vil days;
To take what-e'er the Fa - ther's plea-sure And all dis - cern - ing love have sent;
Trust His rich prom - is - es of grace, So shall they be ful-filled in you;

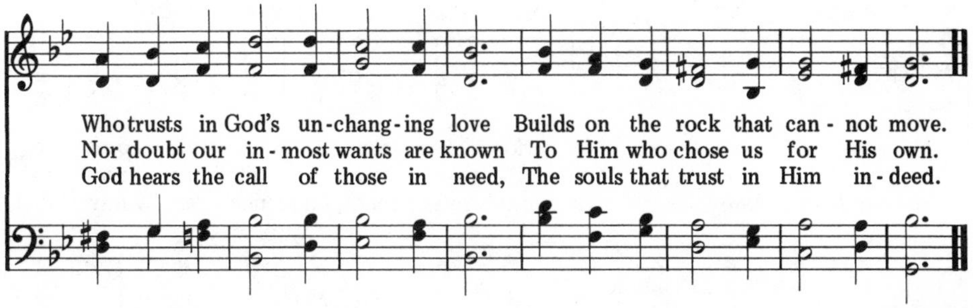

Who trusts in God's un-chang - ing love Builds on the rock that can - not move.
Nor doubt our in - most wants are known To Him who chose us for His own.
God hears the call of those in need, The souls that trust in Him in - deed.

WORDS: Georg Neumark, 1641; tr. Catherine Winkworth, 1855, 1863, alt.; based on Psalm 55
MUSIC: Georg Neumark, 1657

NEUMARK
9.8.9.8.8.8

417 I've Had Many Tears and Sorrows

All things work together for good to them that love God . . . Rom. 8:28

1. I've had man - y tears and sor - rows, I've had ques - tions
2. I've been to lots of plac - es, And I've seen a
3. I thank God for the moun - tains, And I thank Him
for to - mor - row, There've been times I did - n't know right from
lot of fac - es, There've been times I felt so all a -
for the val - leys, I thank Him for the storms He brought me
wrong; But in ev - ery sit - u - a - tion God gave
lone; But in my lone - ly hours, Yes, those
through; For if I'd nev - er had a prob - lem, I
bless - ed con - so - la - tion That my tri - als come to
pre - cious lone - ly hours, Je - sus let me know that
would - n't know that He could solve them, I'd nev - er know what

Refrain
on - ly make me strong.
I was His own.
faith in God could do.
Through it all,
Through it all, I've learned to trust in Je - sus, I've
learned to trust in God; Through it all, Through it all,
I've learned to de - pend up-on His Word.

WORDS and MUSIC: Andraé Crouch, 1971

THROUGH IT ALL
Irregular meter

418 Gentle Shepherd, Come and Lead Us

And when He putteth forth His own sheep, He goeth before them. John 10:4

Gen - tle Shep - herd, come and lead us, For we need You to
help us find our way. Gen - tle Shep - herd, come and feed us,
For we need Your strength from day to day. There's no oth - er
we can turn to Who can help us face an - oth-er day; Gen-tle
Shep - herd, come and lead us, For we need You to help us find our way.

WORDS: Gloria Gaither and William J. Gaither, 1974
MUSIC: William J. Gaither, 1974

GENTLE SHEPHERD
Irregular meter

Guide Me, O Thou Great Jehovah 419

This God is our God . . . He will be our guide even unto death. Psa. 48:14

1. Guide me, O Thou great Je - ho - vah, Pil - grim through this bar - ren land;
2. O - pen now the crys - tal foun - tain, Whence the healing stream doth flow;
3. When I tread the verge of Jor - dan, Bid my anx - ious fears sub - side;
I am weak, but Thou art might - y; Hold me with Thy pow'r - ful hand;
Let the fire and cloud - y pil - lar Lead me all my jour - ney through;
Death of death, and hell's de - struc - tion, Land me safe on Ca - naan's side;
Bread of heav - en, Bread of heav - en, Feed me till I want no
Strong De - liv - erer, strong De - liv - erer, Be Thou still my strength and
Songs of prais - es, songs of prais - es I will ev - er give to
more, (want no more,) Feed me till I want no more.
shield, (strength and shield,) Be Thou still my strength and shield.
Thee, (give to Thee,) I will ev - er give to Thee. A - men.

WORDS: William Williams, 1745; tr. Peter Williams and William Williams. 1771, 1772
MUSIC: John Hughes, 1907

CWM RHONDDA
8.7.8.7.8.7.7

420 Because the Lord Is My Shepherd

The Lord is my shepherd, I shall not want. Psa. 23:1

Unison
Be - cause the Lord is my Shep - herd, I have ev - ery - thing that I
need. He lets me rest in mead-ows green and leads me be - side the
qui - et stream. He keeps on giv - ing life to me, and helps me to
do what hon - ors Him the most. E - ven when walk - ing thro' the dark
val - ley of death, val - ley of death, I will nev - er

be a-fraid, for He is close be - side me. Guard-ing, guid - ing all the
way, He spreads a feast be - fore me in the pres - ence of my
en - e - mies. He wel-comes me as His spe - cial guest with bless-ing ev - er
flow - ing, His good-ness and un - fail - ing kind-ness shall be with me all of my
life, And af - ter-wards I shall live with Him for - ev - er, for - ev - er
in His home, for - ev - er in His home. For - ev - er in His home.

WORDS and MUSIC: Ralph Carmichael, 1969; based on Psalm 23

THE NEW 23RD
Irregular meter

421 I Have Decided to Follow Jesus

Master, I will follow Thee whithersoever Thou goest. Matt. 8:19

Unison

1. I have de - cid - ed to fol - low Je - sus, I have de - cid - ed to fol - low
2. The world be-hind me, the cross be - fore me; The world be-hind me, the cross be-
3. Tho' none go with me, I still will fol - low, Tho' none go with me, I still will
4. Will you de - cide now to fol - low Je - sus? Will you de - cide now to fol - low

Je - sus, I have de - cid - ed to fol - low Je - sus, No turn-ing back, no turn-ing back.
fore me; The world be-hind me, the cross be-fore me, No turn-ing back, no turn-ing back.
fol-low, Tho' none go with me, I still will fol-low, No turn-ing back, no turn-ing back.
Je-sus, Will you de-cide now to fol-low Je - sus? No turn-ing back, no turn-ing back.

WORDS: Source unknown
MUSIC: Folk melody from India

ASSAM
Irregular meter

422 Precious Lord, Take My Hand

... And lead me in the way everlasting. Psa. 139:24

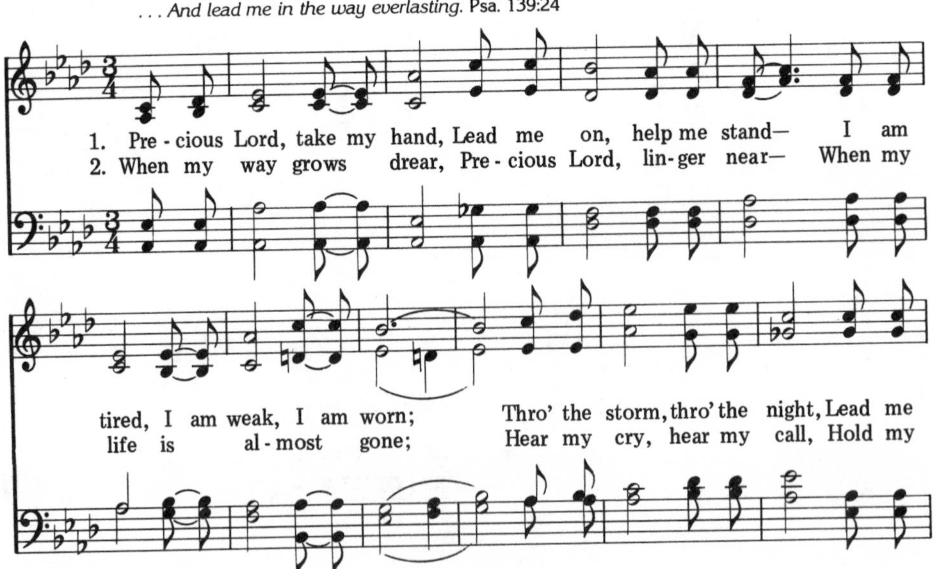
1. Pre - cious Lord, take my hand, Lead me on, help me stand— I am
2. When my way grows drear, Pre - cious Lord, lin - ger near— When my
tired, I am weak, I am worn; Thro' the storm, thro' the night, Lead me
life is al - most gone; Hear my cry, hear my call, Hold my

on to the light— Take my hand, precious Lord, lead me home.
hand lest I fall— Take my hand, precious Lord, lead me home.

WORDS: Thomas A. Dorsey, 1938
MUSIC: George N. Allen, 1844; adapt. Thomas A. Dorsey, 1938

PRECIOUS LORD
6.6.9.6.6.9

Take Thou My Hand, O Father 423

For He hath prepared for them a city. Heb. 11:16

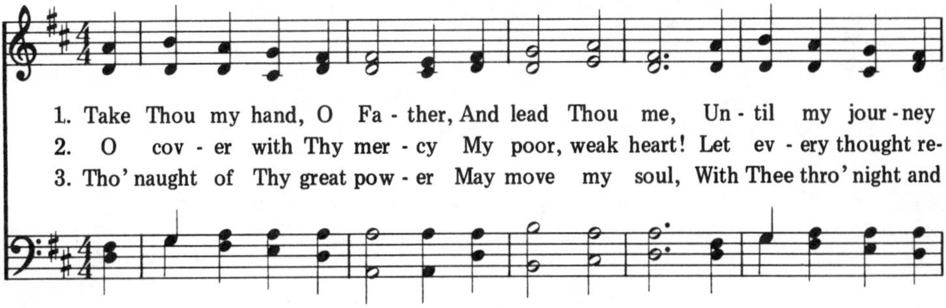

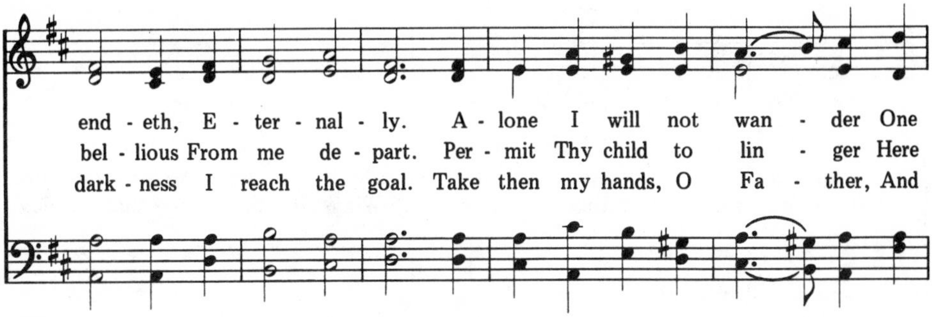

1. Take Thou my hand, O Father, And lead Thou me, Until my journey endeth, Eternally. Alone I will not wander One single day; Be Thou my true companion And with me stay.

2. O cover with Thy mercy My poor, weak heart! Let every thought rebellious From me depart. Permit Thy child to linger Here at Thy feet, And blindly trust Thy goodness With faith complete.

3. Tho' naught of Thy great power May move my soul, With Thee thro' night and darkness I reach the goal. Take then my hands, O Father, And lead Thou me, Until my journey endeth Eternally. Amen.

WORDS: Julie K. Hausmann, 1862; tr. Herman Brückner, 1866-1942
MUSIC: Friedrich Silcher, 1842

SO NIMM DENN MEINE HÄNDE
7.4.5.4 D.

424 All the Way My Savior Leads Me

I will guide thee with mine eye. Psa. 32:8

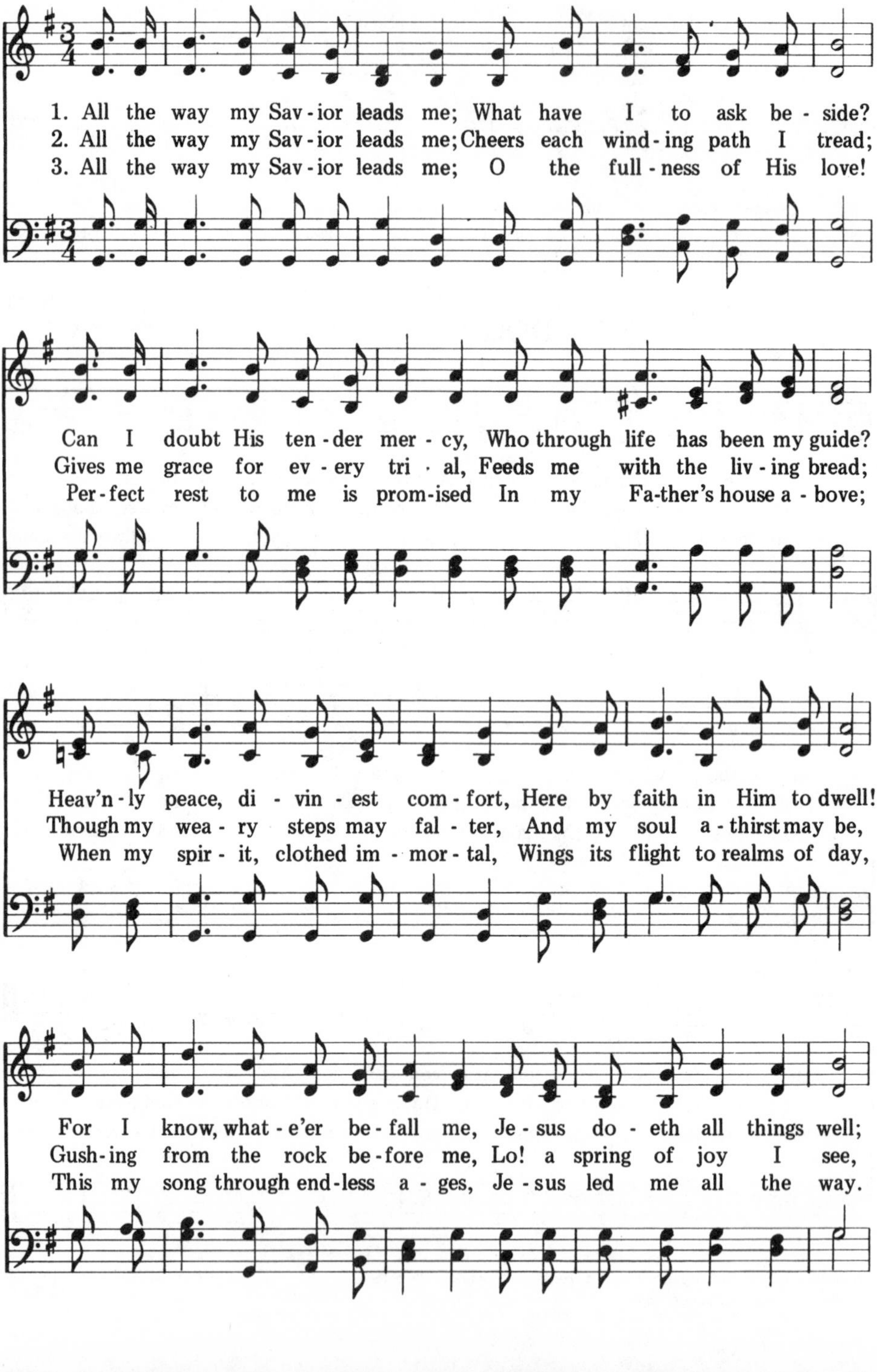

1. All the way my Sav-ior leads me; What have I to ask be - side?
Can I doubt His ten-der mer - cy, Who through life has been my guide?
Heav'n-ly peace, di - vin - est com-fort, Here by faith in Him to dwell!
For I know, what-e'er be-fall me, Je - sus do - eth all things well;

2. All the way my Sav-ior leads me; Cheers each wind-ing path I tread;
Gives me grace for ev - ery tri - al, Feeds me with the liv-ing bread;
Though my wea - ry steps may fal - ter, And my soul a - thirst may be,
Gush-ing from the rock be-fore me, Lo! a spring of joy I see,

3. All the way my Sav-ior leads me; O the full-ness of His love!
Per-fect rest to me is prom-ised In my Fa-ther's house a - bove;
When my spir - it, clothed im - mor - tal, Wings its flight to realms of day,
This my song through end-less a - ges, Je - sus led me all the way.

For I know, what-e'er be-fall me, Je-sus do-eth all things well.
Gush-ing from the rock be-fore me, Lo! a spring of joy I see.
This my song through end-less a-ges, Je-sus led me all the way.
1. Je-sus, Sav-ior, pi-lot me O-ver life's tem-pes-tuous sea;
2. As a moth-er stills her child, Thou canst hush the o-cean wild;
3. When at last I near the shore, And the fear-ful break-ers roar
Un-known waves be-fore me roll, Hid-ing rock and treach-'rous shoal;
Bois-terous waves o-bey Thy will When Thou say'st to them, "Be still!"
'Twixt me and the peace-ful rest, Then, while lean-ing on Thy breast,

WORDS: Fanny J. Crosby, 1875
MUSIC: Robert Lowry, 1875

ALL THE WAY
8.7.8.7 D.

Jesus, Savior, Pilot Me 425

He commandeth even the winds and water, and they obey Him. Luke 8:25

Chart and com-pass came from Thee: Je-sus, Sav-ior, pi-lot me.
Won-drous Sov-'reign of the sea, Je-sus, Sav-ior, pi-lot me.
May I hear Thee say to me, "Fear not, I will pi-lot thee."

WORDS: Edward Hopper, 1871
MUSIC: Traditional Welsh hymn melody

ARFON
7.7.7.7 D.

426 I Want Jesus to Walk with Me

I am with thee, and will keep thee . . . whither thou goest. Gen. 28:15

Unison

1. I want Je - sus to walk with me; I want Je - sus to walk with me; All a - long my pil - grim jour - ney, Lord, I want Je - sus to walk with me.
2. In my tri - als, Lord, walk with me; In my tri - als, Lord, walk with me; When my heart is al - most break - ing, Lord, I want Je - sus to walk with me.
3. When I'm in trou - ble, Lord, walk with me; When I'm in trou - ble, Lord, walk with me; When my head is bowed in sor - row, Lord, I want Je - sus to walk with me.

WORDS and MUSIC: Traditional Spiritual

WALK WITH ME
Irregular meter

427 Children of the Heavenly King

The ransomed of the Lord shall . . . come to Zion with songs and everlasting joy. Isa. 35:10

1. Chil - dren of the heav'n-ly King, As we jour - ney let us sing;
2. We are trav - 'ling home to God In the way our fa - thers trod;
3. Fear not, breth - ren, joy - ful stand On the bor - ders of our land;
4. Lord, o - be - dient - ly we'll go, Glad - ly leav - ing all be - low:

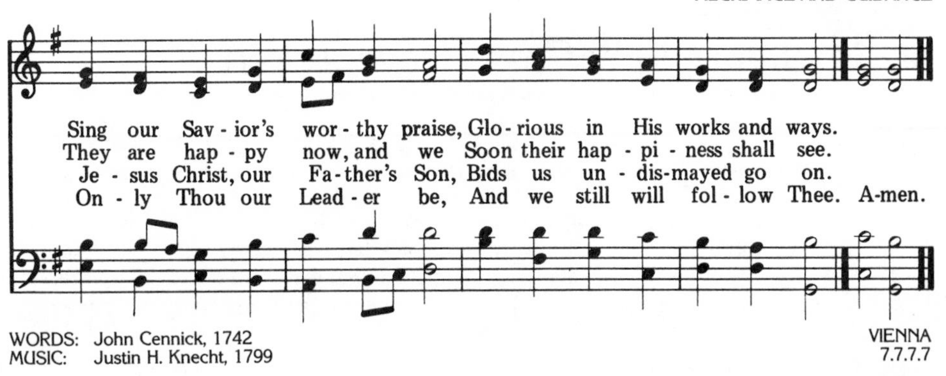
Sing our Sav - ior's wor - thy praise, Glo - rious in His works and ways.
They are hap - py now, and we Soon their hap - pi - ness shall see.
Je - sus Christ, our Fa - ther's Son, Bids us un - dis-mayed go on.
On - ly Thou our Lead - er be, And we still will fol - low Thee. A-men.

WORDS: John Cennick, 1742
MUSIC: Justin H. Knecht, 1799

VIENNA
7.7.7.7

Jesus, Still Lead On 428

Therefore for Thy name's sake lead me, and guide me. Psa. 31:3

1. Je - sus, still lead on, Till our rest be won, And, al - though the
2. If the way be drear, If the foe be near, Let not faith - less
3. When we seek re - lief From a long - felt grief, When op-pressed by
4. Je - sus, still lead on, Till our rest be won; Heav'n - ly lead - er,

way be cheer - less, We will fol - low, calm and fear - less;
fears o'er - take us, Let not faith and hope for - sake us;
new temp - ta - tions, Lord, in - crease and per - fect pa - tience;
still di - rect us, Still sup - port, con - sole, pro - tect us,

Guide us by Thy hand To our fa - ther - land.
For, through man - y a woe, To our home we go.
Show us that bright shore Where we weep no more.
Till we safe - ly stand In our fa - ther - land. A - men.

WORDS: Nikolaus L. von Zinzendorf, 1721;
tr. Jane L. Borthwick, 1846
MUSIC: Adam Drese, 1698

ROCHELLE
5.5.8.8.5.5

429 Jesus, I My Cross Have Taken

Lo, we have left all, and have followed Thee. Mark 10:28

1. Je - sus, I my cross have tak - en, All to leave and fol - low Thee;
2. Let the world de - spise and leave me, They have left my Sav - ior too;
3. Man may trou-ble and dis - tress me, 'Twill but drive me to Thy breast;
4. Has - ten on from grace to glo - ry, Armed by faith and winged by prayer;
Des - ti - tute, de - spised, for - sak - en, Thou from hence my all shalt be:
Hu - man hearts and looks de - ceive me; Thou art not, like man, un - true;
Life with tri - als hard may press me, Heav'n will bring me sweet - er rest.
Heav'n's e - ter - nal day's be - fore me, God's own hand shall guide me there.
Per - ish ev - ery fond am - bi - tion, All I've sought, and hoped, and known;
And, while Thou shalt smile up - on me, God of wis - dom, love, and might,
O 'tis not in grief to harm me, While Thy love is left to me;
Soon shall close my earth - ly mis - sion, Swift shall pass my pil - grim days,
Yet how rich is my con - di - tion, God and heav'n are still my own!
Foes may hate and friends may shun me; Show Thy face, and all is bright.
O 'twere not in joy to charm me, Were that joy un - mixed with Thee.
Hope shall change to glad fru - i - tion, Faith to sight, and prayer to praise. A-men.

WORDS: Henry F. Lyte, 1824
MUSIC: Leavitt's *The Christian Lyre,* 1831; attr. Wolfgang A. Mozart, 1756-1791; arr. Hubert P. Main, c.1868

ELLESDIE
8.7.8.7 D.

Lead, Kindly Light 430

Thou wilt show me the path of life: at Thy right hand there are pleasures . . . Psa. 16:11

1. Lead, kind-ly Light, a - mid th' en-cir-cling gloom, Lead Thou me on;
2. I was not ev - er thus, nor prayed that Thou Shouldst lead me on;
3. So long Thy pow'r hath blest me, sure it still Will lead me on,
The night is dark, and I am far from home; Lead Thou me on:
I loved to choose and see my path; but now Lead Thou me on.
O'er moor and fen, o'er crag and tor - rent, till The night is gone;
Keep Thou my feet; I do not ask to see
I loved the gar - ish day, and, spite of fears,
And with the morn those an - gel fac - es smile,
The dis - tant scene—one step e - nough for me.
Pride ruled my will: re - mem-ber not past years.
Which I have loved long since, and lost a - while. A - men.

WORDS: John H. Newman, 1833
MUSIC: John B. Dykes, 1865

LUX BENIGNA
10.4.10.4.10.10

431 He Leadeth Me, O Blessed Thought

I am the Lord thy God . . . which leadeth thee . . . Isa. 48:17

1. He lead - eth me, O bless - ed thought! O words with heav'n - ly com - fort fraught! What - e'er I do, wher - e'er I be, Still 'tis God's hand that lead - eth me.
2. Some-times 'mid scenes of deep - est gloom, Some-times where E - den's bow - ers bloom, By wa - ters still, o'er trou - bled sea, Still 'tis His hand that lead - eth me.
3. Lord, I would clasp Thy hand in mine, Nor ev - er mur - mur nor re - pine; Con - tent, what - ev - er lot I see, Since 'tis my God that lead - eth me.
4. And when my task on earth is done, When by Thy grace the vic - t'ry's won, E'en death's cold wave I will not flee, Since God through Jor - dan lead - eth me.
Refrain
He lead - eth me, He lead - eth me! By His own hand He lead - eth me! His faith - ful fol - l'wer I would be, For by His hand He lead-eth me.

WORDS: Joseph H. Gilmore, 1862
MUSIC: William B. Bradbury, 1864

HE LEADETH ME
L.M. Ref.

I Must Tell Jesus All of My Trials 432

For in that He Himself hath suffered . . . He is able to succor them . . . Heb. 2:18

1. I must tell Je - sus all of my tri - als; I can - not bear these bur - dens a - lone; In my dis - tress He kind - ly will help me; He ev - er loves and cares for His own.
2. I must tell Je - sus all of my trou - bles; He is a kind, com- pas - sion - ate Friend; If I but ask Him, He will de - liv - er, Make of my trou - bles quick - ly an end.
3. Tempt - ed and tried, I need a great Sav - ior, One who can help my bur - dens to bear; I must tell Je - sus, I must tell Je - sus; He all my cares and sor - rows will share.
4. O how the world to e - vil al - lures me! O how my heart is tempt - ed to sin! I must tell Je - sus, and He will help me O - ver the world the vic - t'ry to win.
Refrain
I must tell Je - sus! I must tell Je - sus! I can - not bear my bur - dens a - lone; I must tell Je - sus! I must tell Je - sus! Je - sus can help me, Je - sus a - lone.

WORDS and MUSIC: Elisha A. Hoffman, 1894

ORWIGSBURG
10.9.10.9 Ref.

433 Our Father, Which Art in Heaven

And when thou hast shut thy door, pray to the Father . . . Matt. 6:6

Unison
Our Fa - ther, which art in heav - en, Hal - low - ed
be Thy name.
Thy king - dom come,
Thy will be done on earth as it is in heav -
en. Give us this day our dai - ly bread, And for - give us our

PRAYER
may be omitted
debts, as we for-give our debt-ors. And
lead us not in-to temp-ta-tion but de-liv-er us from e-vil; For
Thine is the king-dom, and the pow-er, and the glo-ry, For-
ev-er, A-men. A-men.

WORDS: Matthew 6:9-13
MUSIC: Albert Hay Malotte, 1935; arr. Donald P. Hustad, 1984

MALOTTE
Irregular meter

434 What a Friend We Have in Jesus

By prayer . . . with thanksgiving let your requests be made known unto God. Phil. 4:6

1. What a Friend we have in Je - sus, All our sins and griefs to bear!
2. Have we tri - als and temp - ta - tions? Is there trou - ble an - y - where?
3. Are we weak and heav - y - la - den, Cum - bered with a load of care?
What a priv - i - lege to car - ry Ev - ery - thing to God in prayer!
We should nev - er be dis - cour - aged, Take it to the Lord in prayer.
Pre - cious Sav - ior, still our ref - uge— Take it to the Lord in prayer.
O what peace we of - ten for - feit, O what need - less pain we bear,
Can we find a friend so faith - ful Who will all our sor - rows share?
Do thy friends de - spise, for - sake thee? Take it to the Lord in prayer;
All be - cause we do not car - ry Ev - ery - thing to God in prayer!
Je - sus knows our ev - ery weak - ness, Take it to the Lord in prayer.
In His arms He'll take and shield thee, Thou wilt find a sol - ace there.

WORDS: Joseph M. Scriven, 1855
MUSIC: Charles C. Converse, 1868

CONVERSE
8.7.8.7 D.

What a Friend We Have in Jesus 435

For the eyes of the Lord are upon the righteous . . . I Pet. 3:12

1. What a Friend we have in Je - sus, All our sins and griefs to bear!
2. Have we tri - als and temp - ta - tions? Is there trou - ble an - y - where?
3. Are we weak and hea - vy - la - den, Cum - bered with a load of care?

What a pri - vi - lege to car - ry Ev - ery - thing to God in prayer!
We should nev - er be dis - cour - aged: Take it to the Lord in prayer.
Pre - cious Sav - ior, still our ref - uge: Take it to the Lord in prayer.

O what peace we of - ten for - feit, O what need - less pain we bear,
Can we find a friend so faith - ful, Who will all our sor - rows share?
Do thy friends de - spise, for - sake thee? Take it to the Lord in prayer;

All be - cause we do not car - ry Ev - ery - thing to God in prayer!
Je - sus knows our ev - ery weak - ness: Take it to the Lord in prayer.
In His arms He'll take and shield thee! Thou wilt find a so - lace there.

WORDS: Joseph M. Scriven, 1855
MUSIC: William P. Rowlands, 1915

BLAENWERN
8.7.8.7 D.

436 Lord, Listen to Your Children Praying

The effectual fervent prayer of a righteous man availeth much. James 5:16

Refrain - parts
Lord, lis - ten to your chil - dren pray - ing, Lord, send your
Spir - it in this place; Lord, lis - ten to your chil - dren
pray - ing, Send us love, send us pow'r, send us grace.
Fine
Unison
1. Some-thing's gon - na hap - pen like the world has nev - er known, When the
2. He's gon-na take o - ver, He's gon - na take con - trol, When the
3. You're gon - na know it when the Lord stretch-es out His hand, When the
peo - ple of the Lord get down to pray;
peo - ple of the Lord get down to pray;
peo - ple of the Lord get down to pray;

A door's gon-na swing o - pen, and the walls come a - tum-bl - ing
He's gon-na move the moun - tain He's gon-na make the wa - ters
There's gon-na be a brand new song of vic - t'ry in this
D.C.
down, When the peo-ple of the Lord get down to pray.
roll, When the peo-ple of the Lord get down to pray.
land, When the peo-ple of the Lord get down to pray.

WORDS and MUSIC: Ken Medema, 1973

CHILDREN PRAYING
Irregular meter

Come, My Soul, Your Plea Prepare 437

Ask, and it shall be given you . . . Matt. 7:7

1. Come, my soul, your plea pre - pare, Je - sus loves to an - swer prayer;
He Him-self has bid you pray, There-fore will not turn a - way.

2. You are com - ing to a King; Large pe - ti - tions there-fore bring;
For His grace and pow'r are such, None can ev - er ask too much.

3. Lord, I come to Thee for rest; Take pos - ses - sion of my breast;
There Thy blood-bought right maintain, And with - out a ri - val reign.

4. While I am a pil - grim here, Let Thy love my spir - it cheer:
As my guide, my guard, my friend, Lead me to my jour-ney's end. A-men.

WORDS: John Newton, 1779
MUSIC: Carl Maria von Weber, 1826

SEYMOUR
7.7.7.7

438 Jesus, Where'er Thy People Meet

Where two or three are gathered together . . . there am I in the midst. Matt. 18:20

1. Je - sus, wher - e'er Thy peo - ple meet, There they be -
2. For Thou, with - in no walls con - fined, In - hab - it -
3. Here may we prove the power of prayer To strength - en
4. Lord, we are few, but Thou art near; Nor short Thine

hold Thy mer - cy - seat; Wher - e'er they seek Thee Thou art
est the hum - ble mind; Such ev - er bring Thee where they
faith and sweet - en care, To teach our faint de - sires to
arm, nor deaf Thine ear; O rend the heavens, come quick - ly

found, And ev - ery place is hal - lowed ground.
come, And go - ing, take Thee to their home.
rise, And bring all heaven be - fore our eyes.
down, And make a thou - sand hearts Thine own. A - men.

WORDS: William Cowper, 1769
MUSIC: Ralph Harrison, 1784

WARRINGTON
8.8.8.8

439 Prayer Is the Soul's Sincere Desire

Praying always with all prayer and supplication in the Spirit. Eph. 6:18

1. Prayer is the soul's sin - cere de - sire, Un - ut - tered or ex-pressed; The
2. Prayer is the sim - plest form of speech That in - fant lips can try; Prayer,
3. Prayer is the con - trite sin - ner's voice, Re - turn - ing from his ways; While
4. Prayer is the Chris - tian's vi - tal breath, The Chris-tian's na - tive air, His
5. O Thou, by whom we come to God, The Life, the Truth, the Way, The

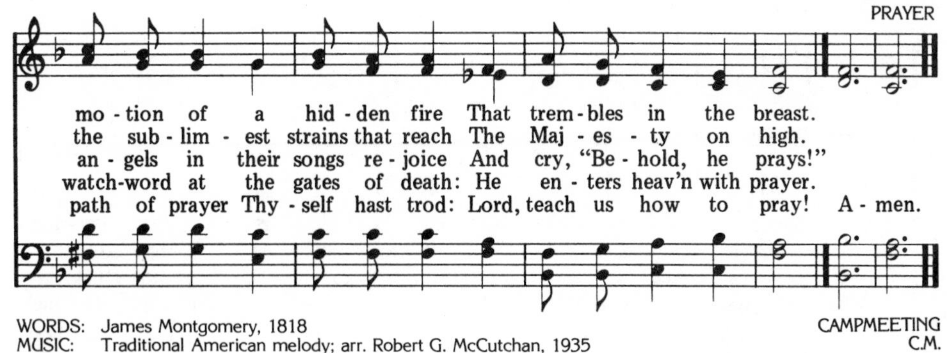
PRAYER
mo - tion of a hid - den fire That trem - bles in the breast.
the sub - lim - est strains that reach The Maj - es - ty on high.
an - gels in their songs re - joice And cry, "Be - hold, he prays!"
watch-word at the gates of death: He en - ters heav'n with prayer.
path of prayer Thy - self hast trod: Lord, teach us how to pray! A - men.

WORDS: James Montgomery, 1818
MUSIC: Traditional American melody; arr. Robert G. McCutchan, 1935

CAMPMEETING
C.M.

Lord, I Have Shut the Door 440

And when thou hast shut thy door, pray to thy Father . . . Matt. 6:6

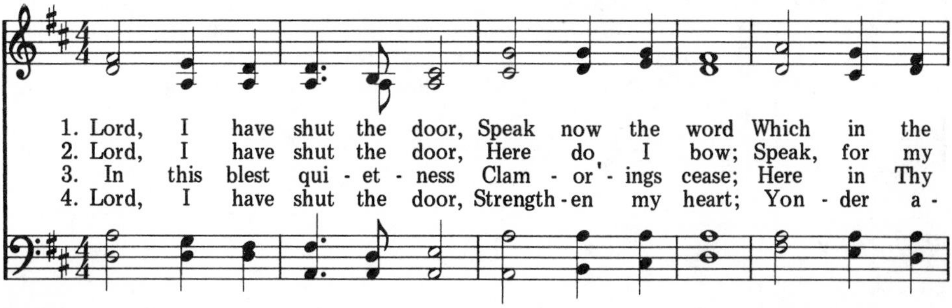

1. Lord, I have shut the door, Speak now the word Which in the
2. Lord, I have shut the door, Here do I bow; Speak, for my
3. In this blest qui - et - ness Clam - or - ings cease; Here in Thy
4. Lord, I have shut the door, Strength - en my heart; Yon - der a -

din and throng Could not be heard; Hushed now my in - ner heart,
soul at - tent Turns to Thee now. Re - buke Thou what is vain,
pres - ence dwells In - fi - nite peace; Yon - der, the strife and cry,
waits the task— I share a part. On - ly through grace be-stowed

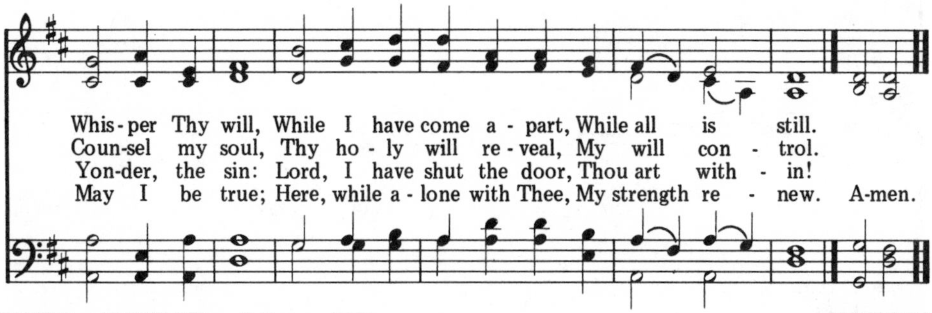

Whis - per Thy will, While I have come a - part, While all is still.
Coun - sel my soul, Thy ho - ly will re - veal, My will con - trol.
Yon - der, the sin: Lord, I have shut the door, Thou art with - in!
May I be true; Here, while a - lone with Thee, My strength re - new. A-men.

WORDS and MUSIC: William M. Runyan, 1923

SANCTUARY
6.4.6.4 D.

441 I Have a Savior, He's Pleading in Glory

He ever liveth to make intercession for them. Heb. 7:25

1. I have a Sav - ior, He's plead - ing in glo - ry, A dear, lov - ing
2. I have a Fa - ther; to me He has giv - en A hope for e-
3. I have a peace; it is calm as a riv - er, A peace that the
4. When He has found you, tell oth - ers the sto - ry, That my lov - ing
Sav - ior, tho' earth-friends be few; And now He is watch - ing in
ter - ni - ty, bless - ed and true; And soon He will call me to
friends of this world nev - er knew: My Sav - ior a - lone is its
Sav - ior is your Sav - ior, too; Then pray that your Sav - ior may
ten - der-ness o'er me, But O, that my Sav - ior were your Sav - ior too!
meet Him in heav - en, But O, that He'd let me bring you with me too!
au - thor and giv - er, And O, could I know it was giv - en for you.
bring them to glo - ry, And prayer will be an-swered—'twas an-swered for you!
Refrain
For you I am pray - ing, For you I am pray - ing,
For you I am pray - ing, I'm pray - ing for you.

WORDS: S. O'Malley Clough, 1860
MUSIC: Ira D. Sankey, 1875

INTERCESSION
11.11.12.11 Ref.

Teach Me to Pray, Lord 442

Lord, teach us to pray . . . Luke 11:1

1. Teach me to pray, Lord, teach me to pray; This is my heart-cry day unto day; I long to know Thy will and Thy way; Teach me to pray, Lord, teach me to pray.

2. Power in prayer, Lord, power in prayer, Here 'mid earth's sin and sorrow and care; Men lost and dying, souls in despair; O give me power, power in prayer!

3. My weakened will, Lord, Thou canst renew; My sinful nature Thou canst subdue; Fill me just now with power anew, Power to pray and power to do!

4. Teach me to pray, Lord, teach me to pray; Thou art my pattern, day unto day; Thou art my surety, now and for aye; Teach me to pray, Lord, teach me to pray.

Refrain

Living in Thee, Lord, and Thou in me; Constant abiding, this is my plea; Grant me Thy power, boundless and free: Power with men and power with Thee.

WORDS and MUSIC: Albert S. Reitz, 1925

REITZ
9.9.9.9 Ref.

443 'Tis the Blessed Hour of Prayer

He shall call upon Me, and I will answer him . . . Psa. 91:15

1. 'Tis the bless - ed hour of prayer, when our hearts low - ly bend,
2. 'Tis the bless - ed hour of prayer, when the Sav - ior draws near,
3. 'Tis the bless - ed hour of prayer, when the tempt - ed and tried
4. At the bless - ed hour of prayer, trust - ing Him we be - lieve
And we gath - er to Je - sus, our Sav - ior and Friend; If we
With a ten - der com - pas - sion His chil - dren to hear; When He
To the Sav - ior who loves them their sor - row con - fide; With a
That the bless - ings we're need - ing we'll sure - ly re - ceive; In the
come to Him in faith, His pro - tec - tion to share, What a balm for the
tells us we may cast at His feet ev - ery care, What a balm for the
sym - pa - thiz - ing heart He re - moves ev - ery care, What a balm for the
full - ness of this trust we shall lose ev - ery care; What a balm for the
wea - ry! O how sweet to be there!
Refrain
Bless - ed hour of prayer, Bless - ed hour of prayer; What a balm for the wea - ry! O how sweet to be there!

WORDS: Fanny J. Crosby, 1880
MUSIC: William H. Doane, 1880

BLESSED HOUR
Irregular meter

Sweet Hour of Prayer 444

Now Peter and John went up together . . . at the hour of prayer. Acts 3:1

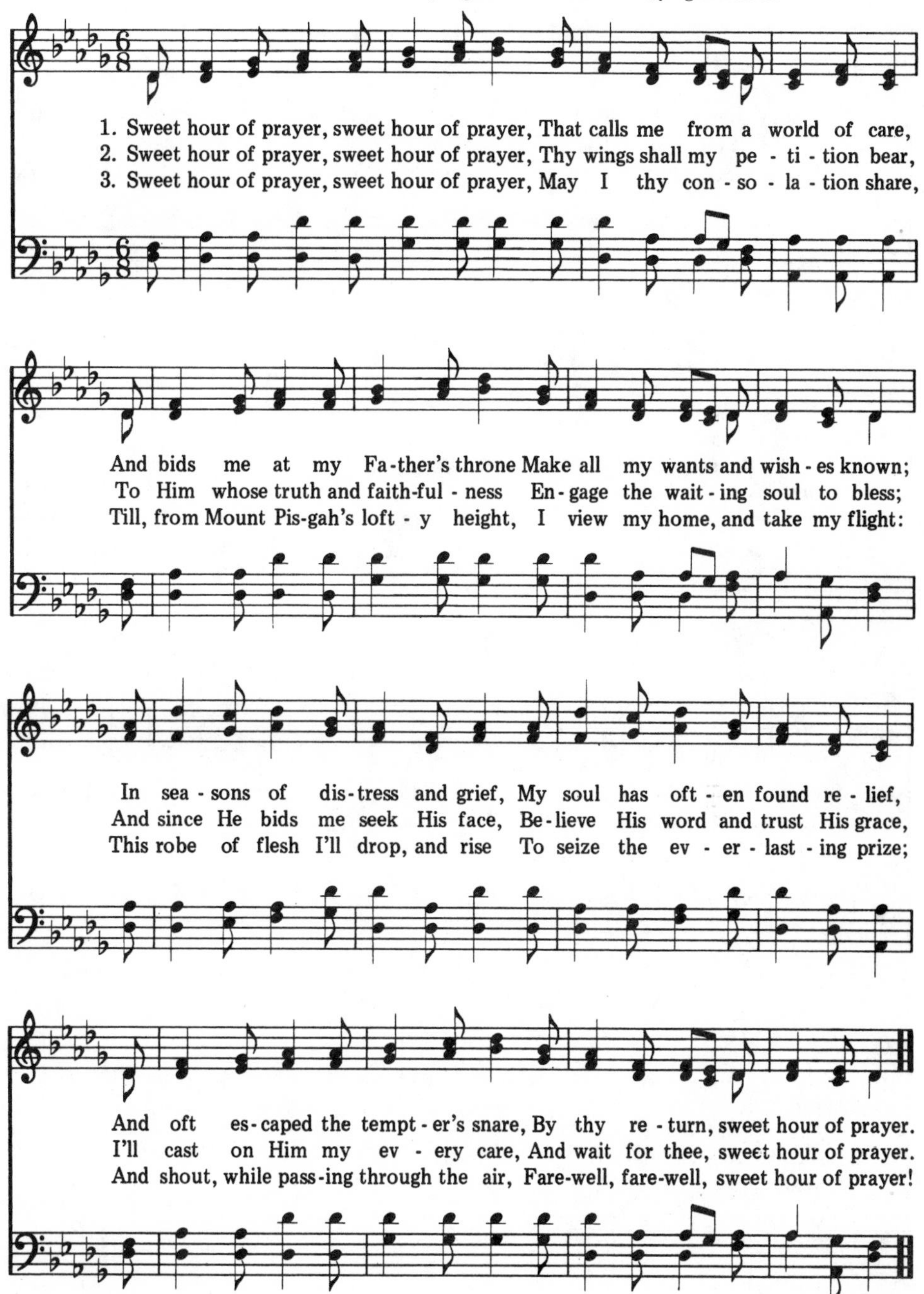
1. Sweet hour of prayer, sweet hour of prayer, That calls me from a world of care,
2. Sweet hour of prayer, sweet hour of prayer, Thy wings shall my pe - ti - tion bear,
3. Sweet hour of prayer, sweet hour of prayer, May I thy con - so - la - tion share,
And bids me at my Fa-ther's throne Make all my wants and wish - es known;
To Him whose truth and faith-ful - ness En-gage the wait - ing soul to bless;
Till, from Mount Pis-gah's loft - y height, I view my home, and take my flight:
In sea - sons of dis-tress and grief, My soul has oft - en found re - lief,
And since He bids me seek His face, Be-lieve His word and trust His grace,
This robe of flesh I'll drop, and rise To seize the ev - er - last - ing prize;
And oft es-caped the tempt - er's snare, By thy re - turn, sweet hour of prayer.
I'll cast on Him my ev - ery care, And wait for thee, sweet hour of prayer.
And shout, while pass-ing through the air, Fare-well, fare-well, sweet hour of prayer!

WORDS: William Walford, 1845
MUSIC: William B. Bradbury, 1861

SWEET HOUR
L.M.D.

445 Soldiers of Christ, Arise

Be strong in the Lord . . . Put on the whole armor of God. Eph. 6:10,11

1. Sol - diers of Christ, a - rise And put your ar - mor on,
2. Stand then in His great might, With all His strength en - dued,
3. Leave no un - guard - ed place, No weak - ness of the soul;
Strong in the strength which God sup - plies, Through His e - ter - nal Son;
And take, to arm you for the fight, The pan - o - ply of God;
Take ev - ery vir - tue, ev - ery grace, And for - ti - fy the whole.
Strong in the Lord of hosts, And in His might - y pow'r, Who
From strength to strength go on, Wres - tle and fight and pray; Tread
That hav - ing all things done, And all your con - flicts past, Ye
in the strength of Je - sus trusts Is more than con - quer - or.
all the pow'rs of dark - ness down, And win the well-fought day.
may o'er - come through Christ a - lone, And stand com - plete at last. A - men.

WORDS: Charles Wesley, 1749
MUSIC: George J. Elvey, 1868

DIADEMATA
S.M.D.

God of Grace and God of Glory 446

Who knoweth whether thou art come to the kingdom for such a time . . . ? Esther 4:14

1. God of grace and God of glory, On Thy people pour Thy pow'r; Crown Thine ancient church's story, Bring her bud to glorious flow'r. Grant us wisdom, Grant us courage For the facing of this hour, For the facing of this hour.
2. Lo! the hosts of evil round us Scorn Thy Christ, assail His ways! Fears and doubts too long have bound us, Free our hearts to faith and praise. Grant us wisdom, Grant us courage For the living of these days, For the living of these days.
3. Set our feet on lofty places; Gird our lives, that they may be Armored with all Christ-like graces In the fight to set men free. Grant us wisdom, Grant us courage That we fail not man nor Thee! That we fail not man nor Thee! A-men.

WORDS: Harry E. Fosdick, 1930
MUSIC: John Hughes, 1907

CWM RHONDDA
8.7.8.7.8.7.7

447 The Son of God Goes Forth to War

Can ye drink of the cup that I drink of . . . ? Mark 10:38

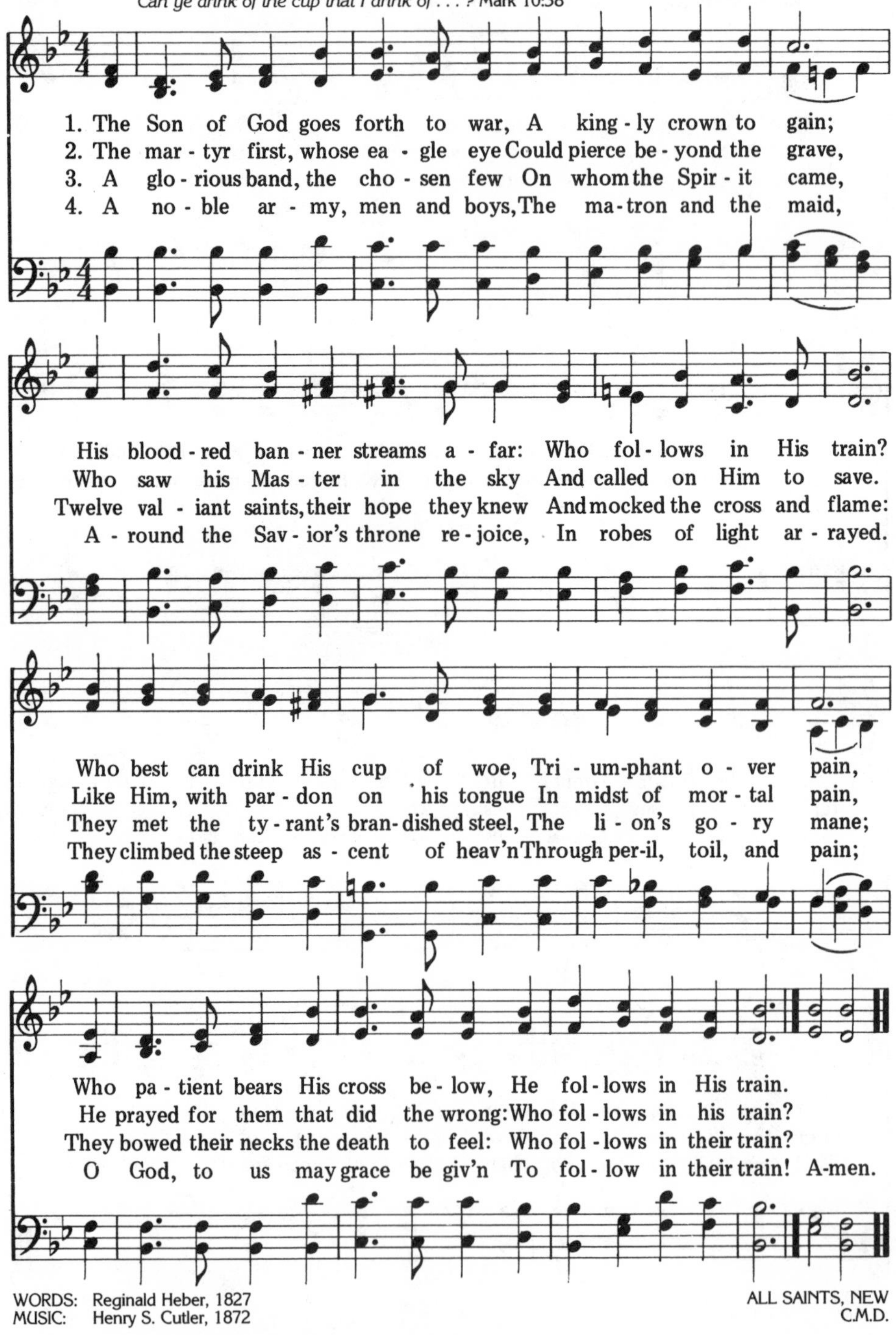
1. The Son of God goes forth to war, A kingly crown to gain;
His blood-red banner streams afar: Who follows in His train?
Who best can drink His cup of woe, Triumphant over pain,
Who patient bears His cross below, He follows in His train.
2. The martyr first, whose eagle eye Could pierce beyond the grave,
Who saw his Master in the sky And called on Him to save.
Like Him, with pardon on his tongue In midst of mortal pain,
He prayed for them that did the wrong: Who follows in his train?
3. A glorious band, the chosen few On whom the Spirit came,
Twelve valiant saints, their hope they knew And mocked the cross and flame:
They met the tyrant's brandished steel, The lion's gory mane;
They bowed their necks the death to feel: Who follows in their train?
4. A noble army, men and boys, The matron and the maid,
Around the Savior's throne rejoice, In robes of light arrayed.
They climbed the steep ascent of heav'n Through peril, toil, and pain;
O God, to us may grace be giv'n To follow in their train! Amen.

WORDS: Reginald Heber, 1827
MUSIC: Henry S. Cutler, 1872

ALL SAINTS, NEW
C.M.D.

Lead On, O King Eternal 448

Henceforth there is laid up for me a crown of righteousness . . . II Tim. 4:8

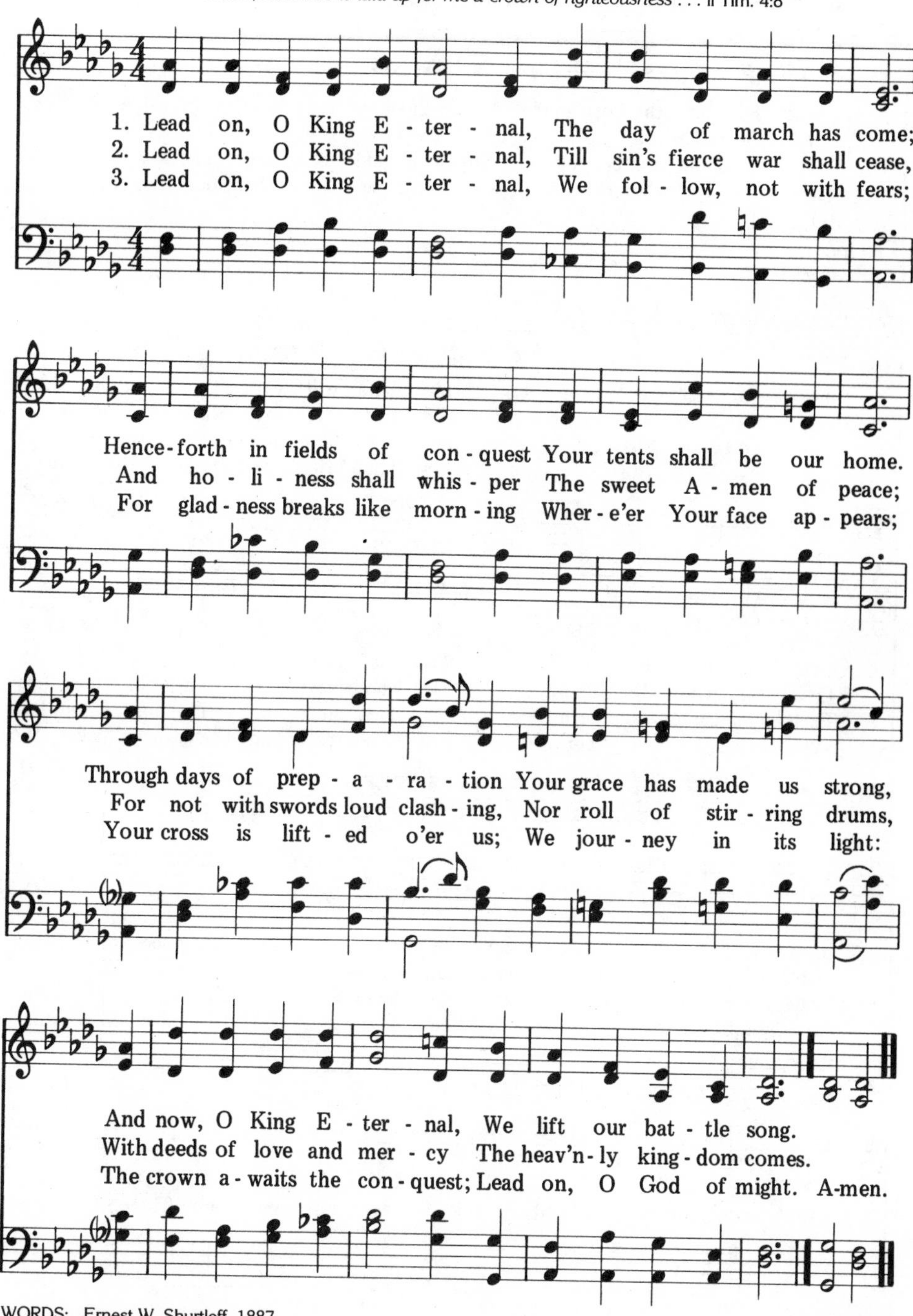
1. Lead on, O King E - ter - nal, The day of march has come;
2. Lead on, O King E - ter - nal, Till sin's fierce war shall cease,
3. Lead on, O King E - ter - nal, We fol - low, not with fears;
Hence-forth in fields of con - quest Your tents shall be our home.
And ho - li - ness shall whis - per The sweet A - men of peace;
For glad - ness breaks like morn - ing Wher - e'er Your face ap - pears;
Through days of prep - a - ra - tion Your grace has made us strong,
For not with swords loud clash - ing, Nor roll of stir - ring drums,
Your cross is lift - ed o'er us; We jour - ney in its light:
And now, O King E - ter - nal, We lift our bat - tle song.
With deeds of love and mer - cy The heav'n - ly king - dom comes.
The crown a - waits the con - quest; Lead on, O God of might. A-men.

WORDS: Ernest W. Shurtleff, 1887
MUSIC: Henry T. Smart, 1835

LANCASHIRE
7.6.7.6 D.

449 Who Is on the Lord's Side?

Who is on the Lord's side? Exo. 32:26

1. Who is on the Lord's side? Who will serve the King? Who will be His helpers, Other lives to bring? Who will leave the world's side? Who will face the foe? Who is on the Lord's side? Who for Him will go? By Thy call of mercy, By Thy grace divine, We are on the Lord's side, Savior, we are Thine.
2. Not for weight of glory, Not for crown and palm, Enter we the army, Raise the warrior psalm; But for love that claimeth Lives for whom He died; He whom Jesus nameth Must be on His side. By Thy love constraining, By Thy grace divine,
3. Jesus, Thou hast bought us, Not with gold or gem, But with Thine own lifeblood, For Thy diadem. With Thy blessing filling Each who comes to Thee, Thou hast made us willing, Thou hast made us free. By Thy grand redemption, By Thy grace divine,
4. Fierce may be the conflict, Strong may be the foe, But the King's own army None can overthrow. Round His standard ranging Vict'ry is secure; For His truth unchanging Makes the triumph sure. Joyfully enlisting By Thy grace divine,
Amen.

WORDS: Frances R. Havergal, 1877
MUSIC: C. Luise Reichardt, 1853; arr. John Goss, 1872

ARMAGEDDON
6.5.6.5 D. Ref.

Once to Every Man and Nation 450

Choose you this day whom ye will serve. Josh. 24:15

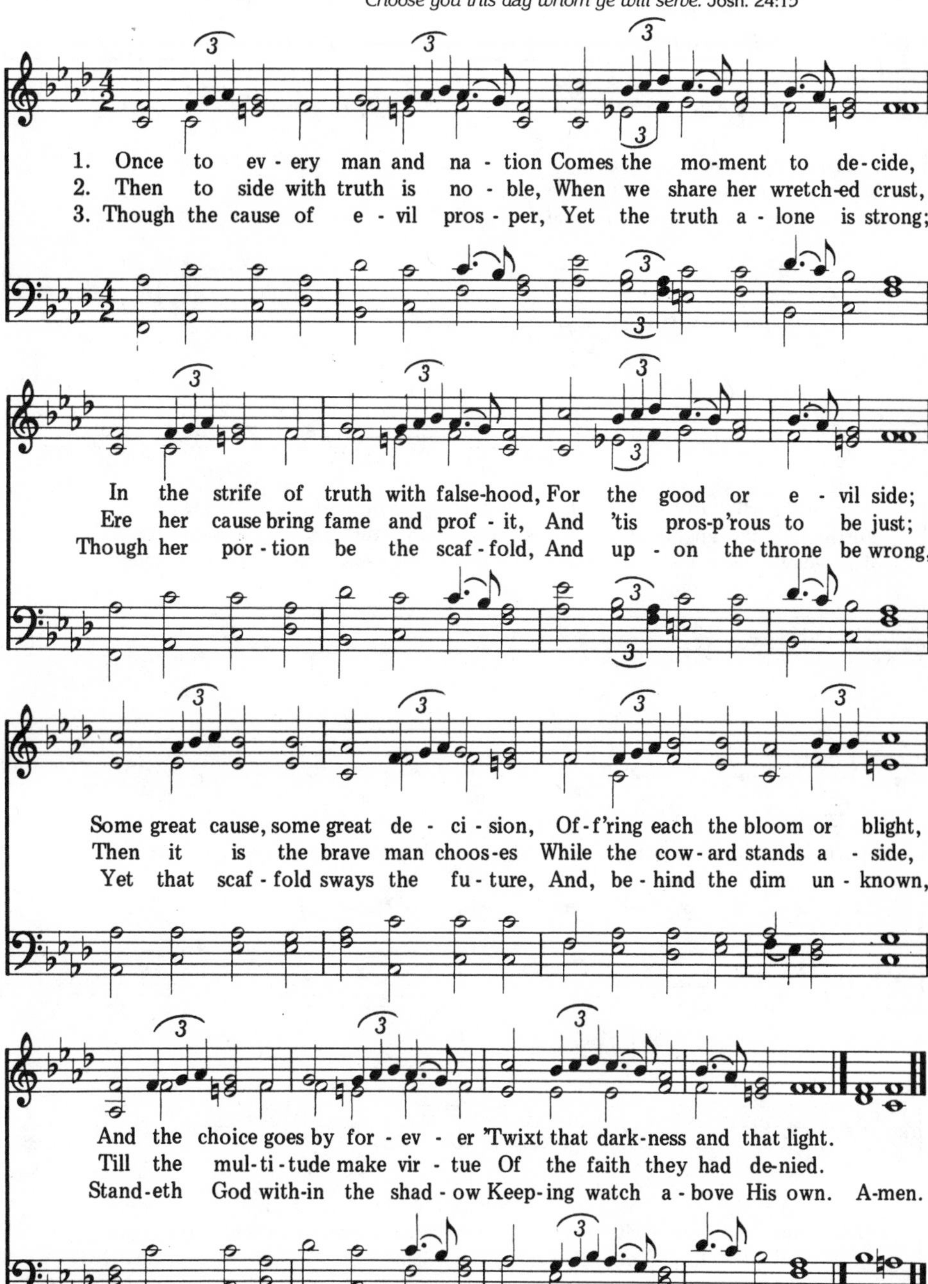
1. Once to ev - ery man and na - tion Comes the mo-ment to de-cide,
2. Then to side with truth is no - ble, When we share her wretch-ed crust,
3. Though the cause of e - vil pros - per, Yet the truth a - lone is strong;
In the strife of truth with false-hood, For the good or e - vil side;
Ere her cause bring fame and prof - it, And 'tis pros-p'rous to be just;
Though her por - tion be the scaf - fold, And up - on the throne be wrong,
Some great cause, some great de - ci - sion, Of-f'ring each the bloom or blight,
Then it is the brave man choos-es While the cow-ard stands a - side,
Yet that scaf - fold sways the fu - ture, And, be - hind the dim un - known,
And the choice goes by for - ev - er 'Twixt that dark-ness and that light.
Till the mul-ti-tude make vir - tue Of the faith they had de-nied.
Stand-eth God with-in the shad - ow Keep-ing watch a - bove His own. A-men.

WORDS: James R. Lowell, 1845
MUSIC: Thomas J. Williams, 1890

TON-Y-BOTEL
8.7.8.7 D.

451 Stand Up, Stand Up for Jesus

Watch ye, stand fast in the faith, quit you like men, be strong. I Cor. 16:13

Unison
1. Stand up, stand up for Je - sus, Ye sol - diers of the cross;
2. Stand up, stand up for Je - sus, The trum - pet call o - bey;
3. Stand up, stand up for Je - sus, The strife will not be long;
Lift high His roy - al ban - ner, It must not suf - fer loss:
Forth to the might - y con - flict In this His glo - rious day:
This day the noise of bat - tle, The next, the vic - tor's song:
From vic - t'ry un - to vic - t'ry His ar - my shall He lead,
"Ye that are men, now serve Him" A- gainst un - num-bered foes;
To Him that o - ver - com - eth A crown of life shall be;
Till ev - ery foe is van - quished And Christ is Lord in - deed.
Let cour - age rise with dan - ger, And strength to strength op - pose.
He with the King of glo - ry Shall reign e - ter - nal - ly.

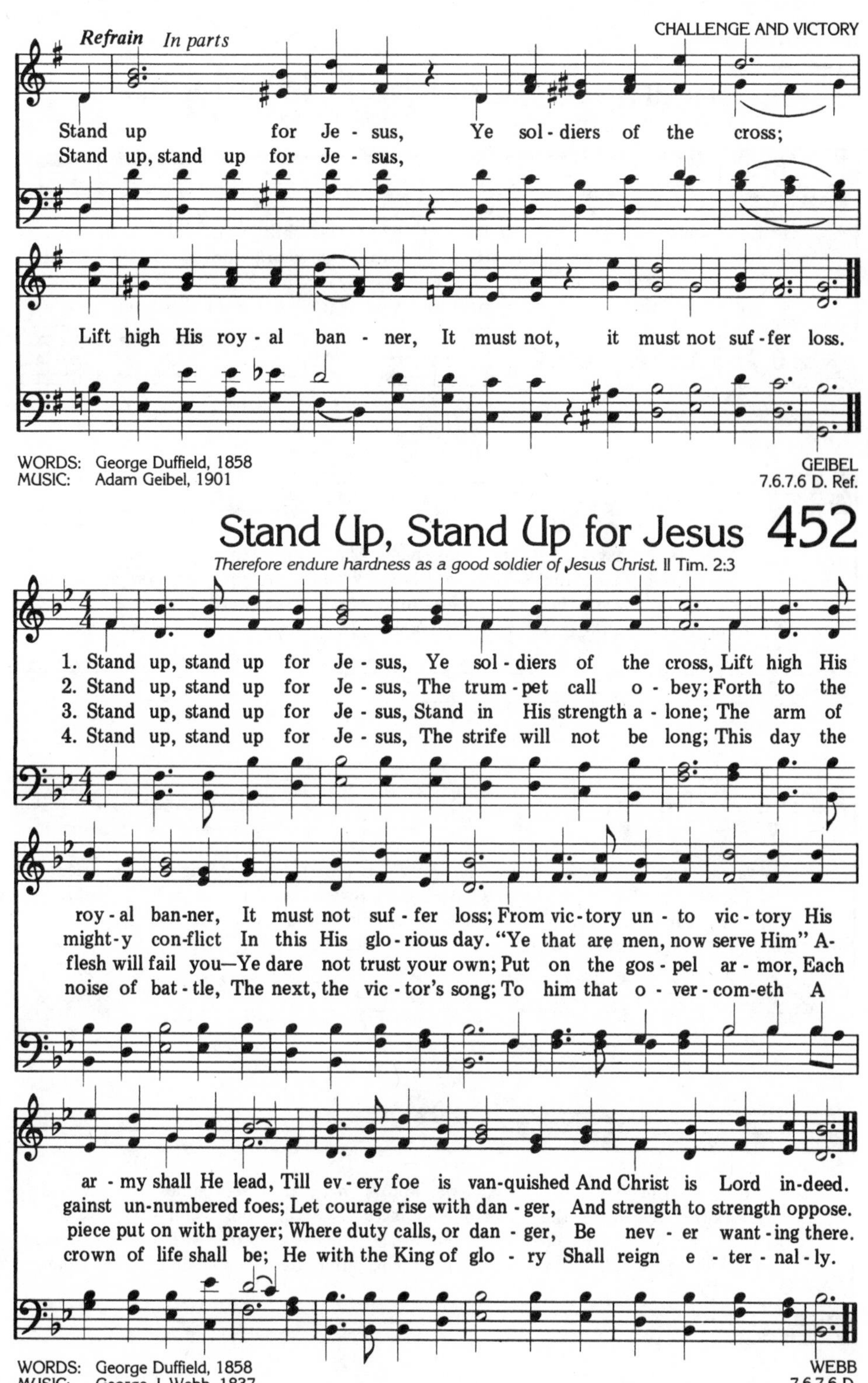
Refrain In parts
Stand up for Je - sus, Ye sol - diers of the cross;
Stand up, stand up for Je - sus,
Lift high His roy - al ban - ner, It must not, it must not suf - fer loss.
WORDS: George Duffield, 1858
MUSIC: Adam Geibel, 1901
GEIBEL
7.6.7.6 D. Ref.
Stand Up, Stand Up for Jesus 452
Therefore endure hardness as a good soldier of Jesus Christ. II Tim. 2:3
1. Stand up, stand up for Je - sus, Ye sol - diers of the cross, Lift high His roy - al ban-ner, It must not suf - fer loss; From vic-tory un - to vic - tory His ar - my shall He lead, Till ev - ery foe is van-quished And Christ is Lord in-deed.
2. Stand up, stand up for Je - sus, The trum - pet call o - bey; Forth to the might-y con-flict In this His glo - rious day. "Ye that are men, now serve Him" A-gainst un-numbered foes; Let courage rise with dan - ger, And strength to strength oppose.
3. Stand up, stand up for Je - sus, Stand in His strength a - lone; The arm of flesh will fail you—Ye dare not trust your own; Put on the gos - pel ar - mor, Each piece put on with prayer; Where duty calls, or dan - ger, Be nev - er want - ing there.
4. Stand up, stand up for Je - sus, The strife will not be long; This day the noise of bat - tle, The next, the vic - tor's song; To him that o - ver - com-eth A crown of life shall be; He with the King of glo - ry Shall reign e - ter - nal - ly.
WORDS: George Duffield, 1858
MUSIC: George J. Webb, 1837
WEBB
7.6.7.6 D.

453 Encamped Along the Hills of Light

This is the victory that overcometh the world, even our faith. I John 5:4

1. En-camped a-long the hills of light, Ye Chris-tian sol-diers, rise,
2. His ban-ner o-ver us is love, Our sword the Word of God;
3. On ev-ery hand the foe we find Drawn up in dread ar-ray;
4. To him that o-ver-comes the foe, White rai-ment shall be giv'n;

And press the bat-tle ere the night Shall veil the glow-ing skies.
We tread the road the saints a-bove With shouts of tri-umph trod.
Let tents of ease be left be-hind, And on-ward to the fray;
Be-fore the an-gels he shall know His name con-fessed in heav'n.

A-gainst the foe in vales be-low Let all our strength be hurled;
By faith they, like a whirl-wind's breath, Swept on o'er ev-ery field;
Sal-va-tion's hel-met on each head, With truth all girt a-bout,
Then on-ward from the hills of light, Our hearts with love a-flame,

Faith is the vic-to-ry, we know, That o-ver-comes the world.
The faith by which they con-quered death Is still our shin-ing shield.
The earth shall trem-ble 'neath our tread, And ech-o with our shout.
We'll van-quish all the hosts of night, In Je-sus' con-quering name.

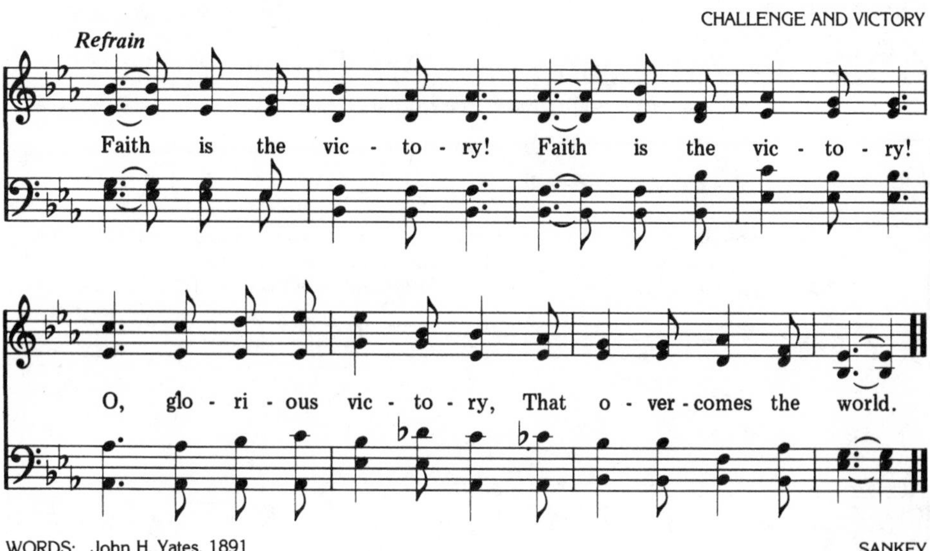
Refrain
Faith is the vic - to - ry! Faith is the vic - to - ry!
O, glo - ri - ous vic - to - ry, That o - ver - comes the world.

WORDS: John H. Yates, 1891
MUSIC: Ira D. Sankey, 1891

SANKEY
C.M.D. Ref.

My Soul, Be on Your Guard 454

Be sober, be vigilant . . . I Pet. 5:8

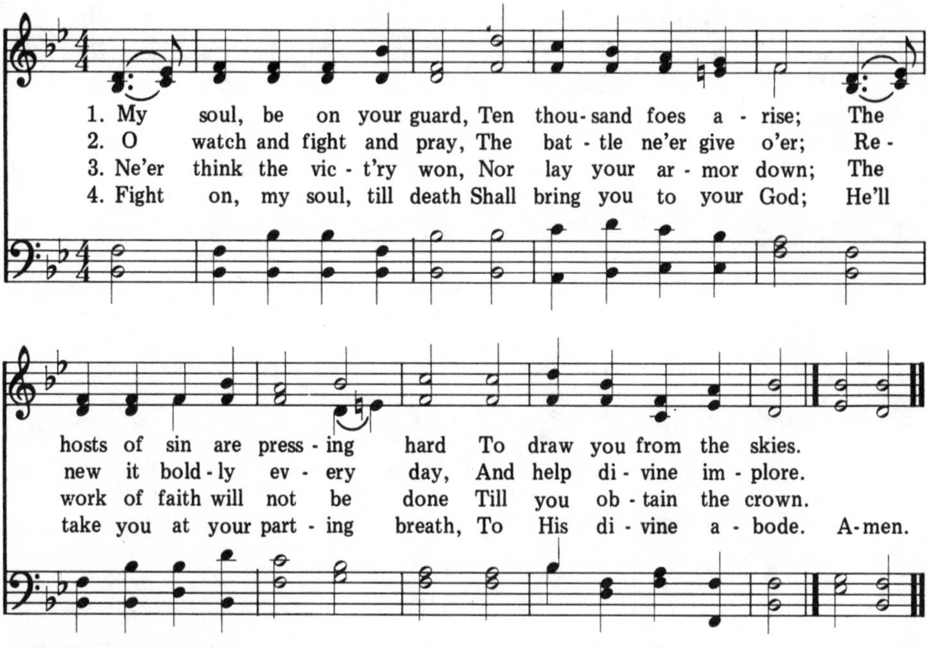

1. My soul, be on your guard, Ten thou - sand foes a - rise; The hosts of sin are press - ing hard To draw you from the skies.
2. O watch and fight and pray, The bat - tle ne'er give o'er; Re - new it bold - ly ev - ery day, And help di - vine im - plore.
3. Ne'er think the vic - t'ry won, Nor lay your ar - mor down; The work of faith will not be done Till you ob - tain the crown.
4. Fight on, my soul, till death Shall bring you to your God; He'll take you at your part - ing breath, To His di - vine a - bode. A-men.

WORDS: George Heath, 1781
MUSIC: Lowell Mason, 1830

LABAN
S.M.

455 We Are Living, We Are Dwelling

For we know that the whole creation groaneth and travaileth in pain . . . until now. Rom. 8:22

1. We are liv - ing, we are dwell - ing In a grand and aw - ful time,
2. Will ye play, then? will ye dal - ly Far be - hind the bat - tle line?
3. Sworn to yield, to wa - ver, nev - er; Con - se - crat - ed, born a - gain;
In an age on a - ges tell - ing; To be liv - ing is sub - lime.
Up! it is Je - ho - vah's ral - ly; God's own arm hath need of thine.
Sworn to be Christ's sol - diers ev - er, On! for Christ at least be men!
Hark! the wak - ing up of na - tions, Hosts ad - vanc - ing to the fray;
Worlds are charg - ing, heav'n be - hold - ing; Thou hast but an hour to fight;
On! let all the soul with - in you For the truth's sake go a - broad!
Hark! what sound - eth is cre - a - tion's Groan - ing for the lat - ter day.
Now, the bla - zoned cross un - fold - ing, On, right on - ward for the right!
Strike! let ev - ery nerve and sin - ew Tell on a - ges, tell for God. A - men.

WORDS: A. Cleveland Coxe, 1840
MUSIC: Franz Joseph Haydn, 1797

AUSTRIAN HYMN
8.7.8.7 D.

Onward, Christian Soldiers 456

Thou therefore endure hardness, as a good soldier of Jesus Christ. II Tim. 2:3

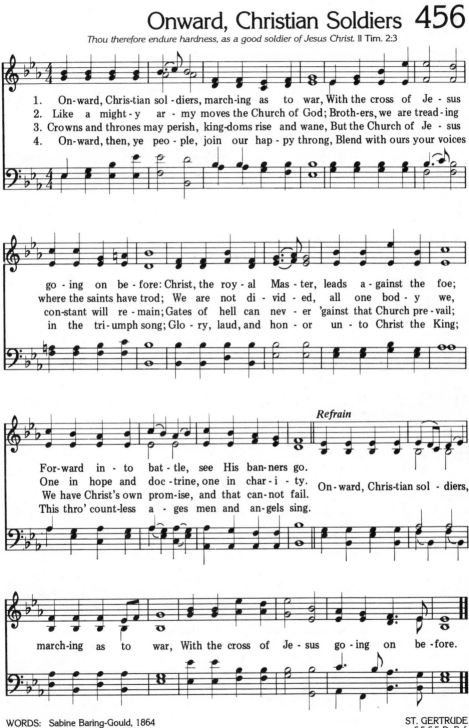

1. On-ward, Chris-tian sol - diers, march-ing as to war, With the cross of Je - sus
2. Like a might - y ar - my moves the Church of God; Broth-ers, we are tread - ing
3. Crowns and thrones may perish, king-doms rise and wane, But the Church of Je - sus
4. On-ward, then, ye peo - ple, join our hap - py throng, Blend with ours your voices

go - ing on be - fore: Christ, the roy - al Mas - ter, leads a - gainst the foe;
where the saints have trod; We are not di - vid - ed, all one bod - y we,
con-stant will re - main; Gates of hell can nev - er 'gainst that Church pre - vail;
in the tri - umph song; Glo - ry, laud, and hon - or un - to Christ the King;

Refrain

For-ward in - to bat - tle, see His ban-ners go.
One in hope and doc - trine, one in char - i - ty.
We have Christ's own prom-ise, and that can-not fail.
This thro' count-less a - ges men and an-gels sing.

On-ward, Chris-tian sol - diers,

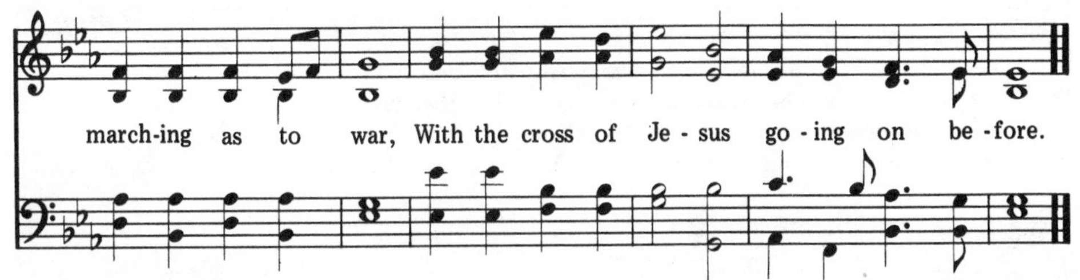
march-ing as to war, With the cross of Je - sus go - ing on be - fore.

WORDS: Sabine Baring-Gould, 1864
MUSIC: Arthur S. Sullivan, 1871

ST. GERTRUDE
6.5.6.5 D. Ref.

457 Rise Up, O Men of God!

Yet a little while, and He . . . will come, and will not tarry. Heb. 10:37

1. Rise up, O men of God! Have done with less - er things;
2. Rise up, O men of God! His King - dom tar - ries long;
3. Rise up, O men of God! The Church for you doth wait,
4. Lift high the cross of Christ! Tread where His feet have trod;
Give heart and soul and mind and strength To serve the King of kings.
Bring in the day of broth - er - hood And end the night of wrong.
Her strength un - e - qual to her task; Rise up, and make her great!
As broth - ers of the Son of Man, Rise up, O men of God! A-men.

WORDS: William P. Merrill, 1911
MUSIC: William H. Walter, 1894

FESTAL SONG
S.M.

458 Fight the Good Fight with All Thy Might

Fight the good fight of faith. I Tim. 6:12

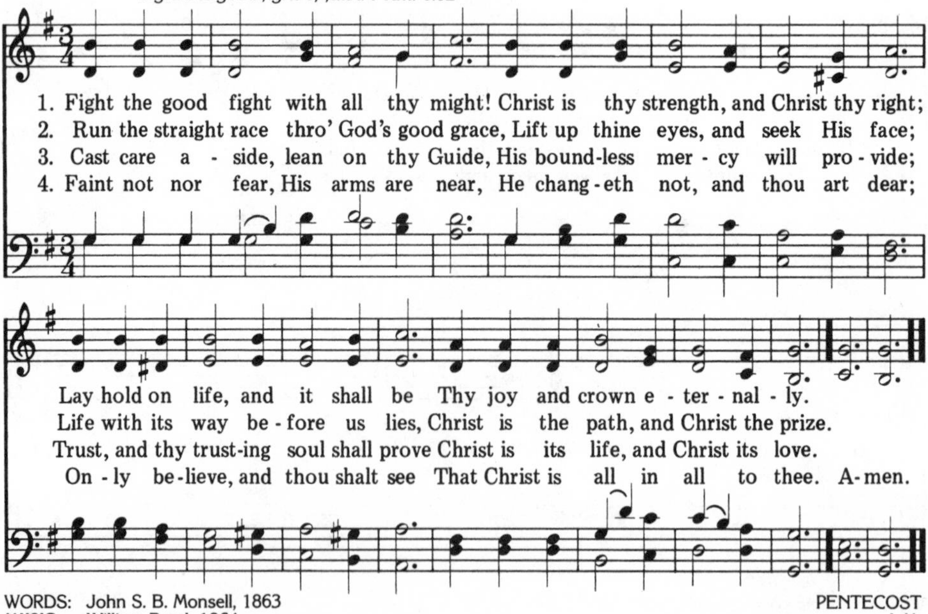

1. Fight the good fight with all thy might! Christ is thy strength, and Christ thy right;
2. Run the straight race thro' God's good grace, Lift up thine eyes, and seek His face;
3. Cast care a - side, lean on thy Guide, His bound-less mer - cy will pro - vide;
4. Faint not nor fear, His arms are near, He chang - eth not, and thou art dear;

Lay hold on life, and it shall be Thy joy and crown e - ter - nal - ly.
Life with its way be - fore us lies, Christ is the path, and Christ the prize.
Trust, and thy trust-ing soul shall prove Christ is its life, and Christ its love.
On - ly be-lieve, and thou shalt see That Christ is all in all to thee. A-men.

WORDS: John S. B. Monsell, 1863
MUSIC: William Boyd, 1864

PENTECOST
L.M.

We've a Story to Tell to the Nations 459

And this gospel . . . shall be preached in all the world for a witness unto all nations. Matt. 24:14

1. We've a sto - ry to tell to the na - tions That shall turn their hearts to the right, A sto - ry of truth and mer - cy, A sto - ry of peace and light, A sto - ry of peace and light.
2. We've a song to be sung to the na - tions That shall lift their hearts to the Lord, A song that shall con - quer e - vil And shat - ter the spear and sword, And shat - ter the spear and sword.
3. We've a mes - sage to give to the na - tions That the Lord who reign - eth a - bove Hath sent us His Son to save us, And show us that God is love, And show us that God is love.
4. We've a Sav - ior to show to the na - tions Who the path of sor - row hath trod, That all of the world's great peo - ples Might come to the truth of God, Might come to the truth of God.

Refrain

For the dark-ness shall turn to dawn-ing, And the dawn-ing to noon-day bright, And Christ's great king-dom shall come to earth, The king - dom of love and light.

WORDS and MUSIC: H. Ernest Nichol, 1896

MESSAGE
10.8.8.7.7 Ref.

460 I'll Tell to All That God Is Love

Wherever this gospel shall be preached throughout the whole world . . . Mark 14:9

1. I'll tell to all that God is love; For the world has nev - er known
The great com - pas - sion of His heart For the way-ward and the lone.

2. I'll tell of mer - cy's bound-less tide, Like the wa - ters of the sea,
That cov - ers ev - ery sin of man; 'Tis sal - va - tion full and free.

3. I'll tell of grace that keeps the soul, Of a - bid - ing peace with - in,
Of faith that o - ver - comes the world, With its tu - mult and its din.

4. E - ter - nal glo - ry is the goal That a - waits the sons of light;
E - ter - nal dark - ness, black as death, For the chil - dren of the night.

Refrain

Till the whole world knows, Till the whole world knows,
Till the world, till the whole world knows, Till the world, till the whole world, whole world knows,
Till the world, the whole world knows,
I will shout and sing of Christ my King, Till the whole world knows.

WORDS: Alfred H. Ackley, 1923
MUSIC: Bentley D. Ackley, 1923

TILL THE WHOLE WORLD KNOWS
8.7.8.7 Ref.

Rescue the Perishing 461

The Son of man is come to seek and to save that which was lost. Luke 19:10

1. Res-cue the per-ish-ing, care for the dy-ing, Snatch them in pit-y from sin and the grave; Weep o'er the err-ing one, lift up the fall-en, Tell them of Je-sus the might-y to save.
2. Though they are slight-ing Him, still He is wait-ing, Wait-ing the pen-i-tent child to re-ceive; Plead with them ear-nest-ly, plead with them gen-tly, He will for-give if they on-ly be-lieve.
3. Down in the hu-man heart, crushed by the tempt-er, Feel-ings lie bur-ied that grace can re-store; Touched by a lov-ing heart, wak-ened by kind-ness, Cords that are bro-ken will vi-brate once more.
4. Res-cue the per-ish-ing, du-ty de-mands it; Strength for thy la-bor the Lord will pro-vide; Back to the nar-row way pa-tient-ly win them; Tell the poor wan-d'rer a Sav-ior has died.
Refrain
Res-cue the per-ish-ing, care for the dy-ing; Je-sus is mer-ci-ful, Je-sus will save.

WORDS: Fanny J. Crosby, 1869
MUSIC: William H. Doane, 1870

RESCUE
11.10.11.10 Ref.

462 Through All the World

Let the whole earth be filled with His glory. Psa. 72:19

Unison
1. Thro' all the world let ev - ery na - tion sing to God the King, As Lord may Christ pre - side where now He is de - fied, And sov -'reign place His throne in lands not yet His own.
2. Thro' all the world let ev - ery man ex - press true right - eous - ness, May Christ now be the norm to which all men con - form, His pas - sion cure the sin that fes - ters from with - in.
3. Thro' all the world let ev - ery man em-brace the gift of grace, May Christ's great light con-sume our dark - est cit - ies' gloom, May Christ's great love ef - face hos - til - i - ties of race.
4. If all the world in ev - ery part shall hear, and God re - vere, We must be moved to care, and in His name to share The lib - er - a - ting word which must be told a - broad.
Thro' all the world let ev-ery na - tion sing to God the King.
Thro' all the world let ev-ery man ex-press true right-eous - ness.
Thro' all the world let ev-ery man em-brace the gift of grace.
Then all the world in ev-ery part shall hear, and God re - vere.

WORDS: Bryan J. Leech, 1970
MUSIC: Paul Liljestrand, 1970

CONRAD
14.12.12.14

Give Me a Passion for Souls, Dear Lord 463

My heart's desire and prayer to God . . . is, that they might be saved. Rom. 10:1

1. Give me a pas-sion for souls, dear Lord, A pas-sion to save the lost;
2. Though there are dan-gers un-told and stern Con-front-ing me in the way,
3. How shall this pas-sion for souls be mine? Lord, make Thou the an-swer clear;
O that Thy love were by all a-dored, And wel-comed at an-y cost.
Will-ing-ly still would I go, nor turn, But trust Thee for grace each day.
Help me to throw out the old life-line To those who are strug-gling near.
Refrain
Je-sus, I long, I long to be win-ning Men who are
lost, and con-stant-ly sin-ning; O may this hour be
one of be-gin-ning The sto-ry of par-don to tell.

WORDS: Herbert G. Tovey, 1914
MUSIC: Foss L. Fellers, 1914

BIOLA
9.7.9.7 Ref.

464 Take Up Thy Cross and Follow Me

Whosoever will come after Me, let him . . . take up his cross and follow Me. Mark 8:34

1. "Take up thy cross and fol - low Me," I heard my Mas - ter say;
"I gave My life to ran - som thee, Sur - ren - der your all to - day."
2. He drew me clos - er to His side, I sought His will to know,
And in that will I now a - bide, Wher - ev - er He leads I'll go.
3. It may be through the shad - ows dim, Or o'er the storm - y sea,
I take my cross and fol - low Him, Wher - ev - er He lead - eth me.
4. My heart, my life, my all I bring To Christ who loves me so;
He is my Mas - ter, Lord, and King, Wher - ev - er He leads I'll go.
Refrain
Wher - ev - er He leads I'll go, Wher - ev - er He leads I'll go,
I'll fol-low my Christ who loves me so, Wher - ev - er He leads I'll go.

WORDS and MUSIC: B. B. McKinney, 1936

FALLS CREEK
8.6.8.7 Ref.

O Christians, Haste, Your Mission High 465

We declare unto you glad tidings. Acts 13:32

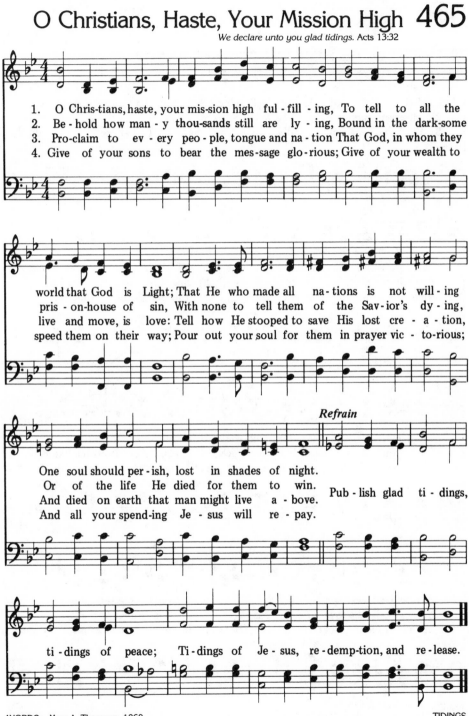

1. O Chris-tians, haste, your mis-sion high ful - fill - ing, To tell to all the
2. Be - hold how man - y thou-sands still are ly - ing, Bound in the dark-some
3. Pro-claim to ev - ery peo - ple, tongue and na - tion That God, in whom they
4. Give of your sons to bear the mes-sage glo-rious; Give of your wealth to

world that God is Light; That He who made all na - tions is not will - ing
pris - on-house of sin, With none to tell them of the Sav - ior's dy - ing,
live and move, is love: Tell how He stooped to save His lost cre - a - tion,
speed them on their way; Pour out your soul for them in prayer vic - to-rious;

Refrain

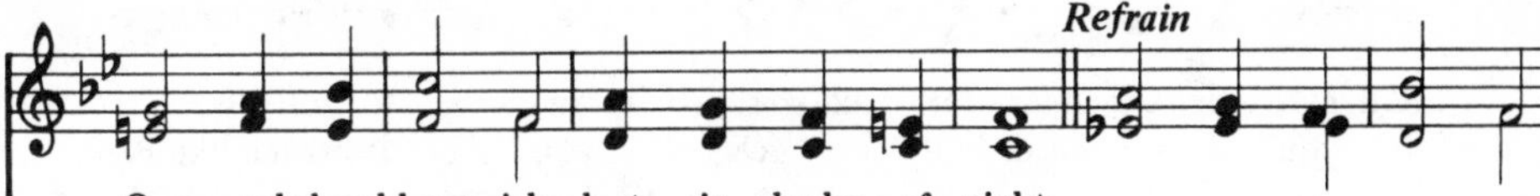

One soul should per - ish, lost in shades of night.
Or of the life He died for them to win.
And died on earth that man might live a - bove.
And all your spend-ing Je - sus will re - pay.

Pub - lish glad ti - dings,

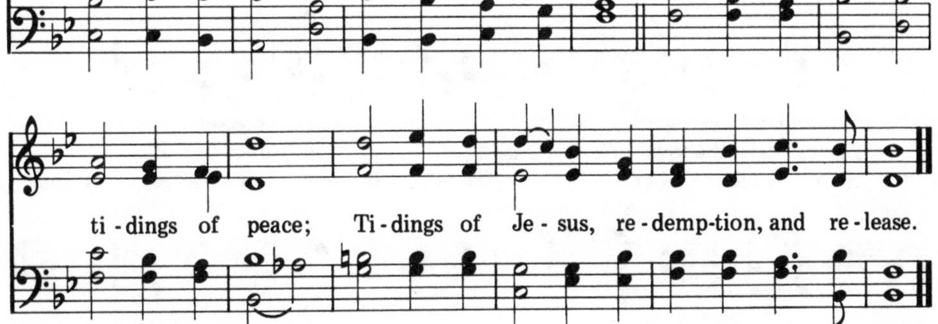

ti - dings of peace; Ti - dings of Je - sus, re - demp-tion, and re - lease.

WORDS: Mary A. Thomson, 1868
MUSIC: James Walch, 1875

TIDINGS
11.10.11.10 Ref.

466 Hark, the Voice of Jesus Calling

The harvest truly is great, but the laborers are few . . . Luke 10:2

1. Hark, the voice of Je - sus call - ing, "Who will go and work to - day?
2. If you can - not be the watch - man Stand - ing high on Zi - on's wall,
3. Let none hear you i - dly say - ing, "There is noth - ing I can do,"

Fields are white, and har - vests wait - ing, Who will bear the sheaves a - way?"
Point - ing out the path to heav - en, Off - 'ring life and peace to all,
While the souls of men are dy - ing, And the Mas - ter calls for you:

Loud and long the Mas - ter call - eth, Rich re - ward He of - fers free;
If you can - not speak like an - gels, If you can - not preach like Paul,
Take the task He gives you glad - ly; Let His work your pleas - ure be;

Who will an - swer, glad - ly say - ing, "Here am I; send me, send me"?
You can tell the love of Je - sus, You can say, "He died for all."
An - swer quick - ly when He call - eth, "Here am I; send me, send me." A - men.

WORDS: Daniel March, 1868
MUSIC: Leavitt's *The Christian Lyre*, 1831; attr. Wolfgang A. Mozart, 1756-1791; arr. Hubert P. Main, c.1868

ELLESDIE
8.7.8.7 D.

The Vision of a Dying World 467

Lift up your eyes, and look on the fields; for they are white . . . John 4:35

1. The vi - sion of a dy - ing world Is vast be - fore our eyes;
2. The sav - age hugs his god of stone And fears de - scent of night;
3. To - day, as un - der-stand-ing's bounds Are stretch'd on ev-ery hand,
4. The warn-ing bell of judg-ment tolls, A - bove us looms the cross;
We feel the heart-beat of its need, We hear its fee - ble cries:
The cit - y dwell - er cring - es lone A - mid the gar - ish light:
O clothe Thy Word in bright, new sounds, And speed it o'er the land;
A - round are ev - er - dy - ing souls— How great, how great the loss!
Lord Je - sus Christ, re - vive Thy church In this, her cru - cial hour!
Lord Je - sus Christ, a - rouse Thy church To see their mute dis - tress!
Lord Je - sus Christ, em - pow - er us To preach by ev - ery means!
O Lord, con-strain and move Thy church The glad news to im - part!
Lord Je - sus Christ, a - wake Thy church With Spir - it - giv - en pow'r.
Lord Je - sus Christ, e - quip Thy church With love and ten - der - ness.
Lord Je - sus Christ, em - bold - en us In near and dis - tant scenes.
And Lord, as Thou dost stir Thy church, Be - gin with - in my heart. A-men.
(♭)

WORDS: Anne Ortlund, 1966
MUSIC: Henry S. Cutler, 1872

ALL SAINTS, NEW
C.M.D.

468 Far, Far Away, in Death and Darkness

Go ye into all the world, and preach the gospel . . . Mark 16:15

1. Far, far a - way, in death and dark-ness dwell-ing, Mil-lions of souls for - ev - er may be lost; Who, who will go, sal - va-tion's sto - ry tell - ing, Look-ing to Je - sus, mind-ing not the cost?
2. See o'er the world wide o - pen doors in - vit - ing, Sol-diers of Christ, a - rise and en - ter in! Chris-tians, a - wake! your forc-es all u - nit - ing, Send forth the gos - pel, break the chains of sin.
3. "Why will ye die?" the voice of God is call - ing, "Why will ye die?" re - ech - o in His name; Je - sus hath died to save from death ap-pall - ing, Life and sal - va - tion there-fore go pro-claim.
4. God speed the day, when those of ev - ery na - tion "Glo - ry to God!" tri - um-phant - ly shall sing; Ran-somed, re-deemed, re - joic - ing in sal - va - tion, Shout Hal - le - lu - jah, for the Lord is King.
Refrain
"All pow'r is giv - en un - to Me, All pow'r is giv - en un - to Me, Go ye in - to all the world and preach the gos - pel, And lo, I am with you al - way."

WORDS and MUSIC: James McGranahan, 1886

GO YE
11.10.11.10 Ref.

Christ Was Born in a Distant Land 469

Behold, I bring you good tidings of great joy . . . Luke 2:10

Unison
1. Christ was born in a dis-tant land, Tell the good news, tell the good news,
2. Christ be-came a man on earth, Tell the good news, tell the good news,
3. Christ a-rose and to heav-en went, Tell the good news, tell the good news,
4. Christ still lives in the world to-day, Tell the good news, tell the good news,
Lived on earth for the good of man, Tell the good news, tell the good news.
Gave His life for man's re-birth, Tell the good news, tell the good news.
All may fol-low who re-pent, Tell the good news, tell the good news.
Giv-ing strength to all souls who pray, Tell the good news, tell the good news.
Refrain
Tell the good news, tell the good news, Tell the good news that Christ has come;
Tell the good news, tell the good news, Tell the good news to ev-ery-one.

WORDS and MUSIC: Gene Bartlett, 1968

RHEA
L.M. Ref.

470 So Send I You

As My Father hath sent Me, even so send I you. John 20:21

1. So send I you to la - bor un - re - ward - ed, To serve un- paid, un - loved, un - sought, un - known, To bear re - buke, to suf - fer scorn and scoff - ing— So send I you to toil for Me a - lone.
2. So send I you to bind the bruised and bro - ken, O'er wand - 'ring souls to work, to weep, to wake, To bear the bur - dens of a world a - wea - ry— So send I you to suf - fer for My sake.
3. So send I you to lone - li - ness and long - ing, With heart a- hung - 'ring for the loved and known, For - sak - ing home and kin - dred, friend and dear one— So send I you to know My love a - lone.
4. So send I you to leave your life's am - bi - tion, To die to dear de - sire, self - will re - sign, To la - bor long, and love where men re - vile you— So send I you to lose your life in Mine.
5. So send I you to hearts made hard by ha - tred, To eyes made blind be - cause they will not see, To spend, though it be blood, to spend and spare not— So send I you to taste of Cal - va - ry.
Refrain (following the final stanza)
"As the Fa - ther hath sent me, So send I you."

WORDS: Margaret Clarkson, 1937
MUSIC: John W. Peterson, 1954

TORONTO
11.10.11.10 Ref.

From Greenland's Icy Mountains 471

Come over . . . and help us. Acts 16:9

1. From Green-land's i - cy moun-tains, From In-dia's cor - al strand,
2. What though the spic - y breez - es Blow soft o'er Cey-lon's isle;
3. Shall we, whose souls are light - ed With wis-dom from on high,
4. Waft, waft, ye winds, His sto - ry, And you, ye wa-ters, roll,
Where Af-ric's sun-ny foun - tains Roll down their gold - en sand,
Though ev - ery pros-pect pleas - es, And on - ly man is vile?
Shall we to men be-night - ed The lamp of life de - ny?
Till, like a sea of glo - ry, It spreads from pole to pole:
From man-y an an-cient riv - er, From man-y a palm - y plain,
In vain with lav - ish kind - ness The gifts of God are strown;
Sal - va - tion! O sal - va - tion! The joy - ful sound pro - claim,
Till o'er our ran-somed na - ture The Lamb for sin-ners slain,
They call us to de - liv - er Their land from er-ror's chain.
The hea-then in his blind-ness Bows down to wood and stone.
Till earth's re-mot-est na - tion Has learned Mes - si - ah's name.
Re-deem - er, King, Cre - a - tor, In bliss re-turns to reign. A - men.

WORDS: Reginald Heber, 1819
MUSIC: Lowell Mason, 1824

MISSIONARY HYMN
7.6.7.6 D.

472 We Have Heard the Joyful Sound

. . . All the ends of the earth shall see the salvation of . . . God. Isa. 52:10

1. We have heard the joy - ful sound: Je - sus saves!
2. Waft it on the roll - ing tide; Je - sus saves!
3. Sing a - bove the bat - tle strife, Je - sus saves!
4. Give the winds a might - y voice, Je - sus saves!
Spread the ti - dings all a - round: Je - sus saves!
Tell to sin - ners far and wide: Je - sus saves!
By His death and end - less life, Je - sus saves!
Let the na - tions now re - joice— Je - sus saves!
Bear the news to ev - ery land, Climb the steeps and
Sing, ye is - lands of the sea; Ech - o back, ye
Sing it soft - ly through the gloom, When the heart for
Shout sal - va - tion full and free, High - est hills and
cross the waves; On - ward! 'tis our Lord's com-mand; Je - sus saves!
o - cean caves; Earth shall keep her ju - bi - lee: Je - sus saves!
mer - cy craves; Sing in tri-umph o'er the tomb: Je - sus saves!
deep - est caves; This our song of vic - to - ry— Je - sus saves!

WORDS: Priscilla J. Owens, 1868
MUSIC: Josiah Booth, 1898

LIMPSFIELD
7.3.7.3.7.7.7.3

We Have Heard the Joyful Sound 473

Tell of His salvation from day to day. Declare His glory . . . Psa. 96:2,3

1. We have heard the joy - ful sound: Je - sus saves! Je - sus saves!
2. Waft it on the roll - ing tide; Je - sus saves! Je - sus saves!
3. Sing a - bove the bat - tle strife, Je - sus saves! Je - sus saves!
4. Give the winds a might - y voice, Je - sus saves! Je - sus saves!
Spread the ti - dings all a - round: Je - sus saves! Je - sus saves!
Tell to sin - ners far and wide: Je - sus saves! Je - sus saves!
By His death and end - less life, Je - sus saves! Je - sus saves!
Let the na - tions now re - joice— Je - sus saves! Je - sus saves!
Bear the news to ev - ery land, Climb the steeps and cross the waves;
Sing, ye is - lands of the sea; Ech - o back, ye o - cean caves;
Sing it soft - ly through the gloom, When the heart for mer - cy craves;
Shout sal - va - tion full and free, High - est hills and deep - est caves;
On - ward! 'tis our Lord's com - mand; Je - sus saves! Je - sus saves!
Earth shall keep her ju - bi - lee: Je - sus saves! Je - sus saves!
Sing in tri - umph o'er the tomb— Je - sus saves! Je - sus saves!
This our song of vic - to - ry— Je - sus saves! Je - sus saves!

WORDS: Priscilla J. Owens, 1868
MUSIC: William J. Kirkpatrick, 1882

JESUS SAVES
7.6.7.6.7.7.7.6

474 The Sending, Lord, Springs

Whom shall I send, and who will go for us? Isa. 6:8

Unison
1. The send-ing, Lord, springs from Thy yearn-ing heart. God, Thou the send - er, Thou the Sent One art, And of Thy mis-sion mak - est us a part. Al - le - lu - ia!
2. Thy bod - y paid for men of ev - ery race; To them we wit - ness, Christ, Thy bound-less grace, With them, one bod - y, kneel be - fore Thy face. Al - le - lu - ia!
3. Where men their broth - ers heart - less - ly op - press, Where peo - ple suf - fer, hope - less in dis - tress, There we Thy name in deed and word con - fess. Al - le - lu - ia!
4. One man in need in bod - y, mind, and soul; One word in Je - sus' name to make him whole; One Lord, one mis - sion leads us to the goal. Al - le - lu - ia!
5. One mis-sion takes me o - ver land and sea And to the Chris - tian broth - er next to me. Help me to lis - ten, Lord, and speak for Thee. Al - le - lu - ia!
6. From ur - ban deeps to or - bits high in space. Thro' cross to glo - ry moves one pil - grim race, Prais - ing the Fa - ther - Son - and Spir - it's grace. Al - le - lu - ia!
1-5
6

WORDS: William J. Danker, 1966
MUSIC: Charles V. Stanford, 1904

ENGELBERG
10.10.10 Alleluias

The Battle Is the Lord's 475

For the battle is the Lord's. I Sam. 17:47

1. The bat - tle is the Lord's! The har - vest fields are white:
2. The bat - tle is the Lord's! Not ours is strength or skill,
3. The bat - tle is the Lord's! The Vic - tor cru - ci - fied
4. The bat - tle is the Lord's! Stand still, my soul, and see
How few the reap - ing hands ap - pear, Their strength how slight!
But His a - lone, in sov - ereign grace, To work His will.
Must with the tra - vail of His soul Be sat - is - fied.
The great sal - va - tion God hath wrought Re - vealed for thee.
Yet vic - to - ry is sure— We face a van-quished foe;
Ours, count - ing not the cost, Un - flinch - ing, to o - bey;
The pow'rs of hell shall fail, And all God's will be done,
Then, rest - ing in His might, Lift high His tri - umph song,
Then for-ward with the ris - en Christ To bat - tle go!
And in His time His ho - ly arm Shall win the day.
Till ev - ery soul whom He hath giv'n To Christ be won.
For pow'r, do - min - ion, king-dom, strength To Christ be - long! A-men.

WORDS: Margaret Clarkson, 1962
MUSIC: Synagogue melody; arr. Meyer Lyon, 1770

LEONI
6.6.8.4 D.

476 Lonely Voices Crying in the City

I . . . am as a sparrow alone upon the housetop. Psa. 102:7

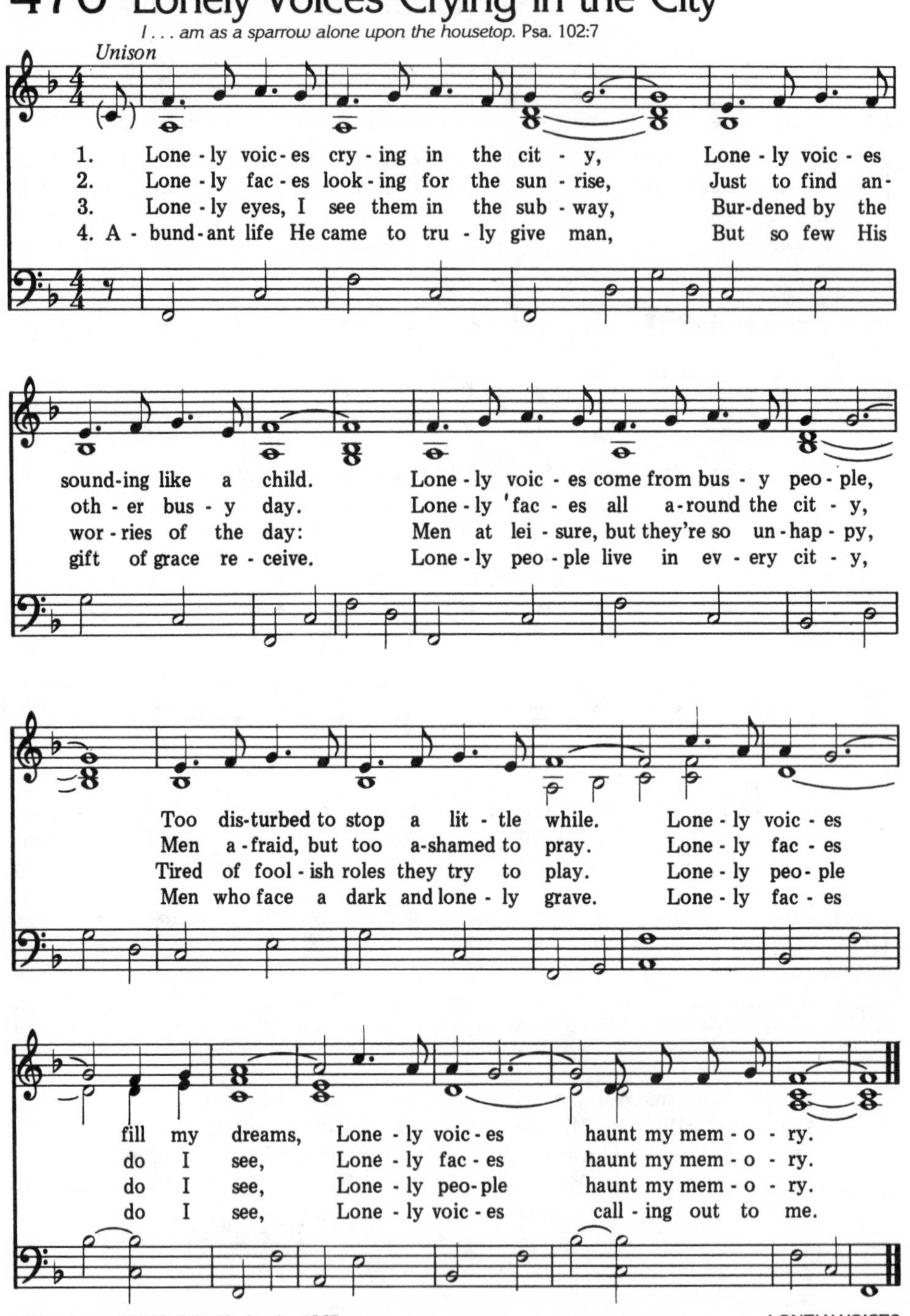
Unison
1. Lone - ly voic - es cry - ing in the cit - y, Lone - ly voic - es
2. Lone - ly fac - es look - ing for the sun - rise, Just to find an-
3. Lone - ly eyes, I see them in the sub - way, Bur-dened by the
4. A - bund - ant life He came to tru - ly give man, But so few His
sound-ing like a child. Lone - ly voic - es come from bus - y peo - ple,
oth - er bus - y day. Lone - ly 'fac - es all a-round the cit - y,
wor - ries of the day: Men at lei - sure, but they're so un - hap - py,
gift of grace re - ceive. Lone - ly peo - ple live in ev - ery cit - y,
Too dis-turbed to stop a lit - tle while. Lone - ly voic - es
Men a - fraid, but too a-shamed to pray. Lone - ly fac - es
Tired of fool - ish roles they try to play. Lone - ly peo - ple
Men who face a dark and lone - ly grave. Lone - ly fac - es
fill my dreams, Lone - ly voic - es haunt my mem - o - ry.
do I see, Lone - ly fac - es haunt my mem - o - ry.
do I see, Lone - ly peo - ple haunt my mem - o - ry.
do I see, Lone - ly voic - es call - ing out to me.

WORDS and MUSIC: Billie Hanks, Jr., 1967

LONELY VOICES
Irregular meter

It Only Takes a Spark 477

If God so loved us, we ought also to love one another. I John 4:11

Unison
1. It only takes a spark to get a fire going,
And soon all those around can warm up in its glowing.
That's how it is with God's love once you've experienced it;
You spread His love to everyone; You want to pass it on.
2. What a wondrous time is spring when all the trees are budding,
The birds begin to sing, the flowers start their blooming,
That's how it is with God's love once you've experienced it;
You want to sing, it's fresh like spring, You want to pass it on.
3. I wish for you, my friend, this happiness that I've found,
You can depend on Him, it matters not where you're bound.
I'll shout it from the mountain top— I want my world to know;
The Lord of love has come to me, I want to pass it on.

WORDS and MUSIC: Kurt Kaiser, 1969

PASS IT ON
Irregular meter

478 All Authority and Power

All authority is given unto Me in heaven and in earth. Matt. 28:18

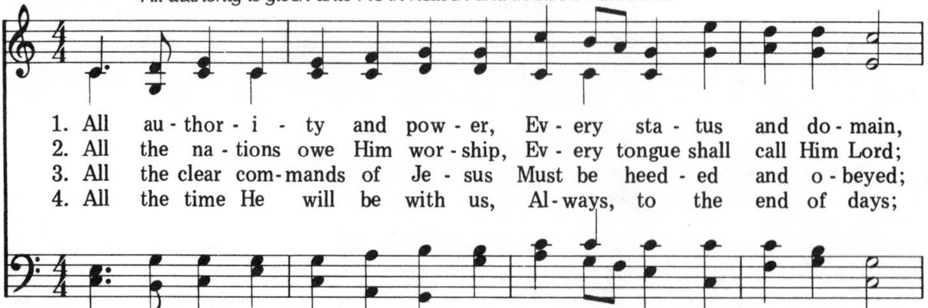

1. All au - thor - i - ty and pow - er, Every sta - tus and do - main,
2. All the na - tions owe Him wor - ship, Ev - ery tongue shall call Him Lord;
3. All the clear com - mands of Je - sus Must be heed - ed and o - beyed;
4. All the time He will be with us, Al - ways, to the end of days;

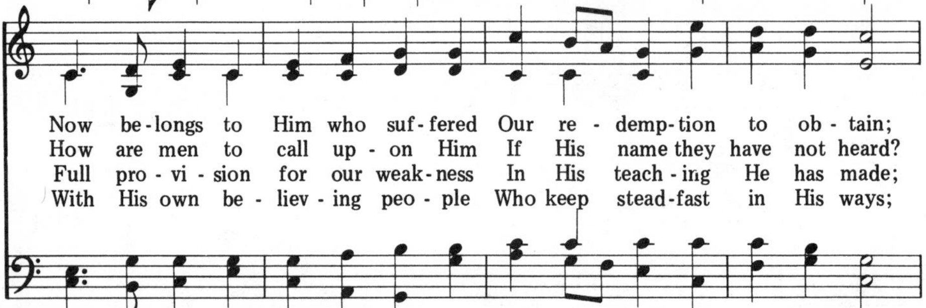

Now be - longs to Him who suf - fered Our re - demp - tion to ob - tain;
How are men to call up - on Him If His name they have not heard?
Full pro - vi - sion for our weak - ness In His teach - ing He has made;
With His own be - liev - ing peo - ple Who keep stead - fast in His ways;

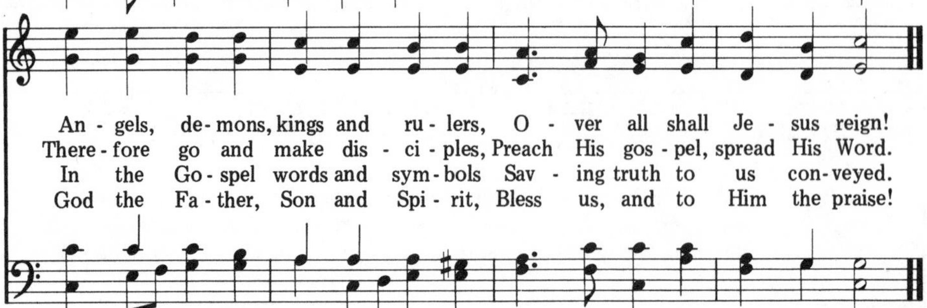

An - gels, de - mons, kings and ru - lers, O - ver all shall Je - sus reign!
There - fore go and make dis - ci - ples, Preach His gos - pel, spread His Word.
In the Go - spel words and sym - bols Sav - ing truth to us con - veyed.
God the Fa - ther, Son and Spi - rit, Bless us, and to Him the praise!

WORDS: Christopher Idle, 1973
MUSIC: Joachim Neander, 1680

UNSER HERRSCHER
8.7.8.7.8.7

479 Jesus Shall Reign Where'er the Sun

All kings shall fall down before Him: all nations shall serve Him. Psa. 72:11

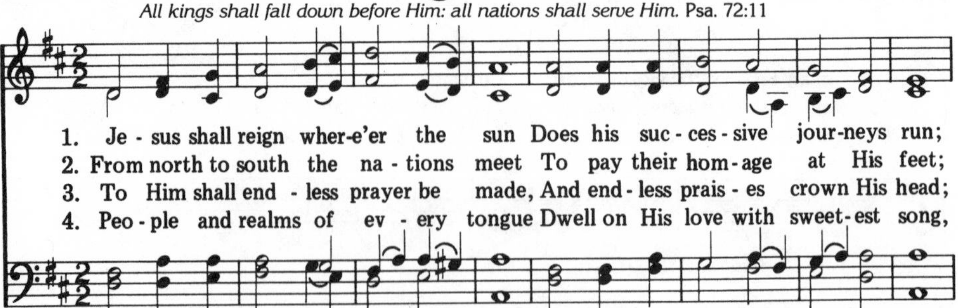
1. Je - sus shall reign wher-e'er the sun Does his suc - ces - sive jour-neys run;
2. From north to south the na - tions meet To pay their hom - age at His feet;
3. To Him shall end - less prayer be made, And end - less prais - es crown His head;
4. Peo - ple and realms of ev - ery tongue Dwell on His love with sweet - est song,

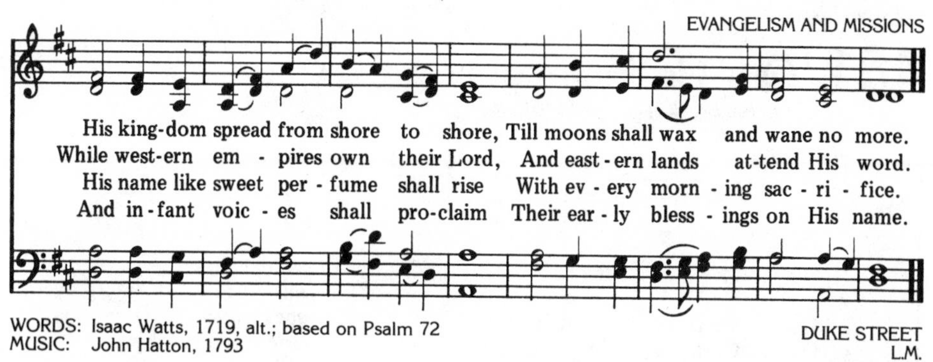
His king-dom spread from shore to shore, Till moons shall wax and wane no more.
While west-ern em - pires own their Lord, And east - ern lands at-tend His word.
His name like sweet per - fume shall rise With ev - ery morn - ing sac - ri - fice.
And in-fant voic - es shall pro-claim Their ear - ly bless - ings on His name.

WORDS: Isaac Watts, 1719, alt.; based on Psalm 72
MUSIC: John Hatton, 1793

DUKE STREET
L.M.

Christ for the World! We Sing 480

Go ye into all the world and preach the gospel . . . Mark 16:15

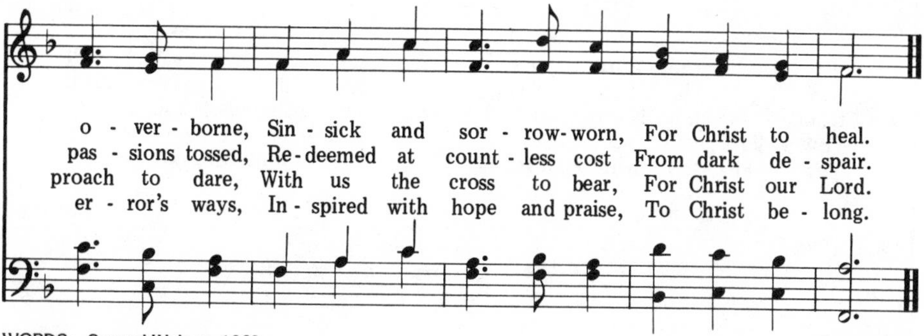

1. Christ for the world! we sing; The world to Christ we bring With lov - ing zeal— The poor and them that mourn, The faint and o - ver - borne, Sin - sick and sor - row-worn, For Christ to heal.

2. Christ for the world! we sing; The world to Christ we bring With fer - vent prayer— The way-ward and the lost, By rest - less pas - sions tossed, Re-deemed at count - less cost From dark de - spair.

3. Christ for the world! we sing; The world to Christ we bring With one ac - cord— With us the work to share, With us re - proach to dare, With us the cross to bear, For Christ our Lord.

4. Christ for the world! we sing; The world to Christ we bring With joy - ful song— The new-born souls whose days, Re-claimed from er - ror's ways, In - spired with hope and praise, To Christ be - long.

WORDS: Samuel Wolcott, 1869
MUSIC: Felice de Giardini, 1769

ITALIAN HYMN
6.6.4.6.6.6.4

481 Our God Is Mighty

Declare His glory among the nations. Psa. 96:3

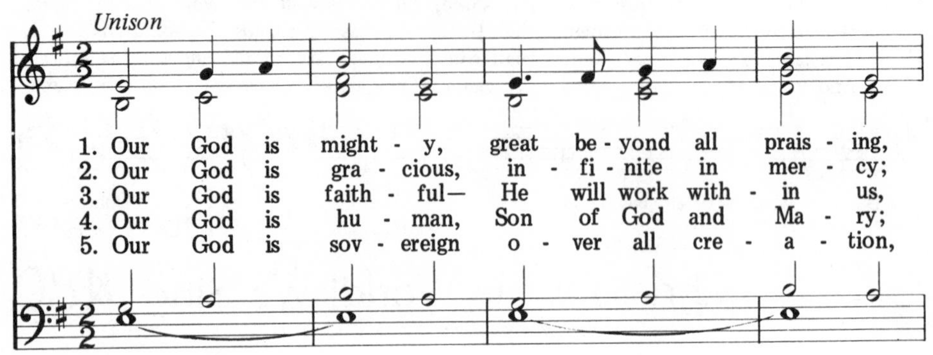
Unison
1. Our God is might - y, great be - yond all prais - ing,
2. Our God is gra - cious, in - fi - nite in mer - cy;
3. Our God is faith - ful— He will work with - in us,
4. Our God is hu - man, Son of God and Ma - ry;
5. Our God is sov - ereign o - ver all cre - a - tion,

Sing un - to Him a glad, tri - um - phant song;
He bridged the hope - less gulf our sin had made;
Ful - fill - ing all the pur - pose He has planned;
He lived our life, He suf - fered all our pain;
And soon His earth shall hear His might - y voice;

He is the Lord, the King of earth and heav - en—
He gave His Son to pur - chase our sal - va - tion—
Cleans - ing our hearts and fill - ing with His Spir - it
Now He calls us to live His love and mer - cy,
His is the King - dom— hail the con-quering Sav - ior!

To Him all maj - es - ty and strength be - long!
In Je - sus Christ we meet God un - a - fraid.
To make us strong to keep His last com - mand.
To show our world God's word made flesh a - gain.
Lift up your hearts, sing out His praise, re - joice!
Refrain
De - clare His glo - ry a-mong the na - tions, Through all cre - a - tion His tri - umph sing, Till all earth's peo - ples bow in ad - o - ra - tion, And Je - sus Christ be ev - er - last - ing King!

WORDS: Margaret Clarkson, 1976
MUSIC: Donald P. Hustad, 1979

JANUS
Irregular meter

482 Remember All the People

Other sheep I have which are not of this fold; them also I must bring. John 10:16

Unison
1. Re - mem - ber all the peo - ple Who live in far off lands,
2. Some work in sul - try for - ests Where apes swing to and fro,
3. God bless the men and wo - men Who serve Him o - ver - sea;
In strange and love - ly cit - ies, Or roam the des - ert sands,
Some fish in might - y riv - ers, Some hunt a - cross the snow.
God raise up more to help them To set the na - tions free,
Or farm the moun - tain pas - tures, Or till the end - less plains
Re - mem - ber all God's chil - dren, Who yet have nev - er heard
Till all the dis - tant peo - ple In ev - ery for - eign place
Where chil - dren wade thro' rice-fields And watch the cam - el trains.
The truth that comes from Je - sus, The glo - ry of His Word.
Shall un - der - stand His king-dom And come in - to His grace. A-men.

WORDS: Percy Dearmer, 1929
MUSIC: *Hemmets Koralbok*, 1921; Traditional Bohemian Brethren melody.

FAR OFF LANDS
7.6.7.6 D.

There Is Joy in Serving Jesus 483

Serve the Lord with gladness: come before His presence with singing. Psa. 100:2

1. There is joy in serv - ing Je - sus, As I jour - ney on my way,
2. There is joy in serv - ing Je - sus, Joy that tri - umphs o - ver pain;
3. There is joy in serv - ing Je - sus, As I walk a - lone with God;
4. There is joy in serv - ing Je - sus, Joy a - mid the dark - est night,
Joy that fills the heart with prais - es, Ev - ery hour and ev - ery day.
Fills my soul with heav - en's mu - sic, Till I join the glad re - frain.
'Tis the joy of Christ, my Sav - ior, Who the path of suf-fering trod.
For I've learned the won-drous se - cret, And I'm walk - ing in the light.
Refrain
There is joy, joy, Joy in serv - ing Je - sus, Joy that throbs with-
in my heart; Ev - ery mo - ment, ev - ery hour, As I draw up-
on His pow'r, There is joy, joy, Joy that nev - er shall de - part.

WORDS: Oswald J. Smith, 1931
MUSIC: Bentley D. Ackley, 1931

JOY IN SERVING JESUS
Irregular meter

484 Reach Out to Your Neighbor

Thou shalt love thy neighbor as thyself. Matt. 22:39

Unison
1. Reach out to your neigh-bor, Let him know you real - ly care, Reach out when he's lone - ly, Let him know some-bod - y's there, Reach out in his dark - ness, When the clouds ob - scure his view, Just walk with him, and talk with him, He's wait - ing there for you.
2. Reach out to a stran - ger, To a man who's lost his way; Like a sheep with-out a shep-herd, Who can't find the light of day; Reach out, your broth - er needs you, Needs to know he's not a - lone! So tell him of God's might - y love, And share with him your own.
3. Reach out, like your Sav - ior, When He gave His life for you, Reach out to all the peo - ple Who don't know what to do; Reach out and tell of Je - sus, Who has done His great - est part; Just share the love I'm sing - ing of; Reach out with all your heart!
Refrain
Reach out in a world filled with hope - less - ness and pain; Reach out with a

(heart)
hand full of love! Reach out, the world is wait-ing for someone to lead the way! Reach out, reach out to find a brand new day!

WORDS and MUSIC: Roger Copeland, 1971

TENKILLER
Irregular meter

We Give Thee but Thine Own 485

Of Thine own have we given Thee. I Chron. 29:14

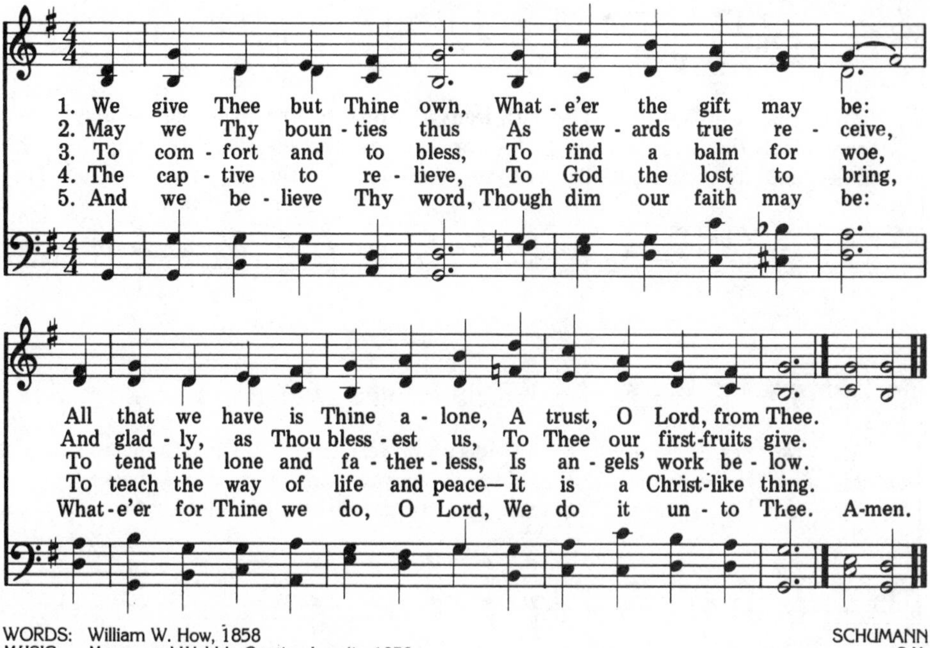

1. We give Thee but Thine own, What-e'er the gift may be:
All that we have is Thine a-lone, A trust, O Lord, from Thee.

2. May we Thy boun-ties thus As stew-ards true re-ceive,
And glad-ly, as Thou bless-est us, To Thee our first-fruits give.

3. To com-fort and to bless, To find a balm for woe,
To tend the lone and fa-ther-less, Is an-gels' work be-low.

4. The cap-tive to re-lieve, To God the lost to bring,
To teach the way of life and peace— It is a Christ-like thing.

5. And we be-lieve Thy word, Though dim our faith may be:
What-e'er for Thine we do, O Lord, We do it un-to Thee. A-men.

WORDS: William W. How, 1858
MUSIC: Mason and Webb's *Cantica Laudis,* 1850

SCHUMANN
S.M.

486 The Master Has Come, and He Calls Us

The Master is come, and calleth for thee. John 11:28

1. The Mas-ter has come, and He calls us to fol - low The track of the
2. The Mas-ter has called us; the road may be drear - y, And dan - gers and
3. The Mas-ter has called us in life's ear - ly morn-ing, With spir - its as
foot-prints He leaves on our way; Far o - ver the moun-tain and
sor - rows are strewn on the track; But God's Ho - ly Spir - it shall
fresh as the dew on the sod; We turn from the world with its
through the deep hol - low, The path leads us on to the man-sions of day: The
com - fort the wea - ry; We fol - low the Sav - ior and can - not turn back; The
smiles and its scorn-ing, To cast in our lot with the peo - ple of God: The
Mas - ter has called us, the chil - dren who fear Him, Who march 'neath Christ's
Mas - ter has called us: tho' doubt and temp-ta - tion May com - pass our
Mas - ter has called us, His sons and His daugh-ters, We plead for His

ban - ner, His own lit - tle band; We love Him and seek Him, we
jour - ney, we cheer - ful - ly sing: "Press on - ward, look up - ward," thro'
bless - ing and trust in His love; And through the green pas - tures, be -
long to be near Him, And rest in the light of His beau - ti - ful land.
much trib - u - la - tion; The chil - dren of Zi - on must fol - low their King.
side the still wa - ters, He'll lead us at last to His king - dom a - bove.

WORDS: Sarah Doudney, 1871
MUSIC: Traditional Welsh melody

ASH GROVE
12.11.12.11 D.

O Master, Let Me Walk with Thee 487

He appeared . . . unto two of them, as they walked . . . Mark 16:12

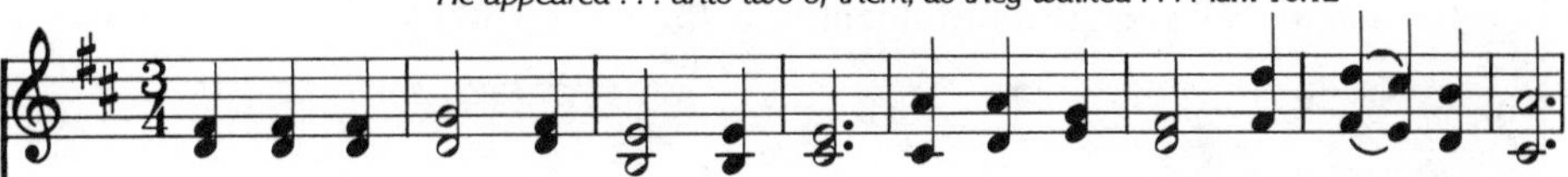

1. O Mas-ter, let me walk with Thee In low - ly paths of ser - vice free;
2. Help me the slow of heart to move By some clear, win-ning word of love;
3. Teach me Thy pa - tience! still with Thee In clos - er, dear - er com - pa - ny,
4. In hope that sends a shin - ing ray Far down the fu-ture's broad-'ning way,

Tell me Thy se - cret; help me bear The strain of toil, the fret of care.
Teach me the way - ward feet to stay, And guide them in the home-ward way.
In work that keeps faith sweet and strong, In trust that tri-umphs o - ver wrong;
In peace that on - ly Thou canst give, With Thee, O Mas - ter, let me live.

WORDS: Washington Gladden, 1879
MUSIC: H. Percy Smith, 1874

MARYTON
L.M.

488 Lord, Make Me an Instrument of Thy Peace

Yield yourselves unto God . . . and your members as instruments of righteousness . . . Rom. 6:13

Unison
Lord, make me an in-stru-ment of Thy peace;
Where there is ha - tred, let me sow love; Where there is in - ju - ry,
par-don; Where there is doubt, faith; Where there is des-pair,
hope; Where there is dark-ness, light; Where there is sad - ness,
joy. O Di-vine Mas-ter, grant that I may not so much

seek to be con-soled as to con-sole, To be un-der-stood
as to un-der-stand, To be loved as to love; For it
is in giv-ing that we re-ceive; It is in
par-d'ning that we are par-doned; It is in
dy-ing that we are born to e-ter-nal life!

WORDS: St. Francis of Assisi, 13th century
MUSIC: Olive Dungan, 1949; arr. Donald Hustad, 1984

ETERNAL LIFE
Irregular meter

489 A Charge to Keep I Have

Walk worthy of the vocation wherewith ye are called. Eph. 4:1

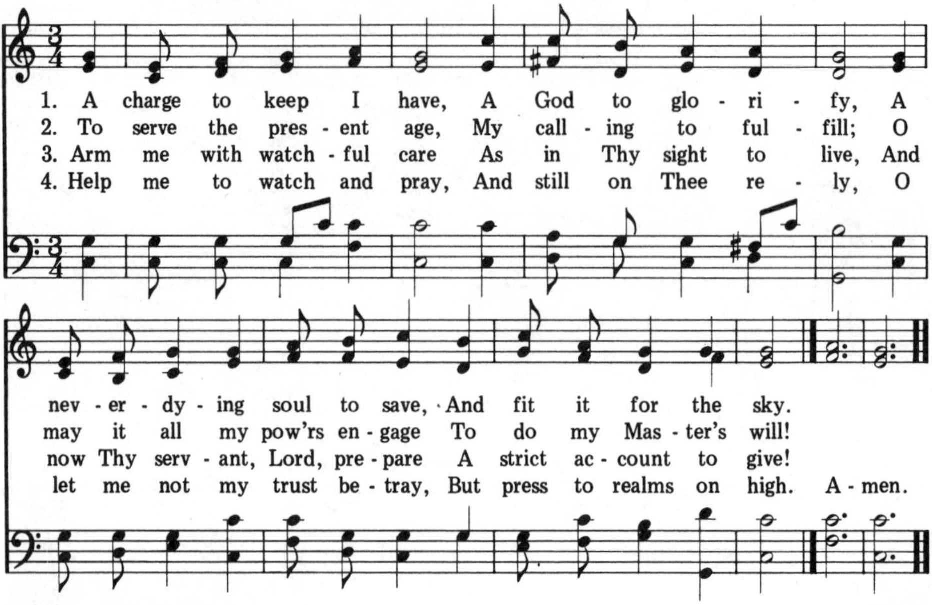

1. A charge to keep I have, A God to glo - ri - fy, A nev - er - dy - ing soul to save, And fit it for the sky.
2. To serve the pres - ent age, My call - ing to ful - fill; O may it all my pow'rs en - gage To do my Mas - ter's will!
3. Arm me with watch - ful care As in Thy sight to live, And now Thy serv - ant, Lord, pre - pare A strict ac - count to give!
4. Help me to watch and pray, And still on Thee re - ly, O let me not my trust be - tray, But press to realms on high. A - men.

WORDS: Charles Wesley, 1762
MUSIC: Lowell Mason, 1832

BOYLSTON
S.M.

490 Am I a Soldier of the Cross?

. . . Endure hardness, as a good soldier of Jesus Christ. II Tim. 2:3

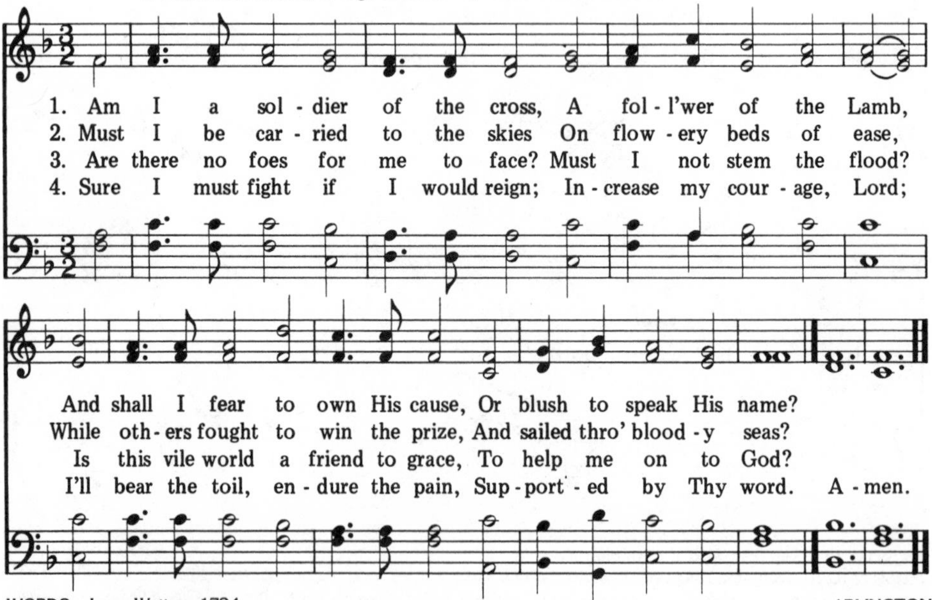

1. Am I a sol - dier of the cross, A fol - l'wer of the Lamb, And shall I fear to own His cause, Or blush to speak His name?
2. Must I be car - ried to the skies On flow - ery beds of ease, While oth - ers fought to win the prize, And sailed thro' blood - y seas?
3. Are there no foes for me to face? Must I not stem the flood? Is this vile world a friend to grace, To help me on to God?
4. Sure I must fight if I would reign; In - crease my cour - age, Lord; I'll bear the toil, en - dure the pain, Sup - port - ed by Thy word. A - men.

WORDS: Isaac Watts, c.1724
MUSIC: Thomas A. Arne, 1762

ARLINGTON
C.M.

Jesus Calls Us; o'er the Tumult 491

He saith unto them, follow Me. Matt. 4:19

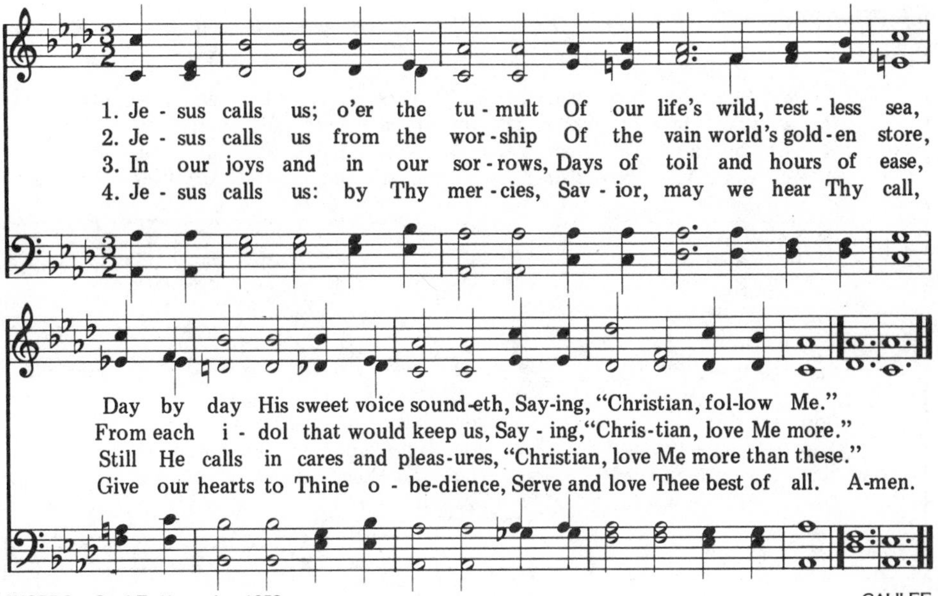

1. Je - sus calls us; o'er the tu - mult Of our life's wild, rest - less sea,
2. Je - sus calls us from the wor - ship Of the vain world's gold - en store,
3. In our joys and in our sor - rows, Days of toil and hours of ease,
4. Je - sus calls us: by Thy mer - cies, Sav - ior, may we hear Thy call,

Day by day His sweet voice sound-eth, Say-ing, "Christian, fol-low Me."
From each i - dol that would keep us, Say - ing, "Chris-tian, love Me more."
Still He calls in cares and pleas-ures, "Christian, love Me more than these."
Give our hearts to Thine o - be-dience, Serve and love Thee best of all. A-men.

WORDS: Cecil F. Alexander, 1852
MUSIC: William H. Jude, 1887

GALILEE
8.7.8.7

Must Jesus Bear the Cross Alone? 492

If any man will come after Me, let him . . . take up his cross. Matt. 16:24

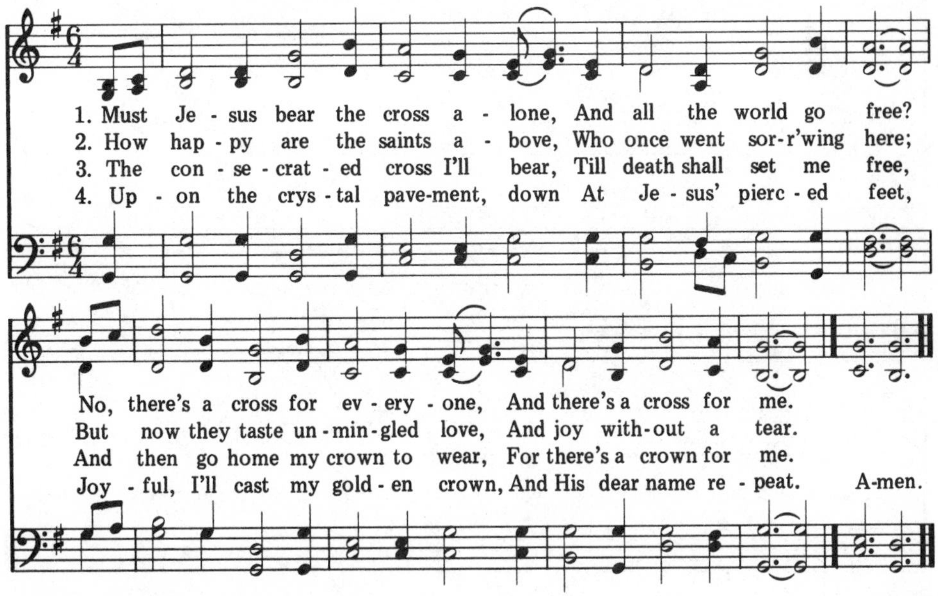

1. Must Je - sus bear the cross a - lone, And all the world go free?
2. How hap - py are the saints a - bove, Who once went sor-r'wing here;
3. The con - se - crat - ed cross I'll bear, Till death shall set me free,
4. Up - on the crys - tal pave-ment, down At Je - sus' pierc - ed feet,

No, there's a cross for ev - ery - one, And there's a cross for me.
But now they taste un - min - gled love, And joy with-out a tear.
And then go home my crown to wear, For there's a crown for me.
Joy - ful, I'll cast my gold - en crown, And His dear name re - peat. A-men.

WORDS: Thomas Shepherd, 1693, and others
MUSIC: George N. Allen, 1844

MAITLAND
C.M.

493 Is Your Life a Channel of Blessing?

A vessel unto honor, sanctified, and meet for the Master's use. II Tim. 2:21

1. Is your life a chan - nel of bless - ing? Is the love of God
2. Is your life a chan - nel of bless - ing? Are you bur - dened for
3. Is your life a chan - nel of bless - ing? Is it dai - ly
4. We can - not be chan - nels of bless - ing If our lives are not
flow - ing through you? Are you tell - ing the lost of the Sav - ior?
those who are lost? Have you urged up - on those who are stray - ing
tell - ing for Him? Have you spo - ken the word of sal - va - tion
free from known sin; We will bar - ri - ers be and a hin-drance
Are you read - y His serv - ice to do?
The Sav - ior who died on the cross?
To those who are dy - ing in sin?
To those we are try - ing to win.
Refrain
Make me a chan - nel of
bless - ing to - day, Make me a chan - nel of bless - ing, I pray; My life pos-
sess - ing, my ser - vice bless - ing, Make me a chan - nel of bless - ing to - day.

WORDS and MUSIC: Harper G. Smyth, 1903

EUCLID
9.9.10.9 Ref.

Out in the Highways and Byways of Life 494

So will I save you and ye shall be a blessing. Zech. 8:13

1. Out in the high-ways and by-ways of life, Man-y are wea-ry and sad;
are wea-ry and sad;
2. Tell the sweet sto-ry of Christ and His love, Tell of His pow'r to for-give;
His pow'r to for-give;
3. Give as 'twas giv-en to you in your need, Love as the Mas-ter loved you;
the Mas-ter loved you;
Car-ry the sun-shine where dark-ness is rife, Mak-ing the sor-row-ing glad.
Oth-ers will trust Him if on-ly you prove True, ev-ery mo-ment you live.
Be to the help-less a help-er in-deed, Un-to your mis-sion be true.
Refrain
Make me a bless-ing, make me a bless-ing, Out of my
life may Je-sus shine; Make me a bless-ing, O Sav-ior,
out of my life
I pray,
I pray Thee, my Sav-ior, Make me a bless-ing to some-one to-day.

WORDS: Ira B. Wilson, 1909
MUSIC: George S. Schuler, 1924

SCHULER
10.7.10.7 Ref.

495 God, Whose Giving Knows No Ending

Freely ye have received, freely give. Matt. 10:8

1. God, whose giv - ing knows no end - ing, From your rich and
2. Skills and time are ours for press - ing Toward the goals of
3. Trea - sure, too, You have en - trust - ed, Gain through pow'rs Your

end - less store: Na - ture's won - der, Je - sus' wis - dom, Cost - ly
Christ, Your Son: All at peace in health and free - dom, Rac - es
grace con - ferred; Ours to use for home and kin - dred, And to

cross, grave's shat - tered door; Gift - ed by You, we turn
joined, the Church made one. Now di - rect our dai - ly
spread the Gos - pel Word. O - pen wide our hands in

to You, Of - f'ring up our - selves in praise; Thank - ful
la - bor, Lest we strive for self a - lone: Born with
shar - ing, As we heed Christ's age - less call, Heal - ing,

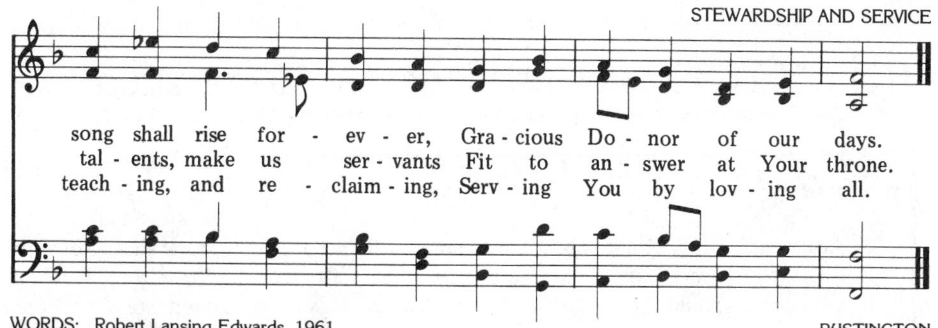
song shall rise for - ev - er, Gra - cious Do - nor of our days.
tal - ents, make us ser - vants Fit to an - swer at Your throne.
teach - ing, and re - claim - ing, Serv - ing You by lov - ing all.

WORDS: Robert Lansing Edwards, 1961
MUSIC: C. Hubert H. Parry, 1897

RUSTINGTON
8.7.8.7 D.

O Jesus, I Have Promised 496

If any man serve Me, let him follow Me . . . John 12:26

1. O Je - sus, I have prom-ised To serve Thee to the end; Be Thou for-ev - er
2. O let me feel Thee near me, The world is ev - er near; I see the sights that
3. O Je - sus, Thou hast prom-ised To all who fol - low Thee, That where Thou art in

near me, My Mas - ter and my Friend: I shall not fear the bat - tle If Thou art
daz - zle, The tempt-ing sounds I hear: My foes are ev - er near me, A-round me
glo - ry, There shall Thy serv-ant be; And, Je - sus, I have prom-ised To serve Thee

by my side, Nor wan - der from the path-way If Thou wilt be my guide.
and with - in; But, Je - sus, draw Thou near-er, And shield my soul from sin.
to the end; O give me grace to fol - low, My Mas - ter and my Friend. A-men.

WORDS: John E. Bode, 1866
MUSIC: Arthur H. Mann, 1881

ANGEL'S STORY
7.6.7.6 D.

497 Come, All Christians, Be Committed

Present your bodies a living sacrifice . . . be ye transformed . . . Rom. 12:1,2

1. Come, all Chris - tians, be com - mit - ted To the ser - vice of the
2. Of your time and tal - ents give ye, They are gifts from God a-
3. God's com - mand to love each oth - er Is re - quired of ev - ery
4. Come in praise and ad - o - ra - tion, All who on Christ's name be-
Lord. Make your lives for Him more fit - ted, Tune your hearts with one ac-
bove, To be used by Chris-tians free - ly To pro-claim His won-drous
man. Show-ing mer - cy to a broth - er Mir - rors His re - demp - tive
lieve. Wor-ship Him with con - se - cra - tion, Grace and love will you record. Come in - to His courts with glad-ness, Each his sa - cred vows re-
love. Come a - gain to serve the Sav - ior, Tithes and off - 'rings with you
plan. In com - pas - sion He has giv - en Of His love that is di-
ceive. For His grace give Him the glo - ry, For the Spir - it and the
new, Turn a - way from sin and sad - ness, Be trans-formed with life a - new.
bring. In your work, with Him find fa - vor, And with joy His prais - es sing.
vine; On the cross sins were for - giv - en; Joy and peace are ful - ly thine.
Word, And re - peat the gos - pel sto - ry Till all men His name have heard.

WORDS: Eva B. Lloyd, 1966
MUSIC: Traditional American melody; *The Sacred Harp,* 1844; arr. James H. Wood, 1958

BEACH SPRING
8.7.8.7 D.

Because I Have Been Given Much 498

. . . Unto whomsoever much is given . . . shall be much required. Luke 12:48

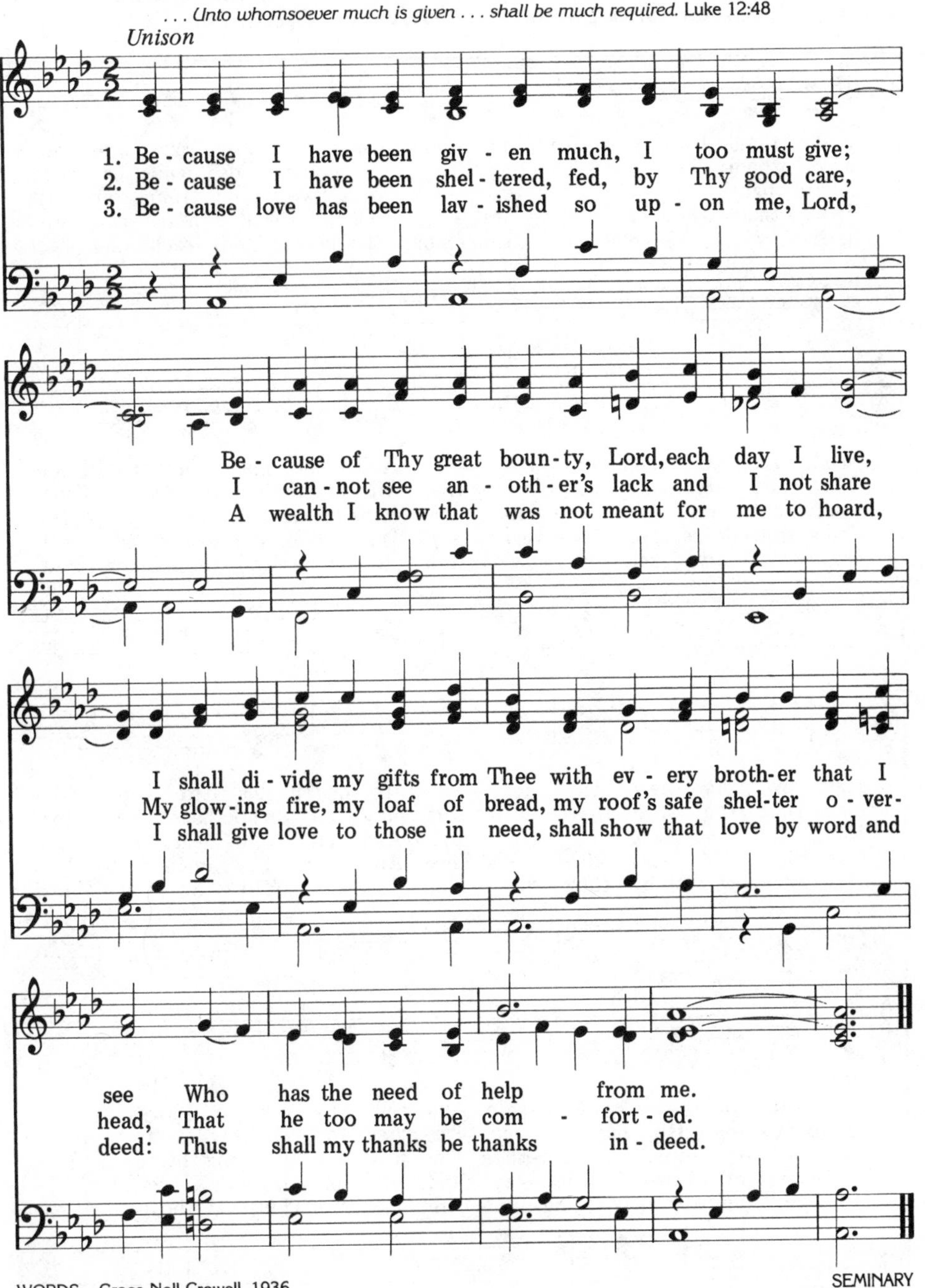
Unison
1. Be - cause I have been giv - en much, I too must give;
2. Be - cause I have been shel - tered, fed, by Thy good care,
3. Be - cause love has been lav - ished so up - on me, Lord,
Be - cause of Thy great boun - ty, Lord, each day I live,
I can - not see an - oth - er's lack and I not share
A wealth I know that was not meant for me to hoard,
I shall di - vide my gifts from Thee with ev - ery broth - er that I
My glow - ing fire, my loaf of bread, my roof's safe shel - ter o - ver-
I shall give love to those in need, shall show that love by word and
see Who has the need of help from me.
head, That he too may be com - fort - ed.
deed: Thus shall my thanks be thanks in - deed.

WORDS: Grace Noll Crowell, 1936
MUSIC: Phillip Landgrave, 1974

SEMINARY
Irregular meter

499 We Thank Thee That Thy Mandate

They went forth and preached . . . confirming the words with signs . . . Mark 16:20

1. We thank Thee that Thy mandate Is every age the same:
To preach and teach the gospel And heal men in Thy Name;
May every new endeavor To match this to our day
Lead men to own Thy Lordship And walk Thy holy way.

2. We thank Thee for Thy preachers, Thy heralds who proclaim
The good news of salvation With hearts and tongues aflame!
Bless Thou the words they utter; May all who hear be blest;
Equipped for earthly living, Prepared for heav'nly rest.

3. Enlighten all Thy teachers With wisdom from on high,
And grant them understanding, Men's minds to edify;
May all who teach the gospel And all who hear be fed,
As every soul is nourished On Christ, the living bread.

4. We thank Thee for the healing Of body, mind and soul,
God's wondrous love revealing That makes the wounded whole;
May those by faith who touch Thee And those Thy touch doth bless
Be cured of their diseases And walk in holiness.

5. As we obey Thy summons To preach and teach and heal,
May every generation Become God's commonweal;
And may this threefold mission Reflect Thy holy love,
Until our earthly kingdoms Are one with Thine above. Amen.

WORDS: Ernest K. Emurian, 1968
MUSIC: Henry T. Smart, 1835

LANCASHIRE
7.6.7.6 D.

Hope of the World 500

. . . Lord Jesus Christ, who is our hope. I Tim. 1:1

Unison
1. Hope of the world, Thou Christ of great com - pas - sion,
2. Hope of the world, God's gift from high - est heav - en,
3. Hope of the world, a - foot on dust - y high - ways,
4. Hope of the world, Who by Thy cross didst save us
5. Hope of the world, O Christ o'er death vic - to - rious,
Speak to our fear - ful hearts by con - flict rent.
Bring - ing to hun - gry souls the bread of life,
Show - ing to wan - dering souls the path of light;
From death and dark de - spair, from sin and guilt;
Who by this sign didst con - quer grief and pain,
Save us, Thy peo - ple, from con - sum - ing pas - sion,
Still let Thy Spir - it un - to us be giv - en
Walk Thou be - side us lest the tempt - ing by - ways
We ren - der back the love Thy mer - cy gave us;
We would be faith - ful to Thy gos - pel glo - rious:
Who by our own false hopes and aims are spent.
To heal earth's wounds and end her bit - ter strife.
Lure us a - way from Thee to end - less night.
Take Thou our lives, and use them as Thou wilt.
Thou art our Lord! Thou dost for - ev - er reign! A-men.

WORDS: Georgia E. Harkness, 1954
MUSIC: V. Earle Copes, 1963

VICAR
11.10.11.10

501 Reach Out and Touch

And Jesus put forth His hand and touched him . . . Matt. 8:3

Unison
1. Reach out and touch a soul that is hun-gry; Reach out and touch a spir - it in de - spair; Reach out and touch a life torn and dirt - y, A man who is lone - ly— If you care! Reach out and touch that neigh-bor who hates you; Reach out and touch that stran-ger who meets you; Reach out and touch the broth-er who needs you; Reach out and
2. Reach out and touch a friend who is wea - ry; Reach out and touch a seek - er un - a - ware; Reach out and touch, tho' touch-ing means los-ing A part of your own self— If you dare! Reach out and give your love to the love-less; Reach out and make a home for the home-less; Reach out and shed God's light in the dark-ness; Reach out and

SOCIAL CONCERN

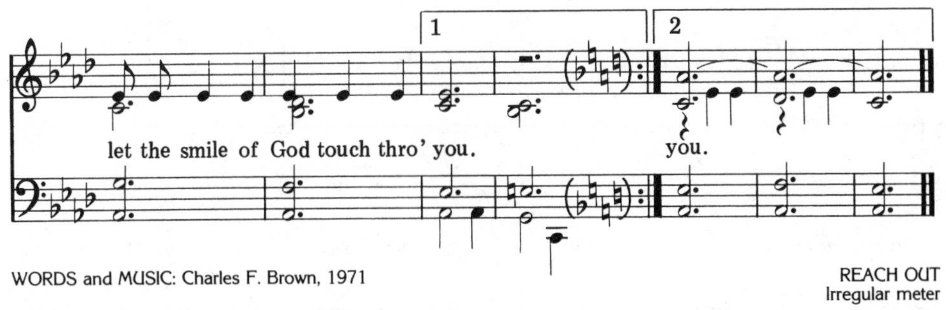
1
2
let the smile of God touch thro' you.
you.

WORDS and MUSIC: Charles F. Brown, 1971

REACH OUT
Irregular meter

Jesu, Jesu, Fill Us with Your Love 502

Love one another as I have loved you. John 15:12

Unison

Je - su, Je - su, Fill us with Your love, Show us how to serve the neigh-bors we have from You. *Fine*

1. Kneels at the feet of His friends, Si - lent-ly wash - es their feet, Mas - ter who acts as a slave to them.
2. Neigh-bors are rich and poor, Neigh-bors are black and white, Neigh- bors are near and far a - way.
3. These are the ones we should serve, These are the ones we should love. All are neigh- bors to us and You.
4. Lov - ing puts us on our knees, Serv - ing as though we are slaves, This is the way we should live with You.
5. Kneel at the feet of our friends, Si - lent-ly wash - ing their feet, This is the way we should live with You.

D. C.

WORDS: Tom Colvin, 1969
MUSIC: Ghana folk song; adapt. Tom Colvin, 1969; arr. Jane Marshall, 1982

CHEREPONI
Irregular meter

503 Whatsoever You Do to the Least

Come, ye blessed of My Father, inherit the kingdom prepared for you . . . Matt. 25:24

Unison
(Ref.) What - so - ev - er you do to the least of my broth - ers,
That you do un - to me.
1. When I was hun - gry, you gave me to eat; When I was thirst - y, you gave me to drink.
When I was home - less, you o - pened your door; When I was na - ked, you gave me your coat.
2. When I was wea - ry, you helped me find rest; When I was anx - ious, you calmed all my fears.
When in a pris - on, you came to my cell; When on a sick - bed, you cared for my needs.
3. When I was Ne - gro, or Chi - nese, or white; Mocked and in - sult - ed, you car - ried my cross.
You saw me cov - ered with spit - tle and blood; You knew my fea - tures, though grim - y with sweat.
Now en - ter in - to the home of my Fa - ther.

WORDS and MUSIC: Willard F. Jabusch, 1966

WHATSOEVER YOU DO
Irregular meter

Father Eternal, Ruler of Creation 504

Thy kingdom come, Thy will be done in earth, as it is in heaven. Matt. 6:10

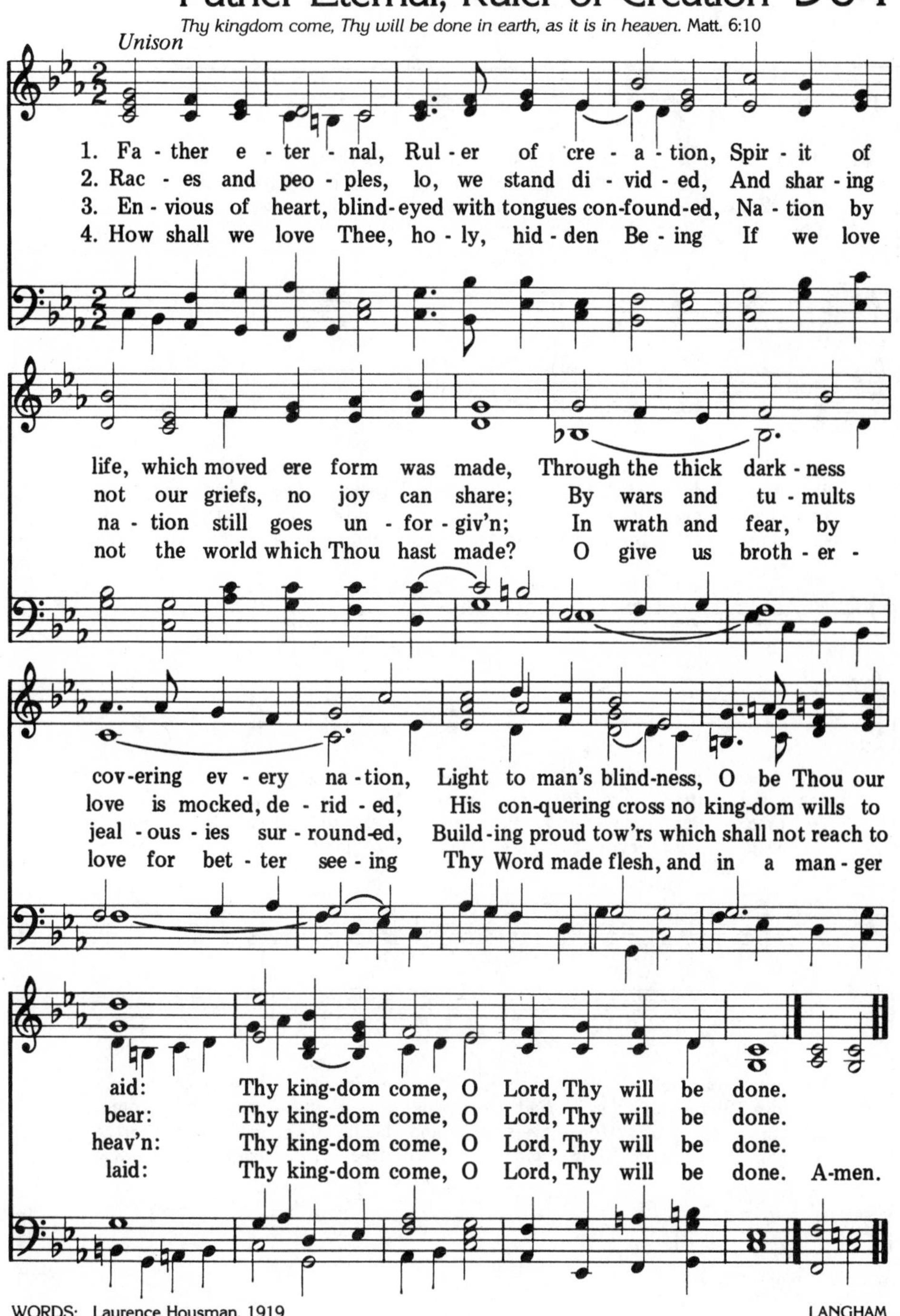
Unison
1. Fa - ther e - ter - nal, Rul - er of cre - a - tion, Spir - it of
2. Rac - es and peo - ples, lo, we stand di - vid - ed, And shar - ing
3. En - vious of heart, blind-eyed with tongues con-found-ed, Na - tion by
4. How shall we love Thee, ho - ly, hid - den Be - ing If we love
life, which moved ere form was made, Through the thick dark - ness
not our griefs, no joy can share; By wars and tu - mults
na - tion still goes un - for - giv'n; In wrath and fear, by
not the world which Thou hast made? O give us broth - er -
cov-ering ev - ery na - tion, Light to man's blind-ness, O be Thou our
love is mocked, de - rid - ed, His con-quering cross no king-dom wills to
jeal - ous - ies sur - round-ed, Build-ing proud tow'rs which shall not reach to
love for bet - ter see - ing Thy Word made flesh, and in a man - ger
aid: Thy king-dom come, O Lord, Thy will be done.
bear: Thy king-dom come, O Lord, Thy will be done.
heav'n: Thy king-dom come, O Lord, Thy will be done.
laid: Thy king-dom come, O Lord, Thy will be done. A-men.

WORDS: Laurence Housman, 1919
MUSIC: Geoffrey Shaw, 1921

LANGHAM
11.10.11.10.10

505 Help Us Accept Each Other

Be kindly affectioned one to another . . . in honor preferring one another. Rom. 12:10

Unison

1. Help us ac - cept each oth - er as Christ ac - cept - ed us;
2. Teach us, O Lord, Your les - sons, as in our dai - ly life
3. Let Your ac - cept - ance change us, so that we may be moved
4. Lord, for to - day's en - coun - ters with all who are in need,

Teach us as sis - ter, broth - er each per - son to em - brace.
We strug - gle to be hu - man and search for hope and faith.
In liv - ing sit - u - a - tions to do the truth in love;
Who hun - ger for ac - cept - ance, for right - eous - ness and bread,

Be pres - ent, Lord, a - mong us and bring us to be - lieve
Teach us to care for peo - ple, for all, not just for some;
To prac - tice Your ac - cept - ance un - til we know by heart
We need new eyes for see - ing, new hands for hold - ing on;

We are our - selves ac - cept - ed and meant to love and live.
To love them as we find them, or as they may be - come.
The ta - ble of for - give - ness and laugh - ter's heal - ing art.
Re - new us with Your Spir - it; Lord, free us, make us one!

WORDS: Fred Kaan, 1975
MUSIC: John Ness Beck, 1977

BECK
7.6.7.6 D.

Let Your Heart Be Broken 506

When He saw the multitudes, He was moved with compassion . . . Matt. 9:36

1. Let your heart be bro - ken For a world in need—
2. Here on earth ap - ply - ing Prin - ci - ples of love—
3. Blest to be a bless - ing, Priv - i - leged to care,
4. Add to your be - liev - ing Deeds that prove it true—
5. Let your heart be ten - der And your vi - sion clear—
Feed the mouths that hun - ger, Soothe the wounds that bleed,
Vis - i - ble ex - pres - sion God still rules a - bove,
Chal - lenged by the need Ap - par - ent ev - ery - where,
Know - ing Christ as Sav - ior, Make Him Mas - ter too:
See man - kind as God sees, Serve Him far and near;
Give the cup of wa - ter And the loaf of bread—
Liv - ing il - lus - tra - tion Of the Liv - ing Word
Where man - kind is want - ing Fill the va - cant place,
Fol - low in His foot - steps, Go where He has trod,
Let your heart be bro - ken By a broth - er's pain,
Be the hands of Je - sus, Serv - ing in His stead.
To the minds of all who've Nev - er seen and heard.
Be the means thro' which the Lord re - veals His grace.
In the world's great trou - ble Risk your - self for God.
Share your rich re - sourc - es— Give and give a - gain.

WORDS: Bryan Jeffery Leech, 1975
MUSIC: James Mountain, 1876

WYE VALLEY
6.5.6.5 D.

507 In Christ There Is No East or West

Ye are all one in Christ Jesus. Gal. 3:28

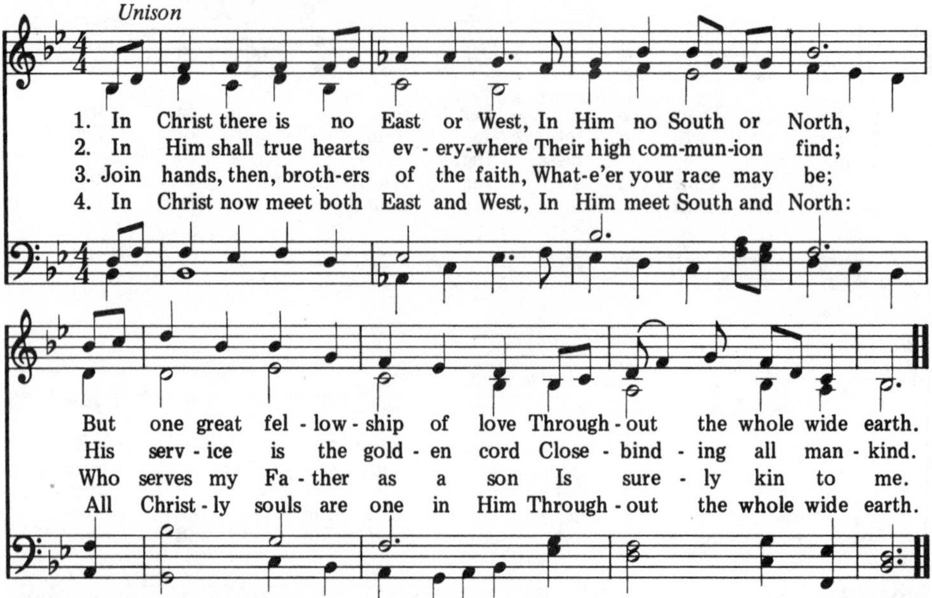

Unison

1. In Christ there is no East or West, In Him no South or North,
2. In Him shall true hearts ev - ery-where Their high com-mun-ion find;
3. Join hands, then, broth-ers of the faith, What-e'er your race may be;
4. In Christ now meet both East and West, In Him meet South and North:

But one great fel - low - ship of love Through - out the whole wide earth.
His serv - ice is the gold - en cord Close - bind - ing all man - kind.
Who serves my Fa - ther as a son Is sure - ly kin to me.
All Christ - ly souls are one in Him Through - out the whole wide earth.

WORDS: John Oxenham, 1908
MUSIC: Traditional Spiritual melody; arr. Harry T. Burleigh, 1939

McKEE
C.M.

Words used by permission of Desmond Dunkerly.

508 Where Cross the Crowded Ways of Life

Whosoever shall give . . . a cup of cold water . . . shall in no wise lose his reward. Matt. 10:42

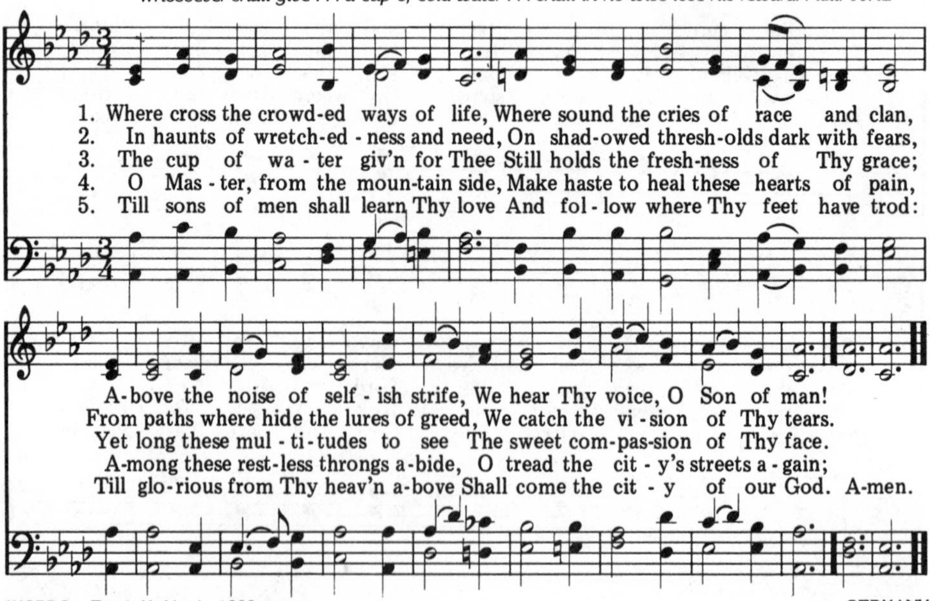

1. Where cross the crowd-ed ways of life, Where sound the cries of race and clan,
2. In haunts of wretch-ed - ness and need, On shad-owed thresh-olds dark with fears,
3. The cup of wa - ter giv'n for Thee Still holds the fresh-ness of Thy grace;
4. O Mas - ter, from the moun-tain side, Make haste to heal these hearts of pain,
5. Till sons of men shall learn Thy love And fol - low where Thy feet have trod:

A-bove the noise of self - ish strife, We hear Thy voice, O Son of man!
From paths where hide the lures of greed, We catch the vi - sion of Thy tears.
Yet long these mul - ti - tudes to see The sweet com-pas-sion of Thy face.
A-mong these rest-less throngs a-bide, O tread the cit - y's streets a - gain;
Till glo-rious from Thy heav'n a-bove Shall come the cit - y of our God. A-men.

WORDS: Frank M. North, 1903
MUSIC: William Gardiner's *Sacred Melodies*, 1815

GERMANY
L.M.

Happy the Home When God Is There 509

As for me and my house, we will serve the Lord. Josh. 24:15

1. Hap - py the home when God is there, And love fills ev - ery breast;
2. Hap - py the home where Je - sus' name Is sweet to ev - ery ear;
3. Hap - py the home where prayer is heard, And praise is wont to rise;
4. Lord, let us in our homes a - gree This bless - ed peace to gain;
When one their wish and one their prayer, And one their heav'n-ly rest.
Where chil-dren ear - ly lisp His fame, And par - ents hold Him dear.
Where par - ents love the sa - cred Word, And all its wis - dom prize.
U - nite our hearts in love to Thee, And love to all will reign. A - men.
WORDS: Henry Ware, Jr., 1846
MUSIC: John B. Dykes, 1866
ST. AGNES
C.M.
O Lord, May Church and Home Combine 510
Thou shalt teach them diligently unto thy children . . . Deut. 6:7
1. O Lord, may church and home com - bine To teach Thy per - fect way,
2. Let us un - wor - thy aims de - part, Im - bue us with Thy grace;
3. Shine, Light Di - vine; re - veal Thy face Where dark - ness else might be.
4. May stead - fast faith and ear - nest prayer Keep sa - cred vows se - cure;
With gen - tle - ness and love like Thine, That none shall ev - er stray.
With - in the home let ev - ery heart Be - come Thy dwell - ing place.
Grant, Love Di - vine, in ev - ery place Glad fel - low - ship with Thee.
Build Thou a hal-lowed dwell - ing where True joy and peace en - dure.
WORDS: Carlton C. Buck, 1961
MUSIC: Alexander R. Reinagle, c.1836
ST. PETER
C.M.

511 O Perfect Love, All Human Thought

. . . And shall be joined unto his wife, and they two shall be one flesh. Eph. 5:31

1. O perfect Love, all human thought transcending,
Lowly we kneel in prayer before Thy throne,
That theirs may be the love which knows no ending,
Whom Thou forevermore dost join in one.

2. O perfect Life, be Thou their full assurance
Of tender charity and steadfast faith,
Of patient hope, and quiet, brave endurance,
With childlike trust that fears not pain nor death.

3. Grant them the joy which brightens earthly sorrow;
Grant them the peace which calms all earthly strife,
And to life's day the glorious, unknown morrow
That dawns upon eternal love and life.

4. Hear us, O Father, gracious and forgiving,
Through Jesus Christ, Thy coeternal Word,
Who, with the Holy Ghost, by all things living
Now and to endless ages art adored. Amen.

WORDS: Dorothy F. Gurney, 1883;
St. 4, John Ellerton, 1875
MUSIC: Joseph Barnby, 1889

SANDRINGHAM
11.10.11.10

O Give Us Homes 512

As for me and my house, we will serve the Lord. Josh. 24:15

1. O give us homes built firm up - on the Sav - ior, Where Christ is head and
2. O give us homes with god - ly fa - thers, moth-ers, Who al - ways place their
3. O give us homes where Christ is Lord and Mas - ter, The Bi - ble read, the
4. O Lord, our God, our homes are Thine for - ev - er! We trust to Thee their
coun - sel - lor and guide; Where ev - ery child is taught His love and fa - vor
hope and trust in Him; Whose ten - der pa-tience tur - moil nev - er both-ers,
pre-cious hymns still sung; Where pray'r comes first in peace or in dis - as - ter,
prob-lems, toil and care; Their bonds of love no en - e - my can sev - er
And gives his heart to Christ, the cru - ci - fied: How sweet to know that,
Whose calm and cour - age trou - ble can - not dim; A home where each finds
And praise is nat - ural speech to ev - ery tongue; Where moun-tains move be-
If Thou art al - ways Lord and Mas - ter there: Be Thou the cen - ter
tho' his foot-steps wa - ver, His faith - ful Lord is walk - ing by his side!
joy in serv - ing oth - ers, And love still shines tho' days be dark and grim.
fore a faith that's vast - er, And Christ suf - fi - cient is for old and young.
of our least en - deav-or— Be Thou our guest, our hearts and homes to share.

WORDS: Barbara B. Hart, 1965
MUSIC: Jean Sibelius, 1899

FINLANDIA
11.10.11.10.11.10

Hymns of Life Eternal

Sing the Wondrous Love of Jesus 513

. . . At Thy right hand there are pleasures for evermore. Psa. 16:11

1. Sing the won - drous love of Je - sus, Sing His mer - cy and His grace; In the man - sions bright and bless - ed He'll pre - pare for us a place.
2. While we walk the pil - grim path - way Clouds will o - ver - spread the sky; But when trav - 'ling days are o - ver, Not a sha - dow, not a sigh.
3. Let us then be true and faith - ful, Trust - ing, serv - ing ev - ery day; Just one glimpse of Him in glo - ry Will the toils of life re - pay.
4. On - ward to the prize be - fore us! Soon His beau - ty we'll be - hold; Soon the pearl - y gates will o - pen, We shall tread the streets of gold.
Refrain
When we all get to heav - en,
When we all
What a day of re - joic - ing that will be!
What a day of re - joic - ing that will be!
When we all see Je - sus, We'll sing and shout the vic - to - ry.
When we all and shout the vic - to - ry.

WORDS: Eliza E. Hewitt, 1898
MUSIC: Emily D. Wilson, 1898

HEAVEN
8.7.8.7 Ref.

514 Behold a Host Arrayed in White

Lo, a great multitude . . . clothed with white robes. Rev. 7:9

1. Be - hold a host ar - rayed in white Like thou - sand
2. On earth their work was not thought wise, But see them
3. O bless - ed saints, now take your rest; A thou - sand
snow - clad moun - tains bright. They stand with palms And
now in heav - en's eyes; Be - fore God's throne Of
times shall you be blest For keep - ing faith Firm
sing their psalms Be - fore the throne of light. These are the
pre - cious stone They shout their vic - t'ry cries. On earth they
un - to death And scorn - ing world - ly trust. For now you
saints who kept God's Word; They are the hon - ored
wept through bit - ter years; Now God has wiped a -
live at home with God; You har - vest seeds once

of the Lord. He is their Prince Who drowned their sins,
way their tears, Trans - formed their strife To heav'n - ly life,
cast a - broad In tears and sighs. See with new eyes
So they were cleansed, re - stored. They now serve God both
And freed them from their fears. For now they have the
The pat - tern in the seed. The myr - iad an - gels
day and night; They sing their songs in end - less light. Their
best at last; They keep their sweet e - ter - nal feast. At
raise their song. O saints, sing with that hap - py throng; Lift
an - thems ring When they all sing With an - gels shin - ing bright.
God's right hand Our Lord com - mands; He is both host and guest.
up one voice; Let heav'n re - joice In our Re - deem - er's song.

WORDS: Hans Adolph Brorson, 1764; tr. Gracia Grindal, 1978; based on Revelation 7:9
MUSIC: Traditional Norse melody, 17th century; harm. Edvard Grieg, 1877

BEHOLD A HOST
Irregular meter

515 When All My Labors and Trials Are O'er

We shall be like Him; for we shall see Him as He is. I John 3:2

1. When all my la - bors and tri - als are o'er, And I am safe on that beau - ti - ful shore, Just to be near the dear Lord I a - dore Will through the a - ges be glo - ry for me.
2. When by the gift of His in - fi - nite grace, I am ac - cord - ed in heav - en a place, Just to be there and to look on His face
3. Friends will be there I have loved long a - go; Joy like a riv - er a- round me will flow; Yet, just a smile from my Sav - ior, I know,
Refrain
O that will be glo - ry for me, Glo - ry for me, glo - ry for me; When by His grace I shall look on His face, That will be glo - ry, be glo - ry for me.
O that will be glo - ry for me, Glo - ry for me, glo - ry for me;
rit.

WORDS and MUSIC: Charles H. Gabriel, 1900

GLORY SONG
10.10.10.10 Ref.

On Jordan's Stormy Banks I Stand 516

For He hath prepared for them a city. Heb. 11:16

1. On Jor-dan's storm-y banks I stand, And cast a wish-ful eye
2. All o'er those wide ex-tend-ed plains Shines one e-ter-nal day;
3. No chill-ing winds nor poi-s'nous breath Can reach that health-ful shore;
4. When shall I reach that hap-py place, And be for-ev-er blest?
To Ca-naan's fair and hap-py land, Where my pos-ses-sions lie.
There God the Son for-ev-er reigns And scat-ters night a-way.
Sick-ness and sor-row, pain and death Are felt and feared no more.
When shall I see my Fa-ther's face, And in His bos-om rest?
Refrain
I am bound for the prom-ised land, I am bound for the prom-ised land;
O who will come and go with me? I am bound for the prom-ised land.

WORDS: Samuel Stennett, 1787
MUSIC: Traditional American melody; arr. Rigdon M. McIntosh, 1895

PROMISED LAND
C.M. Ref.

517 Jerusalem the Golden

. . . That great city . . . Jerusalem, descending out of heaven from God. Rev. 21:10

1. Je - ru - sa - lem the gold - en, With milk and hon - ey blest!
2. They stand, those halls of Zi - on, All ju - bi - lant with song,
3. There is the throne of Da - vid; And there, from care re - leased,
4. O sweet and bless - ed coun - try, The home of God's e - lect!
Be - neath thy con - tem - pla - tion Sink heart and voice op - pressed;
And bright with many an an - gel, And all the mar - tyr throng;
The song of them that tri - umph, The shout of them that feast;
O sweet and bless - ed coun - try That ea - ger hearts ex - pect!
I know not, O I know not What joys a - wait me there;
The Prince is ev - er in them, The day - light is se - rene;
And they, who with their Lead - er Have con-quered in the fight,
Je - sus, in mer - cy bring us To that dear land of rest;
What ra - dian - cy of glo - ry, What bliss be - yond com - pare!
The pas - tures of the bless - ed Are decked in glo - rious sheen.
For - ev - er and for - ev - er Are clad in robes of white.
Who art, with God the Fa - ther, And Spir - it, ev - er blest. A - men.

WORDS: Bernard of Cluny, c.1145; tr. John M. Neale, 1851, and others
MUSIC: Alexander Ewing, 1853

EWING
7.6.7.6 D.

The Sands of Time Are Sinking 518

Behold, the Bridegroom cometh; go ye out to meet Him. Matt. 25:6

1. The sands of time are sink - ing, The dawn of heav - en breaks;
2. O Christ! He is the foun - tain, The deep, sweet well of love!
3. O, I am my Be - lov - ed's, And my Be - lov - ed's mine!
4. The Bride eyes not her gar - ment, But her dear Bride-groom's face;
The sum - mer morn I've sighed for, The fair, sweet morn a - wakes:
The streams on earth I've tast - ed, More deep I'll drink a - bove:
He brings a poor vile sin - ner In - to His "house of wine."
I will not gaze at glo - ry But on my King of grace.
Dark, dark hath been the mid - night, But day - spring is at hand,
There to an o - cean ful - ness His mer - cy doth ex - pand,
I stand up - on His mer - it, I know no oth - er stand,
Not at the crown He giv - eth But on His pierc - ed hand,
And glo - ry, glo - ry dwell - eth In Im - man - uel's land.
And glo - ry, glo - ry dwell - eth In Im - man - uel's land.
Not e'en where glo - ry dwell - eth In Im - man - uel's land.
The Lamb is all the glo - ry Of Im - man - uel's land. A-men.

WORDS: Anne R. Cousin, 1857
MUSIC: Chrétien Urhan, 1834; arr. Edward F. Rimbault, 1867

RUTHERFORD
7.6.7.6.7.6.7.5

519 For All the Saints

These all died in faith . . . and confessed that they were . . . pilgrims. Heb. 11:13

Unison, stanzas 1, 2 and 6.
1. For all the saints who from their la - bors rest, Who Thee by faith be - fore the world con-fessed, Thy name, O Je - sus, be for - ev - er blest.
2. Thou wast their rock, their fort-ress and their might; Thou, Lord, their cap-tain in the well-fought fight; Thou in the dark - ness drear, their one true light.
6. From earth's wide bounds and o-cean's far-thest coast, Thro' gates of pearl stream in the count-less host, Sing - ing to Fa - ther, Son, and Ho - ly Ghost.
Al - le - lu - ia! Al - le - lu - ia!
(after stanza 6)
A - men.
Harmony, stanzas 3, 4, 5.
3. O blest com-mun - ion, fel - low - ship di - vine! We fee - bly strug - gle; they in glo - ry shine. Yet all are one in Thee, for all are Thine.
4. And when the strife is fierce, the war - fare long, Steals on the ear the dis - tant tri-umph song, And hearts are brave a - gain and arms are strong.
5. The gold - en eve - ning bright-ens in the west; Soon, soon to faith - ful war - riors com - eth rest; And sweet the calm of Par - a - dise, the blest.

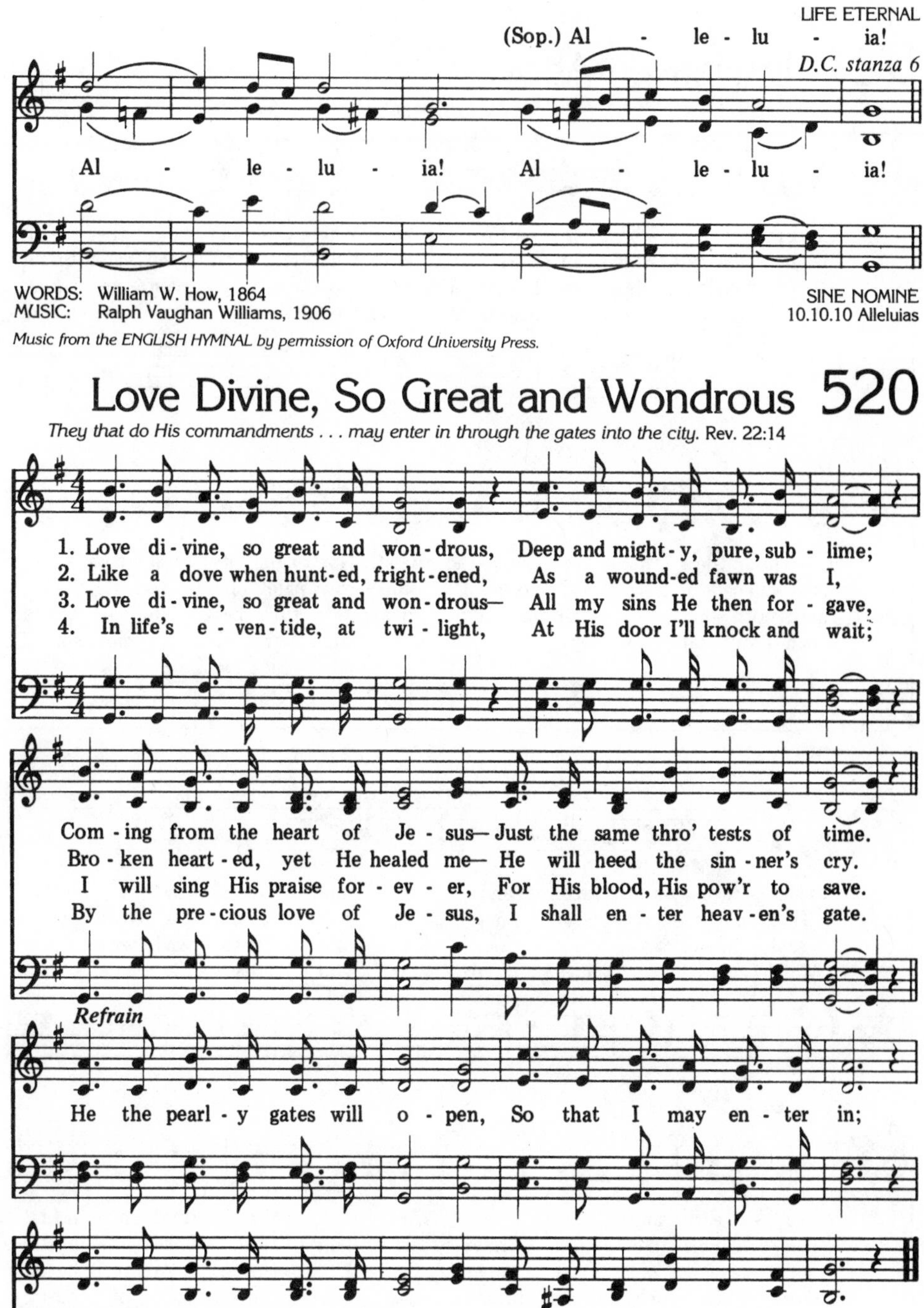
(Sop.) Al - le - lu - ia!
D.C. stanza 6
Al - le - lu - ia! Al - le - lu - ia!
Refrain
1. Love di - vine, so great and won - drous, Deep and might - y, pure, sub - lime;
2. Like a dove when hunt - ed, fright - ened, As a wound - ed fawn was I,
3. Love di - vine, so great and won - drous— All my sins He then for - gave,
4. In life's e - ven - tide, at twi - light, At His door I'll knock and wait;
Com - ing from the heart of Je - sus— Just the same thro' tests of time.
Bro - ken heart - ed, yet He healed me— He will heed the sin - ner's cry.
I will sing His praise for - ev - er, For His blood, His pow'r to save.
By the pre - cious love of Je - sus, I shall en - ter heav - en's gate.
He the pearl - y gates will o - pen, So that I may en - ter in;
For He pur - chased my re - demp - tion, And for - gave me all my sin.

WORDS: William W. How, 1864
MUSIC: Ralph Vaughan Williams, 1906

SINE NOMINE
10.10.10 Alleluias

Music from the ENGLISH HYMNAL by permission of Oxford University Press.

Love Divine, So Great and Wondrous 520

They that do His commandments . . . may enter in through the gates into the city. Rev. 22:14

WORDS: Frederick A. Blom, 1917; tr. Nathaniel Carlson, c.1935
MUSIC: Attr. Elsie Ahlwén, 1930

PEARLY GATES
8.7.8.7 Ref.

521 In Heaven Above

Mine eyes have seen the King, the Lord of hosts. Isa. 6:5

1. In heav'n a - bove, in heav'n a - bove, Where God our Fa - ther dwells,
2. In heav'n a - bove, in heav'n a - bove, What glo - ry deep and bright!
3. In heav'n a - bove, in heav'n a - bove, No tears of pain are shed;
4. In heav'n a - bove, in heav'n a - bove, God hath a joy pre - pared,

How bound-less there the bless - ed - ness! No tongue its great - ness tells;
The splen - dor of the noon - day sun Grows pale be - fore its light;
There noth - ing e'er shall fade or die; Life's full - ness 'round is spread,
Which mor - tal ear hath nev - er heard, Nor mor - tal vi - sion shared,

There face to face, and full and free, Ev - er and
That might - y Sun that ne'er goes down, Be - fore whose
And, like an o - cean, joy o'er - flows, And with im-
Which nev - er en - tered mor - tal breast, By mor - tal

ev - er - more we see— We see the Lord of hosts!
face clouds nev - er frown, Is God the Lord of hosts!
mor - tal mer - cy glows Our God the Lord of hosts!
lips was ne'er ex - pressed, 'Tis God the Lord of hosts!

WORDS: Laurentius Laurentii Laurinus, 1622; adapt. John Aström, 1767-1844; tr. William Maccall, 1812-1888
MUSIC: Traditional Norse melody

HAUGE
8.6.8.6.8.8.6

Ten Thousand Times Ten Thousand 522

Behold, the Lord cometh with ten thousands of His saints. Jude 14

1. Ten thou - sand times ten thou - sand In spark - ling rai - ment bright,
2. What rush of al - le - lu - ias Fills all the earth and sky!
3. O then what rap - tured greet - ings On Ca - naan's hap - py shore!
4. Bring near Thy great sal - va - tion, Thou Lamb for sin - ners slain;
The ar - mies of the ran - somed saints Throng up the steeps of light:
What ring - ing of a thou - sand harps Be - speaks the tri - umph nigh!
What knit - ting sev - ered friend - ships up, Where part - ings are no more!
Fill up the roll of Thine e - lect, Then take Thy pow'r and reign:
Tis fin - ished, all is fin - ished, Their fight with death and sin:
O day, for which cre - a - tion And all its tribes were made;
Then eyes with joy shall spar - kle That brimmed with tears of late,
Ap - pear, De - sire of na - tions, Thine ex - iles long for home;
Fling o - pen wide the gold - en gates, And let the vic - tors in.
O joy, for all its for - mer woes A thou - sand - fold re - paid!
Or - phans no lon - ger fa - ther - less, Nor wid - ows des - o - late.
Show in the heav'ns Thy prom - ised sign; Thou Prince and Sav - ior, come. A - men.

WORDS: Henry Alford, 1867 and 1870
MUSIC: John B. Dykes, 1875

ALFORD
7.6.8.6 D.

523 I'm Just a Poor, Wayfaring Stranger

I am a stranger in the earth. Psa. 119:19

Unison

I'm just a poor, way - far - ing stran - ger, A trav - 'ling through this world of

woe; But there's no sick - ness, no toil or dan - ger, In that bright world to which I

go. I'm go - ing there to see my *(1) moth - er, I'm go - ing there, no more to

roam, I'm just a - go - ing o - ver Jor - dan, I'm just a - go - ing o - ver home.

*(2) fa-ther, (3) Sav-ior,

WORDS: American folk hymn
MUSIC: Traditional American melody

WAYFARING STRANGER
Irregular meter

524 Jerusalem, My Happy Home

Our feet shall stand within thy gates, O Jerusalem. Psa.122:2

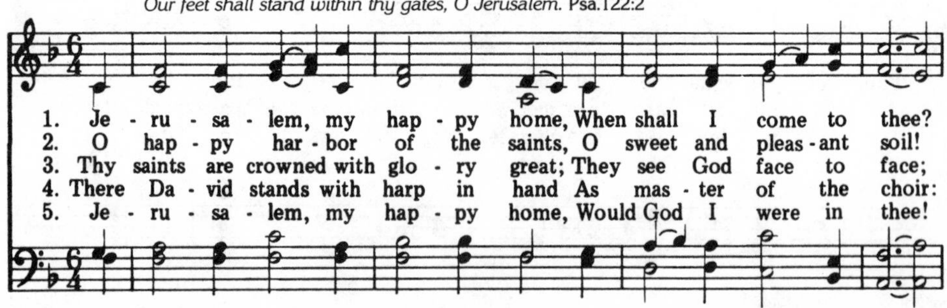
1. Je - ru - sa - lem, my hap - py home, When shall I come to thee?
2. O hap - py har - bor of the saints, O sweet and pleas - ant soil!
3. Thy saints are crowned with glo - ry great; They see God face to face;
4. There Da - vid stands with harp in hand As mas - ter of the choir:
5. Je - ru - sa - lem, my hap - py home, Would God I were in thee!

LIFE ETERNAL
When shall my sor - rows have an end? Thy joys when shall I see?
In thee no sor - row may be found, No grief, no care, no toil.
They tri - umph still, they still re - joice: Most hap - py is their case.
Ten thou - sand times that man were blest That might this mu - sic hear.
Would God my woes were at an end, Thy joys that I might see!
WORDS: "F.B.P.," 16th century; based on anonymous hymn
MUSIC: Traditional American melody; arr. Annabel M. Buchanan, 1938
LAND OF REST
C.M.
Music Copyright © 1962 by J. Fischer & Bros., a division of Belwin-Mills Publishing Corp. All Rights Reserved. Used with permission.
Face to Face with Christ My Savior
525
Now we see through a glass, darkly; but then face to face . . . I Cor. 13:12
1. Face to face with Christ my Sav - ior, Face to face—what will it be—
2. On - ly faint - ly now I see Him, With the dark-ling veil be-tween;
3. What re - joic - ing in His pres - ence When are ban-ished grief and pain;
4. Face to face! O bliss - ful mo - ment! Face to face—to see and know;
When with rap - ture I be - hold Him, Je - sus Christ who died for me?
But a bless - ed day is com - ing When His glo - ry shall be seen.
When the crook - ed ways are straight-ened And the dark things shall be plain.
Face to face with my Re-deem - er, Je - sus Christ who loves me so.
Refrain
Face to face I shall be - hold Him, Far be - yond the star - ry sky;
Face to face in all His glo - ry, I shall see Him by and by!

WORDS: Carrie E. Breck, 1898
MUSIC: Grant C. Tullar, 1898

FACE TO FACE
8.7.8.7 Ref.

Hymns for Special Times and Seasons

O Day of Rest and Gladness 526

Upon the first day of the week . . . the disciples came together. Acts 20:7

1. O day of rest and glad-ness, O day of joy and light,
2. On thee, at the cre - a - tion, The light first had its birth;
3. To - day on wea - ry na - tions The heav'n-ly man-na falls;
4. New grac - es ev - er gain-ing From this our day of rest,
O balm of care and sad-ness, Most beau - ti - ful, most bright;
On thee, for our sal - va - tion, Christ rose from depths of earth;
To ho - ly con - vo - ca - tions The sil - ver trump-et calls,
We reach the rest re - main-ing To spir - its of the blest;
On thee the high and low - ly, Through a - ges joined in tune, Sing
On thee our Lord vic - to - rious The Spir - it sent from heav'n; And
Where gos - pel light is glow-ing With pure and ra-diant beams, And
To Ho - ly Ghost be prais - es, To Fa - ther and to Son; The
"Ho - ly, ho - ly, ho - ly," To the great God Tri - une.
thus on thee most glo-rious A tri - ple light was giv'n.
liv - ing wa - ter flow-ing With soul - re - fresh-ing streams.
Church her voice up - rais - es To Thee, blest Three in One. A-men.

WORDS: Christopher Wordsworth, 1862
MUSIC: Traditional German melody; arr. Lowell Mason, 1839

MENDEBRAS
7.6.7.6 D.

527 Still, Still with Thee

I will sing aloud of Thy mercy in the morning. Psa. 59:16

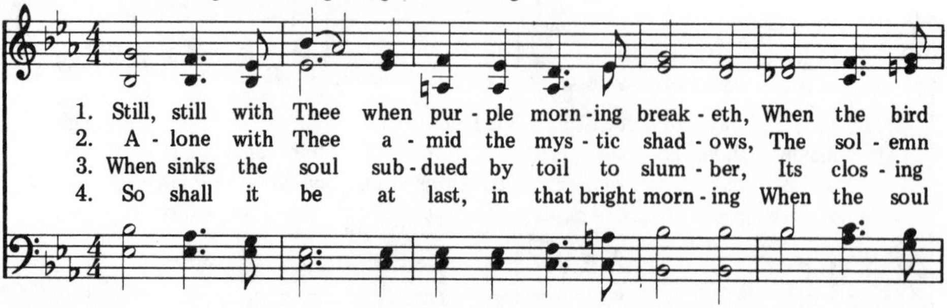

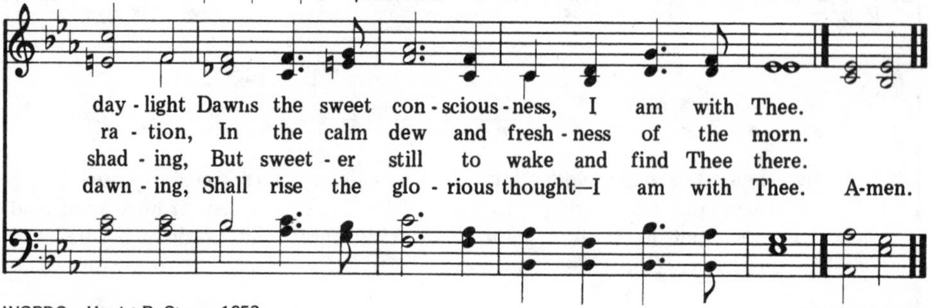

1. Still, still with Thee when pur - ple morn - ing break - eth, When the bird wak - eth and the shad - ows flee; Fair - er than morn - ing, love - lier than the day - light Dawns the sweet con - scious - ness, I am with Thee.
2. A - lone with Thee a - mid the mys - tic shad - ows, The sol - emn hush of na - ture new - ly born; A - lone with Thee in breath-less ad - o - ra - tion, In the calm dew and fresh - ness of the morn.
3. When sinks the soul sub - dued by toil to slum - ber, Its clos - ing eyes look up to Thee in prayer; Sweet the re - pose be-neath Thy wings o'er - shad - ing, But sweet - er still to wake and find Thee there.
4. So shall it be at last, in that bright morn - ing When the soul wak - eth and life's shad - ows flee; O, in that hour, fair - er than day - light dawn - ing, Shall rise the glo - rious thought—I am with Thee. A-men.

WORDS: Harriet B. Stowe, 1853
MUSIC: Felix Mendelssohn, 1834

CONSOLATION
11.10.11.10

528 Awake, My Soul, and with the Sun

I . . . will awake early, I will praise Thee, O Lord. Psa. 108:2,3

1. A-wake, my soul, and with the sun Thy dai - ly stage of du - ty run;
2. Wake and lift up thy - self, my heart, And with the an - gels bear thy part,
3. Lord, I my vows to Thee re - new; Dis-perse my sins as morn-ing dew;
4. Di-rect, con-trol, sug - gest this day, All I de - sign or do or say;
5. Praise God from whom all bless-ings flow, Praise Him, all crea - tures here be - low,

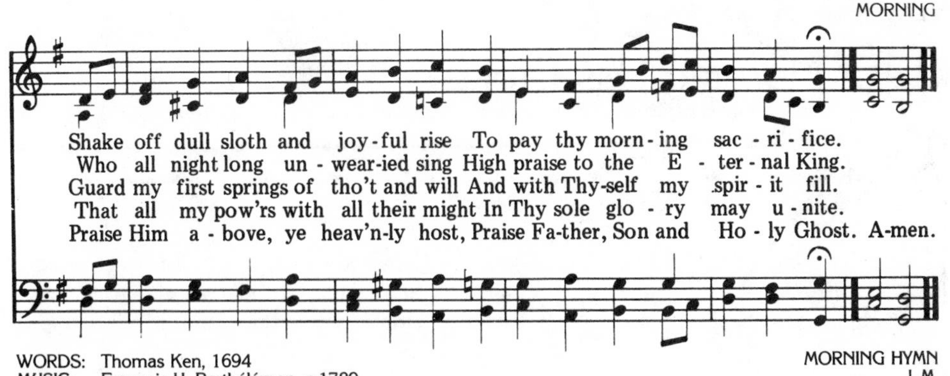
Shake off dull sloth and joy-ful rise To pay thy morn-ing sac-ri-fice.
Who all night long un-wear-ied sing High praise to the E-ter-nal King.
Guard my first springs of tho't and will And with Thy-self my spir-it fill.
That all my pow'rs with all their might In Thy sole glo-ry may u-nite.
Praise Him a-bove, ye heav'n-ly host, Praise Fa-ther, Son and Ho-ly Ghost. A-men.

WORDS: Thomas Ken, 1694
MUSIC: Francois H. Barthélémon, c.1789

MORNING HYMN
L.M.

When Morning Gilds the Skies 529

My voice shalt Thou hear in the morning, O Lord. Psa. 5:3

1. When morning gilds the skies, My heart awaking cries:
May Jesus Christ be praised! Alike at work or prayer
To Jesus I repair: May Jesus Christ be praised!

2. The night becomes as day When from the heart we say:
May Jesus Christ be praised! The pow'rs of darkness fear
When this sweet chant they hear: May Jesus Christ be praised!

3. Sing, suns and stars of space, Sing, ye that see His face,
Sing, Jesus Christ be praised! Let all the earth around
Ring joyous with the sound: May Jesus Christ be praised!

4. Be this while life is mine My canticle divine:
May Jesus Christ be praised! Be this th'eternal song,
Through all the ages long: May Jesus Christ be praised! Amen.

WORDS: *Katholisches Gesangbuch,* Würzburg, 1828; tr. Edward Caswall, 1854
MUSIC: Joseph Barnby, 1868

LAUDES DOMINI
6.6.6.6.6.6

530 Morning Has Broken

In the morning, then ye shall see the glory of the Lord. Exo. 16:7

Unison
1. Morn - ing has bro - ken Like the first morn - ing,
2. Sweet the rain's new fall Sun - lit from heav - en,
3. Mine is the sun - light! Mine is the morn - ing
Black - bird has spo - ken Like the first bird.
Like the first dew - fall On the first grass.
Born of the one light E - den saw play!
Praise for the sing - ing! Praise for the morn - ing!
Praise for the sweet - ness Of the wet gar - den,
Praise with e - la - tion, Praise ev - ery morn - ing,
Praise for them, spring - ing Fresh from the Word!
Sprung in com - plete - ness Where His feet pass.
God's re - cre - a - tion Of the new day!
A-men.

WORDS: Eleanor Farjeon, 1931
MUSIC: Traditional Gaelic melody; arr. David Evans, 1927

BUNESSAN
5.5.5.4 D.

Abide with Me: Fast Falls the Eventide 531

They constrained Him, saying, Abide with us. Luke 24:29

1. A - bide with me: fast falls the e - ven - tide;
2. Swift to its close ebbs out life's lit - tle day;
3. I need Thy pres - ence ev - ery pass - ing hour;
4. I fear no foe, with Thee at hand to bless;
5. Hold Thou Thy cross be - fore my clos - ing eyes;
The dark - ness deep - ens; Lord, with me a - bide!
Earth's joys grow dim, its glo - ries pass a - way;
What but Thy grace can foil the tempt - er's power?
Ills have no weight, and tears no bit - ter - ness.
Shine through the gloom and point me to the skies:
When oth - er help - ers fail, and com - forts flee,
Change and de - cay in all a - round I see.
Who, like Thy - self, my guide and stay can be?
Where is death's sting? Where, grave, thy vic - to - ry?
Heav'n's morn - ing breaks, and earth's vain shad - ows flee;
Help of the help - less, O a - bide with me.
O Thou who chang - est not, a - bide with me.
Through cloud and sun - shine, Lord, a - bide with me.
I tri - umph still, if Thou a - bide with me.
In life, in death, O Lord, a - bide with me. A - men.

WORDS: Henry F. Lyte, 1847
MUSIC: William H. Monk, 1861

EVENTIDE
10.10.10.10

532 Day Is Dying in the West

Holy, holy, holy is the Lord . . . the whole earth is full of His glory. Isa. 6:3

1. Day is dy - ing in the west, Heav'n is touch - ing
2. Lord of life, be - neath the dome Of the u - ni-
3. While the deep - 'ning sha - dows fall, Heart of Love, en-
4. When for - ev - er from our sight Pass the stars, the
earth with rest; Wait and wor - ship while the night Sets her
verse, Thy home, Gath - er us who seek Thy face To the
fold - ing all, Through the glo - ry and the grace Of the
day, the night, Lord of an - gels, on our eyes Let e-
even - ing lamps a - light Through all the sky.
fold of Thy em - brace, For Thou art nigh.
stars that veil Thy face, Our hearts as - cend.
ter - nal morn - ing rise, And shad - ows end.
Refrain
Ho - ly, ho - ly,
ho - ly, Lord God of Hosts! Heav'n and earth are full of Thee!
Heav'n and earth are prais - ing Thee, O Lord most high! A - men.

WORDS: Mary A. Lathbury, 1877
MUSIC: William F. Sherwin, 1877

CHAUTAUQUA
7.7.7.7.4 Ref.

Sun of My Soul, Thou Savior Dear 533

The darkness and the light are both alike to Thee. Psa. 139:12

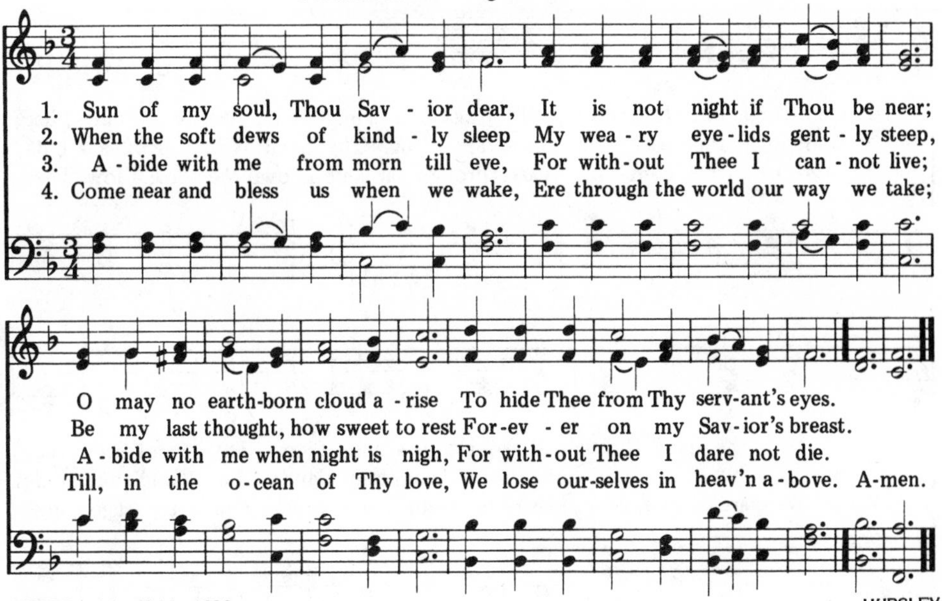

1. Sun of my soul, Thou Sav - ior dear, It is not night if Thou be near;
2. When the soft dews of kind - ly sleep My wea - ry eye - lids gent - ly steep,
3. A - bide with me from morn till eve, For with - out Thee I can - not live;
4. Come near and bless us when we wake, Ere through the world our way we take;
O may no earth-born cloud a - rise To hide Thee from Thy serv-ant's eyes.
Be my last thought, how sweet to rest For - ev - er on my Sav-ior's breast.
A - bide with me when night is nigh, For with - out Thee I dare not die.
Till, in the o - cean of Thy love, We lose our-selves in heav'n a - bove. A-men.

WORDS: John Keble, 1820
MUSIC: *Katholisches Gesangbuch*, Vienna, c. 1774, arr.

HURSLEY
L.M.

Now the Day Is Over 534

Thou shalt lie down, and thy sleep shall be sweet. Prov. 3:24

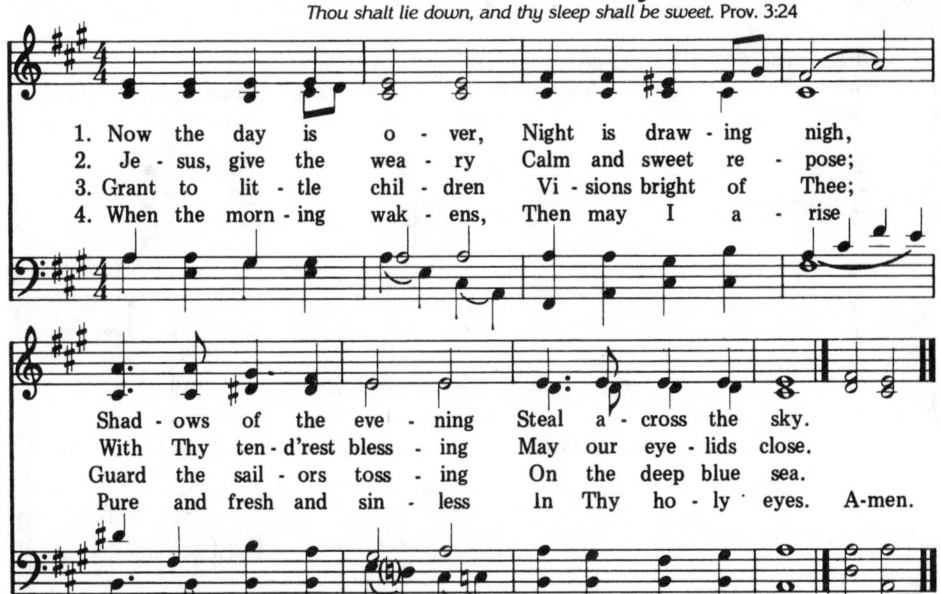

1. Now the day is o - ver, Night is draw - ing nigh,
2. Je - sus, give the wea - ry Calm and sweet re - pose;
3. Grant to lit - tle chil - dren Vi - sions bright of Thee;
4. When the morn - ing wak - ens, Then may I a - rise
Shad - ows of the eve - ning Steal a - cross the sky.
With Thy ten - d'rest bless - ing May our eye - lids close.
Guard the sail - ors toss - ing On the deep blue sea.
Pure and fresh and sin - less In Thy ho - ly eyes. A-men.

WORDS: Sabine Baring-Gould, 1865
MUSIC: Joseph Barnby, 1868

MERRIAL
6.5.6.5

535 God of Our Life, through All the Circling

Thou art the same, and Thy years shall have no end. Psa. 102:27

1. God of our life, through all the cir - cling years, We trust in Thee;
2. God of the past, our times are in Thy hand; With us a - bide.
3. God of the com - ing years, through paths un-known We fol - low Thee;
In all the past, through all our hopes and fears, Thy hand we see.
Lead us by faith to hope's true prom-ised land; Be Thou our guide.
When we are strong, Lord, leave us not a - lone; Our ref - uge be.
With each new day, when morn - ing lifts the veil,
With Thee to bless, the dark - ness shines as light,
Be Thou for us in life our dai - ly bread,
We own Thy mer - cies, Lord, which nev - er fail.
And faith's fair vi - sion chang - es in - to sight.
Our heart's true home when all our years have sped. A - men.

WORDS: Hugh T. Kerr, 1916; alt. 1928
MUSIC: Charles H. Purday, 1860

SANDON
10.4.10.4.10.10

God of the Ages 536

The eternal God is thy refuge . . . Deut. 33:27

Unison
1. God of the a - ges, His - to - ry's Mak - er,
2. God of this morn - ing, Glad - ly Your chil - dren
3. God of to - mor - row, Strong O - ver - com - er,
4. Lord of past a - ges, Lord of this morn - ing,
Plan - ning our path - way, Hold - ing us fast,
Wor - ship be - fore You, Trust - ing - ly bow:
Princ - es of dark - ness Own Your com - mand:
Lord of the fu - ture, Help us, we pray:
Shap - ing in mer - cy All that con - cerns us:
Teach us to know You Al - ways a - mong us,
What then can harm us? We are Your peo - ple,
Teach us to trust You, Love and o - bey You,
Fa - ther, we praise You, Lord of the past.
Qui - et - ly sov - 'reign— Lord of our now.
Now and for - ev - er Kept by Your hand.
Crown You each mo - ment Lord of to - day.

WORDS: Margaret Clarkson, 1982
MUSIC: Traditional Gaelic melody; arr. David Evans, 1927

BUNESSAN
5.5.5.4 D.

537 Day by Day and with Each Passing

As thy days, so shall thy strength be. Deut. 33:25

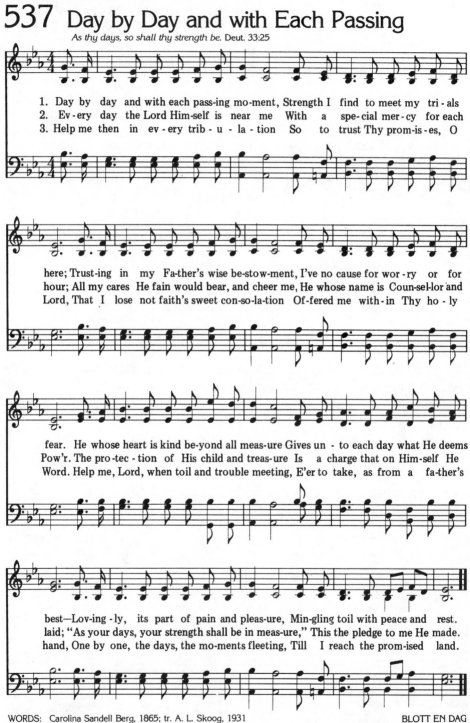

1. Day by day and with each pass-ing mo-ment, Strength I find to meet my tri - als
2. Ev - ery day the Lord Him-self is near me With a spe- cial mer - cy for each
3. Help me then in ev - ery trib - u - la - tion So to trust Thy prom-is - es, O

here; Trust-ing in my Fa-ther's wise be-stow-ment, I've no cause for wor - ry or for
hour; All my cares He fain would bear, and cheer me, He whose name is Coun-sel-lor and
Lord, That I lose not faith's sweet con-so-la-tion Of-fered me with - in Thy ho - ly

fear. He whose heart is kind be-yond all meas-ure Gives un - to each day what He deems
Pow'r. The pro -tec - tion of His child and treas-ure Is a charge that on Him-self He
Word. Help me, Lord, when toil and trouble meeting, E'er to take, as from a fa-ther's

best—Lov-ing - ly, its part of pain and pleas-ure, Min-gling toil with peace and rest.
laid; "As your days, your strength shall be in meas-ure," This the pledge to me He made.
hand, One by one, the days, the mo-ments fleeting, Till I reach the prom-ised land.

WORDS: Carolina Sandell Berg, 1865; tr. A. L. Skoog, 1931
MUSIC: Oscar Ahnfelt, 1872

BLOTT EN DAG
Irregular meter

Another Year Is Dawning 538

So teach us to number our days, that we may apply our hearts unto wisdom. Psa. 90:12

1. An - oth - er year is dawn - ing! Dear Fa - ther, let it be,
2. An - oth - er year of mer - cies, Of faith - ful - ness and grace,
3. An - oth - er year of serv - ice, Of wit - ness for Thy love,
In work - ing or in wait - ing, An - oth - er year with Thee;
An - oth - er year of glad - ness, In the shin - ing of Thy face;
An - oth - er year of train - ing For ho - lier work a - bove;
An - oth - er year of prog - ress, An - oth - er year of praise,
An - oth - er year of lean - ing Up - on Thy lov - ing breast,
An - oth - er year is dawn - ing! Dear Fa - ther, let it be,
An - oth - er year of prov - ing Thy pres - ence all the days.
An - oth - er year of trust - ing, Of qui - et, hap - py rest.
On earth, or else in heav - en, An - oth - er year for Thee. A - men.

WORDS: Frances R. Havergal, 1874
MUSIC: Samuel S. Wesley, 1864

AURELIA
7.6.7.6 D.

539 When upon Life's Billows

Many, O Lord my God, are Thy wonderful works . . . Psa. 40:5

1. When up - on life's bil - lows you are tem - pest-tossed, When you are dis -
2. Are you ev - er bur-dened with a load of care? Does the cross seem
3. When you look at oth - ers with their lands and gold, Think that Christ has
4. So a - mid the con - flict, wheth - er great or small, Do not be dis -
cour - aged, think - ing all is lost, Count your man - y bless - ings—name them
heav - y you are called to bear? Count your man - y bless - ings— ev - ery
prom - ised you His wealth un - told; Count your man - y bless - ings—mon - ey
cour - aged—God is o - ver all; Count your man - y bless - ings— an - gels
one by one, And it will sur - prise you what the Lord has done.
doubt will fly, And you will be sing - ing as the days go by.
can - not buy Your re - ward in heav - en nor your home on high.
will at - tend, Help and com - fort give you to your jour - ney's end.
Refrain
Count your bless-ings—name them one by one; Count your
Count your man-y bless-ings— name them one by one; Count your man-y
bless - ings—see what God has done; Count your bless-ings—
bless - ings— see what God has done; Count your man - y bless-ings—

name them one by one; Count your man - y bless - ings—see what God has done.

WORDS: Johnson Oatman, Jr., 1897
MUSIC: Edwin O. Excell, 1897

BLESSINGS
11.11.11.11 Ref.

We Gather Together 540

If God be for us, who can be against us? Rom. 8:31

1. We gath - er to - geth - er to ask the Lord's bless - ing;
2. Be - side us to guide us, our God with us join - ing,
3. We all do ex - tol Thee, Thou Lead - er tri - um - phant,
He chas - tens and has - tens His will to make known;
Or - dain - ing, main - tain - ing His king - dom di - vine;
And pray that Thou still our De - fend - er wilt be.

The wick - ed op - press - ing now cease from dis - tress - ing,
So from the be - gin - ning the fight we were win - ning:
Let Thy con - gre - ga - tion es - cape trib - u - la - tion:
Sing prais - es to His name: He for - gets not His own.
Thou, Lord, wast at our side, all glo - ry be Thine!
Thy name be ev - er praised! O Lord, make us free! A - men.

WORDS: Netherlands folk hymn; tr. Theodore Baker, 1917
MUSIC: *Nederlandtsch Gedenckelanck,* 1626; arr. Edward Kremser, 1877

KREMSER
12.11.12.11

541 Thanks to God for My Redeemer

In everything give thanks; for this is the will of God . . . I Thess. 5:18

1. Thanks to God for my Re - deem - er, Thanks for all Thou dost pro - vide!
2. Thanks for prayers that Thou hast an-swered,Thanks for what Thou dost de - ny!
3. Thanks for ros - es. by the way - side,Thanks for thorns their stems con - tain!

Thanks for times now but a mem - 'ry, Thanks for Je - sus by my side!
Thanks for storms that I have weath - ered,Thanks for all Thou dost sup - ply!
Thanks for homes and thanks for fire - side, Thanks for hope, that sweet re - frain!

Thanks for pleas - ant, balm - y spring - time, Thanks for dark and drear - y fall!
Thanks for pain and thanks for plea - sure, Thanks for com - fort in de - spair!
Thanks for joy and thanks for sor - row, Thanks for heav'n - ly peace with Thee!

Thanks for tears by now for - got - ten, Thanks for peace with - in my soul!
Thanks for grace that none can meas - ure, Thanks for love be - yond com- pare!
Thanks for hope in the to - mor - row,Thanks thro' all e - ter - ni - ty!

WORDS: August L. Storm, 1891; tr. Carl E. Backstrom, 1931
MUSIC: John A. Hultman, 1891

TACK, O GUD
8.7.8.7 D.

We Plow the Fields, and Scatter 542

Every good gift and every perfect gift is from above. James 1:17

1. We plow the fields, and scat - ter The good seed on the land, But it is
2. He on - ly is the Mak - er Of all things near and far, He paints the
3. We thank Thee then, O Fa - ther, For all things bright and good, The seed-time
fed and wa - tered By God's al - might - y hand; He sends the snow in
way - side flow - er, He lights the eve - ning star; The winds and waves o -
and the har - vest, Our life, our health, our food; Ac - cept the gifts we
win - ter, The warmth to swell the grain, The breez - es and the sun - shine, And
bey Him, By Him the birds are fed; Much more to us, His chil - dren, He
of - fer For all Thy love im - parts, And what Thou most de - sir - est, Our
soft re - fresh - ing rain.
gives our dai - ly bread.
hum - ble, thank - ful hearts.
Refrain
All good gifts a - round us Are sent from heav'n a -
bove; Then thank the Lord, O thank the Lord For all His love. A - men.

WORDS: Matthias Claudius, 1782; tr. Jane M. Campbell, 1861
MUSIC: Johann A. P. Schulz, 1800

WIR PFLÜGEN
7.6.7.6 D. Ref.

543 Come, Ye Thankful People, Come

The harvest is the end of the world; and the reapers are the angels. Matt. 13:39

1. Come, ye thank - ful peo - ple, come, Raise the song of har - vest - home:
2. All the world is God's own field, Fruit un - to His praise to yield;
3. For the Lord our God shall come, And shall take His har - vest home;
4. E - ven so, Lord, quick - ly come To Thy fi - nal har - vest - home;

All is safe - ly gath - ered in, Ere the win - ter storms be - gin;
Wheat and tares to - geth - er sown, Un - to joy or sor - row grown;
From His field shall in that day All of - fens - es purge a - way;
Gath - er Thou Thy peo - ple in, Free from sor - row, free from sin;

God, our Ma - ker, doth pro - vide For our wants to be sup - plied:
First the blade, and then the ear, Then the full corn shall ap - pear:
Give His an - gels charge at last In the fire the tares to cast;
There, for - ev - er pu - ri - fied, In Thy pres - ence to a - bide:

Come to God's own tem - ple, come, Raise the song of har - vest - home.
Lord of har - vest, grant that we Whole - some grain and pure may be.
But the fruit - ful ears to store In His gar - ner ev - er - more.
Come, with all Thine an - gels, come, Raise the glo - rious har - vest - home. A - men.

WORDS: Henry Alford, 1844
MUSIC: George J. Elvey, 1858

ST. GEORGE'S, WINDSOR
7.7.7.7 D.

Now Thank We All Our God 544

Now therefore, our God, we thank Thee, and praise Thy glorious name. I Chron. 29:13

1. Now thank we all our God With heart and hands and voic - es,
2. O may this boun-teous God Through all our life be near us,
3. All praise and thanks to God The Fa - ther now be giv - en,
Who won-drous things hath done, In whom His world re - joic - es;
With ev - er joy - ful hearts And bless - ed peace to cheer us;
The Son, and Him who reigns With them in high - est heav - en,
Who, from our moth - er's arms, Hath blessed us on our way
And keep us in His grace And guide us when per - plexed,
The one e - ter - nal God Whom earth and heav'n a - dore;
With count-less gifts of love, And still is ours to - day.
And free us from all ills In this world and the next.
For thus it was, is now, And shall be ev - er - more. A - men.

WORDS: Martin Rinkart, 1636;
tr. Catherine Winkworth, 1858
MUSIC: Johann Crüger, 1647

NUN DANKET ALLE GOTT
6.7.6.7.6.6.6.6

545 For the Fruit of All Creation

Let them praise the name of the Lord; for He commanded, and they were created. Psa. 148:5

1. For the fruit of all cre - a - tion, Thanks be to God.
2. In the just re - ward of la - bor, God's will is done.
3. For the har - vests of the Spir - it, Thanks be to God.
For His gifts to ev - ery na - tion, Thanks be to God.
In the help we give our neigh - bor, God's will is done.
For the good we all in - her - it, Thanks be to God.
For the plow - ing, sow - ing, reap - ing, Si - lent growth while we are
In our world-wide task of car - ing For the hun - gry and de -
For the won - ders that as-tound us, For the truths that still con -
sleep-ing, Fu - ture needs in earth's safe-keep - ing, Thanks be to God.
spair-ing, In the har - vests we are shar - ing, God's will is done.
found us, Most of all, that love has found us, Thanks be to God.

WORDS: Fred Pratt Green, 1970
MUSIC: Welsh melody; harmonization attr. L. O. Emerson, 1906

AR HYD Y NOS
8.4.8.4.8.8.8.4

Sing to the Lord of Harvest 546

Blessed be the Lord who daily loadeth us with benefits. Psa. 68:19

Unison
1. Sing to the Lord of har - vest, Sing songs of love and praise;
2. God makes the clouds rain good - ness, The des - erts bloom and spring,
3. Bring to this sa - cred al - tar The gifts His good - ness gave,
With joy - ful hearts and voic - es Your al - le - lu - ias raise.
The hills leap up in glad - ness, The val - leys laugh and sing.
The gold - en sheaves of har - vest, The souls Christ died to save.
By Him the roll - ing sea - sons In fruit - ful or - der move;
God fills them with His full - ness, All things with large in - crease;
Your hearts lay down be - fore Him When at His feet you fall,
Sing to the Lord of har - vest A joy - ous song of love.
He crowns the year with bless - ing, With plen - ty and with peace.
And with your lives a - dore Him Who gave His life for all.

WORDS: John Samuel Bewley Monsell, 1866
MUSIC: Johann Steurlein, 1575; harm. Donald P. Hustad, 1984

WIE LIEBLICH IST DER MAIEN
7.6.7.6 D.

547 God of Our Fathers

The Lord of hosts is with us; the God of Jacob is our refuge. Psa. 46:7

3
1. God of our fa - thers, whose al - might - y
2. Thy love di - vine hath led us in the
3. From war's a - larms, from dead - ly pes - ti-
4. Re - fresh Thy peo - ple on their toil - some
hand Leads forth in beau - ty all the star - ry
past; In this free land by Thee our lot is
lence, Be Thy strong arm our ev - er sure de-
way; Lead us from night to nev - er - end - ing
band Of shin - ing worlds in splen - dor through the
cast; Be Thou our Rul - er, Guard - ian, Guide and
fense; Thy true re - lig - ion in our hearts in-
day; Fill all our lives with love and grace di-
skies, Our grate - ful songs be - fore Thy throne a - rise.
Stay, Thy Word our law, Thy paths our cho - sen way.
crease, Thy boun-teous good-ness nour-ish us in peace.
vine; And glo - ry, laud, and praise be ev - er Thine. A- men.

WORDS: Daniel C. Roberts, 1876
MUSIC: George W. Warren, 1892

NATIONAL HYMN
10.10.10.10

O Beautiful for Spacious Skies 548

Blessed is the nation whose God is the Lord. Psa. 33:12
1. O beau - ti - ful for spa - cious skies, For am - ber waves of grain,
2. O beau - ti - ful for pil - grim feet, Whose stern im - pas - sioned stress
3. O beau - ti - ful for he - roes proved In lib - er - at - ing strife,
4. O beau - ti - ful for pa - triot dream That sees be - yond the years
For pur - ple moun - tain maj - es - ties A - bove the fruit - ed plain!
A thor - ough - fare for free - dom beat A - cross the wil - der - ness!
Who more than self their coun - try loved, And mer - cy more than life!
Thine al - a - bas - ter cit - ies gleam, Un - dimmed by hu - man tears!
A - mer - i - ca! A - mer - i - ca! God shed His grace on thee,
A - mer - i - ca! A - mer - i - ca! God mend thine ev - ery flaw,
A - mer - i - ca! A - mer - i - ca! May God thy gold re - fine,
A - mer - i - ca! A - mer - i - ca! God shed His grace on thee,
And crown thy good with broth - er - hood From sea to shin - ing sea!
Con - firm thy soul in self - con - trol, Thy lib - er - ty in law!
Till all suc - cess be no - ble - ness, And ev - ery gain di - vine!
And crown thy good with broth - er - hood From sea to shin - ing sea! A - men.

WORDS: Katharine L. Bates, 1893
MUSIC: Samuel A. Ward, 1882

MATERNA
C.M.D.

549 Mine Eyes Have Seen the Glory

He is terrible to the kings of the earth. Psa. 76:12

1. Mine eyes have seen the glo - ry of the com - ing of the Lord; He is
2. I have seen Him in the watch-fires of a hun-dred cir-cling camps; They have
3. He has sound-ed forth the trum - pet that shall nev - er sound re - treat; He is
4. In the beau - ty of the lil - ies, Christ was born a - cross the sea, With a
tram-pling out the vin - tage where the grapes of wrath are stored; He hath loosed the
build - ed Him an al - tar in the eve - ning dews and damps; I can read His
sift - ing out the hearts of men be - fore His judg-ment seat; O be swift, my
glo - ry in His bos - om that trans - fig - ures you and me; As He died to
fate - ful light - ning of His ter - ri - ble swift sword; His truth is march-ing on.
right - eous sen - tence by the dim and flar - ing lamps; His day is march-ing on.
soul, to an - swer Him! be ju - bi - lant, my feet! Our God is march-ing on.
make men ho - ly, let us live to make men free, While God is march-ing on.
Refrain
Glo - ry! glo - ry, hal - le - lu - jah! Glo - ry! glo - ry, hal - le - lu - jah!
Glo - ry! glo - ry, hal - le - lu - jah! Our God is march - ing on.

WORDS: Julia W. Howe, 1862
MUSIC: Traditional American melody, c.1852

BATTLE HYMN
15.15.15.6 Ref.

My Country, 'Tis of Thee 550

Righteousness exalteth a nation; but sin is a reproach to any people. Prov. 14:34

1. My coun - try, 'tis of thee, Sweet land of lib - er - ty,
2. My na - tive coun - try, thee, Land of the no - ble free,
3. Let mu - sic swell the breeze, And ring from all the trees
4. Our fa - thers' God, to Thee, Au - thor of lib - er - ty,
Of thee I sing: Land where my fa - thers died, Land of the
Thy name I love: I love thy rocks and rills, Thy woods and
Sweet free - dom's song: Let mor - tal tongues a - wake, Let all that
To Thee we sing: Long may our land be bright With free - dom's
pil - grims' pride, From ev - ery moun - tain side Let free - dom ring!
tem - pled hills; My heart with rap - ture thrills Like that a - bove.
breathe par - take; Let rocks their si - lence break, The sound pro - long.
ho - ly light; Pro - tect us by Thy might, Great God, our King! A - men.

WORDS: Samuel F. Smith, 1832
MUSIC: *Thesaurus Musicus*, c.1745

AMERICA
6.6.4.6.6.6.4

God Bless Our Native Land 551

Blessed is the nation whose God is the Lord. Psa. 33:12

1. God bless our native land—
Firm may she ever stand
Through storm and night:
When the wild tempests rave,
Ruler of wind and wave,
Do Thou our country save
By Thy great might.

2. For her our prayers shall rise
To God above the skies—
On Him we wait:
Thou who art ever nigh,
Guarding with watchful eye,
To Thee aloud we cry,
God save the state!

3. And not to us alone,
But be Thy mercies known
From shore to shore:
Lord, make the nations see
That men should brothers be,
And form one family
The wide world o'er.

WORDS: St. 1, 2, Siegfried A. Mahlmann, 1815; tr. Charles T. Brooks and John S. Dwight, 1841;
St. 3, William E. Hickson, 1835

552 O Say, Can You See

It is better to trust in the Lord than to put confidence in princes. Psa. 118:9

1. O say, can you see, by the dawn's ear - ly light, What so
2. O thus be it ev - er, when free men shall stand Be -

proud - ly we hailed at the twi - light's last gleam - ing, Whose broad
tween their loved homes and the war's des - o - la - tion! Blest with

stripes and bright stars, thro' the per - il - ous fight, O'er the
vic - t'ry and peace, may the heav'n - res - cued land Praise the

ram - parts we watched, were so gal - lant - ly stream - ing? And the
Pow'r that hath made and pre - served us a na - tion! Then

rock - ets' red glare, the bombs burst - ing in air, Gave
con - quer we must, when our cause it is just; And
proof thro' the night that our flag was still there. O
this be our mot - to: "In God is our trust!" And the
say, does that star - span - gled ban - ner yet wave O'er the
star - span - gled ban - ner in tri - umph shall wave O'er the
land of the free and the home of the brave?
land of the free and the home of the brave!

WORDS: Francis Scott Key, 1814
MUSIC: Attr. John Stafford Smith, c.1775

STAR-SPANGLED BANNER
Irregular meter

553 O Canada!

In Thee shall all nations be blessed. Gal. 3:8

1. O Can - a - da! our home and na - tive land! True pa - triot
2. Al - might - y Love, by Thy mys - ter - ious pow'r, In wis - dom
love in all thy sons com - mand. With glow - ing hearts we
guide, with faith and free - dom dow'r; Be ours a na - tion
see thee rise, The true north, strong and free. From far and wide, O
ev - er - more That no op - pres - sion blights, Where jus - tice rules from
Can - a - da, We stand on guard for thee. God keep our land
shore to shore, From lakes to north - ern lights. May love a - lone

glo - rious and free, O Can - a - da, we stand on guard for
for wrong a - tone; Lord of the lands, make Can - a - da Thine

thee. O Can - a - da, we stand on guard for thee.
own! Lord of the lands, make Can - a - da Thine own.

WORDS: St. 1, Robert Stanley Weir, 1856-1926; St. 2, Albert C. Watson, 1859-1926
MUSIC: Melody by Calixa Lavallée, 1842-1891; arr. Frederick C. Silvester, 1901-1966

O CANADA
Irregular meter

Lord, While for All Mankind We Pray 554

In righteousness shalt thou be established. Isa. 54:14

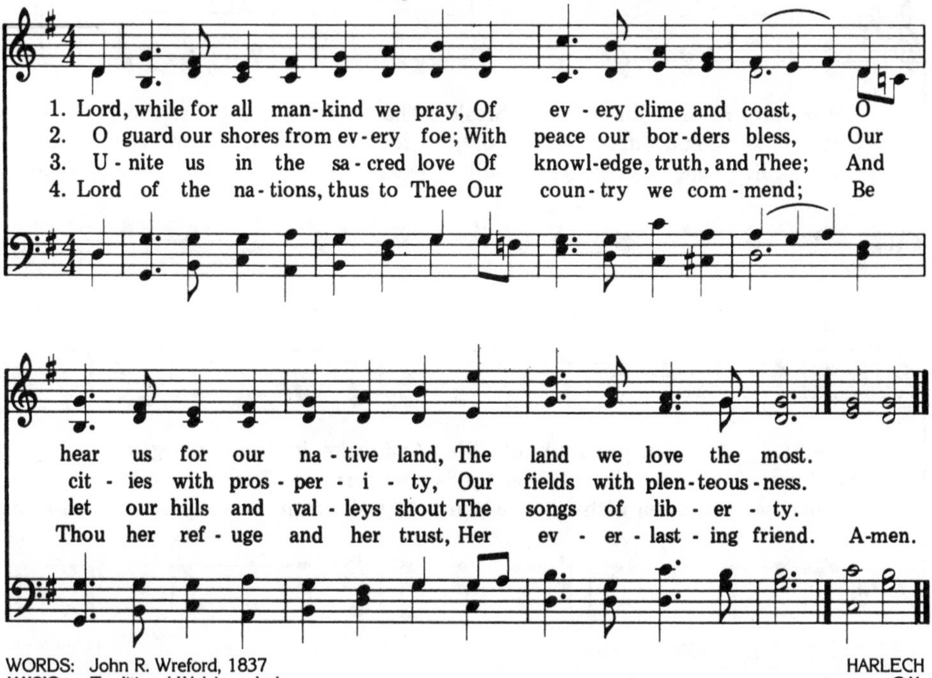

1. Lord, while for all man-kind we pray, Of ev - ery clime and coast, O
2. O guard our shores from ev - ery foe; With peace our bor - ders bless, Our
3. U - nite us in the sa - cred love Of knowl-edge, truth, and Thee; And
4. Lord of the na - tions, thus to Thee Our coun - try we com - mend; Be

hear us for our na - tive land, The land we love the most.
cit - ies with pros - per - i - ty, Our fields with plen - teous - ness.
let our hills and val - leys shout The songs of lib - er - ty.
Thou her ref - uge and her trust, Her ev - er - last - ing friend. A-men.

WORDS: John R. Wreford, 1837
MUSIC: Traditional Welsh melody

HARLECH
C.M.

555 Peace in Our Time, O Lord

And the work of righteousness shall be peace. Isa. 32:17

1. Peace in our time, O Lord, To all the peo - ples, Peace!
2. Too long mis - trust and fear Have held our souls in thrall;
3. O shall we nev - er learn The truth all time has taught,
Peace sure - ly based up - on Your will And built in right - eous - ness.
Sweep thro' the earth, keen Breath of heav'n, And sound a no - bler call!
That with - out God as ar - chi - tect Our build - ing comes to naught?
Your pow'r a - lone can break The fet - ters that en - chain
Come as You did of old, In love so great that men
O liv - ing Christ, who still Does all our bur - dens share,
The sore - ly strick - en soul of life, And make it live a - gain.
Shall cast a - side all oth - er gods And turn to You a - gain!
Come now and dwell with - in the hearts Of all men ev - ery - where! A - men.

WORDS: John Oxenham, 1938
MUSIC: George J. Elvey, 1868

DIADEMATA
S.M.D.

Service Music

556 Praise God from Whom All Blessings

Let everything that hath breath praise the Lord. Psa. 150:6

Praise God from whom all bless - ings flow; Praise Him, all crea - tures here be - low;
Praise Him a - bove, ye heav'n - ly host; Praise Fa - ther, Son, and Ho - ly Ghost. A - men.

WORDS: *Doxology;* Thomas Ken, 1709
MUSIC: *Genevan Psalter,* 1551

OLD HUNDREDTH
L.M.

557 Praise God from Whom All Blessings

(Alternate Rhythm)

Let everything that hath breath praise the Lord. Psa. 150:6

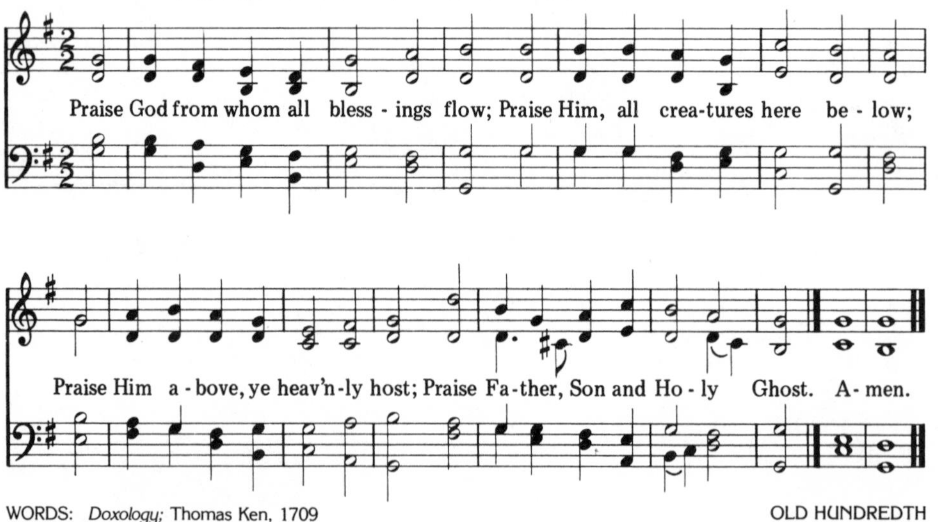
Praise God from whom all bless - ings flow; Praise Him, all crea - tures here be - low;
Praise Him a - bove, ye heav'n - ly host; Praise Fa - ther, Son and Ho - ly Ghost. A - men.

WORDS: *Doxology;* Thomas Ken, 1709
MUSIC: *Genevan Psalter,* 1551

OLD HUNDREDTH
L.M.

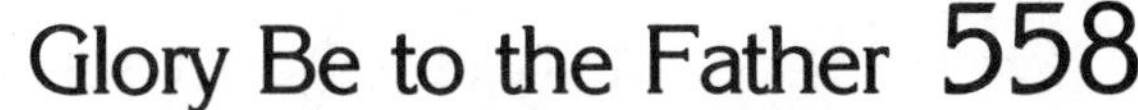

Glory Be to the Father 558

Give unto the Lord the glory due unto His name. I Chron. 16:29

Glo - ry be to the Fa - ther, and to the Son, and to the Ho - ly Ghost; As it was in the be - gin - ning, is now, and ev - er shall be, world with - out end. A - men, A - men.

WORDS: *Gloria Patri;* Traditional, 2nd century
MUSIC: Christoph Meineke, 1844

MEINEKE
Irregular meter

Glory Be to the Father 559

Give unto the Lord the glory due unto His name. I Chron. 16:29

Glo - ry be to the Fa - ther, and to the Son, and to the Ho - ly Ghost; As it was in the be - gin - ning, is now, and ev - er shall be, world with - out end. A - men, A - men.

WORDS: *Gloria Patri;* Traditional, 2nd century
MUSIC: Henry W. Greatorex, 1851

GREATOREX
Irregular meter

560 Holy, Holy, Holy, Lord God of Hosts

There is none holy as the Lord . . . I Sam. 2:2

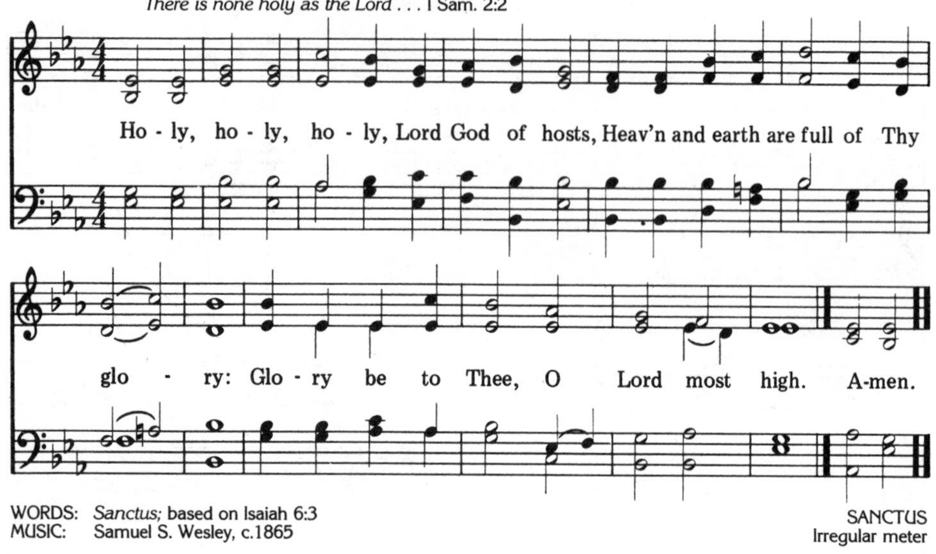
Ho - ly, ho - ly, ho - ly, Lord God of hosts, Heav'n and earth are full of Thy
glo - ry: Glo - ry be to Thee, O Lord most high. A-men.

WORDS: *Sanctus;* based on Isaiah 6:3
MUSIC: Samuel S. Wesley, c.1865

SANCTUS
Irregular meter

561 The Lord Is in His Holy Temple

I will come into Thy house and . . . worship toward Thy holy temple. Psa. 5:7

The Lord is in His ho - ly tem - ple, The Lord is in His ho - ly
tem - ple; Let all the earth keep si - lence, Let all the earth keep si - lence be -
fore Him, Keep si - lence, keep si - lence be - fore Him. A-men.

WORDS: Habakkuk 2:20
MUSIC: George F. Root, 1820-1895

QUAM DILECTA
Irregular meter

Jesus, Stand Among Us 562

The same day at evening . . . came Jesus and stood in the midst. John 20:19

1. Je - sus, stand a - mong us In Thy ris - en power;
2. Breathe the Ho - ly Spir - it In - to ev - ery heart;
Let this time of wor - ship Be a hal - lowed hour.
Bid the fears and sor - rows From each soul de - part. A-men.

WORDS: William Pennefather, 1873
MUSIC: Friedrich Filitz, 1847

BEMERTON
6.5.6.5

Now to the King of Heaven 563

Now unto the King eternal . . . be honor and glory forever . . . I Tim. 1:17

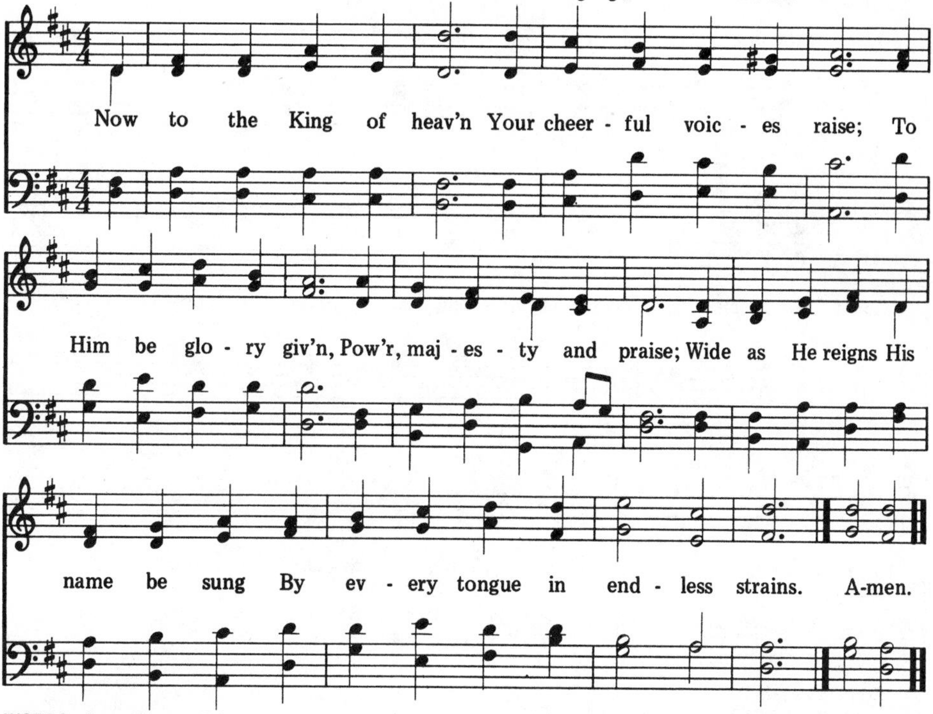

Now to the King of heav'n Your cheer - ful voic - es raise; To
Him be glo - ry giv'n, Pow'r, maj - es - ty and praise; Wide as He reigns His
name be sung By ev - ery tongue in end - less strains. A-men.

WORDS: Isaac Watts, 1719, and Philip Doddridge, 1755
MUSIC: *The Parish Choir,* 1851

ST. JOHN
6.6.6.6.8.8

564 Christ, We Do All Adore Thee

Thou art worthy, O Lord, to receive glory and honor, and power . . . Rev. 4:11

Christ, we do all a - dore Thee, and we do praise Thee for - ev - er;
Christ, we do all a - dore Thee, and we do praise Thee for - ev - er,
For on the ho - ly cross hast Thou the world from sin re - deem - ed.
Christ, we do all a - dore Thee, and we do praise Thee for - ev - er.
(Organ ad lib.)
Christ, we do all a - dore Thee!

WORDS: *Adoramus Te;*
English version, Theodore Baker, 1899
MUSIC: Théodore Dubois, 1867

ADORE THEE
Irregular meter

We Give Thee but Thine Own 565

For all things come of Thee . . . I Chron. 29:14

We give Thee but Thine own, What-e'er the gift may be: All
that we have is Thine a-lone, A trust, O Lord, from Thee. A-men.

WORDS: William W. How, 1858
MUSIC: Mason and Webb's *Cantica Laudis*, 1850

SCHUMANN
S.M.

All Things Come of Thee, O Lord 566

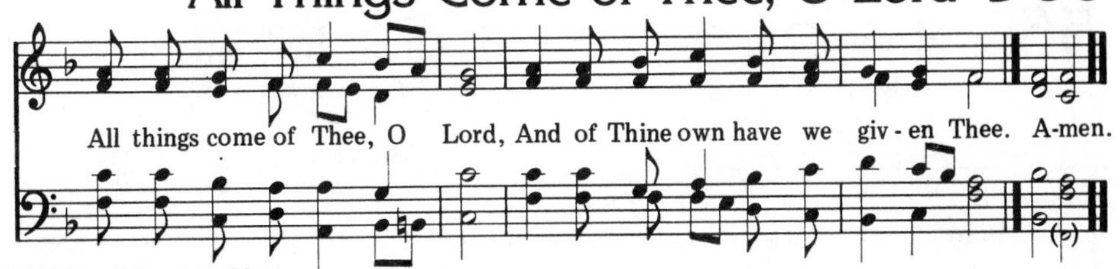
All things come of Thee, O Lord, And of Thine own have we giv-en Thee. A-men.

WORDS: I Chronicles 29:14
MUSIC: John F. Wilson, 1967

All Things Are Thine 567

All things are Thine: no gift have we, Lord of all gifts, to of-fer Thee,
And hence with grate-ful hearts to-day, Thine own be-fore Thy feet we lay.

WORDS: John G. Whittier, 1872
MUSIC: *Pensum Sacrum*, Gorlitz, 1648

HERR JESU CHRIST
L.M.

568 Let the Words of My Mouth

For by thy words thou shalt be justified. Matt. 12:37

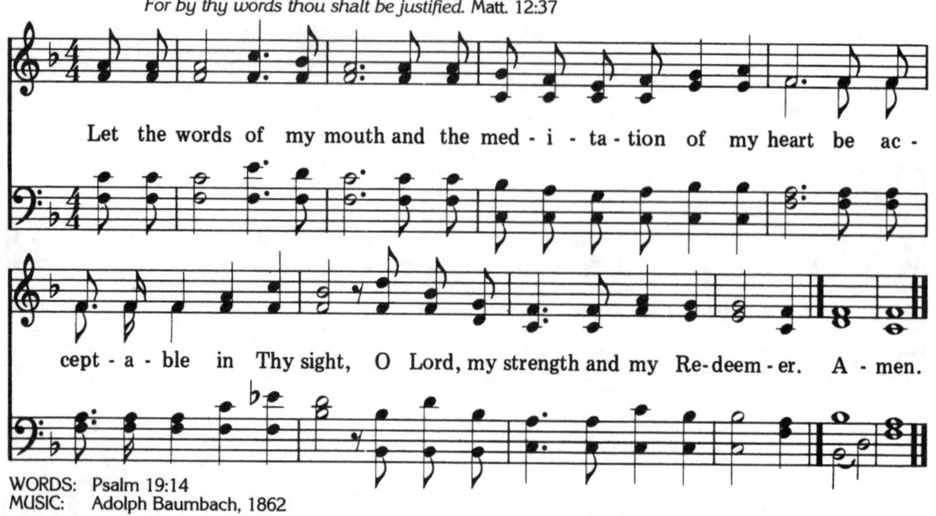
Let the words of my mouth and the med - i - ta - tion of my heart be ac -
cept - a - ble in Thy sight, O Lord, my strength and my Re-deem - er. A - men.

WORDS: Psalm 19:14
MUSIC: Adolph Baumbach, 1862

569 Hear Our Prayer, O Heavenly Father

Whatsoever ye shall ask the Father in My name, He will give it you. John 16:23

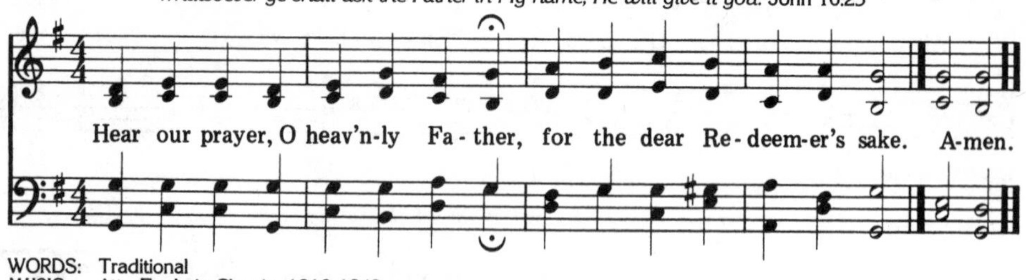
Hear our prayer, O heav'n-ly Fa - ther, for the dear Re-deem-er's sake. A-men.

WORDS: Traditional
MUSIC: Attr. Frederic Chopin, 1810-1849

570 Hear Our Prayer, O Lord

The Lord . . . heareth the prayer of the righteous. Prov. 15:29

Hear our prayer, O Lord, Hear our prayer, O Lord;
In - cline Thine ear to us, And grant us Thy peace. A - men.

WORDS: Psalm 143:1
MUSIC: George Whelpton, 1897

Amens 571

DRESDEN
A - men, A - men.
THREEFOLD
Danish
A - men, A - men, A - men.
THREEFOLD
Traditional
A - men, A - men, A - men.
FOURFOLD
John Stainer, c. 1870
A - men, A - men, A - men, A - men.
SEVENFOLD
John Stainer, 1873
A - men, A - men,
A - men, A - men, A - men, A - men, A -
A - men, A - men,
A - men,
- men, A - men, A - men.
A - men,

572 The Lord Bless You and Keep You

The Lord bless you and keep you. Num. 6:24

The Lord bless you and keep you; The Lord lift His coun-te-nance up-
on you, and give you peace, and give you peace;
and give you peace, and give you peace;
The Lord make His face to shine up - on you,
The Lord make His face to shine up - on you,
the Lord
and be gra - cious un-to you, be gra - cious,
and be gra-cious, and be gra - cious,
1 (optional ending)
The Lord be gra-cious, gra-cious un - to you. A - men.

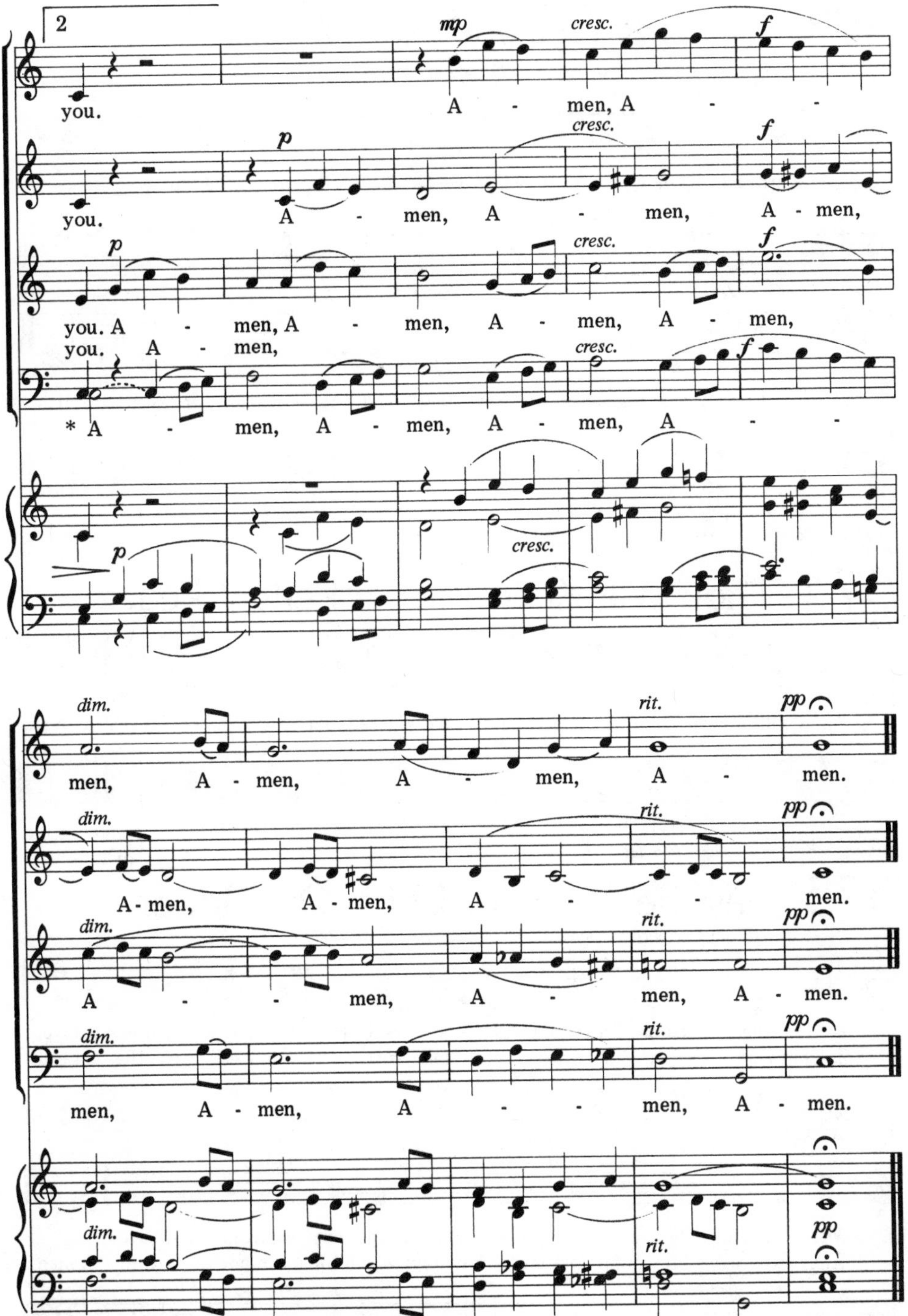

2

you. A - men, A - -

you. A - men, A - men, A - men,

you. A - men, A - men, A - men, A - men,

you. A - men,

* A - men, A - men, A - men, A - -

men, A - men, A - men, A - men.

A - men, A - men, A - - men.

A - - men, A - men, A - men.

men, A - men, A - - men, A - men.

*The Amens may be used separately.

WORDS: From Numbers 6:24-26
MUSIC: Peter C. Lutkin, 1900

BENEDICTION
Irregular meter

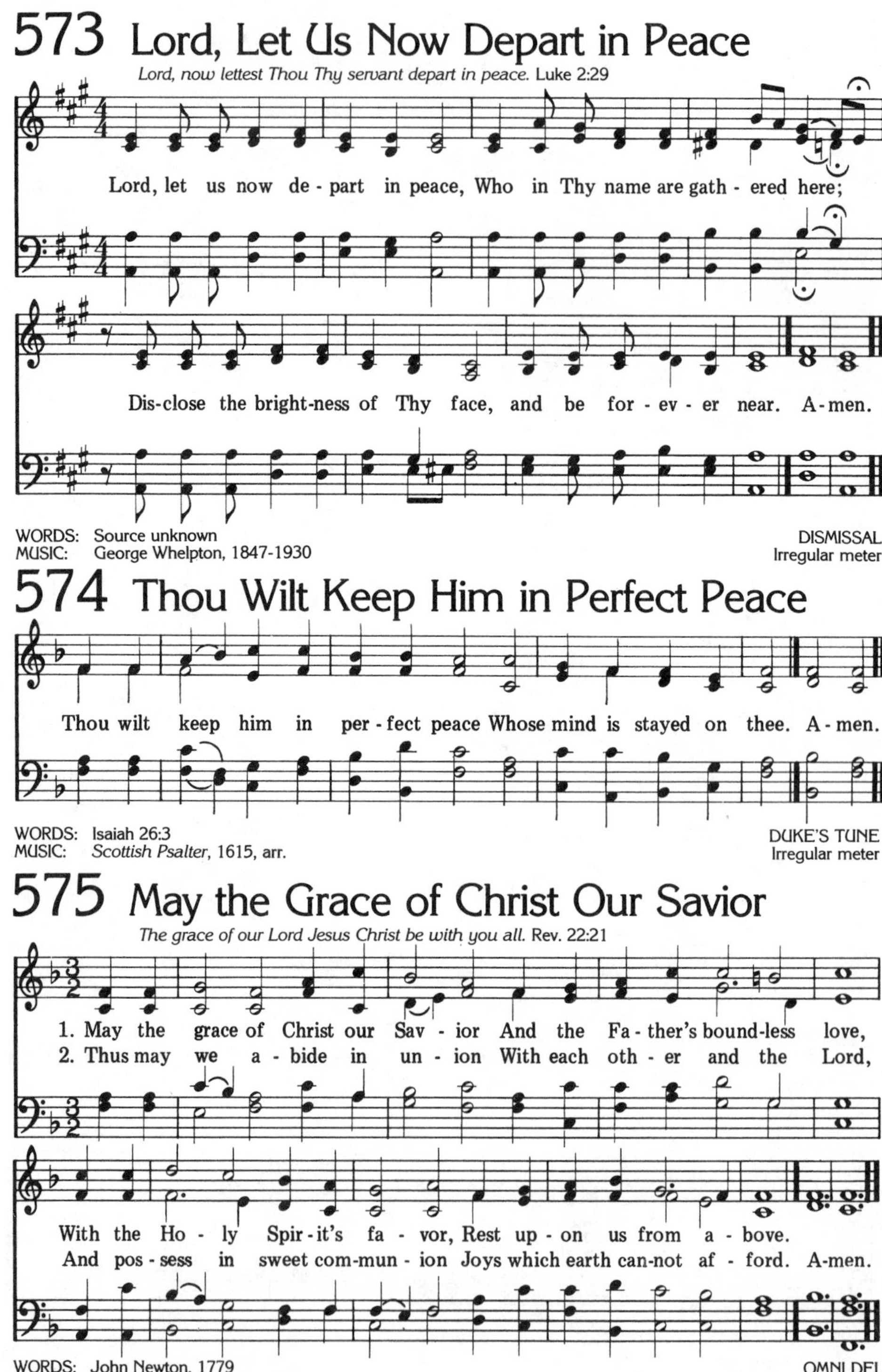
573 Lord, Let Us Now Depart in Peace
Lord, now lettest Thou Thy servant depart in peace. Luke 2:29
Lord, let us now de - part in peace, Who in Thy name are gath - ered here;
Dis-close the bright-ness of Thy face, and be for - ev - er near. A-men.
WORDS: Source unknown
MUSIC: George Whelpton, 1847-1930
DISMISSAL
Irregular meter
574 Thou Wilt Keep Him in Perfect Peace
Thou wilt keep him in per - fect peace Whose mind is stayed on thee. A - men.
WORDS: Isaiah 26:3
MUSIC: Scottish Psalter, 1615, arr.
DUKE'S TUNE
Irregular meter
575 May the Grace of Christ Our Savior
The grace of our Lord Jesus Christ be with you all. Rev. 22:21
1. May the grace of Christ our Sav - ior And the Fa - ther's bound-less love,
2. Thus may we a - bide in un - ion With each oth - er and the Lord,
With the Ho - ly Spir - it's fa - vor, Rest up - on us from a - bove.
And pos - sess in sweet com-mun - ion Joys which earth can-not af - ford. A-men.
WORDS: John Newton, 1779
MUSIC: Corner's Gesangbuch, 1631
OMNI DEI
8.7.8.7

SCRIPTURE READINGS (Translations)

Indexes to the Scripture Readings will be found on pages 574 through 580.

576 GOD, THE CREATOR

In the beginning God created the heavens and the earth.

The earth was without form and void, and darkness was upon the face of the deep; and the Spirit of God was moving over the face of the waters.

And God said, "Let there be light"; and there was light. And God saw that the light was good; and God separated the light from the darkness.

God called the light Day, and the darkness he called Night. And there was evening and there was morning, one day.

Then God said, "Let us make man in our image, after our likeness."

So God created man in his own image, in the image of God he created him; male and female he created them.

And God blessed them, and God said to them, "Be fruitful and multiply, and fill the earth and subdue it; and have dominion over the fish of the sea and over the birds of the air and over every living thing that moves upon the earth."

And God saw everything that he had made, and behold, it was very good. And there was evening and there was morning, a sixth day.

Thus the heavens and the earth were finished, and all the host of them.

And on the seventh day God finished his work which he had done, and he rested on the seventh day from all his work which he had done.

Let all the earth fear the Lord, let all the inhabitants of the world stand in awe of him!

For he spoke, and it came to be; he commanded, and it stood forth.

From Genesis 1 and 2, Psalm 33

577 GOD AND THE FAMILY

So God created man in his own image, in the image of God he created him; male and female he created them.

And God blessed them, and God said to them, "Be fruitful and multiply, and fill the earth and subdue it: and have dominion over every living thing that moves upon the earth."

And you shall love the Lord your God with all your heart, and with all your soul, and with all your might.

And these words which I command you this day shall be upon your heart; and you shall teach them diligently to your children, and you shall talk of them when you sit in your house, and when you walk by the way, and when you lie down, and when you rise.

Be subject to one another out of reverence for Christ. Wives, be subject to your husbands, as to the Lord. For the husband is the head of the wife as Christ is the head of the church, his body, and is himself its Savior.

Husbands, love your wives, as Christ loved the church and gave himself up for her, that he might sanctify her, having cleansed her by the washing of water with the word.

Children, obey your parents in the Lord, for this is right.

"Honor your father and mother" (this is the first commandment with a promise), "that it may be well with you and that you may live long on the earth."

Fathers, do not provoke your children to anger, but bring them up in the discipline and instruction of the Lord.

Finally, be strong in the Lord and in the strength of his might.

From Genesis 1, Deuteronomy 6, Ephesians 5 and 6

578 GOD'S COMMANDMENTS

And God spake all these words, saying, I am the Lord thy God, which have brought thee out of the land of Egypt, out of the house of bondage. Thou shalt have no other gods before me.

Thou shalt not make unto thee any graven image, or any likeness of any thing that is in heaven above, or that is in the earth beneath, or that is in the water under the earth: Thou shalt not bow down thyself to them, nor serve them:

Thou shalt not take the name of the Lord thy God in vain; for the Lord will not hold him guiltless that taketh his name in vain.

Remember the sabbath day to keep it holy. Six days shalt thou labour and do all thy work: But the seventh day is the sabbath of the Lord thy God:

Honour thy father and thy mother: that thy days may be long upon the land which the Lord thy God giveth thee.

Thou shalt not kill.

Thou shalt not commit adultery.

Thou shalt not steal.

Thou shalt not bear false witness against thy neighbour.

Thou shalt not covet thy neighbour's house, nor any thing that is thy neighbour's.

Then one of them, which was a lawyer, asked him a question, tempting him, and saying, Master, which is the great commandment in the law?

Jesus said unto him, Thou shalt love the Lord thy God with all thy heart, and with all thy soul, and with all thy mind. This is the first and great commandment.

And the second is like unto it, Thou shalt love thy neighbour as thyself.

On these two commandments hang all the law and the prophets.

From Exodus 20 and Matthew 22

579 GOD AND THE NATION

Righteousness exalts a nation, but sin is a reproach to any people.

So you shall keep the commandments of the Lord your God, by walking in his ways and by fearing him.

For the Lord your God is bringing you into a good land, a land of brooks of water, of fountains and springs, flowing forth in valleys and hills,

A land of wheat and barley, of vines and fig trees and pomegranates, a land of olive trees and honey,

A land in which you will eat bread without scarcity, in which you will lack nothing, a land whose stones are iron, and out of whose hills you can dig copper.

And you shall eat and be full, and you shall bless the Lord your God for the good land he has given you.

"Take heed lest you forget the Lord your God, by not keeping his commandments and his ordinances and his statutes, which I command you this day.

"Lest when you have eaten and are full, and have built goodly houses and live in them, . . . and all that you have is multiplied, then your heart be lifted up and you forget the Lord your God.

"Beware lest you say in your heart, 'My power and the might of my hand have gotten me this wealth.'

"You shall remember the Lord your God, for it is he who gives you power to get wealth:

"And if you forget the Lord your God and go after other gods and serve them and worship them, I solemnly warn you this day that you shall surely perish.

"Like the nations that the Lord makes to perish before you, so shall you perish, because you would not obey the voice of the Lord your God."

From Proverbs 14 and Deuteronomy 8

580 THE BLESSED LIFE

Blessed is the man that walketh not in the counsel of the ungodly, nor standeth in the way of sinners, nor sitteth in the seat of the scornful.

But his delight is in the law of the Lord: and in his law doth he meditate day and night.

And he shall be like a tree planted by the rivers of water, that bringeth forth his fruit in his season; his leaf also shall not wither; and whatsoever he doeth shall prosper.

The ungodly are not so: but are like the chaff which the wind driveth away.

Therefore the ungodly shall not stand in the judgment, nor sinners in the congregation of the righteous.

For the Lord knoweth the way of the righteous; but the way of the ungodly shall perish.

Psalm 1

* * *

Happy is the man who refuses the advice of evil men, who does not follow the example of sinners, or join those who make fun of God.

Instead, he enjoys reading the law of the Lord, and studying it day and night.

He is like a tree that grows beside a stream; it gives fruit at the right time, and its leaves do not dry up. He succeeds in everything he does.

But evil men are not like this at all; they are like straw that the wind blows away.

Evil men will be condemned by God; sinners will be kept apart from the righteous.

The Lord cares for the righteous man, but the evil man will be lost forever.

Psalm 1

581 GOD'S ATTRIBUTES

The heavens are telling the glory of God; and the firmament proclaims his handiwork.

Day to day pours forth speech, and night to night declares knowledge.

There is no speech, nor are there words; their voice is not heard;

Yet their voice goes out through all the earth, and their words to the end of the world.

The law of the Lord is perfect, reviving the soul;

The testimony of the Lord is sure, making wise the simple;

The precepts of the Lord are right, rejoicing the heart;

The commandment of the Lord is pure, enlightening the eyes;

The fear of the Lord is clean, enduring for ever;

The ordinances of the Lord are true, and righteous altogether.

More to be desired are they than gold, even much fine gold; sweeter also than honey and drippings of the honeycomb.

Moreover by them is thy servant warned; in keeping them there is great reward.

But who can discern his errors? Clear thou me from hidden faults.

Keep back thy servant also from presumptuous sins; let them not have dominion over me!

Then I shall be blameless, and innocent of great transgression.

Let the words of my mouth and the meditation of my heart be acceptable in thy sight, O Lord, my rock and my redeemer.

From Psalm 19

582 THE SHEPHERD PSALM

The Lord is my shepherd; I shall not want.

He maketh me to lie down in green pastures: he leadeth me beside the still waters.

He restoreth my soul: he leadeth me in the paths of righteousness for his name's sake.

Yea, though I walk through the valley of the shadow of death, I will fear no evil: for thou art with me; thy rod and thy staff they comfort me.

Thou preparest a table before me in the presence of mine enemies; thou anointest my head with oil; my cup runneth over.

Surely goodness and mercy shall follow me all the days of my life: and I will dwell in the house of the Lord for ever.

Psalm 23

* * *

The Lord is my shepherd; I have everything I need.

He lets me rest in fields of green grass and leads me to quiet pools of fresh water.

He gives me new strength. He guides me in the right way, as he has promised.

Even if that way goes through deepest darkness, I will not be afraid, Lord, because you are with me! Your shepherd's rod and staff keep me safe.

You prepare a banquet for me, where all my enemies can see me; you welcome me by pouring ointment on my head and filling my cup to the brim.

Certainly your goodness and love will be with me as long as I live; and your house will be my home forever.

Psalm 23

583 THE MAJESTY OF GOD

The earth is the Lord's and the fulness thereof, the world and those who dwell therein;

For he has founded it upon the seas, and established it upon the rivers.

Who shall ascend the hill of the Lord? And who shall stand in his holy place?

He who has clean hands and a pure heart, who does not lift up his soul to what is false, and does not swear deceitfully.

He will receive blessing from the Lord, and vindication from the God of his salvation.

Such is the generation of those who seek him, who seek the face of the God of Jacob.

Lift up your heads, O gates! and be lifted up, O ancient doors! that the King of glory may come in.

Who is the King of glory?

The Lord, strong and mighty, the Lord, mighty in battle!

Lift up your heads, O gates! and be lifted up, O ancient doors! that the King of glory may come in.

Who is this King of glory?

The Lord of hosts, he is the King of glory!

The Lord reigns; let the earth rejoice; let the many coastlands be glad!

His lightnings lighten the world; the earth sees and trembles.

The mountains melt like wax before the Lord, before the Lord of all the earth.

The heavens proclaim his righteousness; and all the peoples behold his glory.

From Psalm 24 and 97

584 CHRISTIAN STEWARDSHIP

The earth is the Lord's, and the fulness thereof; the world, and they that dwell therein.

The silver is mine, and the gold is mine, saith the Lord of hosts.

For every beast of the forest is mine, and the cattle upon a thousand hills.

And all the tithe of the land, whether of the seed of the land, or of the fruit of the tree, is the Lord's: it is holy unto the Lord.

Honour the Lord with thy substance, and with the firstfruits of all thine increase:

So shall thy barns be filled with plenty, and thy presses shall burst out with new wine.

Bring ye all the tithes into the storehouse... and prove me now herewith, saith the Lord of hosts, if I will not open you the windows of heaven, and pour you out a blessing, that there shall not be room enough to receive it.

Render therefore unto Caesar the things which are Caesar's; and unto God the things that are God's.

But this I say, He which soweth sparingly shall reap also sparingly; and he which soweth bountifully shall reap also bountifully.

Every man according as he purposeth in his heart, so let him give; not grudgingly, or of necessity: for God loveth a cheerful giver.

And God is able to make all grace abound toward you; that ye, always having all sufficiency in all things, may abound to every good work:

As every man hath received the gift, even so minister the same one to another, as good stewards of the manifold grace of God.

From Psalm 24 and 50, Haggai 2, Leviticus 27, Proverbs 3, Malachi 3, Matthew 22, 2 Corinthians 9, 1 Peter 4

585 FAITH AND CONFIDENCE

The Lord is my light and my salvation; whom shall I fear? The Lord is the stronghold of my life; of whom shall I be afraid?

When evildoers assail me, uttering slanders against me, my adversaries and foes, they shall stumble and fall.

Though a host encamp against me, my heart shall not fear; though war arise against me, yet I will be confident.

One thing have I asked of the Lord, that will I seek after; that I may dwell in the house of the Lord all the days of my life, to behold the beauty of the Lord, and to inquire in his temple.

For he will hide me in his shelter in the day of trouble; he will conceal me under the cover of his tent, he will set me high upon a rock.

And now my head shall be lifted up above my enemies round about me; and I will offer in his tent sacrifices with shouts of joy; I will sing and make melody to the Lord.

Hear, O Lord, when I cry aloud, be gracious to me and answer me!

Thou hast said, "Seek ye my face." My heart says to thee, "Thy face, Lord, do I seek." Hide not thy face from me.

Turn not thy servant away in anger, thou who hast been my help. Cast me not off, forsake me not, O God of my salvation!

Teach me thy way, O Lord: and lead me on a level path because of my enemies.

I believe that I shall see the goodness of the Lord in the land of the living!

Wait for the Lord; be strong, and let your heart take courage; yea, wait for the Lord!

From Psalm 27

586 DIVINE DELIVERANCE

Rejoice in the Lord, O you righteous! Praise befits the upright.

For the word of the Lord is upright; and all his work is done in faithfulness.

He loves righteousness and justice; the earth is full of the steadfast love of the Lord.

Let all the earth fear the Lord, let all the inhabitants of the world stand in awe of him!

The Lord brings the counsel of the nations to nought; he frustrates the plans of the peoples.

The counsel of the Lord stands for ever, the thoughts of his heart to all generations.

Blessed is the nation whose God is the Lord, the people whom he has chosen as his heritage!

The Lord looks down from heaven, he sees all the sons of men.

From where he sits enthroned he looks forth on all the inhabitants of the earth,

He who fashions the hearts of them all, and observes all their deeds.

A king is not saved by his great army; a warrior is not delivered by his great strength.

The war horse is a vain hope for victory, and by its great might it cannot save.

Behold the eye of the Lord is on those who fear him, on those who hope in his steadfast love,

That he may deliver their soul from death, and keep them alive in famine.

Our soul waits for the Lord; he is our help and shield.

Yea, our heart is glad in him, because we trust in his holy name.

From Psalm 33

587 DIVINE PROVIDENCE

I will bless the Lord at all times; his praise shall continually be in my mouth.

My soul makes its boast in the Lord; let the afflicted hear and be glad.

O magnify the Lord with me, and let us exalt his name together.

I sought the Lord, and he answered me, and delivered me from all my fears.

The angel of the Lord encamps around those who fear him, and delivers them.

O taste and see that the Lord is good! Happy is the man who takes refuge in him!

O fear the Lord, you his saints, for those who fear him have no want!

The young lions suffer want and hunger, but those who seek the Lord lack no good thing.

The eyes of the Lord are toward the righteous, and his ears toward their cry.

The face of the Lord is against evildoers, to cut off the remembrance of them from the earth.

When the righteous cry for help, the Lord hears, and delivers them out of all their troubles.

The Lord is near to the brokenhearted, and saves the crushed in spirit.

Many are the afflictions of the righteous; but the Lord delivers him out of them all.

The Lord redeems the life of his servants; none of those who take refuge in him will be condemned.

From Psalm 34

588 PATIENCE AND TRUST

Don't be worried on account of the wicked; don't be jealous of those who do wrong;

They will disappear like grass that dries up; they will die like plants that wither.

Trust in the Lord and do good; live in the land and be safe.

Seek your happiness with the Lord, and he will give you what you most desire.

Give yourself to the Lord; trust in him, and he will help you;

He will cause your goodness to shine as the light and your righteousness as the noonday sun.

Be calm before the Lord, and wait patiently for him to act;

Don't be worried about those who prosper or those who succeed in their evil plans.

The Lord guides a man safely in the way he should go and is pleased with his conduct.

If he falls, he will not stay down, because the Lord will help him up.

I am old now and no longer a boy, but I have never seen a good man abandoned by the Lord, or his children begging for food.

At all times he gives freely and lends to others, and his children are a blessing.

The good man's words are wise, and he speaks of what is right.

He keeps the law of his God in his heart and never departs from it.

Put your hope in the Lord and obey his commandments;

He will give you the strength to possess the land, and you will see the wicked driven out.

From Psalm 37

589 PRAYER OF PENITENCE

Be merciful to me, God, because of your constant love,

Wipe away my sins, because of your great mercy!

Wash away my evil, and make me clean from my sin!

I recognize my faults; I am always conscious of my sins.

I have sinned against you—only against you, and done what you consider evil.

So you are right in judging me; you are justified in condemning me.

I have been evil from the time I was born; from the day of my birth I have been sinful.

A faithful heart is what you want; fill my mind with your wisdom.

Remove my sin, and I will be clean; wash me, and I will be whiter than snow.

Let me hear the sounds of joy and gladness; and though you have crushed and broken me, I will be happy once again.

Create a pure heart in me, God, and put a new and loyal spirit in me.

Do not banish me from your presence; do not take your holy spirit away from me.

Give me again the joy that comes from your salvation, and make my spirit obedient.

Then I will teach sinners your commands, and they will turn back to you.

You do not want sacrifices, or I would offer them; you are not pleased with burnt offerings.

My sacrifice is a submissive spirit, God; a submissive and obedient heart you will not reject.

From Psalm 51

590 BLESSINGS FROM GOD

Bless the Lord, O my soul; and all that is within me, bless his holy name!

Bless the Lord, O my soul, and forget not all his benefits,

Who forgives all your iniquity, who heals all your diseases,

Who redeems your life from the Pit, who crowns you with steadfast love and mercy,

Who satisfies you with good as long as you live so that your youth is renewed like the eagle's.

The Lord works vindication and justice for all who are oppressed.

He made known his ways to Moses, his acts to the people of Israel.

The Lord is merciful and gracious, slow to anger and abounding in steadfast love. He will not always chide, nor will he keep his anger for ever.

He does not deal with us according to our sins, nor requite us according to our iniquities.

For as the heavens are high above the earth, so great is his steadfast love toward those who fear him;

As far as the east is from the west, so far does he remove our transgressions from us.

As a father pities his children, so the Lord pities those who fear him. For he knows our frame; he remembers that we are dust.

As for man, his days are like grass; he flourishes like a flower of the field; for the wind passes over it; and it is gone, and its place knows it no more.

But the steadfast love of the Lord is from everlasting to everlasting upon those who fear him, and his righteousness to children's children.

From Psalm 103

591 CREATOR AND SUSTAINER

Praise the Lord, my soul! Lord, my God, how great you are!

You are clothed with majesty and glory; you cover yourself with light.

You stretched out the heavens like a tent, and built your home on the waters above. You use the clouds as your chariot, and walk on the wings of the wind.

You use the winds as your messengers, and flashes of lightning as your servants. You have set the earth firmly on its foundations, and it will never be moved.

You make springs flow in the valleys, and water run between the hills.

They provide water for the wild animals; the wild donkeys quench their thirst; in the trees near by the birds make their nests and sing.

From heaven you send rain on the mountains, and the earth is filled with your blessings.

You make grass grow for the cattle, and plants for man to use, so he can grow his crops, and produce wine to make him happy, olive oil to make him cheerful, and bread to give him strength.

Lord, you have made so many things! How wisely you made them all! The earth is filled with your creatures.

All of them depend on you to give them food when they need it. You give it to them, and they eat it; you provide food, and they are satisfied.

May the glory of the Lord last forever! May the Lord be happy with what he made!

I will sing to the Lord all my life; I will sing praises to my God as long as I live. Praise the Lord, my soul! Praise the Lord!

From Psalm 104

592 GOD'S OMNISCIENCE

Lord, you have examined me, and you know me.

You know everything I do; from far away you understand all my thoughts.

You see me, whether I am working or resting; you know all my actions.

Even before I speak you already know what I will say.

You are all around me, on every side; you protect me with your power.

Your knowledge of me is overwhelming; it is too deep for me to understand.

Where could I go to escape from your spirit? Where could I get away from your presence?

If I went up to heaven, you would be there; if I lay down in the world of the dead, you would be there.

If I flew away beyond the east, or lived in the farthest place in the west, you would be there to lead me, you would be there to help me.

I could ask the darkness to hide me, or the light around me to turn into night, but even the darkness is not dark for you, and the night is as bright as the day.

You created every part of me; you put me together in my mother's womb.

I praise you because you are to be feared; all you do is strange and wonderful. I know it with all my heart.

You saw me before I was born. The days that had been created for me had all been recorded in your book, before any of them had ever begun.

Examine me, God, and know my mind; test me, and discover my thoughts. Find out if there is any deceit in me, and guide me in the eternal way. From Psalm 139

593 WORDS OF WISDOM

The blessing of the Lord, it maketh rich, and he addeth no sorrow with it.

The liberal soul shall be made fat: and he that watereth shall be watered also himself.

There is a way which seemeth right unto a man, but the end thereof are the ways of death.

In the fear of the Lord is strong confidence: and his children shall have a place of refuge.

A soft answer turneth away wrath: but grievous words stir up anger.

A man's heart deviseth his way; but the Lord directeth his steps.

A merry heart doeth good like a medicine: but a broken spirit drieth the bones.

A man that hath friends must shew himself friendly: and there is a friend that sticketh closer than a brother.

He that hath pity upon the poor lendeth unto the Lord: and that which he hath given will he pay him again.

Wine is a mocker, strong drink is raging: and whosoever is deceived thereby is not wise.

A good name is rather to be chosen than great riches, and loving favour rather than silver and gold.

Train up a child in the way he should go: and when he is old, he will not depart from it.

He that covereth his sins shall not prosper: But whoso confesseth and forsaketh them shall have mercy.

The fear of man bringeth a snare: but whoso putteth his trust in the Lord shall be safe. From Proverbs

594 CHRIST IN PROPHECY

There shall come forth a shoot from the stump of Jesse, and a branch shall grow out of his roots,

And the Spirit of the Lord shall rest upon him, the spirit of wisdom and understanding, the spirit of counsel and might, the spirit of knowledge and the fear of the Lord.

And his delight shall be in the fear of the Lord. He shall not judge by what his eyes see, or decide by what his ears hear;

But with righteousness he shall judge the poor, and decide with equity for the meek of the earth;

And he shall smite the earth with the rod of his mouth, and with the breath of his lips he shall slay the wicked.

Righteousness shall be the girdle of his waist, and faithfulness the girdle of his loins.

Behold my servant, whom I uphold, my chosen, in whom my soul delights; I have put my Spirit upon him, he will bring forth justice to the nations.

He will not fail or be discouraged till he has established justice in the earth; and the coastlands wait for his law.

"Behold, the days are coming, says the Lord, when I will raise up for David a righteous Branch, and he shall reign as king and deal wisely, and shall execute justice and righteousness in the land.

"In his days Judah will be saved, and Israel will dwell securely. And this is the name by which he will be called: 'The Lord is our righteousness.'

"For behold, the day comes, burning like an oven, when all the arrogant and all evildoers will be stubble;...

"But for you who fear my name the sun of righteousness shall rise, with healing in its wings."

From Isaiah 11 and 42, Jeremiah 23, Malachi 4

595 COMFORT FROM GOD

Comfort, comfort my people, says your God.

Speak tenderly to Jerusalem, and cry to her that her warfare is ended, that her iniquity is pardoned, that she has received from the Lord's hand double for all her sins.

A voice cries: "In the wilderness prepare the way of the Lord, make straight in the desert a highway for our God.

"Every valley shall be lifted up, and every mountain and hill be made low;

"The uneven ground shall become level, and the rough places a plain.

"And the glory of the Lord shall be revealed, and all flesh shall see it together, for the mouth of the Lord has spoken."

Get you up to a high mountain, O Zion, herald of good tidings; lift up your voice with strength, O Jerusalem, herald of good tidings, lift it up, fear not;

Say to the cities of Judah, "Behold your God!" Behold, the Lord God comes with might, and his arm rules for him:

The Lord is the everlasting God, the Creator of the ends of the earth. He does not faint or grow weary, his understanding is unsearchable.

He gives power to the faint, and to him who has no might he increases strength.

Even youths shall faint and be weary, and young men shall fall exhausted; but they who wait for the Lord shall renew their strength.

They shall mount up with wings like eagles, they shall run and not be weary, they shall walk and not faint.

From Isaiah 40

596 THE LAMB OF GOD

Who has believed what we have heard? And to whom has the arm of the Lord been revealed?

For he grew up before him like a young plant, and like a root out of dry ground; he had no form or comeliness that we should look at him, and no beauty that we should desire him.

He was despised and rejected by men; a man of sorrows, and acquainted with grief; and as one from whom men hide their faces he was despised, and we esteemed him not.

Surely he has borne our griefs and carried our sorrows; yet we esteemed him stricken, smitten by God, and afflicted.

But he was wounded for our transgressions, he was bruised for our iniquities; upon him was the chastisement that made us whole, and with his stripes we are healed.

All we like sheep have gone astray; we have turned every one to his own way; and the Lord has laid on him the iniquity of us all.

He was oppressed, and he was afflicted, yet he opened not his mouth; like a lamb that is led to the slaughter, and like a sheep that before its shearers is dumb, so he opened not his mouth.

By oppression and judgment he was taken away; and as for his generation, who considered that he was cut off out of the land of the living, stricken for the transgression of my people?

Yet it was the will of the Lord to bruise him; he has put him to grief: ... Therefore I will divide him a portion with the great, and he shall divide the spoil with the strong;

Because he poured out his soul to death, and was numbered with the transgressors; yet he bore the sin of many, and made intercession for the transgressors.

From Isaiah 53

597 GOD'S INVITATION

"Ho, every one who thirsts, come to the waters; and he who has no money, come, buy and eat! Come, buy wine and milk without money and without price.

"Why do you spend your money for that which is not bread, and your labor for that which does not satisfy?

"Hearken diligently to me, and eat what is good, and delight yourself in fatness.

"Incline your ear, and come to me; hear, that your soul may live; and I will make with you an everlasting covenant.

"Seek the Lord while he may be found, call upon him while he is near;

"Let the wicked forsake his way, and the unrighteous man his thoughts: let him return to the Lord, that he may have mercy on him, and to our God, for he will abundantly pardon.

"For my thoughts are not your thoughts, neither are your ways my ways, says the Lord.

"For as the heavens are higher than the earth, so are my ways higher than your ways and my thoughts than your thoughts.

"For as the rain and the snow come down from heaven, and return not thither but water the earth, making it bring forth and sprout, giving seed to the sower and bread to the eater,

"So shall my word be that goes forth from my mouth: it shall not return to me empty, but it shall accomplish that which I purpose, and prosper in the thing for which I sent it.

"For you shall go out in joy, and be led forth in peace;

"The mountains and the hills before you shall break forth into singing, and all the trees of the field shall clap their hands."

From Isaiah 55

598 PEACE AND RENEWAL

It shall come to pass in the latter days that the mountain of the house of the Lord shall be established as the highest of the mountains, and shall be raised up above the hills; and peoples shall flow to it,

And many nations shall come, and say: "Come, let us go up to the mountain of the Lord, to the house of the God of Jacob that he may teach us his ways and we may walk in his paths."

For out of Zion shall go forth the law, and the word of the Lord from Jerusalem.

He shall judge between many peoples, and shall decide for strong nations afar off;

For all the peoples walk each in the name of its god, but we will walk in the name of the Lord our God for ever and ever.

In that day, says the Lord, I will assemble the lame and gather those who have been driven away, and those whom I have afflicted;

And the lame I will make the remnant; and those who were cast off, a strong nation;

And the Lord will reign over them in Mount Zion from this time forth and for evermore.

Who is a God like thee, pardoning iniquity and passing over transgression for the remnant of his inheritance?

He does not retain his anger for ever because he delights in steadfast love.

And they shall beat their swords into plowshares, and their spears into pruning hooks; nation shall not lift up sword against nation, neither shall they learn war any more:

But they shall sit every man under his vine and under his fig tree, and none shall make them afraid; for the mouth of the Lord of hosts has spoken.

From Micah 4 and 7

599 ADORATION OF THE MAGI

Now when Jesus was born in Bethlehem of Judea in the days of Herod the king, behold, wise men from the East came to Jerusalem, saying,

"Where is he who has been born king of the Jews? For we have seen his star in the East, and have come to worship him."

When Herod the king heard this, he was troubled, and all Jerusalem with him;

And assembling all the chief priests and scribes of the people, he inquired of them where the Christ was to be born.

They told him, "In Bethlehem of Judea; for so it is written by the prophet:

"'And you, O Bethlehem, in the land of Judah, are by no means least among the rulers of Judah; for from you shall come a ruler who will govern my people Israel.'"

Then Herod summoned the wise men secretly and ascertained from them what time the star appeared;

And he sent them to Bethlehem, saying, "Go and search diligently for the child, and when you have found him bring me word, that I too may come and worship him."

When they had heard the king they went their way; and lo, the star which they had seen in the East went before them, till it came to rest over the place where the child was.

When they saw the star, they rejoiced exceedingly with great joy;

And going into the house they saw the child with Mary his mother, and they fell down and worshiped him.

Then, opening their treasures, they offered him gifts, gold and frankincense and myrrh.

From Matthew 2

600 CHRISTIAN BAPTISM

Then Jesus came from Galilee to the Jordan to John, to be baptized by him. John would have prevented him, saying, "I need to be baptized by you, and do you come to me?"

But Jesus answered him, "Let it be so now; for thus it is fitting for us to fulfill all righteousness." Then he consented.

And when Jesus was baptized, he went up immediately from the water, and behold, the heavens were opened and he saw the Spirit of God descending like a dove, and alighting on him;

And lo, a voice from heaven, saying, "This is my beloved Son, with whom I am well pleased."

And Jesus came and said to them, "All authority in heaven and on earth has been given to me. Go therefore and make disciples of all nations.

Baptizing them in the name of the Father and of the Son and of the Holy Spirit, teaching them to observe all that I have commanded you;

And Peter said to them, "Repent, and be baptized every one of you in the name of Jesus Christ for the forgiveness of your sins; and you shall receive the gift of the Holy Spirit.

"For the promise is to you and to your children and to all that are far off, every one whom the Lord our God calls to him."

So those who received his word were baptized, and there were added that day about three thousand souls. And they devoted themselves to the apostles' teaching and fellowship, to the breaking of bread and the prayers.

We were buried therefore with him by baptism into death, so that as Christ was raised from the dead by the glory of the Father, we too might walk in newness of life.

From Matthew 3 and 28, Acts 2, Romans 6

601 THE BEATITUDES

Seeing the crowds, he went up on the mountain, and when he sat down his disciples came to him. And he opened his mouth and taught them, saying: "Blessed are the poor in spirit, for theirs is the kingdom of heaven.

"Blessed are those who mourn, for they shall be comforted.

"Blessed are the meek, for they shall inherit the earth.

"Blessed are those who hunger and thirst for righteousness, for they shall be satisfied.

"Blessed are the merciful, for they shall obtain mercy.

"Blessed are the pure in heart, for they shall see God.

"Blessed are the peacemakers, for they shall be called sons of God.

"Blessed are those who are persecuted for righteousness' sake, for theirs is the kingdom of heaven.

"Blessed are you when men revile you and persecute you and utter all kinds of evil against you falsely on my account.

"Rejoice and be glad, for your reward is great in heaven, for so men persecuted the prophets who were before you.

"You are the salt of the earth; but if salt has lost its taste, how shall its saltness be restored? It is no longer good for anything except to be thrown out and trodden under foot by men.

"You are the light of the world. A city set on a hill cannot be hid.

"Nor do men light a lamp and put it under a bushel, but on a stand, and it gives light to all in the house.

"Let your light so shine before men, that they may see your good works and give glory to your Father who is in heaven."

From Matthew 5

602 HEAVENLY TREASURE

"Do not lay up for yourselves treasures on earth, where moth and rust consume and where thieves break in and steal,

"But lay up for yourselves treasures in heaven, where neither moth nor rust consumes and where thieves do not break in and steal. For where your treasure is, there will your heart be also.

"No one can serve two masters; for either he will hate the one and love the other, or he will be devoted to the one and despise the other. You cannot serve God and mammon.

"Therefore I tell you, do not be anxious about your life, what you shall eat or what you shall drink, nor about your body, what you shall put on. Is not life more than food, and the body more than clothing?

"Look at the birds of the air: they neither sow nor reap nor gather into barns, and yet your heavenly Father feeds them. Are you not of more value than they?

"And why are you anxious about clothing? Consider the lilies of the field, how they grow; they neither toil nor spin; yet I tell you, even Solomon in all his glory was not arrayed like one of these.

"But if God so clothes the grass of the field, which today is alive and tomorrow is thrown into the oven, will he not much more clothe you, O men of little faith?

"Therefore do not be anxious, saying, 'What shall we eat?' or 'What shall we drink?' or 'What shall we wear?'

"For the Gentiles seek all these things; and your heavenly Father knows that you need them all.

"But seek first his kingdom and his righteousness, and all these things shall be yours as well." From Matthew 6

603 THE WAITING HARVEST

And Jesus went about all the cities and villages, teaching in their synagogues and preaching the gospel of the kingdom, and healing every disease and every infirmity.

When he saw the crowds, he had compassion for them, because they were harassed and helpless, like sheep without a shepherd.

Then he said to his disciples, "The harvest is plentiful, but the laborers are few;

"Pray therefore the Lord of the harvest to send out laborers into his harvest."

For there is no distinction between Jew and Greek; the same Lord is Lord of all and bestows his riches upon all who call upon him.

For, "every one who calls upon the name of the Lord will be saved."

But how are men to call upon him in whom they have not believed? And how are they to believe in him of whom they have never heard?

And how are they to hear without a preacher? And how can men preach unless they are sent?

"Do you not say, 'There are yet four months, then comes the harvest?' I tell you, lift up your eyes, and see how the fields are already white for harvest.

"He who reaps receives wages, and gathers fruit for eternal life, so that sower and reaper may rejoice together."

May those who sow in tears reap with shouts of joy!

He that goes forth weeping, bearing the seed for sowing, shall come home with shouts of joy, bringing his sheaves with him.

From Matthew 9, Romans 10, John 4, and Psalm 126

604 THE CHURCH

Now when Jesus came into the district of Caesarea Philippi, he asked his disciples, "Who do men say that the Son of man is?"

And they said, "Some say John the Baptist, others say Elijah, and others Jeremiah or one of the prophets."

He said to them, "But who do you say that I am?"

Simon Peter replied, "You are the Christ, the Son of the living God."

And Jesus answered him, "Blessed are you, Simon Bar-Jona! For flesh and blood has not revealed this to you, but my Father who is in heaven.

"And I tell you, you are Peter, and on this rock I will build my church, and the powers of death shall not prevail against it."

Husbands, love your wives, as Christ loved the church and gave himself up for her, that he might sanctify her, having cleansed her by the washing of water with the word,

That the church might be presented before him in splendor, without spot or wrinkle or any such thing, that she might be holy and without blemish.

So then you are no longer strangers and sojourners, but you are fellow citizens with the saints and members of the household of God,

Built upon the foundation of the apostles and prophets, Christ Jesus himself being the cornerstone . . . .

Now you are the body of Christ and individually members of it.

He is the head of the body, the church; he is the beginning, the first-born from the dead, that in everything he might be preeminent.

From Matthew 16, Ephesians 5 and 2, 1 Corinthians 12, Colossians 1

605 CHRIST AND CHILDREN

At the same time came the disciples unto Jesus, saying, Who is the greatest in the kingdom of heaven?

And Jesus called a little child unto him, and set him in the midst of them, and said,

Verily I say unto you, Except ye be converted, and become as little children, ye shall not enter into the kingdom of heaven.

Whosoever therefore shall humble himself as this little child, the same is greatest in the kingdom of heaven.

And whoso shall receive one such little child in my name receiveth me.

But whoso shall offend one of these little ones which believe in me, it were better for him that a millstone were hanged about his neck, and that he were drowned in the depth of the sea.

Take heed that ye despise not one of these little ones; for I say unto you, that in heaven their angels do always behold the face of my Father which is in heaven.

Whosoever shall receive one of such children in my name, receiveth me: and whosoever shall receive me, receiveth not me, but him that sent me.

And they brought young children to him, that he should touch them: and his disciples rebuked those that brought them.

But when Jesus saw it, he was much displeased, and said unto them, Suffer the little children to come unto me, and forbid them not: for of such is the kingdom of God.

Verily I say unto you, Whosoever shall not receive the kingdom of God as a little child, he shall not enter therein.

And he took them up in his arms, put his hands upon them, and blessed them.

From Matthew 18, Mark 9 and 10

606 JUDGMENT AND REWARD

"When the Son of Man comes as King, and all the angels with him, he will sit on his royal throne, and all the earth's peoples will be gathered before him.

"Then he will divide them into two groups, just as a shepherd separates the sheep from the goats: he will put the sheep at his right and the goats at his left.

"Then the King will say to the people on his right: 'You who are blessed by my Father: come! Come and receive the kingdom which has been prepared for you ever since the creation of the world.

"'I was hungry and you fed me, thirsty and you gave me drink; I was a stranger and you received me in your homes, naked and you clothed me; I was sick and you took care of me, in prison and you visited me.'

"The righteous will then answer him: 'When, Lord, did we ever see you hungry and feed you, or thirsty and give you drink? When did we ever see you a stranger and welcome you in our homes, or naked and clothe you? When did we ever see you sick or in prison, and visit you?'

"The King will answer back, 'I tell you, indeed, whenever you did this for one of the least important of these brothers of mine, you did it for me!'

"Then he will say to those on his left: 'Away from me, you who are under God's curse! Away to the eternal fire which has been prepared for the Devil and his angels!

"'I was hungry but you would not feed me, thirsty but you would not give me drink;

"'I tell you, indeed, whenever you refused to help one of these least important ones, you refused to help me.'

"These, then, will be sent off to eternal punishment; the righteous will go to eternal life." From Matthew 25

607 THE RISEN LORD

After the Sabbath, as Sunday morning was dawning, Mary Magdalene and the other Mary went to look at the grave.

Suddenly there was a strong earthquake; an angel of the Lord came down from heaven, rolled the stone away, and sat on it.

His appearance was like lightning and his clothes were white as snow.

The guards were so afraid that they trembled and became like dead men.

The angel spoke to the women. "You must not be afraid," he said. "I know you are looking for Jesus, who was nailed to the cross.

"He is not here; he has risen, just as he said. Come here and see the place where he lay.

"Quickly, now, go and tell his disciples: 'He has been raised from death, and now he is going to Galilee ahead of you; there you will see him!' Remember what I have told you."

So they left the grave in a hurry, afraid and yet filled with joy, and ran to tell his disciples.

Suddenly Jesus met them and said, "Peace be with you." They came up to him, took hold of his feet, and worshiped him.

"Do not be afraid," Jesus said to them. "Go and tell my brothers to go to Galilee, and there they will see me."

It was late that Sunday evening, and the disciples were gathered together behind locked doors, because they were afraid of the Jews. Then Jesus came and stood among them. "Peace be with you," he said.

After saying this, he showed them his hands and his side. The disciples were filled with joy at seeing the Lord.

From Matthew 28 and John 20

608 THE GREAT COMMISSION

Now the eleven disciples went to Galilee, to the mountain to which Jesus had directed them.

And when they saw him they worshiped him; but some doubted.

And Jesus came and said to them, "All authority in heaven and earth has been given to me. Go therefore and make disciples of all nations, baptizing them in the name of the Father and of the Son and of the Holy Spirit,

"Teaching them to observe all that I have commanded you; and lo, I am with you always, to the close of the age."

Then he opened their minds to understand the scriptures, and said to them, "Thus it is written, that the Christ should suffer and on the third day rise from the dead, and that repentance and forgiveness of sins should be preached in his name to all nations, beginning from Jerusalem.

"You are witnesses of these things. And behold, I send the promise of my Father upon you; but stay in the city, until you are clothed with power from on high."

So when they had come together, they asked him, "Lord, will you at this time restore the kingdom to Israel?"

He said to them, "It is not for you to know times or seasons which the Father has fixed by his own authority.

"But you shall receive power when the Holy Spirit has come upon you; and you shall be my witnesses in Jerusalem and in all Judea and Samaria and to the end of the earth."

And they went forth and preached everywhere, the Lord working with them, and confirming the word with signs following. Amen.

From Matthew 28, Luke 24, Acts 1, and Mark 16

609 THE TRIUMPHAL ENTRY

They were now approaching Jerusalem, and when they reached Bethphage and Bethany, at the Mount of Olives, he sent two of his disciples with these instructions:

'Go to the village opposite, and, just as you enter, you will find tethered there a colt which no one has yet ridden. Untie it and bring it here.

'If anyone asks, "Why are you doing that?", say, "Our Master needs it, and will send it back here without delay."'

So they went off, and found the colt tethered at a door outside in the street.

They were untying it when some of the bystanders asked, 'What are you doing, untying that colt?'

They answered as Jesus had told them, and were then allowed to take it.

So they brought the colt to Jesus and spread their cloaks on it, and he mounted.

And people carpeted the road with their cloaks, while others spread brushwood which they had cut in the fields;

And those who went ahead and the others who came behind shouted, 'Hosanna! Blessings on him who comes in the name of the Lord!

'Blessings on the coming kingdom of our father David! Hosanna in the heavens!'

When he entered Jerusalem the whole city went wild with excitement. 'Who is this?' people asked,

And the crowd replied, 'This is the prophet Jesus, from Nazareth in Galilee.'

From Mark 11 and Matthew 21

610 THE LAST SUPPER

Now on the first day of Unleavened Bread, when the Passover lambs were being slaughtered, his disciples said to him, 'Where would you like us to go and prepare for your Passover supper?'

So he sent out two of his disciples with these instructions: 'Go into the city, and a man will meet you carrying a jar of water. Follow him, and when he enters a house give this message to the householder: "The Master says, 'Where is the room reserved for me to eat the Passover with my disciples?'"

'He will show you a large room upstairs, set out in readiness. Make the preparations for us there.

Then the disciples went off, and when they came into the city they found everything just as he had told them. So they prepared for Passover.

In the evening he came to the house with the Twelve. As they sat at supper Jesus said, 'I tell you this: one of you will betray me—one who is eating with me.

'The Son of Man is going the way appointed for him in the scriptures; but alas for that man by whom the Son of Man is betrayed! It would be better for that man if he had never been born.'

During supper he took bread, and having said the blessing he broke it and gave it to them, with the words: 'Take this; this is my body.

Then he took a cup, and having offered thanks to God he gave it to them; and they all drank from it.

And he said, 'This is my blood of the covenant, shed for many. I tell you this: never again shall I drink from the fruit of the vine until that day when I drink it new in the kingdom of God.

After singing the Passover Hymn, they went out to the Mount of Olives.

From Mark 14

611 THE SAVIOR'S ADVENT

In those days a decree went out from Caesar Augustus that all the world should be enrolled. And all went to be enrolled, each to his own city.

And Joseph also went up from Galilee, from the city of Nazareth, to Judea, to the city of David, which is called Bethlehem, . . . to be enrolled with Mary, his betrothed, who was with child.

And while they were there, the time came for her to be delivered.

And she gave birth to her first-born son and wrapped him in swaddling clothes, and laid him in a manger, because there was no place for them in the inn.

And in that region there were shepherds out in the field, keeping watch over their flock by night.

And an angel of the Lord appeared to them, and the glory of the Lord shone around them, and they were filled with fear.

And the angel said to them, "Be not afraid; for behold, I bring you good news of a great joy which will come to all the people;

"For to you is born this day in the city of David a Savior, who is Christ the Lord. And this will be a sign for you: you will find a babe wrapped in swaddling clothes and lying in a manger."

And suddenly there was with the angel a multitude of the heavenly host praising God and saying,

"Glory to God in the highest, and on earth peace among men with whom He is pleased!"

When the angels went away from them into heaven, the shepherds said to one another, "Let us go over to Bethlehem and see this thing that has happened, which the Lord has made known to us."

And they went with haste, and found Mary and Joseph, and the babe lying in a manger.

From Luke 2

612 THE CHILD JESUS

The child grew big and strong and full of wisdom; and God's favour was upon him.

Now it was the practice of his parents to go to Jerusalem every year for the Passover festival; and when he was twelve, they made the pilgrimage as usual.

When the festive season was over and they started for home, the boy Jesus stayed behind in Jerusalem.

His parents did not know of this; but thinking that he was with the party they journeyed on for a whole day, and only then did they begin looking for him among their friends and relations.

As they could not find him they returned to Jerusalem to look for him; and after three days they found him sitting in the temple surrounded by the teachers, listening to them and putting questions;

And all who heard him were amazed at his intelligence and the answers he gave.

His parents were astonished to see him there, and his mother said to him, 'My son, why have you treated us like this? Your father and I have been searching for you in great anxiety.'

'What made you search?' he said. 'Did you not know that I was bound to be in my Father's house?' But they did not understand what he meant.

Then he went back with them to Nazareth, and continued to be under their authority; his mother treasured up all these things in her heart.

As Jesus grew up he advanced in wisdom and in favour with God and men.

From Luke 2

613 THE GOOD SAMARITAN

Then a certain teacher of the Law came up and tried to trap Jesus. "Teacher," he asked, "what must I do to receive eternal life?"

Jesus answered him, "What do the Scriptures say? How do you interpret them?"

The man answered: "'You must love the Lord your God with all your heart, and with all your soul, and with all your strength, and with all your mind;' and, 'You must love your neighbor as yourself.'"

"Your answer is correct," replied Jesus; "do this and you will live."

But the teacher of the Law wanted to put himself in the right, so he asked Jesus, "Who is my neighbor?"

Jesus answered: "A certain man was going down from Jerusalem to Jericho, when robbers attacked him, stripped him and beat him up, leaving him half dead.

"It so happened that a priest was going down that road; when he saw the man he walked on by, on the other side.

"In the same way a Levite also came there, went over and looked at the man, and then walked on by, on the other side.

"But a certain Samaritan who was traveling that way came upon him, and when he saw the man his heart was filled with pity.

"He went over to him, poured oil and wine on his wounds and bandaged them; then he put the man on his own animal and took him to an inn, where he took care of him."

And Jesus concluded, "Which one of these three seems to you to have been a neighbor to the man attacked by the robbers?" The teacher of the Law answered, "The one who was kind to him."

Jesus replied, "You go, then, and do the same."

From Luke 10

614 CHRIST TEACHES PRAYER

One time Jesus was praying in a certain place. When he finished, one of his disciples said to him, "Lord, teach us to pray, just as John taught his disciples."

Jesus said to them, "This is what you should pray: 'Father, may your name be kept holy, may your Kingdom come. Give us day by day the food we need.

" 'Forgive us our sins, for we forgive everyone who has done us wrong. And do not bring us to hard testing.' "

And Jesus said to his disciples: "Suppose one of you should go to a friend's house at midnight and tell him, 'Friend, let me borrow three loaves of bread. A friend of mine who is on a trip has just come to my house and I don't have a thing to offer him!'

"And suppose your friend should answer from inside, 'Don't bother me! The door is already locked, my children and I are in bed, and I can't get up to give you anything.' Well, what then?

"I tell you, even if he will not get up and give you the bread because he is your friend, yet he will get up and give you everything you need because you are not ashamed to keep on asking.

"And so I say to you: Ask, and you will receive; seek, and you will find; knock, and the door will be opened to you.

"For everyone who asks will receive, and he who seeks will find, and the door will be opened to him who knocks.

"As bad as you are, you know how to give good things to your children. How much more, then, the Father in heaven will give the Holy Spirit to those who ask him!"

"Until now you have not asked for anything in my name; ask and you will receive, so that your happiness may be complete." From Luke 11 and John 16

615 THE INCARNATE CHRIST

In the beginning was the Word, and the Word was with God, and the Word was God.

The same was in the beginning with God.

All things were made by him; and without him was not any thing made that was made.

In him was life; and the life was the light of men.

There was a man sent from God, whose name was John.

The same came for a witness, to bear witness of the Light, that all men through him might believe.

He was not that Light, but was sent to bear witness of that Light.

That was the true Light, which lighteth every man that cometh into the world.

He was in the world, and the world was made by him, and the world knew him not.

He came unto his own, and his own received him not.

But as many as received him, to them gave he power to become the sons of God, even to them that believe on his name:

Which were born, not of blood, nor of the will of the flesh, nor of the will of man, but of God.

And the Word was made flesh, and dwelt among us, and we beheld his glory, the glory as of the only begotten of the Father, full of grace and truth.

No man hath seen God at any time; the only begotten Son, which is in the bosom of the Father, he hath declared him. From John 1

616 GOD'S REDEEMING LOVE

As Moses lifted up the serpent in the wilderness, even so must the Son of man be lifted up: That whosoever believeth in him should not perish, but have eternal life.

For God so loved the world, that he gave his only begotten Son, that whosoever believeth in him should not perish, but have everlasting life.

For God sent not his Son into the world to condemn the world; but that the world through him might be saved.

He that believeth on him is not condemned: but he that believeth not is condemned already, because he hath not believed in the name of the only begotten Son of God.

And this is the condemnation, that light is come into the world, and men loved darkness rather than light, because their deeds were evil.

For every one that doeth evil hateth the light, neither cometh to the light, lest his deeds should be reproved.

But he that doeth truth cometh to the light, that his deeds may be made manifest, that they are wrought in God.

He that believeth on the Son hath everlasting life: and he that believeth not the Son shall not see life; but the wrath of God abideth on him.

In this was manifested the love of God toward us, because that God sent his only begotten Son into the world, that we might live through him.

Herein is love, not that we loved God, but that he loved us, and sent his Son to be the propitiation for our sins.

Beloved, if God so loved us, we ought also to love one another.

We love him, because he first loved us.

From John 3 and 1 John 4

617 THE GOOD SHEPHERD

"Truly, truly, I say to you, he who does not enter the sheepfold by the door but climbs in by another way, that man is a thief and a robber;

"But he who enters by the door is the shepherd of the sheep.

"To him the gatekeeper opens; the sheep hear his voice, and he calls his own sheep by name and leads them out.

"When he has brought out all his own, he goes before them, and the sheep follow him, for they know his voice.

"I am the door; if any one enters by me, he will be saved, and will go in and out and find pasture.

"The thief comes only to steal and kill and destroy; I came that they might have life, and have it abundantly.

"I am the good shepherd. The good shepherd lays down his life for the sheep.

"He who is a hireling and not a shepherd, whose own the sheep are not, sees the wolf coming and leaves the sheep and flees; and the wolf snatches them and scatters them.

"He flees because he is a hireling and cares nothing for the sheep.

"I am the good shepherd; I know my own and my own know me,

"As the Father knows me and I know the Father;

"And I lay down my life for the sheep.

"And I have other sheep, that are not of this fold; I must bring them also, and they will heed my voice. So there shall be one flock, one shepherd.

"My sheep hear my voice, and I know them, and they follow me; and I give them eternal life, and they shall never perish, and no one shall snatch them out of my hand."

From John 10

618 CHRISTIAN UNITY

I am the good shepherd; I know my own and my own know me, as the Father knows me and I know the Father; and I lay down my life for the sheep.

And I have other sheep, that are not of this fold; I must bring them also, and they will heed my voice. So there shall be one flock, one shepherd.

When Jesus had spoken these words, he lifted up his eyes to heaven and said, "Father, the hour has come; glorify thy Son that the Son may glorify thee.

"I have manifested thy name to the men whom thou gavest me out of the world; thine they were, and thou gavest them to me, and they have kept thy word.

"And now I am no more in the world, but they are in the world, and I am coming to thee. Holy Father, keep them in thy name, which thou hast given me, that they may be one, even as we are one.

"That they may all be one; even as thou, Father, art in me, and I in thee, that they also may be in us, so that the world may believe that thou hast sent me."

For just as the body is one and has many members, and all the members of the body, though many, are one body, so it is with Christ.

For by one Spirit we were all baptized into one body—Jews or Greeks, slaves or free—and all were made to drink of one Spirit. For the body does not consist of one member but of many.

There is one body and one Spirit, just as you were called to the one hope that belongs to your call,

One Lord, one faith, one baptism, one God and Father of us all, who is above all and through all and in all.

From John 10 and 17, 1 Corinthians 12, Ephesians 4

619 COMFORT FROM CHRIST

"Let not your hearts be troubled; believe in God, believe also in Me.

"In My Father's house are many dwelling places. If this were not so, I would have told you. For I am going away to prepare a place for you.

"And when I have gone and have prepared a place for you, I will come again, and take you to Myself so that where I am, you also will be.

"And where I am going, you know the way."

Thomas remarked to Him, "Lord, we do not know where you are going. How do we know the way?"

Jesus said to him, "I am the Way and the Truth and the Life; no one comes to the Father except through Me.

"Had you recognized Me, you would have known My Father as well. From now on you do know Him; yes, you have seen Him."

Philip said to Him, "Lord, show us the Father and it is enough for us."

Jesus replied, "How long have I been with you without your knowing Me, Philip? He who has looked on Me has seen the Father. What do you mean by saying, 'Show us the Father'?

"Do you not believe that I am in the Father and the Father in Me? The words that I give to you all, I do not speak just from Myself; the Father, who dwells in Me carries on His works.

"Truly I assure you, the one who believes in Me will himself do the deeds I do and do greater things than these, for I go to the Father.

"And I will bring about whatever you ask in My name, so that the Father may be glorified in the Son.

"I will do whatever you may ask in My name, so that the Father may be glorified in the Son.

"If you love Me, keep My commands."

From John 14

620 THE HOLY SPIRIT PROMISED

"Truly, truly, I say to you, he who believes in me will also do the works that I do; and greater works than these will he do, because I go to the Father.

"Whatever you ask in my name, I will do it, that the Father may be glorified in the Son; if you ask anything in my name, I will do it.

"If you love me, you will keep my commandments. And I will pray the Father, and he will give you another Counselor, to be with you for ever,

"Even the Spirit of truth, whom the world cannot receive, because it neither sees him nor knows him; you know him, for he dwells with you, and will be in you."

"But because I have said these things to you, sorrow has filled your hearts. Nevertheless I tell you the truth: it is to your advantage that I go away,

"For if I do not go away, the Counselor will not come to you; but if I go, I will send him to you."

"I have yet many things to say to you, but you cannot bear them now. When the Spirit of truth comes, he will guide you into all the truth;

"For he will not speak on his own authority; but whatever he hears he will speak, and he will declare to you the things that are to come. He will glorify me, for he will take what is mine and declare it to you."

"These things I have spoken to you, while I am still with you. But the Counselor, the Holy Spirit, whom the Father will send in my name, he will teach you all things, and bring to your remembrance all that I have said to you.

"Peace I leave with you; my peace I give to you; not as the world gives do I give to you. Let not your hearts be troubled, neither let them be afraid."

From John 14 and 16

621 THE VINE AND BRANCHES

"I am the true vine, and my Father is the vinedresser. Every branch of mine that bears no fruit, he takes away, and every branch that does bear fruit he prunes, that it may bear more fruit.

"You are already made clean by the word which I have spoken to you. Abide in me, and I in you. As the branch cannot bear fruit by itself, unless it abides in the vine, neither can you, unless you abide in me.

"I am the vine, you are the branches. He who abides in me, and I in him, he it is that bears much fruit, for apart from me you can do nothing.

"If a man does not abide in me, he is cast forth as a branch and withers; and the branches are gathered, thrown into the fire and burned.

"If you abide in me, and my words abide in you, ask whatever you will, and it shall be done for you.

"By this my Father is glorified, that you bear much fruit, and so prove to be my disciples.

"As the Father has loved me, so have I loved you; abide in my love.

"If you keep my commandments, you will abide in my love, just as I have kept my Father's commandments and abide in his love.

"These things I have spoken to you, that my joy may be in you, and that your joy may be full.

"This is my commandment, that you love one another as I have loved you.

"Greater love has no man than this, that a man lay down his life for his friends. You are my friends if you do what I command you.

"You did not choose me, but I chose you and appointed you that you should go and bear fruit and that your fruit should abide: so that whatever you ask the Father in my name, he may give it to you."

From John 15

622 CRUCIFIXION OF JESUS

Then Pilate handed Jesus over to them to be nailed to the cross. So they took charge of Jesus.

He went out, carrying his own cross, and came to "The Place of the Skull," as it is called. (In Hebrew it is called "Golgotha.")

There they nailed him to the cross; they also nailed two other men to crosses, one on each side, with Jesus between them.

Pilate wrote a notice and had it put on the cross. "Jesus of Nazareth, the King of the Jews," is what he wrote.

After the soldiers had nailed Jesus to the cross, they took his clothes and divided them into four parts, one part for each soldier.

They also took the robe, which was made of one piece of woven cloth, without any seams in it.

The soldiers said to each other, "Let us not tear it; let us throw dice to see who will get it."

This happened to make the scripture come true: "They divided my clothes among themselves, they gambled for my robe."

Standing close to Jesus' cross were his mother, his mother's sister, Mary the wife of Clopas, and Mary Magdalene. Jesus saw his mother, and the disciple he loved standing there; so he said to his mother, "Woman, here is your son."

Then he said to the disciple, "Here is your mother." And from that time the disciple took her to live in his home.

Jesus knew that by now everything had been completed; and in order to make the scripture come true he said, "I am thirsty." They soaked a sponge in the wine, put it on a branch of hyssop, and lifted it up to his lips.

Jesus took the wine and said, "It is finished!" Then he bowed his head and died.

From John 19

623 THE HOLY SPIRIT GIVEN

When the day of Pentecost had come, they were all together in one place.

And suddenly a sound came from heaven like the rush of a mighty wind, and it filled all the house where they were sitting.

And there appeared to them tongues as of fire, distributed and resting on each one of them.

And they were all filled with the Holy Spirit and began to speak in other tongues, as the Spirit gave them utterance.

Now there were dwelling in Jerusalem Jews, devout men from every nation under heaven.

And all were amazed and perplexed, saying to one another, "What does this mean?" But others mocking said, "They are filled with new wine."

But Peter, standing with the eleven, lifted up his voice and addressed them, "Men of Judea and all who dwell in Jerusalem, let this be known to you, and give ear to my words.

"For these men are not drunk, as you suppose, since it is only the third hour of the day;

"But this is what was spoken by the prophet Joel: 'And in the last days it shall be, God declares, that I will pour out my Spirit upon all flesh.

" 'And your sons and your daughters shall prophesy, and your young men shall see visions, and your old men shall dream dreams:

" 'Yea, and on my menservants and my maidservants in those days I will pour out my Spirit; and they shall prophesy.

" 'And it shall be that whoever calls on the name of the Lord shall be saved.' "

From Acts 2

624 REDEMPTION IN CHRIST

Therefore, since we are justified by faith, we have peace with God through our Lord Jesus Christ.

Through him we have obtained access to this grace in which we stand, and we rejoice in our hope of sharing the glory of God.

More than that, we rejoice in our sufferings, knowing that suffering produces endurance, and endurance produces character, and character produces hope,

And hope does not disappoint us, because God's love has been poured into our hearts through the Holy Spirit which has been given to us.

While we were yet helpless, at the right time Christ died for the ungodly.

Why, one will hardly die for a righteous man—though perhaps for a good man one will dare even to die. But God shows his love for us in that while we were yet sinners Christ died for us.

Since, therefore, we are now justified by his blood, much more shall we be saved by him from the wrath of God.

For if while we were enemies we were reconciled to God by the death of his Son, much more, now that we are reconciled, shall we be saved by his life.

Then as one man's trespass led to condemnation for all men, so one man's act of righteousness leads to acquittal and life for all men.

For as by one man's disobedience many were made sinners, so by one man's obedience many will be made righteous.

Law came in, to increase the trespass; but where sin increased, grace abounded all the more,

So that, as sin reigned in death, grace also might reign through righteousness to eternal life through Jesus Christ our Lord. From Romans 5

625 CHRISTIAN ASSURANCE

For all who are led by the Spirit of God are sons of God.

For you did not receive the spirit of slavery to fall back into fear, but you have received the spirit of sonship.

When we cry, "Abba! Father!" it is the Spirit himself bearing witness with our spirit that we are children of God,

And if children, then heirs, heirs of God and fellow heirs with Christ, provided we suffer with him in order that we may also be glorified with him.

I consider that the sufferings of this present time are not worth comparing with the glory that is to be revealed to us.

We know that in everything God works for good with those who love him, who are called according to his purpose.

What, then shall we say to this? If God is for us, who is against us?

He who did not spare his own Son but gave him up for us all, will he not also give us all things with him?

Who shall separate us from the love of Christ? Shall tribulation, or distress, or persecution, or famine, or nakedness, or peril, or sword?

No, in all these things we are more than conquerors through him who loved us.

For I am sure that neither death, nor life, nor angels, nor principalities, nor things present, nor things to come, nor powers,

Nor height, nor depth, nor anything else in all creation, will be able to separate us from the love of God in Christ Jesus our Lord. From Romans 8

626 CALL TO CONSECRATION

So then, my brothers, because of God's many mercies to us, I make this appeal to you: Offer yourselves as a living sacrifice to God, dedicated to his service and pleasing to him. This is the true worship that you should offer.

Do not conform outwardly to the standards of this world, but let God transform you inwardly by a complete change of your mind. Then you will be able to know the will of God—what is good, and is pleasing to him, and is perfect.

Love must be completely sincere. Hate what is evil, hold on to what is good.

Love one another warmly as brothers in Christ, and be eager to show respect for one another.

Work hard, and do not be lazy. Serve the Lord with a heart full of devotion.

Let your hope keep you joyful, be patient in your troubles, and pray at all times.

Share your belongings with your needy brothers, and open your home to strangers.

Ask God to bless those who persecute you; yes, ask him to bless, not to curse.

Rejoice with those who rejoice, weep with those who weep.

Show the same spirit toward all alike. Do not be proud, but accept humble duties. Do not think of yourselves as wise.

If someone does evil to you, do not pay him back with evil. Try to do what all men consider to be good.

Do everything possible, on your part, to live at peace with all men. Do not let evil defeat you; instead, conquer evil with good. From Romans 12

627 CHRISTIAN LOVE

If I could speak the languages of men, of angels too, and have no love, I am only a rattling pan or a clashing cymbal.

If I should have the gift of prophecy, and know all secret truths, and knowledge in its every form, and have such perfect faith that I could move mountains, but have no love, I am nothing.

If I should dole out everything I have for charity, and give my body up to torture in mere boasting pride, but have no love, I get from it no good at all.

Love is so patient and so kind;

Love never boils with jealousy;

It never boasts, is never puffed with pride; It does not act with rudeness, or insist upon its rights;

It never gets provoked, it never harbors evil thoughts;

Is never glad when wrong is done, but always glad when truth prevails;

It bears up under anything;

It exercises faith in everything,

It keeps up hope in everything,

It gives us power to endure in anything.

Love never fails; If there are prophecies, they will be set aside; If now exist ecstatic speakings, they will cease; If there is knowledge, it will soon be set aside; For what we know is incomplete and what we prophesy is incomplete.

And so these three, faith, hope and love endure, but the greatest of them is love. From 1 Corinthians 13

628 CHRIST AND IMMORTALITY

For I delivered to you as of first importance what I also received, that Christ died for our sins in accordance with the scriptures,

That he was buried, that he was raised on the third day in accordance with the scriptures.

Now if Christ is preached as raised from the dead, how can some of you say that there is no resurrection of the dead?

But if there is no resurrection of the dead, then Christ has not been raised; if Christ has not been raised, then our preaching is in vain and your faith is in vain.

But in fact Christ has been raised from the dead, the first fruits of those who have fallen asleep.

For as by a man came death, by a man has come also the resurrection of the dead.

Lo! I tell you a mystery. We shall not all sleep, but we shall all be changed, in a moment, in the twinkling of an eye, at the last trumpet.

For the trumpet will sound, and the dead will be raised imperishable, and we shall be changed.

For this perishable nature must put on the imperishable, and this mortal nature must put on immortality.

When the perishable puts on the imperishable, and the mortal puts on immortality, then shall come to pass the saying that is written: "Death is swallowed up in victory."

"O death, where is thy victory? O death, where is thy sting?"

The sting of death is sin, and the power of sin is the law. But thanks be to God, who gives us the victory through our Lord Jesus Christ.

From 1 Corinthians 15

629 CHRISTIAN CONDUCT

What human nature does is quite plain. It shows itself in immoral, filthy, and indecent actions; in worship of idols and witchcraft.

People become enemies, they fight, become jealous, angry, and ambitious.

They separate into parties and groups; they are envious, get drunk, have orgies, and do other things like these.

I warn you now as I have before: those who do these things will not receive the Kingdom of God.

But the Spirit produces love, joy, peace, patience, kindness, goodness, faithfulness, humility, and self-control. There is no law against such things as these.

And those who belong to Christ Jesus have put to death their human nature, with all its passions and desires.

My brothers, if someone is caught in any kind of wrongdoing, those of you who are spiritual should set him right; but you must do it in a gentle way.

And keep an eye on yourself, so that you will not be tempted, too. Help carry one another's burdens, and in this way you will obey the law of Christ.

Do not deceive yourselves: no one makes a fool of God. A man will reap exactly what he plants.

If he plants in the field of his natural desires, from it he will gather the harvest of death; if he plants in the field of the Spirit, from the Spirit he will gather the harvest of eternal life.

So let us not become tired of doing good; for if we do not give up, the time will come when we will reap the harvest.

From Galatians 5 and 6

630 SPIRITUAL WARFARE

Finally, be strong in the Lord and in the strength of his might.

Put on the whole armor of God, that you may be able to stand against the wiles of the devil.

For we are not contending against flesh and blood, but against the principalities, against the powers, against the world rulers of this present darkness, against the spiritual hosts of wickedness in the heavenly places.

Therefore take the whole armor of God, that you may be able to withstand in the evil day, and having done all, to stand.

Stand therefore, having girded your loins with truth, and having put on the breastplate of righteousness, and having shod your feet with the equipment of the gospel of peace;

Above all taking the shield of faith, with which you can quench all the flaming darts of the evil one.

And take the helmet of salvation, and the sword of the Spirit, which is the word of God.

Pray at all times in the Spirit, with all prayer and supplication.

For though we live in the world we are not carrying on a worldly war, for the weapons of our warfare are not worldly, but have divine power to destroy strongholds.

We destroy arguments and every proud obstacle to the knowledge of God, and take every thought captive to obey Christ.

I have fought the good fight, I have finished the race, I have kept the faith.

Henceforth there is laid up for me the crown of righteousness, which the Lord, the righteous judge, will award to me on that Day, and not only to me but also to all who have loved his appearing.

From Ephesians 6, 2 Corinthians 10, and 2 Timothy 4

631 THE RETURN OF CHRIST

Brothers, we want you to know the truth about those who have died, so that you will not be sad, as are those who have no hope.

We believe that Jesus died and rose again; so we believe that God will bring with Jesus those who have died believing in him.

For this is the Lord's teaching we tell you: we who are alive on the day the Lord comes will not go ahead of those who have died.

There will be the shout of command, the archangel's voice, the sound of God's trumpet, and the Lord himself will come down from heaven!

Those who have died believing in Christ will be raised to life first; then we who are living at that time will all be gathered up along with them in the clouds to meet the Lord in the air. And so we will always be with the Lord.

Therefore, cheer each other up with these words.

There is no need to write you, brothers, about the times and occasions when these things will happen. For you yourselves know very well that the Day of the Lord will come like a thief comes at night.

When people say, "Everything is quiet and safe," then suddenly destruction will hit them! They will not escape.

But you, brothers, are not in the darkness, and the Day should not take you by surprise like a thief.

All of you are people who belong to the light, who belong to the day.

God did not choose us to suffer his wrath, but to possess salvation through our Lord Jesus Christ,

Who died for us in order that we might live together with him, whether we are alive or dead when he comes.

From 1 Thessalonians 4 and 5

632 A CHALLENGE TO FAITH

Now faith is the assurance of things hoped for, the conviction of things not seen. For by it the men of old received divine approval.

By faith Noah, being warned by God concerning events as yet unseen, took heed and constructed an ark for the saving of his household.

By faith Abraham obeyed when he was called to go out to a place which he was to receive as an inheritance; and he went out, not knowing where he was to go.

By faith Moses, when he was grown up, refused to be called the son of Pharaoh's daughter, choosing rather to share ill-treatment with the people of God than to enjoy the fleeting pleasures of sin.

And what more shall I say? For time would fail me to tell of Gideon, Barak, Samson, Jephthah, of David and Samuel and the prophets—

Who through faith conquered kingdoms, enforced justice, received promises, stopped the mouths of lions, quenched raging fire, escaped the edge of the sword.

Others suffered mocking and scourging, and even chains and imprisonment.

They were stoned, they were sawn in two, they were killed with the sword; they went about in skins of sheep and goats, destitute, afflicted, ill-treated—of whom the world was not worthy.

Therefore, since we are surrounded by so great a cloud of witnesses, let us also lay aside every weight, and sin which clings so closely,

And let us run with perseverance the race that is set before us, looking to Jesus the pioneer and perfecter of our faith.

From Hebrews 11 and 12

633 DIVINE DISCIPLINE

"My son, do not regard lightly the discipline of the Lord, nor lose courage when you are punished by him.

"For the Lord disciplines him whom he loves, and chastises every son whom he receives."

It is for discipline that you have to endure. God is treating you as sons; for what son is there whom his father does not discipline?

If you are left without discipline, in which all have participated, then you are illegitimate children and not sons.

Besides this, we have had earthly fathers to discipline us and we respected them. Shall we not much more be subject to the Father of spirits and live?

For they disciplined us for a short time at their pleasure, but he disciplines us for our good, that we may share his holiness.

For the moment all discipline seems painful rather than pleasant;

Later it yields the peaceful fruit of righteousness to those who have been trained by it.

Therefore lift your drooping hands and strengthen your weak knees, and make straight paths for your feet, so that what is lame may not be put out of joint but rather be healed.

Strive for peace with all men, and for the holiness without which no one will see the Lord.

"Behold, happy is the man whom God reproves; therefore despise not the chastening of the Almighty.

"For he wounds, but he binds up; he smites, but his hands heal."

For this slight momentary affliction is preparing for us an eternal weight of glory beyond all comparison,

Because we look not to the things that are seen but to the things that are unseen; for the things that are seen are transient, but the things that are unseen are eternal.

From Hebrews 12, Job 5, 2 Corinthians 4

634 TRIALS AND TEMPTATIONS

Count it all joy, my brethren, when you meet various trials, for you know that the testing of your faith produces steadfastness.

And let steadfastness have its full effect, that you may be perfect and complete, lacking in nothing.

Blessed is the man who endures trial, for when he has stood the test he will receive the crown of life which God has promised to those who love him.

Let no one say when he is tempted, "I am tempted by God"; for God cannot be tempted with evil and he himself tempts no one;

But each person is tempted when he is lured and enticed by his own desire.

Then desire when it has conceived gives birth to sin; and sin when it is full-grown brings forth death.

Blessed be the God and Father of our Lord Jesus Christ! By his great mercy we have been born anew to a living hope through the resurrection of Jesus Christ from the dead,

And to an inheritance which is imperishable, undefiled and unfading, kept in heaven for you, who by God's power are guarded through faith for a salvation ready to be revealed in the last time.

In this you rejoice, though now for a little while you may have to suffer various trials, so that the genuineness of your faith, more precious than gold which though perishable is tested by fire, may redound to praise and glory and honor at the revelation of Jesus Christ.

Without having seen him you love him; though you do not now see him you believe in him and rejoice with unutterable and exalted joy. As the outcome of your faith you obtain the salvation of your souls.

From James 1 and 1 Peter 1

635 THE HOLY SCRIPTURES

First of all you must understand this, that no prophecy of scripture is a matter of one's own interpretation,

Because no prophecy ever came by the impulse of man, but men moved by the Holy Spirit spoke from God.

All scripture is inspired by God and profitable for teaching, for reproof, for correction, and for training in righteousness,

That the man of God may be complete, equipped for every good work.

For the word of God is living and active, sharper than any two edged-sword, piercing to the division of soul and spirit, of joints and marrow, and discerning the thoughts and intentions of the heart.

For whatever was written in former days was written for our instruction, that by steadfastness and by the encouragement of the scriptures we might have hope.

I have laid up thy word in my heart, that I might not sin against thee.

Open my eyes, that I may behold wondrous things out of thy law.

Teach me, O Lord, the way of thy statutes; and I will keep it to the end.

Give me understanding, that I may keep thy law and observe it with my whole heart.

Thy word is a lamp to my feet and a light to my path.

The unfolding of thy words gives light; it imparts understanding to the simple.

Great peace have those who love thy law; nothing can make them stumble.

The grass withers, the flower fades; but the word of our God will stand for ever.

From 2 Peter 1, 2 Timothy 3, Hebrews 4, Romans 15, Psalm 119, Isaiah 40

636 DIVINE JUDGMENT

I want to remind you that in the last days there will come scoffers who will do every wrong they can think of, and laugh at the truth.

This will be their line of argument: "So Jesus promised to come back, did he? Then where is he? He'll never come! Why, as far back as anyone can remember everything has remained exactly as it was since the first day of creation."

They deliberately forget this fact: That God did destroy the world with a mighty flood, long after he had made the heavens by the word of his command, and had used the waters to form the earth and surround it.

And God has commanded that the earth and the heavens be stored away for a great bonfire at the judgment day, when all ungodly men will perish.

The day of the Lord is surely coming, as unexpectedly as a thief, and then the heavens will pass away with a terrible noise and the heavenly bodies will disappear in fire, and the earth and everything on it will be burned up.

And so since everything around us is going to melt away, what holy, godly lives we should be living!

You should look forward to that day and hurry it along—the day when God will set the heavens on fire, and the heavenly bodies will melt and disappear in flames.

But we are looking forward to God's promise of new heavens and a new earth afterwards, where there will be only goodness.

Dear friends, while you are waiting for these things to happen and for him to come, try hard to live without sinning; and be at peace with everyone so that he will be pleased with you when he returns.

And remember why he is waiting. He is giving us time to get his message of salvation out to others.

2 Peter 3

637 LOVE AND DISCIPLESHIP

"A new commandment I give to you, that you love one another; even as I have loved you, that you also love one another.

"By this all men will know that you are my disciples, if you have love for one another."

He who says he is in the light and hates his brother is in the darkness still. He who loves his brother abides in the light, and in it there is no cause for stumbling.

But he who hates his brother is in the darkness and walks in the darkness, and does not know where he is going, because the darkness has blinded his eyes.

See what love the Father has given us, that we should be called children of God; and so we are.

The reason why the world does not know us is that it did not know him.

Beloved, we are God's children now; it does not yet appear what we shall be, but we know that when he appears we shall be like him, for we shall see him as he is.

And every one who thus hopes in him purifies himself as he is pure.

We know that we have passed out of death into life, because we love the brethren. He who does not love remains in death.

By this we know love, that he laid down his life for us; and we ought to lay down our lives for the brethren.

But if any one has the world's goods and sees his brother in need, yet closes his heart against him, how does God's love abide in him?

Little children, let us not love in word or speech but in deed and in truth.

From John 13, 1 John 1 and 3

638 THE HOLY CITY

And I saw a new heaven and a new earth: for the first heaven and the first earth were passed away; and there was no more sea.

And I John saw the holy city, new Jerusalem, coming down from God out of heaven, prepared as a bride adorned for her husband.

Having the glory of God: and her light was like unto a stone most precious, even like a jasper stone, clear as crystal;

And had a wall great and high, and had twelve gates, and at the gates twelve angels, and names written thereon, which are the names of the twelve tribes of the children of Israel.

And the wall of the city had twelve foundations, and in them the names of the twelve apostles of the Lamb.

And the building of the wall of it was of jasper: and the city was pure gold, like unto clear glass.

And I saw no temple therein: for the Lord God Almighty and the Lamb are the temple of it.

And the city had no need of the sun, neither of the moon, to shine in it: for the glory of God did lighten it, and the Lamb is the light thereof.

And the nations of them which are saved shall walk in the light of it: and the kings of the earth do bring their glory and honour into it.

And the gates of it shall not be shut at all by day: for there shall be no night there.

And they shall bring the glory and honour of the nations into it. And there shall in no wise enter into it any thing that defileth,

Neither whatsoever worketh abomination, or maketh a lie: but they which are written in the Lamb's book of life.

From Revelation 21

639 THE FINAL WORD

I John am he who heard and saw these things. And when I heard and saw them, I fell down to worship at the feet of the angel who showed them to me;

But he said to me, "You must not do that! I am a fellow servant with you and your brethren the prophets, and with those who keep the words of this book. Worship God."

And he said to me, "Do not seal up the words of the prophecy of this book, for the time is near.

"Let the evildoer still do evil, and the filthy still be filthy, and the righteous still do right, and the holy still be holy.

"Behold, I am coming soon, bringing my recompense, to repay every one for what he has done.

"I am the Alpha and the Omega, the first and the last, the beginning and the end."

Blessed are those who wash their robes, that they may have the right to the tree of life and that they may enter the city by the gates.

The Spirit and the Bride say, "Come." And let him who hears say, "Come." And let him who is thirsty come, let him who desires take the water of life without price.

I warn every one who hears the words of the prophecy of this book: if any one adds to them, God will add to him the plagues described in this book,

And if any one takes away from the words of the book of this prophecy, God will take away his share in the tree of life and in the holy city, which are described in this book.

He who testifies to these things says, "Surely I am coming soon."

Amen. Come, Lord Jesus!

From Revelation 22

SCRIPTURE READINGS (Paraphrases)

Indexes to the Scripture Readings will be found on pages 574 through 580.

640 LIVING PSALMS

Oh, the joys of those who do not follow evil men's advice, who do not hang around with sinners, scoffing at the things of God:

But they delight in doing everything God wants them to, and day and night are always meditating on his laws and thinking about ways to follow him more closely.

They are like trees along a river bank bearing luscious fruit each season without fail. Their leaves shall never wither, and all they do shall prosper.

But for sinners, what a different story! They blow away like chaff before the wind.

They are not safe on Judgment Day; they shall not stand among the godly.

For the Lord watches over all the plans and paths of godly men, but the paths of the godless lead to doom.

Psalm 1

* * *

Because the Lord is my Shepherd, I have everything I need!

He lets me rest in the meadow grass and leads me beside the quiet streams.

He restores my failing health. He helps me do what honors him the most.

Even when walking through the dark valley of death I will not be afraid, for you are close beside me, guarding, guiding all the way.

You provide delicious food for me in the presence of my enemies. You have welcomed me as your guest; blessings overflow!

Your goodness and unfailing kindness shall be with me all of my life, and afterwards I will live with you forever in your home.

Psalm 23

641 GODLY WOMANHOOD

If you can find a truly good wife, she is worth more than precious gems.

Her husband can trust her, and she will richly satisfy his needs. She will not hinder him, but help him all his life.

She finds wool and flax and busily spins it. She buys imported foods, brought by ship from distant ports.

She gets up before dawn to prepare breakfast for her household, and plans the day's work for her servant girls.

She goes out to inspect a field, and buys it; with her own hands she plants a vineyard. She is energetic, a hard worker, and watches for bargains. She works far into the night!

She sews for the poor, and generously gives to the needy. She has no fear of winter for her household, for she has made warm clothes for all of them.

Her husband is well known, for he sits in the council chamber with the other civic leaders.

She is a woman of strength and dignity, and has no fear of old age.

When she speaks, her words are wise, and kindness is the rule for everything she says.

She watches carefully all that goes on throughout her household, and is never lazy.

Her children stand and bless her; so does her husband. He praises her with these words: "There are many fine women in the world, but you are the best of them all."

Charm can be deceptive and beauty doesn't last, but a woman who fears and reverences God shall be greatly praised.

From Proverbs 31

642 CHALLENGE TO YOUTH

Don't let the excitement of being young cause you to forget about your Creator. Honor him in your youth before the evil days come—when you'll no longer enjoy living.

It will be too late then to try to remember him, when the sun and light and moon and stars are dim to your old eyes, and there is no silver lining left among your clouds.

For there will come a time when your limbs will tremble with age, and your strong legs will become weak, and your teeth will be too few to do their work, and there will be blindness too.

And you will waken at dawn with the first note of the birds; but you yourself will be deaf and tuneless, with quavering voice.

You will be afraid of heights and of falling—a white-haired, withered old man, dragging himself along: without sexual desire, standing at death's door, and nearing his everlasting home.

Yes, remember your Creator now while you are young, before the silver cord of life snaps, and the golden bowl is broken, and the pitcher is broken at the fountain, and the wheel is broken at the cistern; and the dust returns to the earth as it was, and the spirit returns to God who gave it.

The wise man's words are like goads that spur to action. They nail down important truths. Students are wise who master what their teachers tell them.

But, my son, be warned: there is no end of opinions ready to be expressed. Studying them can go on forever, and become very exhausting!

Here is my final conclusion: fear God and obey his commandments, for this is the entire duty of man.

For God will judge us for everything we do, including every hidden thing, good or bad. From Ecclesiastes 12

643 FIRST THINGS FIRST

"You cannot serve two masters: God and money. For you will hate one and love the other, or else the other way around.

"So my counsel is: Don't worry about things—food, drink, and clothes. For you already have life and a body—and they are far more important than what to eat and wear.

"Look at the birds! They don't worry about what to eat—they don't need to sow or reap or store up food—for your heavenly Father feeds them. And you are far more valuable to him than they are.

"Will all your worries add a single moment to your life?

"And why worry about your clothes? Look at the field lilies! They don't worry about theirs. Yet King Solomon in all his glory was not clothed as beautifully as they.

"And if God cares so wonderfully for flowers that are here today and gone tomorrow, won't he more surely care for you, O men of little faith?

"So don't worry at all about having enough food and clothing. Why be like the heathen? For they take pride in all these things and are deeply concerned about them.

"But your heavenly Father already knows perfectly well that you need them, and he will give them to you if you give him first place in your life and live as he wants you to.

"So don't be anxious about tomorrow. God will take care of your tomorrow too.

"Live one day at a time."

"For anyone who keeps his life for himself shall lose it; and anyone who loses his life for me shall find it again.

"What profit is there if you gain the whole world—and lose eternal life? What can be compared with the value of eternal life?" From Matthew 6 and 16

644 THE NEW WAY OF LIFE

"Listen, all of you. Love your enemies. Do good to those who hate you.

"Pray for the happiness of those who curse you; implore God's blessing on those who hurt you.

"If someone slaps you on one cheek, let him slap the other too! If someone demands your coat, give him your shirt besides.

"Give what you have to anyone who asks you for it; and when things are taken away from you, don't worry about getting them back. Treat others as you want them to treat you.

"Do you think you deserve credit for merely loving those who love you? Even the godless do that! And if you do good only to those who do you good—is that so wonderful? Even sinners do that much!

"And if you lend money only to those who can repay you, what good is that? Even the most wicked will lend to their own kind for full return!

"Love your enemies! Do good to them! Lend to them! And don't be concerned about the fact that they won't repay.

"Then your reward from heaven will be very great, and you will truly be acting as sons of God: for he is kind to the unthankful and to those who are very wicked.

"Try to show as much compassion as your Father does. Never criticize or condemn—or it will all come back on you.

"Go easy on others; then they will do the same for you. For if you give, you will get!

"Your gift will return to you in full and overflowing measure, pressed down, shaken together to make room for more, and running over.

"Whatever measure you use to give—large or small—will be used to measure what is given back to you."

From Luke 6

645 THE ONE TRUE GOD

"Men of Athens, I notice that you are very religious, for as I was out walking I saw your many altars, and one of them had this inscription on it—'To the Unknown God.'

"You have been worshiping him without knowing who he is, and now I wish to tell you about him.

"He made the world and everything in it, and since he is Lord of heaven and earth, he doesn't live in man-made temples; and human hands can't minister to his needs—for he has no needs!

"He himself gives life and breath to everything, and satisfies every need there is.

"He created all the people of the world from one man, Adam, and scattered the nations across the face of the earth.

"He decided beforehand which should rise and fall, and when. He determined their boundaries.

"His purpose in all of this is that they should seek after God, and perhaps feel their way toward him and find him—though he is not far from any one of us.

"For in him we live and move and are! As one of your own poets says it, 'We are the sons of God.' If this is true, we shouldn't think of God as an idol made by men from gold or silver or chipped from stone.

"God tolerated man's past ignorance about these things, but now he commands everyone to put away idols and worship only him.

"For he has set a day for justly judging the world by the man he has appointed, and has pointed him out by bringing him back to life again."

From Acts 17

646 FREEDOM FROM SIN

The Ten Commandments were given so that all could see the extent of their failure to obey God's laws. But the more we see our sinfulness, the more we see God's abounding grace forgiving us.

Well then, shall we keep on sinning so that God can keep on showing us more and more kindness and forgiveness?

Of course not! Should we keep on sinning when we don't have to? For sin's power over us was broken when we became Christians and were baptized to become a part of Jesus Christ;

Your old sin-loving nature was buried with him by baptism when he died, and when God the Father, with glorious power, brought him back to life again, you were given his wonderful new life to enjoy.

For you have become a part of him, and so you died with him, so to speak, when he died; and now you share his new life, and shall rise as he did.

Your old evil desires were nailed to the cross with him; that part of you that loves to sin was crushed and fatally wounded, so that your sin-loving body is no longer under sin's control, no longer needs to be a slave to sin;

For when you are deadened to sin you are freed from all its allure and its power over you.

And since your old sin-loving nature "died" with Christ, we know that you will share his new life.

Christ rose from the dead and will never die again. Death no longer has any power over him. He died once for all to end sin's power, but now he lives forever in unbroken fellowship with God.

So look upon your old sin nature as dead and unresponsive to sin, and instead be alive to God, alert to him, through Jesus Christ our Lord.

From Romans 5 and 6

647 COMMUNION OBSERVANCE

For this is what the Lord himself has said about his Table, and I have passed it on to you before: That on the night when Judas betrayed him, the Lord Jesus took bread,

And when he had given thanks to God for it, he broke it and gave it to his disciples and said, "Take this and eat it. This is my body, which is given for you. Do this to remember me."

In the same way, he took the cup of wine after supper, saying, "This cup is the new agreement between God and you that has been established and set in motion by my blood. Do this in remembrance of me whenever you drink it."

For every time you eat this bread and drink this cup you are retelling the message of the Lord's death, that he has died for you. Do this until he comes again.

So if anyone eats this bread and drinks from this cup of the Lord in an unworthy manner, he is guilty of sin against the body and the blood of the Lord.

That is why a man should examine himself carefully before eating the bread and drinking from the cup.

For if he eats the bread and drinks from the cup unworthily, not thinking about the body of Christ and what it means, he is eating and drinking God's judgment upon himself; for he is trifling with the death of Christ.

That is why many of you are weak and sick, and some have even died.

But if you carefully examine yourselves before eating you will not need to be judged and punished.

Yet, when we are judged and punished by the Lord, it is so that we will not be condemned with the rest of the world.

From 1 Corinthians 11

648 ABOUT SPIRITUAL GIFTS

And now, brothers, I want to write about the special abilities the Holy Spirit gives to each of you; for I don't want any misunderstanding about them.

Now God gives us many kinds of special abilities, but it is the same Holy Spirit who is the source of them all.

There are different kinds of service to God, but it is the same Lord we are serving.

There are many ways in which God works in our lives, but it is the same God who does the work in and through all of us who are his.

The Holy Spirit displays God's power through each of us as a means of helping the entire church.

To one person the Spirit gives the ability to give wise advice; someone else may be especially good at studying and teaching, and this is his gift from the same Spirit.

He gives special faith to another, and to someone else the power to heal the sick.

He gives power for doing miracles to some, and to others power to prophesy and preach.

He gives someone else the power to know whether evil spirits are speaking through those who claim to be giving God's messages—or whether it is really the Spirit of God who is speaking.

Still another person is able to speak in languages he never learned; and others, who do not know the language either, are given power to understand what he is saying.

It is the same and only Holy Spirit who gives all these gifts and powers, deciding which each one of us should have.

All of you together are the one body of Christ and each one of you is a separate and necessary part of it.

From 1 Corinthians 12

649 LOVE, THE GREATEST THING

If I had the gift of being able to speak in other languages without learning them, and could speak in every language there is in all of heaven and earth, but didn't love others, I would only be making noise.

If I had the gift of prophecy and knew all about what is going to happen in the future, knew everything about everything, but didn't love others, what good would it do?

Even if I had the gift of faith so that I could speak to a mountain and make it move, I would still be worth nothing at all without love.

If I gave everything I have to poor people, and if I were burned alive for preaching the Gospel but didn't love others, it would be of no value whatever.

Love is very patient and kind, never jealous or envious, never boastful or proud, never haughty or selfish or rude.

Love does not demand its own way. It is not irritable or touchy.

It does not hold grudges and will hardly even notice when others do it wrong.

It is never glad about injustice, but rejoices whenever truth wins out.

If you love someone you will be loyal to him no matter what the cost.

You will always believe in him, always expect the best of him, and always stand your ground in defending him.

All the special gifts and powers from God will someday come to an end, but love goes on forever.

There are three things that remain—faith, hope, and love—and the greatest of these is love.

From 1 Corinthians 13

650 CHRISTIAN SHARING

Dear Brothers, if a Christian is overcome by some sin, you who are godly should gently and humbly help him back onto the right path, remembering that next time it might be one of you who is in the wrong.

Share each other's troubles and problems, and so obey our Lord's command. If anyone thinks he is too great to stoop to this, he is fooling himself. He is really a nobody.

Let everyone be sure that he is doing his very best, for then he will have the personal satisfaction of work well done, and won't need to compare himself with someone else.

Each of us must bear some faults and burdens of his own. For none of us is perfect!

Those who are taught the Word of God should help their teachers by paying them.

Don't be misled; remember that you can't ignore God and get away with it: a man will always reap just the kind of crop he sows!

If he sows to please his own wrong desires, he will be planting seeds of evil and he will surely reap a harvest of spiritual decay and death;

But if he plants the good things of the Spirit, he will reap the everlasting life which the Holy Spirit gives him.

And let us not get tired of doing what is right, for after a while we will reap a harvest of blessing if we don't get discouraged and give up.

That's why whenever we can we should always be kind to everyone, and especially to our Christian brothers.

As for me, God forbid that I should boast about anything except the cross of our Lord Jesus Christ.

Dear brothers, may the grace of our Lord Jesus Christ be with you all.

From Galatians 6

651 HUMILITY AND EXALTATION

Is there any such thing as Christians cheering each other up? Do you love me enough to want to help me?

Does it mean anything to you that we are brothers in the Lord, sharing the same Spirit? Are your hearts tender and sympathetic at all?

Then make me truly happy by loving each other and agreeing wholeheartedly with each other, working together with one heart and mind and purpose.

Don't be selfish; don't live to make a good impression on others. Be humble, thinking of others as better than yourself.

Don't just think about your own affairs, but be interested in others, too, and in what they are doing.

Your attitude should be the kind that was shown us by Jesus Christ, who, though he was God, did not demand and cling to his rights as God, but laid aside his mighty power and glory, taking the disguise of a slave and becoming like men.

And he humbled himself even further, going so far as actually to die a criminal's death on a cross.

Yet it was because of this that God raised him up to the heights of heaven and gave him a name which is above every other name,

That at the name of Jesus every knee shall bow in heaven and on earth and under the earth,

And every tongue shall confess that Jesus Christ is Lord, to the glory of God the Father.

"The more lowly your service to others, the greater you are. To be the greatest, be a servant.

"But those who think themselves great shall be disappointed and humbled; and those who humble themselves shall be exalted."

From Philippians 2 and Matthew 23

652 THE NEW LIFE

If you are then "risen" with Christ, reach out for the highest gifts of Heaven, where Christ reigns in power. Give your heart to the heavenly things, not to the passing things of earth.

For, as far as this world is concerned, you are already dead, and your true life is a hidden one in God, through Christ. In so far, then, as you have to live upon this earth, consider yourself dead to worldly contacts:

But now, put all these things behind you. No more evil temper or furious rage: no more evil thoughts or words about others, no more evil thoughts or words about God, and no more filthy conversation.

Don't tell one another lies any more, for you have finished with the old man and all he did and have begun life as the new man, who is out to learn what he ought to be, according to the plan of God.

As, therefore, God's picked representatives of the new humanity, purified and beloved of God himself, be merciful in action, kindly in heart, humble in mind.

Accept life, and be most patient and tolerant with one another, always ready to forgive if you have a difference with anyone. Forgive as freely as the Lord has forgiven you.

And, above everything else, be truly loving, for love is the golden chain of all the virtues.

Let the peace of Christ rule in your hearts, remembering that as members of the one body you are called to live in harmony, and never forget to be thankful for what God has done for you.

Teach and help one another along the right road with your psalms and hymns and Christian songs, singing God's praises with joyful hearts.

And whatever work you may have to do, do everything in the name of the Lord Jesus, thanking God the Father through him. From Colossians 3

653 THE LORD'S SERVANT

The Lord's servant must not be a man of strife: he must be kind to all, ready and able to teach: he must have patience and the ability gently to correct those who oppose his message.

He must always bear in mind the possibility that God will give them a different outlook, and that they may come to know the truth.

But you must realize that in the last days the times will be full of danger. Men will become utterly self-centered, greedy for money, full of big words.

They will be proud and contemptuous, without any regard for what their parents taught them. They will be utterly lacking in gratitude, purity and normal human affections.

They will be men of unscrupulous speech and have no control of themselves. They will be passionate and unprincipled, treacherous, self-willed and conceited, loving all the time what gives them pleasure instead of loving God.

They will maintain a facade of "religion," but their conduct will deny its validity. You must keep clear of people like this.

Persecution is inevitable for those who are determined to live really Christian lives, while wicked and deceitful men will go from bad to worse, deluding others and deluding themselves.

Yet you must go on steadily in those things that you have learned and which you know are true.

Remember from what sort of people your knowledge has come, and how from early childhood your mind has been familiar with the holy scriptures.

All scripture is inspired by God and is useful for teaching the faith and correcting error, for resetting the direction of a man's life and training him in good living. From 2 Timothy 2 and 3

654 THE DAY OF THE LORD

First of all, you must understand that in the last days some men will appear whose lives are controlled by their own passions.

They will make fun of you and say: "He promised to come, didn't he? Where is he? Our fathers have already died, but everything is still the same as it was since the creation of the world!"

They purposely ignore this fact: long ago God spoke, and the heavens and earth were created. The earth was formed out of water, and by water, and it was by water also, the water of the Flood, that the old world was destroyed.

But the heavens and earth that now exist are being preserved, by the same word of God, for destruction by fire. They are being kept for the day when wicked men will be judged and destroyed.

But the Day of the Lord will come as a thief. On that Day the heavens will disappear with a shrill noise, the heavenly bodies will burn up and be destroyed, and the earth with everything in it will vanish.

Since all these things will be destroyed in this way, what kind of people should you be?

Your lives should be holy and dedicated to God, as you wait for the Day of God, and do your best to make it come soon—

The Day when the heavens will burn up and be destroyed, and the heavenly bodies will be melted by the heat.

But God has promised new heavens and a new earth, where righteousness will be at home, and we wait for these.

And so, my friends, as you wait for that Day, do your best to be pure and faultless in God's sight and to be at peace with him. From 2 Peter 3

655 GOD'S LOVE AND OURS

Dear friends, let us practice loving each other, for love comes from God and those who are loving and kind show that they are the children of God, and that they are getting to know him better.

But if a person isn't loving and kind, it shows that he doesn't know God—for God is love.

God showed how much he loved us by sending his only Son into this wicked world to bring to us eternal life through his death.

In this act we see what real love is: it is not our love for God, but his love for us when he sent his Son to satisfy God's anger against our sins.

Dear friends, since God loved us as much as that, we surely ought to love each other too.

For though we have never yet seen God, when we love each other God lives in us and his love within us grows ever stronger.

We know how much God loves us because we have felt his love and because we believe him when he tells us that he loves us dearly. God is love, and anyone who lives in love is living with God and God is living in him.

And as we live with Christ, our love grows more perfect and complete; so we will not be ashamed and embarrassed at the day of judgment, but can face him with confidence and joy, because he loves us and we love him too.

If anyone says "I love God," but keeps on hating his brother, he is a liar; for if he doesn't love his brother who is right there in front of him, how can he love God whom he has never seen?

And God himself has said that one must love not only God, but his brother too. 1 John 4

ALPHABETICAL INDEX OF SCRIPTURE READINGS

Abbreviations (Index) and Credits for Translations and Paraphrases

SUBJECT INDEX OF SCRIPTURE READINGS

SCRIPTURAL INDEX OF SCRIPTURE READINGS

SCRIPTURAL ALLUSIONS AND QUOTATIONS IN HYMNS

INDEX OF COPYRIGHT OWNERS (Words and Music)

As mentioned in the foreword, we are indebted to the proprietors listed here for permission to include their copyrighted works in THE SINGING CHURCH. The right to use these copyrighted hymns and songs is restricted to this hymnal. Those wishing to use any of the copyrighted words or music contained herein must contact the appropriate owner whose name and address is listed below.

ABINGDON PRESS, 201 Eighth Avenue, South, P.O. Box 801, Nashville, TN 37202—(615) 749-6432: Hymns 22, 222, 500.

ALBERT E. BRUMLEY AND SONS, Powell, MO 65730—(417) 435-2225: Hymn 277.

AUGSBURG PUBLISHING HOUSE, 426 S. Fifth Street, Box 1209, Minneapolis, MN 55440—(612) 330-3300: Hymns 125, 130, 164, 203, 215, 514.

BELL & HYMAN LIMITED, Denmark House, 37/39 Queen Elizabeth Street, London, SE1 2QB, England—01 407 0709: Hymn 101.

BOARD OF PUBLICATION, Lutheran Church in America, 2900 Queen Lane, Philadelphia, PA 19129—(215) 848-6800: Hymn 37.

BREITKOPF & HÄRTEL, Postfach 1707, D-6200 Wiesbaden 1, Germany: Hymns 318, 395, 512.

BROADMAN PRESS, 127 Ninth Avenue North, Nashville, TN 37234—(615) 251-2000: Hymns 223, 282, 346, 442, 464, 469, 497, 498.

CARL FISCHER, INC., 62 Cooper Square, New York, NY 10003—(212) 777-0900: Hymn 100.

CHARLES SCRIBNER'S SONS, 597 Fifth Avenue, New York, NY 10017: Hymn 14.

CHRISTIAN PUBLICATIONS, INC., 3825 Hartzdale Drive, P.O. Box 8070, Camp Hill, PA 17011-8870—(717) 761-7044: Hymn 475.

CHRISTIANITY TODAY, 465 Gundersen Drive, Carol Stream, IL 60188—(312) 260-6200: Hymn: 474.

CLARKE IRWIN INC., Box 200, Agincourt, Ontario, Canada M1S 3B6—(416) 293-4175: Hymn 401.

CONCORDIA PUBLISHING HOUSE, 3558 S. Jefferson Avenue, St. Louis, MO 63118—(314) 664-7000: Hymn 335.

CRESCENDO PUBLICATIONS, INC., P.O. Box 28218, Dallas, TX 75228—(214) 579-7700: Hymn 436.

CROWELL, REID, 719 Lowell Street, Dallas, TX 75214: Hymn 498.

CRUMP, ELUNED and DILYS EVANS, Tan-y-Coed, Uxbridge Square, Caernarvon, North Wales LL552 RE: Hymns 242, 450.

DUNKERLEY, DESMOND, 23 Haslemere Road, Southsea, Portsmouth, Hants. PO4 8BB, England: Hymns 507, 555.

EDITOR'S LITERARY ESTATE/CHATTO & WINDUS, 40 William IV Street, London, WC2N 4DF, England—01 379 6637: Hymn 359.

EMURIAN, THE REV. ERNEST K., The Cherrydale United Methodist Church, 3701 Lorcom Lane, Arlington, VA 22207: Hymn 499.

EVANGELICAL COVENANT CHURCH, 5101 North Francisco Avenue, Chicago, IL 60625—(312) 784-3000: Hymn 506.

F.E.L. PUBLICATIONS, LTD., 1925 Pontius Avenue, Los Angeles, CA 90025—(213) 478-0053: Hymn 212.

FRANKLIN HOUSE PUBLISHING, P.O. Box 989, Franklin, TN 37064—(615) 790-2812: Hymn 187.

G.I.A. PUBLICATIONS, INC., 7404 S. Mason Avenue, Chicago, IL 60638—(312) 496-3800: Hymns 13, 478.

G. SCHIRMER, INC., 866 Third Avenue, New York, NY 10022—(212) 935-5100: Hymns 25, 43, 104, 433.

GABE, GLYN A., Seaward, Lamb's Well Close, Langland, Swansea, Wales SA3 4HJ: Hymn 435.

GAITHER, WILLIAM J., Gaither Music Company, Box 300, Alexandria, IN 46001—(317) 724-4441: Hymns 73, 81, 159, 281, 306, 418.

HAROLD OBER ASSOCIATES, 40 East 49th Street, New York, NY 10017: Hymn 530.
HILL AND RANGE SONGS, INC., c/o Hal Leonard Publishing Corporation, 8112 West Bluemound Rd., P.O. Box 13819, Milwaukee, WI 53213—(414) 774-3630: Hymn 422.
HOLLIS MUSIC, INC., c/o The Richmond Organization, 10 Columbus Circle, New York, NY 10019—(212) 765-9889: Hymn 103.
HOPE PUBLISHING COMPANY, Carol Stream, IL 60188—(312) 665-3200. Listed for your convenience.
HYMN SOCIETY OF AMERICA—contact Hope Publishing Company: Hymns 45, 239, 462, 495, 500, 510.
HYMNS ANCIENT & MODERN LIMITED, St. Mary's Works, St. Mary's Plain, Norwich, Norfolk, England NR3 3BH—(0603) 612914: Hymns 143, 150.
INTERVARSITY CHRISTIAN FELLOWSHIP, InterVarsity Press, Box F, Downers Grove, IL 60515—(312) 964-5700: Hymn 67.
J. FISCHER & BROS., a division of Belwin-Mills Publishing Corporation, 1776 Broadway, New York, NY 10019—(212) 245-1100: Hymn 524.
JABUSCH, WILLARD F., St. Mary of the Lake Seminary, Mundelein, IL 60060—(312) 566-6401: Hymn 503.
JOHN CHURCH COMPANY, THE, c/o Theodore Presser Company, Presser Place, Bryn Mawr, PA 19010—(215) 525-3636: Hymn 488.
JOHN W. PETERSON MUSIC COMPANY, c/o Good Life Publications, 8655 East Via De Ventura, Suite G-151, Scottsdale, AZ 85258—(602) 998-7788: Hymns 56, 168, 189, 285, 331.
JUDSON PRESS, American Baptist Churches, U.S.A., Valley Forge, PA 19481: Hymn 204.
LATTER RAIN MUSIC, c/o Sparrow Records, Inc., 8025 Deering Avenue, Canoga Park, CA 91304—(213) 703-6599: Hymn 153.
LEXICON MUSIC INC., P.O. Box 2222, Newbury Park, CA 91320—(805) 499-5881: Hymns 12, 23, 198, 240, 295, 407, 420, 477.
LILLENAS PUBLISHING COMPANY, Box 527, Kansas City, MO 64141—(816) 931-1900: Hymns 21, 208, 291.
MANNA MUSIC, INC., 2111 Kenmere Avenue, Burbank, CA 91504—(213) 843-8100: Hymns 1, 79, 186, 243, 417.
MARANATHA MUSIC, P.O. Box 1396, Costa Mesa, CA 92626—(714) 979-8536: Hymns 202, 270.
MOODY PRESS, 2101 West Howard Street, Chicago, IL 60645—(312) 973-7800: Hymn 183.
NORMAN CLAYTON PUBLISHING—contact Word Music: Hymns 304, 311.
NOVELLO & COMPANY LTD., Borough Green, Sevenoaks, Kent, TN15 8DT, England—Borough Green 3261: Hymn 131.
ORTLUND, ANNE, 32 Whitewater Drive, Corona Del Mar, CA 92625: Hymn 467.
OXFORD UNIVERSITY PRESS, Ely House, 37 Dover Street, London, W1X 4AH, England—01 629 8494: Hymns 24, 41, 48, 51, 86, 121, 164, 323, 482, 504, 519, 530, 536.
PEARCE, MRS. ROWAN, 502 Elizabeth Drive, Lancaster, PA 17601: Hymn 178.
PRESBYTERIAN OUTLOOK, THE, 512 East Main Street, Richmond, VA 23219—(804) 649-1371: Hymn 457.
RODEHEAVER COMPANY, THE—contact Word Music: Hymns 47, 122, 149, 174, 192, 251, 280, 287, 349, 374, 380, 460, 483, 494.
SACRED SONGS—contact Word Music: Hymns 265, 378.
SINGSPIRATION MUSIC, INC., 1415 Lake Drive, S.E., Grand Rapids, MI 49506—(616) 459-6900: Hymns 31, 138, 140, 171, 173, 256, 266, 302, 394, 406, 470.
THORNTON, JAMES D., 10A North Road, Hertford, Hertfordshire, SG14 1LS, England: Hymn 172.
TRUSTEES OF VINCENT (HAZEON) TRUST, c/o Crossman, Block & Keith, Imperial Life House, Cross Lanes, London Road, Guildford, GU1 1TG, England—Guildford 33811: Hymn 339.
WESTMINSTER PRESS, 925 Chestnut Street, Philadelphia, PA 19107—(215) 928-2700: Hymn 535.
WORD MUSIC, a division of Word, Inc., Winona Lake, IN 46590—(219) 267-5116: Hymns 257, 501.
WORK, MRS. JOHN W. III, 1030 17th Avenue North, Nashville, TN 37208: Hymn 107.
WORLD COUNCIL OF CHURCHES, P.O. Box 66, 150 Route De Ferney, 1211 Geneva 20, Switzerland: Hymn 84.
WORLD STUDENT CHRISTIAN FEDERATION, 27 Ch. des Crets de Pregny, 1218 Grand-Saconnex, Geneva, Switzerland—(022) 98 89 53: Hymn 161.

ALPHABETICAL INDEX OF TUNES

Code:
S.M. (Short Meter)
C.M. (Common Meter)
L.M. (Long Meter)
Ref. (with Refrain)
D. (Doubled)
A. (with Alleluias)
Rep. (with Repeats)
Irr. (Irregular)

METRICAL INDEX OF TUNES

Note: This index is commonly used in choosing alternate tunes for a particular hymn text. For this reason only those meters are listed that are represented by at least two tunes. This index also does not include hymns with irregular meters or hymns with refrains. Every tune (with its meter) is listed in the Alphabetical Index of Tunes.

INDEX OF AUTHORS, COMPOSERS AND SOURCES

C

S

T

U

V

W

Y

Z

TOPICAL INDEX OF HYMNS

CHRIST

WITNESS, HYMNS OF

WITNESSING

WORD OF GOD

WORSHIP

YOUTH HYMNS

ZEAL

ALPHABETICAL INDEX OF HYMNS

The basic listing is of first lines;
common titles are in capital letters.